Exam 70-294: *Planning, Implementing, and Maintaining a Microsoft Windows Server 2003 Active Directory Infrastructure*

Objective	Pages
Planning and Implementing an Active Directory Infrastructure (1.0)	
Plan a strategy for placing global catalog servers.	1-4 to 1-20, 5-41 to 5-47, 15-5 to 15-9
■ Evaluate network traffic considerations when placing global catalog servers.	5-41 to 5-47
■ Evaluate the need to enable universal group caching.	5-41 to 5-47
Plan flexible operations master role placement.	4-18 to 4-22, 15-10 to 15-16
■ Plan for business continuity of operations master roles.	4-18 to 4-22
■ Identify operations master role dependencies.	4-18 to 4-22
Implement an Active Directory directory service forest and domain structure.	2-3 to 2-37, 4-3 to 4-17, 15-17 to 15-36
■ Create the forest root domain.	2-3 to 2-37
■ Create a child domain.	4-3 to 4-17
■ Create and configure Application Data Partitions.	5-48 to 5-58
■ Install and configure an Active Directory domain controller.	2-3 to 2-37
■ Set an Active Directory forest and domain functional level based on requirements.	3-3 to 3-16
■ Establish trust relationships. Types of trust relationships might include external trusts, shortcut trusts, and cross-forest trusts.	4-39 to 4-73
Implement an Active Directory site topology.	5-3 to 5-40, 15-28 to 15-31
■ Configure site links.	5-25 to 5-40
■ Configure preferred bridgehead servers.	5-25 to 5-40
Plan an administrative delegation strategy.	6-3 to 6-23, 15-32 to 15-36
■ Plan an organizational unit (OU) structure based on delegation requirements.	6-3 to 6-9
■ Plan a security group hierarchy based on delegation requirements.	8-3 to 8-21
Managing and Maintaining an Active Directory Infrastructure (2.0)	
Manage an Active Directory forest and domain structure.	4-3 to 4-18, 16-6 to 16-13
■ Manage trust relationships.	4-23 to 4-38
■ Manage schema modifications.	3-3 to 3-17
■ Add or remove a UPN suffix.	3-3 to 3-17
Manage an Active Directory site.	5-3 to 5-40, 16-14 to 16-20
■ Configure replication schedules.	5-25 to 5-40
■ Configure site link costs.	5-25 to 5-40
■ Configure site boundaries.	5-11 to 5-24
Monitor Active Directory replication failures. Tools might include Replication Monitor, Event Viewer, and support tools.	5-48 to 5-58, 16-21 to 16-27
■ Monitor Active Directory replication.	5-48 to 5-58
■ Monitor File Replication service (FRS) replication.	14-2 to 14-18
Restore Active Directory directory service.	3-44 to 3-55, 16-28 to 16-32
■ Perform an authoritative restore operation.	3-44 to 3-55
■ Perform a nonauthoritative restore operation.	3-44 to 3-55
Troubleshoot Active Directory.	4-18 to 4-22, 5-41 to 5-47, 16-33 to 16-37
■ Diagnose and resolve issues related to Active Directory replication.	5-59 to 5-73
■ Diagnose and resolve issues related to operations master role failure.	4-18 to 4-22
■ Diagnose and resolve issues related to the Active Directory database.	4-23 to 4-38

Objective	Pages
Planning and Implementing User, Computer, and Group Strategies (3.0)	
Plan a security group strategy.	8-3 to 8-34, 17-5 to 17-13
Plan a user authentication strategy.	7-3 to 7-12, 13-3 to 13-12, 17-14 to 17-19
■ Plan a smart card authentication strategy.	7-3 to 7-12, 13-3 to 13-12
■ Create a password policy for domain users.	3-3 to 13-12
Implement an OU structure.	6-3 to 6-9, 17-20 to 17-27
■ Create an OU.	6-3 to 6-9
■ Delegate permissions for an OU to a user or to a security group.	6-3 to 6-9
■ Move objects within an OU hierarchy.	
Planning and Implementing Group Policy (4.0)	
Plan Group Policy strategy.	10-3 to 10-48, 18-5 to 18-14
■ Plan a Group Policy strategy by using Resultant Set of Policy (RSoP) Planning mode.	10-3 to 10-48
■ Plan a strategy for configuring the user environment by using Group Policy.	10-3 to 10-48
■ Plan a strategy for configuring the computer environment by using Group Policy.	10-3 to 10-48
Configure the user environment by using Group Policy.	10-3 to 10-48, 11-3 to 11-60, 12-3 to 12-48, 13-3 to 13-80, 18-15 to 18-23
■ Distribute software by using Group Policy.	12-3 to 12-48
■ Automatically enroll user certificates by using Group Policy.	13-3 to 13-44
■ Redirect folders by using Group Policy.	11-29 to 11-50
■ Configure user security settings by using Group Policy.	13-3 to 13-44
Deploy a computer environment by using Group Policy.	10-3 to 10-48, 11-3 to 11-60, 12-3 to 12-48, 13-3 to 13-85, 18-15 to 18-23
■ Distribute software by using Group Policy.	12-3 to 12-48
■ Automatically enroll computer certificates by using Group Policy.	13-3 to 13-44
■ Configure computer security settings by using Group Policy.	13-3 to 13-44
Managing and Maintaining Group Policy (5.0)	
Troubleshoot issues related to Group Policy application deployment. Tools might include RSoP and the gpresult command.	12-42 to 12-48, 19-5 to 19-13
Maintain installed software by using Group Policy.	12-35 to 12-41, 19-14 to 19-23
■ Distribute updates to software distributed by Group Policy.	12-35 to 12-41
■ Configure automatic updates for network clients by using Group Policy.	12-35 to 12-41
Troubleshoot the application of Group Policy security settings. Tools might include RSoP and the gpresult command.	13-45 to 13-80, 19-24 to 19-30

Note: Exam objectives are subject to change at any time without prior notice and at Microsoft's sole discretion. Please visit the Microsoft Learning Certification Web site (*www.microsoft.com/learning/mcp/*) for the most current listing of exam objectives.

Microsoft®

MCSE Self-Paced Training Kit (Exam 70-294):

Planning, Implementing, and Maintaining a Microsoft® Windows Server™ 2003 Active Directory® Infrastructure, Second Edition

Jill Spealman, Kurt Hudson, and Melissa Craft with Anthony Steven of Content Master

PUBLISHED BY
Microsoft Press
A Division of Microsoft Corporation
One Microsoft Way
Redmond, Washington 98052-6399

Copyright © 2006 by Microsoft Corporation

Library of Congress Control Number 2006922559

Printed and bound in the United States of America.

3 4 5 6 7 8 9   QWT   1 0 9 8 7

Distributed in Canada by H.B. Fenn and Company Ltd.

A CIP catalogue record for this book is available from the British Library.

Microsoft Press books are available through booksellers and distributors worldwide. For further information about international editions, contact your local Microsoft Corporation office or contact Microsoft Press International directly at fax (425) 936-7329. Visit our Web site at www.microsoft.com/mspress. Send comments to *tkinput@microsoft.com*.

Microsoft, Active Directory, ActiveX, Excel, IntelliMirror, JScript, Microsoft Press, MS-DOS, MSN, NetMeeting, Tahoma, Verdana, Visual Basic, Visual C++, Visual Studio, Windows, Windows Media, Windows NT, and Windows Server are either registered trademarks or trademarks of Microsoft Corporation in the United States and/or other countries. Other product and company names mentioned herein may be the trademarks of their respective owners.

The example companies, organizations, products, domain names, e-mail addresses, logos, people, places, and events depicted herein are fictitious. No association with any real company, organization, product, domain name, e-mail address, logo, person, place, or event is intended or should be inferred.

This book expresses the author's views and opinions. The information contained in this book is provided without any express, statutory, or implied warranties. Neither the authors, Microsoft Corporation, nor its resellers, or distributors will be held liable for any damages caused or alleged to be caused either directly or indirectly by this book.

Product Planner: Ken Jones
Content Development Manager: Maureen Zimmerman
Project Manager: Maria Gargiulo, Karen Szall

Body Part No. X12-21272

About the Authors

Jill Spealman

Jill, a technical writer and instructional designer, is the owner of Wordsmith, Inc., a Chicago-area company that develops training materials. Jill has written six training and certification books for Microsoft Press on Microsoft Windows NT and Microsoft Windows 2000, and she has received national awards for these works from the Society for Technical Communication. She has 16 years of experience developing documentation and training, and has worked for Thomson NETG, Wallace, Waste Management, Rockwell FirstPoint Contact, GAB Robins, and National Forwarding.

Kurt Hudson

Kurt is an instructor, author, and consultant for computer technologies. In recent years, he has concentrated on the areas of computer networking, Active Directory, integrating UNIX and Microsoft Windows, and computer security. Kurt regularly teaches summer programs at Northern Arizona University in Flagstaff, Arizona. He also has taught several courses through Microsoft Research for several other universities, including the University of Colorado (Boulder), Texas A&M, Duke University—Fuqua College of Business, the University of Iowa, the University of California (San Diego), the University of Virginia, the University of North Carolina, Kansas State University (Manhattan), Case Western Reserve University, and the University of Florida (Gainesville).

Kurt has earned many technical certifications, including Microsoft Certified Systems Engineer (MCSE) in Windows 2000, Windows NT 4.0+I, and Windows NT 3.51; Microsoft Certified Systems Administrator (MCSA); Cisco Certified Network Associate (CCNA); Certified Technical Trainer (CTT+); Security+; Network+; A+; and i-Net+. He also has a graduate degree in business management (Masters of Management) from Troy State University in Troy, Alabama. Further, he has written many books on computer-related topics and has contributed to numerous other publications.

Melissa Craft

Melissa (CCNA, MCNE, MCSE, Network+, CNE-3, CNE-4, CNE-GW, CNE-5, CCA) is the vice president and CIO for Dane Holdings, Inc., a financial services corporation in Phoenix, Arizona, where she manages the Web development, local area network (LAN), and wide area network (WAN) for the company. During her career, Melissa has focused her expertise on developing enterprise-wide technology solutions and methodologies focused on client organizations. These technology solutions touch every part of a system's lifecycle, from assessing the need, determining the return on investment, network design, testing, and implementation to operational management and strategic planning. In 1997, Melissa began writing magazine articles on networking and the information technology industry. In 1998, Syngress hired Melissa to contribute to an MCSE certification guide. Since then, Melissa has continued to write about various technology and certification subjects.

Melissa holds a bachelor's degree from the University of Michigan and is a member of the Institute of Electrical and Electronics Engineers (IEEE), the Society of Women Engineers, and American Mensa, Ltd. Melissa currently resides in Glendale, Arizona, with her family: Dan, Justine, and Taylor.

Content Master

Anthony Steven is a technology manager with Content Master, part of the CM Group Ltd. Content Master is a Microsoft Gold Certified Partner that specializes in developing technical content. Anthony is a trainer and consultant, and has worked with the Windows Server family of products for many years, specializing in messaging and management technologies. He has contributed to many technical articles for Microsoft, including the "Security Monitoring and Attack Detection Guide" and the "Identity and Access Management Series." Anthony is married with two children and lives in Nidderdale, Yorkshire, in the United Kingdom.

David Coombes is an associate writer for Content Master. David is a trainer, consultant, and technical author, and has worked with Windows Server products going back to the Windows NT 3.1 days. He has contributed to other Microsoft technical articles and training materials. David is married with two children and lives near Bristol in the United Kingdom.

Paul Captainino is an associate writer for Content Master and a freelance IT consultant and trainer. Paul has worked in IT for more than 20 years, currently specializing in secure infrastructure design and messaging technologies. He has contributed to several Microsoft courses and Microsoft white papers. He has been an MCT for more than 10 years and is an MCSE, an MCSA, and an MCDST. Paul lives with his wife and three children in a small village in Buckinghamshire in the United Kingdom.

Contents at a Glance

Practices

Tables

Troubleshooting Labs

Case Scenario Exercises

Contents

> **What do you think of this book? We want to hear from you!**
>
> Microsoft is interested in hearing your feedback about this publication so we can continually improve our books and learning resources for you. To participate in a brief online survey, please visit: *www.microsoft.com/learning/booksurvey/*

4   Installing and Managing Domains, Trees, and Forests

Part 2   Prepare for the Exam

15   Planning and Implementing an Active Directory Infrastructure (1.0)

**What do you think
of this book?
We want to hear from you!**

Microsoft is interested in hearing your feedback about this
publication so we can continually improve our books and learning
resources for you. To participate in a brief online survey, please visit:
www.microsoft.com/learning/booksurvey/

About This Book

Welcome to *MCSE Self-Paced Training Kit (Exam 70-294): Planning, Implementing, and Maintaining a Microsoft Windows Server 2003 Active Directory Infrastructure,* Second Edition. This training kit introduces you to the Active Directory directory service in Windows Server 2003 with Service Pack 1 (SP1) and prepares you to plan, configure, and administer your Active Directory infrastructure. You will learn to use the Active Directory directory service to centrally manage users, groups, shared folders, and network resources, and to administer the user environment and software with Group Policy. This training kit shows you how to implement and troubleshoot security in a directory services infrastructure and how to monitor and troubleshoot Active Directory performance.

Planning The 70-294 exam includes simulation questions. Simulating a computer running the Windows Server 2003 operating system, these challenging questions provide you with a virtual computer interface through which you need to perform a number of administrative procedures. A simulation question presents a scenario with a list of requirements that you must translate into a set of procedures to perform. For a demonstration of a simulation, see the "Answering Simulation Questions" demo on the companion CD.

Note In this book, the use of "Windows Server 2003 family" and "Windows Server 2003" refers to the family of four products: Microsoft Windows Server 2003, Standard Edition; Microsoft Windows Server 2003, Enterprise Edition; Microsoft Windows Server 2003, Datacenter Edition; and Microsoft Windows Server 2003, Web Edition. However, Windows Server 2003, Web Edition, only partially supports the use of Active Directory. Windows Server 2003, Web Edition, can participate as a member server in an Active Directory–enabled network, but it cannot be used as an Active Directory domain controller.

Intended Audience

This book was developed for information technology (IT) professionals who plan to take the related Microsoft Certified Professional (MCP) exam 70-294, *Planning, Implementing, and Maintaining a Microsoft Windows Server 2003 Active Directory Infrastructure,* as well as IT professionals who need to install, configure, administer, monitor, and troubleshoot Microsoft Windows Server 2003 Active Directory.

> **Note** Exam skills are subject to change without prior notice and at the sole discretion of Microsoft.

Prerequisites

To complete this training kit, you should have the following:

- Experience implementing and administering a network operating system in environments where: from 250 to 5,000 or more users are supported; three or more physical locations are supported; typical network services and resources include messaging, database, file and print, proxy server or firewall, Internet and intranet, remote access, and client computer management; three or more domain controllers are supported; and connectivity needs include connecting branch offices and individual users in remote locations to the corporate network and connecting corporate networks to the Internet

- Experience implementing and administering a desktop operating system

- Experience designing a network infrastructure

About the CD-ROM

For your use, this book includes a companion CD-ROM. This CD-ROM contains a variety of informational aids to complement the book content:

- The Microsoft Press Readiness Review Suite Powered by MeasureUp. This suite of practice tests and objective reviews contains questions of varying degrees of complexity and offers multiple testing modes. You can assess your understanding of the concepts presented in this book and use the results to develop a learning plan that meets your needs.

- An electronic version of this book (eBook). For information about using the eBook, see the section "The eBook" later in this introduction.

- Installation scripts and example files that you will use to perform the hands-on exercises in this book. These include files that demonstrate key concepts and illustrate a specific point, as well as files that are there for your convenience, such as scripts that can be used to reduce the amount of time you spend setting up your system to perform a particular exercise.

- Sample chapters from several Microsoft Press books that give you additional information about Windows Server 2003 and introduce you to other resources that are available from Microsoft Press.

- An overview of Windows Server 2003 Service Pack 1 and Windows Server 2003 R2.

- A free demo: "Answering Simulation Questions."

- Bonus material including white papers and links to a free e-learning course and clinic.

Two additional CD-ROMs contain a 180-day Evaluation Edition of Microsoft Windows Server 2003 with SP1 and R2, Enterprise Edition. You will use SP1 to complete the exercises in this training kit. Do not install R2 until you have completed the training kit exercises; R2 is for your reference only.

> **Important**   The 180-day Evaluation Edition provided with this training is not the full retail product and is provided only for the purposes of training and evaluation. Microsoft Technical Support does not support this Evaluation Edition.

For additional support information regarding this book and the CD-ROM (including answers to commonly asked questions about installation and use), visit the Microsoft Press Technical Support Web site at *http://www.microsoft.com/learning/support/books/*. You can also e-mail *tkinput@microsoft.com* or send a letter to Microsoft Press, Attention: Microsoft Press Technical Support, One Microsoft Way, Redmond, WA 98052-6399.

Features of This Book

This book has two parts. Use Part 1 to learn at your own pace and practice what you've learned with practical exercises. Part 2 contains questions and answers that you can use to test yourself on what you've learned.

Part 1: Learn at Your Own Pace

Each chapter identifies the exam objectives that are covered within the chapter, provides an overview of why the topics matter by identifying how the information applies in the real world, and lists any prerequisites that must be met to complete the lessons presented in the chapter.

The chapters are divided into lessons. Lessons contain practices made up of one or more hands-on exercises. These exercises give you an opportunity to use the skills being presented or explore the part of the application being described. Each lesson also has a set of review questions to test your knowledge of the material covered in that lesson.

After the lessons, you are given an opportunity to apply what you've learned in a case scenario exercise. In this exercise, you work through a multistep solution for a realistic case scenario. You are also given an opportunity to work through a troubleshooting lab that explores difficulties you might encounter when applying what you've learned on the job.

Each chapter ends with a short summary of key concepts and a short section listing key topics and terms that you need to know before taking the exam, summarizing the key learning points with a foucs on the exam.

> **Real World   Helpful Information**
> You will find sidebars like this one that contain related information you might find helpful. "Real World" sidebars contain specific information gained through the experience of IT professionals just like you.

Part 2: Prepare for the Exam

Part 2 helps to familiarize you with the types of questions that you will encounter on the MCP exam. By reviewing the objectives and the sample questions, you can focus on the specific skills that you need to improve before taking the exam.

> **See Also**   For a complete list of Microsoft certification exams and their related objectives, go to *http://www.microsoft.com/learning/mcp/default.asp*.

Part 2 is organized by the exam's objectives. Each chapter covers one of the primary groups of objectives, called *Objective Domains*. Each chapter lists the tested skills you need to master to answer the exam questions and includes a list of further reading to help you improve your ability to perfom the tasks or skills specified by the objectives.

Within each Objective Domain, you will find the related objectives that are covered on the exam. Each objective provides you with several practice exam questions. The answers are accompanied by explanations of each correct and incorrect answer.

> **On the CD**   These questions are also available on the companion CD as a practice test.

Informational Notes

Several types of reader aids appear throughout the training kit.

- **Tip** contains methods of performing a task more quickly or in a not-so-obvious way.

- **Important** contains information that is essential to completing a task.

- **Note** contains supplemental information.

- **Caution** contains valuable information about possible loss of data; be sure to read this information carefully.

- **Warning** contains critical information about possible physical injury; be sure to read this information carefully.

- **See Also** contains references to other sources of information.

- **Planning** contains hints and useful information that should help you plan the implementation.

- **Security Alert** highlights information you need to know to maximize security in your work environment.

- **Exam Tip** flags information you should know before taking the certification exam.

- **Off the Record** contains practical advice about the real-world implications of information presented in the lesson.

Notational Conventions

The following conventions are used throughout this book.

- Characters or commands that you type appear in **bold** type.

- *Italic* in syntax statements indicates placeholders for variable information. *Italic* is also used for newly introduced terms and book titles.

- Names of files and folders appear in Title caps, except when you are to type them directly. Unless otherwise indicated, you can use all lowercase letters when you type a file name in a dialog box or at a command prompt.

- File name extensions appear in all lowercase.

- Acronyms appear in all uppercase.

- Monospace type represents code samples, examples of screen text, or entries that you might type at a command prompt or in initialization files.

- Square brackets [ ] are used in syntax statements to enclose optional items. For example, *[filename]* in command syntax indicates that you can choose to type a file name with the command. Type only the information within the brackets, not the brackets themselves.

- Braces { } are used in syntax statements to enclose required items. Type only the information within the braces, not the braces themselves.

Keyboard Conventions

- A plus sign (+) between two key names means that you must press those keys at the same time. For example, "Press ALT+TAB" means that you hold down ALT while you press TAB.

- A comma (,) between two or more key names means that you must press each of the keys consecutively, not together. For example, "Press ALT, F, X" means that you press and release each key in sequence. "Press ALT+W, L" means that you first press ALT and W at the same time, and then release them and press L.

Getting Started

This training kit contains hands-on exercises to help you learn about Active Directory in a Windows Server 2003 SP1 environment. Use this section to prepare your self-paced training environment. Your environment should meet the system requirements listed at *http://www.microsoft.com/windowsserver2003/evaluation/sysreqs/default.mspx.*

To complete some of these procedures, you must have two networked computers or be connected to a larger network. Both computers must be running Windows Server 2003 SP1, Enterprise Edition.

Caution   Several exercises may require you to make changes to your servers. This may have undesirable results if you are connected to a larger network. If you are connected to a larger network, check with your network administrator before attempting these exercises.

Hardware Requirements

Each computer must have the following minimum hardware configuration.

- Minimum CPU: 133 MHz processor (550 MHz recommended)

- Minimum RAM: 128 MB RAM (256 MB recommended)

- Hard disk space for setup: 1.5 GB–2.0 GB

- CD-ROM or DVD-ROM drive

- Display monitor capable of 800 × 600 resolution or higher

- High-density floppy disk drive

- Microsoft Mouse or compatible pointing device

- Network interface adapter

Software Requirements

The following software is required to complete the procedures in this training kit:

- A copy of the Windows Server 2003 SP1 installation CD-ROM (A 180-day Evaluation Edition of Microsoft Windows Server 2003 with SP1 and R2, Enterprise Edition, is included with this training kit.)

Caution   The 180-day Evaluation Edition provided with this training kit is not the full retail product and is provided only for the purposes of training and evaluation. Microsoft Technical Support does not support these Evaluation Editions. For additional support information regarding this book and the CD-ROMs (including answers to commonly asked questions about installation and use), visit the Microsoft Press Technical Support Web site at *http://www.microsoft.com/learning/support/books/*. You can also e-mail *tkinput@microsoft.com* or send a letter to Microsoft Press, Attn: Microsoft Press Technical Support, One Microsoft Way, Redmond, WA 98502-6399.

Setup Instructions

Set up your computers according to the manufacturer's instructions. Then install Windows Server 2003 SP1, Enterprise Edition, according to the instructions in the next section.

Important   The Evaluation Edition software provided with this training includes SP1. Install SP1 (CD1) to complete the exercises in this training kit. Do not install R2 (CD2) until you have completed the exercises. This version of R2 is for your reference only. It is not covered in the 70-294 exam and, therefore, is not covered in this training kit.

Caution   If your computers are part of a larger network, you must verify with your network administrator that the computer names, domain name, and other information used in setting up your computers as described in Chapter 2, "Installing and Configuring Active Directory," does not conflict with network operations. If it does conflict, ask your network administrator to provide alternative values and use those values throughout the exercises in this book.

Installing Windows Server 2003

To complete the exercises in this training kit, you should install Windows Server 2003 SP1 on two networked computers according to the instructions provided on the installation CD-ROM. During installation, you can use the Windows Server 2003 Setup program to create a partition on your hard disks, on which you should install Windows Server 2003 as a stand-alone server in a workgroup.

> **Note**   You can use an automated installation file, Winnt.sif, on the CD-ROM to install your computers. You'll find a copy of the file in the Unattended folder in the Server1 and Server2 subfolders. If you use these automated installation files, simply copy the appropriate Winnt.sif file onto a floppy disk. Start your computer from the CD-ROM drive. After the system begins to start from CD-ROM, insert the floppy disk with the Winnt.sif file. The installation should proceed without your intervention. The only thing that you must do is type the product key when prompted. Otherwise, the installation of your server is automated. Install Server1 before you install Server2. Otherwise, follow the manual installation method described next.

To install Windows Server 2003

1. Insert the Microsoft Windows Server 2003, Enterprise Edition, CD-ROM into the CD-ROM drive.

2. On the Welcome To Microsoft Windows Server 2003 screen, select Install Windows Server 2003, Enterprise Edition.

3. On the Welcome To Windows Setup page on the Windows Setup dialog box, select New Installation in the Installation Type list, and then click Next.

4. On the License Agreement page on the Windows Setup dialog box, read the license agreement. To proceed, you must select I Accept This Agreement. Click Next.

5. On the Your Product Key page, type the product key that appears on the sticker attached to the installation CD-ROM case, and then click Next.

6. On the Setup Options page, select the appropriate setup options for your organization, and then click Next.

7. On the Upgrade To The Windows NTFS File System page, select the appropriate file system for your setup, and then click Next.

8. On the Get Updated Setup Files, select No, Skip This Step and Continue Installing Windows, and then click Next. The installation procedure copies setup files and restarts your computer in text mode.

9. On the Setup Notification page, press ENTER.

10. On the Welcome To Setup page, press ENTER. Setup searches for previously installed versions of Windows.

11. A new page appears if Setup finds previously installed versions of Windows. Press ESC to continue.

12. On the next page, select the partition on which you want to install Windows Server 2003 SP1, Enterprise Edition, press ENTER, and then press C to continue Setup using

the selected partition. Or, to create a new partition in unpartitioned space, just press c. Then you can install Windows Server 2003 SP1, Enterprise Edition, in the newly partitioned space. Specify the size of the partition (at least 2 GB is recommended) and press ENTER to continue. Be sure to format the partition as NTFS.

Setup examines your disks, copies additional files, and then restarts your computer.

13. Setup installs Windows files and displays messages about the benefits of using Windows Server 2003 SP1, Enterprise Edition. On the Regional and Language Options page, select the appropriate settings for your organization, and then click Next.

14. On the Personalize Your Software page, type your name in the Name box and your organization name in the Organization box, and then click Next.

15. On the Licensing Modes page, click Next.

16. On the Computer Name And Administrator Password page, type **SERVER1** in the Computer Name box. (Type **SERVER2** in the Computer Name box if you are installing Windows Server 2003 SP1, Enterprise Edition on your second computer.) Then type a password in the Administrator Password and Confirm Password boxes. Click Next.

17. On the Modem Dialing Information page, enter the appropriate information about your modem, and then click Next.

18. On the Date And Time Settings page, enter the appropriate information about the date and time and your time zone, and then click Next.

19. Setup installs Windows files and displays messages about the benefits of using Windows Server 2003. On the Networking Settings page, ensure that Typical Settings is selected, and then click Next.

20. On the Workgroup Or Computer Domain page, ensure that No, This Computer Is Not On a Network Or Is On A Network Without A Domain is selected, and that the workgroup name is WORKGROUP, and then click Next.

Setup installs Windows files, displays messages about the benefits of using Windows Server 2003, and then restarts your computer. The newly installed version of Windows Server 2003 SP1, Enterprise Edition is now running.

21. Remove the Windows Server 2003 SP1 installation CD-ROM from the CD-ROM drive.

The Microsoft Press Readiness Review Suite

The companion CD-ROM includes a practice test of 300 sample exam questions and an objective review with an additional 125 questions. Use these tools to reinforce your learning and to identify any areas in which you need to gain more experience before taking the exam.

To install the practice test and objective review

1. Insert the companion CD-ROM into your CD-ROM drive.

> **Note** If AutoRun is disabled on your machine, refer to the Readme.txt file on the companion CD-ROM.

2. Click Readiness Review Suite on the user interface menu and follow the prompts.

The eBook

The companion CD-ROM includes an electronic version of this training kit, as well as bonus material, including sample chapters from several Microsoft Press books and relevant white papers. The eBook and bonus materials are in Portable Document Format (PDF) and can be viewed using Adobe Reader (*http://www.adobe.com*).

To use the eBook

1. Insert the companion CD into your CD-ROM drive.

> **Note** If AutoRun is disabled on your computer, refer to the Readme.txt file on the CD.

2. Click eBook on the user interface menu and follow the prompts. You can also review any of the other PDF files that are provided for your use.

The Microsoft Certified Professional Program

The Microsoft certifications provide the best method to prove your command of current Microsoft products and technologies. The exams and corresponding certifications are developed to validate your mastery of critical competencies as you design and develop, or implement and support, solutions with Microsoft products and technologies. Computer professionals who become Microsoft certified are recognized as experts and are sought after industry-wide. Certification brings a variety of benefits to the individual and to employers and organizations.

> **Off the Record** or a full list of Microsoft certifications, go to *http://www.microsoft.com /learning/itpro/default.asp.*

Technical Support

Every effort has been made to ensure the accuracy of this book and the contents of the companion disc. If you have comments, questions, or ideas regarding this book or the companion disc, please send them to Microsoft Press using either of the following methods:

E-mail: *tkinput@microsoft.com*

Postal Mail: Microsoft Press
Attn: *MCSE Self-Paced Training Kit (Exam 70-294): Planning, Implementing, and Maintaining a Microsoft Windows Server 2003 Active Directory Infrastructure*, Second Edition, Editor
One Microsoft Way
Redmond, WA 98052-6399

For additional support information regarding this book and the CD-ROM (including answers to commonly asked questions about installation and use), visit the Microsoft Press Technical Support Web site at *http://www.microsoft.com/learning/support/books/*. To connect directly to the Microsoft Press Knowledge Base and enter a query, visit *http://www.microsoft.com/mspress/support/search.asp*. For support information regarding Microsoft software, please connect to *http://support.microsoft.com/*.

Evaluation Edition Software Support

The 180-day Evaluation Edition provided with this training is not the full retail product and is provided only for the purposes of training and evaluation. Microsoft and Microsoft Technical Support do not support this Evaluation Edition.

> **Caution**   The Evaluation Edition of Microsoft Windows Server 2003 with SP1 and R2, Enterprise Edition, that is included with this book should not be used on a primary work computer. The Evaluation Edition is unsupported. For online support information relating to the full version of Microsoft Windows Server 2003 R2, Enterprise Edition, that might also apply to the Evaluation Edition, you can connect to *http://support.microsoft.com*.

Information about any issues relating to the use of this Evaluation Edition with this training kit is posted to the Support section of the Microsoft Press Web site (*http://www.microsoft.com/learning/support/books/*). For information about ordering the full version of any Microsoft software, please call Microsoft Sales at (800) 426-9400 or visit *http://www.microsoft.com*.

Microsoft Press Online:
Resources for Microsoft Windows Server 2003
Training Kits, Second Edition

This site provides you with resources that work with your training kit to keep you current and help you prepare for one of the core MCSA (Microsoft Certified Systems Administrator) or MCSE (Microsoft Certified Systems Engineer) certification exams.

Go to http://www.microsoft.com/learning/books/windowsserver2003trainingkits/ to find:

- Updated information for your training kit, when available
- Sample content from additional Microsoft Press books
- A brief survey to provide feedback about your books
- Special offers

At the site, you may also join the Microsoft Press Insiders' club, with the following additional benefits:

- Microsoft Press book in searchable e-Reference form
- Discounts on popular Microsoft Press books
- Updates on changes to the certification exam covered by this Training Kit, when available

Charter membership in the Microsoft Press Insiders' club, which includes e-mail updates about the latest offerings in learning products, special offers, advance notices about discounts at participating booksellers, and exclusive offers. It is the one e-mail you'll be glad to see in your inbox!

Visit *http://www.microsoft.com/learning/books/windowsserver2003trainingkits/*.

Part 1
Learn at Your Own Pace

1 Introduction to Active Directory

Active Directory directory service provides a single point of network resource management, allowing you to add, remove, and relocate users and resources easily. This chapter introduces you to Active Directory concepts and administration tasks and walks you through the steps involved in planning an Active Directory infrastructure.

> **Note** In this book, the use of "Windows Server 2003 family" and "Windows Server 2003" refers to the family of four products: Microsoft Windows Server 2003, Standard Edition; Microsoft Windows Server 2003, Enterprise Edition; Microsoft Windows Server 2003, Datacenter Edition; and Microsoft Windows Server 2003, Web Edition. However, Windows Server 2003, Web Edition only partially supports the use of Active Directory. Windows Server 2003, Web Edition can participate as a member server in an Active Directory-enabled network but cannot be used as an Active Directory domain controller.

Why This Chapter Matters

This chapter introduces you to Active Directory. As you read through the lessons in this chapter, keep in mind that the concepts introduced here are examined in greater detail in later chapters as you learn how to implement and administer Windows Server 2003 Active Directory.

Lessons in this Chapter:

Before You Begin

To complete this chapter, you must be familiar with basic administration concepts used in Microsoft Windows NT or Microsoft Windows 2000.

Lesson 1: Active Directory Overview

Active Directory provides a method for designing a directory structure that meets the needs of your organization. This lesson introduces the concept of a directory service, the use of objects in Active Directory, and the function of each of the Active Directory components.

After this lesson, you will be able to

- Explain the function of a directory service
- Explain the purpose of Active Directory
- Explain the purpose of the schema in Active Directory
- Identify the components of Active Directory
- Describe the function of Active Directory components
- Explain the purpose of the global catalog in Active Directory

Estimated lesson time: 30 minutes

Understanding Directory Services

A directory is a stored collection of information about objects that are related to one another in some way. For example, an e-mail address book stores names of users or entities and their corresponding e-mail addresses. The e-mail address book listing might also contain a street address or other information about the user or entity.

In a distributed computing system or a public computer network such as the Internet, there are many objects stored in a directory, such as file servers, printers, fax servers, applications, databases, and users. Users must be able to locate and use these objects. Administrators must be able to manage how these objects are used. A directory service stores all the information needed to use and manage these objects in a centralized location, simplifying the process of locating and managing these resources. A directory service differs from a directory in that it is both the source of the information and the mechanism that makes the information available to the users.

A directory service acts as the main switchboard of the network operating system. It is the central authority that manages the identities and brokers the relationships between distributed resources, enabling them to work together. Because a directory service supplies these fundamental operating system functions, it must be tightly coupled with the management and security mechanisms of the operating system to ensure the integrity and privacy of the network. It also plays a critical role in an organization's ability to define and maintain the network infrastructure, perform system administration, and control the overall user experience of a company's information systems.

Why Have a Directory Service?

A directory service provides the means to organize and simplify access to resources of a networked computer system. Users and administrators might not know the exact name of the objects they need. However, they might know one or more characteristics of the objects in question. As illustrated in Figure 1-1, they can use a directory service to query the directory for a list of objects that match known characteristics. For example, "Find all color printers on the third floor" queries the directory for all color printer objects that are associated with the third floor characteristic (or maybe a location characteristic that has been set to "third floor"). A directory service makes it possible to find an object based on one or more of its characteristics.

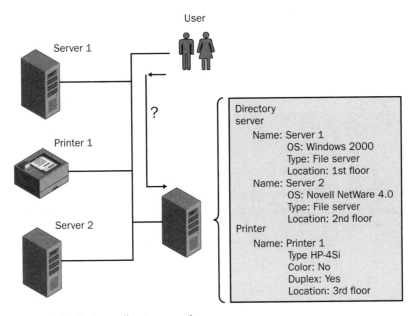

Figure 1-1   Using a directory service

A directory service is both an administration tool and an end user tool. As a network becomes larger, more objects must be managed and the directory service becomes a necessity.

The Windows Server 2003 Directory Service

Active Directory is the directory service included in the Windows Server 2003 family. Active Directory includes the directory, which stores information about network resources, as well as all the services that make the information available and useful. Active Directory is also the directory service included in Windows 2000.

Active Directory Services Features

Active Directory in the Windows Server 2003 family is a significant enhancement over the flat domain model provided in Windows NT. Active Directory is integrated within the Windows Server 2003 family and offers the following features:

- **Centralized data store** All data in Active Directory resides in a single, distributed data repository, allowing users easy access to the information from any location. A single distributed data store requires less administration and duplication and improves the availability and organization of data.

- **Scalability** Active Directory enables you to scale the directory to meet business and network requirements through the configuration of domains and trees and the placement of domain controllers. Active Directory allows millions of objects per domain and uses indexing technology and advanced replication techniques to speed performance.

- **Extensibility** The structure of the Active Directory database (the schema) can be expanded to allow customized types of information.

- **Manageability** In contrast to the flat domain model used in Windows NT, Active Directory is based on hierarchical organizational structures. These organizational structures make it easier for you to control administrative privileges and other security settings, and to make it easier for your users to locate network resources such as files and printers.

- **Integration with the Domain Name System (DNS)** Active Directory uses DNS, an Internet standard service that translates easily readable host names to numeric Internet Protocol (IP) addresses. Although separate and implemented differently for different purposes, Active Directory and DNS have the same hierarchical structure. Active Directory clients use DNS to locate domain controllers. When using the Windows Server 2003 DNS service, primary DNS zones can be stored in Active Directory, enabling replication to other Active Directory domain controllers.

- **Client configuration management** Active Directory provides new technologies for managing client configuration issues, such as user mobility and hard disk failures, with a minimum of administration and user downtime.

- **Policy-based administration** In Active Directory, policies are used to define the permitted actions and settings for users and computers across a given site, domain, or organizational unit. Policy-based management simplifies tasks such as operating system updates, application installation, user profiles, and desktop-system lock down.

- **Replication of information** Active Directory provides multimaster replication technology to ensure information availability, fault tolerance, load balancing, and other performance benefits. Multimaster replication enables you to update the directory at any domain controller and replicates directory changes to any other domain controller. Because multiple domain controllers are employed, replication continues, even if any single domain controller stops working.

- **Flexible, secure authentication and authorization**   Active Directory authentication and authorization services provide protection for data while minimizing barriers to doing business over the Internet. Active Directory supports multiple authentication protocols, such as the Kerberos version 5 protocol, Secure Sockets Layer (SSL) version 3, and Transport Layer Security (TLS) using X.509 version 3 certificates. In addition, Active Directory provides security groups that span domains.

- **Security integration**   Active Directory is integrated with Windows Server 2003 security. Access control can be defined for each object in the directory and on each property of each object. Security policies can be applied locally, or to a specified site, domain, or organizational unit.

- **Directory-enabled applications and infrastructure**   Features within Active Directory make it easier for you to configure and manage applications and other directory-enabled network components. In addition, Active Directory provides a powerful development environment through Active Directory Service Interfaces (ADSI).

- **Interoperability with other directory services**   Active Directory is based on standard directory access protocols, including *Lightweight Directory Access Protocol (LDAP)* version 3, and the *Name Service Provider Interface (NSPI)*, and can interoperate with other directory services employing these protocols. Because the LDAP directory access protocol is an industry-standard directory service protocol, programs can be developed using LDAP to share Active Directory information with other directory services that also support LDAP. The NSPI protocol, which is used by Microsoft Exchange Server 4 and 5.*x* clients, is supported by Active Directory to provide compatibility with the Exchange directory.

- **Signed and encrypted LDAP traffic**   By default, Active Directory tools in Windows Server 2003 sign and encrypt all LDAP traffic by default. Signing LDAP traffic guarantees that the packaged data comes from a known source and that it has not been tampered with.

See Also   For those readers already familiar with the features of Active Directory for Windows 2000, a detailed listing of the new Active Directory features available in the Windows Server 2003 family is located in Appendix A, "Active Directory Features in the Windows Server 2003 Family."

Active Directory Objects

The data stored in Active Directory, such as information about users, printers, servers, databases, groups, computers, and security policies, is organized into objects. An *object* is a distinct named set of attributes that represents a network resource. Object attributes are characteristics of objects in the directory. For example, the attributes of a user account object might include the user's first name, last name, and logon name, while the attributes of a computer account object might include the computer name and description (see Figure 1-2).

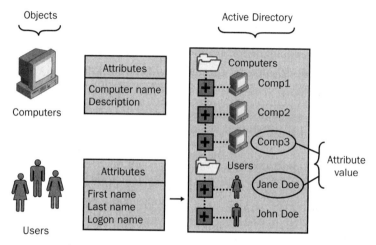

Figure 1-2   Active Directory objects and attributes

Some objects, known as *containers*, can contain other objects. For example, a domain is a container object that can contain objects such as user and computer accounts. In Figure 1-2, the Users folder is a container that contains user account objects.

Active Directory Schema

The Active Directory schema defines objects that can be stored in Active Directory. The *schema* is a list of definitions that determines the kinds of objects and the types of information about those objects that can be stored in Active Directory. Because the schema definitions themselves are stored as objects, they can be administered in the same manner as the rest of the objects in Active Directory.

The schema is defined by two types of objects: schema class objects (also referred to as schema classes) and schema attribute objects (also referred to as schema attributes). As shown in Figure 1-3, class objects and attribute objects are defined in separate lists within the schema. Schema class objects and attribute objects are collectively referred to as *schema objects* or *metadata*.

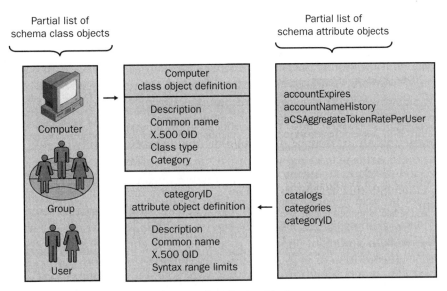

Figure 1-3 Schema class objects and attribute objects

Schema class objects describe the possible Active Directory objects that can be created. A schema class functions as a template for creating new Active Directory objects. Each schema class is a collection of schema attribute objects. When you create a schema class, the schema attributes store the information that describes the object. The User class, for example, is composed of many schema attributes, including Network Address and Home Directory. Every object in Active Directory is an instance of a schema class object.

Schema attribute objects define the schema class objects with which they are associated. Each schema attribute is defined only once and can be used in multiple schema classes. For example, the Description attribute is used in many schema classes, but is defined only once in the schema, which ensures consistency.

A set of basic schema classes and attributes is shipped with Active Directory. Experienced developers and network administrators can dynamically extend the schema by defining new classes and attributes for existing classes. For example, if you need to provide information about users that is not currently defined in the schema, you must extend the schema for the User class. However, extending the schema is an advanced operation that could have serious consequences. Because schema cannot be deleted, but only deactivated, and a schema is automatically replicated, you must plan and prepare carefully before extending the schema.

Active Directory Components

Various Active Directory components are used to build a directory structure that meets the needs of your organization. The following Active Directory components represent logical structures in an organization: domains, organizational units (OUs), trees, and forests. The following Active Directory components represent physical structures in an organization: sites (physical subnets) and domain controllers. Active Directory completely separates the logical structure from the physical structure.

Logical Structures

In Active Directory, you organize resources in a logical structure—a structure that mirrors organizational models—using domains, OUs, trees, and forests. Grouping resources logically allows you to easily find a resource by its name rather than by remembering its physical location. Because you group resources logically, Active Directory makes the network's physical structure transparent to users. Figure 1-4 illustrates the relationship of the Active Directory domains, OUs, trees, and forests.

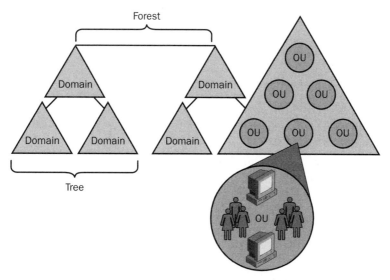

Figure 1-4   The relationship of Active Directory domains, OUs, trees, and forests

Domains   The core unit of logical structure in Active Directory is the *domain*, which can store millions of objects. Objects stored in a domain are those considered vital to the network. These vital objects are items the members of the networked community need in order to do their jobs: printers, documents, e-mail addresses, databases, users, distributed components, and other resources. All network objects exist within a domain, and each domain stores information only about the objects it contains. Active Directory is made up of one or more domains. A domain can span more than one physical location. Domains share the following characteristics:

- All network objects exist within a domain, and each domain stores information only about the objects that it contains.

- Access to domain objects is governed by access control lists (ACLs), which contain the permissions associated with the objects. Such permissions control which users can gain access to an object and what type of access they can gain. In the Windows Server 2003 family, objects include files, folders, shares, printers, and other Active Directory objects. None of the security policies and settings—such as administrative rights, security policies, and ACLs—can cross from one domain to another. You, as the domain administrator, have absolute rights to set policies only within your domain.

The *domain functional level* (known as *domain mode* in Windows 2000) provides a way to enable domain-wide Active Directory features within your network environment. Four domain functional levels are available: Windows 2000 mixed (default), Windows 2000 native, Windows Server 2003 interim, and Windows Server 2003. The Windows 2000 mixed functional level allows a Windows Server 2003 domain controller to interact with domain controllers in the same domain running Windows NT 4, Windows 2000, or the Windows Server 2003 family. The Windows 2000 native functional level allows a Windows Server 2003 domain controller to interact with domain controllers in the domain running Windows 2000 or Windows Server 2003. The Windows Server 2003 interim functional level allows a Windows Server 2003 domain controller to interact with domain controllers in the domain running Windows NT 4 or Windows Server 2003. The Windows Server 2003 functional level allows a Windows Server 2003 domain controller to interact only with domain controllers in the domain running Windows Server 2003. You can raise the functional level of a domain only if the domain controllers in the domain are running the appropriate version of Windows. See Chapter 3, "Administering Active Directory," for details about raising domain functional levels.

As an administrator, you must create a domain structure to reflect your company's organization. See Lesson 3, "Planning the Active Directory Infrastructure Design," to learn the basics of domain design. See Chapter 4, "Installing and Managing Domains, Trees, and Forests," for details about creating domains.

OUs   An *OU* is a container used to organize objects within a domain into a logical administrative group. OUs provide a means for handling administrative tasks, such as the administration of users and resources, as they are the smallest scope to which you can delegate administrative authority. An OU can contain objects such as user accounts, groups, computers, printers, applications, file shares, and other OUs from the same domain. The OU hierarchy within a domain is independent of the OU hierarchy structure of other domains—each domain can implement its own OU hierarchy. By adding OUs to other OUs, or *nesting*, you can provide administrative control in a hierarchical fashion.

As an administrator, you must create an OU structure to reflect your company's organization. See Lesson 3, "Planning the Active Directory Infrastructure Design," to learn the basics of OU design. See Chapter 6, "Implementing an OU Structure," to learn about implementing an OU structure.

In Figure 1-5, the *microsoft.com* domain mirrors the organization of a shipping company and contains three OUs: US, Orders, and Disp, where Orders and Disp are nested within the US OU. In the summer months the number of shipping orders taken increases, and management has requested the addition of a subadministrator for the Orders department. The subadministrator must have permission only to create user accounts and provide users with access to Orders department files and shared printers. Rather than creating another domain, the request can be met by assigning the subadministrator the appropriate permissions within the Orders OU.

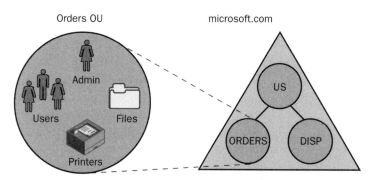

Figure 1-5   Using an OU to handle administrative tasks

If the subadministrator is later required to create user accounts in the US, Orders, and Disp OUs, you could grant the administrator the appropriate permissions separately within each OU. However, because the Orders and Disp OUs are nested in the US OU, a more efficient method is to assign permissions once in the US OU, and allow them to be inherited by the Orders and Disp OUs. By default, all child objects (the Orders and Disp OUs) within Active Directory inherit permissions from their parents (the US OU). Granting permissions at a higher level and using inheritance capabilities can reduce administrative tasks.

Trees   A *tree* is a grouping or hierarchical arrangement of one or more Windows Server 2003 domains that you create by adding one or more child domains to an existing parent domain. Domains in a tree share a contiguous namespace and a hierarchical naming structure. Namespaces are covered in detail in the next lesson. Following DNS standards, the domain name of a child domain is the relative name of that child domain appended with the name of the parent domain. In Figure 1-6, *microsoft.com* is the parent domain and *us.microsoft.com* and *uk.microsoft.com* are its child domains. The child domain of *uk.microsoft.com* is *sls.uk.microsoft.com*. By creating a hierarchy of domains in a tree, you can retain security and allow for administration within an OU or within a single domain of a tree. The tree structure easily accommodates organizational changes.

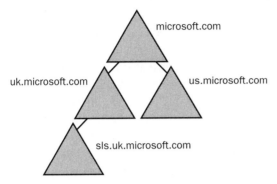

Figure 1-6   A domain tree

As an administrator, you must create a tree structure to reflect your company's organization. See Lesson 3, "Planning the Active Directory Infrastructure Design," to learn the basics of tree design. See Chapter 4, "Installing and Managing Domains, Trees, and Forests," for details about creating trees.

Forests   A *forest* is a grouping or hierarchical arrangement of one or more separate, completely independent domain trees. As such, forests have the following characteristics:

- All domains in a forest share a common schema.
- All domains in a forest share a common global catalog.
- All domains in a forest are linked by implicit two-way transitive trusts.
- Trees in a forest have different naming structures, according to their domains.
- Domains in a forest operate independently, but the forest enables communication across the entire organization.

In Figure 1-7, the *microsoft.com* and *msn.com* trees form a forest. The namespace is contiguous only within each tree.

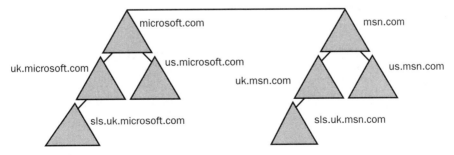

Figure 1-7   A forest of trees

The *forest functional level* provides a way to enable forest-wide Active Directory features within your network environment. Three forest functional levels are available: Windows 2000 (default), Windows Server 2003 interim, and Windows Server 2003. If you are upgrading your first Windows NT domain so that it becomes the first domain in a new Windows Server 2003 forest, you can choose Windows Server 2003 interim. The Windows Server 2003 interim forest functional level supports more features than the Windows 2000 forest functional level but fewer features than the Windows Server 2003 forest functional level. To enable all the forest-wide features, all domain controllers in the forest must be running Windows Server 2003, and the forest functional level must be raised to Windows Server 2003. Before raising the forest functional level to Windows Server 2003, you must verify that all domains in the forest are set to the domain functional level of Windows 2000 native or Windows Server 2003. Note that domains that are set to the domain functional level of Windows 2000 native will automatically be raised to Windows Server 2003 at the same time the forest functional level is raised to Windows Server 2003. See Chapter 3, "Administering Active Directory," for details about raising forest functional levels.

As an administrator, you must create a forest structure to reflect your company's organization. See Lesson 3, "Planning the Active Directory Infrastructure Design," to learn the basics of forest design. See Chapter 4, "Installing and Managing Domains, Trees, and Forests," for details about creating forests.

Physical Structures

The physical components of Active Directory are sites and domain controllers. As an administrator, you use these components to develop a directory structure that mirrors the physical structure of your organization.

Sites A *site* is a combination of one or more IP subnets connected by a highly reliable and fast link to localize as much network traffic as possible. Typically, a site has the same boundaries as a local area network (LAN). When you group subnets on your network, you should combine only subnets that have fast, cheap, and reliable network connections with one another. "Fast" network connections are at least 512 kilobits per second (Kbps). An available bandwidth (the average amount of bandwidth that is available for use after normal network traffic is handled) of 128 Kbps and higher is sufficient for a site.

With Active Directory, sites are not part of the namespace. When you browse the logical namespace, you see computers and users grouped into domains and OUs, not sites. Sites contain only computer objects and connection objects used to configure replication between sites. As shown in Figure 1-8, a single domain can span one or more geographical sites, and a single site can include user accounts and computers belonging to multiple domains.

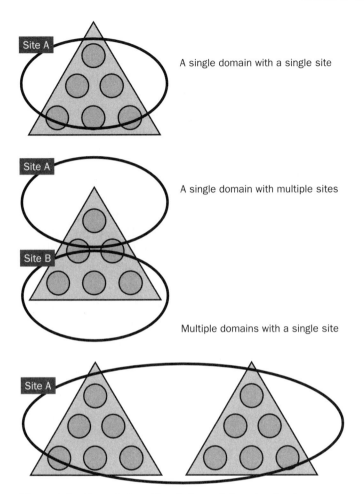

A single domain with a single site

A single domain with multiple sites

Multiple domains with a single site

Figure 1-8   The relationship of site and domain structures

As an administrator, you must create a site structure to reflect your company's organization. See Lesson 3, "Planning the Active Directory Infrastructure Design," to learn the basics of site design. See Chapter 5, "Configuring Sites and Managing Replication," for details about configuring sites.

Domain Controllers   A *domain controller* is a computer running Windows Server 2003 that stores a replica of the domain directory (local domain database). Because a domain can contain one or more domain controllers, each domain controller in a domain has a complete replica of the domain's portion of the directory. A domain controller can service only one domain. A domain controller also authenticates user logon attempts and maintains the security policy for a domain.

The following list describes the functions of domain controllers:

■ Each domain controller stores a complete copy of all Active Directory information for that domain, manages changes to that information, and replicates those changes to other domain controllers in the same domain.

- Domain controllers in a domain automatically replicate directory information for all objects in the domain to each other. When you perform an action that causes an update to Active Directory, you are actually making the change at one of the domain controllers. That domain controller then replicates the change to all other domain controllers within the domain. You can control replication of traffic between domain controllers in the network by specifying how often replication occurs and the amount of data that each domain controller replicates at one time.

- Domain controllers immediately replicate certain important updates, such as the disabling of a user account.

- Active Directory uses multimaster replication, in which no one domain controller is the master domain controller. Instead, all domain controllers within a domain are peers, and each domain controller contains a copy of the directory database that can be written to. Domain controllers can hold different information for short periods of time until all domain controllers have synchronized changes to Active Directory.

- Although Active Directory supports multimaster replication, some changes are impractical to perform in multimaster fashion. One or more domain controllers can be assigned to perform single-master replication (operations not permitted to occur at different places in a network at the same time). *Operations master roles* are special roles assigned to one or more domain controllers in a domain to perform single-master replication.

- Domain controllers detect collisions, which can occur when an attribute is modified on a domain controller before a change to the same attribute on another domain controller is completely propagated. Collisions are detected by comparing each attribute's property version number, a number specific to an attribute that is initialized upon creation of the attribute. Active Directory resolves the collision by replicating the changed attribute with the higher property version number.

- Having more than one domain controller in a domain provides fault tolerance. If one domain controller is offline, another domain controller can provide all required functions, such as recording changes to Active Directory.

- Domain controllers manage all aspects of users' domain interaction, such as locating Active Directory objects and validating user logon attempts.

As an administrator, you must place domain controllers in sites to reflect your organization's physical structure and optimize replication and authentication. See Lesson 3, "Planning the Active Directory Infrastructure Design," to learn the basics of domain controller placement. See Chapter 2, "Installing and Configuring Active Directory," for details about creating domain controllers.

Catalog Services—The Global Catalog

Active Directory allows users and administrators to find objects such as files, printers, or users in their own domain. However, finding objects outside of the domain and across the enterprise requires a mechanism that allows the domains to act as one entity. A catalog service contains selected information about every object in all domains in the directory, which is useful in performing searches across an enterprise. The global catalog is the catalog service provided by Active Directory.

The *global catalog* is the central repository of information about objects in a tree or forest. By default, a global catalog is created automatically on the initial domain controller in the first domain in the forest. A domain controller that holds a copy of the global catalog is called a *global catalog server*. You can designate any domain controller in the forest as a global catalog server. Active Directory uses multimaster replication to replicate the global catalog information between global catalog servers in other domains. It stores a full replica of all object attributes in the directory for its host domain and a partial replica of all object attributes contained in the directory for every domain in the forest. The partial replica stores attributes most frequently used in search operations (such as a user's first and last names, logon name, and so on). Attributes are marked or unmarked for replication in the global catalog when they are defined in the Active Directory schema. Object attributes replicated to the global catalog inherit the same permissions as in source domains, ensuring that data in the global catalog is secure.

Global Catalog Functions

The global catalog performs the following two key functions:

- It enables a user to log on to a network by providing universal group membership information to a domain controller when a logon process is initiated.

- It enables finding directory information regardless of which domain in the forest actually contains the data.

When a user logs on to the network, the global catalog provides universal group membership information for the account to the domain controller processing the user logon information. If there is only one domain controller in a domain, the domain controller holds the global catalog server. If there are multiple domain controllers in the network, one domain controller is configured to hold the global catalog. If a global catalog is not available when a user initiates a network logon process, the user is able to log on only to the local computer unless the site has been specifically configured to cache universal group membership lookups when processing user logon attempts.

 Tip   If a user is a member of the Domain Admins group, he or she is able to log on to the network even when the global catalog is not available.

The global catalog is designed to respond to user and programmatic queries about objects anywhere in the domain tree or forest with maximum speed and minimum network traffic. Because a single global catalog contains information about all objects in all domains in the forest, a query about an object that is not contained in the local domain can be resolved by a global catalog server in the domain in which the query is initiated. Thus, finding information in the directory does not produce unnecessary query traffic across domain boundaries.

The Query Process

A *query* is a specific request made by a user to the global catalog in order to retrieve, modify, or delete Active Directory data. The following steps, illustrated in Figure 1-9, describe the query process:

1. The client queries its DNS server for the location of the global catalog server.

2. The DNS server searches for the global catalog server location and returns the IP address of the domain controller designated as the global catalog server.

3. The client queries the IP address of the domain controller designated as the global catalog server. The query is sent to port 3268 on the domain controller; standard Active Directory queries are sent to port 389.

4. The global catalog server processes the query. If the global catalog contains the attribute of the object being searched for, the global catalog server provides a response to the client. If the global catalog does not contain the attribute of the object being searched for, the query is referred to Active Directory.

You can configure any domain controller or designate additional domain controllers as global catalog servers. When considering which domain controllers to designate as global catalog servers, base your decision on the ability of your network structure to handle replication and query traffic.

As an administrator, you must place global catalog servers in sites to provide quick responses to user inquiries, as well as redundancy. See Lesson 3, "Planning the Active Directory Infrastructure Design," to learn the basics of designing global catalog server placement. See Chapter 5, "Configuring Sites and Managing Replication," for details about configuring global catalog servers.

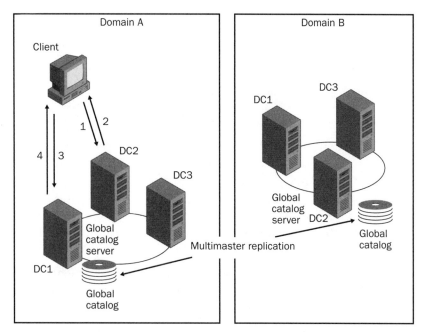

Figure 1-9   The query process

Lesson Review

The following questions are intended to reinforce key information presented in this lesson. If you are unable to answer a question, review the lesson and then try the question again. Answers to the questions can be found in the "Questions and Answers" section at the end of this chapter.

1. How is a directory service different from a directory?

_____

_____

2. How is Active Directory scalable?

_____

_____

3. What is multimaster replication?

_____

_____

4. Name the Active Directory components used to represent an organization's logical structure.

_____

_____

5. Name the physical components of Active Directory.

_____

_____

6. What is the function of the global catalog?

_____

_____

Lesson Summary

- A directory service stores all the information needed to use and manage system objects in a centralized location, simplifying the process of locating and managing these resources.

- Data stored in Active Directory is organized into objects, which have attributes. The Active Directory schema defines objects that can be stored in Active Directory. Schema classes and attributes define the Active Directory schema.

- The logical structures in an organization are represented by the following Active Directory components: domains, OUs, trees, and forests.

- The physical components of Active Directory are sites and domain controllers.

- The global catalog is the central repository of information about objects in a tree or forest.

Lesson 2: Understanding Active Directory Concepts and Administration Tasks

In the Windows Server 2003 family and Active Directory, there are several new concepts and some changes to the concepts used in Windows NT. These concepts include replication, trust relationships, change and configuration management, group policies, DNS, and object naming. It is important that you understand the meaning of these concepts as they apply to Active Directory. In addition, you should also familiarize yourself with the Active Directory administration tasks, which correspond to the chapters in this training kit.

After this lesson, you will be able to

- Explain Active Directory replication
- Explain the security relationships between domains in a tree (trusts)
- Explain the components of change and configuration management
- Explain the purpose and function of Group Policy
- Describe how DNS is used by Active Directory
- Describe how objects are named in Active Directory
- Describe the tasks required for Active Directory administration

Estimated lesson time: 20 minutes

Replication

Users and services should be able to access directory information at any time from any computer in the domain tree or forest. *Replication* ensures that changes to a domain controller are reflected in all domain controllers within a domain. Directory information is replicated to domain controllers both within and among sites.

What Information Is Replicated

The information stored in the directory (in the Ntds.dit file) is logically partitioned into four categories. Each of these information categories is referred to as a *directory partition*. A directory partition is also referred to as a *naming context*. These directory partitions are the units of replication. The directory contains the following partitions:

- **Schema partition**   This partition defines the objects that can be created in the directory and the attributes those objects can have. This data is common to all domains in a forest and is replicated to all domain controllers in a forest.

- **Configuration partition**   This partition describes the logical structure of the deployment, including data such as domain structure or replication topology. This data is common to all domains in a forest and is replicated to all domain controllers in a forest.

- **Domain partition**   This partition describes all of the objects in a domain. This data is domain-specific and is not replicated to any other domains. However, the data is replicated to every domain controller in that domain.

- **Application Directory partition**   This partition stores dynamic application-specific data in Active Directory without significantly affecting network performance by enabling you to control the scope of replication and the placement of replicas. The application directory partition can contain any type of object except security principals (users, groups, and computers). Data can be explicitly rerouted to administrator-specified domain controllers within a forest in order to prevent unnecessary replication traffic, or it can be set to replicate everything to all domain controllers in the same fashion as the schema, configuration, and domain partitions.

A domain controller stores and replicates:

- The schema partition data for a forest.

- The configuration partition data for all domains in a forest.

- The domain partition data (all directory objects and properties) for its domain. This data is replicated to additional domain controllers in the domain. For the purpose of finding information, a partial replica containing commonly used attributes of all objects in the domain is replicated to the global catalog.

A global catalog stores and replicates:

- The schema partition data for a forest

- The configuration partition data for all domains in a forest

- A partial replica containing commonly used attributes for all directory objects in the forest (replicated between global catalog servers only)

- A full replica containing all attributes for all directory objects in the domain in which the global catalog is located

> **Caution**   Extensions to schema in a global catalog should be approached carefully. Schema extensions can have disastrous effects on large networks because the extensions cannot be deleted (only disabled) and because of the large amount of network traffic generated as the extensions are synchronized throughout the forest.

How Information Is Replicated

Active Directory replicates information in two ways: *intrasite* (within a site) and *intersite* (between sites). The need for up-to-date directory information is balanced with the limitations imposed by available network bandwidth.

Intrasite Replication   Within a site, a Windows Server 2003 service known as the *knowledge consistency checker (KCC)* automatically generates a topology for replication among domain controllers in the same domain using a ring structure. The KCC is a built-in process that runs on all domain controllers. The topology defines the path for directory updates to flow from one domain controller to another until all domain controllers in the site receive the directory updates. The KCC determines which servers are best suited to replicate with each other, and designates certain domain controllers as replication partners on the basis of connectivity, history of successful replication, and the matching of full and partial replicas. Domain controllers can have more than one replication partner. The KCC then builds connection objects that represent replication connections between the replication partners.

The ring structure ensures that there are at least two replication paths from one domain controller to another; if one domain controller is down temporarily, replication still continues to all other domain controllers, as shown in Figure 1-10.

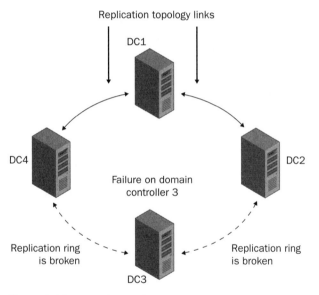

Figure 1-10   Intrasite replication topology

The KCC analyzes the replication topology within a site every 15 minutes to ensure that it still works. If you add or remove a domain controller from the network or a site, the KCC reconfigures the topology to reflect the change.

When more than seven domain controllers are added to a site, the KCC creates additional connection objects across the ring structure so that if a change occurs at any one domain controller, replication partners are available to ensure that no domain controller is more than three replication hops from another domain controller, as shown in Figure 1-11. These optimizing connections are created at random and are not necessarily created on every domain controller.

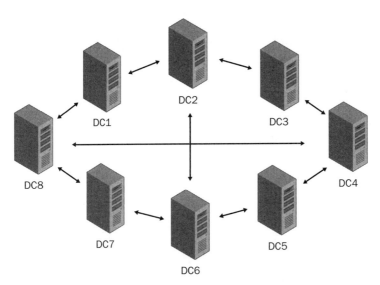

Figure 1-11   A maximum of three replication hops between domain controllers, due to the addition of connection objects by the KCC

Intersite Replication   To ensure replication between sites, you must connect them manually by creating site links. Site links represent network connections and allow replication to occur. A single KCC per site generates all connections between sites. Active Directory uses the network connection information to generate connection objects that provide efficient replication and fault tolerance, as shown in Figure 1-12.

You provide information about the replication transport used, cost of a site link, times when the link is available for use, and how often the link should be used. Active Directory uses this information to determine which site link is used to replicate information. Customizing replication schedules so replication occurs during specific times, such as when network traffic is light, makes replication more efficient.

As an administrator, you must configure sites and replication to ensure that the most up-to-date information is available to users. Replication and site link configuration are discussed in more detail in Chapter 5, "Configuring Sites and Managing Replication."

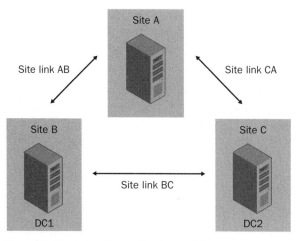

Figure 1-12   Intersite replication topology

Trust Relationships

A *trust* relationship is a link between two domains in which the trusting domain honors the logon authentication of the trusted domain, as shown in Figure 1-13. Users and applications are authenticated in the Windows Server 2003 family using one of two trust protocols: Kerberos version 5 or NT LAN Manager (NTLM). The Kerberos version 5 protocol is the default protocol for computers running Windows Server 2003. If any computer involved in a transaction does not support Kerberos version 5, the NTLM protocol is used. A trust relationship is also permitted with any MIT Kerberos version 5 realm. There are two domains in a trust relationship—the trusting and the trusted domain.

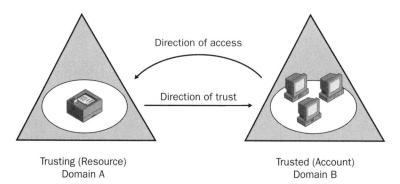

Figure 1-13   Trusting and trusted domains linked with a one-way trust

Trusts have the following characteristics:

- **Method of creation**   Trusts can be created manually (explicitly) or automatically (implicitly). Not all trusts can be created both ways.

- **Transitivity**   Trusts can be not bound by the domains in the trust relationship (transitive), or they can be bound by the domains in the trust relationship (non-transitive). For example, a transitive trust means that if a Domain A trusts Domain

B and Domain B trusts Domain C, then Domain A trusts Domain C. Similarly, a nontransitive trust means that if Domain A trusts Domain B and Domain B trusts Domain C, there is no trust relationship between Domain A and Domain C.

- **Direction**   Trusts can be one-way or two-way. A one-way trust is a single trust relationship, where Domain A trusts Domain B, as shown in Figure 1-13. One-way relationships can be nontransitive or transitive depending on the type of trust being created. In a two-way trust, Domain A trusts Domain B and Domain B trusts Domain A. This means that authentication requests can be passed between the two domains in both directions.

In the Windows Server 2003 family, Active Directory supports the following forms of trust relationships:

- **Tree-root trust**   A *tree-root trust* is implicitly established when you add a new tree root domain to a forest. For example, in Figure 1-14, a tree-root trust is established between Domain A and Domain 1 when Domain 1, a new tree root domain, is added to the forest. The trust is created between the domain you are creating (the new tree root) and the existing forest root domain. A tree-root trust can be set up only between the roots of two trees in the same forest. The trust is transitive and two-way.

- **Parent-child trust**   A *parent-child trust* relationship is implicitly established when you create a new child domain in a tree. For example, in Figure 1-14, a parent-child trust is established between Domain 1 and Domain 2 when Domain 2, a new child domain, is added to the tree. The Active Directory installation process automatically creates a trust relationship between the new domain and the domain that immediately precedes it in the namespace hierarchy (for example, *uk.microsoft.com* is created as the child of *microsoft.com*). As a result, a domain joining a tree immediately has trust relationships established with every domain in the tree. These trust relationships make all objects in the domains of the tree available to all other domains in the tree. The trust is transitive and two-way.

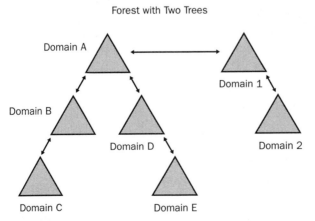

Figure 1-14   Domain structure showing tree-root and parent-child trusts

- **Shortcut trust**   A *shortcut trust* must be explicitly created by a systems administrator between two domains in a forest. This trust is used to improve user logon times, which can be slow when two domains are logically distant from each other in a forest or tree hierarchy. The trust is transitive and can be one-way or two-way.

- **External trust**   An *external trust* must be explicitly created by a systems administrator between Windows Server 2003 domains that are in different forests, or between a Windows Server 2003 domain and a domain whose domain controller is running Windows NT 4 or earlier. This trust is used when users need access to resources located in a Windows NT 4 domain or in a domain located within a separate forest, which cannot be joined by a forest trust. The trust is nontransitive and can be one-way or two-way.

- **Forest trust**   A *forest trust* must be explicitly created by a systems administrator between two forest root domains. This trust allows all domains in one forest to transitively trust all domains in another forest. A forest trust is not transitive across three or more forests. For example, forest A trusts forest B and forest B trusts forest C. There is no trust relationship between forest A and forest C. The trust is transitive between two forests only and can be one-way or two-way. Forest trusts are only available when the forest is at the Windows Server 2003 functional level.

- **Realm trust**   A *realm trust* must be explicitly created by a systems administrator between a non–Windows Kerberos realm and a Windows Server 2003 domain. This trust provides interoperability between the Windows Server 2003 domain and any realm used in Kerberos version 5 implementations. The trust can be transitive or nontransitive and one-way or two-way.

As an administrator, you must plan trust relationships to provide users with the access to resources they require. See Chapter 4, "Installing and Managing Domains, Trees, and Forests," for details about planning trust relationships.

Change and Configuration Management

Change and configuration management is a set of Windows Server 2003 features that simplify computer management tasks such as

- Managing the configuration of each user's desktop
- Managing how software is deployed and installed on personal computers to ensure that users have the software that they require to perform their jobs
- Installing an initial operating system on a new computer
- Replacing computers

Change and configuration management includes the User Data Management, Software Installation and Maintenance, User Settings Management, and Computer Settings Management features, which are collectively known as the IntelliMirror management technologies. Change and configuration management also includes the Remote Operating System (OS) Installation technologies.

The IntelliMirror Management Technologies can be described as follows:

- **User Data Management**   Data and documents follow the users so they can access the data they need to do their jobs. Technologies used include Active Directory, Group Policy, Offline Files, Synchronization Manager, Disk Quotas, and Roaming user profiles.

- **Software Installation and Maintenance**   Software follows the users so they have the software they need to do their jobs. Technologies used include Active Directory, Group Policy, Windows Installer, and Add/Remove Programs in Control Panel.

- **User Settings Management**   User settings follow users and the users can see their preferred desktop arrangements. Technologies used include Active Directory and Roaming user profiles.

- **Computer Settings Management**   Administrators can define how computers are customized and restricted on the network. Technologies used include Active Directory user and computer accounts and Group Policy.

- **Remote Installation Services**   Administrators can enable remote installation of Microsoft Windows XP; Windows Server 2003, Standard Edition; Windows Server 2003, Enterprise Edition; Microsoft Windows 2000 Professional; Microsoft Windows 2000 Server; and Windows 2000 Advanced Server on new or replacement computers without pre-installation or on-site technical support. Technologies used include Active Directory, Group Policy, and Remote Installation Services.

IntelliMirror is a set of Windows Server 2003 features that assist with managing user and computer information, settings, and applications. When IntelliMirror is used in both server and client, the users' data, applications, and settings follow them when they move to another computer. IntelliMirror uses Active Directory and Group Policy to manage users' desktops based on users' business roles, group memberships, and locations. You can configure desktops to meet a new user's requirements each time that user logs on to the network.

Group Policies

Group policies are collections of user and computer configuration settings that can be linked to computers, sites, domains, and OUs to specify the behavior of users' desktops. For example, using group policies, you can set the programs that are available to users, the programs that appear on the user's desktop, and Start menu options.

To create a specific desktop configuration for a particular group of users, you create Group Policy Objects (GPOs). GPOs are collections of Group Policy settings. Each computer running Windows Server 2003 has one local GPO and might, in addition, be subject to any number of nonlocal (Active Directory-based) GPOs. Local GPOs are overridden by nonlocal GPOs. Nonlocal GPOs are linked to Active Directory objects (sites, domains, or OUs). Nonlocal GPOs can be applied to either users (regardless of which computer they log on to) or computers (regardless of who logs on to them). Following the inheritance properties of Active Directory, nonlocal GPOs are applied hierarchically from the least restrictive group (site) to the most restrictive group (OU) and are cumulative.

Because nonlocal GPOs are applied hierarchically, the user or computer's configuration is a result of the GPOs linked to its site, domain, and OU. GPOs are applied in the following order:

1. **Local GPO**   Each server running Windows Server 2003 has exactly one GPO stored locally.

2. **GPOs linked to sites**   Any GPOs that have been linked to the site are applied next. GPO application is synchronous; the administrator specifies the order of GPOs linked to a site.

3. **GPOs linked to domains**   Multiple domain-linked GPOs are applied synchronously; the administrator specifies the order of GPOs linked to a domain.

4. **GPOs linked to OUs**   GPOs linked to the OU highest in the Active Directory hierarchy are applied first, followed by GPOs linked to its child OU, and so on. Finally, the GPOs linked to the OU that contains the user or computer are applied. At the level of each OU in the Active Directory hierarchy, one, many, or no GPOs can be linked. If several group policies are linked to an OU, then they are applied synchronously in an order specified by the administrator.

Figure 1-15 shows how Group Policy is applied for the example Marketing and Servers OUs.

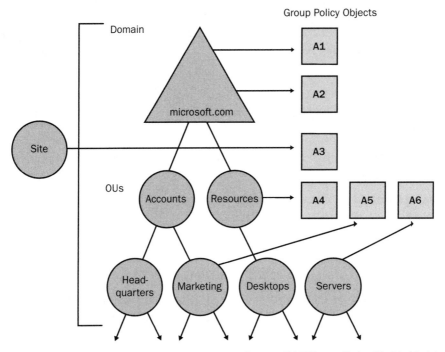

Servers OU GPOs applied = A3, A1, A2, A4, A6
Marketing OU GPOs applied = A3, A1, A2, A5

Figure 1-15 How Group Policy is applied

The default order of processing Group Policy settings can be subject to exceptions if the computer is a member of a workgroup or if any of the No Override, Block Policy Inheritance, or Loopback settings are invoked for a GPO.

The *Resultant Set of Policy (RSoP) Wizard* is provided to make policy implementation and troubleshooting easier. The RSoP Wizard is a query engine that works in two modes: logging mode and planning mode. In logging mode, the wizard polls existing policies and any applications associated with a particular user or computer, and then reports the results of the query. In planning mode, the wizard asks questions about a planned policy implementation, and then reports the results of the query.

Note Under Windows Server 2003 Service Pack 1, RSoP will not work through the Windows Firewall unless you enable and apply both the "Windows Firewall: Allow remote administration exception" and "Windows Firewall: Allow file and printer sharing exception" Group Policy settings on the target computers.

As an administrator, you must be able to administer Group Policy to provide users with the access to resources they require. See Chapter 10, "Implementing Group Policy," Chapter 11, "Administering Group Policy," and Chapter 12, "Deploying Software with Group Policy," for details about Group Policy administration.

DNS

DNS is a service used in *Transmission Control Protocol/Internet Protocol (TCP/IP)* networks, such as the Internet, to locate computers and services through user-friendly names. DNS provides a method of naming computers and network services using a hierarchy of domains. When a user enters a user-friendly DNS name in an application, DNS services can resolve the name to other information associated with the name, such as an IP address. For example, it's easy for most users who want to locate a computer on a network to remember and learn a friendly name such as *example.microsoft.com*. However, computers communicate over a network by using numeric addresses. DNS provides a way to map the user-friendly name for a computer or service to its numeric address. If you have used a Web browser, you have used DNS.

Active Directory uses DNS as its domain naming and location service. DNS provides the following benefits:

- DNS names are user-friendly, which means they are easier to remember than IP addresses.

- DNS names remain more constant than IP addresses. An IP address for a server can change, but the server name remains the same.

- DNS allows users to connect to local servers using the same naming convention as the Internet.

> **See Also**   To read more about DNS, launch an Internet search engine and run a search for RFC 1034 and RFC 1035. Requests For Comments (RFCs) are the official documents of the Internet Engineering Task Force (IETF) that specify the details for new Internet specifications or protocols. RFC 1034 is titled "Domain Names—Concepts and Facilities," and RFC 1035 is titled "Domain Names—Implementation and Specification."

Object Naming

Because Active Directory is an LDAP-compliant directory service, network clients use LDAP to query the Active Directory database. Every object in Active Directory is identified by a name, and LDAP standards determine how the objects are named. Active Directory uses a variety of object naming conventions: distinguished names, relative distinguished names, globally unique identifiers, and user principal names.

> **See Also**   To read more about LDAP, launch an Internet search engine and run a search for RFC 1779, RFC 2247, and RFC 2251. RFC 1779 is titled "A String Representation of Distinguished Names," RFC 2247 is titled "Using Domains in LDAP/X.500 Distinguished Names," and RFC 2251 is titled "Lightweight Directory Access Protocol (v3)."

Distinguished Name

Every object in Active Directory has a *distinguished name (DN)* that uniquely identifies the object and contains sufficient information for a client to retrieve the object from the directory. The DN includes the name of the domain that holds the object, as well as the complete path through the container hierarchy to the object. For example, the following DN identifies the user object Scott Cooper in the *microsoft.com* domain:

```
CN=Scott Cooper,OU=Promotions,OU=Marketing,DC=Microsoft,DC=Com
```

In the DN, three LDAP abbreviations, CN, OU, and DC, are used for the naming attribute. CN indicates the object's common name, OU indicates the organizational unit name, and DC indicates the domain component name. DNs must be unique, because Active Directory does not allow duplicate DNs.

Relative Distinguished Name

Active Directory supports querying by attributes, so you can locate an object even if the exact DN is unknown or has changed. The *relative distinguished name (RDN)* of an object is the part of the name that is an attribute of the object itself. In the preceding example, the RDN of the Scott Cooper user object is Scott Cooper. The RDN of the parent object is Promotions.

> **Note**   Active Directory does not display the LDAP abbreviations for the naming attributes common name (CN), organizational unit (OU), and domain component (DC). These abbreviations are shown here only to illustrate how LDAP recognizes the portions of the distinguished name. Most Active Directory tools display object names in canonical form, which lists the RDNs from the root, or the DNS domain name, downwards.

Globally Unique Identifier

A *globally unique identifier (GUID)* is a 128-bit hexadecimal number that is guaranteed to be unique within the enterprise. GUIDs are assigned to objects when the objects are created. The GUID never changes, even if you move or rename the object. Applications can store the GUID of an object and use the GUID to retrieve that object regardless of its current DN.

In Windows NT, each domain resource was associated with a security identifier (SID) that was generated within the domain. This meant that the SID was guaranteed to be unique only within the domain. A GUID is unique across all domains, meaning that you can move objects from domain to domain and they will still have a unique identifier.

User Principal Name

Each user account has a "friendly" name, known as the *user principal name (UPN)*. The UPN consists of a user account name (sometimes referred to as the *user logon name*) and a domain name identifying the domain in which the user account is located. For example, the user object Scott Cooper in the *microsoft.com* tree might have a UPN of *ScottC@microsoft.com* (using the full first name and the first letter of the last name).

Active Directory Administration Tasks

Administering Windows Server 2003 Active Directory involves both configuration and day-to-day maintenance tasks. Administrative tasks can be grouped into the categories described in Table 1-1. These administrative categories roughly correspond to chapters in this training kit.

Table 1-1   Active Directory Administration Tasks

Administrative Category	Specific Tasks
Planning the Active Directory infrastructure design	Assemble a design team. Analyze the business and technical environment. Create a forest plan. Create a domain plan. Create an OU plan. Create a site topology plan.
Installing and configuring Active Directory	Gather pre-installation information. Install Active Directory. Verify the Active Directory installation. Remove Active Directory. Use tools to troubleshoot the Active Directory installation.
Administering Active Directory	Use Active Directory administration tools. Use and customize Microsoft Management Consoles (MMCs). Back up and restore Active Directory.
Installing and managing domains, trees, and forests	Plan and create additional domains, trees, and forests. Transfer operations master roles. Seize operations master roles. Plan and implement trust relationships.
Configuring sites and managing replication	Plan, create, and configure sites. Configure intersite replication. Configure global catalog servers. Use tools to manage, monitor, and troubleshoot replication.
Implementing an OU structure	Plan, create, and manage an OU structure.
Administering user accounts	Create user accounts, user profiles, and home directories. Maintain user accounts.

Table 1-1   Active Directory Administration Tasks

Administrative Category	Specific Tasks
Administering group accounts	Plan, create, and manage group accounts.
Administering Active Directory objects	Locate Active Directory objects. Publish resources in Active Directory. Control access to Active Directory objects. Delegate administrative control of Active Directory objects. Move Active Directory objects. Use scripting to manage Active Directory objects.
Implementing Group Policy	Plan and create GPOs. Link GPOs to sites, domains, and OUs.
Administering Group Policy	Use the RsoP Wizard to check the results of GPOs. Redirect special folders with Group Policy. Use tools to manage and troubleshoot Group Policy.
Deploying software with Group Policy	Deploy software using Group Policy. Deploy a software upgrade or security patch using Group Policy. Use tools to manage and troubleshoot the software deployment.
Administering Active Directory security	Implement software restriction policies. Implement an audit policy to log security events. Administer the security log and view security events. Manage security templates. Use the Security Configuration and Analysis tool to analyze system security.
Managing Active Directory performance	Use Active Directory performance monitoring tools to monitor Active Directory performance. Optimize and troubleshoot Active Directory performance.

Lesson Review

The following questions are intended to reinforce key information presented in this lesson. If you are unable to answer a question, review the lesson and then try the question again. Answers to the questions can be found in the "Questions and Answers" section at the end of this chapter.

1. List the four directory partitions of the Active Directory database.

   _____

   _____

2. What is the function of the KCC?

   _____

   _____

3. List the six types of trusts used in Active Directory.

   _____

   _____

4. What is change and configuration management? What is IntelliMirror?

_____

_____

5. Explain the function of group policies.

_____

_____

6. Define each of the following names: DN, RDN, GUID, UPN.

_____

_____

Lesson Summary

- The information stored in the directory is logically partitioned into four units of replication in the following partitions: schema partition, configuration partition, domain partition, and application partition.

- Active Directory replicates information in two ways: intrasite (within a site), and intersite (between sites).

- A trust relationship is a link between two domains in which the trusting domain honors the logon authentication of the trusted domain. Windows Server 2003 supports the following trust relationships: tree-root trust, parent-child trust, shortcut trust, external trust, forest trust, and realm trust.

- Group policies are collections of user and computer configuration settings that can be linked to computers, sites, domains, and OUs to specify the behavior of users' desktops. GPOs are collections of Group Policy settings.

- DNS is a service used in TCP/IP networks, such as the Internet, to locate computers and services through user-friendly names. Active Directory uses DNS as its domain naming and location service.

Lesson 3: Planning the Active Directory Infrastructure Design

This lesson introduces you to the Active Directory infrastructure design. It also explains the tools you need to create an infrastructure design and provides an overview of the design process. In each stage of the design process, the basic reasons for defining each component of Active Directory in the design are discussed. It is important that you understand the value of planning your Active Directory infrastructure before you attempt implementation. You should also have basic knowledge of the reasons for defining Active Directory components in a design.

After this lesson, you will be able to

- State the function of an Active Directory infrastructure design
- Name the resources necessary to create an Active Directory infrastructure design
- Name the steps in the Active Directory infrastructure design process
- Discuss the reasons for using multiple forests
- Discuss the reasons for using multiple domains
- Discuss the reasons for defining OUs
- Discuss the reasons for defining sites
- Discuss the reasons for placing domain controllers in sites

Estimated lesson time: 30 minutes

What Is an Active Directory Infrastructure Design?

Before you implement Active Directory in your organization, you need to devise some type of plan. An *Active Directory infrastructure design* is a plan you create that represents your organization's network infrastructure. You use this plan to determine how you will configure Active Directory to store information about objects on your network and make the information available to users and network administrators.

Because your Active Directory infrastructure design is key to the success of your Windows Server 2003 deployment, you must thoroughly gather information for, develop, and test your design before deployment. A significant amount of rethinking, redevelopment, and retesting might also be necessary at various points during the design process to ensure that your design meets the needs of your organization. An effective infrastructure design helps you provide a cost-effective deployment, eliminating the need to spend time and money reworking your infrastructure.

Design Tools

To develop an effective Active Directory infrastructure design, you must assemble the following tools:

- Design team
- Business and technical analyses
- Test environment

Assembling a Design Team

Before you begin designing your Active Directory infrastructure, you must identify the people in your organization who should be involved in the design process and assemble them into a design team. To ensure that all aspects of your organization are addressed in your Active Directory implementation, you might want to employ a multi-level team design consisting of the following three panels:

- **Infrastructure designers**   The key personnel involved in designing your Active Directory infrastructure
- **Staff representatives**   The personnel throughout the organization who are responsible for carrying out daily operations
- **Management representatives**   The management level personnel who are responsible for approving business decisions within the organization

The design team members selected for each panel must be willing and be permitted to commit their time and talents throughout the design process to ensure that the infrastructure design effectively meets the requirements of their organization.

Analyzing Business and Technical Environments

After you've assembled a design team, the next design tools you need to assemble are analyses of your organization's business and technical environments. An analysis of an organization's business environment defines how it organizes and manages its nontechnical resources, such as its products and customers, business structure, business processes, company strategies, and the information technology (IT) management organization. An analysis of an organization's technical environment defines how it organizes and manages its technical resources, such as its network architecture, hardware, software, technical standards, DNS environment (if applicable), and Windows NT environment (if applicable). Most often, your organization will have a business infrastructure or network already in place; it's up to you as an infrastructure designer to call on members of the design team to help you assemble documentation about these environments.

Testing Environment

After you complete your infrastructure design, you should be prepared to test it in a test environment. A test environment is a simulation of your production environment that allows you to test parts of your Windows Server 2003 deployment, such as your Active Directory infrastructure design, without risk to your organization's network. To ensure the success of your organization's Windows Server 2003 deployment, your organization should establish a test environment.

By setting up your infrastructure design in a test environment, you can see how the design actually works and determine whether any changes are necessary for improvement. Setting up your design in a test environment is an invaluable tool in the development of an effective design.

The Design Process

After you've assembled your design team, gathered business and network analyses, and established a test environment, you're ready to begin planning your infrastructure design. The Active Directory infrastructure design process consists of the following four stages:

1. Creating a forest plan
2. Creating a domain plan
3. Creating an OU plan
4. Creating a site topology plan

During each stage, you consult your business and technical analysis documents and assess your organization's requirements. You also assess any changes planned to address growth and scalability issues.

Stage One—Creating a Forest Plan

After analyzing your organization's requirements, the first step in creating a forest plan is to determine the number of Active Directory forests required. Because using more than one forest requires administrators to maintain multiple schemas, configuration containers, global catalogs, and trusts, and requires users to take complex steps to use the directory, you should strive to create only one forest for your organization. However, you might need to consider using multiple forests in the following situations:

- Network administration is separated into autonomous groups that do not trust each other.

- Business units are politically separated into autonomous groups.

- Business units must be maintained separately.

- There is a need to isolate the schema, configuration container, or global catalog.

- There is a need to limit the scope of the trust relationship between domains or domain trees.

In this stage you also create a *schema modification policy*, a plan that outlines who has control of the schema and how modifications that affect the entire forest are administered. Adhering to the schema modification policy, you assess an organization's schema needs and determine whether to modify the schema. If it is necessary to modify the schema, you design a schema modification plan.

Stage Two—Creating a Domain Plan

After analyzing your organization's requirements, the first step in creating a domain plan is to determine the number of domains required. Because adding domains to the forest increases management and hardware costs, you should minimize the number of domains. Once you've created a domain, the domain cannot be easily moved or renamed. However, you might need to consider using multiple domains in the following situations:

- To meet required security policy settings, which are linked to domains

- To meet special administrative requirements, such as legal or privacy concerns

- To optimize replication traffic

- To retain Windows NT domains

- To establish a distinct namespace

The second step in creating a domain plan is to define the forest root domain. You can choose an existing domain for the forest root or designate a new domain to serve as a dedicated forest root domain. Using a dedicated forest root domain provides advantages in security administration, replication traffic, and scalability. Define your forest root domain with caution, because once you've named the forest root domain you cannot change it without renaming and reworking the entire Active Directory tree.

The third step in creating a domain plan is to define a domain hierarchy and name domains. To define the domain hierarchy, you must perform the following actions:

- Determine the number of domain trees

- Designate tree root domains for each of the trees

- Arrange the remaining subdomains in a hierarchy under the root domains

To name domains, you must perform the following actions:

- Assign a DNS name to the forest root domain for each forest in the organization

- Assign a DNS name to each tree root domain

- Assign DNS names to each remaining subdomain, according to its position in the hierarchy

Finally, you determine the placement of DNS servers. You also plan additional zones, determine the existing DNS services employed on DNS servers, and determine the zone replication method to use. The end result of a domain plan is a domain hierarchy diagram that includes domain names and planned zones.

Stage Three—Creating an OU Plan

After analyzing your organization's requirements, to create an OU plan you must define an OU structure. There are three reasons for defining an OU:

- To delegate administration
- To hide objects
- To administer Group Policy

The primary reason for defining an OU is to delegate administration. Delegating administration is the assignment of IT management responsibility for a portion of the namespace, such as an OU, to an administrator, a user, or a group of administrators or users.

After you've determined the OU structure, you must place user accounts in the appropriate OUs. The end result of an OU plan is a diagram of OU structures for each domain and a list of users in each OU.

Stage Four—Creating a Site Topology Plan

After analyzing your organization's requirements, the first step in creating a site topology plan is to define sites. The main purpose of a site is to physically group computers to optimize network traffic. In Active Directory, site structure mirrors the location of user communities. You must define a site for each of the following:

- Each LAN or set of LANs that are connected by a high-speed backbone
- Each location that does not have direct connectivity to the rest of the network and is reachable only by using SMTP mail

The second step in creating a site topology plan is to place domain controllers. Because the availability of Active Directory depends on the availability of domain controllers, a domain controller must always be available so users can be authenticated. For optimum network response time and application availability, you must place at least

- One domain controller in each site
- Two domain controllers in each domain

In addition, you might need to place additional domain controllers in a site if

■ There are a large number of users in a site and the link to the site is slow or near capacity

■ The link to a site is historically unreliable or only intermittently available

The third step in creating a site topology plan is to define a replication strategy. An effective replication strategy ensures efficient replication and fault tolerance. In this step you configure site links, which includes designating the method of replication transport, site link cost, replication frequency, and replication availability. You also have the option to specify preferred bridgehead servers.

The final step in creating a site topology plan is to place global catalog servers and operations masters within a forest. The end result of a site topology plan is a site diagram that includes site links and a site link table that provides details about site link configurations, as well as locations of domain controllers and operations masters roles. Depending on the needs of the organization, a site topology plan might also include a table that provides details about site link bridges and preferred bridgehead servers.

Lesson Review

The following questions are intended to reinforce key information presented in this lesson. If you are unable to answer a question, review the lesson and then try the question again. Answers to the questions can be found in the "Questions and Answers" section at the end of this chapter.

1. What three tools are necessary to develop an effective Active Directory infrastructure design?

   _____

   _____

2. List the four stages in the Active Directory design process.

   _____

   _____

3. Why should you strive to create only one forest for your organization?

   _____

   _____

4. Why should you try to minimize the number of domains in your organization?

   _____

   _____

5. Why should you define the forest root domain with caution?

_____

_____

6. What is the primary reason for defining an OU?

_____

_____

Lesson Summary

- The Active Directory infrastructure design process consists of four stages: (1) creating a forest plan, (2) creating a domain plan, (3) creating an OU plan, and (4) creating a site topology plan.

- Strive to create only one forest for an organization to avoid administering multiple schemas, configuration containers, global catalogs, and trusts, and requiring users to take complex steps to use the directory.

- Minimize the number of domains to avoid increased management and hardware costs. Once you've named the forest root domain you cannot change it without rebuilding the entire Active Directory tree.

- There are three reasons for defining an OU: (1) to delegate administration, (2) to hide objects, and (3) to administer Group Policy. The primary reason for defining an OU is to delegate administration.

- The main purpose of a site is to physically group computers to optimize network traffic. In Active Directory, site structure mirrors the location of user communities.

Chapter Summary

- The logical structures in an organization are represented by the following Active Directory components: domains, OUs, trees, and forests.

- The physical components of Active Directory are sites and domain controllers.

- The global catalog is the central repository of information about objects in a tree or forest.

- The information stored in the directory is logically partitioned into four units of replication in the following partitions: schema partition, configuration partition, domain partition, and application partition.

- Active Directory replicates information in two ways: intrasite (within a site), and intersite (between sites).

- Windows Server 2003 supports the following trust relationships: tree-root trust, parent-child trust, shortcut trust, external trust, forest trust, and realm trust.

- Group policies are collections of user and computer configuration settings that can be linked to computers, sites, domains, and OUs to specify the behavior of users' desktops.

- The Active Directory infrastructure design process consists of four stages: (1) creating a forest plan, (2) creating a domain plan, (3) creating an OU plan, and (4) creating a site topology plan.

Exam Highlights

Before taking the exam, review the key points and terms that are presented in this chapter. You need to know this information.

Key Points

- The logical structures in an organization are represented by the following Active Directory components: domains, OUs, trees, and forests.

- The physical components of Active Directory are sites and domain controllers.

- Active Directory replicates information in two ways: intrasite (within a site), and intersite (between sites).

- Group policies are collections of user and computer configuration settings that can be linked to computers, sites, domains, and OUs to specify the behavior of users' desktops.

- The primary reason for defining an OU is to delegate administration.

- The main purpose of a site is to physically group computers to optimize network traffic.

Key Terms

Active Directory   A Windows-based directory service. Active Directory stores information about objects on a network and makes this information usable to users and network administrators. Active Directory gives network users access to permitted resources anywhere on the network using a single logon process. It provides network administrators with an intuitive, hierarchical view of the network and a single point of administration for all network objects.

domain   A collection of computer, user, and group objects defined by the administrator. These objects share a common directory database, security policies, and security relationships with other domains.

forest   One or more Active Directory domains that share the same class and attribute definitions (schema), site, and replication information (configuration), and forest-wide search capabilities (global catalog). Domains in the same forest are linked with two-way, transitive trust relationships.

organizational unit (OU)   An Active Directory container object used within domains. An OU is a logical container into which users, groups, computers, and other OUs are placed. It can contain objects only from its parent domain. An OU is the smallest scope to which a GPO can be linked, or over which administrative authority can be delegated.

site   One or more well-connected (highly reliable and fast) TCP/IP subnets. A site allows administrators to configure Active Directory access and replication topology to take advantage of the physical network.

Page
1-19

Lesson 1 Review

1. How is a directory service different from a directory?

A directory service differs from a directory in that it is both the source of the information and the mechanism that makes the information available to the users.

2. How is Active Directory scalable?

Active Directory enables you to scale the directory to meet business and network requirements through the configuration of domains and trees, and the placement of domain controllers. Active Directory allows millions of objects per domain and uses indexing technology and advanced replication techniques to speed performance.

3. What is multimaster replication?

Multimaster replication is a replication model in which any domain controller accepts and replicates directory changes to any other domain controller. Because multiple domain controllers are employed, replication continues, even if any single domain controller stops working.

4. Name the Active Directory components used to represent an organization's logical structure.

The Active Directory components used to represent an organization's logical structure are domains, organizational units (OUs), trees, and forests.

5. Name the physical components of Active Directory.

The physical components of Active Directory are sites and domain controllers.

6. What is the function of the global catalog?

The global catalog has two main functions: (1) it enables a user to log on to a network by providing universal group membership information to a domain controller when a logon process is initiated, and (2) it enables finding directory information regardless of which domain in the forest actually contains the data.

Page
1-34

Lesson 2 Review

1. List the four directory partitions of the Active Directory database.

The four directory partitions of the Active Directory database are schema partition, configuration partition, domain partition, and application partition.

2. What is the function of the KCC?

The KCC is a built-in process that runs on all domain controllers. The KCC configures connection objects between domain controllers. Within a site, each KCC generates its own connections. For replication between sites, a single KCC per site generates all connections between sites.

3. List the six types of trusts used in Active Directory.

The six types of trusts used in Active Directory are tree-root trust, parent-child trust, shortcut trust, external trust, forest trust, and realm trust.

4. What is change and configuration management? What is IntelliMirror?

Change and configuration management is a set of Windows Server 2003 features that simplify computer management tasks. IntelliMirror is a set of Windows Server 2003 features that assist with managing user and computer information, settings, and applications. When IntelliMirror is used in both server and client, the users' data, applications, and settings follow them when they move to another computer.

5. Explain the function of group policies.

Group policies are collections of user and computer configuration settings that can be linked to computers, sites, domains, and OUs to modify computer settings and specify the behavior of users' desktops.

6. Define each of the following names: DN, RDN, GUID, UPN.

The distinguished name (DN) uniquely identifies the object and contains the name of the domain that holds the object, as well as the complete path through the container hierarchy to the object. The relative distinguished name (RDN) is the part of an object's DN that is an attribute of the object itself. The globally unique identifier (GUID) is a 128-bit hexadecimal number that is guaranteed to be unique within the enterprise. The user principal name (UPN) consists of a user account name (sometimes referred to as the user logon name) and a domain name identifying the domain in which the user account is located.

Page 1-41 **Lesson 3 Review**

1. What three tools are necessary to develop an effective Active Directory infrastructure design?

The following tools are necessary to develop an effective Active Directory infrastructure design: design team, business and technical analyses, and test environment.

2. List the four stages in the Active Directory design process.

The stages in the design process are creating a forest plan, creating a domain plan, creating an OU plan, and creating a site topology plan.

3. Why should you strive to create only one forest for your organization?

Using more than one forest requires administrators to maintain multiple schemas, configuration containers, global catalogs, and trusts, and requires users to take complex steps to use the directory.

4. Why should you try to minimize the number of domains in your organization?

Adding domains to the forest increases management and hardware costs.

5. Why should you define the forest root domain with caution?

Define your forest root domain with caution, because once you've named the forest root domain you cannot change it without renaming and reworking the entire Active Directory tree.

6. What is the primary reason for defining an OU?

The primary reason for defining an OU is to delegate administration.

2 Installing and Configuring Active Directory

Exam Objectives in this Chapter:

- Implement an Active Directory directory service forest and domain structure.
- Create the forest root domain.
- Install and configure an Active Directory domain controller.

Why This Chapter Matters

The information in this chapter shows you how to install, remove, and verify Active Directory, and troubleshoot an Active Directory installation. Determining whether to install a new forest, domain tree, or domain are some of the first decisions you'll have to make when installing Active Directory. Understanding exactly what is involved when you make these choices is critical to the success of your installation. Planning the Active Directory structure and Domain Name System (DNS) structure is essential.

It's important to be familiar with the various installation methods so you can choose the one that best meets your needs. Once you've installed Active Directory, you should expect that some changes might still be necessary. This could involve the installation of additional domain controllers or the removal of others. You must be able to remove Active Directory if you find that a particular server no longer needs to be a domain controller. Verifying proper Active Directory installation is important to ensure the installation turned out the way you intended before you continue with your Active Directory deployment. Finally, as an administrator, you must be able to use tools to troubleshoot problems you may encounter during the Active Directory installation and removal processes.

Lessons in this Chapter:

Before You Begin

To complete the lessons in this chapter, you must

- Have a general understanding of Active Directory components and concepts as discussed in Chapter 1, "Introduction to Active Directory"

- Prepare your test environment according to the descriptions given in the "Getting Started" section of "About This Book"

Lesson 1: Preparing for Active Directory Installation

There are a number of prerequisites you must consider before you begin installing Active Directory. These prerequisites include the design of your organization's domain structure and domain name; the storage location of the database, log, and shared system volume files; and the method of DNS configuration. This lesson shows you how to prepare for Active Directory installation.

After this lesson, you will be able to

- Describe the Active Directory installation prerequisites

Estimated lesson time: 15 minutes

Active Directory Installation Prerequisites

Before you can install Active Directory, you should take some time to be sure that you are prepared by determining in advance:

- The domain structure
- The domain name
- The storage location of the database and log files
- The location of the shared system volume folder
- The DNS configuration method
- The DNS configuration

You must determine all of these installation prerequisites because they are required to complete the Active Directory installation process.

Determining the Domain Structure

To determine the domain structure, you must assess your company's physical environment, determine the forest root domain, determine the number of domains, and organize domains in a hierarchy.

Assessing the Physical Environment

The physical environment of your organization's network includes

- The current location of points on the network
- The current number of users at each location
- The current network type used at each location

- The current location, link speed, and percentage of available bandwidth of remote network links

> **Note** Available bandwidth is the amount of bandwidth that remains when you take the total bandwidth available for a link and subtract the amount of network traffic that occurs on the link during peak traffic.

- The current Transmission Control Protocol/Internet Protocol (TCP/IP) subnets at each location
- The current speed of local network links
- The current location of domain controllers
- The current list of servers at each location and the services that run on them
- The current location of firewalls in the network

> **Note** In this scenario, "firewalls" refers to the corporate or enterprise firewalls and not to any host firewalls, such as Windows Firewall.

For example, Figure 2-1 shows the physical environment for Contoso Pharmaceuticals. Employees are distributed fairly evenly among the four locations. In the next five years, growth for all locations is estimated at 3 percent. The Chicago office is the hub of the Contoso Pharmaceuticals' wide area network (WAN). Network connections are utilized moderately; however, the Kansas City–Chicago connection has a high degree of utilization.

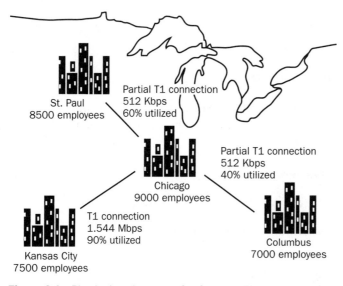

Figure 2-1 Physical environment for Contoso Pharmaceuticals

In addition to your assessment of the organization's physical environment, you should also consider other infrastructures currently employed in the organization. For example, if your organization has already invested in a DNS structure, you should probably retain this structure. Similarly, if your organization is using a large Microsoft Exchange operation, you might want to base your domain structure on the same model. Before you change existing infrastructures, you must weigh the cost of the change against the potential benefits.

Real World   Integrating DNS Structures

Most organizations have existing DNS structures they must maintain. This is especially true for any organization that already has a Windows 2000 Active Directory installation. Further, companies that manage medium to large TCP/IP networks usually have existing DNS servers. In these organizations, you'll probably need to integrate the Windows 2003 Server Active Directory domain and any DNS configuration into the existing environment.

Organizations that already have Windows 2000 Active Directory implementations should be the easiest to integrate because the DNS structure will likely remain the same when the domain is upgraded to the Windows 2003 Server Active Directory domain. Organizations that do not have an existing Active Directory implementation are likely to have a lot more planning to do. For example, the most prevalent non-Windows DNS implementation is the Berkeley Internet Name Domain (BIND), which is maintained by the Internet Software Consortium (ISC). If an organization chooses to keep their BIND DNS servers, there are three main methods for integrating an existing BIND and Active Directory:

- Configure BIND DNS to handle all DNS records for Active Directory. In this case, you'd ensure that the BIND DNS server version could support SRV records (BIND 4.9.7 and later versions work properly for this purpose). Also, it is highly desirable to use a BIND server that supports Dynamic DNS (BIND versions 8.2.2 and later will do so).

- Configure BIND DNS to delegate an Active Directory specific subdomain. For example, if the company uses *contoso.com*, the Active Directory name space might be *ad.contoso.com*. This is a very popular choice for many companies.

- Configure the BIND DNS server to delegate the _msdcs, _sites, tcp, and _udp portions of the DNS namespace to your Windows 2003 Server configured as a DNS server.

For more information on this subject, search the Microsoft Web site for "Domain Name System (DNS) Center Knowledge Base Articles." Also, anyone using BIND DNS should visit *http://www.isc.org* to review the latest notes and updates for BIND.

Determining the Forest Root Domain

As you learned in Chapter 1, the *forest root domain* is the first domain you create in an Active Directory forest. The forest root domain must be centrally managed by an IT organization that is responsible for making domain hierarchy, naming, and policy decisions. When planning a domain structure, you should start with a *dedicated* forest root domain. A forest root domain is dedicated when it is set up exclusively to administer the forest infrastructure. A dedicated forest root domain is recommended for the following reasons:

- You can control the number of administrators allowed to make forest-wide changes. By limiting the number of administrators in the forest root domain, you reduce the likelihood that an administrative error will impact the entire forest.

- You can easily replicate the forest root across the enterprise. Because a dedicated root domain is small, it can be easily replicated anywhere on your network to provide protection against catastrophes.

- The forest root never becomes obsolete. Because the only purpose of the forest root domain is to serve as the root, there is little chance of it becoming obsolete.

- You can easily transfer ownership of the root. Transferring ownership of the root domain does not involve migrating production data or resources.

The role of a dedicated forest root domain is to define and manage the infrastructure. Therefore, when you plan domains, you should reserve the dedicated forest root domain for forest administration only. Avoid including users or resources not dedicated to forest administration in the forest root domain.

Determining the Number of Domains

After you've planned the dedicated forest root domain, you should begin planning your domain structure with a single child domain under the root, and add more domains only when the single child domain model no longer meets your needs. One domain can span multiple sites and contain millions of objects. Keep in mind that site and domain structures are separate and flexible. A single domain can span multiple geographical sites, and a single site can include users and computers belonging to multiple domains. Planning your site structure is covered in Chapter 5, "Configuring Sites and Managing Replication."

You should not create separate domains to reflect your company's organization of divisions and departments. Because functional structures such as divisions, departments, or project teams are always subject to change, defining domains based on these structures in the organization is strongly discouraged. Within each domain, you can model your organization's management hierarchy for delegation or administration using organizational units (OUs) for this purpose. You can then assign Group Policy and place users, groups, and computers into the OUs. Planning OU structure is covered in Chapter 6, "Implementing an OU Structure."

If you are upgrading from Microsoft Windows NT, it is likely that you will need to consolidate domains. The principles for defining multiple domains in Windows NT no longer apply in Windows Server 2003. These principles are the following:

- **Security Accounts Manager (SAM) size limitations**   In Windows NT, the SAM database had a limitation of about 40,000 objects per domain. In Windows Server 2003, each domain can contain more than one million objects, so it is no longer necessary to define a new domain just to handle more objects.

- **Primary domain controller (PDC) availability requirements**   In Windows NT, only one computer in a domain, the PDC, could accept updates to the domain database. In Windows Server 2003, all domain controllers accept updates, eliminating the need to define new domains just to provide fault tolerance.

- **Limited delegation of administration within domains**   In Windows NT, domains were the smallest units of administrative delegation. In Windows Server 2003, OUs allow you to partition domains to delegate administration, eliminating the need to define domains just for delegation.

Reasons to create more than one child domain under the forest root include the following:

- To meet required security policy settings that are linked to domains
- To meet special administrative requirements, such as legal or privacy concerns
- To optimize replication traffic
- To retain Windows NT domains
- To establish a distinct namespace

> **Exam Tip**   Make sure you know why using a dedicated root domain is important. Also, make sure you know the reasons for creating more than one child domain.

In the example, Contoso Pharmaceuticals requires stricter password requirements at the Chicago office, and there is a need to control replication traffic on the highly utilized Chicago–Kansas City network connection. In addition, the company plans to add a new office in Winnipeg, Canada within two years and anticipates having to address requirements of the government of Canada. Therefore, the Active Directory infrastructure designers have planned to implement a dedicated forest root domain and a domain for each of the company's present locations; a total of five domains, as shown in Figure 2-2.

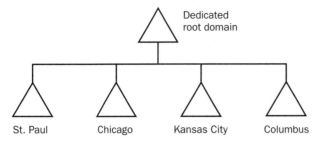

Figure 2-2 The domains planned for Contoso Pharmaceuticals

Defining a Domain Hierarchy

If you've determined that your company requires more than one domain, you must organize the domains into a hierarchy that fits the needs of your organization. Recall that domains in a forest share the same configuration, schema, and global catalog. As domains are placed in a hierarchy, the two-way transitive trust relationship allows the domains to share resources.

The primary difference between domain trees and forests is in their DNS name structure. All domains in a domain tree have a contiguous DNS namespace. Unless your organization operates as a group of several entities, such as a partnership or conglomerate, your network probably lends itself to a contiguous DNS namespace and you should set up multiple domains in a single domain tree in a forest. If you need to combine organizations with unique domain names, create an additional forest. You can also create additional forests to separate DNS zones. Each tree in the forest has its own unique namespace.

In the example, the Contoso Pharmaceuticals physical structure maps to a group of domains in a domain tree. Contoso Pharmaceuticals is not a part of any other entity, nor are there any known plans for creating multiple entities in the future. There is one dedicated root domain. Therefore, Contoso Pharmaceuticals will set up its multiple domains in a single tree in a single forest, as shown in Figure 2-2.

See Also The "Active Directory Step-by-Step Guides" are an excellent guide for developing an Active Directory, and are available on the Microsoft TechNet Web site at: *http: //www.microsoft.com/technet/prodtechnol/windowsserver2003/technologies/directory /activedirectory/stepbystep/default.mspx*. These guides provides a step-by-step methodology for Active Directory design based on practices learned from customers who have already deployed Active Directory in their organizations.

Determining the Domain Name

In Windows Server 2003 and Active Directory, a *domain name* is a name given to a collection of networked computers that share a common directory. Because Active Directory uses DNS as its domain naming and location service, Windows Server 2003 domain names are also DNS names. When logging on to the network or when domain controllers are locating replication partners, Active Directory clients query their DNS servers to locate domain controllers.

> **Note**   Domain controllers that run Windows Server 2003 with Service Pack 1 (SP1) can request several variations of the server name that might be registered, which results in fewer failures from DNS delays and misconfiguration. For more information about DNS name resolution under Windows Server 2003 SP1, see "Fixing Replication DNS Lookup Problems" on the Microsoft Web site at *http://www.microsoft.com/technet/prodtechnol/windowsserver2003 /library/Operations/43e6f617-fb49-4bb4-8561-53310219f997.mspx.*

In DNS, names are arranged in a hierarchy and can be partitioned according to the hierarchy. The hierarchy allows parent-child relationships where the name of the child domain is designated by the name of the parent domain, preceded by a label for the child domain. For example, *uk.microsoft.com* is a child domain of the *microsoft.com* domain; for the child name the "uk" label is placed before the name of the parent domain, *microsoft.com*. Thus, a domain's name identifies its position in the hierarchy.

In the example shown in Figure 2-3, the root domain is named *contoso.com*, while each of the child domains have been named for the physical locations that represent the domains.

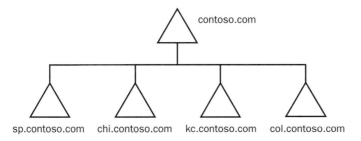

Figure 2-3   Domain naming for Contoso Pharmaceuticals

Because domain names designated in Active Directory are employed by users as they navigate the forest, the names you select are very important. Select an easily identifiable name for the forest root domain, which is the basis for its child and grandchild domains. If you adhere to some basic guidelines, you should be able to determine domain names that meet the needs of your organization. The following are guidelines for naming domains:

- Use only the Internet standard characters. Internet standard characters are defined as: A–Z, a–z, 0–9, and the hyphen (-). Although Windows Server 2003 DNS supports the use of almost any Unicode character in a name, by using only Internet standard characters you ensure that your Active Directory domain names will be compatible with other versions of DNS.

- Differentiate between internal and external namespaces. Because most organizations have an Internet presence, you should use different names for the internal and external root domains to clearly delineate public resources from private resources and prevent unauthorized users from accessing resources on the internal network. For example, Microsoft is represented on the Internet by the DNS name *microsoft.com*. However, the organization might use *corp.microsoft.com* to represent their Active Directory forest root domain name.

- Base the internal DNS name on the Internet DNS name. If you use an internal DNS name that is related to the Internet DNS name, it will be easier for users to understand the navigational structure. Consider using the Internet DNS name as a suffix for Active Directory domain names. For example, *corp.microsoft.com* is easily understandable as an extension to *microsoft.com*.

- Never use the same domain name twice. For example, Microsoft should not use the name *microsoft.com* for both its Internet and intranet root domains. If a *microsoft.com* client attempts to connect to either the Internet or the intranet *microsoft.com* site, the domain that answers first is the one to which the client is connected.

- Use only registered domain names. Register all second-level domain names, whether they are internal or external namespaces, with the InterNIC or other authorized naming authority. For example, Microsoft should register its second-level domain name as *microsoft.com*. The company does not need to register *corp.microsoft.com* because it is not a second-level domain name. Internal names that are second-level domain names should be registered to ensure access from outside the corporate firewall. You can find more information about registering domain names at *http://www.internic.net*.

Tip   Be sure to register and receive verification for domain names *before* creating your Active Directory domain namespace to avoid having to change domain names. Changing a domain name can take time and waste resources.

- Use short, distinct, meaningful names. Use domain names that are easy to use and are representative of your organization's identity.

- Use names that have been reviewed internationally. Review domain names to ensure that they are not derogatory or offensive in other languages.

- Use names that will remain static. Use generic names rather than specific ones. For example, Microsoft might use *hq.corp.microsoft.com* for its Redmond headquarters domain rather than *redmond.corp.microsoft.com* to avoid the need for change if the headquarters is moved.

- Use the International Organization for Standardization (ISO) standards for names that include countries and U.S. states. The ISO defines two-letter country codes and U.S. state codes, as presented in ISO 3166. You can find more information about ISO 3166 at *http://www.iso.org/iso/en/prods-services/iso3166ma/index.html*.

Determining the Storage Location of the Database and Log Files

Installing Active Directory creates the database and database log files. The Active Directory database is the directory for the new domain. The default location for the database and database log files is *%Systemroot%*\Ntds, where *%Systemroot%* is the path and folder name where the Microsoft Windows Server 2003 system files are located, typically, C:\Windows. However, you can specify a different location when installing Active Directory using the Active Directory Installation Wizard. For best performance and fault tolerance, it's recommended that you place the database and the log file on separate hard disks that are NT file system (NTFS) drives, although NTFS is not required. It's also recommended that you have 1 gigabyte (GB) of space to install Active Directory, although the Active Directory Installation Wizard requires only a minimum of 200 megabytes (MB) of disk space for the Active Directory database and 50 MB for the log files.

The directory database is stored in a file named Ntds.dit, which contains all of the information stored in the Active Directory data store. The directory database is an Extensible Storage Engine (ESE) database that contains the schema, global catalog, and objects stored on a domain controller. When Active Directory is installed, Ntds.dit is copied from the *%Systemroot%*\System32 directory into the directory you specify. Active Directory services are started from the new copy of the file, and if there are other domain controllers present, the replication process updates the file to the other domain controllers.

Determining the Location of the Shared System Volume Folder

Installing Active Directory creates the shared system volume, a folder structure that exists on all Windows Server 2003 domain controllers. It stores public files that must be replicated to other domain controllers, such as logon scripts and some of the Group Policy Objects (GPOs), for both the current domain and the enterprise. The default location for the shared system volume is *%Systemroot%*\Sysvol. However, you can specify a different location during Active Directory installation. The shared system volume must be located on a partition or volume formatted with NTFS.

Replication of the shared system volume occurs on the same schedule as Active Directory replication. As a result, you might not notice file replication to or from the newly created system volume until two replication periods have elapsed (typically, 10 minutes). This is because the first file replication period updates the configuration of other system volumes so that they are aware of the newly created system volume.

Determining the DNS Configuration Method

You can configure your Windows Server 2003 DNS server manually or you can allow it to be configured automatically during Active Directory installation. Manual configuration of DNS to support Active Directory is required if you are using a non–Windows Server 2003 DNS server or if you want to set up a configuration other than the default configuration set up during Active Directory installation. You can configure DNS manually using the DNS console. For details about manually configuring DNS for Active Directory, refer to the *MCSA/MCSE Self-Paced Training Kit (Exam 70-291): Implementing, Managing, and Maintaining a Microsoft Windows Server 2003 Network Infrastructure*, Second Edition (Microsoft Press, 2006).

Although Active Directory requires that the DNS service be installed on your network, you can install DNS implementations other than Microsoft Windows Server 2003 DNS service. However, these other implementations might not have all of the features of Windows Server 2003 DNS. Therefore, you might not be able to take advantage of full DNS integration with Active Directory. For details about Active Directory interoperability with other DNS services, refer to the *MCSA/MCSE Self-Paced Training Kit (Exam 70-291): Implementing, Managing, and Maintaining a Microsoft Windows Server 2003 Network Infrastructure*.

Determining the DNS Configuration

If you allow DNS to be configured automatically during Active Directory installation, the server is automatically set to meet the DNS requirements for joining Active Directory. However, if you have installed DNS manually or if your DNS solution does not support dynamic update, you must ensure that your configuration meets the DNS requirements for joining an Active Directory domain as described in this section.

Computers joining an Active Directory domain must satisfy the following DNS requirements:

- The computer must be configured with a static Internet Protocol (IP) address and the IP address of a preferred DNS server.

- The _ldap._tcp.dc._msdcs. *DNSDomainName* service (SRV) resource record must exist in DNS. *DNSDomainName* is the DNS name of the Active Directory domain the computer is attempting to join.

- The host (A) resource record for the DNS name of the domain controllers specified in the data field of the _ldap._tcp.dc._msdcs. *DNSDomainName* service (SRV) resource record must exist in DNS.

Configuring a Static IP Address and Preferred DNS Server

Before you install Active Directory on a server, you should configure a static IP address for the server and designate a preferred DNS server. To configure a static IP address for a server and designate a preferred DNS server, complete the following steps:

1. Click Start, point to Control Panel, right-click Network Connections, and click Open.

2. Right-click Local Area Connection and then click Properties.

3. Click Internet Protocol (TCP/IP) and then click Properties.

4. In the Internet Protocol (TCP/IP) Properties dialog box, shown in Figure 2-4, click Use The Following IP Address. To specify a static IP address for the DNS server, type the IP address, subnet mask, and default gateway IP addresses in the IP Address, Subnet Mask, and Default Gateway boxes, respectively.

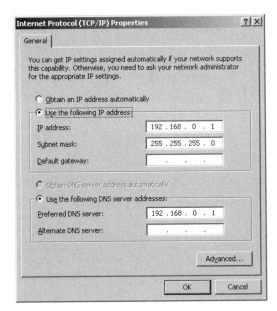

Figure 2-4   The Internet Protocol (TCP/IP) Properties dialog box, showing configuration for a static IP address

5. Click the Use The Following DNS Server Addresses button and type the IP address of the preferred DNS server in the Preferred DNS Server box. It is a best practice

to use a preferred DNS server in the same site. Optionally, you can specify the IP address of an alternate DNS server that this server will use if the preferred DNS server does not respond.

6. Click OK.

7. Click OK again.

> **Off the Record**   You should always configure a Preferred and Alternate DNS server for all client computers, member servers, and domain controllers whenever possible. Without DNS, domain member computers are unable to find domain controllers. If you only configure a Preferred DNS server on (a) domain member computer(s) and that DNS server is unavailable for any reason, those domain member computers will be unable to locate a domain controller. If a client computer is unable to locate a domain controller, a large variety of connectivity and logon issues can occur.

Configuring the Required DNS Resource Records

Computers joining an Active Directory domain require the following resource records in DNS to locate an Active Directory domain controller:

- _ldap._tcp.dc._msdcs. *DNSDomainName* service (SRV) resource record, which identifies the names of the domain controllers that serve the Active Directory domain. *DNSDomainName* is the DNS name of the Active Directory domain the computer is attempting to join.

- A corresponding address (A) resource record that identifies the IP addresses for the domain controllers listed in the _ldap._tcp.dc._msdcs. *DNSDomainName* SRV resource record.

To verify the presence of DNS resource records needed to join an Active Directory domain, complete the following steps:

1. Click Start, and then click Command Prompt.

2. Type **nslookup** and press ENTER.

3. At the Nslookup (">") prompt, type **set q=srv** and press ENTER.

4. At the next prompt, type **_ldap._tcp.dc._msdcs.** *DNSDomainName*. The DNS query for resource records specified in the Nslookup command **set q=srv** returns both SRV and A resource records.

5. Review the output and determine if all domain controllers in the Active Directory domain that this computer is attempting to join are included and registered using valid IP addresses. In some cases, you might need to manually add or

verify registration of the service (SRV) resource records used to support Windows Server 2003 domain controllers.

6. If you need to add the SRV resource records that have been created for a domain controller, open and view the Netlogon.dns file, created by the Active Directory Installation Wizard when a server computer is promoted to a domain controller. Netlogon.dns can be found at the following location on a domain controller: *%Systemroot%*\System32\Config\Netlogon.dns. If you have installed DNS manually or if your DNS solution does not support dynamic update, you must manually enter these records on your DNS server(s).

Practice: Configuring a Static IP Address and Preferred DNS Server

In this practice, you configure a static IP address and preferred DNS Server for your two practice servers, Server1 and Server2. You will use these servers to complete exercises throughout this training kit.

> **Caution**   The exercises in this training kit are designed to be completed on servers set up on their own practice network. The exercises require you to make changes to your server configuration and can produce undesirable results if you are connected to a larger network. If you are connected to a larger network, check with your administrator before attempting these exercises.

Exercise: Configuring a Static IP Address and Preferred DNS Server

In this exercise, you configure a static IP address and a preferred DNS server to prepare your servers for Active Directory service installation in Lesson 2.

▶ **To configure a static IP address and preferred DNS server**

1. Log on to both servers as Administrator using **password** as your password.

> **Security Alert**   In a real-world environment, always be sure to use a complex password. Microsoft recommends mixing uppercase and lowercase letters, numbers, and symbols (for example, Lp6*g9F2).

2. Use the procedure provided earlier in this lesson to configure a static IP address for Server1. Configure Server1 as its own preferred DNS server. See your network administrator for valid IP addresses or use 192.168.1.1.

3. Use the procedure provided earlier in this lesson to configure a static IP address for Server2. Configure Server1 as the preferred DNS server. See your network administrator for valid IP addresses or use 192.168.1.2.

Lesson Review

The following questions are intended to reinforce key information presented in this lesson. If you are unable to answer a question, review the lesson and then try the question again. Answers to the questions can be found in the "Questions and Answers" section at the end of the chapter.

1. What are the reasons to create more than one child domain under a dedicated root domain?

   _____

   _____

2. What is a forest root domain?

   _____

   _____

3. For best performance and fault tolerance, where should you store the database and log files?

   _____

   _____

4. What is the function of the shared system volume folder and where is the default storage location of the folder?

   _____

   _____

5. Which of the following is not a valid reason for creating an additional domain?

   a. To meet SAM size limitations

   b. To meet required security policy settings, which are linked to domains

   c. To meet special administrative requirements, such as legal or privacy concerns

   d. To optimize replication traffic

Lesson Summary

- Before you can install Active Directory, you must determine the domain structure, domain names, storage location of the database and log files, location of the shared system volume folder, and the DNS configuration method.

- Begin your domain structure with a single dedicated root domain, and add child domains only to meet required security policy settings, which are linked to domains; to meet special administrative requirements, such as legal or privacy concerns; to optimize replication traffic; to retain Windows NT domains; or to establish a distinct namespace.

■ A forest root domain is the first domain you create in an Active Directory forest. The forest root domain must be centrally managed by an IT organization that is responsible for making domain hierarchy, naming, and policy decisions.

■ The default location for the database and database log files is *%Systemroot%\Ntds*, although you can specify a different location during Active Directory installation. For best performance and fault tolerance, place the database and the log file on separate hard disks that are NTFS drives.

■ The default location for the shared system volume is *%Systemroot%\Sysvol*, although you can specify a different location during Active Directory installation. The shared system volume must be located on a partition or volume formatted with NTFS.

Lesson 2: Installing and Removing Active Directory

After you've completed your preparation work with the installation prerequisites described in Lesson 1, you're ready to install Active Directory. Removing Active Directory follows a process similar to installation. This lesson shows you how to install and remove Active Directory.

After this lesson, you will be able to

- Install Active Directory using the Active Directory Installation Wizard
- Install Active Directory using an unattended installation
- Install Active Directory using the network or backup media
- Install Active Directory using the Configure Your Server Wizard
- Remove Active Directory

Estimated lesson time: 40 minutes

Installing Active Directory

There are four ways to install Active Directory:

- Using the Active Directory Installation Wizard (to install Active Directory in most situations)

- Using an answer file to perform an unattended installation (to install Active Directory remotely)

- Using the network or backup media (to install Active Directory on additional domain controllers in the network using media)

- Using the Configure Your Server Wizard (an additional way to install the first domain controller in a network only)

All these methods promote the computer to the role of domain controller, install Active Directory, and, if desired, install and configure the DNS server.

Installing Active Directory Using the Active Directory Installation Wizard

The Active Directory Installation Wizard is the main tool used to install Active Directory. The wizard presents a set of pages, on which you must input the following:

- Domain controller type—either the first domain controller for a new domain or a new domain controller added to an existing domain

- Domain type—a new domain in a new forest, a child domain in an existing domain tree, or a new domain tree in an existing forest

- Domain name

- NetBIOS name for the domain

- Active Directory database and log folder location

- Shared system volume folder location

- Default permissions for user and group objects

- Directory services restore mode administrator password

After you input this information, the wizard installs Active Directory, creates the full domain name, assigns the NetBIOS name for the domain, sets the Active Directory database and log folder location, sets the shared system volume folder location, and installs DNS and a preferred DNS server if you requested automatic DNS installation. The Active Directory Installation Wizard does not install Dynamic Host Configuration Protocol (DHCP), assign the static IP address, assign the subnet mask, create a DHCP scope, or set up an application naming context in Active Directory for use by Telephony Application Programming Interface (TAPI) client applications.

As you begin installing Active Directory using the Active Directory Installation Wizard, you must choose whether to create the first domain controller for a new domain or add the new domain controller to an existing domain. You portray the domain structure by making these choices as they are presented in the wizard.

Creating the First Domain Controller for a New Domain   If you choose to create the first domain controller for a new domain, you create both the domain controller and a new domain. You can then specify whether you want to create a new domain in a new forest, a child domain in an existing domain tree, or a new domain tree in an existing forest, as illustrated in Figure 2-5.

When you create a new domain in a new forest, either the new domain is the first domain in the organization or it is a new domain that you want to be completely independent from your existing forest. When you create a new child domain in an existing domain tree, the new domain is a child domain of an existing domain. Recall that domains in a tree share a contiguous namespace and a hierarchical naming structure. When you create a new domain tree in an existing forest, the new domain is not part of an existing domain. Recall that trees in a forest have different naming structures, according to their domains, but the forest enables communication across the entire organization.

Domain controller for a new domain

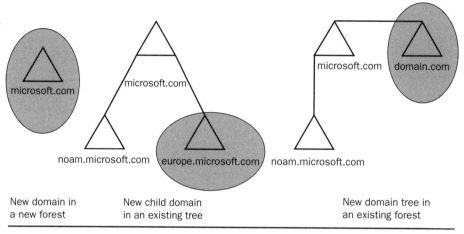

New domain in a new forest   New child domain in an existing tree   New domain tree in an existing forest

Additional domain controller for an existing domain

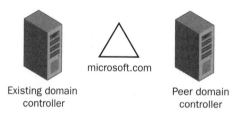

Figure 2-5   Domain controller roles and domain structure selections available during Active Directory installation

Adding a New Domain Controller to an Existing Domain   If you choose to add a domain controller to an existing domain, you create a *peer domain controller,* as shown in Figure 2-5. Peer domain controllers provide redundancy and reduce the load on the existing domain controllers. Peer domain controllers are often placed in different geographic locations to minimize Active Directory access traffic.

Off the Record   Whenever you configure Active Directory, it's very important to consider two domain controllers per domain the absolute minimum. If you only have one domain controller, you can lose the entire domain and all accounts if a serious hardware issue occurs. Of course, if you take the time to back up your Active Directory domain, the domain is not lost entirely, but it can still cause a significant problem. For example, users may not be able to log on properly and no new accounts can be created until Active Directory is restored. Further, you'll only have the data that is current as of your last backup of Active Directory. Any accounts created since that backup will be lost. To avoid this issue, always install a minimum of two domain controllers for each domain.

Using the Active Directory Installation Wizard   The Active Directory Installation Wizard is started by typing **dcpromo** in the Run dialog box.

> **Exam Tip**   Know how to invoke the Active Directory Installation Wizard.

To install Active Directory for a new domain using the Active Directory Installation Wizard, complete the following steps:

1. Click Start and then click Run. In the Run dialog box, type **dcpromo** in the Open box and click OK.

2. On the Welcome To The Active Directory Installation Wizard page, click Next.

3. On the Operating System Compatibility page, click Next.

4. On the Domain Controller Type page, shown in Figure 2-6, select Domain Controller For A New Domain, and then click Next.

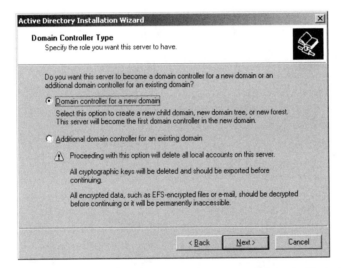

Figure 2-6   Active Directory Installation Wizard, Domain Controller Type page

5. On the Create New Domain page, shown in Figure 2-7, ensure that Domain In A New Forest is selected, and then click Next.

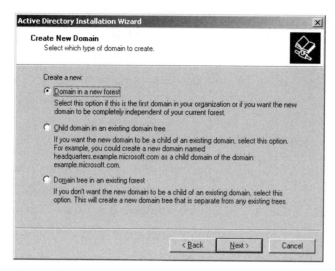

Figure 2-7   Active Directory Installation Wizard, Create New Domain page

6. On the New Domain Name page, shown in Figure 2-8, in the Full DNS Name For New Domain box, type the name of the domain and then click Next.

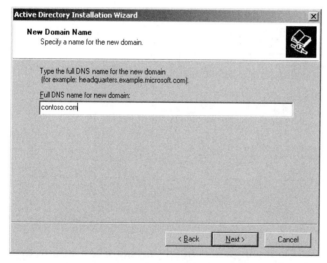

Figure 2-8   Active Directory Installation Wizard, New Domain Name page

7. After a few moments, the NetBIOS Domain Name page appears, as shown in Figure 2-9. It's recommended that you use the default NetBIOS name. Click Next.

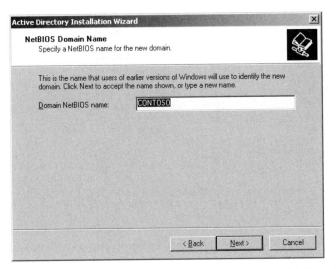

Figure 2-9   Active Directory Installation Wizard, NetBIOS Domain Name page

8. On the Database and Log Folders page, shown in Figure 2-10, type the location of the Active Directory database in the Database Folder box and the Active Directory log in the Log Folder box. It's recommended that you place the database and the log file on separate hard disks that are NTFS drives. Click Next.

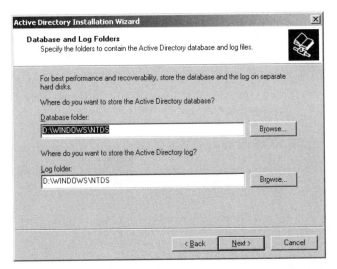

Figure 2-10   Active Directory Installation Wizard, Database And Log Folders page

9. On the Shared System Volume page, shown in Figure 2-11, type the location of the Sysvol folder in the Folder Location box. The shared system volume must be located on a partition or volume formatted with NTFS. Click Next.

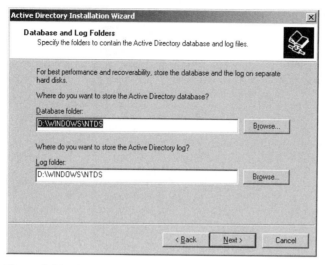

Figure 2-11   Active Directory Installation Wizard, Shared System Volume page

10. On the DNS Registration Diagnostics page, shown in Figure 2-12, view the details of the diagnostic test. Then select the appropriate option, as follows:

   ❑ If you have configured DNS but there is a problem and you have fixed it, select I Have Corrected The Problem. Perform The DNS Diagnostic Test Again, and then click Next.

   ❑ If you have not yet configured DNS and you want the wizard to configure it, select Install And Configure The DNS Server On This Computer, and then click Next.

   ❑ If you have configured DNS but there is a problem and you would like to correct the problem later, select I Will Correct The Problem Later By Configuring DNS Manually, and then click Next.

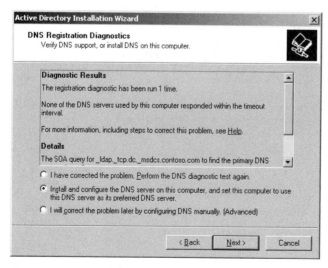

Figure 2-12   Active Directory Installation Wizard, DNS Registration Diagnostics page

11. On the Permissions page, shown in Figure 2-13, select the appropriate default permissions for user and group objects, and then click Next.

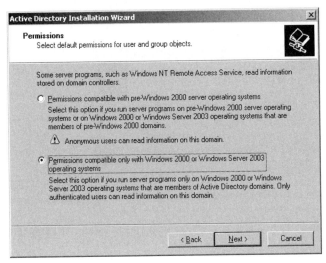

Figure 2-13   Active Directory Installation Wizard, Permissions page

12. On the Directory Services Restore Mode Administrator Password page, shown in Figure 2-14, type the password you want to assign to this server's Administrator account in the event the computer is started in directory services restore mode in the Restore Mode Password box. Confirm the password in the Confirm Password box. Click Next.

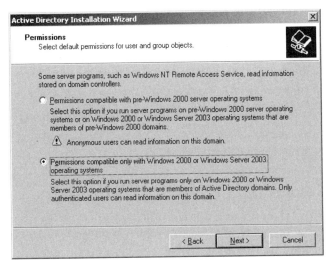

Figure 2-14   Active Directory Installation Wizard, Directory Services Restore Mode Administrator Password page

13. On the Summary page, shown in Figure 2-15, the options that you selected are listed. Review the contents of the Summary page, and then click Next. The wizard takes a few minutes to configure Active Directory components. If you have not configured a static IP address for the server, you will be prompted to do so.

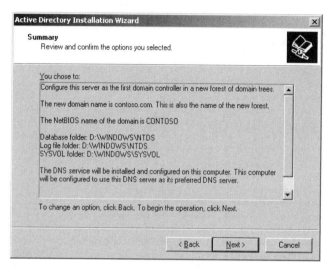

Figure 2-15   Active Directory Installation Wizard, Summary page

14. When the Completing The Active Directory Installation Wizard page appears, click Finish, and then click Restart Now.

15. On the This Server Is Now A Domain Controller page, click Finish. Active Directory is now installed on the server.

> **Note**   Before you attempt to install Active Directory on a server, you must have an edition (other than Windows Server 2003 Web Edition) of the Windows Server 2003 family installed and a static IP address configured for the server. Refer to Lesson 1 for instructions on configuring a static IP address for a server.

Installing Active Directory Using an Answer File

You can create an answer file to run the Active Directory Installation Wizard without having to respond to the screen prompts. An *answer file* is a file that contains answers to questions that should be automated during installation. The answer file must contain all of the parameters that the Active Directory Installation Wizard needs to install Active Directory. An answer file that is used to install Windows Server 2003 can also include the installation of Active Directory, or you can create an answer file that installs only

Active Directory and is run after the Windows Server 2003 setup is complete and you have logged on to the system.

To create the answer file, refer to the instructions located in the "Microsoft Windows Preinstallation Reference," viewable by opening the Ref.chm compiled HTML help file on the Windows Server 2003 CD-ROM. The Ref.chm file is located in the Deploy.cab file in the \Support\Tools folder on the CD. The parameters required for the Active Directory setup answer file are described in Appendix B, "Active Directory Setup Answer File Parameters."

To install Active Directory using an answer file, complete the following steps:

1. Restart your computer and log on as Administrator.

2. Click Start and then click Run. In the Run dialog box, type **dcpromo/answer: answer file**, where *answer file* is the name of the answer file, in the Open box and click OK.

Installing Active Directory Using the Network or Backup Media

In Windows 2000, promoting a member server to become an additional domain controller in an existing domain required replicating the entire directory database to the new domain controller. In case of low network bandwidth or a large directory database, this replication could take hours or even days to complete. Servers running Windows Server 2003 can be promoted using a restored backup taken from a Windows Server 2003 domain controller. This backup can be stored on any backup media (Tape, CD, or DVD) or a network share. You can find more information about backing up Active Directory in Chapter 3, "Administering Active Directory."

Using backup media to create an additional domain controller in your domain reduces the amount of replication required to copy the directory database across your LAN or WAN and will create an additional domain controller faster. This is because Active Directory only needs to replicate the changes that occurred after that backup was taken. The amount of replication that transpires depends on the age of the backup. The backup cannot be older than the tombstone lifetime of the domain, which is set to a default value of 60 days. Therefore, it is always recommended to use the most recent backup available.

If the domain controller that was backed up contained an application directory partition, it will not be restored on the new domain controller. For information about creating an application directory partition on a new domain controller, refer to Chapter 5, "Configuring Sites and Managing Replication."

Note   Windows Server 2003 with SP1 enables you to include application directory partitions in the backup media that you use to install Active Directory. To do this, you increase the forest functional level and then install Windows Server 2003 SP1 on the domain controller that you back up and on any servers that you intend to install as domain controllers. For more information, see "How to use the Install from Media feature to promote Windows Server 2003–based domain controllers" on the Microsoft Web site at *http://support.microsoft.com/?id=311078.*

Although network bandwidth requirements will be greatly reduced by using this mechanism, network connectivity is still necessary so that

- All critical objects are replicated to the new domain controller

- Non-critical objects created after the backup was taken and other changes can be replicated to the new domain controller

- Data stored in the Sysvol folder is replicated to the new domain controller

To install Active Directory using the network or backup media, complete the following steps:

1. Click Start, click Run, and then type **dcpromo /adv** in the Open box and click OK.

2. On the Operating System Compatibility page, click Next.

3. On the Domain Controller Type page, select Additional Domain Controller For An Existing Domain, and then click Next.

4. On the Copying Domain Information page, select one of the following options:

   ❑ Over The Network to copy domain information to this server over the network.

   ❑ From These Restored Backup Files and type the path to the backup files in the box to copy domain information to this server from backup files.

Note   To copy domain information to the server from backup files, you must first back up the system state of a domain controller belonging to the domain in which this server will become an additional domain controller. Second, the system state backup must be restored locally on the server you are promoting. To do this using Windows Server 2003 backup, choose the option Restore Files To: Alternate Location.

If the domain controller from which you restored the system state was also a global catalog, the Active Directory Installation Wizard will ask if you would like this domain controller to become a global catalog as well.

See Also   For more information about backing up Active Directory, refer to Chapter 3.

❏ On the Network Credentials page, specify your user name and password in the User Name and Password boxes, respectively. In the Domain box, type in the domain name and then click Next.

5. On the Database and Log Folders page, ensure that the correct locations for the database folder and the log folder appear in the Database Folder box and the Log Folder box, respectively. Click Next.

6. On the Shared System Volume page, ensure that the correct location for the shared system volume folder appears in the Folder Location box. Click Next.

7. On the Directory Services Restore Mode Administrator Password page, type the password you want to assign to this server's Administrator account in the event the computer is started in directory services restore mode in the Restore Mode Password box. Confirm the password in the Confirm Password box. Click Next.

8. On the Summary page, review your selections. Click Next to proceed with the installation. Restart the computer when prompted.

Installing Active Directory Using the Configure Your Server Wizard

The *Configure Your Server Wizard* provides a central location for you to install many services, including Active Directory, on a computer running Windows Server 2003. The Configure Your Server Wizard is available from the Manage Your Server screen, which opens automatically the first time you log on to a server by using administrative permissions. You can use the Configure Your Server Wizard to install Active Directory only if the computer is the first server on the network and has not yet been configured. Otherwise, if you attempt to use the Configure Your Server Wizard to install additional domain controllers on the network, the wizard simply accesses the Active Directory Installation Wizard to perform the actual installation.

If the computer is the first server on the network and has not yet been configured, the Configure Your Server Wizard provides the Configuration Options page to promote the server to a domain controller and install Active Directory. The Configuration Options page configures your server in the following ways:

■ Promotes the computer to domain controller.

■ Creates a full domain name for your network.

■ Assigns a static IP address.

■ Installs Active Directory, DNS server, DHCP server, and Routing and Remote Access.

- Assigns a subnet mask, if none has been configured on this server. By default, the Configure Your Server Wizard assigns a subnet mask of 255.255.255.0.

- Assigns a preferred DNS server, if none has been configured on this server. By default, the Configure Your Server Wizard assigns a preferred DNS server with the same IP address as the one specified for this server.

- Assigns a DNS forwarder that you specify.

- Configures and activates a DHCP scope.

- Authorizes a DHCP server in Active Directory.

- Sets up an application-naming context on the domain controller in Active Directory for use by TAPI client applications.

> **Note**   Unlike the Active Directory Installation Wizard, the Configure Your Server Wizard does not allow you to set the Active Directory database and log folder location or set the shared system volume folder location. It also does not allow you to select a Directory Services Restore Mode Administrator Password.

When you use the Configure Your Server Wizard, the Configuration Options page is not available if the following points are true:

- The computer is already configured as a DNS or DHCP server.

- The computer has been set up to receive a dynamically configured IP address from a DHCP server on the network.

- The current session is a remote session.

- The computer is running Routing and Remote Access.

- No IP-enabled network adapters are installed.

- More than one IP-enabled network adapter has been installed.

- The computer does not have at least one NTFS partition.

- The computer is joined to a domain.

- The computer is already a domain controller.

- The computer is not a domain controller yet, but the Active Directory Installation Wizard has already been started.

- The computer is a certificate authority (CA).

- There is another computer on the network running the Windows Server 2003 family.

- The computer is running Windows Server 2003, Datacenter Edition.

- The computer is running Windows Server 2003, Web Edition.

Note   If the Configuration Options page is not available and you attempt to use the Configure Your Server Wizard to install Active Directory, the wizard simply starts the Active Directory Installation Wizard. Refer to the "Installing Active Directory Using the Active Directory Installation Wizard" section earlier in this chapter for details.

If the Configuration Options page is available, the Configure Your Server Wizard presents a set of pages, on which you must input:

- Domain name
- NetBIOS name
- IP address of a forwarder, if desired

Removing Active Directory Services from a Domain Controller

Running Dcpromo on an existing domain controller allows you to remove Active Directory from the domain controller and demotes it to either a stand-alone server or a member server. If the domain controller is the last domain controller in the domain, it will become a stand-alone server. If other domain controllers will remain in the domain, it will become a member server. A *stand-alone server* is a computer that runs the Windows Server 2003 operating system but does not participate in a domain. It does not share account information with any other computer and cannot provide access to domain accounts. A *member server* is a computer that runs the Windows Server 2003 operating system and participates in a domain, but does not store a copy of the directory database. For a member server, permissions can be set on resources that allow users to connect to the server and use its resources.

If you remove Active Directory from all domain controllers in a domain, you also delete the directory database for the domain, and the domain no longer exists. Computers joined to this domain can no longer log on to the domain or use domain services.

To remove Active Directory, you must have administrative credentials as follows:

- To remove Active Directory from a domain controller that is the last domain controller in a tree-root or a child domain, you must provide enterprise administrator credentials or be a member of the Enterprise Admins group.

- To remove Active Directory from a domain controller that is the last domain controller in the forest, you must log on to the domain as Administrator or as a member of the Domain Admins group.

■ To remove Active Directory from a domain controller that is not the last domain controller in the domain, you must be logged on as a member of either the Domain Admins group or the Enterprise Admins group.

To remove Active Directory from a domain controller, complete the following steps:

1. Log on as the appropriate administrator.

2. Click Start, click Run, and then type **dcpromo** in the Open box and then click OK.

3. On the Welcome To The Active Directory Installation Wizard page, click Next.

4. If the domain controller is a global catalog server, a message appears telling you to make sure other global catalogs are accessible to users of the domain before removing Active Directory from this computer. Click OK.

5. On the Remove Active Directory page, select the check box if the server is the last domain controller in the domain. Click Next.

6. If the server is the last domain controller in the domain, the Application Directory Partitions page appears. If you want to remove all application directory partitions listed on this page, click Next. Otherwise, click Back. If you clicked Next, the Confirm Deletion page appears. Select the check box if you want the wizard to delete all the application directory partitions on the domain controller, and then click Next.

> **Note**   Because removing the last replica of an application directory partition will result in the permanent loss of any data contained in the partition, the Active Directory Installation Wizard will not remove application directory partitions unless you confirm the deletion. You must decide when it is safe to delete the last replica of a particular partition. If the domain controller holds a TAPI application directory partition, you may need to use the Tapicfg.exe command-line tool to remove the TAPI application directory partition. For more information on using Tapicfg.exe, refer to Windows Server 2003 help.

7. On the Administrator Password page, type and confirm the administrator password, and then click Next.

8. On the Summary page, click Next. The Configuring Active Directory progress indicator appears as Active Directory is removed from the server. This process will take several minutes. Click Finish.

9. On the Active Directory Installation Wizard dialog box, click Restart Now to restart the computer and complete the removal of Active Directory from the computer.

Practice: Installing and Removing Active Directory

In this practice, you install and remove Active Directory on your two practice servers, Server1 and Server2.

> **Note**   To complete this practice successfully, you must have completed the practice in Lesson 1.

Exercise 1: Installing Active Directory

In this exercise, you install Active Directory on Server1, a stand-alone server, making it the first domain controller in a new domain.

▶ **To install Active Directory**

1. On Server1, click Start, point to Control Panel, click Add Or Remove Programs, and then click Add/Remove Windows Components. The Windows Components Wizard opens.

2. In the Components box in the Windows Components window, scroll down and clear Networking Services, and then click Next.

3. In the Completing the Windows Components Wizard window, click Finish.

4. Close the Add or Remove Programs window.

5. Restart Server1 and log on as Administrator.

> **Tip**   Ensure that the IP address for Server1 is the preferred DNS server as specified in Lesson 1.

6. Use the procedure provided earlier in this lesson for installing Active Directory using the Active Directory Installation Wizard to install Active Directory on Server1. Use the Active Directory domain name *contoso.com*. Ensure that the Net-BIOS name is contoso.

7. On the Database and Log Folders page, ensure that the correct locations for the database folder and the log folder appear in the Database Folder box and the Log Folder box, respectively. Click Next.

8. On the Shared System Volume page, ensure that the correct location for the shared system volume folder appears in the Folder Location box. Click Next.

9. On the Directory Services Restore Mode Administrator Password page, type the password you want to assign to this server's Administrator account in the Restore

Mode Password box in the event the computer is started in directory services restore mode. Confirm the password in the Confirm Password box. Click Next.

10. Use the default entries for the remaining wizard pages. On the Summary page, review your selections. Click Next to proceed with the installation.

11. Restart Server1 when the wizard prompts you.

> ## Real World   Verifying DNS Configuration Settings
>
> DNS configuration errors are one of the most common Active Directory installation issues. Issues such as the DNS client pointing to the wrong IP address will prevent you from installing Active Directory. If you have difficulty installing Active Directory, you should verify your DNS settings on both the client and the server, especially if you see a message that indicates the domain or domain controller could not be contacted.

Practice: Fixing a DNS Configuration and Installing Active Directory

In this practice, you configure DNS server settings on Server2 so that you can install Active Directory, and then uninstall Active Directory from the server.

Exercise 1: Fixing a DNS Configuration

In this exercise, you'll incorrectly configure your DNS server settings for Server2. Then, you'll attempt to install Active Directory on Server2. Finally, you'll correct the DNS server settings so you can properly install Active Directory on Server2.

▶ **To fix a DNS configuration and install Active Directory**

1. Log on to Server2 as Administrator.

2. Click Start, point to Control Panel, point to Network Connections, and then click Local Area Connection.

3. In the Local Area Connection Status dialog box, click Properties.

4. In the Local Area Connection Properties dialog box, select Internet Protocol (TCP/IP), and then click Properties.

5. Ensure DNS is not installed by clicking Start, pointing to Administrative Tools, and then checking for DNS in the tree.

6. In the Internet Protocol (TCP/IP) Properties dialog box, set Preferred DNS Server setting to 127.0.0.1.

7. Clear all IP Addresses in the Alternative DNS server setting box, and then click OK.

8. Log off Administrator.

9. Log on using the local administrator's user name and password. In the Log On To Windows dialog box, ensure that you have the Log On To box set to SERVER2 (this computer). You may need to click Options in order to see the Log On To box. Click OK.

10. Click Start, and then click Run. Type **dcpromo** in the Open dialog box. Click OK.

11. When the Active Directory Installation Wizard starts, click Next to begin installing Active Directory.

12. Read the Operating System Compatibility page, and then click Next.

13. On the Domain Controller Type page, select Additional Domain Controller For An Existing Domain, and then click Next.

14. On the Network Credentials page, type the user name and password of the domain administrator account. Type **contoso.com** as the domain, and then click Next.

15. You should see an Active Directory Installation Wizard message box indicating an error. The message box tells you that the domain controller for *contoso.com* cannot be located. This is because your Preferred DNS server is incorrectly configured. Click Details to read more about this error, and then click OK.

16. On the Network Credentials screen, click Cancel to cancel the Active Directory installation, and then click Yes to confirm the cancellation.

17. To correct your DNS configuration, click Start, point to Control Panel, point to Network Connections, and then click Local Area Connection.

18. In the Local Area Connection Properties dialog box, select Internet Protocol (TCP/IP) and click Properties.

19. In the Internet Protocol (TCP/IP) Properties dialog box, set the Preferred DNS Server setting to the IP Address of Server1. Click OK.

20. Click OK to close the Local Area Connection Properties dialog box.

21. Install Active Directory on Server2 as described earlier in this exercise.

Exercise 2: Removing Active Directory from a Domain Controller

In this exercise, you remove Active Directory from Server2, a domain controller, making it a member server for a domain.

▶ **To remove Active Directory from a domain controller**

1. On Server2, use the procedure provided earlier in this lesson to remove Active Directory from a domain controller.

2. Restart Server2 when the wizard prompts you.

Lesson Review

The following questions are intended to reinforce key information presented in this lesson. If you are unable to answer a question, review the lesson and then try the question again. Answers to the questions can be found in the "Questions and Answers" section at the end of this chapter.

1. What command must you use to install Active Directory using the Active Directory Installation Wizard?

   _____

   _____

2. What items are installed when you use the Active Directory Installation Wizard to install Active Directory?

   _____

   _____

3. Explain the two ways you can use an answer file to install Active Directory.

   _____

   _____

4. What command must you use to install Active Directory using the network or backup media?

   _____

   _____

5. Which of the following commands is used to demote a domain controller?

   a. Dcdemote

   b. Dcinstall

   c. Dcpromo

   d. Dcremove

Lesson Summary

- You can install Active Directory using the Active Directory Installation Wizard by using an answer file to perform an unattended installation, by using the network or backup media, or by using the Configure Your Server Wizard.

- The Active Directory Installation Wizard is the main tool used to install Active Directory. You use the Dcpromo command to start the Active Directory Installation Wizard.

- You can create an answer file to run the Active Directory Installation Wizard. The answer file can be a part of the answer file used to install Windows Server 2003, or it can install only Active Directory and run after Windows Server 2003 Setup is complete.

- You can use the network or backup media to install Active Directory on additional domain controllers for an existing domain. Using backup media reduces bandwidth requirements for Active Directory installation.

- You can remove Active Directory from an existing domain controller and demote it to either a stand-alone server or a member server by using the Dcpromo command.

Lesson 3: Verifying Active Directory Installation

Verifying Active Directory installation involves verifying the domain configuration, DNS configuration, DNS integration with Active Directory, installation of the shared system volume, and operation of the Directory Services Restore Mode boot option. This lesson shows you how to verify your Active Directory installation.

After this lesson, you will be able to

■ Verify Active Directory installation

Estimated lesson time: 15 minutes

Verifying an Active Directory Installation

After you have completed the installation of Active Directory, you must verify that Active Directory has been correctly installed. You can do this by verifying the following:

■ Domain configuration

■ DNS configuration

■ DNS integration with Active Directory

■ Installation of the shared system volume

■ Operation of the Directory Services Restore Mode boot option

Verifying Domain Configuration

After the domain controller is installed, various Active Directory administrative tools are added to the administrative tools menu. You can verify that Active Directory is functioning properly and that your domain controller is placed properly by opening the Active Directory Users And Computers console and checking for the presence of the domain and domain controller.

To verify domain configuration, complete the following steps:

1. Click Start, point to Administrative Tools, and then click Active Directory Users And Computers.

2. On the Active Directory Users And Computers console, verify that your domain is correctly named by finding it in the console tree.

3. Double-click the domain. Click the Domain Controllers container. Verify that your domain controller appears and is correctly named by finding it in the details pane.

4. Double-click the server. Verify that all information is correct on the tabs in the Properties dialog box for the server.

Verifying the DNS Configuration

If you allow the Active Directory Installation Wizard to configure DNS for you, and your DNS solution supports dynamic update, the Netlogon service registers a set of default SRV resource records on the DNS server, as shown in Figure 2-16. SRV records are required for clients to find hosts that provide required services.

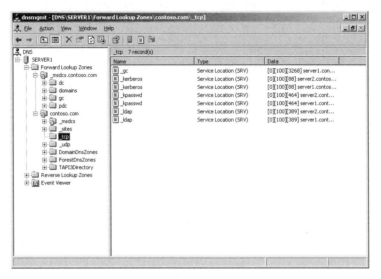

Figure 2-16   Set of default SRV records on Server1 and Server2

To verify the DNS configuration, complete the following steps:

1. Click Start, point to Programs, point to Administrative Tools, and then click DNS.

2. In the DNS console tree, double-click the DNS server, double-click Forward Lookup Zones, and double-click the zone. Expand the _msdcs, _sites, _tcp, and _udp folders to view the default resource records.

Notice that the set of default SRV resource records is registered in multiple layers. The structure shown in Figure 2-16 is for two domain controllers; more complex environments will appear as such, with multiple records in the multiple layers. Records are provided for the global catalog, Kerberos, Kpasswd (Kerberos password change), and Lightweight Directory Access Protocol (LDAP) services.

The Netlogon service creates a log file that contains all the SRV resource records and places the log file in *%Systemroot%*\System32\Config\Netlogon.dns. An example Netlogon.dns file is shown in Figure 2-17. If your DNS solution does not support dynamic update, you must manually enter these records on your DNS server(s).

Figure 2-17 Example Netlogon.dns file

Verifying DNS Integration with Active Directory

If you allow the Active Directory Installation Wizard to configure a basic DNS setup for you, and your DNS solution supports dynamic update, the wizard configures an *Active Directory–integrated forward lookup zone* with the name of the domain. The configuration of this zone changes the storage location of zone data from the zone file to Active Directory on the server. You can verify DNS integration by viewing the properties for the DNS zone and the DNS server.

To verify DNS integration with Active Directory, complete the following steps:

1. Click Start, point to Administrative Tools, and then click DNS.

2. In the DNS console tree, double-click the DNS server, double-click Forward Lookup Zones, right-click the zone, and select Properties from the menu. The Properties dialog box for the zone appears.

3. In the General Tab, verify that Active Directory–Integrated appears after Type. Verify that Nonsecure And Secure appears in the Dynamic Updates box. Notice that the Security tab now exists to set the security for secure dynamic update. Click OK.

4. In the DNS console tree, right-click the DNS server and then select Properties from the menu. The Properties dialog box for the DNS server appears.

5. In the Advanced tab, verify that the Load Zone Data On Startup box is set to From Active Directory And Registry. Click OK.

Verifying Installation of the Shared System Volume

The Active Directory Installation Wizard builds the shared system volume, Sysvol, during the creation of a domain controller. Sysvol is a tree of folders containing files that need to be available and synchronized between domain controllers in a domain or forest, including

- Sysvol shared folder
- Netlogon shared folder
- Microsoft Windows 95, Microsoft Windows 98, Microsoft Windows Millennium Edition (Windows Me), and Microsoft Windows NT 4 system policies
- Windows 2000 and Windows Server 2003 Group Policy settings
- User logon and logoff scripts

For example, the default folder structure contains the following folders for policies or scripts used by network clients:

%Systemroot%\Sysvol\Sysvol\domain_name\Policies

%Systemroot%\Sysvol\Sysvol\domain_name\Scripts

You can verify the installation of the shared system volume by viewing the Sysvol folders in the location you specified during Active Directory installation.

To verify installation of the shared system volume, complete the following steps:

1. Open My Computer.
2. Open *%Systemroot%\Sysvol* or the location you specified during Active Directory installation.
3. Verify that the Sysvol folder contains a shared Sysvol folder. Verify that the shared Sysvol folder contains a folder for the domain, which contains a shared Scripts and a Policies folder.

Verifying Operation of the Directory Services Restore Mode Boot Option

The Directory Services Restore Mode boot option allows restores of Active Directory on a domain controller. This option is not available on member servers. You should verify that this boot option is operational and runs with the password you specified during Active Directory installation to ensure its availability if needed during troubleshooting or restore operations.

To verify operation of the directory services restore mode boot option, complete the following steps:

1. Restart your computer and press F8 when you see the Boot menu.

2. On the Windows Advanced Options menu, use the arrow keys to select Directory Services Restore Mode, and then press ENTER.

3. The Boot menu is displayed again, with the words "Directory Services Restore Mode" displayed in color at the bottom. Select the operating system installation that you want to start, and then press ENTER. The computer restarts in directory services restore mode. This can take a few minutes.

4. On the Welcome To Windows screen, press CTRL+ALT+DELETE. Log on to the local computer using the server's Administrator account name (specified during server setup) and directory services restore mode administrator password (specified during Active Directory installation). Click OK.

Note   You cannot use the name and password of the Active Directory administrator because Active Directory is offline and account verification cannot occur. Rather, the SAM database is used to control access to Active Directory on the local computer while Active Directory is offline.

5. In the Windows Is Running In Safe Mode warning message box, click OK to run the domain controller in safe mode.

6. To return to normal Active Directory operation, restart the computer.

Practice: Verifying Active Directory Installation

In this practice, you verify Active Directory installation on the domain controller you created in Lesson 2.

Note   To complete this practice successfully, you must have completed the practices in Lessons 1 and 2.

Exercise: To Verify Active Directory Installation

In this exercise, you verify Active Directory installation by verifying the domain configuration, the DNS configuration, DNS integration with Active Directory, installation of the shared system volume, and operation of the Directory Services Restore Mode boot option.

▶ **To verify Active Directory installation**

1. Log on to Server1 as Administrator using **password** as your password.

2. Use the procedures provided earlier in this lesson to verify the following:

   ❏ Domain configuration

   ❏ DNS configuration

❑ DNS integration with Active Directory

❑ Installation of the shared system volume

❑ Operation of the Directory Services Restore Mode boot option

Lesson Review

The following questions are intended to reinforce key information presented in this lesson. If you are unable to answer a question, review the lesson and then try the question again. Answers to the questions can be found in the "Questions and Answers" section at the end of this chapter.

1. After Active Directory has been installed, how can you verify the domain configuration?

_____

_____

2. After Active Directory has been installed, how can you verify the DNS configuration?

_____

_____

3. After Active Directory has been installed, how can you verify DNS integration with Active Directory?

_____

_____

4. After Active Directory has been installed, how can you verify installation of the shared system volume?

_____

_____

Lesson Summary

■ You can verify that Active Directory has been correctly installed by verifying domain configuration, DNS configuration, DNS integration with Active Directory, installation of the shared system volume, and the operation of the Directory Services Restore Mode boot option.

Lesson 4: Troubleshooting Active Directory Installation and Removal

In order to install or remove Active Directory you must be able to troubleshoot Active Directory installation and removal. Troubleshooting Active Directory installation and removal involves using the Directory Service log; the Netdiag, Dcdiag, and Ntdsutil command-line tools; and the Dcpromo*xx*.log files to solve Active Directory installation and removal-related problems. This lesson shows you how to troubleshoot the installation and removal of Active Directory.

After this lesson, you will be able to

■ Troubleshoot the installation and removal of Active Directory

Estimated lesson time: 20 minutes

Troubleshooting Active Directory Installation

Some of the common problems you might encounter when installing and removing Active Directory include the following:

■ You cannot reach the server from which you are installing, perhaps because the DNS name is not registered yet.

■ The name of the domain you are authenticating against is incorrect or not available yet.

■ The user name and password you supplied are incorrect.

■ The DNS server settings are not configured correctly.

■ You are unable to remove data in Active Directory after an unsuccessful removal of Active Directory.

Windows Server 2003 provides the following tools to diagnose and resolve problems encountered during Active Directory installation and removal:

■ Directory Service log

■ Netdiag.exe: Network Connectivity Tester

■ Dcdiag.exe: Domain Controller diagnostic tool

■ Dcpromoui.log, Dcpromos.log, and Dcpromo.log files

■ Ntdsutil.exe: Active Directory diagnostic tool

Troubleshooting with the Directory Service Log

Active Directory records events, including errors, warnings, and information that Active Directory generates, in the Directory Service log in Event Viewer. You can use the log to monitor the activity level of Active Directory or to investigate problems.

To view the Directory Service log, complete the following steps:

1. Click Start, point to Administrative Tools, and then click Event Viewer.

2. In the console tree, select Directory Service. In the details pane, Event Viewer displays a list of events and summary information for each item, as shown in Figure 2-18. Information events appear with an "i" icon, warnings appear with a yellow triangle icon, and errors appear with a red circle and white "x" icon.

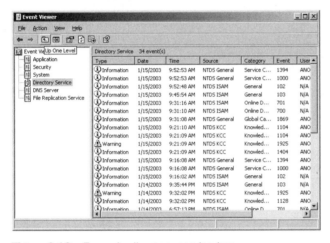

Figure 2-18   Example directory service log

3. To view additional information for any event, double-click the event.

Troubleshooting with Netdiag.exe: Network Connectivity Tester

The Network Connectivity Tester (Netdiag) is a command-line, diagnostic tool included with the Windows Support Tools on the Windows Server 2003 Setup CD-ROM that helps isolate networking and connectivity problems by performing a series of tests to determine the state of a network client. *Netdiag* diagnoses network problems by checking all aspects of a host computer's network configuration and connections. These tests and the network information they provide give support personnel a more direct means of identifying and isolating network problems. In addition, because this tool does not require parameters or switches to be specified, support personnel can focus on analyzing the output, rather than using the tool.

Netdiag has the following syntax:

```
netdiag [/q] [/v] [/l] [/debug] [/d:DomainName] [/fix] [/DcAccountEnum]
[/test:testname] [/skip:testname] [/?]
```

Each of the command parameters is explained in Table 2-1.

Table 2-1 Netdiag Command Switches

Parameter	Function
/q	Lists only tests that return errors
/v	More extensive listing of test data as tests are performed
/l	Stores output in Netdiag.log, in the default directory
/debug	Complete list of test data with reasons for success or failure
/d:*DomainName*	Finds a domain controller in the specified domain
/fix	Fixes minor problems
/DcAccountEnum	Enumerates domain controller computer accounts
/test:*testname*	Runs only the test specified by *testname*. For a complete list, type **netdiag /?**
/skip:*testname*	Skips the named test
/?	Displays the netdiag syntax, including a list of tests.

Run Netdiag whenever a computer is having network problems. The utility tries to diagnose the problem and can even flag problem areas for closer inspection. It can fix simple DNS problems with the optional /fix switch.

To use Windows Support Tools, including Netdiag, you must first install them on your computer. To install the Windows Support Tools, complete the following steps:

1. Start Windows Server 2003. You must log on as a member of the Administrators group to install the support tools.

2. Insert the Windows Server 2003 CD into your CD-ROM drive.

3. Click Start, and then select Run.

4. In the Run dialog box, type **E:\Support\Tools\suptools.msi**, where *E:* is the drive letter of your CD-ROM drive. Click OK.

5. Follow the instructions that appear on your screen.

Note The Setup program requires a maximum of 22 megabytes (MB) of free space to install all Windows Support Tools files onto your hard disk. Setup creates a Support Tools folder within the Program Files folder on the system drive. Support Tools are available from the Start Menu by selecting All Programs followed by the Windows Support Tools option. For detailed information about individual tools, click the Support Tools Help menu item. Graphical user interface (GUI) tools can be invoked from the Tools menu. Command-line tools must be invoked at the command prompt.

See Also   You can find more information about Windows Support Tools in Chapter 3, "Administering Active Directory."

To use Netdiag to check domain controller connectivity, complete the following steps:

1. Click Start, and then click Command Prompt.

2. At the command prompt, type **netdiag / debug** and press ENTER. The test runs and displays the results in the command-prompt window.

For more information about Netdiag, see Windows Support Tools Help.

Troubleshooting with Dcdiag.exe: Domain Controller Diagnostic Tool

The Domain Controller Diagnostic tool (Dcdiag) is a command-line, diagnostic tool included with the Windows Support Tools on the Windows Server 2003 Setup CD-ROM that analyzes the state of domain controllers in a forest or enterprise and reports any problems. *Dcdiag* runs a series of tests to verify different functional areas of Active Directory. The user specifies which domain controllers are tested, such as all domain controllers within an enterprise or site, or just a single domain controller. The user can also select domain controllers holding a directory partition. In the default mode, minimum output is displayed—a confirmation of each test. In the verbose mode, the collected data for each test is displayed. Dcdiag is a read-only tool that does not affect the state of the enterprise, and performs an automatic analysis of the domain controller with little user intervention. Although the Dcdiag tool has many other uses, you can use it to perform a test that diagnoses domain controller connectivity, which is a common Active Directory installation troubleshooting issue. The test for connectivity in the Dcdiag tool verifies that

- DNS names for the server are registered

- The server can be reached by means of IP at its IP address, LDAP, and a remote procedure call (RPC)

Note   Windows Server 2003 with SP1 enhances Dcdiag.exe to include new DNS functionality for reporting on the overall DNS health of domain controllers and to assist with identifying security configurations that can cause Active Directory replication to fail.

See Also   For more information, see "Windows Server 2003 Service Pack 1 32-bit Support Tools" on the Microsoft Web site at *http://www.microsoft.com/downloads/details.aspx? familyid=6EC50B78-8BE1-4E81-B3BE-4E7AC4F0912D&displaylang=en*.

Dcdiag has the following syntax:

```
dcdiag /s:DomainController [/ n:NamingContext] [/u:Domain\Username /p:{* | Password |
""}] [{/a | /e}] [{/q | /v}] [/i] [/f:LogFile] [/ferr:ErrLog] [/c [/skip:Test]] [/
test:Test] [/fix] [{/h|/?}]
```

Each of the command parameters is explained in Table 2-2.

Table 2-2   Dcdiag Command Switches

Parameters	Function
/s:*DomainController*	Uses *DomainController* as a home server. This is a required parameter.
/n:*NamingContext*	Uses *NamingContext* as the naming context to test. Domains can be specified in NetBIOS, DNS, or distinguished name format.
/u:*Domain**Username* /p: {*	*Password*	""}	Uses *Domain**Username* credentials for binding, with *Password* as the password. "" is an empty or null password. * prompts for the password.
/a	Tests all the servers on this site.
/e	Tests all the servers in the entire enterprise. Overrides /a.
/q	(Quiet) Prints only error messages.
/v	(Verbose) Prints extended information.
/i	Ignores superfluous error messages.
/f:*LogFile*	Redirects all output to *LogFile*. /f: operates independently of /ferr:.
/ferr:*ErrLog*	Redirects fatal error output to a separate file *ErrLog*. /ferr: operates independently of /f:.
/c	(Comprehensive) Runs all tests except DCPromo and RegisterInDNS, including non-default tests. Optionally, can be used with /skip to skip specified tests. The following tests are not run by default: Topology, CutoffServers, and OutboundSecureChannels.
/skip:*Test*	Skips the specified *Test*. Must be used with /c. Should not be run in the same command line with /test. The only *Test* that cannot be skipped is Connectivity.
/test:*Test*	Runs only this test. The non-skippable Connectivity test is also run. Should not be run in the same command line with /skip. For a complete list, type **dcdiag /?**.
/fix	Fixes the Service Principal Names (SPNs) on the domain controller's Machine Account Object. Affects only the *MachineAccount* test.
{/h	/?}	Displays a syntax screen at the command prompt.

> **Note**   To use Windows Support Tools, including Dcdiag, you must first install them on your computer. You can find the complete installation procedure in Chapter 3, "Administering Active Directory."

To use Dcdiag to check domain controller connectivity, complete the following steps:

1. Click Start, and then click Command Prompt.

2. At the command prompt, type **dcdiag /s:domain_controller_name/ test:connectivity** and press ENTER. The connectivity test runs and displays the results in the command-prompt window.

> **See Also**   For more information about Dcdiag, see the Windows Support Tools Help.

Troubleshooting with the Dcpromo Log Files

Windows Server 2003 maintains Dcpromo log files that pertain to Active Directory installation. When installing or removing Active Directory using the Active Directory Installation Wizard, the following log files are created in the *%Systemroot%*\Debug folder:

- Dcpromoui.log
- Dcpromos.log
- Dcpromo.log

You need to be familiar with the information provided in these log files because they provide facts about Active Directory installation and removal performance and services.

Dcpromoui.log   The Dcpromoui.log file contains a detailed progress report of the Active Directory installation and removal processes from a graphical interface perspective. Logging begins when the Active Directory Installation Wizard is opened and continues until the summary page appears; regardless of whether it terminated prematurely or completed successfully. If the installation or removal fails, detailed error messages appear in the log immediately after the step that caused the failure. When the installation or removal process is successful, the log provides positive confirmation of that fact. The Dcpromoui.log file includes the following information about the installation or removal of Active Directory:

- The name of the source domain controller for replication
- The directory partitions that were replicated to the target server

- The number of items that were replicated in each directory partition
- The services configured on the target domain controller
- The access control entries (ACEs) set on the registry and files
- The Sysvol directories
- Applicable error messages
- Applicable selections that were entered by the Administrator during the installation or removal process

Dcpromos.log   The Dcpromos.log file is similar to Dcpromoui.log. Dcpromos.log is created by the user interface during the graphical user interface mode setup when a Microsoft Windows 3.*x*–based or Microsoft Windows NT 4–based domain controller is promoted to a Windows 2000 domain controller.

Dcpromo.log   The Dcpromo.log file records settings used for promotion or demotion, such as the site name, the path for the Active Directory database and log files, time synchronization, and information about the computer account. The Dcpromo.log file captures the creation of the Active Directory database, Sysvol trees and the installation, modification, and removal of services. This file is created by using the Active Directory Installation Wizard.

To view the dcpromo logs, complete the following steps:

1. Open My Computer.
2. Open *%Systemroot%*\Debug. Double-click the desired log file.

Troubleshooting with Ntdsutil.exe: Active Directory Diagnostic Tool

The Active Directory diagnostic tool (Ntdsutil) is a command-line tool that provides management facilities for Active Directory. By default, the Ntdsutil.exe file is installed in the *%Systemroot%*\System32 folder. If you are an experienced administrator, you can use Ntdsutil to remove metadata left behind by domain controllers that were removed from the network without being properly uninstalled.

> **Caution**   Ntdsutil is intended for use by experienced administrators only. Improper use of Ntdsutil can result in partial or complete loss of Active Directory functionality. In a production environment, it's recommended that you have a current backup of the system state data before using Ntdsutil. For information on backups, refer to Chapter 3, "Administering Active Directory."

Note   Windows Server 2003 with SP1 updates the Active Directory diagnostic tool (Ntd-sutil), significantly improving the usability of this tool and enhancing the Metadata cleanup functionality.

See Also   For more information, see "Active Directory Directory Services Maintenance Utility" on the Microsoft Web site at *http://technet2.microsoft.com/WindowsServer/en/Library /819bea8b-3889-4479-850f-1f031087693d1033.mspx.*

As part of the removal of Active Directory from a domain controller, the Active Directory Installation Wizard removes the configuration data for the domain controller from Active Directory. This data takes the form of the NTDS Settings object, which exists as a child of the server object. You can view these objects in the Sites container in the Active Directory Sites And Services console. The attributes of the NTDS Settings object include data that represent how the domain controller is identified to its replication partners, the directory partitions that are maintained on the computer, and whether or not the domain controller is a global catalog server. The NTDS Settings object is also a container that can have child objects that represent the domain controller's direct replication partners. This data is required for the domain controller to operate within the environment, but the NTDS Settings object is removed upon the removal of Active Directory.

Removing Orphaned Metadata   If the NTDS Settings object is not properly removed during the process of removing Active Directory, you can use Ntdsutil with the Metadata Cleanup option to manually remove the NTDS Settings object. Windows Server 2003 with SP1 significantly improves the functionality of the NTDS Metadata Cleanup option. Before manually removing the NTDS Settings object from any server, you must also check if replication has occurred because of the removal of Active Directory.

Note   You can learn more about using Ntdsutil to manage orphaned metadata in Chapter 3, "Administering Active Directory." For more information about using Ntdsutil, refer to the *Microsoft Windows Server 2003 Resource Kit,* located on the Microsoft Web site at *http: //www.microsoft.com/windows/reskits/default.asp.*

Removing the Domain Controller Object   After you remove Active Directory from a domain controller, the object that represents the server in the Active Directory Sites And Services console remains. This condition occurs because the server object is a container object that can hold child objects that represent configuration data for other services installed on your computer. For this reason, the wizard does not automatically remove the server object.

If the server object contains any child objects named NTDS Settings, these objects represent the server as a domain controller and must be removed automatically when Active Directory is removed. If these objects are not removed automatically, or if removal of Active Directory cannot be performed (for example, if a computer has malfunctioning hardware), these objects must be removed by using Ntdsutil before you can delete the server object. You can safely delete the server object in the Active Directory Sites And Services console only after all services have been removed and no child objects exist.

To remove the domain controller object, complete the following steps:

1. Click Start, point to Administrative Tools, and then click Active Directory Sites And Services.

2. In the Active Directory Sites And Services console, double-click the Sites container to expand it, and then double-click the appropriate site object (the site in which the server resides) to expand the site object.

3. Double-click the Servers container, right-click the server object, and then click Delete.

4. When you are prompted to confirm deleting the object, click Yes. This process might not complete successfully for either of the following reasons:

   ❑ If you receive a message that states the server is a container that contains other objects, verify that the appropriate services have been stopped before you continue.

   ❑ If you receive a message that states the NTDS Settings object cannot be deleted, you might be attempting to delete an active domain controller. However, this message would only occur if the NTDS Settings object is the computer that you are trying to delete. Otherwise, the delete operation will succeed.

Troubleshooting Scenarios

Table 2-3 describes some Active Directory installation and removal troubleshooting scenarios.

Table 2-3   Active Directory Installation and Removal Troubleshooting Scenarios

Cause	Solution
Error: The computer successfully resolved the DNS service (SRV) resource record required to locate a domain controller, but it failed to locate a domain controller for the Active Directory domain.	
The required A (address) resource records that map the name of the domain controller to its IP address do not exist in DNS.	Verify that the required A resource records exist in DNS by using Nslookup.
The domain controller advertised in DNS might not be connected to the network or is connected to the network but is not running.	Verify connectivity using ping and then verify that the domain controller is running.
Error: The server could not dynamically register Domain Controller Locator records because the DNS servers it uses for name resolution did not find a primary authoritative zone for these resource records.	
The preferred or alternate DNS servers used by this computer for name resolution contain incorrect root hints.	Update the root hints for the DNS servers.
There are incorrect delegations in the DNS zones starting at the root and descending to the zone with same name as the Active Directory domain name you specified.	Verify DNS zone delegations by using Nslookup.
Error: The computer receives "Domain not found," "Server not found," or "RPC server is unavailable" messages.	
Name registration or name resolution is not functioning correctly. This could be caused by a NetBIOS or DNS name registration or resolution problem, or a network connectivity problem.	Run Netdiag /debug on the server that is experiencing the problem to evaluate NetBIOS, DNS, registration, and services. Run Dcdiag on the domain controller to evaluate network connectivity.
Error: This computer could not locate a domain controller for the Active Directory domain displayed in the error message because the DNS servers used by this computer for name resolution failed to look up the service (SRV) resource record.	
The DNS SRV resource record is not registered in DNS.	Verify that the service (SRV) resource record for the requested domain and service type exists in DNS by using Nslookup on a domain controller for the Active Directory domain you entered.
One or more of the zones listed in the error message do not include a delegation to its child zone.	Verify DNS zone delegations by using Nslookup.

Practice: Using Active Directory Installation Troubleshooting Tools

In this practice, you use Active Directory installation troubleshooting tools to perform routine troubleshooting tasks on the domain controller you created in Lesson 2.

> **Note**   To complete this practice successfully, you must have completed the practices in Lesson 1 and Lesson 2.

Exercise 1: Performing Routine Troubleshooting Tasks

In this exercise, you perform routine troubleshooting tasks, including viewing the directory service log, using Netdiag to check domain controller connectivity, using Dcdiag to check domain controller connectivity, and viewing the Dcpromo logs.

▶ **To perform routine troubleshooting tasks**

1. Log on to Server1 as Administrator using **password** as your password.

2. Use the procedure provided earlier in this lesson to

   ❑ View the directory service log

   ❑ Use Netdiag to check domain controller connectivity

   ❑ Use Dcdiag to check domain controller connectivity

   ❑ View the Dcpromo logs

> **Off the Record**   In Lesson 3 of this chapter, you learned how to verify the installation of Active Directory using a variety of tools in the interface. Now that you've seen Dcdiag in action, you probably realize that it can also be used to verify the installation of Active Directory as well as check the system's status. If you try to run Dcdiag on a non-domain controller, the utility will fail, telling you that the computer is not a domain controller. You should consider the utilities that are part of the Windows Support Tools a primary troubleshooting resource. Windows XP and Windows 2000 also include Support Tools that are useful in troubleshooting client, server, and domain controller computers.

Lesson Review

The following questions are intended to reinforce key information presented in this lesson. If you are unable to answer a question, review the lesson and then try the question again. Answers to the questions in the "Questions and Answers" section can be found at the end of this chapter.

1. What information is recorded in the directory service log?

   _____

   _____

2. How can you fix data left behind after an unsuccessful removal of Active Directory?

_____

_____

3. Which of the following tools are best used to evaluate network connectivity? Choose all that apply.

    a. Dcpromoui.log file

    b. Dcpromo.log file

    c. Ntdsutil

    d. Netdiag

    e. Dcdiag

Lesson Summary

- The Directory Service log records events, including errors, warnings, and information generated by Active Directory.

- The Network Connectivity Tester (Netdiag) is a command-line, diagnostic tool that helps isolate networking and connectivity problems by performing a series of tests to determine the state of a network client.

- The Domain Controller Diagnostic tool (Dcdiag) is a command-line, diagnostic tool that analyzes the state of domain controllers in a forest or enterprise and reports any problems.

- The Dcpromoui.log, Dcpromos.log, and Dcpromo.log files are created when installing or removing Active Directory using the Active Directory Installation Wizard.

- The Active Directory diagnostic tool (Ntdsutil) is a command-line tool that provides management facilities for Active Directory. Ntdsutil is designed to be run by an experienced administrator.

Case Scenario Exercise

You are a network consultant. You are consulting for an educational institution called Graphic Design Institute. The institute has four different departments: Information Technology Services (ITS), Administration, Marketing, and Research. The ITS department maintains the institute's Web site (*http://www.graphicdesigninstitute.com*) and connection to the Internet. The Administration department primarily handles student services, such as the enrollment and transcript management and student user account creation and maintenance. The Marketing department is responsible for public awareness, sales, and advertising for the institute. Table 2-4 describes the significant details concerning the Graphic Design Institute's network infrastructure.

Table 2-4   Graphic Design Institute Network Description

Department	Number of Users	Number of Computers	Operating Systems Used
ITS	10	25	UNIX
Administration	5,000	5,030	Windows 2000 Advanced Server, Windows 2000 Professional, and Windows XP
Marketing	15	20	Windows NT 4 Workstation and Windows NT 4 Server

The Research department is newly formed. The Research department has only two employees, Mary Baker, VP of Research, and Bob Gage, Manager of Research. The Research department currently has four computers. Two of the computers are running Windows XP Professional. The other two are expected to run Windows Server 2003. Mary and Bob use the Windows XP Professional computers as their personal workstations. This department is expected to grow significantly in the near future. The ITS department has already installed a sufficient network infrastructure to support up to 200 computers. Bob plans to hire 25 new employees in the next month and another 75 in the next several months. Mary expects that her department will grow only to about 100 to 150 computers. Mary would like to centralize the department's network administrative services and hire two people to manage the network.

The network structure for the Graphic Design Institute is outlined in Figure 2-19.

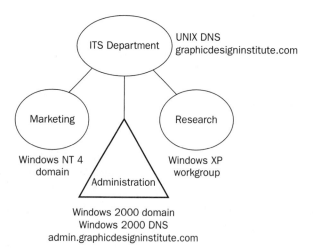

Figure 2-19   Network structure for the Graphic Design Institute

The Director of the Graphic Design Institute, Laura Steele, asks you to assist Mary with the implementation of an Active Directory infrastructure in the Research department. She tells you that the company as a whole is not ready to even consider moving to Active Directory right now. Laura wants you to consider setting up Active Directory using Windows Server 2003 for only the Research department at this time. If that goes well, she says she'll discuss doing further upgrades that involve other departments.

Given this information, answer the following questions:

1. Before you install Active Directory for the Research department, what Active Directory domain structure decisions must be made?

2. Assuming that Mary wants a separate forest for the Research department, what DNS decisions should be made before you install Active Directory?

3. If the ITS department decides to manage the Research department's namespace, what requirements will their UNIX DNS servers need to meet?

4. If the ITS department decides that it will manage the Research department's namespace, but it won't allow dynamic DNS updates, what must be done manually? How often must this be done?

5. If the Research department is expected to support the DNS records required by Active Directory, what options would you have?

6. If the Research department decides to handle its own DNS namespace and they want the most secure dynamic DNS configuration possible, what would you expect to configure?

7. If the Research department wants to allow non-domain members or even non-Microsoft computers to update Windows Server 2003 computers configured as DNS servers, what type of updates must you allow?

Troubleshooting Lab

You are troubleshooting connectivity problems reported by the network administrator for the Research department, which has two Windows Server 2003 computers and 100 Windows XP Professional client computers. One of the administrators for Research reports that he sees DNS registration errors in the Event Viewer and also sees errors when he runs the Netdiag utility.

In this section, you'll troubleshoot this problem using the DNS console and the Netdiag utility. To make this lab more realistic, you'll actually create a problem by deleting the PDC emulator DNS record. You'll learn the significance of the PDC emulator in Chapter 4.

To delete the PDC emulator DNS record, perform the following steps:

1. On Server1, log on as Administrator to the *contoso.com* domain.

2. Open the DNS console. (You can do this in one of two ways: Click Start, select Administrative Tools, and then click DNS; or click Start, then Run, and type **dnsmgmt.msc** in the Open dialog box. Click OK.)

3. Expand the SERVER1 object. Expand the following objects: Forward lookup Zones, _msdcs.contoso.com, pdc, and then the tcp object.

4. Select the _ldap record in the right-hand pane. Right-click the record and then select Delete. Click Yes to confirm the deletion.

5. Right-click _msdcs.contoso.com object and click Properties on the resulting context menu. You'll see the _msdcs.contoso.com Properties dialog box General tab appear.

6. Change the Dynamic Updates option box to read None.

7. Click OK.

8. Close the DNS console.

9. Restart Server1.

At this point you've purposely created a connectivity issue and deleted a significant DNS record. Typically, an administrator wouldn't purposely cause such a problem. However, DNS problems due to mistakes, lack of administrator knowledge, and network connectivity issues are quite common. For example, changing the domain membership of a domain controller could potentially result in a DNS configuration error as documented in Microsoft Knowledge Base Article 311354: "Event 5781 Occurs After DC Changes Domain."

To fix such a problem, perform the following steps:

1. On Server1, log on as Administrator.

2. Open the Event Viewer application. (You can do this in one of two ways: Click Start, click All Programs, Administrative Tools, and then click Event Viewer; or click Start, click Run, and then type **eventvwr.msc** in the Open dialog box. Click OK.)

3. Click on the System log. You should see some Warning events in the right-hand pane that display a source of Netlogon. The time on these events should be the time you restarted Server1. There should be at least two unique messages, but there could be four or more of these events in a row. The Event IDs are 5773 and 5781, which you can see by double-clicking each Warning event. Review the information inside each Warning event and then close it. Once you've reviewed all of these messages, close the Event Viewer.

4. Open a command prompt.

5. In the Command Prompt window, type **netdiag** and press ENTER. Remember, the Windows Support Tools must be installed in order for this command to work.

6. Once this utility has finished running, scroll up in the Command Prompt window until you see the DNS test section. Notice that the DNS test shows a failure. Read that message.

7. Now, you'll attempt to repair this issue by typing **netdiag /fix** and then pressing ENTER. Scroll up in the Command Prompt window until you see the DNS test section. Notice all of the [FATAL] messages.

   Your attempt to fix the issue at this point fails because your DNS server is not accepting dynamic updates. Now you'll switch your DNS server back to allowing dynamic updates in order to correct this issue. Remember, if you don't allow dynamic updates, the only way to correct this issue is to enter the records manually in DNS based on the contents of the Netlogon.dns file (as described earlier in this chapter).

8. Open the DNS console and expand the SERVER1 object, Forward Lookup Zones object, and the _msdcs.contoso.com object.

9. Right-click _msdcs.contoso.com object and click Properties on the resulting context menu. You'll see the _msdcs.contoso.com Properties dialog box General tab appear.

10. Change the Dynamic Updates option box to read Secure Only. Leave the DNS console open.

11. Now, you'll use the Netdiag utility to fix this issue. Return to the Command Prompt window and type **netdiag /fix** and press ENTER. Once this utility has finished running, scroll up until you see the DNS test section. Notice that Netdiag has repaired the problem. The utility may still report one failure, but that issue is actually solved. You'll see this if you run the utility one more time.

12. Type **netdiag** and press ENTER. Scroll up to the DNS test and notice that the DNS test is entirely successful.

13. You can also verify the fix by checking the DNS console. Return to the DNS console and press the F5 key to refresh the screen. Notice that the _ldap record appears on the right-hand pane.

The Windows Support Tools are invaluable when troubleshooting configuration issues. Netdiag is one of the first troubleshooting tools experienced administrators use because it can diagnose and even correct several issues.

Chapter Summary

- To prepare for Active Directory installation, you must determine the domain structure, domain names, storage location of the database and log files, location of the shared system volume folder, and the DNS configuration method.

❑ Begin your domain structure with a single domain, called the forest root domain. Add domains to meet required security policy settings, which are linked to domains; to meet special administrative requirements, such as legal or privacy concerns; to optimize replication traffic; to retain Windows NT domains; or to establish a distinct namespace.

❑ The default location for the database and the database log files is *%Systemroot%* Ntds, although you can specify a different location during Active Directory installation. For best performance and fault tolerance, place the database and the log file on separate hard disks that are NTFS drives.

❑ The default location for the shared system volume is *%Systemroot%\Sysvol*, although you can specify a different location during Active Directory installation. The shared system volume must be located on a partition or volume formatted with NTFS.

❑ You can configure a Windows Server 2003 DNS server manually or you can allow it to be configured automatically during Active Directory installation. Manual configuration of DNS to support Active Directory is required if you are using a non-Windows Server 2003 DNS server or if you want to set up a configuration other than the default configuration set up automatically during Active Directory installation.

■ You can install Active Directory using the Active Directory Installation Wizard by using an answer file to perform an unattended installation, by using the network or backup media, or by using the Configure Your Server Wizard.

❑ The Active Directory Installation Wizard is the main tool used to install Active Directory. You use the dcpromo command to start the Active Directory Installation Wizard.

❑ You can create an answer file to run the Active Directory Installation Wizard. The answer file can be a part of the answer file used to install Windows Server 2003, or it can install only Active Directory and run after Windows Server 2003 Setup is complete. You can use the network or backup media to install Active Directory on additional domain controllers for an existing domain.

❑ You can remove Active Directory from an existing domain controller and demote it to either a stand-alone server or a member server by using the dcpromo command.

■ Troubleshooting Active Directory installation and removal involves using the directory service log; the Netdiag, Dcdiag, and Ntdsutil command-line tools; and the Dcpromo*xx*.log files to solve Active Directory installation and removal-related problems.

Exam Highlights

Before taking the exam, review the key points and terms that are presented in this chapter. You need to know this information.

Key Points

- Before you can install Active Directory, you must determine the domain structure, domain names, storage location of the database and log files, location of the shared system volume folder, and the DNS configuration method.

- You can install Active Directory using the Configure Your Server Wizard or the Active Directory Installation Wizard, by using an answer file to perform an unattended installation, or by using the network or backup media.

- You can remove Active Directory from an existing domain controller and demote it to either a stand-alone server or a member server by using the Dcpromo command.

- You can troubleshoot Active Directory installation and removal by using the Directory Service log; the Netdiag, Dcdiag, and Ntdsutil command-line tools; and the Dcpromo*xx*.log files.

Key Terms

Active Directory Installation Wizard   The tool that is used to install and remove Active Directory.

Configure Your Server Wizard   The tool that helps assign roles to a server, including the role of domain controller.

domain name   The name given by an administrator to a collection of networked computers that share a common directory. Part of the DNS naming structure, domain names consist of a sequence of name labels separated by periods.

forest root domain   The first domain created in a new forest.

Questions and Answers

Page
2-16
Lesson 1 Review

1. What are the reasons to create more than one child domain under a dedicated root domain?

    The reasons to create more than one child domain under the dedicated root are to meet required security policy settings, which are linked to domains; to meet special administrative requirements, such as legal or privacy concerns; to optimize replication traffic; to retain Windows NT domains; and to establish a distinct namespace.

2. What is a forest root domain?

    A forest root domain is the first domain you create in an Active Directory forest. The forest root domain must be centrally managed by an IT organization that is responsible for making domain hierarchy, naming, and policy decisions.

3. For best performance and fault tolerance, where should you store the database and log files?

    For best performance and fault tolerance, it's recommended that you place the database and the log file on separate hard disks that are NTFS drives, although NTFS is not required.

4. What is the function of the shared system volume folder and where is the default storage location of the folder?

    The shared system volume folder stores public files that must be replicated to other domain controllers, such as logon scripts and some of the GPOs, for both the current domain and the enterprise. The default location for the shared system volume folder is *%Systemroot%*\Sysvol. The shared system folder must be placed on an NTFS drive.

5. Which of the following is not a valid reason for creating an additional domain?

    a. To meet SAM size limitations

    b. To meet required security policy settings, which are linked to domains

    c. To meet special administrative requirements, such as legal or privacy concerns

    d. To optimize replication traffic

    The correct answer is a. In Windows NT, the SAM database had a limitation of about 40,000 objects per domain. In Windows Server 2003, each domain can contain more than 1 million objects, so it is no longer necessary to define a new domain just to handle more objects.

Page
2-36
Lesson 2 Review

1. What command must you use to install Active Directory using the Active Directory Installation Wizard?

    Use the Dcpromo command to install Active Directory using the Active Directory Installation Wizard.

2. What items are installed when you use the Active Directory Installation Wizard to install Active Directory?

The Active Directory Installation Wizard installs Active Directory, creates the full domain name, assigns the NetBIOS name for the domain, sets the Active Directory database and log folder location, sets the shared system volume folder location, and installs DNS and a preferred DNS server if you requested DNS installation.

3. Explain the two ways you can use an answer file to install Active Directory.

An answer file that is used to install Windows Server 2003 can also include the installation of Active Directory. Or, you can create an answer file that installs only Active Directory and is run after Windows Server 2003 Setup is complete and you have logged on to the system.

4. What command must you use to install Active Directory using the network or backup media?

Use the Dcpromo /adv command to install Active Directory using the network or backup media.

5. Which of the following commands is used to demote a domain controller?

    a. Dcdemote

    b. Dcinstall

    c. Dcpromo

    d. Dcremove

The correct answer is c. You use the Dcpromo command to demote a domain controller.

Page
2-43

Lesson 3 Review

1. After Active Directory has been installed, how can you verify the domain configuration?

You can verify the domain configuration in three steps by using the Active Directory Users And Computers console. First, you verify that your domain is correctly named by finding it in the console tree. Second, you double-click the domain, click the Domain Controllers container, and verify that your domain controller appears and is correctly named by finding it in the details pane. Third, you double-click the server and verify that all information is correct on the tabs in the Properties dialog box for the server.

2. After Active Directory has been installed, how can you verify the DNS configuration?

You can verify DNS configuration by viewing the set of default SRV resource records on the DNS server in the DNS console.

3. After Active Directory has been installed, how can you verify DNS integration with Active Directory?

You can verify DNS integration by viewing the Type setting and the Dynamic Updates setting in the General tab in the Properties dialog box for the DNS zone and the Load Zone Data On Startup setting in the Advanced tab in the Properties dialog box for the DNS server.

4. After Active Directory has been installed, how can you verify installation of the shared system volume?

You can verify installation of the shared system volume by opening *%Systemroot%*\Sysvol or the location you specified during Active Directory installation and verifying that the Sysvol folder contains a shared Sysvol folder and that the shared Sysvol folder contains a folder for the domain, which contains a shared Scripts and a Policies folder.

Page 2-54

Lesson 4 Review

1. What information is recorded in the directory service log?

Active Directory records events, including errors, warnings, and information that it generates, in the directory service log in Event Viewer.

2. How can you fix data left behind after an unsuccessful removal of Active Directory?

First, you must remove the orphaned metadata—NTDS Settings objects—using Ntdsutil. Then you must remove the domain controller object in the Active Directory Sites And Services console. You can safely delete the domain controller object only after all services have been removed and no child objects exist.

3. Which of the following tools are best used to evaluate network connectivity? Choose all that apply.

   a. Dcpromoui.log file

   b. Dcpromo.log file

   c. Ntdsutil

   d. Netdiag

   e. Dcdiag

The correct answers are d and e. Netdiag and Dcdiag are the tools best suited to evaluate network connectivity. The Dcpromoui and Dcpromo log files log events during the installation process, and Ntdsutil provides management facilities for Active Directory.

Page 2-55

Case Scenario Exercise

1. Before you install Active Directory for the Research department, what Active Directory domain structure decisions must be made?

Mary must decide whether they want to install a completely new forest, install a domain tree, or become part of an existing domain. For example, the Research department could become part of the Windows 2000 Administrative domain, using their Windows Server 2003 domain controllers as replica servers. Given what Laura told you, the decision will probably be to install a new forest root.

2. Assuming that Mary wants a separate forest for the Research department, what DNS decisions should be made before you install Active Directory?

You must determine whether Research or the ITS department will manage that namespace. You also need to know what namespace the new Research domain will use. For example, does Mary want the new domain known as *research.graphicdesigninstitute.com* or something else?

3. If the ITS department decides to manage the Research department's namespace, what requirements will their UNIX DNS servers need to meet?

The UNIX DNS servers must be able to support SRV records.

4. If the ITS department decides that it will manage the Research department's namespace, but it won't allow dynamic DNS updates, what must be done manually? How often must this be done?

The SRV records must be entered manually from each domain controller's Netlogon.dns file. This will have to be done each time there is an infrastructure change to domain or any domain controller. For example, if the IP address or server name of a domain controller changes, you'll have to update the DNS SRV records as well as the DNS A (Host) Records. If you add or remove a site or global catalog server, the SRV records will also require an update.

5. If the Research department is expected to support the DNS records required by Active Directory, what options would you have?

Probably the most obvious, and certainly the most simple, is to ask the ITS department to delegate the domain name *research.graphicdesigninstitute.com* namespace to the Research department. The other option would be to have the Research department manage those portions of the namespace that include SRV records. Those portions begin with _msdcs, _sites, _tcp, and _udp. Delegation is only necessary if other departments and/or users from the Internet need to be able to contact the Research domain resources and hosts using host names.

6. If the Research department decides to handle its own DNS namespace and they want the most secure dynamic DNS configuration possible, what would you expect to configure?

Set the Research department's DNS servers to support Secure Only updates. This will work as long as all Research department computers are members of the Active Directory domain.

7. If the Research department wants to allow non-domain members or even non-Microsoft computers to update Windows Server 2003 computers configured as DNS servers, what type of updates must you allow?

Secure and non-secure.

3 Administering Active Directory

Exam Objectives in this Chapter:

- Set an Active Directory forest and domain functional level based upon requirements.
- Manage schema modifications.
- Add or remove a UPN suffix.
- Restore Active Directory directory service.
- Perform an authoritative restore operation.
- Perform a nonauthoritative restore operation.
- Diagnose and resolve issues related to the Active Directory database.

Why This Chapter Matters

The information in this chapter shows you how to use various tools to administer Active Directory. Both graphical and command-line tools are available. The graphical tools are typically easier to use, especially for simple and unique tasks. Many of the command line tools are quite useful when troubleshooting or automating processes. No matter how you decide to administer Active Directory, you should be sure to back up your Active Directory database routinely. Despite many technological advances, people still make mistakes and equipment sometimes fails. If someone accidentally deletes an Active Directory container object, or if a server crashes, you might need to restore from backup.

Microsoft Windows Server 2003 with Service Pack 1 (SP1) includes new functionality that provides notification of the backup status of the directory service partitions. Windows Server 2003 with SP1 also increases the duration of the tombstone lifetime, the time after which deleted objects in Active Directory are permanently removed from the directory service.

The Active Directory Domains And Trusts console, the Active Directory Sites And Services Console, and the Active Directory Users And Computers console are the main tools for handling Active Directory—it's important to know what function each console serves. Windows Support Tools are also available; you must know how to install them to be able to administer the fine points of Active Directory. Microsoft Management Consoles (MMCs) allow you to administer Active Directory from remote locations or to allow other administrators to manage Active Directory. This chapter shows you how to create and work with MMCs. Finally, you use the Backup Or Restore Wizard to create backups of Active Directory and perform a restore. Being able to maintain effective backups and having the ability to restore Active Directory from backup is vital for effective system administration.

Lessons in this Chapter:

Before You Begin

To complete the lessons in this chapter, you must

- Prepare your test environment according to the descriptions given in the "Getting Started" section of "About This Book"
- Complete the practices for installing and configuring Active Directory as discussed in Chapter 2, "Installing and Configuring Active Directory"

Lesson 1: Using Active Directory Administration Tools

The powerful and flexible Active Directory administration tools that are included with Windows Server 2003 simplify directory service administration. The Active Directory administrative consoles enable you to administer Active Directory directory service. A number of additional Active Directory administration tools are available in the Windows Support Tools. This lesson introduces the Active Directory administrative consoles and Windows Support Tools that are used to configure, manage, and debug Active Directory.

After this lesson, you will be able to

- Describe the functions of the Active Directory Users And Computers administrative console
- Describe the functions of the Active Directory Sites And Services administrative console
- Describe the functions of the Active Directory Domains And Trusts administrative console
- Describe the functions of the Active Directory Schema snap-in
- Change the domain functional level
- Change the forest functional level
- Add or remove a UPN suffix
- Explain the purpose of each of the Windows Support Tools that pertain to Active Directory

Estimated lesson time: 20 minutes

Active Directory Administration Tools

Two main tools are used to administer Active Directory:

- Active Directory administrative consoles
- Active Directory-specific tools in Windows Support Tools

Active Directory Administrative Consoles

The Active Directory administrative consoles are installed automatically on computers configured as Windows Server 2003 domain controllers when Active Directory is installed. The administrative consoles can also be installed on other servers running Windows Server 2003 using the optional Administrative Tools package. This enables you to administer Active Directory from a computer that is not a domain controller. The following administrative consoles are available on the Administrative Tools menu of all Windows Server 2003 domain controllers:

- Active Directory Domains And Trusts console
- Active Directory Sites And Services console

- Active Directory Users And Computers console

The Active Directory Schema snap-in is also available on a computer configured as a domain controller, but must be installed manually.

Active Directory Domains And Trusts Console   The Active Directory Domains And Trusts console provides the interface to manage domains and manage trust relationships between forests and domains. Using Active Directory Domains And Trusts, you can:

- Provide interoperability with other domains (such as pre–Microsoft Windows 2000 domains or domains in other Windows Server 2003 forests) by managing explicit domain trusts. Trusts are discussed in detail in Chapter 4, "Installing and Managing Domains, Trees, and Forests."

- Change the domain functional level (formerly known as a domain mode) of a Windows Server 2003 domain from Windows 2000 mixed to the Windows 2000 native or Windows Server 2003 functional level.

- Change the forest functional level from Windows 2000 to Windows Server 2003 functional level.

- Add and remove alternate user principal name (UPN) suffixes used to create user logon names.

- Transfer the domain naming operations master role from one domain controller to another. Operations master roles are discussed in detail in Chapter 4, "Installing and Managing Domains, Trees, and Forests."

Domain Functional Levels   As you learned in Chapter 1, *domain functional levels* (formerly known as domain modes) provide a way to enable domain-wide Active Directory features within your network environment. Four domain functional levels are available: Windows 2000 mixed (default), Windows 2000 native, Windows Server 2003 interim, and Windows Server 2003.

- **Windows 2000 mixed**   When you first install or upgrade a domain controller to a Windows Server 2003 operating system, the domain controller is set to run in Windows 2000 mixed functionality. The Windows 2000 mixed functional level allows a Windows Server 2003 domain controller to interact with domain controllers in the domain running Microsoft Windows NT 4, Windows 2000, or Windows Server 2003.

- **Windows 2000 native**   The Windows 2000 native functional level allows a domain controller running the Windows Server 2003 operating system to interact with domain controllers in the domain running Windows 2000 or Windows Server 2003. You can raise the functional level of a domain to Windows 2000 native if the domain controllers in the domain are all running Windows 2000 Server or later.

- **Windows Server 2003 interim**   The Windows Server 2003 interim functional level allows a domain controller running the Windows Server 2003 operating system to interact with domain controllers in the domain running Windows NT 4 or Windows Server 2003. The Windows Server 2003 interim functional level is an option only when upgrading the first Windows NT domain to a new forest and can be manually configured after the upgrade. This functional level does not support domain controllers running Windows 2000.

- **Windows Server 2003**   The Windows Server 2003 functional level allows a domain controller running the Windows Server 2003 operating system to interact only with domain controllers in the domain running Windows Server 2003. You can raise the functional level of a domain to Windows Server 2003 only if all domain controllers in the domain are running Windows Server 2003.

Real World   Integrating Windows Server 2003 into Existing Domains

If you plan to install Windows Server 2003 servers configured as domain controllers into an existing Windows 2000 domain, you'll have to run the Adprep.exe command line utility. This utility is located in the I386 directory of the Windows 2003 Server installation CD-ROM. You'll have to run the command **adprep /forestprep** on your existing Windows 2000 Server domain controller holding the schema operations master role. You'll have to run **adprep /domainprep** on the Windows 2000 Server domain controller holding Infrastructure Operations Master role. Be sure to search for articles concerning ADPREP at *http://support.microsoft.com* before you actually run these commands.

Note that the Adprep.exe tool in Windows Server 2003 with SP1 has been improved to reduce the impact of File Replication service (FRS) synchronization that results from updating SYSVOL files during the upgrade. The tool allows you to perform SYSVOL operations in a separate step when preparing the domain for upgrade. The **adprep /domainprep** command, which formerly performed both directory and SYSVOL updates, now updates only the directory. A new switch, /gpprep, has been added to accommodate the SYSVOL updates, which can be performed at a convenient time following the upgrade. Adprep.exe also now detects third-party schema extensions that can block an upgrade, identifies the blocking extensions, and recommends fixes. Adprep.exe also detects Microsoft Exchange Server schema objects so that the Exchange Server schema can be prepared appropriately to accommodate InetOrgPerson naming.

When you convert from Windows 2000 mixed or Windows Server 2003 interim functional level to the Windows 2000 native or Windows Server 2003 functional level, keep in mind the following:

- Support for pre–Windows 2000 replication ceases. Because pre–Windows 2000 replication is gone, you can no longer have any domain controllers in your domain that are not running Windows 2000 Server or later.

- You can no longer add new pre–Windows 2000 domain controllers to the domain.

- The server that served as the primary domain controller during migration is no longer the domain master; all domain controllers begin acting as peers.

 Note   The change in domain functional level is one-way only; you cannot change from the Windows 2000 native or Windows Server 2003 functional level to the Windows 2000 mixed or Windows Server 2003 interim functional level.

Table 3-1 describes the domain-wide features that are enabled for their corresponding domain functional level.

Table 3-1   Features Enabled by Domain Functional Level

Domain Feature	Windows 2000 Mixed	Windows 2000 Native	Windows Server 2003
Domain controller rename tool	Disabled	Disabled	Enabled
Update logon timestamp	Disabled	Disabled	Enabled
User password on InetOrgPerson object	Disabled	Disabled	Enabled
Universal Groups	Disabled for security groups. Enabled for distribution groups.	Enabled. Allows security and distribution groups.	Enabled. Allows security and distribution groups.
Group Nesting	Enabled for distribution groups. Disabled for security groups, except for domain local security groups that can have global groups as members.	Enabled. Allows full group nesting.	Enabled. Allows full group nesting.
Converting Groups	Disabled. No group conversions allowed.	Enabled. Allows conversion between security groups and distribution groups.	Enabled. Allows conversion between security groups and distribution groups.

Table 3-1 Features Enabled by Domain Functional Level

Domain Feature	Windows 2000 Mixed	Windows 2000 Native	Windows Server 2003
SID History	Disabled	Enabled. Allows migration of security principals from one domain to another.	Enabled. Allows migration of security principals from one domain to another.

Exam Tip Be able to distinguish between the domain functional levels.

To change the domain functional level to Windows 2000 native or Windows Server 2003, complete the following steps:

1. Click Start, select Administrative Tools, and then click Active Directory Domains And Trusts.

2. Right-click the domain and then click Raise Domain Functional Level.

3. On the Raise Domain Functional Level dialog box, in the Select An Available Domain Functional Level list, select the domain functionality you want. Click Raise.

4. In the Raise Domain Functional Level message box, click OK.

Forest Functional Levels Forest functional levels provide a way to enable forest-wide Active Directory features within your network environment. Three forest functional levels are available: Windows 2000 (default), Windows Server 2003 interim, and Windows Server 2003.

- **Windows 2000** When you first install or upgrade a domain controller to a Windows Server 2003 operating system, the forest is set to run in the Windows 2000 functional level. The Windows 2000 functional level allows a Windows Server 2003 domain controller to interact with domain controllers in the forest running Windows NT 4, Windows 2000, or Windows Server 2003.

- **Windows Server 2003 interim** The Windows Server 2003 interim functional level allows a domain controller running the Windows Server 2003 operating system to interact with domain controllers in the domain running Windows NT 4 or Windows Server 2003. The Windows Server 2003 interim functional level is an option only when upgrading the first Windows NT domain to a new forest and can be manually configured after the upgrade. This functional level does not support domain controllers running Windows 2000.

■ **Windows Server 2003** The Windows Server 2003 functional level allows a domain controller running the Windows Server 2003 operating system to interact only with domain controllers in the domain running Windows Server 2003. You can raise the functional level of a forest to Windows Server 2003 only if all domain controllers in the forest are running Windows Server 2003 and all domain functional levels in the forest have been raised to Windows Server 2003.

Once the forest functional level has been raised, domain controllers running earlier operating systems cannot be introduced into the forest. Table 3-2 describes the forest-wide features that are enabled for their corresponding functional levels.

Table 3-2   Features Enabled by Forest Functional Levels

Forest Feature	Windows 2000	Windows Server 2003
Global catalog replication improvements	Enabled if both replication partners are running Windows Server 2003. Otherwise, disabled.	Enabled
Defunct schema objects	Disabled	Enabled
Forest trusts	Disabled	Enabled
Linked value replication	Disabled	Enabled
Domain rename	Disabled	Enabled
Improved Active Directory replication algorithms	Disabled	Enabled
Dynamic auxiliary classes	Disabled	Enabled
InetOrgPerson objectClass change	Disabled	Enabled

Exam Tip Be able to distinguish between the forest functional levels.

To change the forest functional level to Windows Server 2003, complete the following steps:

1. Click Start, select Administrative Tools, and then click Active Directory Domains And Trusts.

2. Right click the Active Directory Domains And Trusts node and then click Raise Forest Functional Level.

3. On the Raise Forest Functional Level dialog box, click Raise.

4. In the Raise Forest Functional Level message box, click OK.

UPN Suffixes   A *UPN suffix* is the part of a UPN to the right of the @ character. The default UPN suffix for a user account is the Domain Name System (DNS) domain name of the domain that contains the user account. You can add alternative UPN suffixes to simplify administration and user logon processes by providing a single UPN suffix for all users. The UPN suffix is only used within the Active Directory forest and is not required to be a valid DNS domain name.

Using alternative domain names as the UPN suffix can provide additional logon security and simplify the names used to log on to another domain in the forest. For example, if your organization uses a deep domain tree, such as one organized by department and region, the domain name can be long. The default user UPN for a user in such a domain might be *sales.chi.contoso.com*. Creating a UPN suffix of "contoso" would allow the user to log on using the much simpler logon name of *user@contoso*. If you create an alternative UPN, the UPN is then available when you create users by using Active Directory Users And Computers.

To add or remove UPN suffixes, complete the following steps:

1. Click Start, select Administrative Tools, and then click Active Directory Domains And Trusts.

2. Right click the Active Directory Domains And Trusts node and then click Properties.

3. On the Active Directory Domains And Trusts dialog box, in the UPN Suffixes tab, shown in Figure 3-1, do one of the following:

   ❑ To add a UPN suffix, type an alternative UPN suffix in the Alternative UPN Suffixes box, and then click Add.

   ❑ To remove a UPN suffix, select the suffix from the Alternative UPN Suffixes box, and then click Remove. On the Active Directory Domains and Trusts message box, click Yes.

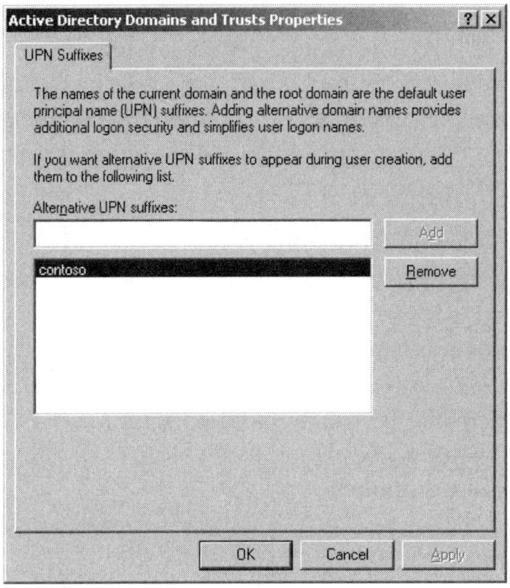

Figure 3-1 UPN Suffixes tab

4. Click OK.

Active Directory Sites And Services Console You provide information about the physical structure of your network by publishing sites to Active Directory using the Active Directory Sites And Services console. Active Directory uses this information to determine how to replicate directory information and handle service requests. Sites are discussed in more detail in Chapter 5, "Configuring Sites and Managing Replication."

Active Directory Users And Computers Console The Active Directory Users And Computers console allows you to add, modify, delete, and organize Windows Server 2003 user accounts, computer accounts, security and distribution groups, and published resources in your organization's directory. It also allows you to manage domain controllers and organizational units (OUs).

Note Windows Server 2003 with SP1 extends the default period that Active Directory retains a deleted object, called the *tombstone lifetime*, from 60 days to 180 days. The longer tombstone lifetime increases the shelf life of system state backups and decreases the chance that a deleted object will reappear in the directory service. This reappearance can occur if a domain controller is reconnected to the network after a directory service object has been permanently deleted from the online domain controllers.

The tombstone lifetime does not change automatically when you upgrade to Windows Server 2003 with SP1, but you can change the tombstone lifetime manually after the upgrade.

New forests created with domain controllers running Windows Server 2003 with SP1 have a default tombstone lifetime of 180 days.

Active Directory Schema Snap-In The Active Directory Schema snap-in is available so you can view and modify Active Directory schema. By default, the snap-in is not available on the Administrative Tools menu. You must install it using the command line and by creating an MMC for it. This action is required to ensure that the schema cannot be modified by accident.

To install the Active Directory Schema snap-in, complete the following steps:

1. Log on as an Administrator.

2. Click Start, and then click Command Prompt.

3. Type **regsvr32 schmmgmt.dll**.

4. Click Start, and then click Run.

5. In the Run box, type **mmc** and then click OK.

6. On the File menu, click Add/Remove Snap-In.

7. In the Add/Remove Snap-In dialog box, click Add.

8. In the Add Standalone Snap-In dialog box, in the Snap-In column, double-click Active Directory Schema, and then click Close.

9. In the Add/Remove Snap-In dialog box, click OK.

10. To save this console, on the File menu, click Save. In the Save As dialog box, ensure that Administrative Tools is shown in the Save In box. Then type **Active Directory Schema** in the File Name box and click Save. The Active Directory Schema snap-in is now available from the Administrative Tools menu.

11. Close the Active Directory Schema snap-in.

> **See Also** Modifying the Active Directory schema is an advanced operation that is best performed by experienced programmers or system administrators. For detailed information about modifying the Active Directory schema, see the Microsoft Windows Server 2003 Resource Kit, located on the Microsoft Web site at *http://www.microsoft.com/windows/reskits/ default.asp*.

For further information about using MMCs, refer to Lesson 2.

Active Directory-Specific Windows Support Tools

In Chapter 2, you installed the Windows Support Tools to assist you in troubleshooting Active Directory installation. In addition, several tools that can be used to configure, manage, and debug Active Directory are available in the Windows Support Tools. The Windows Support Tools are included on the Windows Server 2003 CD in the

\Support\Tools folder. These tools are intended for use by Microsoft support personnel and experienced users.

Table 3-3 describes the Windows Support Tools that pertain to Active Directory.

Table 3-3   Active Directory-Specific Windows Support Tools

Tool	Used to
Acldiag.exe: ACL Diagnostics[*]	Determine whether a user has been granted or denied access to an Active Directory object. It can also be used to reset access control lists (ACLs) to their default state.
Adsiedit.msc: ADSI Edit[†]	Add, delete, and move objects in the directory (including schema and configuration naming contexts). Object attributes can be viewed, modified, and deleted.
Dcdiag.exe: Domain Controller Diagnostic Tool[*]	Analyze the state of domain controllers in a forest or enterprise and report any problems. Note that Dcdiag.exe in Windows Server 2003 with SP1 includes a new DNS health check, and a new security check that can detect security configurations that can cause replication to fail.
Dfscmd.exe: Distributed File System Command Tool[*]	Manage a distributed file system from the command line. Note that Dfscmd.exe in Windows Server 2003 with SP1 includes new commands to move or rename links.
Dfsutil.exe: Distributed File System Utility[*]	Manage all aspects of Distributed File System (DFS), check the configuration concurrency of DFS servers, and display the DFS topology. Note that Dfsutil.exe in Windows Server 2003 with SP1 includes the ability to implement failback settings for roots and links.
Dsacls.exe[*]	View or modify the ACLs of objects in Active Directory.
Dsastat.exe: Directory Services Utility[*]	Compare naming contexts on domain controllers and detect differences.
Ldp.exe: LDP Tool[‡]	Allow Lightweight Directory Access Protocol (LDAP) operations, such as connect, bind, search, modify, add, and delete, to be performed against Active Directory.
Movetree.exe: Active Directory Object Manager[*]	Move Active Directory objects such as OUs and users between domains in a single forest to support domain consolidation or organizational restructuring operations.
Netdom.exe: Windows Domain Manager[*]	Manage Windows Server 2003 domains and trust relationships from the command line.
Nltest.exe[*]	Provide a list of primary domain controllers, force a remote shutdown, provide information about trusts and replication.

Table 3-3   Active Directory-Specific Windows Support Tools

Tool	Used to
Ntfrsutl.exe[*]	Dump internal tables, thread, and memory information for the NT File Replication Service (NTFRS). It runs against local and remote servers.
Repadmin.exe: Replication Diagnostics Tool[*]	Diagnose replication problems between domain controllers. See Chapter 5, "Configuring Sites and Managing Replication," for more information about using Repadmin.
Replmon.exe: Active Directory Replication Monitor[‡]	Graphically display replication topology, monitor replication status, force synchronization between domain controllers. See Chapter 5, "Configuring Sites and Managing Replication," for more information about using Replmon.
Sdcheck.exe: Security Descriptor Check Utility[*]	Display the security descriptor for any object stored in Active Directory. This tool enables an administrator to determine if ACLs are being inherited correctly and if ACL changes are being replicated from one domain controller to another.
Search.vbs: Active Directory Search Tool[*]	Perform searches against an LDAP server to get information from Active Directory.
Setspn.exe: Manipulate Service Principal Names for Accounts[*]	Read, modify, and delete the Service Principal Names (SPN) directory property for an Active Directory service account.
SIDwalker Security Administration Tools	Manage access control policies on Windows Server 2003 and Windows NT systems. SIDwalker consists of three separate programs: Showaccs.exe[*] and Sidwalk.exe[*] for examining and changing access control entries, and Security Migration Editor for editing mapping between old and new security identifiers (SIDs).

[*]   command-line tool

[†]   MMC snap-in

[‡]   GUI tool

See Windows Support Tools help for more information about using the Windows Support Tools that pertain to Active Directory.

Active Directory Service Interfaces (ADSI) provides a simple, powerful, object-oriented interface to Active Directory. ADSI makes it easy for programmers and administrators to create programs utilizing directory services by using high-level tools such as Microsoft Visual Basic, Java, C, C#, or Visual C++ as well as scripted languages such as VBScript, JScript, or PerlScript without having to worry about the underlying differences between the different namespaces. ADSI is a fully programmable Automation object for use by administrators.

ADSI enables you to build or buy programs that give you a single point of access to multiple directories in your network environment, whether those directories are based on LDAP or another protocol.

> **Note**   A detailed discussion of ADSI is beyond the scope of this training kit. For further information about ADSI, refer to the Microsoft Windows Server 2003 Resource Kit located on the Microsoft Web site at *http://www.microsoft.com/windows/reskits/default.asp*.

Practice: Viewing Active Directory Administration Tools

In this practice, you view the Active Directory administrative consoles and some of the Active Directory support tools.

Exercise 1: Viewing Active Directory Administrative Consoles

In this exercise, you view the Active Directory administrative consoles.

▶ **To view Active Directory administrative consoles**

1. Log on to Server01 as Administrator.

2. Click Start, point to Administrative Tools, and then click Active Directory Domains And Trusts.

3. In the console tree, right-click the *contoso.com* domain and then select Properties. In the Properties dialog box for the *contoso.com* domain, click the Trusts tab. Notice the trust information boxes that would contain information about trusts if there were other domains in the forest. Click Cancel.

4. In the console tree, right-click the *contoso.com* domain and then select Raise Domain Functional Level. On the Raise Domain Functional Level dialog box, notice the list in which you can raise domain functionality. Click Cancel. In the console tree, right-click the Active Directory Domains And Trusts node and then select Raise Forest Functional Level. On the Raise Forest Functional Level dialog box, notice that you cannot raise forest functionality until you have raised the domain functional level to Windows Server 2003. Click OK.

5. In the console tree, right-click the Active Directory Domains And Trusts node and then select Properties. On the UPN Suffixes tab, notice where you can enter alternate UPN suffixes. Click OK and then close the Active Directory Domains And Trusts console.

6. Click Start, point to Administrative Tools, and then click Active Directory Sites And Services. In the console tree, double-click the Sites folder. Notice that a site called Default-First-Site is present. This site is created automatically when Active Directory is installed. Close the Active Directory Sites And Services console.

7. Click Start, point to Administrative Tools, and then click Active Directory Users And Computers. In the console tree, double-click the Builtin folder and examine all the default groups. Double-click the Users folder and examine all the default users. Close the Active Directory Users And Computers console.

Exercise 2: Installing and Viewing the Active Directory Schema Snap-In

In this exercise, you install the Active Directory Schema snap-in and view its contents.

▶ **To install and view the Active Directory Schema snap-in**

1. Use the procedure provided earlier in this lesson to install the Active Directory Schema snap-in.

2. Open the Active Directory Schema snap-in. In the console tree, double-click Active Directory Schema. Double-click the Classes folder. Notice the list of classes provided in the details pane.

3. In the console tree, double-click any class. Notice the list of attributes for that class provided in the Details pane. Close the Active Directory Schema snap-in.

4. On the Microsoft Management Console message box, click No.

Exercise 3: Installing and Viewing the Active Directory-Specific Windows Support Tools

In this exercise, you install Windows Support Tools and view some of the Active Directory-specific support tools.

▶ **To install and view the Active Directory-specific Windows Support Tools**

1. If you haven't already installed the Windows Support Tools, use the procedure provided in Chapter 2 to install them.

2. Click Start, point to All Programs, point to Windows Support Tools, then click Support Tools Help.

3. Access the Dsacls.exe tool in the alphabetical list of tools by file name. View Help for this tool.

4. In help, click Open Command Prompt. At the command prompt, type **dsacls \\server1\DC=contoso,DC=com** and press ENTER. The output shows the access control list for Active Directory on Server01.

5. Close the command prompt. Close Dsacls Help.

Lesson Review

The following questions are intended to reinforce key information presented in this lesson. If you are unable to answer a question, review the lesson and then try the question

again. Answers to the questions can be found in the "Questions and Answers" section at the end of this chapter.

1. What is the purpose of the Active Directory Domains And Trusts console?

   _____

   _____

2. What is the purpose of the Active Directory Sites And Services console?

   _____

   _____

3. What is the purpose of the Active Directory Users And Computers console?

   _____

   _____

4. Why isn't the Active Directory Schema snap-in provided automatically on the Administrative Tools menu after you install Active Directory?

   _____

   _____

5. Which Active Directory-specific Windows Support Tool enables you to manage Windows Server 2003 domains and trust relationships?

   a. Ntdsutl.exe

   b. Netdom.exe

   c. Active Directory Domains And Trusts console

   d. Nltest.exe

Lesson Summary

- Three Active Directory administrative consoles are available on the Administrative Tools menu of all Windows Server 2003 domain controllers. The Active Directory Schema snap-in is also available on a domain controller, but must be installed manually to ensure the schema is not modified by accident.

- Domain functional level (formerly known as the domain mode) provides a way to enable domain-wide Active Directory features within your network environment. Four domain functional levels are available: Windows 2000 mixed (default), Windows 2000 native, Windows Server 2003 interim, and Windows Server 2003. The change in domain functional level is one-way only.

■ Forest functional level provides a way to enable forest-wide Active Directory features within your network environment. Three forest functional levels are available: Windows 2000 (default), Windows Server 2003 interim, and Windows Server 2003. You can raise the functional level of a forest to Windows Server 2003 only if all domain controllers in the forest are running Windows Server 2003.

■ You can add alternative UPN suffixes to simplify administration and user logon processes by providing a single UPN suffix for all users. Using alternative domain names as the UPN suffix can provide additional logon security and simplify the names used to log on to another domain in the forest.

■ Several additional tools that can be used to configure, manage, and debug Active Directory are available in the Windows Support Tools. To use these tools you must first install the Windows Support Tools on your computer.

Lesson 2: Customizing MMCs

In the previous lesson, you learned how to use the standard administrative consoles provided when you install Active Directory. You can also create custom consoles that focus on management tasks you specify by using the MMC. This lesson explains how you can create, use, and modify custom consoles.

***

After this lesson, you will be able to

- Create customized MMCs
- Modify customized MMCs

Estimated lesson time: 25 minutes

***

The MMC

The MMC is a tool used to create, save, and open collections of administrative tools, which are called *consoles*. When you access the Active Directory administrative consoles discussed in Lesson 1, you are accessing the MMC for that tool. The Active Directory Domains And Trusts, Active Directory Sites And Services, and Active Directory Users And Computers administrative tools are each a console. The console does not provide management functions itself, but is the program that hosts management applications called *snap-ins*. Snap-ins are programs used by administrators to manage network services.

There are two types of MMCs: preconfigured and custom. Preconfigured MMCs contain commonly used snap-ins, and they appear on the Administrative Tools menu. You create custom MMCs to perform a unique set of administrative tasks, such as the MMC for the Active Directory schema discussed in the previous lesson. You can use both preconfigured and custom MMCs for remote administration.

Preconfigured MMCs

Preconfigured MMCs contain snap-ins that you use to perform the most common administrative tasks. The Windows Server 2003 family installs a number of preconfigured MMCs during installation. The following are characteristics of preconfigured MMCs:

- They contain a stand-alone snap-in that provides the functionality to perform a related set of administrative tasks.

- They function in user mode. Because preconfigured MMCs are in user mode, you cannot modify them, save them, or add additional snap-ins. However, when you create custom consoles, you can add as many preconfigured consoles as you want as snap-ins to your custom console.

■ They might be added by Windows Server 2003 when you install additional components. Optional Windows Server 2003 components might include additional preconfigured MMCs that Windows Server 2003 adds when you install a component. For example, when you install the DNS service, Windows Server 2003 also installs the DNS Management console.

Custom MMCs

You can use many of the preconfigured MMCs for administrative tasks. However, there will be times when you need to create your own custom MMCs. Although you can't modify preconfigured consoles, you can combine multiple preconfigured snap-ins with third-party snap-ins provided by independent software vendors that perform related tasks to create custom MMCs. You can then do the following:

■ Save the custom MMCs to use again.

■ Distribute the custom MMCs to other administrators.

■ Use the custom MMCs from any computer to centralize and unify administrative tasks.

Creating custom MMCs allows you to meet your administrative requirements by combining snap-ins that you use to perform common administrative tasks. By creating a custom MMC, you do not have to switch between different programs or different preconfigured MMCs because all of the snap-ins that you need to perform your job are located in the custom MMC.

Consoles are saved as files and have an .msc extension. All the settings for the snap-ins contained in the console are saved and restored when the file is opened, even if the console file is opened on a different computer or network.

Console Tree and Details Pane

Every MMC has a *console tree*, which displays the hierarchical organization of its associated snap-ins. The MMC in Figure 3-2, for example, contains Device Manager on the local computer and the Disk Defragmenter snap-ins.

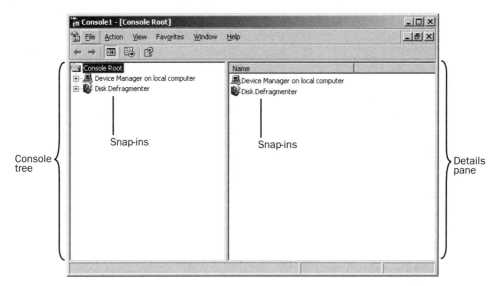

Figure 3-2   A sample MMC

The console tree organizes snap-ins that are part of an MMC. This allows you to easily locate a specific snap-in. Items that you add to the console tree appear under the console root. The *details pane* lists the contents of the active snap-in.

Every MMC contains an Action menu and a View menu. The choices on these menus vary, depending on the current selection in the console tree.

Snap-Ins

Snap-ins are applications that are designed to work in an MMC. Use snap-ins to perform administrative tasks. There are two types of snap-ins: stand-alone snap-ins and extension snap-ins.

Stand-alone snap-ins are usually referred to simply as *snap-ins*. Use stand-alone snap-ins to perform Windows Server 2003 administrative tasks. Each snap-in provides one function or a related set of functions. Windows Server 2003 comes with many standard snap-ins.

Extension snap-ins are usually referred to simply as *extensions*. They are snap-ins that provide additional administrative functionality to another snap-in. The following are characteristics of extensions.

- Extensions are designed to work with one or more stand-alone snap-ins, based on the function of the stand-alone snap-in. For example, the Group Policy extension is available in the Active Directory Users And Computers console; however, it is not available in the Disk Defragmenter snap-in, because Group Policy does not relate to the administrative task of disk defragmentation.

- When you add an extension, Windows Server 2003 displays only extensions that are compatible with the stand-alone snap-in. Windows Server 2003 places the extensions into the appropriate location within the stand-alone snap-in.

- When you add a snap-in to a console, MMC adds all available extensions by default. You can remove any extension from the snap-in.

- You can add an extension to multiple snap-ins.

Figure 3-3 demonstrates the concept of snap-ins and extensions. A toolbox (an MMC) holds a drill (a snap-in). You can use a drill with its standard drill bit, and you can perform additional functions with different drill bits (extensions). Extensions are pre-assigned to snap-ins, and multiple snap-ins can use the same extension.

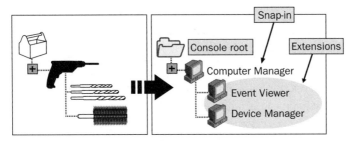

Figure 3-3   Snap-ins and extensions

Some stand-alone snap-ins can use extensions that provide additional functionality, for example, Computer Management. However, some snap-ins, like Event Viewer, can act as either a snap-in or an extension.

Console Options

Use console options to determine how each MMC operates by selecting the appropriate console mode. The console mode determines the MMC functionality for the person who is using a saved MMC. The two available console modes are author mode and user mode.

> **Note**   Additional console options can be set using Group Policy. For information on setting group policies, see Chapter 11, "Administering Group Policy."

When you save an MMC in author mode, you enable full access to all MMC functionality, which includes modifying the MMC. Save the MMC using author mode to allow those using it to do the following:

- Add or remove snap-ins.
- Create new windows.

- View all portions of the console tree.

- Save MMCs.

> **Note**   By default, all new MMCs are saved in author mode.

Usually, if you plan to distribute an MMC to other administrators, you save the MMC in user mode. When you set an MMC to user mode, users cannot add snap-ins to, remove snap-ins from, or save the MMC.

There are three types of user modes that allow different levels of access and functionality. Table 3-4 describes when to use each type of user mode.

Table 3-4   MMC User Mode Types

User mode	Use when
Full access	You want to allow users to navigate between snap-ins, open new windows, and gain access to all portions of the console tree.
Limited access, multiple windows	You do not want to allow users to open new windows or gain access to a portion of the console tree. You want to allow users to view multiple windows in the console.
Limited access, single window	You do not want to allow users to open new windows or gain access to a portion of the console tree. You want to allow users to view only one window in the console.

Using MMCs for Remote Administration

When you create custom MMCs, you can set up a snap-in for remote administration. Remote administration allows you to perform administrative tasks from any location. For example, you can use a computer running Windows XP Professional with Service Pack 1 or the 329357 hotfix applied to perform administrative tasks on a computer running Windows Server 2003. You cannot use all snap-ins for remote administration; the design of each snap-in dictates whether or not you can use it for remote administration.

To perform remote administration:

- You can use snap-ins from computers running different editions of the Windows Server 2003 family.

- You must use specific snap-ins designed for remote administration. If the snap-in is available for remote administration, Windows Server 2003 prompts you to choose the target computer to administer.

Suppose you need to administer Windows Server 2003 from a Windows XP Professional desktop. Because Windows XP Professional does not provide the same level of administrative tools as Windows Server 2003, you will need to install a more complete set of tools on the Professional desktop. By accessing the server and executing the Adminpak.msi file located at *%Systemroot%*\System32, you can copy the administrative tools onto the Professional desktop. Then configure each tool for use with the server. One benefit of installing the entire package is that it includes the Active Directory Management MMC, which contains the three major Active Directory MMCs and the DNS MMC. Note that some tools may be installed that are not actually running on the server; the Windows Server 2003 Administration Tools Setup Wizard is simply a means for loading administrative tools to a remote machine.

Off the Record   The Adminpak.msi can be used to repair console issues related to file corruption. For example, if you find that you can no longer open a console, such as the DNS console, you should try reinstalling Adminpak.msi.

Creating Custom MMCs

To create a custom MMC, you must open an empty console and then add the snap-ins needed to perform the desired administrative tasks.

To create a custom MMC, complete the following steps:

1. Click Start and point to Run.

2. Type **mmc** in the Run box, and then click OK. An MMC window opens, titled Console1 and containing a window titled Console Root. This is an empty MMC.

3. Maximize the Console1 and Console Root windows.

4. On the File menu, click Add/Remove Snap-In.

5. In the Standalone tab in the Add/Remove Snap-In dialog box, click Add.

6. In the Add Standalone Snap-In dialog box, shown in Figure 3-4, select the snap-in you want to add and click Add. In some instances, the snap-in is simply added to the MMC. In other cases, MMC requires you to specify additional details for the snap-in in a dialog box or through a wizard.

Figure 3-4 Add Standalone Snap-In dialog box

7. Enter additional details for the snap-in as needed.

8. If the snap-in supports remote administration, a dialog box for the snap-in appears, as shown in Figure 3-5. Do one of the following:

   ❑ Select Local Computer to manage the computer on which the console is running.

   ❑ Select Another Computer to manage a remote computer. Then click Browse. In the Select Computer dialog box, type the name of the remote computer, then click OK.

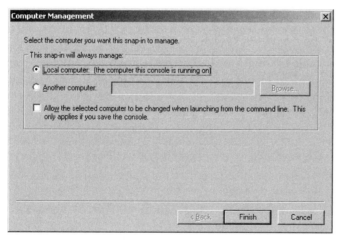

Figure 3-5 Dialog box indicating type of management for the Computer Management snap-in

9. Click Finish.

10. When you are finished adding snap-ins, click Close in the Add Standalone Snap-In dialog box. The snap-ins you have added appear in the list in the Add/Remove Snap-In dialog box.

11. In the Add/Remove Snap-In dialog box, click OK. MMC displays the snap-ins you have added in the console tree below Console Root.

12. Select the Console Root.

13. On the File menu, click Options. MMC displays the Options dialog box with the Console tab active, as shown in Figure 3-6.

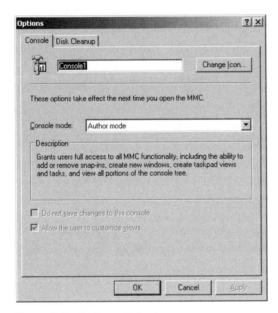

Figure 3-6   Options dialog box

14. Select the console mode in the Console Mode box, and then click OK.

15. On the File menu, click Save As.

16. In the File Name box in the Save As dialog box, type the name for your customized MMC and then click Save. The name of your console appears in the MMC title bar.

17. On the File menu, click Exit. The customized console has been created and saved and can now be accessed on the Administrative Tools menu.

Modifying Custom MMCs

You can modify a custom MMC by adding or removing snap-ins or extensions. Not all snap-ins have extensions. You can add or remove extensions from a console when you need to expand or limit administrative tasks. This allows you to include only those extensions that are relevant to the computer being administered.

To add a snap-in to an existing MMC, complete the following steps:

1. Click Start, point to All Programs, point to Administrative Tools, and then click the name of the custom MMC.

2. On the File menu, click Add/Remove Snap-In.

3. In the Standalone tab in the Add/Remove Snap-In dialog box, click Add.

4. In the Add Standalone Snap-In dialog box, select the snap-in you want to add to the existing MMC and click Add.

5. Enter additional details for the snap-in as described in the previous procedure.

6. When you are finished adding snap-ins, click Close in the Add Standalone Snap-In dialog box. The snap-ins you have added appear in the list in the Add/Remove Snap-In dialog box.

7. In the Add/Remove Snap-In dialog box, click OK. MMC displays the snap-ins you have added in the console tree below Console Root.

To remove a snap-in from an existing MMC, complete the following steps:

1. Click Start, point to All Programs, point to Administrative Tools, then click the name of the custom MMC.

2. On the File menu, click Add/Remove Snap-In.

3. In the Standalone tab in the Add/Remove Snap-In dialog box, select the snap-in you want to delete and click Remove. Then click OK. The snap-in is removed from the console.

To add or remove an extension to a snap-in on an existing MMC, complete the following steps:

1. Click Start, point to All Programs, point to Administrative Tools, and then click the name of the custom MMC.

2. On the File menu, click Add/Remove Snap-In.

3. In the Standalone tab in the Add/Remove Snap-In dialog box, click the Extensions tab. Then select the snap-in for which you want to add or remove an extension.

4. In the Extensions tab, shown in Figure 3-7, indicate the extension(s) you want to add or delete, as follows:

   ❑ To add an extension, click the desired extension.

   ❑ To remove an extension, clear the Add All Extensions check box and then in the Available Extensions box, clear the check box for the desired extension.

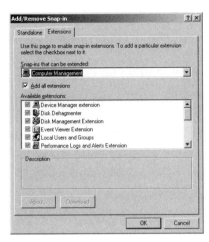

Figure 3-7   Add/Remove Snap-In dialog box, Extensions tab

5. Click OK.

6. Expand the snap-in to confirm that the desired extension has been added or removed.

Practice: Customizing an MMC

In this practice, you customize an MMC.

Exercise 1: Creating a Custom MMC

In this exercise, you create a custom MMC.

▶ **To create a custom MMC**

1. Log on to Server1 as Administrator.

2. Use the procedure provided earlier in this lesson to create a custom MMC. Add the Computer Management snap-in to the MMC. Although the Computer Management snap-in supports remote administration, set up the snap-in to manage the local computer. Set the console mode to author mode. Save the MMC with the name Administrator A.

   Do not use any of the tools at this point.

Exercise 2: Adding a Snap-In to an Existing MMC

In this exercise, you add a snap-in to an existing MMC.

▶ **To add a snap-in to an existing MMC**

1. Use the procedure provided earlier in this lesson to add the Event Viewer snap-in to the Administrator A MMC.

2. Set this snap-in to manage the local computer.

3. Confirm that the Event Viewer snap-in has been added to the Administrator A MMC.

Exercise 3: Removing an Extension to a Snap-In on an Existing MMC

In this exercise, you remove an extension to a snap-in on an existing MMC.

▶ **To remove an extension to a snap-in on an existing MMC**

1. Use the procedure provided earlier in this lesson to remove the Disk Management extension from the Computer Management snap-in on the Administrator A MMC.

2. Confirm that the Disk Management extension has been removed from the Computer Management snap-in.

Lesson Review

The following questions are intended to reinforce key information presented in this lesson. If you are unable to answer a question, review the lesson and then try the question again. Answers to the questions can be found in the "Questions and Answers" section at the end of this chapter.

1. What is the function of an MMC? Why is it necessary to create customized MMCs?

_____

_____

2. What is a snap-in?

_____

_____

3. What is the function of a console tree?

_____

_____

4. What are extensions?

_____

_____

5. Which of the following console mode types allows users to create new windows in the console?

   a. Author mode

   b. User mode—full access

      c. User mode—limited access, multiple window

      d. User mode—limited access, single window

Lesson Summary

- There are two types of MMCs: preconfigured and custom. Preconfigured MMCs contain commonly used snap-ins and appear on the Administrative Tools menu. You create custom MMCs to perform a unique set of administrative tasks.

- Snap-ins are applications that work within an MMC and are used to perform administrative tasks. There are two types of snap-ins: stand-alone and extension. Stand-alone snap-ins are referred to simply as snap-ins, and provide one function or a related set of functions. Extension snap-ins are referred to as extensions, and provide additional administrative functionality to another snap-in.

- The console mode determines how an MMC is used. There are two console modes: author and user. Author mode provides full access to all MMC functionality, which includes modifying the MMC. In user mode, users cannot add snap-ins to, remove snap-ins from, or save the MMC.

- For custom MMCs, you can set up a snap-in for remote administration, allowing you to perform administrative tasks from any location. Not all snap-ins are available for remote administration.

Lesson 3: Backing Up Active Directory

This lesson guides you through the steps required to back up Active Directory data. When you create a backup, you need to conduct several preliminary tasks, and then perform a number of tasks using the Backup Or Restore Wizard. In this lesson you will learn how to back up Active Directory data, how to schedule and run an unattended backup, and how to delete an unattended backup.

After this lesson, you will be able to

- Back up Active Directory data at a local computer
- Schedule and run an unattended backup of Active Directory data
- Delete an unattended backup of Active Directory data

Estimated lesson time: 25 minutes

Preliminary Backup Tasks

An important part of backing up Active Directory data is performing the preliminary tasks. You must prepare the files that you want to back up, and, if you are using a removable media device, you must prepare the device. If you use a removable media device, you must ensure that:

- The backup device is attached to a computer on the network and is turned on. If you are backing up to tape, you must attach the tape device to the computer on which you run Windows Backup.

- The media device is listed on the Windows Server 2003 Hardware Compatibility List (HCL).

- The medium is loaded in the media device. For example, if you are using a tape drive, ensure that a tape is loaded in the tape drive.

You must be a member of the Administrators or the Backup Operators groups to perform a backup.

Creating an Active Directory Backup

After you have completed the preliminary tasks, you can perform the Active Directory backup using the Backup Or Restore Wizard. When you back up Active Directory, the Backup Or Restore Wizard automatically backs up all the system components and all the distributed services that Active Directory requires. Collectively, these components and services are known as *system state data*.

For Windows Server 2003, the system state data comprises the registry, COM+ Class Registration database, system boot files, files under Windows File Protection, and the

Certificate Services database (if the server is a certificate server). If the server is a domain controller, Active Directory and the Sysvol directory are also contained in the system state data. When you choose to back up system state data, all of the system state data that is relevant to your computer is backed up; you cannot choose to back up individual components of the system state data. This is due to dependencies among the system state components. You can back up only the system state data on a local computer. You cannot back up the system state data on a remote computer.

To assist with your backup strategy, Windows Server 2003 with SP1 includes event ID 2089 in the Directory Service event log. Event ID 2089 provides the backup status of each directory partition that a domain controller stores. This event appears in the Directory Service event log if a directory partition has not been backed up for a period greater than half the backup latency interval (tombstone lifetime). The event is logged daily until the partition is backed up.

To create an Active Directory backup, complete the following steps:

1. Log on to your domain as Administrator, point to Start, point to All Programs, point to Accessories, point to System Tools, and select Backup.

2. On the Welcome To The Backup Or Restore Wizard page, click Next.

3. On the Backup Or Restore page, shown in Figure 3-8, select Backup Files And Settings, and then click Next.

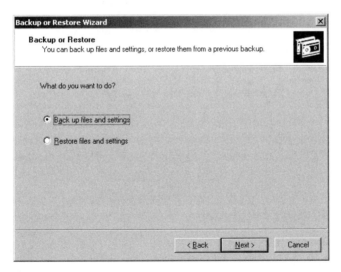

Figure 3-8   Backup Or Restore page

4. On the What To Back Up page, shown in Figure 3-9, select Let Me Choose What To Back Up, and then click Next.

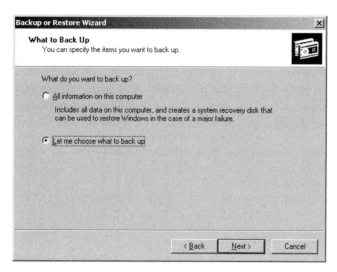

Figure 3-9   What To Back Up page

5. On the Items To Back Up page, shown in Figure 3-10, expand the My Computer item, and then select System State. Click Next.

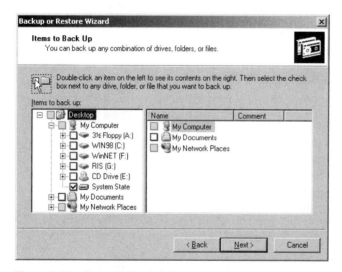

Figure 3-10   Items To Back Up page

6. On the Backup Type, Destination, And Name page, shown in Figure 3-11, complete the following steps:

❑ Select Tape in the Select The Backup Type list if you are using tape; otherwise this option defaults to File.

❑ In the Choose A Place To Save Your Backup list, choose the location where Windows Backup will store the data. If you are saving to a tape, select the tape name. If you are saving to a file, browse to the path for the backup file location.

❑ In the Type A Name For This Backup box, enter a name for the backup you are going to do.

❑ Click Next.

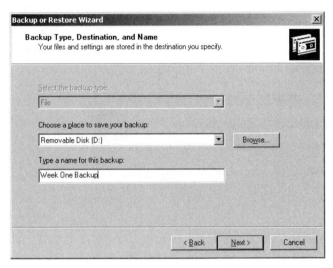

Figure 3-11   Backup Type, Destination, And Name page

7. On the Completing The Backup Or Restore Wizard page, click Advanced.

8. On the Type Of Backup page, shown in Figure 3-12, select Normal as the backup type used for this backup job. Normal is the only backup type supported by Active Directory. If the Hierarchical Storage Manager (HSM) has moved data to remote storage and you want to back it up, select the Backup Migrated Remote Storage Data check box. Click Next.

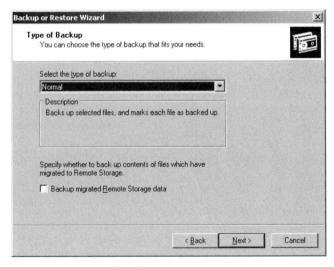

Figure 3-12   Type Of Backup page

9. On the How To Back Up page, shown in Figure 3-13, select the Verify Data After Backup check box. This option causes the backup process to take longer but it confirms that files are correctly backed up. If you are using a tape device and it supports hardware compression, select the Use Hardware Compression, If Available check box to enable hardware compression. It's recommended that you do not select the Disable Volume Shadow Copy check box. By default, Backup creates a volume shadow copy of your data to create an accurate copy of the contents of the hard drive, including open files or files in use by the system. Click Next.

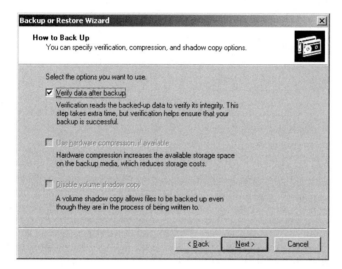

Figure 3-13   How To Back Up page

10. On the Backup Options page, shown in Figure 3-14, select the Replace The Existing Backups option, then select the Allow Only The Owner And The Administrator Access To The Backup Data And To Any Backups Appended To This Medium check box. This action saves only the most recent copy of Active Directory and allows you to restrict who can gain access to the completed backup file or tape. Click Next.

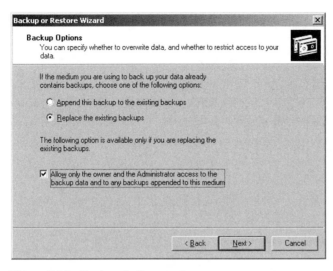

Figure 3-14   Backup Options page

11. On the When To Back Up page, shown in Figure 3-15, select Now. Click Next.

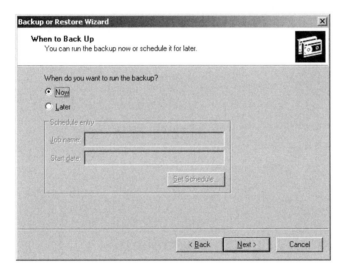

Figure 3-15   When To Back Up page

12. On the Completing The Backup Or Restore Wizard page, click Finish to start the backup operation.

13. The Backup Progress window shows the progress of the backup.

14. When the backup operation is complete, the Backup Progress window, shown in Figure 3-16, shows that the backup is complete. You can click the Report button to see a report about the backup operation, as shown in Figure 3-17. The report is stored on the hard disk of the computer on which you are running the backup.

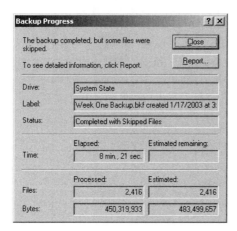

Figure 3-16   Backup Progress window showing completed backup

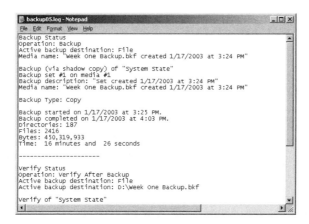

Figure 3-17   Backup operation report

15. Close the report when you have finished viewing it and then click Close to close the backup operation.

Scheduling Active Directory Backup Operations

Scheduling an Active Directory backup operation means that you can have an unattended backup job occur later when users are not at work and files are closed. You can also schedule Active Directory backup operations to occur at regular intervals. To enable this, Windows Server 2003 integrates the backup operation with the Task Scheduler service. To schedule a backup operation, you must access the advanced backup settings as described in the following procedure.

To schedule an Active Directory backup operation, complete the following steps:

1. Follow steps 1–10 in the previous section, "Creating an Active Directory Backup."

2. On the When To Back Up page, shown in Figure 3-18, select Later. Then type the job name in the Job Name box and click Set Schedule.

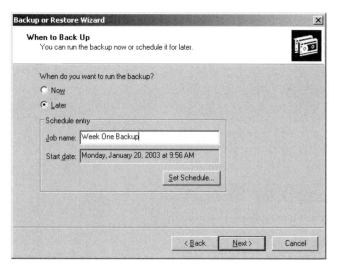

Figure 3-18   When To Back Up page

3. In the Schedule tab in the Schedule Job dialog box, shown in Figure 3-19, select the frequency of the backup operation: Daily, Weekly, Monthly, Once, At System Startup, At Logon, or When Idle from the Schedule Task list. Indicate the time the backup operation will begin in the Start Time list. Indicate when the task will occur in the Schedule Task box for the selected frequency. Click Advanced.

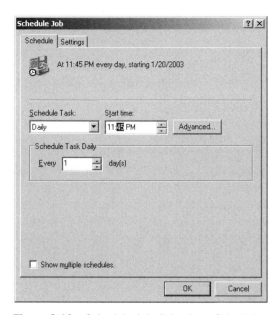

Figure 3-19   Schedule Job dialog box, Schedule tab

4. In the Advanced Schedule Options dialog box, shown in Figure 3-20, you can specify when the backup operations should begin, end, or how often they should be repeated in the Start Date, End Date, and Repeat Task boxes, respectively. Enter information as necessary and click OK.

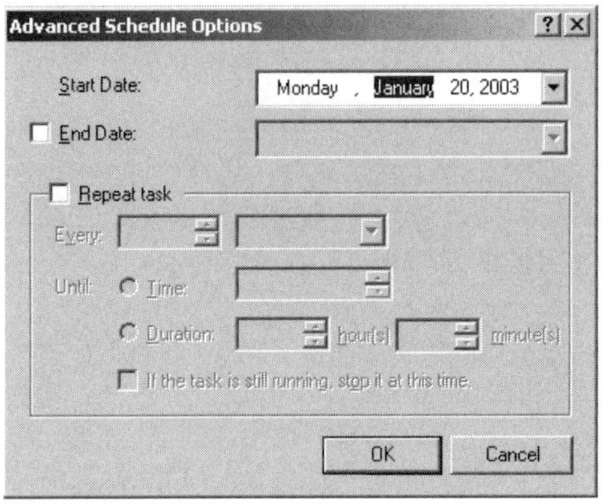

Figure 3-20   Advanced Schedule Options dialog box

5. In the Schedule tab in the Schedule Job dialog box, select the Show Multiple Schedules check box if you wish to set up more than one schedule for the backup operation. Repeat steps 1–4 for each schedule. Click the Settings tab when you are finished setting up schedules.

6. In the Settings tab in the Schedule Job dialog box, shown in Figure 3-21, specify whether to delete the task file from your computer's hard disk after the backup operation has finished running and is not scheduled to run again in the Scheduled Task Completed box. Specify whether to start or stop the backup operation based on the computer's idle time in the Idle Time box. Specify whether to start or stop the backup operation based on the computer's power status in the Power Management box. Click OK.

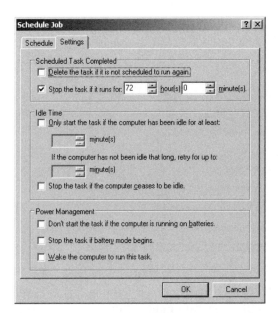

Figure 3-21   Schedule Job dialog box, Settings tab

7. On the When To Back Up page, click Next.

8. In the Set Account Information dialog box, shown in Figure 3-22, type the password for the account shown in the Password box and confirm the password in the Confirm Password box. Click OK.

Figure 3-22   Set Account Information dialog box

9. Confirm your selections on the Completing The Backup Or Restore Wizard page, then click Finish to schedule the backup.

Deleting Scheduled Active Directory Backup Operations

To delete a scheduled Active Directory backup operation, you must access the advanced backup settings as described in the following procedure.

To delete a scheduled Active Directory backup operation, complete the following steps:

1. Log on to your domain as Administrator, point to Start, point to All Programs, point to Accessories, point to System Tools, and select Backup.

2. On the Welcome To The Backup Or Restore Wizard page click the Advanced Mode link.

3. On the Welcome To The Backup Utility Advanced Mode page, shown in Figure 3-23, click the Schedule Jobs tab.

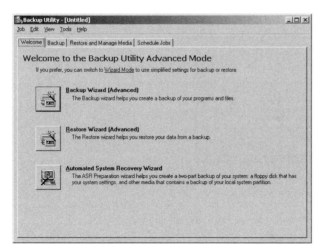

Figure 3-23   Welcome To The Backup Utility Advanced Mode page

4. In the Schedule Jobs tab, shown in Figure 3-24, icons for the scheduled backup operation(s) appear on the schedule for the date(s) the operation is specified to be performed. In this example, a backup operation is scheduled daily. Click the backup operation you want to delete.

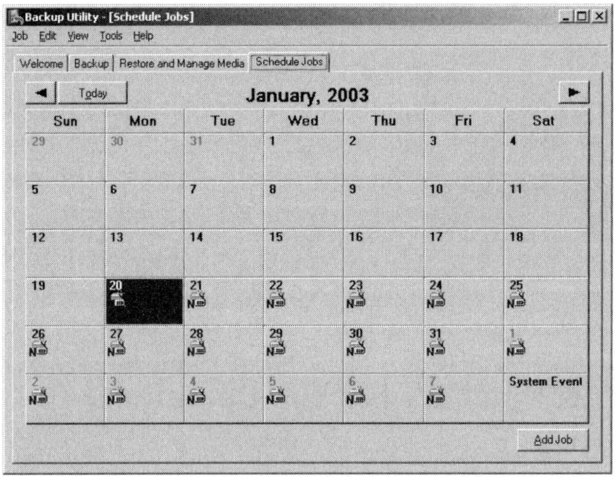

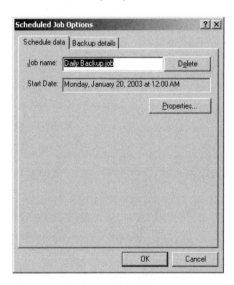

Figure 3-24   Schedule Jobs tab

5. In the Scheduled Job Options dialog box that appears, shown in Figure 3-25, ensure that the job you want to delete appears in the Job Name box. Click Delete.

Figure 3-25   Scheduled Job Options dialog box

6. In the Removing a Scheduled Job message box that appears, click Yes. The backup operation has been deleted from the schedule.

Practice: Backing Up Active Directory

In this practice, you back up Active Directory and perform tasks related to backup scheduling.

Exercise 1: Creating an Active Directory Backup

In this exercise, you create an Active Directory backup.

▶ **To create an Active Directory backup**

1. Log on to Server1 as Administrator.

2. Open the Active Directory Users And Computers console. Create a new, empty OU by right-clicking the domain in the console tree, pointing to New, and then clicking Organizational Unit. In the New Object-Organizational Unit dialog box, type **TEST1** in the Name box, then click OK. Verify that the TEST1 OU appears in the console tree.

3. Use the procedure provided earlier in this lesson to create an Active Directory backup. Name this backup Active Directory Backup1. Check with your administrator to ensure the availability of disks or tapes for backup storage.

4. When you have finished the backup operation for Active Directory Backup1, return to Active Directory Users And Computers and delete the TEST1 OU you created in step 2.

> **Note**   In this exercise, you backed up Active Directory when it contained the TEST1 OU and then deleted the TEST1 OU. In the next lesson you will restore Active Directory to contain the TEST1 OU.

Exercise 2: Scheduling an Active Directory Backup Operation

In this exercise, you schedule an Active Directory backup operation.

▶ **To schedule an Active Directory backup operation**

1. Use the procedure provided earlier in this lesson to schedule an Active Directory backup operation. Name this backup Active Directory Backup2.

2. Schedule this backup to occur daily at 12:00 A.M.

3. Check with your administrator to ensure the availability of disks or tapes for backup storage at the specified time.

Exercise 3: Deleting a Scheduled Active Directory Backup Operation

In this exercise, you delete a scheduled Active Directory backup operation.

▶ **To delete a scheduled Active Directory backup operation**

Use the procedure provided earlier in this lesson to delete Active Directory Backup2 after you have completed the exercise and the backup operation runs.

Lesson Review

The following questions are intended to reinforce key information presented in this lesson. If you are unable to answer a question, review the lesson and then try the question again. Answers to the questions can be found in the "Questions and Answers" section at the end of this chapter.

1. What tasks should you complete before attempting to back up Active Directory data?

   _____

   _____

2. What is system state data and why is it significant to backing up Active Directory?

   _____

   _____

3. Can you restrict who can gain access to a completed backup file or tape? If so, how?

   _____

   _____

4. When you specify the items you want to back up in the Backup Or Restore Wizard, which of the following should you select to successfully back up Active Directory data?

   a. System state data

   b. Shared system volume folder

   c. Database and log files

   d. Registry

Lesson Summary

- Before you can back up Active Directory data, you must prepare the files that you want to back up, and, if you are using a removable media device, you must prepare the device.

- Active Directory and the Sysvol directory are also contained in the system state data. Therefore, when you back up Active Directory data, you must specify that you want to back up only system state data.

■ You can perform a backup of Active Directory data on demand, or you can schedule the backup operation to occur daily, weekly, monthly, once, at system startup, at logon, or when idle.

Lesson 4: Restoring Active Directory

There are two ways to restore Active Directory: nonauthoritatively and authoritatively. This lesson shows you how to perform both methods of restoring Active Directory.

After this lesson, you will be able to

- Explain the difference between nonauthoritative and authoritative restore
- Restore Active Directory

Estimated lesson time: 35 minutes

Restoring Active Directory

Like the backup process, when you choose to restore Active Directory, you can only restore all of the system state data that was backed up, including the registry, the COM+ Class Registration database, system boot files, files under Windows File Protection; the Sysvol directory and Active Directory (if the server is a domain controller); and the Certificate Services database (if the server is a certificate server). You cannot choose to restore individual components (for example, only the Active Directory) of the system state data.

If you are restoring the system state data to a domain controller, you must choose whether you want to perform a nonauthoritative restore or an authoritative restore. The default method of restoring the system state data to a domain controller is nonauthoritative. You must be a member of the Administrators or the Backup Operators groups to perform a restore.

Nonauthoritative Restore

In nonauthoritative restore, the distributed services on a domain controller are restored from backup media and the restored data is then updated through normal replication. Each restored directory partition is updated with that of its replication partners by replication after you restore the data. For example, if the last backup was performed a week ago, and the system state is restored nonauthoritatively, any changes made subsequent to the backup operation will be replicated from the other domain controllers. The Active Directory replication system will update the restored data with newer data from your other servers. Nonauthoritative restore is typically performed when a domain controller has completely failed due to hardware or software problems.

Authoritative Restore

An authoritative restore brings a domain or a container back to the state it was in at the time of backup and overwrites all changes made since the backup. If you do not want to replicate the changes that have been made subsequent to the last backup operation, you must perform an authoritative restore. For example, you must perform an authoritative restore if you inadvertently delete users, groups, or OUs from Active Directory and you want to restore the system so that the deleted objects are recovered and replicated. Authoritative restore is typically used to restore a system to a previously known state, for example, before Active Directory objects were erroneously deleted.

To authoritatively restore Active Directory data, you must run the Ntdsutil utility after you have performed a nonauthoritative restore of the system state data but before you restart the server. The Ntdsutil utility allows you to mark objects as authoritative. Marking objects as authoritative changes the update sequence number of an object so it is higher than any other update sequence number in the Active Directory replication system. This ensures that any replicated or distributed data that you have restored is properly replicated or distributed throughout your organization. The Ntdsutil utility can be found in the *%Systemroot%*\System32 directory and accompanying documentation within the Windows Server 2003 Help files (available from the Start menu).

Using Windows Server 2003 SP1 to Remove Domain Controller Metatdata

Ntdsutil in Windows Server 2003 with SP1 has two commands that make it easier to remove domain controller metadata. Preliminary steps, such as connecting to a server, domain, and site, are no longer required. You simply specify the server to remove. These two commands have the following syntax:

- **Ntdsutil "metadata cleanup" "remove selected server"***ServerObject*   When using this command, specify the distinguished name (DN) path of the server object (*ServerObject*) of the domain controller whose metadata you want to remove. The server object is the parent of the NTDS settings object in the configuration container. For example, for the domain controller named DC1 located in the Default-First-Site-Name of the contoso.com forest, the DN path of the server object would be cn=DC1,cn=servers,cn=default-first-site-name ,cn=configuration,dc=contoso,dc=com. If the DN path contains any spaces, enclose the entire DN path in quotes.

- **Ntdsutil "metadata cleanup" "remove selected server"***ServerObject* **on** ***TargetDC***   This command is identical to the preceding one, except it allows the administrator to specify the domain controller (*TargetDC*) on which the removal is performed. *TargetDC* must be entered as the DNS or NetBIOS name of the domain controller.

For example, suppose you back up the system on Monday, and then create a new user called Ben Smith on Tuesday, which replicates to other domain controllers in the domain, but on Wednesday, another user, Nancy Anderson, is accidentally deleted. To authoritatively restore Nancy Anderson without reentering information, you can non-authoritatively restore the domain controller with the backup created on Monday. Then, using Ntdsutil you can mark the Nancy Anderson object as authoritative. The result is that Nancy Anderson is restored without any effect on Ben Smith.

> **Exam Tip**   Know when to use authoritative or nonauthoritative restore.

Preliminary Restore Tasks

Like the backup process, an important part of restoring Active Directory data is performing the preliminary tasks. Before you can restore Active Directory, you must perform the following tasks:

- Ensure that you can access all locations that require the restoration of files.

- Ensure that the appropriate device for the storage medium containing the data to be restored is attached to a computer on the network and is turned on.

- Ensure that the medium containing the data to be restored is loaded in the device.

Performing a Nonauthoritative Restore

To restore the system state data on a domain controller, you must first start your computer in a special safe mode called directory services restore mode. This allows you to restore the Sysvol directory and Active Directory directory services database. You can only restore system state data on a local computer. You cannot restore the system state data on a remote computer.

However, you can restore backed up system state data to an alternate location—a folder you designate. By restoring to an alternate location, you preserve the file and folder structure of the backed up data—all folders and subfolders appear in the alternate folder you specify.

> **Note**   If you restore the system state data and you do not designate an alternate location for the restored data, Backup will erase the system state data that is currently on your computer and replace it with the system state data you are restoring. Also, if you restore the system state data to an alternate location, only the registry files, Sysvol directory files, Cluster database information files (if applicable), and system boot files are restored to the alternate location. The Active Directory database, Certificate Services database (if applicable), and COM+ Class Registration database are not restored if you designate an alternate location.

To nonauthoritatively restore Active Directory, complete the following steps:

1. Restart the computer.

2. During the phase of startup where the operating system is normally selected, press F8.

3. On the Windows Advanced Options Menu, select Directory Services Restore Mode and press ENTER. This ensures that the domain controller is offline and is not connected to the network.

4. At the Please Select The Operating System To Start prompt, select the appropriate Microsoft Windows Server 2003 operating system and press ENTER.

5. Log on to your domain as Administrator.

> **Note**   When you restart the computer in directory services restore mode, you must log on as an Administrator by using a valid Security Accounts Manager (SAM) account name and password, *not* the Active Directory Administrator's name and password. This is because Active Directory is offline, and account verification cannot occur. Rather, the SAM accounts database is used to control access to Active Directory while it is offline. You specified this password when you set up Active Directory.

6. In the Desktop message box that warns you that Windows is running in safe mode, click OK.

7. Point to Start, point to All Programs, point to Accessories, point to System Tools, and then select Backup.

8. On the Welcome To The Backup Or Restore Wizard page, click Next.

9. On the Backup Or Restore page, shown previously in Figure 3-8, select Restore Files And Settings. Click Next.

10. On the What To Restore page, shown in Figure 3-26, expand the media type that contains the data that you want to restore in the Items To Restore box or click Browse. The media can be either tape or file. Expand the appropriate media set until the data that you want to restore is visible. Select the data you want to restore, such as system state, then click Next.

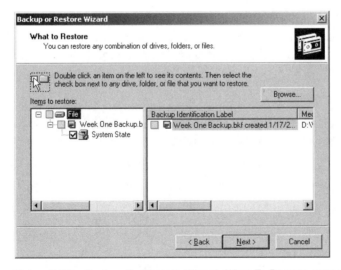

Figure 3-26   Backup Or Restore Wizard, What To Restore page with system state data selected for restore

11. Ensure that media containing the backup file is in the correct location.

12. On the Completing The Backup Or Restore Wizard page, do one of the following:

    ❑ Click Finish to start the restore process. The Backup Or Restore Wizard requests verification for the source of the restore data and then performs the restore. During the restore, the Backup Or Restore Wizard displays status information about the restore.

    ❑ Click Advanced to specify advanced restore options. Refer to the next section, "Specifying Advanced Restore Settings for a Nonauthoritative Restore" for details.

13. In the Warning message box that warns you that restoring system state will always overwrite current system state, click OK.

14. The Restore Progress dialog box displays status information about the restore process. As with the backup process, when the restore is complete, you can choose to view the report of the restore. The report contains information about the restore, such as the number of files that have been restored and the duration of the restore process.

15. Close the report when you have finished viewing it and then click Close to close the restore operation.

16. When prompted to restart the computer, click Yes.

Real World   Shutdown Event Tracker

You've probably noticed that Windows Server 2003 has a new feature that requests a shutdown reason each time you restart the server. This feature is called the Shutdown Event Tracker. If you are working in a test environment, you might choose to disable this feature to avoid the hassle of typing in a reason each time you restart. To disable this feature, you can perform the following steps:

1. Click Start, click Run, and type **gpedit.msc** and press ENTER.

2. Expand the Computer Configuration and then Administrative Templates objects. Click on the System object. In the right-hand pane you'll see several settings appear.

3. Locate and double-click that Display Shutdown Event Tracker setting. The Display Shutdown Event Tracker Properties dialog box opens.

4. Click the Disabled radio button to disable the Shutdown Event Tracker. Click OK. Close the Group Policy Editor console.

Now when you shut down this server, you won't be asked to enter a reason.

Specifying Advanced Restore Settings for a Nonauthoritative Restore

The Advanced settings in the Backup Or Restore Wizard vary, depending on the type of backup media from which you are restoring.

To specify advanced restore settings for a nonauthoritative Active Directory restore, complete the following steps:

1. On the Where to Restore page, in the Restore Files To list, select the target location for the data that you are restoring. The choices in the list are the following:

   ❑ *Original Location*—Replaces corrupted or lost data. This is the default and must be selected to restore Active Directory.

   ❑ *Alternate Location*—Restores an older version of a file to a folder you designate.

   ❑ *Single Folder*—Consolidates the files from a tree structure into a single folder. For example, use this option if you want copies of specific files but do not want to restore the hierarchical structure of the files.

> **Note**   If you select either an alternate location or a single folder, you must also provide the path to the location or folder.

2. Click Next.

3. On the How to Restore page, select how you want to restore the system state data from the following:

   ❑ *Leave Existing Files (Recommended)*—Prevents accidental overwriting of existing data. This is the default.

   ❑ *Replace Existing Files If They Are Older Than The Backup Files*—Verifies that the most recent copy exists on the computer.

   ❑ *Replace Existing Files*—Windows Backup does not provide a confirmation message if it encounters a duplicate file name during the restore operation.

4. Click Next.

5. On the Advanced Restore Options page, select whether or not to restore security or special system files from the following:

   ❑ *Restore Security Settings*—Applies the original permissions to files that you are restoring to a Windows NTFS file service volume. Security settings include access permissions, audit entries, and ownership. This option is available only if you have backed up data from an NFTS volume and are restoring to an NTFS volume.

   ❑ *Restore Junction Points, But Not The Folders And File Data They Reference*—Restores junction points on your hard disk but not the data to which the junction points refer. If you have any mounted drives and you want to restore the data that mounted drives point to, you should *not* select this check box.

❑ *Preserve Existing Volume Mount Points*—Prevents the restore operation from writing over any volume mount points on the destination volume. If you are restoring data to a replacement drive, and you have partitioned and formatted the drive and restored volume mount points, you should select this option so your volume mount points are not restored. If you are restoring data to a partition or drive that you have just reformatted, and you want to restore the old volume mount points, you should not select this option.

❑ *Restore The Cluster Registry To The Quorum Disk And All Other Nodes*—Makes certain that the cluster quorum database is restored and replicated on all nodes in a server cluster. If selected, the Backup Or Restore Wizard will stop the Cluster service on all other nodes of the server cluster after the node that was restored reboots.

❑ *When Restoring Replicated Data Sets, Mark The Restored Data As The Primary Data For All Replicas*—Ensures that restored File Replication service (FRS) data is replicated to your other servers. If you are restoring FRS data, you should choose this option. If you do not choose this option, the FRS data that you are restoring may not be replicated to other servers because the restored data will appear to be older than the data already on the servers. This will cause the other servers to overwrite the restored data, preventing you from restoring the FRS data.

6. Click Next.

7. On the Completing The Backup Or Restore Wizard page, click Finish to start the restore process. The Backup Or Restore Wizard requests verification for the source of the restore data and then performs the restore. During the restore, the Backup Or Restore Wizard displays status information about the restore.

Performing an Authoritative Restore

An authoritative restore occurs after a nonauthoritative restore and designates the entire directory, a subtree, or individual objects to be recognized as authoritative with respect to replica domain controllers in the forest. The Ntdsutil utility allows you to mark objects as authoritative so that they are propagated through replication, thereby updating existing copies of those objects throughout the forest.

To authoritatively restore Active Directory, complete the following steps:

1. Perform a nonauthoritative restore as described previously.

2. Restart the computer.

3. During the phase of startup where the operating system is normally selected, press F8.

4. On the Windows Advanced Startup Options Menu, select Directory Services Restore Mode and press ENTER. This ensures that the domain controller is offline and is not connected to the network.

5. At the Please Select The Operating System To Start prompt, select the appropriate Microsoft Windows Server 2003 operating system and press ENTER.

6. Log on as Administrator.

> **Note**   When you restart the computer in directory services restore mode, you must log on as an Administrator by using a valid SAM account name and password, *not* the Active Directory Administrator's name and password. This is because Active Directory is offline and account verification cannot occur. Rather, the SAM accounts database is used to control access to Active Directory while it is offline.

7. In the Desktop message box that warns you that Windows is running in safe mode, click OK.

8. Point to Start, then select Command Prompt.

9. At the command prompt, type **ntdsutil** and press ENTER.

10. At the Ntdsutil prompt, type **authoritative restore** and press ENTER.

11. At the authoritative restore prompt, do the following:

   ❑ To authoritatively restore the entire directory, type **restore database** and press ENTER.

   ❑ To authoritatively restore a portion or subtree of the directory, such as an OU, use the OU's distinguished name, type **restore subtree** *subtree_distinguished_name* and press ENTER.

   For example, to restore the Security1 OU in the *microsoft.com* domain, the commands would be

   ```
   ntdsutil
   authoritative restore
   restore subtree OU=Security1,DC=Microsoft,DC=COM
   ```

   ❑ To authoritatively restore the entire directory *and* override the version increase, type **restore database verinc** *version_increase* and press ENTER.

   ❑ To authoritatively restore a subtree of the directory *and* override the version increase, type **restore subtree** *subtree_distinguished_name* **verinc** *version_increase* and press ENTER.

The authoritative restore opens the Ntds.dit file, increases version numbers, counts the records that need updating, verifies the number of records updated, and reports completion. If a version number increase is not specified, one is automatically calculated.

12. Type **quit** and press ENTER to exit the Ntdsutil utility and close the Command Prompt window.

13. Restart the domain controller in normal mode and connect the restored domain controller to the network. When the restored domain controller is online and connected to the network, normal replication brings the restored domain controller up to date with any changes from the additional domain controllers that were not overridden by the authoritative restore. Replication also propagates the authoritatively restored object(s) to other domain controllers in the forest. The deleted objects that were marked as authoritative are replicated from the restored domain controller to the additional domain controllers. Because the objects that are restored have the same object globally unique identifier (GUID) and object SID, security remains intact, and object dependencies are maintained.

14. Ensure the integrity of the computer's Group Policy by performing one of the following:

❑ If you authoritatively restored the entire Active Directory database, copy the Sysvol directory on the alternate location over the existing one *after* the Sysvol share is published.

❑ If you authoritatively restored specific Active Directory objects, copy only the policy folders (identified by the GUID) corresponding to the restored policy objects from the alternate location *after* the Sysvol share is published. Then, copy them over the existing ones.

When authoritatively restoring either the entire Active Directory database or selected objects, it is important that you copy the Sysvol and policy data from the alternate location *after* the Sysvol share is published. If the computer is in a replicated domain, it may take several minutes before the Sysvol share is published because it needs to synchronize with its replication partners. If all computers in the domain are authoritatively restored and restarted at the same time, then each will be waiting (indefinitely) to synchronize with each other. In this case, restore one of the domain controllers first so that its Sysvol share can be published; then restore the other computers nonauthoritatively.

Impact of Authoritative Restore on Trust Relationships and Network Connections

Both parent and child trust relationships in Windows domains and Kerberos and NTLM trust relationships to other Windows domains reside in the domain directory partition. Because trust relationship and computer account passwords are renegotiated at a specified interval, if you authoritatively restore an entire domain directory partition, computer passwords and trust relationship passwords are restored to the values at the time of the backup. If the password values are different from the current values, trust relationships and computer accounts might be invalidated. For trust relationships, domain controllers may no longer be able to communicate with domain controllers from other domains. If an older computer account password is restored, the member's workstation may no longer be able to communicate with the server and the domain controller. If you authoritatively restore objects that affect trust relationships or computer account passwords, you must reset the passwords. Therefore, you should restore only those portions of the domain directory partition that are absolutely necessary. The more of the domain hierarchy included in the restore, the greater chance that trust relationships are affected.

> **Note**   By default, passwords are reset every seven days; except for computer accounts. The previous password is also maintained. Therefore, performing authoritative restore with a backup that is older than 14 days can affect the trust relationships.

To minimize the effort involved with resetting trusts and rejoining computers, you must perform regular backups.

Practice: Restoring Active Directory

In this practice, you restore Active Directory from the backup you made in Lesson 3.

> **Note**   To complete this practice, you must have successfully completed the practice in Lesson 3.

Exercise 1: Restoring Active Directory

In this exercise, you perform an authoritative restore to restore Active Directory.

▶ **To restore Active Directory**

1. Use the procedure provided earlier in this lesson to authoritatively restore Active Directory using Active Directory Backup1. Hint: Use the **restore subtree** command parameter with **OU=TEST1,DC=contoso,DC=com** as the subtree distinguished name.

2. Verify that the TEST1 OU you created, backed up, and deleted in Lesson 3 has been restored in the Active Directory Users And Computers console.

Lesson Review

The following questions are intended to reinforce key information presented in this lesson. If you are unable to answer a question, review the lesson and then try the question again. Answers to the questions can be found in the "Questions and Answers" section at the end of this chapter.

1. Describe what happens in a nonauthoritative restore.

   _____

   _____

2. Describe what happens in an authoritative restore.

   _____

   _____

3. Which method of restore should you use if you accidentally delete an OU?

   _____

   _____

4. Which method of restore should you use if a domain controller has completely failed due to hardware or software problems?

   _____

   _____

5. Which of the following Ntdsutil command parameters should you use if you want to restore the entire directory?

   a. Restore database

   b. Restore subtree

   c. Database restore

   d. Subtree restore

Lesson Summary

- You restore Active Directory data by performing a nonauthoritative restore (default) or an authoritative restore.

- In nonauthoritative restore, the distributed services on a domain controller are restored from backup media and the restored data is then updated through normal replication. Each restored directory partition is updated with that of its replication partners.

- An authoritative restore brings a domain or a container back to the state it was in at the time of backup and overwrites all changes made since the backup.

- Before you can restore Active Directory, you must ensure that you can access all locations that require the restoration of files, the appropriate device for the storage medium containing the data to be restored is attached to a computer on the network and is turned on, and the medium containing the data to be restored is loaded in the device.

- To restore the system state data on a domain controller, you must start your computer in directory services restore mode. To perform a nonauthoritative restore, use the Backup Or Restore Wizard. To perform an authoritative restore, use the Backup Or Restore Wizard and the Ntdsutil command.

Case Scenario Exercise

You are a network consultant. You are consulting for an educational institution called Graphic Design Institute as described in Chapter 2. You've just finished installing the Research department's forest root domain controller. The Research department is using a server running Windows Server 2003 configured as a domain controller. You've installed a primary DNS server and configured those records to be stored in Active Directory.

As you are working, Laura Steele, the director of the institute, asks you to discuss potential upgrades for the Administrative and Marketing departments. The following list describes significant details about the departments and network environment of the Graphic Design Institute:

- **Information Technology Services (ITS)**   This department utilizes UNIX client and server operating systems. The ITS department maintains DNS servers and Internet access for the entire institute. There are 10 users and 25 computers in this department. The ITS department also maintains the institute's physical network infrastructure which includes 100 Mbps and gigabit Ethernet capable cables, hubs, switches, and routers.

- **Administration department**   This department has a Windows 2000 Active Directory domain structure. The operating systems in use include Windows 2000 Advanced Server, Windows 2000 Professional, and Windows XP Professional. There are 12 domain controllers, eight file servers, and 5,000 users in this department. Ten of those domain controllers are also hosting the domain's Active Directory-integrated DNS zone. The ITS department delegated the *admin.graphicdesigninstitute.com* namespace to the Administration department.

- **Marketing department**   This department has a Windows NT 4 domain that includes one primary domain controller (PDC) and one backup domain controller (BDC). The operating systems in use are Windows NT 4 Server, Windows NT 4 Workstation, and Windows 2000 Professional. The department has 15 users and 20 computers.

- **Research department**   At this time the Research department has 25 employees and 30 computers. You've installed a forest root domain controller and DNS server on one computer. Most of the employees haven't yet been issued computers. They are still putting together their office furniture. However, you've suggested installing a Remote Installation Services (RIS) server to deploy Windows XP Professional. Steve Masters, the newly hired network manager for Research, plans to install the client computers once you are finished configuring the directory structure.

Given this information, answer the following questions:

1. Before you move on to upgrading the other departments, what should you do to ensure the Research department's Active Directory data is protected? What should you ensure that Steve will continue to do in order to protect the Research department's data?

2. What similarities exist between the implementation of Active Directory in the Research and Marketing departments?

3. If you must install an additional Windows Server 2003 domain controller in the existing Administration domain, what must you first do to the Administration domain?

4. If you're asked to upgrade the PDC of the Marketing domain, but hold off on the upgrade of the BDC, what functional level should you use on the new Windows 2003 Server domain?

5. The network administrators of the Marketing domain want to know what the equivalent of the User Manager for Domains and the Server Manager applications are on Windows Server 2003 domain controller. What would you tell them?

Troubleshooting Lab

You are a network administrator for Contoso Pharmaceuticals. You recently lost one of your domain controllers, named Server2, due to a hardware failure. This domain controller cannot be repaired and there was no recent backup. You notice many replication errors start to appear in the Directory Service log of the Event Viewer on your other domain controller. You need to install a new server to replace Server2. You attempt to install a new domain controller named Server2, but the installation fails, reporting Server2 already exists. You must resolve this issue.

You'll begin this lab by installing Server2 as a domain controller. Then, you'll pretend that Server2 has experienced an unrecoverable error by reinstalling the entire operating system without first demoting Server2.

1. Install Active Directory on Server2. You can do this manually or by using the Server2dc.txt answer file on the Supplemental CD-ROM. Place the companion CD-ROM in your CD-ROM drive. To use the answer file, run the command **dcpromo /answer:d:\70-294\labs\chapter03\Server2dc.txt** (this command makes the assumption that your CD-ROM drive is D; if not, substitute the drive letter of your CD-ROM drive). If you'd prefer to install Active Directory manually, use the written steps in Chapter 2 to install an additional domain controller for the *contoso.com* domain.

Caution   What you are about to do is not the recommended method for removing a domain controller from your Active Directory infrastructure. The recommended method is to run DCPROMO to uninstall the domain controller first. You are performing these steps to simulate an unexpected failure of your domain controller.

2. Ensure that you allow Server2 to fully complete the installation of Active Directory. You are now about to reinstall Server2 using the Windows 2003 Enterprise Server installation CD-ROM. You can use an unattended setup file to install Server2. For directions on using the unattended installation, see the Setup.txt file in the D:\70-394\Labs\Unattend\ folder.

3. Then, place the Windows Server 2003 CD-ROM in the CD-ROM drive. When you see the Press Any Key To Boot From The CD-ROM message, press the Space bar. If you want to use the unattended installation method, insert the floppy disk with the Winnt.sif immediately following this prompt. Otherwise, install manually, choosing options that are appropriate for your network.

Note   Whether you are using the unattended or manual method, you should not fully complete the Server2 reinstallation at this point. Just begin the installation, but don't go past the point of entering the Product Key code until you finish your work on Server1 (in the steps that follow). You need to be sure that you've removed all references of Server2 from Active Directory before you rejoin the domain.

4. Log on to Server1 using the domain administrator name and password.

Important   If you are completing this exercise on a domain controller running Windows Server 2003 SP1, replace the following steps (5–18) with this new step 5:

Open a command prompt. Type **Ntdsutil "metadata cleanup" "remove selected server" cn=Server2,cn=servers,cn=default-first-site-name ,cn=configuration,dc=contoso,dc=com**.

5. Open a command prompt. Type **ntdsutil** and press ENTER. The Ntdsutil prompt is displayed.

6. Type **metadata cleanup** and press ENTER. The metadata cleanup prompt is displayed.

7. Type **connections** and press ENTER. The server connections prompt is displayed.

8. Type **connect to server server1** and press ENTER.

9. Type **quit** and press ENTER. The metadata cleanup prompt appears again.

10. Type **select operation target**.

11. Type **list domains**. You should see only one domain and it should be numbered zero (0). If this is not the case, take note of which object and number represents *contoso.com* and use that number in the next step.

12. Type **select domain 0** and press ENTER.

13. Type **list sites** and press ENTER. You should see only one site and it should be numbered zero (0). If this is not the case, take note of which object and number represents your site and use that number in the next step.

14. Type **select site 0** and press ENTER.

15. Type **list servers in site** and press ENTER. You should see two servers. Take note of which number represents Server2, probably the number one (1). If that is not the case, then substitute the actual number of Server2 in the following step (instead of typing 1).

16. Type **select server 1** and press ENTER.

17. Type **quit** and press ENTER. The metadata cleanup prompt is displayed.

18. Type **remove selected server** and press ENTER. A prompt appears asking you to confirm the removal of Server2. Read this prompt carefully and then click Yes to remove the object.

19. Type **quit** and press ENTER twice. This closes the metadata cleanup and Ntdsutil prompts. Then type **exit** to close the command prompt.

20. You've now successfully removed the NTDS Setting object. However, there are still remnants of Server2 in the database. Therefore, you'll have to delete additional items using the DNS console and ADSIEdit.

21. Open the DNS console. Expand the structure as necessary to locate the *contoso.com* domain object and click on it.

22. In the right-hand pane, locate the (same as parent folder) Host (A) record that has the same IP address as Server2. Right-click that record and select Delete. Click Yes to confirm deletion.

23. Also in the right-hand pane, right-click the Server2 host record and select Delete. Click Yes to confirm deletion. You've now removed the DNS record for Server2. Close the DNS console.

24. Click Start, click Run, and then type **ADSIEdit.msc** and press ENTER. The ADSIEdit console opens.

25. Expand the following structure: Domain\DC=contoso,DC=com\OU=Domain Controllers. Click on the CN=Server2 object, and then press DELETE. Click Yes to confirm this deletion. You've now removed the Server object from the Active Directory Domain Name Context.

26. Expand the following structure: Configuration\CN=Configuration,DC=contoso, DC=com\CN=Sites\CN=Default-First-Site-Name\CN=Servers. Click on the CN=Server2 object, and then press DELETE. Click Yes to confirm this deletion.

You've now removed the Server object from the Configuration Name Context. Close the ADSIEdit console.

You've now successfully removed the references to Server2 in the Active Directory domain hosted by Server1. This is how you would clean up Active Directory after the loss of a domain controller. Now you should finish the installation of Server2. Then, join Server2 to the *contoso.com* domain as a member server. Directions on how to do that are covered in Chapter 2.

Chapter Summary

- The Active Directory administration tools include the Active Directory Domains And Trusts console, the Active Directory Sites And Services console, the Active Directory Users And Computers console, the Active Directory Schema snap-in, and the Active Directory-specific Windows Support Tools.

- Domain functional level (formerly known as the domain mode) provides a way to enable domain-wide Active Directory features within your network environment. Four domain functional levels are available: Windows 2000 mixed (default), Windows 2000 native, Windows Server 2003 interim, and Windows Server 2003.

- Forest functional level provides a way to enable forest-wide Active Directory features within your network environment. Three forest functional levels are available: Windows 2000 (default), Windows Server 2003 interim, and Windows Server 2003.

- Alternative UPN suffixes simplify administration and user logon processes by providing a single UPN suffix for all users. Using alternative domain names as the UPN suffix can provide additional logon security and simplify the names used to log on to another domain in the forest.

- Several additional tools that can be used to configure, manage, and debug Active Directory are available in the Windows Support Tools. To use these tools you must first install the Windows Support Tools on your computer.

- The MMC is a tool used to create, save, and open collections of administrative tools, called consoles. There are two types of MMCs: preconfigured and custom. Preconfigured MMCs contain commonly used snap-ins and appear on the Administrative Tools menu. You create custom MMCs to perform a unique set of administrative tasks.

- You use the Backup Or Restore Wizard to back up Active Directory.

- When you back up Active Directory data, you must specify that you want to back up only system state data. You can only back up the system state data on a local computer. You cannot back up the system state data on a remote computer.

- You restore Active Directory data by performing a nonauthoritative restore (default) or an authoritative restore. To restore the system state data on a domain controller, you must start your computer in directory services restore mode.

- In a nonauthoritative restore, the distributed services on a domain controller are restored from backup media and the restored data is then updated through normal replication. Each restored directory partition is updated with that of its replication partners. An authoritative restore brings a domain or a container back to the state it was in at the time of backup and overwrites all changes made since the backup.

Exam Highlights

Before taking the exam, review the key points and terms that are presented in this chapter. You need to know this information.

Key Points

- The Active Directory Domains And Trusts console provides the interface for setting the domain and forest functional levels and for specifying alternative UPN suffixes.

- Domain functional level provides a way to enable domain-wide Active Directory features within your network environment. Four domain functional levels are available: Windows 2000 mixed (default), Windows 2000 native, Windows Server 2003 interim, and Windows Server 2003.

- Forest functional level provides a way to enable forest-wide Active Directory features within your network environment. Three forest functional levels are available: Windows 2000 (default), Windows Server 2003 interim, and Windows Server 2003.

- Alternative UPN suffixes simplify administration and user logon processes by providing a single UPN suffix for all users. Using alternative domain names as the UPN suffix can provide additional logon security and simplify the names used to log on to another domain in the forest.

- You use the Backup Or Restore Wizard to back up Active Directory. To back up Active Directory data, you must specify that you want to back up only system state data. You can only back up the system state data on a local computer. You cannot back up the system state data on a remote computer.

- You restore Active Directory data by performing a nonauthoritative restore (default) or an authoritative restore. You must start your computer in directory services restore mode to initiate a restore.

Key Terms

authoritative restore   In Backup, a type of restore operation performed on an Active Directory domain controller in which the objects in the restored directory are treated as authoritative, replacing (through replication) all existing copies of those objects.

domain functional level   The level on which a domain running Windows Server 2003 is running. The functional level of a domain can be raised to enable new Active Directory features that will apply to that domain only.

forest functional level   The level on which a forest running Windows Server 2003 is running. The functional level of a forest can be raised to enable new Active Directory features that will apply to every domain in the forest.

nonauthoritative restore   A restore operation performed on an Active Directory domain controller in which the objects in the restored directory are not treated as authoritative. The restored objects are updated with changes held on other domain controllers in the domain.

UPN suffix   The part of the UPN to the right of the @ character. The default UPN suffix for a user account is the DNS domain name of the domain that contains the user account. The UPN suffix is only used within the Active Directory forest, and it is not required to be a valid DNS name.

Questions and Answers

Page
3-15

Lesson 1 Review

1. What is the purpose of the Active Directory Domains And Trusts console?

    The Active Directory Domains And Trusts console provides the interface to manage domains and manage trust relationships between forests and domains.

2. What is the purpose of the Active Directory Sites And Services console?

    The Active Directory Sites And Services console contains information about the physical structure of your network.

3. What is the purpose of the Active Directory Users And Computers console?

    The Active Directory Users And Computers console allows you to add, modify, delete, and organize Windows Server 2003 user accounts, computer accounts, security and distribution groups, and published resources in your organization's directory. It also allows you to manage domain controllers and OUs.

4. Why isn't the Active Directory Schema snap-in provided automatically on the Administrative Tools menu after you install Active Directory?

    By default, the Active Directory Schema snap-in is not available on the Administrative Tools menu and must be installed. This action is required to ensure that the schema cannot be modified by accident.

5. Which Active Directory-specific Windows Support Tool enables you to manage Windows Server 2003 domains and trust relationships?

    a. Ntdsutl.exe

    b. Netdom.exe

    c. Active Directory Domains And Trusts console

    d. Nltest.exe

    The correct answer is b. The Netdom.exe tool enables you to manage Windows Server 2003 domains and trust relationships. While the Active Directory Domains And Trusts console also provides this capability, this tool is not an Active Directory-specific Windows Support Tool.

Page
3-28

Lesson 2 Review

1. What is the function of an MMC? Why is it necessary to create customized MMCs?

    The MMC is a tool used to create, save, and open collections of administrative tools, which are called consoles. The console does not provide management functions itself, but is the program that hosts management applications called snap-ins. You create custom MMCs to perform a unique set of administrative tasks.

2. What is a snap-in?

Snap-ins are programs used by administrators to manage network services.

3. What is the function of a console tree?

A console tree displays the hierarchical organization of the snap-ins contained with an MMC.

4. What are extensions?

Extensions are snap-ins that provide additional administrative functionality to another snap-in.

5. Which of the following console mode types allows users to create new windows in the console?

    a. Author mode

    b. User mode—full access

    c. User mode—limited access, multiple window

    d. User mode—limited access, single window

The correct answer is a. Author mode allows users to add or remove snap-ins, create new windows in the console, view all portions of the console tree, and save MMCs.

Lesson 3 Review

Page 3-42

1. What tasks should you complete before attempting to back up Active Directory data?

Before attempting to back up Active Directory data, you must prepare the files that you want to back up, and, if you are using a removable media device, you must prepare the device.

2. What is system state data and why is it significant to backing up Active Directory?

For the Windows Server 2003 operating system, the system state data comprises the registry, COM+ Class Registration database, system boot files, files under Windows File Protection, and the Certificate Services database (if the server is a certificate server). If the server is a domain controller, Active Directory and the Sysvol directory are also contained in the system state data. To back up Active Directory, you must back up the system state data.

3. Can you restrict who can gain access to a completed backup file or tape? If so, how?

You can restrict who can gain access to a completed backup file or tape by selecting the Replace The Data On The Media With This Backup option and the Allow Only The Owner And The Administrator Access To The Backup Data And To Any Backups Appended To This Medium option on the Backup Options page in the Backup Or Restore Wizard.

4. When you specify the items you want to back up in the Backup Or Restore Wizard, which of the following should you select to successfully back up Active Directory data?

    a. System state data

    b. Shared system volume folder

   c. Database and log files

   d. Registry

The correct answer is a. When you specify the items you want to back up in the Backup Or Restore Wizard, you must specify system state data to successfully back up Active Directory data.

Page
3-53
Lesson 4 Review

   1. Describe what happens in a nonauthoritative restore.

   In a nonauthoritative restore, the distributed services on a domain controller are restored from backup media and the restored data is then updated through normal replication. Each restored directory partition is updated with that of its replication partners.

   2. Describe what happens in an authoritative restore.

   An authoritative restore brings a domain or a container back to the state it was in at the time of backup and overwrites all changes made since the backup.

   3. Which method of restore should you use if you accidentally delete an OU?

   Authoritative.

   4. Which method of restore should you use if a domain controller has completely failed due to hardware or software problems?

   Nonauthoritative.

   5. Which of the following Ntdsutil command parameters should you use if you want to restore the entire directory?

   a. Restore database

   b. Restore subtree

   c. Database restore

   d. Subtree restore

The correct answer is a. Database restore and subtree restore are not Ntdsutil command parameters. Restore subtree is used to restore a portion or a subtree of the directory.

Page
3-55
Case Scenario Exercise

   1. Before you move on to upgrading the other departments, what should you do to ensure the Research department's Active Directory data is protected? What should you ensure that Steve will continue to do in order to protect the Research department's data?

   First, the Research department should have a minimum of two domain controllers, so they have an online redundant copy of the Active Directory database. Second, they should be sure to back up the system state of the domain controllers routinely. Backing up system state data monthly is probably the bare minimum. Remember, the default lifespan of an Active Directory backup is 60 days due to the tombstone lifetime.

> **Note**   Remember that Windows Server 2003 with SP1 extends the tombstone lifetime from 60 days to 180 days.

Performing system state backups on a weekly basis is common. They should also perform a backup anytime major changes are made to the Active Directory database, such as when large numbers of accounts are added, modified, or deleted. Also, they would be wise to run a system state backup if sites or domains are added, modified, or removed.

> **Note**   Also remember that Windows Server 2003 with SP1 includes event ID 2089, which provides the backup status of each directory partition that a domain controller stores, including application directory partitions. Monitoring for this event ID would indicate whether a directory service partition had not been backed up for a period of at least half the tombstone lifetime.

2. What similarities exist between the implementation of Active Directory in the Research and Marketing departments?

   The need to determine which department will manage the DNS namespace. Also, what will that namespace be? (The answer is *marketing.graphicdesigninstitute.com.*) You should also install at least two Active Directory domain controllers and tell the network administration team for Research to make regular backups of Active Directory.

3. If you must install an additional Windows Server 2003 domain controller in the existing Administration domain, what must you do first to the Administration domain?

   You must run Adprep.exe on the Windows 2000 domain so that it can support servers running Windows Server 2003 configured as domain controllers.

4. If you're asked to upgrade the PDC of the Marketing domain, but hold off on the upgrade of the BDC, what functional level should you use on the new Windows 2003 Server domain?

   The best option is Windows Server 2003 interim, since this domain is meant to interact only with Windows NT 4 domain controllers. That is all that is required in the Marketing department. Another option is the Windows 2000 mixed functional level because this option allows a Windows Server 2003 to interact with Windows 2000, Windows NT 4, and Windows Server 2003 products.

5. The network administrators of the Marketing domain want to know what the equivalent of the User Manager for Domains and the Server Manager applications are on Windows Server 2003 domain controller. What would you tell them?

User Manager for Domains and Server Manager allow you to add computer and user accounts. In Active Directory there is a single interface for doing this called Active Directory Users And Computers. The snap-in is Dsa.msc. Server Manager allows you to also control some items like shared directories. You can do that by accessing the Computer Management console. The fastest way to do so is to click Start, click Run, type **compmgmt.msc**, and then press ENTER.

4 Installing and Managing Domains, Trees, and Forests

Exam Objectives in this Chapter:

- Plan flexible operations master role placement.
- Plan for business continuity of operations master roles.
- Identify operations master role dependencies.
- Implement an Active Directory directory service forest and domain structure.
- Create a child domain.
- Establish trust relationships. Types of trust relationships might include external trusts, shortcut trusts, and cross-forest trusts.
- Manage an Active Directory forest and domain structure.
- Manage trust relationships.
- Troubleshoot Active Directory.
- Diagnose and resolve issues related to operations master role failure.

Why This Chapter Matters

This chapter shows you how to create the domains, trees, and forests that make up your Active Directory structure. Large organizations or those that have multiple autonomous departments often require Active Directory structures that include multiple domains. Other organizations may have the need to share data between previously autonomous business units or companies that have separate Active Directory forests. The Microsoft Windows Server 2003 Active Directory implementation has the ability to better conform to these situations than did the Microsoft Windows 2000 Active Directory implementation. As network administrator, you may be faced with situations in which you must be able to create multiple domains, rename domains, or restructure existing domains. You must also know how to protect your Active Directory structure from potential disasters and mistakes, so that you can restore data if necessary.

Lessons in this Chapter:

Before You Begin

To complete the lessons in this chapter, you must

- Prepare your test environment according to the descriptions given in the "Getting Started" section of "About This Book"

- Complete the practices for installing and configuring Active Directory as discussed in Chapter 2, "Installing and Configuring Active Directory"

- Learn to use Active Directory administration tools as discussed in Chapter 3, "Administering Active Directory"

- Install the Windows Support Tools on Server2 as explained in Chapter 2

Lesson 1: Creating Multiple Domains, Trees, and Forests

In Chapter 2, you learned to install Active Directory, which actually creates the initial domain, tree, and forest for an organization. However, some organizations might require multiple domains, trees, or forests for Active Directory to effectively meet their needs. This lesson shows you how to create additional domains, trees, and forests.

After this lesson, you will be able to

- Create additional domains, trees, and forests
- Explain the reasons for using multiple domains, trees, and forests
- Explain the implications for using multiple domains, trees, and forests

Estimated lesson time: 20 minutes

Creating Multiple Domains

You must determine the number of domains for each forest in your organization. Although one domain might effectively represent the structure of small or medium-sized organizations, larger and more complex organizations might find that one domain is not sufficient. Before adding any domains you should be able to state the purpose of the new domain and justify it in terms of administrative and hardware costs.

Reasons to Create Multiple Domains

As stated in Chapter 2, you should create multiple domains to

- Meet security requirements
- Meet administrative requirements
- Optimize replication traffic
- Retain Microsoft Windows NT domains

Tip Do not create multiple domains to accommodate polarized groups or for isolated resources that are not easily assimilated into other domains. Both the groups and the resources are usually better candidates for organizational units (OUs).

Creating Domains to Meet Security Requirements   The settings in the Account Policies subdirectory in the Security Settings node of a Group Policy Object (GPO) can be specified only at the domain level. If the security requirements set in the Account Policies subdirectory vary throughout your organization, you need to define separate domains to handle the different requirements. The Account Policies subdirectory contains the following policies:

- **Password policy** Contains settings for passwords, such as password history, age, length, complexity, and storage

- **Account lockout policy** Contains settings for account lockout, such as lockout duration, threshold, and the lockout counter

- **Kerberos policy** Contains Kerberos-related settings, such as user logon restrictions, service and user ticket lifetimes, and enforcement

Note You can learn more about Account Policies in Chapter 13, "Administering Security with Group Policy."

Creating Domains to Meet Administrative Requirements Some organizations might need to establish boundaries to meet special administrative requirements that cannot be accommodated by establishing OUs in one domain. Special requirements might include satisfying specific legal or privacy concerns. For example, an organization might have a privacy requirement that outside administrators not be given control over sensitive product development files. In a one-domain scenario, members of the Domain Admins predefined global group would have complete control over all objects in the domain, including the sensitive files. By establishing a new domain containing the files, the first Domain Admins group is outside of the new domain and no longer has control of the files.

Creating Domains to Optimize Replication Traffic In organizations with one or more sites, you must consider whether site links can handle the replication traffic associated with a single domain. In a forest with one domain, all objects in the forest are replicated to every domain controller in the forest. If objects are replicated to locations where they are not used, bandwidth is used unnecessarily. By defining multiple small domains and replicating only those objects that are relevant to a location, you can reduce network traffic and optimize replication. However, you must weigh the savings achieved by optimizing replication against the cost of hardware and administration for the additional domains.

To determine whether you should define a domain to optimize replication traffic, you must consider

- **Link capacity and availability** If a link is operating near capacity or is not available for replication traffic during specific times of the day, it might not be able to handle replication traffic, and you should consider defining another domain. However, if links are idle at specific times, replication could be scheduled to occur during these times, provided the appropriate bandwidth is available.

- **Whether replication traffic will compete with other traffic**   If a link carries other, more important traffic that you do not want disturbed by replication traffic, you should consider defining another domain.

- **Whether links are pay-by-usage**   If replication traffic will cross an expensive pay-by-usage link, you should consider defining another domain.

- **Whether links are limited to Simple Mail Transport Protocol (SMTP)**   If a location is connected by SMTP-only links, it must have its own domain. Mail-based replication can occur only between domains; it cannot be used between domain controllers in the same domain.

Creating Domains to Retain Windows NT Domains   Organizations that have large Windows NT infrastructures might choose to retain an existing Windows NT domain. Existing Windows NT domains can be upgraded to Windows Server 2003, sometimes referred to as an in-place upgrade. You must weigh the costs of upgrading the Windows NT domain or consolidating the domain against the savings of maintaining and administering fewer domains. It is recommended that you minimize the number of domains by consolidating Windows NT domains before upgrading to Windows Server 2003.

Implications of Creating Multiple Domains   Adding a domain increases administrative and hardware costs. When determining whether to create multiple domains, keep the following cost issues in mind:

- **Domain administrators**   Each time a domain is added, a Domain Admins predefined global group is added as well. More administration is required to monitor the members of this group.

- **Security principals**   As domains are added, the likelihood that security principals will need to be moved between domains becomes greater. Although moving a security principal between OUs within a domain is a simple operation, moving a security principal between domains is more complex and can negatively affect users.

> **Note**   A *security principal* is a user, group, computer, or service that is assigned a unique *security identifier (SID)*. Security principals are discussed in more detail in Chapter 9, "Administering Active Directory Objects."

- **Group policy and access control**   Because group policy and access control are applied at the domain level, if your organization uses group policies or delegated administration across the enterprise or many domains, the measures must be applied separately to each domain.

- **Domain controller hardware and security facilities**   Each Windows Server 2003 domain requires at least two domain controllers to support fault-tolerance and multimaster requirements. In addition, it is recommended that domain controllers be located in a secure facility with limited access to prevent physical access by intruders.

■ **Trust links**   If a user from one domain must log on in another domain, the domain controller from the second domain must be able to contact the domain controller in the user's original domain. In the event of a link failure, the domain controller might not be able to maintain service. More trust links, which require setup and maintenance, might be necessary to alleviate the problem.

Creating Additional Domains

When creating additional domains, you use the Active Directory Installation Wizard.

To create an additional domain, complete the following steps:

1. Restart your computer and log on as Administrator.

2. Click Start and then click Run. In the Run dialog box, type **dcpromo** in the Run box and click OK.

3. On the Welcome To The Active Directory Installation Wizard page, click Next.

4. On the Operating System Compatibility page, click Next.

5. On the Domain Controller Type page, shown in Figure 4-1, select Domain Controller For A New Domain, and then click Next.

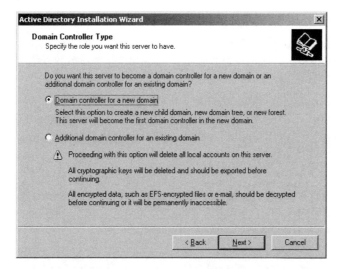

Figure 4-1   Active Directory Installation Wizard, Domain Controller Type page

6. On the Create New Domain page, shown in Figure 4-2, select Child Domain In An Existing Domain Tree, and then click Next.

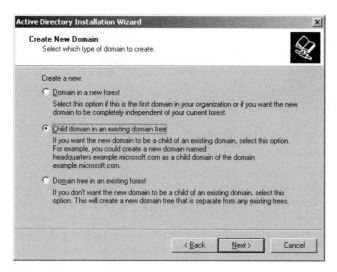

Figure 4-2   Active Directory Installation Wizard, Create New Domain page

7. On the Network Credentials page, shown in Figure 4-3, type the user name, password, and domain of the user account that has permission to create the domain in the User Name, Password, and Domain boxes, respectively. Click Next.

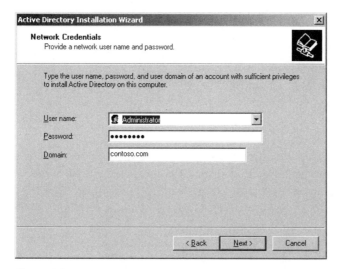

Figure 4-3   Active Directory Installation Wizard, Network Credentials page

8. On the Child Domain Installation page, shown in Figure 4-4, type the name of the parent domain in the Parent Domain box, and then type the name of the child domain in the Child Domain box. Ensure that the full Domain Name System (DNS) name of the child appears the way you want it in the Complete DNS Name Of New Domain box, and then click Next.

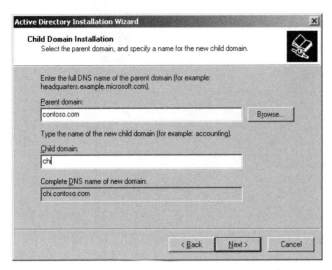

Figure 4-4   Active Directory Installation Wizard, Child Domain Installation page

9. Proceed through the following Active Directory Installation Wizard pages the same way you did in the "Installing Active Directory Using the Active Directory Installation Wizard" section of Chapter 2:

   ❑ NetBIOS Domain Name

   ❑ Database And Log Folders

   ❑ Shared System Volume

   ❑ DNS Registration Diagnostics

   ❑ Permissions

   ❑ Directory Services Restore Mode Administrator Password

10. On the Summary page, shown in Figure 4-5, the options that you selected are listed. Note that the new child domain is indicated. Review the contents of the Summary page, and then click Next. The Configuring Active Directory progress indicator appears as the Active Directory service is installed on the server. This process takes several minutes.

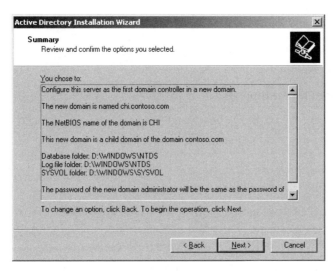

Figure 4-5   Active Directory Installation Wizard, Summary page

Creating Multiple Trees

Recall that a tree is a grouping or hierarchical arrangement of one or more Windows Server 2003 domains with contiguous names that you create by adding one or more child domains to an existing parent domain. A forest can have one or more trees. However, one tree per forest is considered ideal because it requires fewer administrative activities. Although the recommended number of trees in a forest is one, you might need to define more than one tree if your organization has more than one DNS name. Create a new tree only when you need to create a domain whose DNS namespace is not related to the other domains in the forest.

Real World   DNS Consideration for New Domains

As mentioned in Chapter 2, one of the most important issues when configuring Active Directory concerns DNS structure. When you create additional domains in the existing forest, you should consider your existing DNS structure and how it might change. The primary consideration is determining which servers should handle name resolution for the new domain. If the parent or forest root domain DNS servers are designated to handle name resolution for the new domain, you need to ensure that the DNS zone for the new domain exists on those DNS servers. You must also configure the computers for the new domain to utilize the parent or forest root domain DNS servers as their Preferred and Alternate DNS servers.

If, instead, you decide to install DNS servers in the new domain to handle name resolution, then you must delegate the new domain's namespace to those DNS servers. You should also consider creating a stub zone for the delegated name

> space on the parent or forest root domain's DNS servers. To learn more about DNS delegation and stub zones, review the topics "Delegating Zones" and "Understanding Stub Zones" in the Windows Server 2003 Help and Support Center.

Implications of Creating Multiple Trees

Creating multiple trees increases administrative costs. When determining whether to create multiple trees, keep the following items in mind:

- **DNS names**   Because each tree requires a separate DNS name, your organization will be responsible for maintaining more DNS names.

- **Proxy client exclusion list or proxy autoconfiguration (PAC) file**   Because each tree requires a separate DNS name, you must add these names to the list or file.

- **Non-Microsoft LDAP clients**   Such Lightweight Directory Access Protocol (LDAP) clients might not be able to perform a global catalog search and instead might need to perform an LDAP search of subtree scope that searches each tree separately.

Designating Tree Root Domains

Once you've determined the number of trees in each forest for your organization, you should determine which domain will serve as the *tree root domain* for each tree. The tree root domain is the highest-level domain in the tree; child and grandchild domains are arranged under it. Typically, the domain you select should be the one that is most critical to the operation of the tree. A tree root domain can also be the forest root domain, as shown in Figure 4-6.

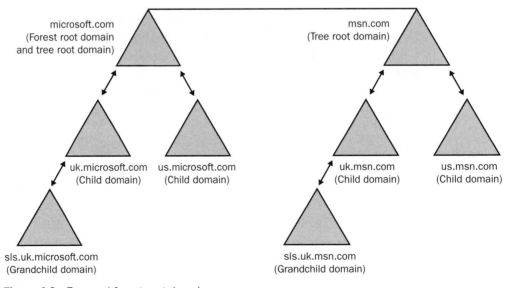

microsoft.com
(Forest root domain
and tree root domain)

msn.com
(Tree root domain)

uk.microsoft.com
(Child domain)

us.microsoft.com
(Child domain)

uk.msn.com
(Child domain)

us.msn.com
(Child domain)

sls.uk.microsoft.com
(Grandchild domain)

sls.uk.msn.com
(Grandchild domain)

Figure 4-6   Tree and forest root domains

Creating Additional Trees

When creating additional trees, you use the Active Directory Installation Wizard.

To create an additional tree, complete the following steps:

1. Restart your computer and log on as Administrator.

2. Click Start and then click Run. In the Run dialog box, type **dcpromo** in the Run box and click OK.

3. On the Welcome To The Active Directory Installation Wizard page, click Next.

4. On the Operating System Compatibility page, click Next.

5. On the Domain Controller Type page, shown previously in Figure 4-1, select Domain Controller For A New Domain, and then click Next.

6. On the Create New Domain page, shown previously in Figure 4-2, select Domain Tree In An Existing Forest, and then click Next.

7. On the Network Credentials page, shown previously in Figure 4-3, type the user name, password, and domain of the user account that has permission to create the new domain in the User Name, Password, and Domain boxes, respectively. Click Next.

8. On the New Domain Tree page, shown previously in Figure 4-7, type the complete DNS name of the new tree root domain in the Full DNS Name For New Domain box, and then click Next.

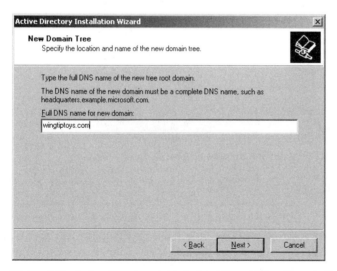

Figure 4-7   Active Directory Installation Wizard, New Domain Tree page

9. Proceed through the following Active Directory Installation Wizard pages in the same way you did in the "Installing Active Directory Using the Active Directory Installation Wizard" section of Chapter 2:

   ❑ NetBIOS Domain Name

   ❑ Database And Log Folders

   ❑ Shared System Volume

   ❑ DNS Registration Diagnostics

   ❑ Permissions

   ❑ Directory Services Restore Mode Administrator Password

10. On the Summary page, shown in Figure 4-8, the options that you selected are listed. Note that the new domain tree is indicated. Review the contents of the Summary page, and then click Next. The Configuring Active Directory progress indicator appears as the Active Directory service is installed on the server. This process takes several minutes.

Figure 4-8   Active Directory Installation Wizard, Summary page

Creating Multiple Forests

Because Windows Server 2003 domains in a forest share a single schema, configuration container, and global catalog, and are linked by two-way transitive trusts, you should strive to have only one forest for your organization. Ideally, the use of multiple forests should be temporary and reserved for situations such as a merger, acquisition, or partnership where two or more organizations must be joined. By defining multiple forests, you add substantial administrative and usability costs to your organization.

Reasons to Create Multiple Forests

Although you should strive to define only one forest for your organization, there are some situations that might warrant the creation of multiple forests. You might need to consider creating multiple forests:

- **Secure data**   Sensitive data can be protected so that only users within that forest can access it, such as a situation where business units must be separately maintained or when there is a need to isolate the schema, configuration container, or global catalog.

- **Isolate directory replication**   Schema changes, configuration changes, and the addition of new domains to a forest affect only that forest.

- **Accommodate development/lab environments**   New or test environments that may not yet be ready for production can be isolated from the rest of the organization.

If you want to separate business units or keep specific users from accessing resources and you cannot achieve this through your domain or OU structure, a multiple forest model can be an effective tool for creating privacy and security.

Implications of Creating Multiple Forests

Adding a forest dramatically increases administrative and usability costs. When determining whether to create multiple forests, keep the following administrative issues in mind:

- **Schema**   Each forest has its own schema. You need to maintain the contents and administration group memberships for each schema separately even if they are similar.

- **Configuration container**   Each forest has its own configuration container. You need to maintain the contents and administration group memberships for each configuration container separately even if they are similar.

- **Trusts**   A one-way or two-way forest trust is permitted between forest root domains in two different forests. You must explicitly (manually) set up and maintain this trust, which allows all domains in one forest to transitively trust all domains in another forest. A forest trust is not transitive across three or more forests.

- **Replication**   Replication of objects between forests is manual and requires the development of new administrative policies and procedures.

- **Merging forests or moving domains**   Forests cannot be merged in a one-step operation; you must clone security principals, migrate objects, decommission domain controllers, downgrade them to member servers, and add each to the new forest domain.

- **Moving objects**   Although objects can be moved between forests, you must use the ClonePrincipal tool to clone security principals in the new forest, or the Ldifde.exe command-line tool to move other objects.

- **Smart card logon**   Default user principal names (UPNs) must be maintained for smart cards to be able to log on across forests.

- **Additional domains**   Each forest must contain at least one domain. Additional domains increase hardware and administrative costs.

When determining whether to create multiple forests, keep the following usability issues in mind:

- **User logon**   Unless a forest trust is created, when a user logs on to a computer outside his or her own forest, he or she must specify the default UPN, which contains the full domain path for the user account, rather than just the easy-to-remember abstracted UPN. The default UPN is required because the domain controller in the forest will not be able to find the abstracted UPN in its global catalog. The user's abstracted UPN resides only in the global catalog in the user's forest.

- **User queries**   Unless a forest trust is created, users must be trained to make explicit queries across all of an organization's forests. Incomplete or incorrect queries can affect how users perform their work.

All the reasons for creating multiple forests involve administrative issues. However, the negative effects of a multiple forest scenario have the greatest impact on users. Unless you plan to create and administer forest trusts to make the use of multiple forests in your organization appear transparent to users, you should try not to create separate forests.

Creating Additional Forests

When creating additional forests, you use the Active Directory Installation Wizard.

To create an additional forest, complete the following steps:

1. Restart your computer and log on as Administrator.

2. Click Start and then click Run. In the Run dialog box, type **dcpromo** in the Run box and then click OK.

3. On the Welcome To The Active Directory Installation Wizard page, click Next.

4. On the Operating System Compatibility page, click Next.

5. On the Domain Controller Type page, shown previously in Figure 4-1, select Domain Controller For A New Domain, and then click Next.

6. On the Create New Domain page, shown previously in Figure 4-2, select Domain In A New Forest, and then click Next.

7. On the New Domain Name page, shown in Figure 4-9, type the complete DNS name of the new forest root domain in the Full DNS Name For New Domain box, and then click Next.

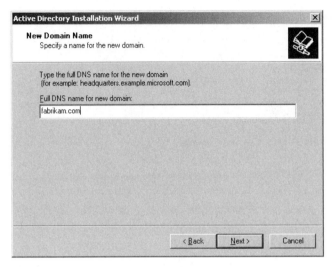

Figure 4-9 Active Directory Installation Wizard, New Domain Name page

8. Proceed through the following Active Directory Installation Wizard pages the same way you did in the "Installing Active Directory Using the Active Directory Installation Wizard" section of Chapter 2:

   ❑ NetBIOS Domain Name

   ❑ Database And Log Folders

   ❑ Shared System Volume

   ❑ DNS Registration Diagnostics

   ❑ Permissions

   ❑ Directory Services Restore Mode Administrator Password

9. On the Summary page, shown in Figure 4-10, the options that you selected are listed. Note that the new forest is indicated. Review the contents of the Summary page, and then click Next. The Configuring Active Directory progress indicator appears as the Active Directory service is installed on the server. This process takes several minutes.

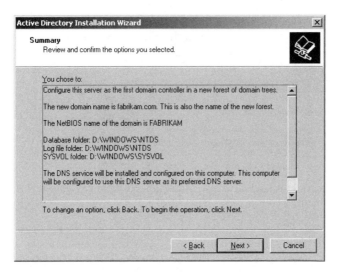

Figure 4-10   Active Directory Installation Wizard, Summary page

Practice: Creating a Child Domain

In this practice, you create a child domain for the domain *contoso.com.*

Exercise 1: Creating a Child Domain

In this exercise, you create the child domain *chi.contoso.com.*

▶ **To create a child domain**

1. Log on to Server1 and Server2 as Administrator. If you completed the exercises in Chapter 2, Server2 should currently be a member server.

2. Use the procedure provided earlier in this lesson to create a child domain named *chi.contoso.com* on Server2. The parent domain is *contoso.com.*

3. Verify that the domain has been installed correctly on Server2 by verifying the domain configuration, the DNS configuration, DNS integration with Active Directory, installation of the shared system volume, and operation of the Directory Services Restore Mode boot option, as described in Chapter 2.

4. On Server1, click Start, point to Administrative Tools, and then click Active Directory Domains And Trusts. Note the presence of the *chi.contoso.com* domain when you expand the *contoso.com* domain.

Lesson Review

The following questions are intended to reinforce key information presented in this lesson. If you are unable to answer a question, review the lesson and then try the question

again. Answers to the questions can be found in the "Questions and Answers" section at the end of this chapter.

1. What is the main consequence of creating multiple domains and trees?

   _____

   _____

2. Why would you need to create additional trees in your Active Directory forest?

   _____

   _____

3. What is a tree root domain?

   _____

   _____

4. What are the reasons for creating multiple forests in an organization?

   _____

   _____

5. Which of the following is not a reason for creating multiple domains?

   a. To meet security requirements

   b. To meet administrative requirements

   c. To optimize replication traffic

   d. To meet delegation requirements

   e. To retain Windows NT domains

Lesson Summary

- Create multiple domains to meet security requirements, meet administrative requirements, optimize replication traffic, or retain Windows NT domains.

- Although the recommended number of trees in a forest is one, you might need to define more than one tree if your organization has more than one DNS name. Adding a domain or tree increases administrative and hardware costs.

- The recommended number of forests is one. Consider creating multiple forests if you need to secure data or you need to isolate directory replication.

- Adding a forest dramatically increases administrative and usability costs and can directly affect users during the logon and query processes.

- To create additional domains, trees, or forests, you use the Dcpromo command and the Active Directory Installation Wizard.

Lesson 2: Renaming and Restructuring Domains and Renaming Domain Controllers

Windows Server 2003 allows you to rename any domain that has domain controllers running Windows Server 2003, move existing domains to other locations in the domain hierarchy, and rename domain controllers without first demoting them. This lesson shows you how to rename and restructure domains and how to rename domain controllers.

After this lesson, you will be able to

- Name the tool used to rename and restructure a domain
- Rename a domain controller

Estimated lesson time: 15 minutes

Renaming and Restructuring Domains

Windows Server 2003 allows you to rename a domain, which provides you with the flexibility to make important forest-wide infrastructure changes as the needs of your organization change. Renaming domains can accommodate acquisitions, mergers, name changes, or reorganizations.

> **Note**   In Windows Server 2003, the domain renaming function provides a supported method to rename domains only when necessary. Domain renaming is a complex process, and the renaming function is not intended for use as a routine operation.

Windows Server 2003 also allows you to restructure the hierarchy of domains in your forest so that a domain residing in one domain tree can be moved to another domain tree. Restructuring a forest allows you to move a domain anywhere within the forest it resides in (except the forest root domain); this includes the ability to move a domain so that it becomes the root of its own domain tree.

> **Note**   You can rename or restructure the domains in a forest only if all domain controllers in the forest are running Windows Server 2003, all domain functional levels in the forest have been raised to Windows Server 2003, and the forest functional level has been raised to Windows Server 2003.

You can use the domain rename utility (Rendom.exe) to rename or restructure a domain. Domain rename allows you to

- Change the DNS and NetBIOS names of the forest-root domain
- Change the DNS and NetBIOS names of any tree-root domains

- Change the DNS and NetBIOS names of any parent and child domains

- Restructure a domain's position in the forest

The Rendom.exe utility can be found in the \Valueadd\Msft\Mgmt\Domren directory on the Windows Server 2003 CD-ROM. A domain rename will affect every domain controller in your forest and is a thorough multistep process that requires a detailed understanding of the operation. For detailed information about the domain rename function, see the Readme file found in the same directory.

Renaming a Domain Controller

Windows Server 2003 allows you to rename domain controllers running Windows Server 2003. You might want to rename a domain controller to

- Use an existing domain controller to serve a large number of clients whose inaccessibility could overload the remaining domain controllers

- Restructure your network for organizational and business needs

- Make management and administrative control easier

Only Domain Admins have sufficient permissions to rename a domain controller.

Note   You can rename a domain controller only if the domain functional level of the domain to which the domain controller is joined is set to Windows Server 2003.

When a domain controller is renamed, the new name is automatically updated to DNS and Active Directory. Once the new name propagates to DNS and Active Directory, clients are then capable of locating and authenticating to the renamed domain controller. DNS and Active Directory replication latency may cause a temporary inability of clients to locate or authenticate to the renamed domain controller. The length of time this takes depends on specifics of the network and the replication topology of the organization. This might be acceptable for clients who try to locate and authenticate to a particular domain controller since other domain controllers should be available to process the authentication request.

Note   If the new domain controller name contains a primary DNS suffix different from the name of the domain to which it is joined, the domain should be properly configured for the new primary DNS suffix. The new primary DNS suffix is written to the dnsHostName attribute of the computer account in Active Directory.

You rename a domain controller by using the Netdom.exe: Windows Domain Manager command-line tool, included with the Windows Support Tools on the Windows Server

2003 Setup CD-ROM. You use the Netdom Computername command to manage the primary and alternate names for a computer.

> **Note**   For detailed instructions on installing the Windows Support Tools, refer to Chapter 3, "Administering Active Directory."

To rename a domain controller, complete the following steps:

1. Click Start, and then click Command Prompt.

2. At the command prompt, type: **netdom computername *CurrentComputerName* /add:*NewComputerName***, where *CurrentComputerName* is the current full computer name or IP address of the domain controller you are renaming and *NewComputerName* is the new full name for the domain controller. This action updates the service principal name (SPN) attributes in Active Directory for this domain controller account and registers DNS resource records for the new domain controller name.

3. Wait for replication latency time interval to ensure replication of the registered DNS host (A) resource record(s) to all authoritative DNS servers.

4. At the command prompt type: **netdom computername *CurrentComputerName* /makeprimary: *NewComputerName*** where *CurrentComputerName* is the current full computer name or IP address of the domain controller you are renaming and *NewComputerName* is the new full name for the domain controller. This action updates the domain controller account in the Active Directory with the new domain controller name (the name you added in step 2).

5. Restart the computer.

6. Wait for the replication of the domain controller locator resource records to occur on all authoritative DNS servers. These records are registered by the domain controller after the renamed domain controller has been restarted and contain the new computer name. The records that are registered are available on the domain controller in the %*Systemroot*%\System32\Config\Netlogon.dns file.

7. To ensure that the domain controller has been successfully renamed, make the following checks:

   ❑ Click Start, point to Control Panel, and then click System. On the Computer Name tab, verify that the correct name appears after Full Computer Name. Click Cancel.

   ❑ Click Start, and then click Command Prompt. At the command prompt, validate the names that the computer is currently configured with by typing: **netdom computername *NewComputerName* /enumerate:**, where *NewComputerName* is the new name of the domain controller. Note that the domain controller has two names.

8. At the command prompt, type: **netdom computername** *NewComputerName* **/remove:***OldComputerName*, where *NewComputerName* is the new name of the domain controller and *OldComputerName* is the old name of the domain controller. This action removes the old domain controller name.

> **Note**   Both the old and new domain controller names are maintained until you remove the old domain controller name (shown in step 8). This function ensures that there is no interruption in the ability of clients to locate or authenticate to the renamed domain controller, except when the domain controller is restarted.

The new computer name must not coincide with the name of the computer object that already exists in the domain. Microsoft recommends using computer names that are shorter than 16 bytes. If you rename your computer or workgroup when it is disconnected from the network, duplicate computer names might result. Check with your network administrator before renaming your computer.

Practice: Renaming a Domain Controller

In this practice, you rename Server1.

Exercise 1: Renaming a domain controller

In this exercise, you rename Server1 to be Server9.

▶ **To rename a domain controller**

1. Log on to Server1 as Administrator.

2. Use the procedure provided earlier in this lesson to change the name of *server1.contoso.com* to *server9.contoso.com*.

3. Use the procedure provided earlier in this lesson to ensure that the domain controller has been successfully renamed to *server9.contoso.com*.

4. Use the procedure provided earlier in this lesson to change the name of *server9.contoso.com* back to *server1.contoso.com*.

Lesson Review

The following questions are intended to reinforce key information presented in this lesson. If you are unable to answer a question, review the lesson and then try the question again. Answers to the questions can be found in the "Questions and Answers" section at the end of this chapter.

1. Under what domain and forest functional levels can you rename or restructure domains in a forest?

   _____

   _____

2. What utility is used to rename or restructure a domain in a forest?

   _____

   _____

3. Under what domain functional level can you rename a domain controller?

   _____

   _____

4. What tool is used to rename a domain controller?

   _____

   _____

Lesson Summary

- You can rename the domains in a forest only if all domain controllers in the forest are running Windows Server 2003, all domain functional levels in the forest have been raised to Windows Server 2003, and the forest functional level has been raised to Windows Server 2003.

- You use the domain rename utility (Rendom.exe) to rename or restructure a domain.

- You can rename a domain controller only if the functional level of the domain to which the domain controller is joined is set to Windows Server 2003.

- You rename a domain controller by using the Netdom.exe: Windows Domain Manager command-line tool, included with the Windows Support Tools on the Windows Server 2003 Setup CD-ROM. You use the Netdom Computername command to manage the primary and alternate names for a computer.

Lesson 3: Managing Operations Master Roles

This lesson introduces you to operations master roles and the tasks involved in the management of master role assignments. Operations master roles (also known as flexible single master operations, or FSMO) are special roles assigned to one or more domain controllers in an Active Directory domain. The domain controllers assigned these roles perform single-master replication. In this lesson, you learn how to plan operations master locations and to view, transfer, and seize operations master role assignments.

After this lesson, you will be able to

- Describe the forest-wide operations master roles
- Describe the domain-wide operations master roles
- Plan operations master locations
- View operations master role assignments
- Transfer operations master role assignments
- Seize operations master role assignments

Estimated lesson time: 30 minutes

Operations Master Roles

As discussed in Chapter 1, "Introduction to Active Directory," Active Directory supports multimaster replication of the Active Directory database between all domain controllers in the domain. However, some changes are impractical to perform in multimaster fashion, so one or more domain controllers can be assigned to perform operations that are *single-master* (not permitted to occur at different places in a network at the same time). *Operations master roles* are assigned to domain controllers to perform single-master operations.

In any Active Directory forest, five operations master roles must be assigned to one or more domain controllers. Some roles must appear in every forest. Other roles must appear in every domain in the forest. You must be aware of operations master roles assigned to a domain controller if problems develop on the domain controller or if you plan to take it out of service.

Note   Windows Server 2003 with Service Pack 1 (SP1) logs events in the Directory Service event log when an operation that requires a domain controller with a specific operations master role cannot be performed. These events identify role holders that do not exist, exist but are not available, or are available but have not replicated recently with the contacting domain controller.

Forest-Wide Operations Master Roles

Every Active Directory forest must have the following roles:

- Schema master
- Domain naming master

These roles must be unique in the forest. This means that throughout the entire forest there can be only one schema master and one domain naming master.

Schema Master Role

The domain controller assigned the *schema master* role controls all updates and modifications to the schema. To update the schema of a forest, you must have access to the schema master. At any time, there can be only one schema master in the entire forest.

Domain Naming Master Role

The domain controller holding the *domain naming master* role controls the addition or removal of domains in the forest. There can be only one domain naming master in the entire forest at any time.

Domain-Wide Operations Master Roles

Every domain in the forest must have the following roles:

- Relative identifier (RID), or relative ID, master
- Primary domain controller (PDC) emulator
- Infrastructure master

These roles must be unique in each domain. This means that each domain in the forest can have only one RID master, PDC emulator master, and infrastructure master.

RID Master Role

The domain controller assigned the *RID master* role allocates sequences of relative IDs to each of the various domain controllers in its domain. At any time, there can be only one domain controller acting as the RID master in each domain in the forest.

Whenever a domain controller creates a user, group, or computer object, it assigns the object a unique security ID. The security ID consists of a domain security ID (that is the same for all security IDs created in the domain) and a relative ID that is unique for each security ID created in the domain.

To move an object between domains (using Movetree.exe: Active Directory Object Manager), you must initiate the move on the domain controller acting as the RID master of the domain that currently contains the object.

PDC Emulator Role

If the domain contains computers operating without Windows Server 2003 client software or if it contains Windows NT backup domain controllers (BDCs), the domain controller assigned the *PDC emulator* role acts as a Windows NT PDC. It processes password changes from clients and replicates updates to the BDCs. At any time, there can be only one domain controller acting as the PDC emulator in each domain in the forest.

Even after all systems are upgraded to Windows Server 2003, and the Windows Server 2003 domain is operating at the Windows Server 2003 functional level, the PDC emulator receives preferential replication of password changes performed by other domain controllers in the domain. If a password was recently changed, that change takes time to replicate to every domain controller in the domain. If a logon authentication fails at another domain controller due to a bad password, that domain controller forwards the authentication request to the PDC emulator before rejecting the logon attempt.

Infrastructure Master Role

The domain controller assigned the *infrastructure master* role is responsible for updating the group-to-user references whenever the members of groups are renamed or changed. At any time, there can be only one domain controller acting as the infrastructure master in each domain.

When you rename or move a member of a group (and the member resides in a different domain from the group), the group might temporarily appear not to contain that member. The infrastructure master of the group's domain is responsible for updating the group so it knows the new name or location of the member. The infrastructure master distributes the update via multimaster replication.

There is no compromise to security during the time between the member rename and the group update. Only an administrator looking at that particular group membership would notice the temporary inconsistency.

> **Note**   If there is more than one domain controller in the domain, the infrastructure master role should not be assigned to any domain controller that is hosting the global catalog. For more information, refer to the "Planning Operations Master Locations" section of this chapter.

Figure 4-11 shows how the operations master roles are distributed throughout a forest by default. Domain A was the first domain created in the forest (the forest root domain). It holds both of the forest-wide operations master roles. The first domain controller in each of the other domains is assigned the three domain-specific roles.

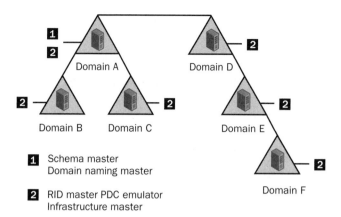

Figure 4-11   Operations master role default distribution in a forest

Exam Tip   Know which operations master roles are forest-wide and which are domain-wide.

Managing Operations Master Roles

There are two ways to manage operations master roles: transfer and seizure.

Transferring Operations Master Roles

To transfer an operations master role is to move it with the cooperation of its current owner. You transfer an operations master role when you want to move a role from one server to another. The transfer of an operations master role is secured by standard Windows Server 2003 access controls, and should be limited to only those that might need to move it. For example, an organization with a substantial Information Technology (IT) department might place the schema master role on a server in the IT group and configure its access control list (ACL) so that it cannot be moved at all.

Seizing Operations Master Roles

To seize an operations master role is to move it without the cooperation of its current owner. You seize an operations master role assignment when a server that is holding a role fails and you do not intend to restore it. The operations master role assignment is seized (reassigned) to a domain controller you select to act as a standby operations master. Some operations master roles are crucial to the operation of your network. Others can be unavailable for quite some time before their absence becomes a problem. Generally, you will notice that a single master operations role holder is unavailable when you try to perform some function controlled by the particular operations master. Remember that Windows Server 2003 with SP1 will log events in the Directory Service event log if you carry out an operation that requires a particular operations master role and that operations master is not available.

Before seizing the operations master role, determine the cause and expected duration of the computer or network failure, using the Directory Service events if available. If the cause is a networking problem or a server failure that will be resolved soon, wait for the role holder to become available again. If the domain controller that currently holds the role has failed, you must determine if it can be recovered and brought back online. You must also determine which domain controller can effectively serve as a standby operations master. In general, seizing an operations master role is a drastic step that should be considered only if the current operations master will never be available again. The decision depends upon the role and how long the particular role holder will be unavailable. The impact of various role holder failures is discussed in the following topics.

> **Caution**   A domain controller whose schema, domain naming, or RID master role has been seized must *never* be brought back online without first reformatting the drives and reloading Windows Server 2003. Before proceeding with the role seizure, you must ensure that the outage of this domain controller is permanent by physically disconnecting the domain controller from the network.

Schema Master Failure   Temporary loss of the schema operations master is not visible to network users. It is not visible to network administrators either, unless they are trying to modify the schema or install an application that modifies the schema during installation. If the schema master will be unavailable for an unacceptable length of time, you can seize the role to the domain controller you've chosen to act as the standby schema master. However, seizing this role is a step that you should take only when the failure of the schema master is permanent.

Domain Naming Master Failure   Temporary loss of the domain naming master is not visible to network users. It is not visible to network administrators either, unless they are trying to add a domain to the forest or remove a domain from the forest. If the domain naming master will be unavailable for an unacceptable length of time, you can seize the role to the domain controller you've chosen to act as the standby domain naming master. However, seizing this role is a step that you should take only when the failure of the domain naming master is permanent.

RID Master Failure   Temporary loss of the RID operations master is not visible to network users. It is not visible to network administrators either, unless they are creating objects and the domain in which they are creating the objects runs out of relative identifiers. If the RID master will be unavailable for an unacceptable length of time, you can seize the role to the domain controller you've chosen to act as the standby RID master.

However, seizing this role is a step that you should take only when the failure of the RID master is permanent.

PDC Emulator Failure   The loss of the PDC emulator affects network users. Therefore, when the PDC emulator is not available, you might need to immediately seize the role. If the current PDC emulator will be unavailable for an unacceptable length of time and its domain has clients without Windows Server 2003 client software, or if it contains Windows NT backup domain controllers, seize the PDC emulator role to the domain controller you've chosen to act as the standby PDC emulator. When the original PDC emulator is returned to service, you can return the role to the original domain controller.

Infrastructure Master Failure   Temporary loss of the infrastructure master is not visible to network users. It is not visible to network administrators either, unless they have recently moved or renamed a large number of accounts. If the infrastructure master will be unavailable for an unacceptable length of time, you can seize the role to a domain controller that is not a global catalog but is well connected to a global catalog (from any domain), ideally in the same site as a global catalog server. When the original infrastructure master is returned to service, you can transfer the role back to the original domain controller.

Planning Operations Master Locations

When you create the first domain in a new forest, all of the operations master roles are automatically assigned to the first domain controller in that domain. When you create a new child domain or the root domain of a new domain tree in an existing forest, the first domain controller in the new domain is automatically assigned the RID master, PDC emulator, and infrastructure master roles. Because there can be only one schema master and one domain naming master in the forest, these roles remain in the first domain on the first domain controller created in the forest.

The default operations master locations work well for a forest deployed on a few domain controllers in a single site. In a forest with more domain controllers, or in a forest that spans multiple sites, you need to transfer the default operations master role assignments to other domain controllers in the domain or forest to

- Balance the load among domain controllers, or

- Accommodate domain controller maintenance and hardware upgrades

Planning the Operations Master Role Assignments by Domain

Follow these guidelines when assigning operations master roles for a domain:

- If a domain has only one domain controller, that domain controller must hold all of the domain roles.

- If a domain has more than one domain controller

    □ Choose two well-connected domain controllers that are direct replication partners. Make one of the domain controllers the operations master domain controller, to which you should assign the RID master, the PDC emulator, and the infrastructure master roles. The other domain controller functions as a standby operations master domain controller, used in case of failure of the operations master domain controller.

    □ In domains that are not large, assign both the RID master and PDC emulator roles to the domain controller you selected as the operations master domain controller.

    □ In very large domains, you can reduce the peak load on the PDC emulator by placing RID master and PDC emulator roles on separate domain controllers, both of which are direct replication partners of the domain controller you selected as the standby operations master domain controller. However, to avoid the administrative tasks associated with separating the two roles, you should keep the two roles together unless the load on the domain controller you selected as the operations master domain controller justifies separating the roles.

    □ The infrastructure master role should not be assigned to any domain controller that is hosting the global catalog. However, you should assign the infrastructure master role to any domain controller that is well connected to a global catalog (from any domain) in the same site. If the domain controller you selected as the operations master domain controller meets these requirements, use it unless the load justifies the extra management burden of separating the roles. If the infrastructure master and global catalog are on the same domain controller, the infrastructure master will not function. The infrastructure master will never find data that is out of date, so it will never replicate any changes to the other domain controllers in the domain. If all of the domain controllers in a domain are also hosting the global catalog, all of the domain controllers have the current data and it does not matter which domain controller holds the infrastructure master role.

Planning the Operations Master Roles for the Forest

Once you have planned all of the domain roles for each domain, consider the forest roles. The schema master and the domain naming master roles should always be assigned to the same domain controller. For best performance, assign them to a domain controller that is well connected to the computers used by the administrator or group responsible for schema updates and the creation of new domains. The load of these operations master roles is very light, so, to simplify management, place these roles on the operations master domain controller of one of the domains in the forest.

Planning for Growth

Normally, as your forest grows, you will not need to change the locations of the various operations master roles. But when you are planning to decommission a domain controller, to change the global catalog status of a domain controller, or to reduce the connectivity between parts of your network, you should review your plan and revise the operations master role assignments, as necessary.

Viewing Operations Master Role Assignments

Before you can revise operations master role assignments, you need to view the current operations master role assignments for your domain.

To view the RID master, the PDC emulator, or the infrastructure master role assignments, complete the following steps:

1. Open the Active Directory Users And Computers console.

2. In the console tree, right-click the Active Directory Users And Computers node, point to All Tasks, and then click Operations Masters.

3. In the Operations Masters dialog box, select one of the following choices:

   ❑ Click the RID tab, and the name of the RID master appears in the Operations Master box.

   ❑ Click the PDC tab, and the name of the PDC emulator appears in the Operations Master box.

   ❑ Click the Infrastructure tab, and the name of the infrastructure master appears in the Operations Master box.

4. Click Close to close the Operations Master dialog box.

To view the domain naming master role assignment, complete the following steps:

1. Open the Active Directory Domains And Trusts console.

2. In the console tree, right-click the Active Directory Domains And Trusts node, then click Operations Master. In the Change Operations Master dialog box, the name of the current domain naming master appears in the Domain Naming Operations Master box.

3. Click Close to close the Change Operations Master dialog box.

To view the schema master role assignment, complete the following steps:

1. Open the Active Directory Schema snap-in.

Note   The Active Directory Schema snap-in must be installed separately after Active Directory is installed. See Chapter 3 for details on installing the Active Directory Schema snap-in.

2. In the console tree, right-click Active Directory Schema, and then click Operations Master. In the Change Schema Master dialog box, the name of the current schema master appears in the Current Schema Master (Online) box.

3. Click Close to close the Change Schema Master dialog box.

Transferring an Operations Master Role Assignment

To perform a role transfer, both domain controllers must be available and connected to each other through the network. Depending upon the operations master role to be transferred, you perform the role transfer using one of the three Active Directory consoles.

To transfer the RID master, the PDC emulator, or the infrastructure master role assignments, complete the following steps:

1. Open the Active Directory Users and Computers console.

2. In the console tree, right-click the Active Directory Users And Computers node, and then click Connect To Domain.

3. In the Connect To Domain dialog box, type the domain name or click Browse to select the domain from the list, and then click OK.

4. In the console tree, right-click the Active Directory Users And Computers node, and then click Connect To Domain Controller.

5. In the Connect To Domain Controller dialog box, shown in Figure 4-12, in the Or Select An Available Domain Controller list, select the domain controller that will become the new RID master, PDC emulator, or infrastructure master, and then click OK.

Figure 4-12   Connect To Domain Controller dialog box

6. In the console tree, right-click the Active Directory Users And Computers node, point to All Tasks, and then click Operations Masters.

7. In the Operations Masters dialog box, shown in Figure 4-13, select one of the following choices:

   ❑ Click the RID tab, and then click Change.

   ❑ Click the PDC tab, and then click Change.

   ❑ Click the Infrastructure tab, and then click Change.

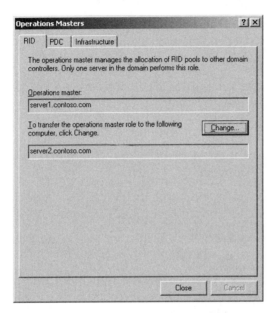

Figure 4-13 Operations Masters dialog box

8. On the Active Directory message box, click Yes to confirm that you want to transfer the operations master role. On the second Active Directory message box, click OK.

9. Click Close to close the Operations Master dialog box.

To transfer the domain naming master role assignment, complete the following steps:

1. Open the Active Directory Domains And Trusts console.

2. In the console tree, right-click the Active Directory Domains And Trusts node, and then click Connect To Domain Controller.

3. In the Connect To Domain Controller dialog box, in the Or Select An Available Domain Controller list, select the domain controller that will become the new domain naming master, and then click OK.

4. In the console tree, right-click the Active Directory Domains And Trusts node, and then click Operations Master.

5. In the Change Operations Master dialog box, shown in Figure 4-14, click Change.

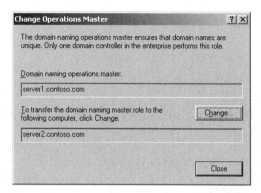

Figure 4-14   Change Operations Master dialog box

6. Click Close to close the Change Operations Master dialog box.

To transfer the schema master role assignment, complete the following steps:

1. Open the Active Directory Schema snap-in.

> **Note**   The Active Directory Schema snap-in must be installed separately after Active Directory is installed. See Chapter 3 for details on installing the Active Directory Schema snap-in.

2. In the console tree, right-click Active Directory Schema, and then click Change Domain Controller.

3. In the Change Domain Controller dialog box, shown in Figure 4-15, click either

   ❑ Any DC, to let Active Directory select the new schema operations master, or

   ❑ Specify Name, and then type the name of the new schema master to specify the new schema operations master

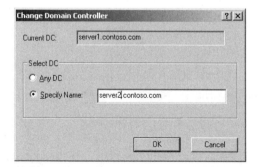

Figure 4-15   Change Domain Controller dialog box

4. Click OK.

5. In the console tree, right-click Active Directory Schema, and then click Operations Master.

6. In the Change Schema Master dialog box, click Change.

7. Click OK to close the Change Schema Master dialog box.

Seizing an Operations Master Role Assignment

A role seizure is controlled through the same per-role object permissions that controls role transfers, plus the Write fsmoRoleOwner property permission at the new role owner. To seize a role, you need both the per-role object permission and the Write fsmoRoleOwner property permission. By default, the Write fsmoRoleOwner property permission is granted to the same groups that are granted the per-role object permissions.

A role seizure is a two-step process. In the first step, you must determine whether the domain controller that seizes the role is fully up-to-date with the updates performed on the previous role owner by using the Repadmin command-line tool. After you have determined the status of the domain controller seizing the role, you can seize the operations master role by using the Ntdsutil utility.

> **Caution** Do not seize an operations master role if you can transfer it instead. Seizing an operations master role is a drastic step that should be considered only if the current operations master will never be available again.

Determining the Status of the Domain Controller Seizing the Role

The domain controller that seizes the role must be fully up-to-date with the updates performed on the previous role owner. Because of replication latency, it is possible that the domain controller might not be up-to-date. To check the status of updates for a domain controller, use the Repadmin.exe: Replication Diagnostics command-line tool, included with the Windows Support Tools on the Windows Server 2003 CD-ROM in the \Support\Tools folder.

> **Note** For detailed instructions on installing the Windows Support Tools, refer to Chapter 3, "Administering Active Directory."

For example, to make sure a domain controller is fully up-to-date, suppose that "server1" is the RID master of the domain *microsoft.com*, "server2" is the standby operations master domain controller, and "server3" is the only other domain controller in the *microsoft.com* domain. Using the Repadmin tool along with the /Showutdvec argument, you would issue the following commands, shown in bold:

```
C:\> repadmin/showutdvec server2.microsoft.com dc=microsoft,dc=com
New-York\server1   @ USN 2604 @ Time 2003-01-22 12:50:44
San-Francisco\server3 @ USN 2706 @ Time 2003-01-22 12:53:36

C:\>repadmin/showutdvec server3.microsoft.com dc=microsoft,dc=com
New-York\server1 @ USN 2590 @ Time 2003-01-22 12:50:44
Chicago\server2 @ USN 3110 @ Time 2003-01-22 12:57:55
```

The output for server1 is especially relevant. Server2's up-to-date status value with respect to server1 (server1 @ USN 2604) is larger than server3's up-to-date status value with respect to server1 (server1 @ USN 2590), making it safe for server2 to seize the RID master role formerly held by server1. If the up-to-date status value for server2 was less than the value for server3, you would wait for normal replication to update server2, or use the Repadmin tool's /Syncall commands to make the replication happen immediately. You can learn more about using Repadmin in Windows Support Tools help.

Seizing the Role

The Ntdsutil tool allows you to transfer and seize operations master roles. When you use the Ntdsutil command-line tool to seize an operations master role, the tool attempts a transfer from the current role owner first. Then, if the existing operations master is unavailable, it performs the seizure.

To seize the operations master role assignments, complete the following steps:

1. Click Start, and then click Command Prompt.

2. At the command prompt, type **ntdsutil** and press ENTER.

3. At the ntdsutil prompt, type **roles** and press ENTER.

4. At the fsmo maintenance prompt, type **connections** and press ENTER.

5. At the server connections prompt, type **connect to server**, followed by the fully qualified domain name (FQDN), and press ENTER.

6. At the server connections prompt, type **quit** and press ENTER.

7. At the fsmo maintenance prompt, type one of the following and press ENTER:

   ❑ **seize schema master**

   ❑ **seize domain naming master**

   ❑ **seize RID master**

   ❑ **seize PDC**

   ❑ **seize infrastructure master**

8. At the fsmo maintenance prompt, type **quit** and press ENTER.

9. At the ntdsutil prompt, type **quit** and press ENTER.

The following is an example of seizing an operations master role using the Ntdsutil command:

```
C:\>ntdsutil
ntdsutil: roles
fsmo maintenance: connections
server connections: connect to server server2.microsoft.com
Binding to server2.microsoft.com ...
Connected to server2.microsoft.com
 using credentials of locally logged on user
server connections: quit
fsmo maintenance: seize RID master
Server "server2.microsoft.com" knows about 5 roles
Schema - CN=NTDS Settings,CN=server01,CN=Servers,
 CN=New-York,CN=Sites,CN=Configuration,DC=microsoft,DC=com
Domain - CN=NTDS Settings,CN=server01,CN=Servers,
 CN=New-York,CN=Sites,CN=Configuration,DC=microsoft,DC=com
PDC - CN=NTDS Settings,CN=server2,CN=Servers,
 CN=Chicago,CN=Sites,CN=Configuration,DC=microsoft,DC=com
RID - CN=NTDS Settings,CN=server2,CN=Servers,
 CN=Chicago,CN=Sites,CN=Configuration,DC=microsoft,DC=com
Infrastructure - CN=NTDS Settings,CN=server3,CN=Servers,
 CN=San-Francisco,CN=Sites,CN=Configuration,DC=microsoft,DC=com
fsmo maintenance: quit
ntdsutil: quit
C:\>
```

Off the Record You can use several methods to determine the operations master role holders of the forest and domain. For example, you can query these roles using the Replication Monitor (Replmon.exe), Netdom, and Ntdsutil. You can also use the Windows Script Host (WSH) to query the Active Directory Services Interface (ADSI) to find the operations masters, as documented in Microsoft Knowledge Base article 235617, "How to Find the FSMO Role Owners Using ADSI and WSH" (available from *http://support.microsoft.com*).

Practice: Viewing and Transferring Operations Master Role Assignments

In this practice, you manage operations master role assignments.

Note To complete this practice, you must have successfully completed the practice in Lesson 1.

Exercise 1: Viewing Operations Master Role Assignments

In this exercise, you view operations master role assignments.

▶ **To view operations master role assignments**

1. Log on to Server1 and Server2 as Administrator.

2. Use the procedure provided earlier in this lesson to view the RID master, the PDC emulator, and the infrastructure master role assignments for the *contoso.com* domain.

3. Use the procedure provided earlier in this lesson to view the domain naming master role assignment for the *contoso.com* domain.

4. Use the procedure provided earlier in this lesson to view the schema master role assignment for the *contoso.com* domain.

Exercise 2: Transferring an Operations Master Role Assignment

In this exercise, you transfer the domain naming master role assignment from Server1 to Server2.

▶ **To transfer an operations master role assignment**

1. Use the procedure provided earlier in this lesson to transfer the domain naming master role assignment from Server1 (*contoso.com* domain) to Server2 (*chi.contoso.com* domain).

2. When you have finished viewing the domain naming master role assignment on Server2, transfer the domain naming master role assignment back to Server1.

3. Demote Server2 so it becomes a member server for the *contoso.com* domain and the *chi.contoso.com* domain no longer exists.

Lesson Review

The following questions are intended to reinforce key information presented in this lesson. If you are unable to answer a question, review the lesson and then try the question again. Answers to the questions can be found in the "Questions and Answers" section at the end of this chapter.

1. What is the purpose of the operations master roles?

   _____

   _____

2. Which operations master roles must be unique in each forest?

   _____

   _____

3. Which operations master roles must be unique in each domain?

_____

_____

4. When should you seize an operations master role?

_____

_____

5. Which of the following operations master roles should not be assigned to the domain controller hosting the global catalog?

   a. Schema master

   b. Domain naming master

   c. RID master

   d. PDC emulator

   e. Infrastructure master

Lesson Summary

- Operations master roles are assigned to domain controllers to perform single-master operations.

- Every Active Directory forest must have the schema master and domain naming master roles. Every domain in the forest must have the RID master, the PDC emulator, and the infrastructure master roles.

- There are two ways to manage operations master roles: transfer and seizure.

- To transfer an operations master role is to move it with the cooperation of its current owner. You transfer an operations master role to other domain controllers in the domain or forest to balance the load among domain controllers, or accommodate domain controller maintenance and hardware upgrades.

- To seize an operations master role is to move it without the cooperation of its current owner. You seize an operations master role assignment when a server holding the role fails and you do not intend to restore it. If the cause of the failure is a networking problem or a server failure that will be resolved soon, wait for the role holder to become available again. Do not seize an operations master role if you can transfer it instead. Seizing an operations master role is a drastic step that should be considered only if the current operations master will never be available again. The decision depends upon the role and how long the particular role holder will be unavailable.

Lesson 4: Managing Trust Relationships

This lesson introduces you to trust relationships and the tasks involved in the management of trusts. In Chapter 1, you learned that a trust relationship is a link between two domains in which the trusting domain honors the logon authentication of the trusted domain. Trust relationships can be created automatically (implicitly) or manually (explicitly). Trust relationships created implicitly do not need management. In this lesson, you learn how to plan, create, and administer explicit trust relationships.

After this lesson, you will be able to

- Name the trust protocols used in Windows Server 2003
- Describe the trust types used in Windows Server 2003
- Explain when it is necessary to create a shortcut, realm, external, or forest trust
- Create shortcut, realm, external, and forest trusts
- Administer shortcut, realm, external, and forest trusts

Estimated lesson time: 30 minutes

Trust Relationships

A trust relationship is a logical relationship established between domains to allow pass-through authentication, in which a trusting domain honors the logon authentications of a trusted domain. There are two domains in a trust relationship—the trusting and the trusted domain.

In Windows NT, trusts are one-way and nontransitive, and can require a great deal of administrator maintenance. Trusts were limited to the two domains involved in the trust and the trust relationship was one-way. In Windows Server 2003, trusts have three characteristics.

- Trusts can be created manually (explicitly) or automatically (implicitly).
- Trusts can be either transitive (not bound by the domains in the trust relationship) or nontransitive (bound by the domains in the trust relationship).
- Trusts can be one-way or two-way.

Trust Protocols

Windows Server 2003 authenticates users and applications using either the Kerberos version 5 or NTLM protocol. The Kerberos version 5 protocol is the default protocol for computers running Windows Server 2003. If any computer involved in a transaction does not support Kerberos version 5, the NTLM protocol is used.

When using the Kerberos version 5 protocol, the client requests a ticket from a domain controller in its account domain for presentation to the server in the trusting domain. This ticket is issued by an intermediary trusted by the client and the server. The client presents this trusted ticket to the server in the trusting domain for authentication.

When a client tries to access resources on a server in another domain using NTLM authentication, the server containing the resource must contact a domain controller in the client's account domain to verify the account credentials. A trust relationship can also be created with any MIT version 5 Kerberos realm.

Trust Types

The following forms of trust relationships are supported by Windows Server 2003:

- **Tree-root trust** Implicitly established when you add a new tree root domain to a forest. The trust is transitive and two-way.

- **Parent-child trust** Implicitly established when you add a new child domain to a tree. The trust is transitive and two-way.

- **Shortcut trust** Explicitly created by a systems administrator between two domains in a forest to improve user logon times. This is useful when two domains are separated by two domain trees. The trust is transitive and can be one-way or two-way. A shortcut trust may also be referred to as a cross-link trust.

- **Realm trust** Explicitly created by a systems administrator between a non–Windows Kerberos realm and a Windows Server 2003 domain. This trust provides interoperability between Windows Server 2003 and any realm used in Kerberos version 5 implementations. It can be transitive or nontransitive and one-way or two-way.

- **External trust** Explicitly created by a systems administrator between Windows Server 2003 domains that are in different forests or between a Windows Server 2003 domain and a domain whose domain controller is running Windows NT 4 or earlier. This trust provides backward compatibility with Windows NT environments and communications with domains located in other forests not joined by forest trusts. The trust is nontransitive and can be one-way or two-way.

- **Forest trust** Explicitly created by a systems administrator between two forest root domains. If a forest trust is two-way, it effectively allows all authentication requests made from one forest to reach another. The trust is transitive between two forests only and can be one-way or two-way.

 Note When a user is authenticated by a domain controller, the presence of a trust does not guarantee access to resources in that domain. Access to resources is determined solely by the rights and permissions granted to the user account by the domain administrator for the trusting domain. For information about providing access to resources, refer to Chapter 9, "Administering Active Directory Objects."

Understanding Forest Trusts

In Windows NT and Windows 2000, if users in one forest needed access to resources in a second forest, an administrator had to create an external trust relationship between the two domains. Because external trusts are one-way and nontransitive, they require administrator resources and limit the ability for trust paths to extend to other domains. Forest trusts are a new feature in Windows Server 2003, extending transitivity beyond the scope of a single forest to a second Windows Server 2003 forest. Forest trusts provide the following benefits:

- Simplified management. Forest trusts reduce the number of external trusts necessary to share resources with a second forest.

- Two-way trust relationships between all domains in two forests.

- UPN authentications can be used across two forests.

- Both the Kerberos and NTLM authentication protocols can be used to help improve the trustworthiness of authorization data transferred between forests.

- Administrative flexibility. Administrators can choose to split collaborative delegation efforts with other administrators into forest-wide administrative units.

Forest trusts can be created and are transitive between only two forests. Therefore, if a forest trust is created between Forest1 and Forest2, and a forest trust is also created between Forest2 and Forest3, Forest1 does not have an implicit trust with Forest3.

Planning Trust Relationships

As an administrator, you must plan trust relationships to provide users with the access to resources they require. When you add a Windows Server 2003 domain to an existing Windows Server 2003 forest, a tree-root or a parent-child trust is established automatically. Both of these trust relationships are two-way and transitive and are established at the time that the domain is created. Once established, these trust relationships do not need to be managed.

The four remaining types of trusts must be managed. They are

- Shortcut trusts
- Realm trusts
- External trusts
- Forest trusts

When to Create a Shortcut Trust

Shortcut trusts are transitive one-way or two-way trusts that can be used to optimize the authentication process between domains that are logically distant from each other. In Windows Server 2003, authentication requests must travel an established trust path between domain trees. A *trust path* is a series of trust relationships that must be traversed in order to pass authentication requests between any two domains. In a complex forest, following the trust path can take time and affect query response performance; each time clients are referred to another domain controller, the chances of a failure or of encountering a slow link are increased. Windows Server 2003 provides a means for improving query response performance through shortcut trusts. Shortcut trusts help to shorten the path traveled for authentication requests made between domains located in two separate trees.

Shortcut trusts can be created only between Windows Server 2003 domains in the same forest. Figure 4-16 illustrates a shortcut trust created to shorten the trust path and improve query response performance between Domain M and Domain P. If the shortcut trust were not created, the client in Domain M would have to "walk" the trust path through domains L, K, J, N, and O before being able to communicate with the domain controller in Domain P to verify the authentication request.

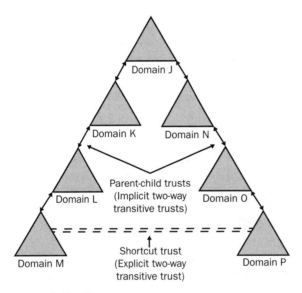

Figure 4-16   Shortcut trust

One-Way Shortcut Trusts   A one-way shortcut trust established between two domains located in separate domain trees can reduce the time needed to fulfill authentication requests, but from only one direction. If a one-way shortcut trust is established between Domain M and Domain P, authentication requests made in Domain M to Domain P can take full advantage of the new one-way trust path. However, when authentication requests from Domain P to Domain M are made, they cannot utilize the shortcut trust path that was created between Domain M and Domain P, and default to walking up the trust path hierarchy in order to find Domain M.

Two-Way Shortcut Trusts   A two-way shortcut trust directly established between two domains located in separate domain trees can help optimize authentication requests made from users located in either domain. Therefore, authentication requests made from either Domain M to Domain P or from Domain P to Domain M can utilize the shortened shortcut trust path.

Accessing Resources Across Domains Joined by Shortcut Trust   Using Active Directory Domains and Trusts, you can determine the scope of authentication between two domains that are joined by a external trust. You can set *selective authentication* differently for outgoing and incoming external trusts, which allows you to make flexible access control decisions between domains. You set selective authentication on the Outgoing Trust Authentication Level page when you set up a shortcut trust using the New Trust Wizard.

If you use domain-wide authentication on the incoming external trust, users in the second domain have the same level of access to resources in the local domain as users who belong to the local domain. For example, if Domain A has an incoming shortcut trust from Domain B and domain-wide authentication is used, any user from Domain B can access any resource in Domain A (assuming the user has the required permissions).

If you set selective authentication on an incoming shortcut trust, you need to manually assign permissions on each resource to which you want users in the second domain to have access. To do this, set an access control right Allowed To Authenticate on an object for that particular user or group from the second domain.

When a user authenticates across a trust with the Selective authentication option enabled, an Other Organization SID is added to the user's authorization data. The presence of this SID prompts a check on the resource domain to ensure that the user is allowed to authenticate to the particular service. Once the user is authenticated, if the Other Organization SID is not already present, the server to which the user authenticates adds the This Organization SID. Only one of these special SIDs can be present in an authenticated user's context.

Administrators in each domain can add objects from one domain to ACLs on shared resources in the other domain. You can use the ACL editor to add or remove objects residing in one domain to ACLs on resources in the other domain. For more information about how to set permissions on resources, refer to Chapter 9, "Administering Active Directory Objects."

Requirements To create a shortcut trust, you must have Enterprise Admin or Domain Admin privileges in both domains within the forest. Each trust is assigned a password that must be known to the administrators of both domains in the relationship.

When to Create a Realm Trust

A realm trust can be established between any non–Windows Kerberos version 5 realm and a Windows Server 2003 domain to allow cross-platform interoperability with security services based on other Kerberos version 5 implementations, such as UNIX or MIT. Realm trusts can be switched from nontransitive to transitive and back and can be either one-way or two-way.

Requirements To create a realm trust, you must have Enterprise Admin or Domain Admin privileges for the domain in the Windows Server 2003 forest and the appropriate administrative privileges in the target Kerberos realm.

When to Create an External Trust

You can create an external trust to form a one-way or two-way nontransitive relationship with domains outside of your forest. External trusts are sometimes necessary when users need access to resources located in a Windows NT 4 domain or in a domain located within a separate forest that is not joined by a forest trust.

When a trust is established between a domain in a forest and a domain outside of that forest, security principals from the external domain can access resources in the internal domain. Active Directory creates a foreign security principal object in the internal domain to represent each security principal from the trusted external domain. These foreign security principals can become members of domain local groups in the internal domain. You can view foreign security principals in the Active Directory Users And Computers console when Advanced Features are enabled. To enable Advanced Features, select Advanced Features from the View menu on the Active Directory Users And Computers console.

> **Note** If you upgrade a Windows NT 4 domain to a Windows Server 2003 domain, the existing trust relationship remains in the same state.

Accessing Resources Across Domains Joined by an External Trust Using Active Directory Domains And Trusts, you can determine the scope of authentication between two domains that are joined by an external trust. You can set selective authentication differently for outgoing and incoming external trusts, which allows you to make flexible authentication decisions between external domains. You select domain-wide or selective authentication on the Outgoing Trust Authentication Level page when you set up an external trust using the New Trust Wizard.

If you apply domain-wide authentication to an external trust, users in the trusted domain have the same level of access to resources in the local domain as users who belong to the local domain. For example, if Domain A trusts Domain B and domain-wide authentication is used, any user from Domain B can access any resource in Domain A (assuming the user has the required permissions).

If you apply selective authentication to an external trust, you need to manually designate which users in the trusted domain can authenticate for specific computers in the trusting domain. To do this, use Active Directory Users And Computers to open the access control list for each computer in the trusting domain that hosts resources that may be accessed by any users in the trusted domain. Grant users in the trusted domain (or groups that include users in the trusted domain) the access control right Allowed To Authenticate.

> **Exam Tip**   Allowed To Authenticate is a new access control right that allows you to control which users from other domains can authenticate to a particular type of object or service.

When a user authenticates across a trust with the Selective authentication option enabled, an Other Organization SID is added to the user's authorization data. The presence of this SID prompts a check on the resource domain to ensure that the user is allowed to authenticate to the particular service. Once the user is authenticated, if the Other Organization SID is not already present, the server to which the user authenticates adds the This Organization SID. Only one of these special SIDs can be present in an authenticated user's context.

Administrators in each domain can add objects from one domain to ACLs on shared resources in the other domain. You can use the ACL editor to add or remove objects residing in one domain to ACLs on resources in the other domain. For more information about how to set permissions on resources, refer to Chapter 9, "Administering Active Directory Objects."

Requirements   To create an external trust, you must have Enterprise Admin or Domain Admin privileges for the domain in the Windows Server 2003 forest, and Enterprise Admin or Domain Admin privileges for the domain outside of the forest. Each trust must be assigned a password that is known to the administrators of both domains in the relationship.

When to Create a Forest Trust

Creating a trust between two forest root domains provides a transitive relationship between every domain residing within each forest, and can be one-way or two-way. Forest trusts are useful for application service providers, organizations undergoing mergers or acquisitions, collaborative business extranets, and organizations seeking solutions for administrative autonomy.

One-Way Forest Trusts In a one-way forest trust, all domains in the trusted forest can utilize resources in the trusting forest, although members in the trusting forest cannot access resources in the trusted forest. For example, if you create a one-way forest trust between Forest1 (the trusted forest) and Forest2 (the trusting forest), then users in Forest1 can access resources in Forest2 (assuming the users have permissions on resources). However, users in Forest2 will not be able to access resources in Forest1 until a second forest trust is established.

Two-Way Forest Trusts In a two-way forest trust, every domain in one forest trusts every domain in its partner forest implicitly. Users in either forest can access any resource located anywhere in either forest (assuming the users have permissions to the resource).

Accessing Resources Across Forests Joined by a Forest Trust Using Active Directory Domains and Trusts, you can determine the scope of authentication between two forests that are joined by a forest trust. You can set selective authentication differently for outgoing and incoming forest trusts, which allows you to make flexible access control decisions between forests. You set selective authentication on the Outgoing Trust Authentication Level page when you set up a forest trust using the New Trust Wizard.

If you use forest-wide authentication on the incoming external trust, users from the outside forest have the same level of access to resources in the local forest as users who belong to the local forest. For example, if ForestA has an incoming forest trust from ForestB and forest-wide authentication is used, any user from ForestB can access any resource in ForestA (assuming the user has the required permissions).

If you set selective authentication on an incoming forest trust, you must manually assign permissions on each domain and resource to which you want users in the second forest to have access. To do this, set the access control right Allowed To Authenticate on an object for that particular user or group from the second forest.

When a user authenticates across a trust with the Selective Authentication option enabled, an Other Organization SID is added to the user's authorization data. The presence of this SID prompts a check on the resource domain to ensure that the user is allowed to authenticate to the particular service. Once the user is authenticated, if the Other Organization SID is not already present, the server to which the user authenticates adds the This Organization SID. Only one of these special SIDs can be present in an authenticated user's context.

Administrators in each forest can add objects from one forest to ACLs on shared resources in the other forest. You can use the ACL editor to add or remove objects residing in one forest to ACLs on resources in another forest. For more information about how to set permissions on resources, refer to Chapter 9, "Administering Active Directory Objects."

Requirements   To create a forest trust, you must have Enterprise Admin privileges in both forests. Each trust must be assigned a password that is known to the administrators of both forests in the relationship. Before creating a forest trust, you need to verify that you have the correct DNS infrastructure in place and that the appropriate functional level for the Active Directory forest has been established. For more information on what to verify before creating a forest trust, refer to the "Creating a Forest Trust" section of this chapter.

> **Exam Tip**   Know when to create each type of trust.

Creating Trust Relationships

After you determine the trusts required by your organization, you must create the trusts. This section contains procedures for creating shortcut, realm, external, and forest explicit trusts. You use the New Trust Wizard to create explicit trusts.

Creating a Shortcut Trust

A shortcut trust is a trust between two domains in a forest, created to improve user logon times.

To create a shortcut trust, complete the following steps:

1. Click Start, point to Administrative Tools, and then click Active Directory Domains And Trusts.

2. In the console tree, right-click the domain node for the domain for which you want to create a shortcut trust, and then click Properties.

3. In the Properties dialog box, click the Trusts tab.

4. In the Trusts tab, shown in Figure 4-17, click New Trust to launch the New Trust Wizard.

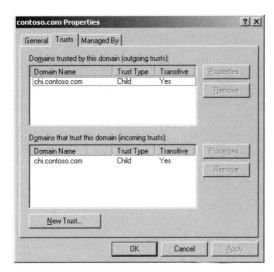

Figure 4-17   Properties dialog box for a domain, Trusts tab

5. On the Welcome To The New Trust Wizard page, click Next.

6. On the Trust Name page, shown in Figure 4-18, type the DNS name of the target domain with which you want to establish a trust in the Name box, then click Next.

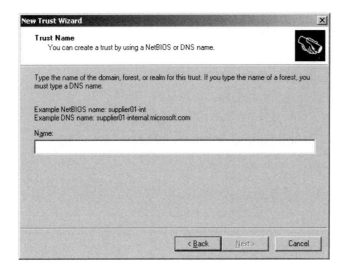

Figure 4-18   New Trust Wizard, Trust Name page

7. On the Direction Of Trust page, shown in Figure 4-19, select one of the following choices.

❑ If you want all users in both domains to be able to access all resources anywhere in either domain, click Two-Way, and then click Next.

❑ If you want only users in this domain to be able to access resources anywhere in the other domain, click One-Way: Incoming, and then click Next.

❑ If you want only users in the other domain to be able to access resources anywhere in this domain, click One-Way: Outgoing, and then click Next.

Note By selecting the One-Way: Incoming option, users in the other domain will not be able to access any resources in this domain. By selecting the One-Way: Outgoing option, users in this domain will not be able to access any resources in the other domain.

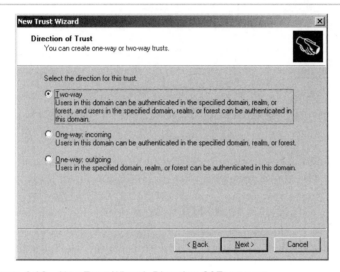

Figure 4-19 New Trust Wizard, Direction Of Trust page

8. On the Sides Of Trust page, shown in Figure 4-20, select one of the following choices:

❑ Select This Domain Only to create the trust relationship in the local domain. Click Next.

❑ Select Both This Domain And The Specified Domain to create a trust relationship in the local domain and a trust relationship in the specified domain. If you select this option, you must have trust creation privileges in the specified domain. Click Next.

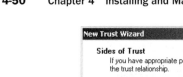

Figure 4-20   New Trust Wizard, Sides Of Trust page

9. Select one of the following paths, depending on your choices in steps 7 and 8:

❑ If you selected Two-Way or One-Way: Outgoing in step 7, and This Domain Only in step 8, the Outgoing Trust Authentication Level page, shown in Figure 4-21, appears. Select Domain Wide Authentication to automatically authenticate all users in the specified domain for all resources in the local domain. Select Selective Authentication to not automatically authenticate all users in the specified domain for all resources in the local domain. Click Next. On the Trust Password page, shown in Figure 4-22, type a password for the trust in the Trust Password and Confirm Trust Password boxes. Click Next.

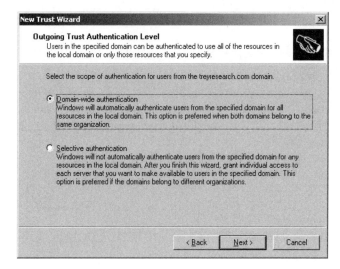

Figure 4-21   New Trust Wizard, Outgoing Trust Authentication Level page

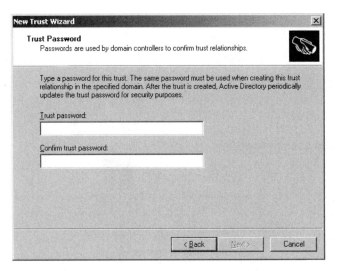

Figure 4-22   New Trust Wizard, Trust Password page

❑ If you selected One-Way: Incoming in step 7, and This Domain Only in step 8, the Trust Password page, shown in Figure 4-22, appears. Type a password for the trust in the Trust Password and Confirm Trust Password boxes. Click Next.

❑ If you selected Both This Domain And The Specified Domain in step 8, the User Name And Password page, shown in Figure 4-23, appears. Type the user name and password of an account that has administrative privileges in the specified domain. Click Next.

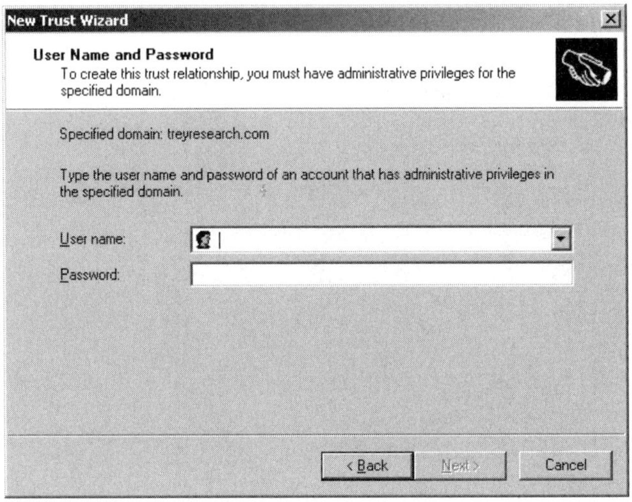

Figure 4-23   New Trust Wizard, User Name And Password page

10. On the Trust Selections Complete page, verify that the correct trust settings are configured, and then click Next. The wizard creates the trust.

11. On the Trust Creation Complete page, verify the settings, and then click Next.

12. On the Confirm Outgoing Trust page, shown in Figure 4-24, select Yes, Confirm The Outgoing Trust if you created both sides of the trust. If you only created one side, choose No, Do Not Confirm The Outgoing Trust. Click Next.

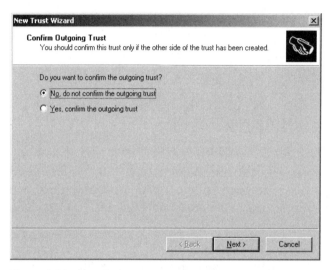

Figure 4-24   New Trust Wizard, Confirm Outgoing Trust page

13. On the Confirm Incoming Trust page, shown in Figure 4-25, select Yes, Confirm The Incoming Trust if you created both sides of the trust. If you only created one side, choose No, Do Not Confirm The Incoming Trust. Click Next.

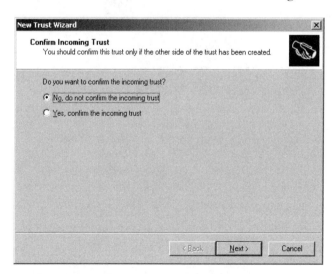

Figure 4-25   New Trust Wizard, Confirm Incoming Trust page

14. On the Completing The New Trust Wizard page, verify the settings, and then click Finish.

15. Note the presence of the shortcut trust you just set up in the Trusts tab of the Properties dialog box for the domain. An example is shown in Figure 4-26. Click OK.

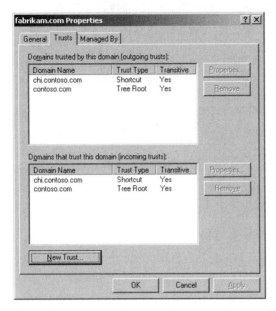

Figure 4-26   Properties dialog box for a domain, Trusts tab, showing shortcut trust between fabrikam.com and chi.contoso.com, domains in separate trees in the same forest

Creating a Realm Trust

A realm trust is a trust between a non–Windows Kerberos realm and a Windows Server 2003 domain, created to allow cross-platform interoperability with security services based on other Kerberos version 5 implementations.

To create a realm trust, complete the following steps:

1. Click Start, point to Administrative Tools, and then click Active Directory Domains And Trusts.

2. In the console tree, right-click the domain node for the domain for which you want to create a realm trust, and then click Properties.

3. In the Properties dialog box, click the Trusts tab.

4. In the Trusts tab, shown previously in Figure 4-17, click New Trust.

5. On the Welcome To The New Trust Wizard page, click Next.

6. On the Trust Name page, shown previously in Figure 4-18, type the DNS name of the target realm with which you want to establish a trust in the Name box, and then click Next.

7. On the Trust Type page, shown in Figure 4-27, select the Realm Trust option, and then click Next.

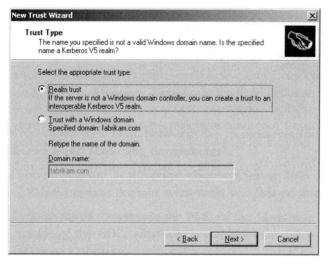

Figure 4-27   New Trust Wizard, Trust Type page

8. On the Transitivity Of Trust page, shown in Figure 4-28, select one of the following choices:

❑ If you want only this domain and the specified realm to form a trust relationship, click Nontransitive, and then click Next.

❑ If you want this domain and all trusted domains to form a trust relationship with the specified realm and all trusted realms, click Transitive, and then click Next.

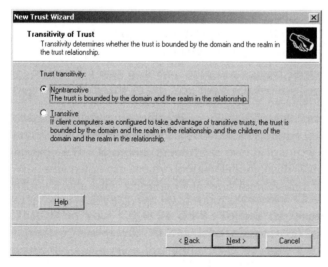

Figure 4-28   New Trust Wizard, Transitivity Of Trust page

9. On the Direction Of Trust page, shown previously in Figure 4-19, select one of the following choices:

   ❑ If you want all users in both the domain and the realm to be able to access all resources anywhere in either the domain or the realm, click Two-Way, and then click Next.

   ❑ If you want only users in this domain to be able to access resources anywhere in the realm, click One-Way: Incoming, and then click Next.

   ❑ If you want only users in the realm to be able to access resources anywhere in this domain, click One-Way: Outgoing, and then click Next.

Note   By selecting the One-Way: Incoming option, users in the realm will not be able to access any resources in this domain. By selecting the One-Way: Outgoing option, users in this domain will not be able to access any resources in the realm.

10. On the Trust Password page, shown previously in Figure 4-22, type the trust password in the Trust Password and Confirm Trust Password boxes. This password must match the password used in the realm. Click Next.

11. On the Trust Selections Complete page, verify that the correct trust settings appear, and then click Next.

12. On the Completing The New Trust Wizard page, verify the settings, and then click Finish.

13. Note the presence of the realm trust you just set up in the Trusts tab of the Properties dialog box for the domain. Click OK.

Creating an External Trust

An external trust is a trust between Windows Server 2003 domains in different forests or between a Windows Server 2003 domain and a domain whose domain controller is running Windows NT 4 or earlier. This trust is created to provide backward compatibility with Windows NT environments or communications with domains located in other forests not joined by forest trusts. Before you can create an external trust, you must configure a DNS forwarder *on both* of the DNS servers that are authoritative for the trusting forests.

Note   Windows 2000 DNS does not support conditional forwarding. If you configure domains to forward to each other in Windows 2000, the resulting traffic may overwhelm many networks. You should forward domains to each other only if both servers support conditional forwarding, as in the Windows Server 2003 family.

To configure a DNS forwarder, complete the following steps on both authoritative DNS servers:

1. Click Start, point to Administrative Tools, and then click DNS.

2. In the console tree, right click the DNS server you want to configure, and then click Properties.

3. In the Properties dialog box for the DNS server, click the Forwarders tab.

4. In the Forwarders tab, specify the DNS domain names that require queries to be forwarded (conditional forwarding) in the Domain box by clicking New and typing the domain name. Type the IP address(es) of the server(s) to which the queries are forwarded in the Selected Domain's IP Address List, and then click Add.

5. Click OK in the Forwarders tab.

To create an external trust, complete the following steps:

1. Click Start, point to Administrative Tools, and then click Active Directory Domains And Trusts.

2. In the console tree, right-click the domain node for the domain in the first forest for which you want to create an external trust, and then click Properties.

3. In the Properties dialog box, click the Trusts tab.

4. In the Trusts tab, shown previously in Figure 4-17, click New Trust.

5. On the Welcome To The New Trust Wizard page, click Next.

6. On the Trust Name page, shown previously in Figure 4-18, type the DNS name of the target domain in the second forest with which you want to establish a trust in the Name box, and then click Next.

7. If the forest functional level is set to Windows Server 2003, the Trust Type page appears, shown in Figure 4-29. Select the External Trust option, and then click Next. Otherwise, skip to the next step.

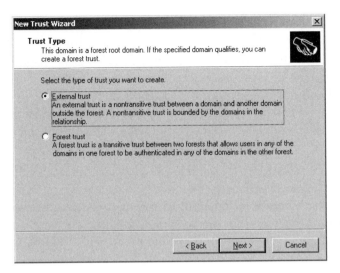

Figure 4-29   New Trust Wizard, Trust Type page

8. On the Direction Of Trust page, shown previously in Figure 4-19, select one of the following choices:

❑ If you want all users in both domains to be able to access all resources anywhere in either domain, click Two-Way, and then click Next.

❑ If you want only users in this domain to be able to access resources anywhere in the second domain, click One-Way: Incoming, and then click Next.

❑ If you want only users in the second domain to be able to access resources anywhere in this domain, click One-Way: Outgoing, and then click Next.

Note   By selecting the One-Way: Incoming option, users in the domain in the second forest will not be able to access any resources in the domain in this forest. By selecting the One-Way: Outgoing option, users in the domain in this forest will not be able to access any resources in the domain in the second forest.

9. On the Sides Of Trust page, shown previously in Figure 4-20, select one of the following choices:

❑ Select This Domain Only to create the trust relationship in the local domain. Click Next.

❑ Select Both This Domain And The Specified Domain to create a trust relationship in the local domain and a trust relationship in the specified domain. If you select this option you must have trust creation privileges in the specified domain. Click Next.

10. Select one of the following paths, depending on your choices in steps 8 and 9:

   ❑ If you selected Two-Way or One-Way: Outgoing in step 8, and This Domain Only in step 9, the Outgoing Trust Authentication Level page, shown previously in Figure 4-21, appears. Select Domain Wide Authentication to automatically authenticate all users in the specified domain for all resources in the local domain. Select Selective Authentication to not automatically authenticate all users in the specified domain for all resources in the local domain. Click Next. On the Trust Password page, shown previously in Figure 4-22, type a password for the trust in the Trust Password and Confirm Trust Password boxes. Click Next.

   ❑ If you selected One-Way: Incoming in step 8, and This Domain Only in step 9, the Trust Password page, shown previously in Figure 4-22, appears. Type a password for the trust in the Trust Password and Confirm Trust Password boxes. Click Next.

   ❑ If you selected Both This Domain And The Specified Domain in step 9, the User Name And Password page, shown previously in Figure 4-23, appears. Type the user name and password of an account that has administrative privileges in the specified domain. Click Next.

11. On the Trust Selections Complete page, verify that the correct trust settings are configured, and then click Next. The wizard creates the trust.

12. On the Trust Creation Complete page, verify the settings, and then click Next.

13. On the Confirm Outgoing Trust page, shown previously in Figure 4-24, select Yes, Confirm The Outgoing Trust if you created both sides of the trust. If you only created one side, choose No, Do Not Confirm The Outgoing Trust. Click Next.

14. On the Confirm Incoming Trust page, shown previously in Figure 4-25, select Yes, Confirm The Incoming Trust if you created both sides of the trust. If you only created one side, choose No, Do Not Confirm The Incoming Trust. Click Next.

15. On the Completing the New Trust Wizard page, verify the settings, and then click Finish.

16. Note the presence of the external trust you just set up in the Trusts tab of the Properties dialog box for the domain. An example is shown in Figure 4-30. Click OK.

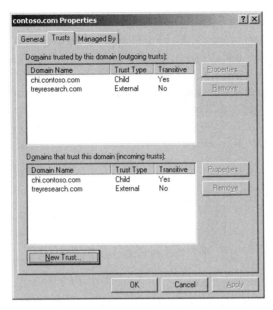

Figure 4-30 Properties dialog box for a domain, Trusts tab, showing external trust between treyresearch.com and contoso.com, domains in different forests

Creating a Forest Trust

A forest trust is a trust between two forest root domains, created to allow all authentication requests made from one forest to reach another. The procedure for creating a forest trust is similar to the one used for creating an external trust. However, before you can create a forest trust, you must complete the following preliminary tasks.

■ Configure a DNS root server that is authoritative over both forest DNS servers that you want to form a trust with, or configure a DNS forwarder on both of the DNS servers that are authoritative for the trusting forests.

■ Ensure that the forest functional level for both forests is Windows Server 2003.

Note You can raise the functional level of a forest to Windows Server 2003 only if all domain controllers in the forest are running Windows Server 2003 and all domain functional levels in the forest have been raised to Windows Server 2003. To change the forest functional level to Windows Server 2003, refer to Chapter 3, "Administering Active Directory."

To configure a DNS forwarder, complete the following steps:

1. Click Start, point to Administrative Tools, and then click DNS.

2. In the console tree, right click the DNS server you want to configure, and then click Properties.

3. In the Properties dialog box for the DNS server, click the Forwarders tab.

4. In the Forwarders tab, specify the DNS domain names that require queries to be forwarded (conditional forwarding) in the Domain box by clicking New and typing the domain name. Type the IP address(es) of the server(s) to which the queries are forwarded in the Selected Domain's IP Address List, and then click Add.

5. Click OK in the Forwarders tab.

To create a forest trust, complete the following steps:

1. Click Start, point to Administrative Tools, and then click Active Directory Domains And Trusts.

2. In the console tree, right-click the domain node for the domain in the first forest for which you want to create a forest trust, and then click Properties.

3. In the Properties dialog box, click the Trusts tab.

4. In the Trusts tab, shown previously in Figure 4-17, click New Trust.

5. On the Welcome To The New Trust Wizard page, click Next.

6. On the Trust Name page, shown previously in Figure 4-18, type the DNS name of the target domain in the second forest with which you want to establish a trust in the Name box, and then click Next.

7. On the Trust Type page, shown previously in Figure 4-29, select the Forest Trust option, and then click Next.

> **Note**   If the Forest Trust option does not appear, you must confirm that you have completed the preliminary tasks for creating a forest trust.

8. On the Direction Of Trust page, shown previously in Figure 4-19, select one of the following choices:

   ❑ If you want all users in both forests to be able to access all resources anywhere in either forest, click Two-Way, and then click Next.

   ❑ If you want only users in this forest to be able to access resources anywhere in the second forest, click One-Way: Incoming, and then click Next.

   ❑ If you want only users in the second forest to be able to access resources anywhere in this forest, click One-Way: Outgoing, then click Next.

> **Note**   By selecting the One-Way: Incoming option, users in the second forest will not be able to access any resources in this forest. By selecting the One-Way: Outgoing option, users in this forest will not be able to access any resources in the second forest.

9. On the Sides Of Trust page, shown previously in Figure 4-20, select one of the following choices:

   ❑ Select This Domain Only to create the trust relationship in the local forest. Click Next.

   ❑ Select Both This Domain And The Specified Domain to create a trust relationship in the local forest and a trust relationship in the specified forest. If you select this option, you must have trust creation privileges in the specified forest. Click Next.

10. Select one of the following paths, depending on your choices in steps 8 and 9:

    ❑ If you selected Two-Way or One-Way: Outgoing in step 8, and This Domain Only in step 9, the Outgoing Trust Authentication Level page, shown previously in Figure 4-21, appears. Select Domain Wide Authentication to automatically authenticate all users in the specified forest for all resources in the local forest. Select Selective Authentication to not automatically authenticate all users in the specified forest for all resources in the local forest. Click Next. On the Trust Password page, shown previously in Figure 4-22, type a password for the trust in the Trust Password and Confirm Trust Password boxes. Click Next.

    ❑ If you selected One Way: Incoming in step 8, and This Domain Only in step 9, the Trust Password page, shown previously in Figure 4-22, appears. Type a password for the trust in the Trust Password and Confirm Trust Password boxes. Click Next.

    ❑ If you selected Both This Domain And The Specified Domain in step 9, the User Name And Password page, shown previously in Figure 4-23, appears. Type the user name and password of an account that has administrative privileges in the specified forest. Click Next.

11. On the Trust Selections Complete page, verify that the correct trust settings are configured, and then click Next. The wizard creates the trust.

12. On the Trust Creation Complete page, verify the settings, and then click Next.

13. On the Confirm Outgoing Trust page, shown previously in Figure 4-24, select Yes, Confirm The Outgoing Trust if you created both sides of the trust. If you only created one side, choose No, Do Not Confirm The Outgoing Trust. Click Next.

14. On the Confirm Incoming Trust page, shown previously in Figure 4-25, select Yes, Confirm The Incoming Trust if you created both sides of the trust. If you only created one side, choose No, Do Not Confirm The Incoming Trust. Click Next.

15. On the Completing the New Trust Wizard page, verify the settings, and then click Finish.

16. Note the presence of the forest trust you just set up in the Trusts tab of the Properties dialog box for the domain. An example is shown in Figure 4-31. Click OK.

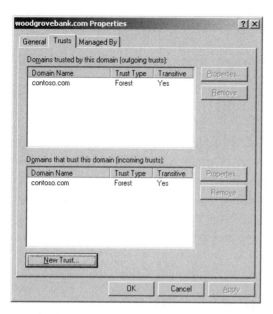

Figure 4-31   Properties dialog box for a domain, Trusts tab, showing forest trust between woodgrovebank.com and contoso.com, domains in different forests

    Exam Tip   Know how to create each type of trust.

Administering Trust Relationships

To administer trust relationships, you use the New Trust Wizard. You can verify and remove shortcut, realm, external, and forest trusts.

To verify a trust, complete the following steps:

1. Click Start, point to Administrative Tools, and then click Active Directory Domains And Trusts.

2. In the console tree, right-click one of the domains involved in the trust you want to verify, and then click Properties.

3. In the Properties dialog box, click the Trusts tab.

4. In the Trusts tab, shown previously in Figure 4-17, click the trust to be verified in either the Domains Trusted By This Domain (Outgoing Trusts) box or the Domains That Trust This Domain (Incoming Trusts) box, and then click Properties.

5. In the Properties dialog box for the trust, shown in Figure 4-32, click Validate.

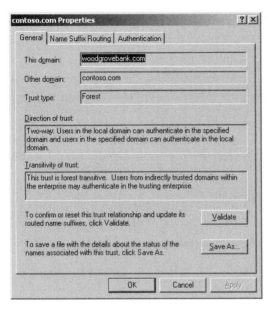

Figure 4-32   Properties dialog box for a trust

6. In the Active Directory dialog box, shown in Figure 4-33, select one of the following choices:

   ❑ Select No, Do Not Validate The Incoming Trust to validate only the outgoing trust, and then click OK.

   ❑ Select Yes, Validate The Incoming Trust, to validate the outgoing and the incoming trust. Type the user name and password of an account with administrative privileges in the other domain in the User Name and Password boxes respectively. Click OK.

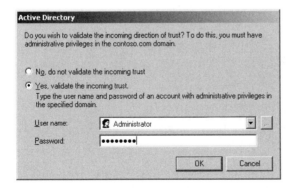

Figure 4-33   Active Directory dialog box

7. In the Active Directory message box, a message indicates that the trust has been verified. Click OK.

8. In the Properties dialog box for the trust, click OK.

9. In the Trusts tab, click OK.

To remove a trust, complete the following steps:

1. Click Start, point to Administrative Tools, and then click Active Directory Domains And Trusts.

2. In the console tree, right-click one of the domain nodes involved in the trust you want to remove, and then click Properties.

3. In the Properties dialog box, click the Trusts tab.

4. In the Trusts tab, click the trust to be removed in the Domains Trusted By This Domain (Outgoing Trusts) box, then click Remove.

5. In the Active Directory dialog box, shown in Figure 4-34, select one of the following choices:

   ❑ Select No, Remove The Trust From The Local Domain Only to remove the trust from the local domain, and then click OK.

   ❑ Select Yes, Remove The Trust From Both The Local Domain And The Other Domain, to remove the trust from both domains. Type the user name and password of an account with administrative privileges in the other domain in the User Name and Password boxes respectively. Click OK.

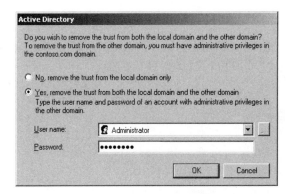

Figure 4-34 Active Directory dialog box

6. In the Active Directory message box, confirm that you want to remove the trust by clicking Yes.

7. In the Trusts tab, click the trust to be removed in the Domains That Trust This Domain (Incoming Trusts) box, then click Remove.

8. Repeat steps 4 and 5 to remove the incoming trusts.

9. In the Trusts tab, note that the trusts have been removed, and then click OK.

> **Note**   If you need to delete an external trust in a domain using Windows 2000 mixed functionality, the trust should always be deleted from a domain controller running Windows Server 2003. External trusts to Windows NT 4 or 3.51 domains can be deleted by authorized administrators on the Windows NT 4 or 3.51 domain controllers. However, only the trusted side of the relationship can be deleted on Windows NT 4 or 3.51 domain controllers. The trusting side of the relationship (created in the Windows Server 2003 domain) is not deleted, and although it will not be operational, the trust will continue to display in the Active Directory Domains And Trusts console. To remove the trust completely, you delete the trust from a domain controller running Windows Server 2003 in the trusting domain. If an external trust is inadvertently deleted from a Windows NT 4 or 3.51 domain controller, you must recreate the trust from any domain controller running Windows Server 2003 in the trusting domain.

> **Note**   It is not possible to remove the default two-way transitive trusts between domains in a forest. Only explicitly created trusts can be deleted.

Creating and Administering Trusts Using the Command Line

In addition to creating and administering trusts using the Windows interface, you can also create and administer most trusts by using the Netdom.exe: Windows Domain Manager command line tool, included with the Windows Support Tools on the Windows Server 2003 Setup CD-ROM. You use the netdom trust command to create, verify, or reset a trust relationship between domains.

Netdom trust has the following syntax:

```
netdom trust TrustingDomainName /d: TrustedDomainName [/ud:[Domain\]User]
[/pd:{Password|*}] [/uo: User] [/ po:{Password|*}] [/verify] [/reset] [/ passwordt:
NewRealmTrustPassword] [/add [/realm]] [/remove [/force]] [/twoway] [/kerberos]
[/transitive[:{YES|NO}]] [/verbose]
```

Each of the command parameters are explained in Table 4-1.

Table 4-1   Netdom Trust Command Parameters

Parameter	Description
TrustingDomainName	Specifies the name of the trusting domain.
/d: TrustedDomainName	Specifies the name of the trusted domain. If the parameter is omitted, then the domain that the current computer belongs to is used.
/uo: User	Specifies the user account that makes the connection with the trusting domain. If this parameter is omitted, the current user account is used.

Table 4-1   Netdom Trust Command Parameters

Parameter	Description
/po:{*Password*|*}	Specifies the password of the user account that is specified in the /uo parameter. Use * to be prompted for the password.
/verify	Verifies the secure channel secrets upon which a specific trust is based.
/reset	Resets the trust secret between trusted domains or between the domain controller and the workstation.
/passwordt: *NewRealmTrustPassword*	Specifies a new trust password. This parameter is valid only with the /add parameter and only if one of the domains specified is a non–Windows Kerberos realm. The trust password is set on the Windows domain only, which means that credentials are not needed for the non-Windows domain.
/add	Specifies to create a trust.
/realm	Indicates that the trust is created to a non–Windows Kerberos realm. The /realm parameter is valid only with the /add and /passwordt parameters.
/remove	Specifies to break a trust.
/force	Removes both the trusted domain object and the cross-reference object for the specified domain from the forest. This is used to clean up decommissioned domains that are no longer in use and were not able to be removed by using the Active Directory Installation wizard. This can occur if the domain controller for that domain was disabled or damaged and there were no domain controllers or it was not possible to recover the domain controller from backup media. This parameter is valid only when the /remove parameter is specified.
/twoway	Specifies to establish a two-way trust relationship rather than a one-way trust relationship.
/kerberos	Specifies to exercise the Kerberos protocol between a workstation and a target domain. This parameter is valid only when the /verify parameter is specified.
/transitive[:{YES|NO}]	Specifies whether to set a transitive or nontransitive trust. This parameter is valid only for a non–Windows Kerberos realm. Non–Windows Kerberos trusts are created as nontransitive. If a value is omitted, then the current transitivity state is displayed. Yes sets the realm to a transitive trust. No sets the realm to a nontransitive trust.
/verbose	Specifies verbose output. By default, only the result of the operation is reported. If /verbose is specified, the output lists the success or failure of each transaction necessary to perform the operation as well as returning an error level based on the success (0) or failure (1) of the operation.

> **Note**   Netdom cannot be used to create a forest trust. You can type the command **netdom query trust** to see a list of existing trust relationships.

For further information about using Netdom to create and administer trusts, refer to Windows Support Tools help.

> **Off the Record**   The Nltest tool can also be used to manage trusts. Nltest is an older tool typically utilized for troubleshooting issues relating to Windows NT 4.0 clients and domains. Still, you can use it with Windows Server 2003 computers and domains. For example, try typing the following command at a Command Prompt on Server1: **nltest/server:Server1 /trusted_domains**. For more information on the capabilities of Nltest, see Support Tools Help (part of the Windows Support Tools).

Practice: Managing Trust Relationships

In this practice, you manage trust relationships by creating, validating, and removing a forest trust.

> **Note**   To complete this practice, you must have successfully completed the practices in Lessons 1 and 3.

Exercise 1: Creating an Additional Forest

In this exercise, you create another forest in addition to the *contoso.com* forest you created in Chapter 2.

▶   **To create an additional forest**

1. Use the procedure provided in Lesson 1 to create a new domain in a new forest on Server2. Name the domain *woodgrovebank.com.*

2. Verify that the domain has been installed correctly on Server2 by verifying the domain configuration, the DNS configuration, DNS integration with Active Directory, installation of the shared system volume, and operation of the Directory Services Restore Mode boot option as described in Chapter 2.

3. On Server1, click Start, point to Administrative Tools, and then click Active Directory Domains And Trusts. Note that the *woodgrovebank.com* domain is not visible.

Exercise 2: Creating, Validating, and Deleting a Forest Trust

In this exercise, you create, validate, and finally delete a forest trust between the *contoso.com* forest root domain you created in Chapter 2 and the *woodgrovebank.com* forest root domain you created in Exercise 1.

▶ **To create, validate, and delete a forest trust**

1. Use the procedure provided earlier in this lesson to create a forest trust between the *contoso.com* forest root domain and the *woodgrovebank.com* forest root domain.

2. Use the procedure provided earlier in this lesson to validate the forest trust.

3. When you have finished exploring the forest trust, use the procedure provided earlier in this lesson to delete the forest trust.

Lesson Review

The following questions are intended to reinforce key information presented in this lesson. If you are unable to answer a question, review the lesson and then try the question again. Answers to the questions can be found in the "Questions and Answers" section at the end of this chapter.

1. Which type of trust provides transitive trusts between domains in two forests?

   _____

   _____

2. What is the purpose of a shortcut trust?

   _____

   _____

3. What is the purpose of an external trust?

   _____

   _____

4. What preliminary tasks must you complete before you can create a forest trust?

   _____

   _____

5. Which of the following trust types are created implicitly? Choose all that apply.

   a. Tree-root

   b. Parent-child

   c. Shortcut

   d. Realm

   e. External

   f. Forest

Lesson Summary

- A trust relationship is a link between two domains in which the trusting domain honors the logon authentication of the trusted domain.

- In Windows Server 2003, trusts can be created manually or automatically, can be transitive or nontransitive, and can be one-way or two-way.

- Windows Server 2003 supports the following types of trusts: tree-root, parent-child, shortcut, realm, external, and forest.

- You use the New Trust Wizard to create explicit trusts, which is accessed from the Active Directory Domains and Trusts administrative tool.

Troubleshooting Lab

To prepare for this lab, you must first remove the *woodgrovebank.com* Active Directory installation. You should also remove the DNS server service. The following steps guide you through this task.

> **Note**   The commands in this lab assume that your CD-ROM drive is D. If it is something else, use that letter in place of D in the steps below.

1. Manually or automatically remove the *woodgrovebank.com* Active Directory install. To remove it automatically, insert the Supplemental CD into the CD-ROM drive on Server2. Click Start, click Run, type:

    dcpromo/answer:D:\70-294\Labs\Chapter04\RemoveWoodgroveDC.txt
    and then press ENTER.

2. Log on to Server2 using the local administrator user name and password.

3. To remove the DNS server service, click Start, point to Control Panel, and click Add or Remove Programs.

4. On the Add Or Remove Programs window, click the Add/Remove Windows Components icon. Wait for the Windows Components Wizard to load.

5. Clear the Networking Services checkbox and click Next. This will remove all Networking Services, including the DNS server service.

6. Click Finish to complete this process. Close the Add or Remove Programs window.

7. Now configure Server2 as a member server of *contoso.com*, as you learned to do in Chapter 2.

Once this is complete, you are ready to begin the troubleshooting lab. The troubleshooting scenario follows:

You are a network administrator for Contoso Pharmaceuticals. Another member of your network administration team returns from a temporary assignment that lasted several weeks. Her computer was offline the entire time she was away. She returns to the office and starts her computer. She has trouble logging on and then she finds an error in the Event Viewer console's System log. She asks you to look at the error. (To see this error, you must open a saved Event Log on your Supplemental CD-ROM.)

1. Log on to Server2 as the local administrator. Place your Supplemental CD-ROM into the CD-ROM drive of Server2 if you have not already done so.

2. Click Start, click Run, type **eventvwr.msc**, and then press ENTER.

3. On the Event Viewer console, right click the Event Viewer (Local) icon, and then click Open Log File. The Open dialog box is displayed.

4. In the File Name list, type **D:\70-294\Labs\Chapter04\3210.evt**. In the Log Type box, click the down arrow and select System. Click Open. A Saved System Log appears in your Event Viewer.

5. In the right window pane, scroll to the only error event in the saved log and double-click it. The Event Properties dialog box opens. Review the error message and then click OK. Close the Event Viewer.

> **Note**   This type of error can occur if a member server is unable to synchronize its machine password with the domain controller. If you haven't done so already, install the Windows Support Tools on Server2. The Netdom commands in the following steps show you how to diagnose and repair this issue. Before you attempt any of the following commands, ensure that your domain controller has been on for at least 15 minutes.

1. At the command prompt, reset the secure channel by typing **netdom reset server2 /domain:contoso**. You should see a confirmation message that reads: "The secure channel from SERVER2 to the domain CONTOSO.COM has been reset." You've now solved the problem.

2. Now verify that the secure channel between the member server and domain controller is functioning properly. At the command prompt, type **netdom verify**

server2 /domain:contoso.com. The following message appears: "The secure channel from SERVER2 to the domain CONTOSO.COM has been verified. The connection is with the machine \\SERVER1.CONTOSO.COM," indicating the channel is functioning properly.

> ### Real World   Troubleshooting Secure Channels
>
> Both the Nltest and Netdom tools can be used to verify and reset secure channels between domain controller and domain member computers. If either utility indicates that a secure channel doesn't exist for the domain member computer, try the following:
>
> 1. Remove the computer from the domain by making it a member of a workgroup.
>
> 2. Delete the computer account from the Active Directory Users And Computers console.
>
> 3. Join the computer to the domain once again.

Case Scenario Exercise

You are a computer consultant working for the Graphic Design Institute. In the past year you've helped the institute implement Active Directory in three different departments: Marketing, Administration, and Research. See the Case Scenario Exercises in Chapter 2 and Chapter 3 for more information about this company. Today, the company's network infrastructure is host to three different forests. These forests are

■ *marketing.graphicdesigninstitute.com*

■ *administration.graphicdesigninstitute.com*

■ *research.graphicdesigninstitute.com*

The Information Technology Services (ITS) department is still running UNIX servers and hosting the company's Internet connection. ITS has delegated the applicable DNS namespace for each domain to the Marketing, Administration, and Research departments. Each department has its own network administration team.

Laura Steele, the director of the institute, wants to discuss some issues she and the department directors have experienced.

Answer the following questions based on this information:

1. Right now, Research and Marketing are sharing data by burning CD-ROMs and DVD-ROMs. Under the current structure, how could Research and Marketing share information over the network?

2. Laura asks you: "What if we decided that ITS should handle the entire institute's network administration? If we were building the entire administrative structure right now using Windows Server 2003 and Active Directory, how would it be different than what we have now?"

_____

_____

3. What are the potential issues of simply moving the management function of the existing structure to the ITS department, without modifying anything?

_____

_____

Chapter Summary

- You can create multiple domains, trees, and forest by using dcpromo and the Active Directory Installation Wizard.

- Create multiple domains to meet security requirements, meet administrative requirements, optimize replication traffic, or retain Windows NT domains. Create multiple trees if your organization has more than one DNS name. Create multiple forests if you need to secure data or you need to isolate directory replication.

- In Windows Server 2003, you can now rename any domain that has domain controllers running Windows Server 2003 and move existing domains to other locations in the domain hierarchy if all domain functional levels in the forest have been raised to Windows Server 2003, and the forest functional level has been raised to Windows Server 2003. Use the domain rename utility (Rendom.exe) to rename or restructure a domain.

- You can rename domain controllers without first demoting them if the functional level of the domain to which the domain controller is joined is set to Windows Server 2003. Use the Netdom.exe: Windows Domain Manager command-line tool, included with the Windows Support Tools on the Windows Server 2003 Setup CD-ROM, to rename a domain controller.

- Operations master roles are assigned to domain controllers to perform single-master operations. Every Active Directory forest must have the schema master and domain naming master roles. Every domain in the forest must have the RID master, the PDC emulator, and the infrastructure master roles. There are two ways to manage operations master roles: transfer and seizure.

- A trust relationship is a link between two domains in which the trusting domain honors the logon authentication of the trusted domain. Windows Server 2003 supports the following types of trusts: tree-root, parent-child, shortcut, realm, external, and forest.

Exam Highlights

Before taking the exam, review the key points and terms that are presented in this chapter. You need to know this information.

Key Points

- Before implementing a forest and domain structure, plan the structure. Create child domains to meet security requirements, meet administrative requirements, optimize replication traffic, or retain Windows NT domains. Create multiple trees if your organization has more than one DNS name. Create multiple forests if you need to secure data or you need to isolate directory replication. You implement an Active Directory forest and domain structure by using dcpromo and the Active Directory Installation Wizard.

- The default FSMO role configuration works well for most organizations. In a forest with more than a few domain controllers, or in a forest that spans multiple sites, you might want to transfer the default operations master role assignments to other domain controllers in the domain or forest to balance the load among domain controllers, or accommodate domain controller maintenance and hardware upgrades.

- Every Active Directory forest must have the schema master and domain naming master roles. Every domain in the forest must have the RID master, the PDC emulator, and the infrastructure master roles. The infrastructure master role should not be assigned to the domain controller that is hosting the global catalog.

- To handle FSMO role failure, you can transfer or seize an operations master role.

- Tree-root and parent-child trusts are established automatically when you add a new tree root domain to a forest or a new child domain to a tree. There are four other trusts which must be planned and established explicitly: shortcut trusts, realm trusts, external trusts, and forest trusts. You use the New Trust Wizard to create explicit trusts, which is accessed from the Active Directory Domains and Trusts administrative tool.

Key Terms

operations master   A domain controller that has been assigned one or more special roles in an Active Directory domain. The domain controllers assigned these roles perform operations that are single-master (not permitted to occur at different places on the network at the same time).

selective authentication   A method of setting the scope of authentication differently for outgoing and incoming external and forest trusts. Selective trusts allow you to make flexible access control decisions between external domains in a forest.

trust relationship   A logical relationship established between domains to allow pass-through authentication, in which a trusting domain honors the logon authentications of a trusted domain. User accounts and global groups defined in a trusted domain can be given rights and permissions in a trusting domain, even though the user accounts or groups don't exist in the trusting domain's directory.

Questions and Answers

Page
4-16

Lesson 1 Review

1. What is the main consequence of creating multiple domains and trees?

   Adding domains and trees increases administrative and hardware costs.

2. Why would you need to create additional trees in your Active Directory forest?

   You might need to define more than one tree if your organization has more than one DNS name.

3. What is a tree root domain?

   A tree root domain is the highest-level domain in the tree; child and grandchild domains are arranged under it. Typically, the domain you select for a tree root should be the one that is most critical to the operation of the tree. A tree root domain can also be the forest root domain.

4. What are the reasons for creating multiple forests in an organization?

   Some of the reasons for creating multiple forests include to secure data and to isolate directory replication.

5. Which of the following is not a reason for creating multiple domains?

   a. To meet security requirements

   b. To meet administrative requirements

   c. To optimize replication traffic

   d. To meet delegation requirements

   e. To retain Windows NT domains

   The correct answer is d. In Windows NT, domains were the smallest units of administrative delegation. In Windows Server 2003, OUs allow you to partition domains to delegate administration, eliminating the need to define domains just for delegation.

Page
4-21

Lesson 2 Review

1. Under what domain and forest functional levels can you rename or restructure domains in a forest?

   You can rename or restructure the domains in a forest only if all domain controllers in the forest are running Windows Server 2003, all domain functional levels in the forest have been raised to Windows Server 2003, and the forest functional level has been raised to Windows Server 2003.

2. What utility is used to rename or restructure a domain in a forest?

   You can use the domain rename utility (Rendom.exe) to rename or restructure a domain.

3. Under what domain functional level can you rename a domain controller?

You can rename a domain controller only if the domain functionality of the domain to which the domain controller is joined is set to Windows Server 2003.

4. What tool is used to rename a domain controller?

You rename a domain controller by using the Netdom.exe: Windows Domain Manager command-line tool, included with the Windows Support Tools on the Windows Server 2003 Setup CD-ROM. You use the Netdom Computername command to manage the primary and alternate names for a computer.

Page 4-37

Lesson 3 Review

1. What is the purpose of the operations master roles?

The domain controllers assigned operations master roles perform operations that are single-master (not permitted to occur at different places in the network at the same time).

2. Which operations master roles must be unique in each forest?

The schema master and the domain naming master roles must be unique in each forest.

3. Which operations master roles must be unique in each domain?

The RID master, the PDC emulator, and the infrastructure master roles must be unique in each domain.

4. When should you seize an operations master role?

Consider seizing an operations master role assignment when a server that is holding a role fails and you do not intend to restore it. Before seizing the operations master role, determine the cause and expected duration of the computer or network failure. If the cause is a networking problem or a server failure that will be resolved soon, wait for the role holder to become available again. If the domain controller that currently holds the role has failed, you must determine if it can be recovered and brought back online. In general, seizing an operations master role is a drastic step that should be considered only if the current operations master will never be available again.

5. Which of the following operations master roles should not be assigned to the domain controller hosting the global catalog?

  a. Schema master

  b. Domain naming master

  c. RID master

  d. PDC emulator

  e. Infrastructure master

The correct answer is e. The infrastructure master role should not be assigned to the domain controller that is hosting the global catalog. If the infrastructure master and global catalog are on the same domain controller, the infrastructure master will not function. The infrastructure master will never find data that is out of date, so it will never replicate any changes to the other domain controllers in the domain.

Page
4-68

Lesson 4 Review

1. Which type of trust provides transitive trusts between domains in two forests?

A forest trust.

2. What is the purpose of a shortcut trust?

A shortcut trust is a trust between two domains in a forest, created to improve user logon times.

3. What is the purpose of an external trust?

An external trust is a trust between Windows Server 2003 domains in different forests or between a Windows Server 2003 domain and a domain whose domain controller is running Windows NT 4 or earlier. This trust is created to provide backward compatibility with Windows NT environments or communications with domains located in other forests not joined by forest trusts.

4. What preliminary tasks must you complete before you can create a forest trust?

Before you can create a forest trust, you must

a. Configure a DNS root server that is authoritative over both forest DNS servers that you want to form a trust with, or configu=re a DNS forwarder on both of the DNS servers that are authoritative for the trusting forests.

b. Ensure that the forest functionality for both forests is Windows Server 2003.

5. Which of the following trust types are created implicitly? Choose all that apply.

a. Tree-root

b. Parent-child

c. Shortcut

d. Realm

e. External

f. Forest

The correct answers are a and b. Shortcut, realm, external, and forest trusts must all be created manually (explicitly).

Page
4-71

Case Scenario Exercise

1. Right now, Research and Marketing are sharing data by burning CD-ROMs and DVD-ROMs. Under the current structure, how could Research and Marketing share information over the network?

There are two main options: 1) The departments could share resources to Everyone and allow unauthenticated access to their resources. This could pose a security risk as they'd be allowing anyone access to their data, instead of just users in the Research or Marketing departments. 2) Research and Marketing could create trust relationships between their separate forests and share information to specific users in a more secure way.

2. Laura asks you, "What if we decided that ITS should handle the entire institute's network administration? If we were building the entire administrative structure right now using Windows Server 2003 and Active Directory, how would it be different than what we have now?"

The institute's network resources would probably be configured as a single forest. The single forest model allows the company to share a common set of administrators called Enterprise Admins. These administrators would have the user rights to handle issues throughout the entire institute. If you wanted separate domains for each department, you'd probably configure them as child domains. The forest root and parent of all these child domains would be the ITS department. Another option would be to configure a single domain and create OUs to subdivide the domain when there are unique administrative requirements. For example, you might create a separate OU for each department, if they required separate management.

3. What are the potential issues of simply moving the management function of the existing structure to the ITS department, without modifying anything?

Centralized management of resources would be more complicated than necessary because there are currently three separate forests with no trust relationships. The administrative team would have to use three separate sets of Enterprise Admin accounts. Many tasks would have to be performed three times instead of only once.

5 Configuring Sites and Managing Replication

Exam Objectives in this Chapter:

- Plan a strategy for placing global catalog servers.
- Evaluate network traffic considerations when placing global catalog servers.
- Evaluate the need to enable universal group membership caching.
- Create and configure application directory partitions.
- Implement an Active Directory site topology.
- Configure site links.
- Configure preferred bridgehead servers.
- Manage an Active Directory site.
- Configure replication schedules.
- Configure site link costs.
- Configure site boundaries.
- Monitor Active Directory replication failures. Tools might include Replication Monitor, Event Viewer, and support tools.
- Monitor Active Directory replication.
- Troubleshoot Active Directory.
- Diagnose and resolve issues related to Active Directory replication.

Why This Chapter Matters

This chapter shows you how to configure your Active Directory physical structure by configuring sites and replication. When you are faced with managing a geographically spread out Active Directory infrastructure, you'll need to understand replication. There are two types of replication: intersite and intrasite. Intrasite is the default replication type that occurs as soon as you place the second domain controller in a domain. Intersite replication occurs when you create sites. You use sites to control data replication between domain controllers. To implement a site topology, you'll need to know how to configure sites and intersite replication. To configure intersite replication, you must be familiar with site links and their attributes of cost, frequency, and scheduling. You must know why it's not always necessary to designate a preferred bridgehead server, site link bridges, or connection objects.

Lessons in this Chapter:

Before You Begin

To complete the lessons in this chapter, you must

- Prepare your test environment according to the descriptions given in the "Getting Started" section of "About This Book"

- Complete the practices for installing and configuring Active Directory as discussed in Chapter 2, "Installing and Configuring Active Directory"

- Learn to use Active Directory administration tools as discussed in Chapter 3, "Administering Active Directory"

Lesson 1: Understanding Sites and Replication

Understanding how sites and replication work is a prerequisite for being able to configure and manage sites and replication for Active Directory. This lesson introduces you to how sites and replication work to represent the physical structure of Active Directory.

After this lesson, you will be able to

- Explain the purpose of sites
- Explain how information is replicated within sites and between sites
- Explain the purpose of site links, site link bridges, and bridgehead servers
- Explain site link transitivity

Estimated lesson time: 20 minutes

Understanding Sites

Recall from Chapter 1, "Introduction to Active Directory," that a *site* is a set of Internet Protocol (IP) subnets connected by a highly reliable and fast link, usually a local area network (LAN). A *subnet* is a subdivision of an IP network. Typically, networks with a bandwidth of at least 512 kilobits per second (Kbps) are considered fast networks. An available bandwidth of 128 Kbps and higher is sufficient for designating a site. *Available bandwidth* is the amount of bandwidth that is actually available for use during peak traffic after normal network traffic is handled.

In Active Directory, site structure mirrors the location of user communities. Site structure corresponds to the physical environment and is maintained separately from the logical environment, which is represented by the domain structure. Because sites are independent of the domain structure, a single domain can include a single site or multiple sites, and a single site can include multiple domains.

The main purpose of a site is to physically group computers to optimize network traffic. Sites act to confine authentication and replication traffic to only the devices within a site. Because network traffic is prevented from unnecessarily crossing slow wide area network (WAN) links, WAN traffic is limited. Sites have two main roles:

- To facilitate authentication by determining the nearest domain controller when a user logs on from a workstation
- To facilitate the replication of data between sites

Because site names are used in the records registered in the Domain Name System (DNS) by the domain locator, they must be valid DNS names. Recall that valid DNS names consist of the standard characters A–Z, a–z, 0–9, and hyphen (-).

Understanding Replication

In Active Directory, all of the objects in the forest are represented in the *directory tree*, a hierarchy of objects and containers. For each forest, the directory tree is partitioned to allow sections to be distributed to domain controllers in different domains within the forest. Each domain controller stores a copy of a specific part of the directory tree, called a *directory partition*. A directory partition is also known as a *naming context*. The copy of the directory partition is called a *replica*. A replica contains all attributes for each directory partition object and is readable and writable. In the Microsoft Windows Server 2003 operating system, the replication process ensures that changes made to a replica on one domain controller are synchronized to replicas on all other domain controllers within the domain.

Information Replicated

At least three types of directory partition replicas are stored on each domain controller:

- **Schema partition**   Contains definitions of objects that can be created in the forest and the attributes those objects can have. Objects in the schema partition must be replicated to all domain controllers in all domains in the forest.

- **Configuration partition**   Contains objects that represent the logical structure of the forest deployment, including the domain structure and replication topology. Objects in the configuration partition must be replicated to all domain controllers in all domains in the forest.

- **Domain partition**   Contains all of the objects stored in a domain. Objects in the domain partition can be replicated only to domain controllers within the domain.

In addition, a new type of directory partition—the Application directory partition—is available only to domain controllers in the Windows Server 2003 operating system. This partition is used by applications and services to store application-specific data, which can include any type of object except security principals (users, groups, and computers). The application partition can be configured to replicate objects to any set of domain controllers in the forest, not necessarily all in the same domain. This partition provides the capability to host data in Active Directory without significantly impacting network performance by providing control over the scope of replication and placement of replicas. Therefore, dynamic data from network services such as Remote Access Service (RAS), RADIUS, Dynamic Host Configuration Protocol (DHCP), and Common Open Policy Service (COPS) can reside in a directory, allowing applications to access them uniformly with one access methodology.

Some domain controllers are global catalog servers. On these domain controllers, there is also stored a partial replica of directory partition objects from other domains, for the purpose of finding information throughout the domain tree or forest. A partial replica contains a subset of the attributes of a directory partition replica and is read-only. To be stored in a partial replica, an attribute must have the *isMemberOfPartialAttributeSet* value on its *attributeSchema* object set to TRUE.

Replication Triggers

The following actions trigger replication between domain controllers:

- Creating an object
- Modifying an object
- Moving an object
- Deleting an object

How Information Is Replicated

Active Directory replicates information in two ways: *intrasite* (within a site) and *intersite* (between sites). Table 5-1 compares intrasite and intersite replication.

Table 5-1 Intrasite and Intersite Replication Comparison

	Intrasite Replication	**Intersite Replication**
Compression	To save CPU time, replication data is not compressed.	To save WAN bandwidth, replication data greater than 50 kilobytes (KB) is compressed.
Replication model	To reduce replication latency, replication partners notify each other when changes need to be replicated and then pull the information for processing.	To save WAN bandwidth, replication partners do not notify each other when changes need to be replicated.
Replication frequency	Replication partners poll each other periodically.	Replication partners poll each other at specified intervals, only during scheduled periods. If updates are necessary, operations are scheduled to pull the information for processing.
Transport protocols	Remote procedure call (RPC).	IP or Simple Mail Transport Protocol (SMTP).

For intrasite replication, the knowledge consistency checker (KCC) on each domain controller helps to automatically generate and optimize a replication topology among domain controllers in the same domain. To accomplish this, the KCC automatically creates connection objects between domain controllers. A *connection object* is an Active Directory object that represents an inbound-only connection to a domain controller. Under normal conditions, Active Directory automatically creates and deletes connection objects. However, you can manually create connection objects to force replication if you are certain the connection is required and you want the connection to persist until you manually remove it.

Real World   Initiating Replication

You can use several different methods to force replication. Microsoft Knowledge Base article 232072, "Initiating Replication Between Active Directory Direct Replication Partners" (available from *http://support.microsoft.com*), discusses the following four methods:

1. Using the Active Directory Sites and Services MMC snap-in (Dssite.msc)

2. Using Repadmin

3. Using Replmon

4. Using a script

All of these methods, except for using a script, are illustrated in the exercises and examples in this chapter. A sample script for initiating replication named Replicate.vbs can be found in the \70-294\Labs\Chapter05 folder on the Supplemental CD-ROM.

Site Links

For intersite replication to occur, you must customize how Active Directory replicates information by setting up site links. *Site links* are logical, transitive connections between two or more sites that mirror the network links and allow replication to occur. Once you have created site links, the KCC will then automatically generate the replication topology by creating the appropriate connection objects. It is important to note the difference between site links and connection objects. Site links are used by the KCC to determine replication paths between two sites and *must* be created manually. Connection objects actually connect domain controllers and are created by the KCC, though you can also manually create them if necessary.

Real World   Site Link Availability Schedule

If you work for an organization that spans multiple time zones, you must consider this when configuring your site link schedule. Although the site link schedule interface displays the schedule based on local time, this information is stored in Coordinated Universal Time (UTC). This means that someone in another time zone looking at the same schedule will see different link availability. Ensure that when you schedule site link availability for two locations in different time zones, you take into account what is happening at both locations at the scheduled time.

Site Link Transitivity   By default, all site links are transitive, which simply means that if sites A and B are linked and sites B and C are linked, then site A and site C are transitively linked. Site link transitivity is enabled or disabled by selecting the Bridge All Site Links check box in the Properties dialog box for either the IP or the SMTP intersite transport. By default, site link transitivity is enabled for each transport.

> **Note**   If site link transitivity is enabled and connections are created between sites that span firewalls, replication errors will occur if the firewall allows packets to travel only between specific domain controllers.

If you disable site link transitivity for a transport, all site links for that transport are affected and none of them are transitive. You must manually create site link bridges to provide transitive replication. The following are some reasons why you might want to disable site link transitivity:

- To have total control over replication traffic patterns
- To avoid a particular replication path, such as a path that involves a firewall
- If your IP network is not fully routed

> **Caution**   Carefully consider the needs of your organization before disabling site link transitivity.

Site Link Bridges   A *site link bridge* connects two or more site links in a transport where transitivity has been disabled in order to create a transitive and logical link between two sites that do not have an explicit site link. For example, in Figure 5-1, site link Ber-Lu connects the Bern and Lucerne sites. Site link Lu-Zur connects the Lucerne and Zurich sites. Site link bridge Ber-Lu-Zur connects site links Ber-Lu and Lu-Zur.

Because site links are transitive by default, it is seldom necessary to create site link bridges. In other words, if site link transitivity is enabled, then manually creating a site link bridge is redundant and has no effect. However, if site link transitivity is disabled, you need to manually create a site link bridge if a transitive link is required to handle your organization's replication strategy.

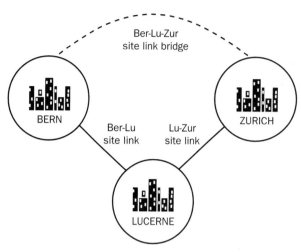

Figure 5-1   A site link bridge

Bridgehead Servers

After you have configured sites and site links, the KCC automatically designates a domain controller in each site, for each intersite transport, as the *bridgehead server*. A bridgehead server is a single domain controller in a site, the contact point, used for replication between sites. The KCC automatically creates connection objects between bridgehead servers. When a bridgehead server receives replication updates from another site, it replicates the data to the other domain controllers within its site.

A bridgehead server is designated automatically by the KCC. You can also specify a *preferred bridgehead server* if you have a computer with appropriate bandwidth to transmit and receive information. If you specify a preferred bridgehead server rather than use the one designated by the KCC, you can select the optimum conditions for the connection between sites. You can specify multiple preferred bridgehead servers, but only one is active at any time in a single site.

Caution   By specifying preferred bridgehead servers, you limit the ability of the KCC to provide failover if the bridgehead servers you designated as preferred go offline. If an active preferred bridgehead server fails, Active Directory selects another preferred bridgehead server from the set you designated. If no other preferred bridgehead servers are specified or no other preferred bridgehead servers are available, replication does not occur to that site even if there are servers that can act as bridgehead servers.

How Intersite Replication Works

The following steps, illustrated in Figure 5-2, show how intersite replication works:

1. At the interval determined by the selected replication frequency, the bridgehead server in the Zurich site polls the bridgehead server in the Lucerne site for any updated data.

2. If the bridgehead server in the Lucerne site finds that it has updated Active Directory data, it compresses the data (if larger than 50 KB) and sends it to the bridgehead server in the Zurich site.

3. When the bridgehead server in the Zurich site has received all of the data, it then replicates the data to the other domain controllers in the site without compressing the information.

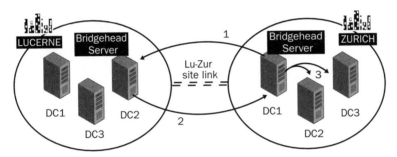

Figure 5-2   The intersite replication process

Note that polling and pull replication, rather than notification and push replication, are used between bridgehead servers during intersite replication. Pull replication is more efficient for intersite replication because the destination domain controller knows which replication data to request. In contrast, notification and push replication are more efficient for intrasite replication, when domain controllers are well connected and not restrained by site link schedules.

Lesson Review

The following questions are intended to reinforce key information presented in this lesson. If you are unable to answer a question, review the lesson and then try the question again. Answers to the questions can be found in the "Questions and Answers" section at the end of this chapter.

1. What is a site?

_____

_____

2. Which directory partition replica type must be replicated to all domain controllers within the domain?

_____

_____

3. Which type of replication compresses data to save WAN bandwidth?

_____

_____

4. What is the difference between a site link and a connection object?

_____

_____

5. Which of the following actions does not trigger replication?

   a. Accessing an object

   b. Creating an object

   c. Deleting an object

   d. Modifying an object

   e. Moving an object

Lesson Summary

- A site is a set of IP subnets connected by a highly reliable and fast link (usually a LAN). Site structure mirrors the location of user communities. Sites have two main roles: to facilitate authentication and to replicate data between sites.

- The replication process ensures that changes made to a replica on one domain controller are synchronized to replicas on all other domain controllers within the domain. Creating, modifying, moving, or deleting an object triggers replication between domain controllers. Active Directory replicates information in two ways: intrasite (within a site) and intersite (between sites).

- There are four types of directory partition replicas: schema, configuration, domain, and application.

- A site link is a logical, transitive connection between two or more sites that mirrors the network links and allows replication to occur. By default, all site links are transitive. A site link bridge connects two or more site links in a transport where transitivity has been disabled in order to create a transitive and logical link between two sites that do not have an explicit site link.

- A bridgehead server is a single domain controller in a site, the contact point, used for replication between sites, and is designated automatically by the KCC.

Lesson 2: Configuring Sites

This lesson discusses the configuration of sites, which includes the creation of sites, subnets, and domain controller objects and the designation of a site license server. It also discusses when to create sites and where to place domain controllers. In this lesson, you learn how to create and rename a site, to create subnets and associate them with sites, to create, move, or remove domain controller objects in a site, and to view and change a site license server.

After this lesson, you will be able to

- Determine when to create a site
- Create a site
- Rename a site
- Create a subnet
- Associate a subnet with a site
- Determine when to place a domain controller in a site
- Create a domain controller object in a site
- Move a domain controller object between sites
- Remove a domain controller object from a site
- View a site license server
- Change a site license server

Estimated lesson time: 20 minutes

Configuring Sites

To configure a site, you must complete the following tasks:

1. Create a site
2. Create a subnet and associate it with the site
3. Create or move a domain controller object into the site
4. Designate a site license server for the site

You can complete each of these tasks by using the Active Directory Sites And Services console.

The Active Directory Sites And Services Console

You use the Active Directory Sites And Services console to configure sites. The hierarchy of objects used by the KCC to represent the replication topology are displayed as the contents of the Sites container, as shown in Figure 5-3.

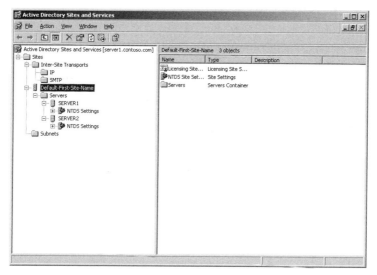

Figure 5-3   Sites container in the Active Directory Sites And Services console

The Sites container contains an object for each site in the forest. The Sites container stores the following objects, arranged in a hierarchy:

- Varying numbers of Site objects, each of which contains three child objects:

    ❑ The Licensing Site object, which stores the licensing settings for the site.

    ❑ The NTDS Site Settings object, which stores directory properties common to all domain controllers in the site, such as the schedule for replication.

    ❑ The Servers container, which stores a server object for each domain controller in the site. Each server object contains an NTDS Settings object. Each NTDS Settings object represents the presence of Active Directory on the server. If Active Directory is removed from a server, its NTDS Settings object is deleted, but the server object remains. Each NTDS Settings object contains connection objects that represent the inbound connections from other domain controllers in the forest that are currently available to send changes to this domain controller.

- Inter-Site Transports container, which stores site link objects.

- Subnets container, which stores subnet objects.

Creating Sites

When you install Active Directory on the first domain controller in a domain, a site object named Default-First-Site-Name is automatically created in the Sites container on the Active Directory Sites And Services console. The first domain controller for the domain is then installed into this site. Subsequent domain controllers are installed either into the site of the source domain controller (assuming the IP address maps to the site) or into an existing site. When your first domain controller has been installed, you can rename Default-First-Site-Name to the name you want to use for the site.

When you install Active Directory on subsequent servers, if alternate sites have been defined in Active Directory and the IP address of the installation computer matches an existing subnet in a defined site, the domain controller is added to that site. Newly installed domain controllers that do not have a subnet identifier matching one of the previously defined sites will be placed in the site named Default-First-Site-Name. If you rename the Default-First-Site-Name site to something different, you'll find the new domain controllers in that location.

Define a site for

- Each LAN or set of LANs that are connected by a high-speed backbone.

- Each location that does not have direct connectivity to the rest of the network and is reachable only by SMTP mail.

- Networks separated by links that are heavily used during some parts of the day and idle during other parts of the day. You can then schedule replication between sites to prevent replication traffic from competing with other traffic during high usage hours.

Tip   A multihomed computer (a computer with more than one IP address) with subnet addresses in different sites can belong to only one site. To avoid confusion, you should assign all the addresses for a multihomed computer to the same site.

If an entire network consists of fast, reliable links, the network can be considered a single site. Similarly, if bandwidth between networks is plentiful and it is acceptable for a client on one network to communicate with a server on another network, the networks can together be considered a single site.

To create a site, complete the following steps:

1. Click Start, point to Administrative Tools, and then click Active Directory Sites And Services.

2. Right-click the Sites container, and then click New Site.

3. In the New Object–Site dialog box, shown in Figure 5-4, type the name of the new site in the Name box. Assign a site link to the site by selecting a site link in the Link Name column, and then click OK.

Note   If you want to assign a site link that has not yet been created for the site, you can create and assign this link after the site is created. However, you must assign a site link at the creation of the site, so use DEFAULTIPSITELINK until you change it. To learn more about creating and assigning site links, refer to Lesson 3, "Configuring Intersite Replication."

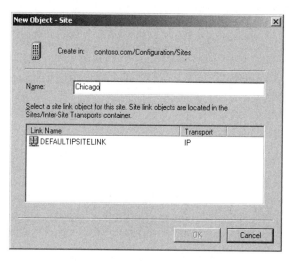

Figure 5-4   New Object–Site dialog box

4. In the Active Directory message box, shown in Figure 5-5, note that to finish the configuration of a site, you must

❏ Ensure that the site is linked to other sites with site links as appropriate.

❏ Add subnets for the site to the Subnets container.

❏ Install one or more domain controllers in the site or move existing domain controllers into the site.

❏ Select the licensing computer for the site.

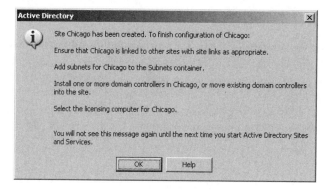

Figure 5-5   Active Directory message box

5. Click OK.

To rename a site, complete the following steps:

1. Click Start, point to Administrative Tools, and then click Active Directory Sites And Services.

2. Click the Sites folder.

3. Right-click the site you want to rename, and then click Rename.

4. Type the new site name over the existing site name. Click in an empty part of the console tree.

Creating Subnets

Computers on TCP/IP networks are assigned to sites based on their location in a subnet or a set of subnets. Subnet information is used to find a domain controller in the same site as the computer that is authenticated during the logon process, and is used during Active Directory replication to determine the best routes between domain controllers. Subnets must be defined in Active Directory to ensure accurate and efficient directory replication and resource usage. Each site must have at least one subnet, but a subnet can be assigned to only one site.

When you create a subnet, you must specify the subnet address and mask. Then you must assign the subnet to a specific site. A subnet name is automatically assigned based on the subnet address you entered and the number of subnet mask bits you specified in the subnet mask. For example, if you specify a subnet address of 192.168.16.0 and a subnet mask of 255.255.255.0, the subnet name assigned is 192.168.16.0/24.

To create a subnet, complete the following steps:

1. Click Start, point to Administrative Tools, and then click Active Directory Sites And Services.

2. Double-click the Sites folder.

3. Right-click the Subnets folder, and then click New Subnet.

4. In the New Object–Subnet dialog box, shown in Figure 5-6, type the subnet address in the Address box. In the Mask box, type the subnet mask that describes the range of addresses included in this site's subnet. Choose a site to associate this subnet, and then click OK.

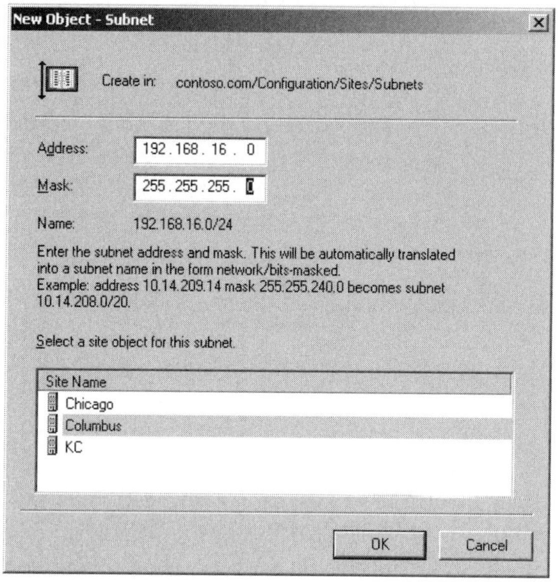

Figure 5-6   New Object–Subnet dialog box

To associate an existing subnet with a site, complete the following steps:

1. Click Start, point to Administrative Tools, and then click Active Directory Sites And Services.

2. Open the Subnets folder, and then click the subnet.

3. Right-click the subnet, and then click Properties.

4. In the Properties dialog box for the subnet, shown in Figure 5-7, select a site with which to associate this subnet from the choices available in the Site list, and then click OK.

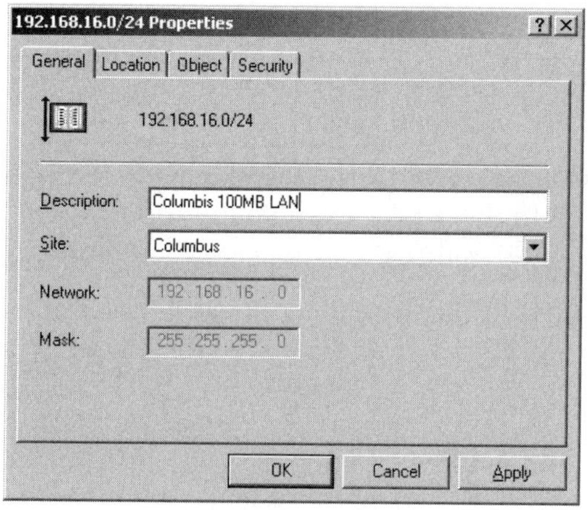

Figure 5-7   Properties dialog box for a subnet

Creating, Moving, and Removing Domain Controller Objects in a Site

As discussed earlier in this lesson, when you install Active Directory on the first domain controller in a domain, a site object named Default-First-Site-Name is automatically created in the Sites container, and the first domain controller for the domain is installed into this site. Subsequent domain controllers are installed either into the site of the source domain controller (assuming the IP address maps to the site) or into an existing site. Domain controllers might also need to be demoted. Therefore, it is often necessary to create, move, or remove domain controller objects in a site. However, you must first consider the location of domain controllers for each site.

Determining the Location of Domain Controllers

For optimum network response time and application availability, place at least

- **One domain controller in each site**   A domain controller in each site provides users with a local computer that can service query requests for their domain over LAN connections.

- **Two domain controllers in each domain**   By placing at least two domain controllers in each domain, you provide redundancy and reduce the load on the existing domain controller in the domain. Recall that a domain controller can service only one domain.

> **Note**   When a single site includes multiple domains, you cannot place a domain controller in the site and expect it to service more than one domain.

Reasons for placing additional domain controllers in a site are the following:

- **There are a large number of users in the site, and the link to the site is slow or near capacity.**   If a site has slow logon times and slow authentication when attempting to access user resources, capacity might be insufficient. By monitoring domain controller usage, you can determine whether there is enough processing power and bandwidth to service requests. If performance is lagging, you should consider adding another domain controller to the site.

- **The link to the site is historically unreliable or only intermittently unavailable.**   If a single domain controller in a site fails, clients can connect to other domain controllers in other sites in the domain by crossing site links. However, if site links are unreliable, users on that site may not be able to log on to their computers. In this case, you should consider adding another domain controller to the site.

In some situations, it might *not* be efficient to place a domain controller in a site. These situations include

- **Sites with small numbers of users**   For sites with a small number of users, using available bandwidth to log on and query the directory might be more economical than adding a domain controller.

- **Small sites that have client computers but no servers**   For sites with no servers, a domain controller is not necessary. Users can still log on using cached credentials if the site link fails. Because there are no server-based resources at the site, there is no need for further authentication.

> **Note**   The following procedures are used to create, move, and remove domain controller objects in a site, which is not the same as installing or demoting a domain controller. To install or demote a domain controller, you must use the Active Directory Installation Wizard. These procedures associate or disassociate a domain controller with a site.

To create a domain controller object in a site, complete the following steps:

1. Click Start, point to Administrative Tools, and then click Active Directory Sites And Services.

2. In the Active Directory Sites And Services console tree, double-click the site that you want to contain the new domain controller object.

3. Right-click the Servers folder, point to New, and then click Server.

4. In the New Object–Server dialog box, type the name for the new domain controller object in the Name box, and then click OK.

To move a domain controller object into a site, complete the following steps:

1. Click Start, point to Administrative Tools, and then click Active Directory Sites And Services.

2. In the Active Directory Sites And Services console tree, right-click the domain controller object that you want to move to a different site, and then click Move.

3. In the Move Server dialog box, click the site to which you want to move the domain controller object, and then click OK.

To remove a domain controller object from a site, complete the following steps:

Note Use this procedure only if you want to permanently remove a server object from a site. If you plan to reactivate the server, delete the NTDS Settings object for the server rather than the server object itself. When you bring the server back online, Active Directory automatically creates a new NTDS Settings object, inserting the server into the replication topology as appropriate.

1. Click Start, point to Administrative Tools, and then click Active Directory Sites And Services.

2. In the Active Directory Sites And Services console tree, right-click the domain controller object that you want to remove, and then click Delete.

3. In the Active Directory message box, click Yes.

Designating a Site License Server

An administrator can ensure an organization's legal compliance with software license agreements for the Windows Server 2003 operating system by monitoring license purchases, deletions, and usage. The License Logging service on each server in a site collects and replicates this licensing information to a centralized database on a server for the site called the *site license server*. A site administrator or administrator for the site license server can then use the Licensing utility in Administrative Tools to view the licensing history for the entire site stored on the site license server.

The default site license server is the first domain controller created for the site; however, the site license server does not have to be a domain controller. For optimal performance, however, the site license server should be in the same site. In a large organization with multiple sites, licensing information for each site is collected separately by the site license server in each site.

To view the site license server for a site, complete the following steps:

1. Click Start, point to Administrative Tools, and then click Active Directory Sites And Services.

2. In the console tree, click the site.

3. In the details pane, click Licensing Site Settings.

4. On the Action menu, click Properties.

5. In the Licensing Site Settings Properties dialog box, shown in Figure 5-8, the current site license server is listed in the Computer and Domain boxes.

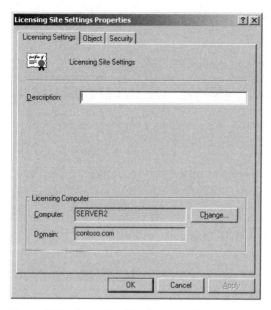

Figure 5-8   Licensing Site Settings Properties dialog box

To change a license server for a site, complete the following steps:

1. Click Start, point to Administrative Tools, and then click Active Directory Sites And Services.

2. Click the site for which you want to assign a licensing computer.

3. In the details pane, right-click Licensing Site Settings, and then click Properties.

4. In the Licensing Site Settings Properties dialog box, shown previously in Figure 5-8, click Change in the Licensing Computer box.

5. In the Select Computer dialog box, shown in Figure 5-9, select the computer you want to designate as the licensing computer for this site, and then click OK.

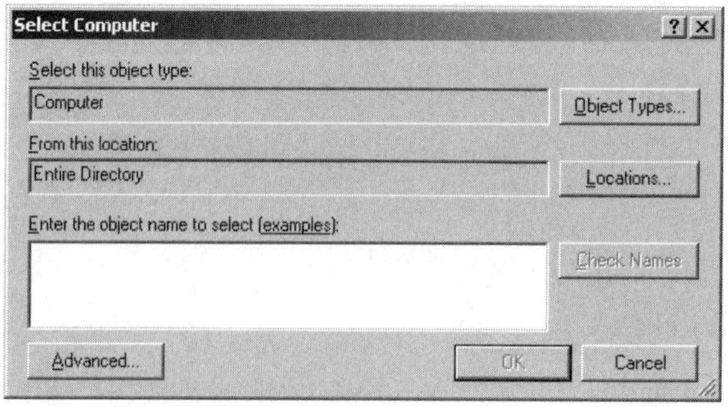

Figure 5-9   Select Computer dialog box

6. In the Licensing Site Settings Properties dialog box, click OK.

Practice: Configuring Sites

In this practice, you configure sites, including renaming and creating sites, creating subnets and associating them with sites, moving and creating a domain controller object, and changing the site licensing server for a site.

> **Note**   To complete this practice, you must make Server2 an additional domain controller in the *contoso.com* domain. If you didn't complete the Troubleshooting Lab in Chapter 4, Server2 is still a domain controller for *woodgrovebank.com*. In that case, you must demote Server2 and then promote it to be an additional domain controller in the *contoso.com* domain. If necessary, refer to Chapter 2, "Installing and Configuring Active Directory," for instructions on removing and installing Active Directory.

Exercise 1: Renaming and Creating Sites

In this exercise, you rename the Default-First-Site-Name site and create two other sites.

▶ **To rename and create sites**

1. Log on to Server1 and Server2 as Administrator.

2. On Server1, use the procedure provided earlier in this lesson to rename the Default-First-Site-Name site to Columbus.

3. On Server2, use the procedure provided earlier in this lesson to create a new site named Chicago. Assign the DEFAULTIPSITELINK object to the Chicago site for now. You will work with site links in the next lesson when you configure replication.

4. On Server1, use the procedure provided earlier in this lesson to create a new site named KC. Assign the DEFAULTIPSITELINK object to the KC site for now.

> **Note**   You might have to wait up to 15 minutes for replication to occur before you can see the results of the changes you made in steps 2–4 in the Active Directory Sites And Services console on the opposite server.

Exercise 2: Creating Subnets and Associating Them with Sites

In this exercise, you create subnets and associate them with the sites you created in Exercise 1.

▶ **To create subnets and associate them with sites**

1. On Server1, use the procedure provided earlier in this lesson to create a subnet with the address 192.168.16.0 and subnet mask 255.255.255.0. Associate the subnet to the Columbus site.

2. On Server2, use the procedure provided earlier in this lesson to create a subnet with the address 10.100.1.0 and subnet mask 255.255.255.0. Associate the subnet to the Chicago site.

3. On Server1, use the procedure provided earlier in this lesson to create a subnet with the address 172.16.1.0 and subnet mask 255.255.255.0. Associate the subnet to the KC site.

Note   You might have to wait up to 15 minutes for replication to occur before you can see the results of the changes you made in steps 1–3 in the Active Directory Sites And Services console on the opposite server.

Exercise 3: Moving a Domain Controller Object to a Site

In this exercise, you move a domain controller object to a site you created in Exercise 1.

▶ **To move a domain controller object to a site**

1. Note how Server1 has been installed in the Default-First-Site-Name site, which is now the Columbus site. By default, Server2 has been installed into the Columbus site as well because its IP address maps to the Columbus site.

2. On Server1, use the procedure provided earlier in this lesson to move Server2 to the Chicago site. Do not be concerned that the IP address of Server2 does not match the subnet of the Chicago site at this time.

Exercise 4: Creating a Domain Controller Object in a Site

In this exercise, you create a domain controller object in a site you created in Exercise 1.

▶ **To create a domain controller object in a site**

On Server1, use the procedure provided earlier in this lesson to create the domain controller object for Server1 in the KC site. Do not be concerned that Server1 is used in both the Columbus and KC sites and that the IP address of Server1 does not match the subnet of the KC site at this time.

Exercise 5: Changing the Site License Server

In this exercise, you change the site license server for a site you created in Exercise 1.

▶ **To change the site license server**

On Server1, use the procedure provided earlier in this lesson to change the site license server for the Chicago site to Server2 in the *contoso.com* domain.

Lesson Review

The following questions are intended to reinforce key information presented in this lesson. If you are unable to answer a question, review the lesson and then try the question again. Answers to the questions can be found in the "Questions and Answers" section at the end of this chapter.

1. What site is created automatically in the Sites container when you install Active Directory on the first domain controller in a domain?

   _____

   _____

2. How many subnets must each site have? To how many sites can a subnet be assigned?

   _____

   _____

3. What is the minimum number of domain controllers you should place in a site?

   _____

   _____

4. What is the purpose of a site license server?

   _____

   _____

5. Which of the following administrative tools is used to configure sites?

   a. Active Directory Users And Computers console

   b. Active Directory Domains And Trusts console

   c. Active Directory Sites And Services console

   d. Licensing console

Lesson Summary

- To configure a site, you must create the site, create a subnet and associate it with the site, create or move a domain controller object into the site, and designate a site license server for the site.

- When you install Active Directory on the first domain controller in the domain, a site object named Default-First-Site-Name is automatically created in the Sites container on the Active Directory Sites And Services console.

■ Subnet information is used to find a domain controller in the same site as the computer that is authenticated during the logon process, and is used during Active Directory replication to determine the best routes between domain controllers. Each site must have at least one subnet, but a subnet can be assigned to only one site.

■ When you install additional domain controllers in an Active Directory domain, they are installed either into the site of the source domain controller (assuming the IP address maps to the site) or into an existing site.

■ For optimum network response time and application availability, place at least one domain controller in each site or two domain controllers in each domain.

Lesson 3: Configuring Intersite Replication

This lesson introduces you to the tasks involved in the configuration of intersite replication. By creating site links and configuring their cost, replication frequency, and replication availability, you provide Active Directory with information about how to use these connections to replicate directory data. Optionally, you can also designate a preferred bridgehead server, create site link bridges, and create and configure connection objects to meet your organization's replication needs.

After this lesson, you will be able to

- Create site links
- Configure site link attributes
- Designate a preferred bridgehead server
- Create site link bridges
- Create and configure connection objects

Estimated lesson time: 35 minutes

Configuring Intersite Replication

To configure intersite replication, you must complete the following tasks:

1. Create site links.

2. Configure site link attributes.

3. Designate a preferred bridgehead server (optional).

4. Create site link bridges (optional).

5. Create and configure connection objects (optional).

Creating Site Links

When you install Active Directory on the first domain controller in a site, the Active Directory Installation Wizard automatically creates an object named DEFAULTIP-SITELINK in the IP container for the first default site, also created by the Active Directory Installation Wizard. You must create subsequent site links separately. When your first domain controller has been installed, you can rename the DEFAULTIPSITELINK to the name you want to use for the site link.

Replication Transport Protocols

Directory information can be exchanged over site links using one of the following protocols:

- **Directory Service Remote Procedure Call (DS-RPC)** Designated in the Windows Server 2003 operating system as IP. Choose IP replication for a site link when there is a live, reliable connection between two or more domain controllers in different sites. IP site links communicate synchronously, meaning each replication transaction must complete before another can start. By default, intersite IP replication adheres to replication schedules and does not require a certificate authority (CA).

- **Inter-Site Messaging–Simple Mail Transport Protocol (ISM-SMTP)** Designated in the Windows Server 2003 operating system as SMTP. Choose SMTP replication when the network connections are unreliable or not always available. SMTP site links communicate asynchronously, meaning each replication transaction does not need to complete before another can start because the transaction can be stored until the destination server is available. Because SMTP is asynchronous, it does not adhere to replication schedules and requires the installation and configuration of a CA. The CA signs SMTP messages that are exchanged between domain controllers, ensuring the authenticity of directory updates.

Note Installing a CA is beyond the scope of this training kit. Refer to the *Microsoft Windows Server 2003 Resource Kit* (located on the Microsoft Web site at *http://www.microsoft.com /windows/reskits/default.asp*) for more information on this topic.

The following rules apply to the replication transports:

- Intrasite replication always uses RPC over IP.

- Intersite replication can use either RPC over IP or SMTP.

- Intersite replication using SMTP is supported only for domain controllers in different domains. Domain controllers in the same domain must replicate using RPC over IP.

Use the Inter-Site Transports container to map the site link to the replication transport. If you create the site link in the IP container, it will use RPC over IP as its transport protocol. If you create the site link in the SMTP container, it will use SMTP as its transport protocol.

To create a site link, complete the following steps:

1. Click Start, point to Administrative Tools, and then click Active Directory Sites And Services.

2. Open the Inter-Site Transports folder and right-click either the IP or SMTP folder, depending on which protocol you want the site to use. Select New Site Link.

> **Caution**   If you create a site link that uses SMTP, you must have an enterprise CA available and SMTP must be installed on all domain controllers that use the site link.

3. In the New Object–Site Link dialog box, shown in Figure 5-10, type the name to be given to the site link in the Name field. Use a name that includes the sites that you are linking.

Figure 5-10   New Object–Site Link dialog box

4. In the Sites Not In This Site Link box, click two or more sites to connect, and then click Add. Click OK.

To rename a site link, complete the following steps:

1. Click Start, point to Administrative Tools, and then click Active Directory Sites And Services.

2. Open the Inter-Site Transports folder and double-click either the IP or SMTP folder, depending on the location of the site link you want to rename.

3. In the details pane, right-click the site link you want to rename, and then click Rename.

4. Type the new site link name over the existing site link name. Click in an empty part of the details pane.

To add a site to an existing site link, complete the following steps:

1. Click Start, point to Administrative Tools, and then click Active Directory Sites And Services.

2. Open the Inter-Site Transports folder and either the IP or SMTP folder, and then right-click the site link to which you want to add the site. Click Properties.

3. In the Properties dialog box for the site link, in the Sites Not In This Site Link box, click the site you want to add to this site link, and then click Add. Click OK.

Configuring Site Link Attributes

To ensure efficient replication and fault tolerance, you must configure site link cost, replication frequency, and replication availability information for all site links.

Configuring Site Link Cost

Configure site link cost to indicate the cost of the connection in relation to the speed of the link. Higher costs are used for slow links, and lower costs are used for fast links. For example, if you have a high-speed T1 line and a dial-up network connection in case the T1 line is unavailable, configure a lower cost for the T1 line and a higher cost for the dial-up network connection. Active Directory always chooses the connection on a per-cost basis, so the least expensive connection is used as long as it is available.

Configuring Site Link Replication Frequency

Configure site link replication frequency for site links by providing an integer value that tells Active Directory how many minutes it should wait before using a connection to check for replication updates. The replication interval must be at least 15 and no more than 10,080 minutes (equal to one week). A site link must be available for any replication to occur, so if a site link is scheduled as unavailable when the number of minutes between replication updates has passed, no replication occurs.

Configuring Site Link Replication Availability

Configure site link replication availability to determine when a site link will be available for replication. Because SMTP is asynchronous and ignores all schedules, do not configure site link replication availability on SMTP site links unless

■ The site links use scheduled connection objects

■ The SMTP queue is not on a schedule and information is being exchanged directly from one server to another and not through intermediaries, as is the case, for example, on a network backbone

To configure site link attributes, complete the following steps:

1. Click Start, point to Administrative Tools, and then click Active Directory Sites And Services.

2. Open the Inter-Site Transports folder and either the IP or SMTP folder, and then right-click the site link for which you want to configure site link cost. Click Properties.

3. In the Properties dialog box for the site link, shown in Figure 5-11, enter a value for the cost of replication in the Cost box. The default cost is 100; the lower the value, the higher the priority. For example, the cost of a T1 link might be 100, while the cost of a dial-up link might be 120.

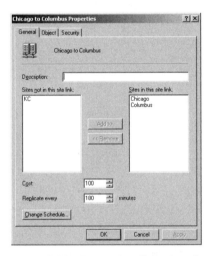

Figure 5-11   Properties dialog box for a Site Link

4. In the Replicate Every box, type the number of minutes between replications. The default time is 180; the value is processed as the nearest multiple of 15, ranging from a minimum of 15 to a maximum of 10,080 minutes (one week).

5. Click Change Schedule.

6. In the Schedule For dialog box for the site link, shown in Figure 5-12, select the block of time when this site link is or is not available to replicate directory information, and then click OK.

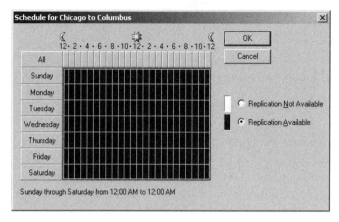

Figure 5-12 Schedule For dialog box for a Site Link

7. In the Properties dialog box for the site link, click OK.

Note Steps 5 and 6 have no effect if you have enabled Ignore Schedules in the Properties dialog box for the intersite transport.

To ignore schedules, complete the following steps:

1. Click Start, point to Administrative Tools, and then click Active Directory Sites And Services.

2. Open the Inter-Site Transports folder and right-click either the IP or SMTP folder, and then click Properties.

3. On the General tab in the IP Properties or SMTP Properties dialog box, shown in Figure 5-13, select the Ignore Schedules check box. Click OK.

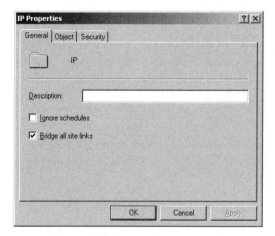

Figure 5-13 IP Properties dialog box, General tab

Designating a Preferred Bridgehead Server

Bridgehead servers are the contact point for exchange of directory information between sites. Replication occurs between bridgehead servers in different sites. When two sites are connected by a site link, the KCC automatically selects bridgehead servers—one in each site for each domain that has domain controllers in the site. The KCC then creates inbound-only connection objects between bridgehead servers. You can designate bridgehead servers manually if you want the same servers to be always used as bridgehead servers.

You can specify a preferred bridgehead server if you have a computer with appropriate bandwidth to transmit and receive information. If there's typically a high level of directory information exchange, a computer with more bandwidth can ensure these exchanges are handled promptly. Matching the demands of your Active Directory deployment with a domain controller having the capacity to handle those demands can help to enable efficient updates of directory information. You can specify multiple preferred bridgehead servers, but only one in each site is the active preferred bridgehead server at any time.

You must specify a preferred bridgehead server if your deployment uses a firewall to protect a site. Establish your firewall proxy server as the preferred bridgehead server, making it the contact point for exchanging information with servers outside the firewall. If you do not do this, directory information might not be successfully exchanged.

The Implications of Using a Preferred Bridgehead Server

If the active preferred bridgehead server fails, Active Directory selects another preferred bridgehead server to be the active preferred bridgehead server from the set you designate. If no other preferred bridgehead servers are specified or no other preferred bridgehead servers are available, replication does not occur to that site even if there are servers that can act as bridgehead servers.

In addition, if you specify preferred bridgehead servers, you must assign one bridgehead server for each domain and writable directory partition combination in your forest, which might result in high costs in a large organization.

Replacement of a Failed Preferred Bridgehead Server

If a preferred bridgehead server fails and you want the KCC to be able to fail over to other domain controllers but there are no other preferred bridgehead servers available, you must perform one of the following tasks at a domain controller in each site:

- Add new domain controllers and designate them as preferred bridgehead servers for the corresponding directory partitions, site, and transport. If there is more than one domain represented in the site, you must add a preferred bridgehead server for each domain.

- Remove all preferred bridgehead designations that you have made for the corresponding directory partition, site, and transport, and allow the KCC to select new bridgehead servers automatically.

Because the KCC creates only inbound connections, a bridgehead server cannot create an outbound connection to another bridgehead server. This is the reason why changes to preferred bridgehead server status must be made on a domain controller in each affected site so that inbound connections are created in each site. This process might require two administrators if the site locations are far away from each other.

> **Note**   If preferred bridgehead servers are available and you want to add another preferred bridgehead server to the site, you do not have to add the server in both sites because the change replicates to the other site through the currently available bridgehead servers.

To designate a preferred bridgehead server, complete the following steps:

1. Click Start, point to Administrative Tools, and then click Active Directory Sites And Services.

2. In the Active Directory Sites And Services console tree, click the site that contains the domain controller that you want to make a preferred bridgehead server.

3. In the Active Directory Sites And Services console tree, right-click the domain controller that you want to make a bridgehead server, and then click Properties.

4. In the Properties dialog box for the domain controller, shown in Figure 5-14, in the Transports Available For Inter-Site Data Transfer box, select the intersite transport or transports for which this computer will be a preferred bridgehead server. Click Add, and then click OK.

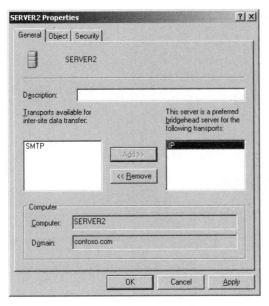

Figure 5-14   Properties dialog box for a domain controller

Creating Site Link Bridges

As discussed in Lesson 1, when more than two sites are linked for replication and use the same transport, by default, all of the site links are "bridged" in terms of cost, assuming the site links have common sites. If site link transitivity is enabled, which it is by default, creating a site link bridge has no effect. It is seldom necessary to create site link bridges. However, if site link transitivity has been disabled, you need to create a site link bridge manually if a transitive link is required to handle your organization's replication strategy.

> **Note**   If site link transitivity is enabled and connections are created between sites that span firewalls, replication errors will occur if the firewall allows packets to travel only between specific domain controllers.

To create a site link bridge, complete the following steps:

1. Click Start, point to Administrative Tools, and then click Active Directory Sites And Services.

2. Open the Inter-Site Transports folder and right-click either the IP or SMTP folder, and then click New Site Link Bridge.

3. In the New Object–Site Link Bridge dialog box, shown in Figure 5-15, type a name for the site link bridge in the Name box.

Figure 5-15   New Object–Site Link Bridge dialog box

4. In the Site Links Not In This Site Link Bridge box, click two or more sites to connect, and then click Add. Click OK.

Tip   If site link transitivity is enabled, which it is by default, this procedure is redundant and has no effect.

To disable site link transitivity, complete the following steps:

1. Click Start, point to Administrative Tools, and then click Active Directory Sites And Services.

2. Open the Inter-Site Transports folder and right-click either the IP or SMTP folder, then click Properties.

3. On the General tab in the IP Properties or SMTP Properties dialog box, shown previously in Figure 5-13, clear the Bridge All Site Links check box. Click OK.

Exam Tip   Know how to configure site links, site link costs, replication schedules, and preferred bridgehead servers.

Creating and Configuring Connection Objects

As discussed in Lesson 1, a connection object is an Active Directory object that represents an inbound-only connection to a domain controller. When there is a single site, all KCCs generate connection objects for replication within the site. When there is more than one site, a single KCC in each site generates all connection objects for replication between sites. Connection objects can also be created manually by an administrator. Connection objects created by the KCC are "owned" by the KCC. Connection objects created or modified by an administrator are owned by the administrator.

Although you can create or configure connection objects manually to force replication over a particular connection, normally you should allow replication to be automatically optimized by the KCC based on information you provide in the Active Directory Sites And Services console about your deployment. Create connection objects manually only if the connections that are automatically configured by the KCC do not connect specific domain controllers that you want to connect. Adding redundant manual connection objects to the optimal connection objects created by the KCC can increase replication traffic.

Connection Transport

Each connection object has a replication transport, which is assigned to the RPC transport by default. The RPC transport is used for uniform high-speed, synchronous RPC over IP within a site. Because the IP and SMTP transports are used for intersite replication, it is unlikely that you will need to use them when configuring a connection object.

Connection Schedule

Each connection object has a schedule that is set automatically by the KCC. The connection schedule controls the frequency of intrasite replication on the connection, with a minimum increment of 15 minutes. The default intrasite replication schedule for automatically generated connection objects is once per hour, which is set in the NTDS Site Settings object, available at the site level. Here you can set a default schedule of None (no replication), Once Per Hour (default), Twice Per Hour, or Four Times Per Hour.

You can override the default schedule set on the NTDS Site Settings object only if you create a connection object manually. The default intrasite replication schedule for manually created connection objects is four times per hour. If you attempt to modify the schedule on an automatically generated connection object (owned by the KCC), you receive a warning message asking if you want to turn the connection object into a manually created connection object. If you select Yes, the automatically generated connection object will be turned into a manual one. If you select No, the KCC reverts to the schedule on the NTDS Site Settings object the next time it runs.

Intrasite replication begins when you make a directory update on a domain controller. By default, the source domain controller waits 15 seconds and then sends an update notification to its closest replication partner. If the source domain controller has more than one replication partner, subsequent notifications go out by default at 3-second intervals to each partner. If no changes occur on the domain controller during the time allowed by the connection schedule, replication is triggered according to the default schedule set on the NTDS Site Settings object.

To create and configure a connection object, complete the following steps:

1. Click Start, point to Administrative Tools, and then click Active Directory Sites And Services.

2. Double-click the site that contains the domain controller for which you want to create a connection object.

3. Open the Servers folder, select the domain controller for which you are enabling the inbound connection, right-click NTDS Settings, and then click New Active Directory Connection.

4. In the Find Domain Controllers dialog box, shown in Figure 5-16, select the domain controller and click OK.

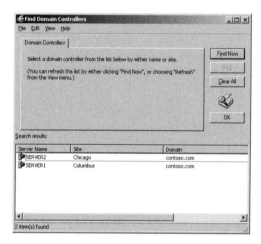

Figure 5-16 Find Domain Controllers dialog box

5. In the New Object–Connection dialog box, type a name for the new Connection object in the Name field. It is best to use the name of the domain controller for which you are enabling the inbound connection. Click OK.

6. Right-click the connection object in the details pane and select Properties.

7. In the Properties dialog box for the connection object, shown in Figure 5-17, type a description of the connection object in the Description box. Ensure that RPC appears in the Transport box. Click Change Schedule to change the default intra-site replication schedule (four times per hour).

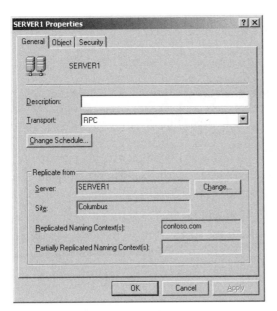

Figure 5-17   Properties dialog box for a connection object

8. In the Schedule For dialog box for the connection object, shown in Figure 5-18, select the intrasite replication frequency for this connection object, then click OK.

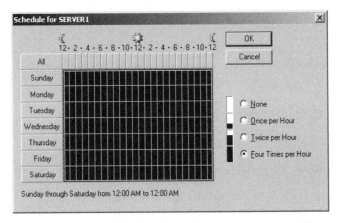

Figure 5-18   Schedule For dialog box for a connection object

9. In the Properties dialog box for the connection object, click OK.

Practice: Configuring Intersite Replication

In this practice, you configure intersite replication, including renaming a site link, creating additional site links, configuring site link attributes, designating a preferred bridgehead server, and configuring a connection object.

> **Note**   To complete this practice, you must have successfully completed the exercises in Lesson 2.

Exercise 1: Renaming and Creating Sites

In this exercise, you rename DEFAULTIPSITELINK and create two other site links.

▶ **To rename and create sites**

1. Use the procedure provided earlier in this lesson to rename the DEFAULTIP-SITELINK "Columbus to Chicago."

2. Use the procedure provided earlier in this lesson to create two new site links. Name the first site link "Columbus to KC," and link the Columbus and KC sites. Name the second site link "Chicago to KC," and link the Chicago and KC sites.

Exercise 2: Configuring Site Links

In this exercise, you configure the site links you renamed and created in Exercise 1.

▶ **To configure site links**

1. Use the procedure provided earlier in this lesson to configure site link attributes for each of the site links you created in Exercise 1. Examine the Properties dialog box for each site link. Experiment with the settings for cost and replication frequency.

2. Click the Change Schedule button to experiment with setting replication availability. Make one of the site links available at all times except 8–9 A.M. and 4–5 P.M.

Exercise 3: Designating a Preferred Bridgehead Server

In this exercise, you designate a preferred bridgehead server for a site.

▶ **To designate a preferred bridgehead server**

Use the procedure provided earlier in this lesson to designate Server1 as a preferred bridgehead server. In the Description box, type **Bridgehead Server Columbus to Chicago**.

Exercise 4: Creating and Configuring a Connection Object

In this exercise, you create and configure a connection object for a domain controller.

▶ **To create and configure a connection object**

1. Use the procedure provided earlier in this lesson to create a connection object for Server1. Although you will receive a message stating that there is already a

connection from Server1 to the destination server, create another connection for this exercise. Name the connection object SERVER1.

2. Configure the connection object to use RPC protocol. Schedule the intrasite replication frequency for this connection object to be once per hour from 8 A.M. to 5 P.M. on weekdays. Leave the replication frequency for the remaining days and times as default.

Lesson Review

The following questions are intended to reinforce key information presented in this lesson. If you are unable to answer a question, review the lesson and then try the question again. Answers to the questions can be found in the "Questions and Answers" section at the end of this chapter.

1. What object is created automatically in the IP container when you install Active Directory on the first DC in a domain?

   _____

   _____

2. You specified a preferred bridgehead server for your network. It fails and there are no other preferred bridgehead servers available. What is the result?

   _____

   _____

3. Why is it seldom necessary to create site link bridges?

   _____

   _____

4. Which type of replication does the connection schedule control?

   _____

   _____

5. Which of the following protocols should you use when network connections are unreliable?

   a. IP

   b. SMTP

   c. RPC

   d. DHCP

6. You have a high-speed T1 link and a dial-up network connection in case the T1 link is unavailable. You assign the T1 link to have a cost of 100. What cost value should you assign to the dial-up link?

    a. 0

    b. 50

    c. 100

    d. 150

Lesson Summary

- To configure intersite replication, you must create site links and configure site link attributes. Optionally, you can designate a preferred bridgehead server, create site link bridges, and create and configure connection objects. Directory information can be exchanged over site links using the DS-RPC or the ISM-SMTP protocols.

- Site link attributes of cost, replication frequency, and replication availability are set in the Properties dialog box for a site link.

- Bridgehead servers are the contact point for exchange of directory information between sites. When two sites are connected by a site link, the KCC automatically selects bridgehead servers. You can designate bridgehead servers manually; these are known as "preferred" bridgehead servers.

- A site link bridge is the linking of more than two sites for replication using the same transport. When more than two sites are linked for replication and use the same transport, by default, all of the site links are "bridged" in terms of cost, assuming the site links have common sites. If site link transitivity is enabled, which it is by default, creating a site link bridge has no effect. Therefore, it is seldom necessary to create site link bridges.

- A connection object is an Active Directory object that represents an inbound-only connection to a domain controller and is created automatically by the KCC. You can also create connection objects manually.

Lesson 4: Configuring Global Catalog Servers

This lesson introduces you to the tasks involved in configuring global catalog servers. It also discusses when to designate a domain controller as a global catalog server and introduces you to the universal group membership caching feature.

> **After this lesson, you will be able to**
>
> - Determine when to designate a domain controller as a global catalog server
> - Create a global catalog server
> - Remove a global catalog server
> - Enable the universal group membership caching logon feature
>
> **Estimated lesson time: 10 minutes**

Understanding Global Catalog Servers

Recall from Chapter 1, "Introduction to Active Directory," that the *global catalog* is the central repository of information about objects in a tree or forest. By default, a global catalog is created automatically on the initial domain controller in the first domain in the forest, known as the global catalog server. A *global catalog server* stores a full copy of all objects in the directory for its host domain and a partial copy of all objects for all other domains in the forest. This storage strategy provides efficient searches without unnecessary referrals to other domain controllers.

The global catalog performs three key functions:

- It enables a user to log on to a network by providing universal group membership information to a domain controller when a logon process is initiated.

- It enables finding directory information regardless of which domain in the forest actually contains the data.

- It resolves user principal names (UPNs) when the authenticating domain controller does not have knowledge of the account.

If a global catalog is not available when a user in a universal security group logs on to a domain, the computer uses cached credentials to allow access if the user has logged on to the domain previously. If the user has not logged on to the domain previously, the user can log on only to the local computer unless the universal group membership caching feature has been enabled.

Although the initial domain controller in a forest is designated as a global catalog server, you can configure any domain controller or designate additional domain controllers to serve this function.

Universal Group Membership Caching Feature

Due to network bandwidth and server hardware limitations, it might not be practical to have a global catalog in small remote office locations. The *universal group membership caching* feature, new in Windows Server 2003, allows a site that does not contain a global catalog server to be configured to cache universal group memberships for users who log on to the domain controller in the site. This ability allows a domain controller to process user logon requests without contacting a global catalog server when a global catalog server is unavailable. The cache is refreshed periodically as determined in the replication schedule. This feature eliminates the need to deploy global catalog servers into smaller remote office locations in order to avoid logon failures in the event that the network link connecting the remote site to the rest of the organization is disconnected. The universal group membership caching feature must be set for each site and requires a domain controller to run a Windows Server 2003 operating system. When a user attempts to log on the first time after a Windows Server 2003 domain controller has been configured to enable the universal group membership caching feature, the domain controller obtains the universal group membership information for the user from a global catalog. The universal group membership information is then cached on the domain controller for the site indefinitely and is periodically refreshed. The next time the user attempts to log on, the authenticating Windows Server 2003 domain controller obtains the universal group membership information from its local cache without contacting a global catalog.

By default, the universal group membership information contained in the cache of each domain controller is refreshed every eight hours. To refresh the cache, domain controllers running Windows Server 2003 send a universal group membership confirmation request to a designated global catalog. Up to 500 universal group memberships can be updated at once.

The universal group membership caching feature provides the following benefits to remote office locations:

- Faster logon times because the authenticating domain controllers no longer need to access a global catalog to obtain universal group membership information

- No need to upgrade hardware of existing domain controllers to handle the extra system requirements necessary for hosting a global catalog

- Minimized network bandwidth usage because a domain controller does not have to handle replication for all of the objects located in the forest

Determining the Location of Global Catalog Servers

For optimum network response time and application availability, designate at least one domain controller in each site as the global catalog server. A global catalog server in each site provides users with a local computer that can service query requests for their domain over LAN connections. When considering which domain controllers to designate as global catalog servers, base your decision on the ability of your network structure to handle replication and query traffic. Network traffic related to global catalog queries generally requires more network resources than normal directory replication traffic.

Off the Record   As you learned in earlier chapters, domain member computers use DNS servers to locate domain controllers. Therefore, you should consider placing a DNS server in each site. If you use Active Directory integrated DNS and you already have domain controllers in each site, you could install the DNS server service on one or more domain controllers in each site. DNS record replication would follow the same replication as Active Directory. If you cannot use that option, you might choose to create standard secondary DNS servers or caching-only DNS servers in each location.

To optimize replication in a multiple site environment, you might need to consider adding global catalogs for specific sites. Table 5-2 shows some reasons for adding a global catalog, along with their consequences.

Table 5-2   Reasons for Adding a Global Catalog and Their Consequences

Add a global catalog when	Advantage	Disadvantage
A commonly used application in the site utilizes port 3268 to resolve global catalog queries.	Performance improvement	Additional network traffic due to replication
A slow or unreliable WAN connection is used to connect to other sites. Use the same failure and load distribution rules that you use for individual domain controllers to determine whether additional global catalog servers are necessary in each site.	Fault tolerance	Additional network traffic due to replication
Users in the site belong to a Microsoft Windows 2000 or Windows Server 2003 domain running in native mode. In this case, all users must obtain universal group membership information from a global catalog server. If a global catalog is not located within the same site, all logon requests must be routed over your WAN connection to a global catalog located in another site. (If the domain controller is a Windows Server 2003 domain controller and it has the universal group membership caching option enabled, then all users obtain a current cached listing of their universal group memberships from the domain controller located within their site, and an additional global catalog is not needed.)	Fast user logon implementation	Additional network traffic due to replication

> **Note**   You might want to continue using a global catalog in branch office locations if an application in a site is sending global catalog queries to port 3268. Universal group membership caching feature does not intercept calls made to port 3268.

If your organization uses Microsoft Exchange 2000 Server, you should try to place a global catalog server in each site that contains an Exchange server. This is because Exchange 2000 uses Active Directory as its directory service, and all mailbox names are resolved by queries through Active Directory to the global catalog server. In a large Exchange environment, a global catalog server might need to handle a large number of queries, so placing a global catalog server in each site that contains an Exchange server can ensure that all queries are handled promptly.

> **Exam Tip**   Know the reasons for adding a global catalog server.

Creating or Removing a Global Catalog

Global catalogs can be created or removed using the Active Directory Sites And Services console.

> **Caution**   Do not create a global catalog unless you are certain it will provide value in your deployment. For this option to be useful, your deployment must have multiple domains, and even then only one global catalog server is typically useful in each site.

To create or remove a global catalog, complete the following steps:

1. Click Start, point to Administrative Tools, and then click Active Directory Sites And Services.

2. In the Active Directory Sites And Services console tree, double-click the domain controller hosting the global catalog.

3. Right-click NTDS Settings, and then click Properties.

4. In the NTDS Settings Properties dialog box, shown in Figure 5-19, perform one of the following actions:

   ❑ To create a global catalog, select the Global Catalog check box, and then click OK.

   ❑ To remove a global catalog, clear the Global Catalog check box, and then click OK.

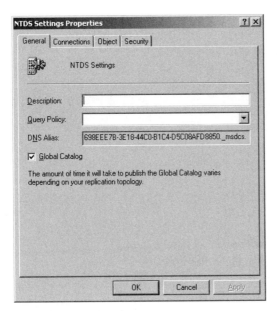

Figure 5-19   NTDS Settings Properties dialog box

Enabling the Universal Group Membership Caching Feature

The universal group membership caching feature can be enabled using the Active Directory Sites And Services console.

To enable the universal group membership caching feature, complete the following steps:

1. Click Start, point to Administrative Tools, and then click Active Directory Sites And Services.

2. In the Active Directory Sites And Services console tree, click the site for which you want to enable universal group membership caching.

3. In the details pane, right-click NTDS Site Settings, and then click Properties.

4. In the NTDS Site Settings Properties dialog box, shown in Figure 5-20, select the Enable Universal Group Membership Caching check box. Although you can choose a site from which this site will refresh its cache in the Refresh Cache From list, it is recommended that you leave this list clear (the default setting), in which case the most efficient route to a site with a global catalog is used. Click OK.

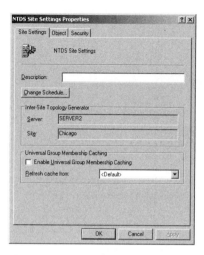

Figure 5-20   NTDS Site Settings Properties dialog box

Lesson Review

The following questions are intended to reinforce key information presented in this lesson. If you are unable to answer a question, review the lesson and then try the question again. Answers to the questions can be found in the "Questions and Answers" section at the end of this chapter.

1. What is the function of the global catalog?

2. What is a global catalog server?

3. What must you do to allow a domain controller to process user logon requests without contacting a global catalog server?

4. For optimum network response time, how many domain controllers in each site should you designate as a global catalog server?

5. The universal group membership caching feature is set for which of the following?

   a. Forest

   b. Domain

   c. Site

   d. Domain controller

Lesson Summary

- The global catalog is the central repository of information about objects in a tree or forest and is created automatically on the initial domain controller in the first domain in the forest, known as the global catalog server. A global catalog server is a domain controller that stores a full copy of all objects in the directory for its host domain and a partial copy of all objects for all other domains in the forest.

- Universal group membership caching, a new feature in the Windows Server 2003 operating system, allows a site that does not contain a global catalog server to be configured to cache universal group memberships for users who log on to the domain controller in the site. The universal group membership caching feature must be set for each site and requires a domain controller to run a Windows Server 2003 operating system.

- For optimum network response time and application availability, designate at least one domain controller in each site as the global catalog server. To optimize replication in a multiple site environment, you might need to consider adding global catalogs for specific sites.

Lesson 5: Configuring Application Directory Partitions

This lesson introduces you to application directory partitions, a new feature in Windows Server 2003. It also walks you through the tasks involved in configuring and managing application directory partitions.

After this lesson, you will be able to

- Explain the purpose of an application directory partition
- Configure an application directory partition
- Manage an application directory partition

Estimated lesson time: 30 minutes

Application Directory Partitions

An *application directory partition* is a directory partition that is replicated only to specific domain controllers. Only domain controllers running Windows Server 2003 can host a replica of an application directory partition. Applications and services can use application directory partitions to store application-specific data. Application directory partitions can contain any type of object except security principals (users, groups, and computers). Telephony Application Programming Interface (TAPI) is an example of a service that stores its application-specific data in an application directory partition.

Using application directory partitions provides the following benefits:

- Provides redundancy, availability, or fault tolerance by replicating data to a specific domain controller or any set of domain controllers anywhere in the forest.

- Reduces replication traffic because the application data is only replicated to specific domain controllers.

- Applications or services that use Lightweight Directory Access Protocol (LDAP) can continue using it to access and store their application data in Active Directory.

Application directory partitions are usually created by the applications that use them to store and replicate data. For testing and troubleshooting purposes, members of the Enterprise Admins group can manually create or manage application directory partitions using the Ntdsutil command-line tool.

Application Directory Partition Naming

An application directory partition is part of the overall forest namespace just like a domain directory partition. It follows the same DNS and distinguished names naming conventions as a domain directory partition. An application directory partition can appear anywhere in the forest namespace that a domain directory partition can appear.

An application directory partition can be placed in the following areas in the forest namespace:

- A child of a domain directory partition
- A child of an application directory partition
- A new tree in the forest

For example, if you created an application directory partition called example1 as a child of the *microsoft.com* domain, the DNS name of the application directory partition would be *example1.microsoft.com*. The distinguished name of the application directory partition would be dc=example1, dc=microsoft, dc=com. If you then created an application directory partition called example2 as a child of *example1.microsoft.com*, the DNS name of the application directory partition would be *example2.example1.microsoft.com* and the distinguished name would be dc=example2, dc=example1, dc=microsoft, dc=com.

However, if the domain *microsoft.com* were the root of the only domain tree in your forest, and you created an application directory partition with the DNS name of example1 and the distinguished name of dc=example1, this application directory partition would not be in the same tree as the *microsoft.com* domain. This application directory partition would be the root of a new tree in the forest.

Domain directory partitions cannot be children of an application directory partition. For example, if you created an application directory partition with the DNS name of *example1.microsoft.com*, you could not create a domain with the DNS name of *domain.example1.microsoft.com*.

Application Directory Partition Replication

The KCC automatically generates and maintains the replication topology for all application directory partitions in the enterprise. When an application directory partition has replicas in more than one site, those replicas follow the same intersite replication schedule as the domain directory partition. Objects stored in an application directory partition are never replicated to the global catalog as read-only replicas. Any domain controller running Windows Server 2003 can hold a replica, including domain controllers that also act as global catalog servers.

In addition, if an application requests data through the global catalog port (with LDAP, port 3268, or with LDAP/SSL port 3269), that query will not return any objects from an application directory partition, even if the computer hosting the application directory partition is also hosting the global catalog. This is done so that LDAP queries to different global catalogs will not return inconsistent results because the application directory partition is replicated to only one of the servers hosting the global catalogs.

Application Directory Partitions and Domain Controller Demotion

If you must demote a domain controller, consider the following:

- If a domain controller holds a replica of an application directory partition, then you must remove the domain controller from the replica set of the application directory partition or delete the application directory partition before you can demote the domain controller.

- If a domain controller holds the last replica of an application directory partition, then before you can demote the domain controller, you must do one of the following: specify that you want the Active Directory Installation Wizard to remove all replicas from the domain controller, remove the replica manually by using the utility provided by the application that installed it, or remove the replica manually by using the Ntdsutil command.

> **Note**   Under Windows Server 2003 with Service Pack 1 (SP1), replication metadata for former domain controllers from which Active Directory has been removed is no longer retained by default, although a waiting period can be configured. This change improves replication security and eliminates replication error messages caused by failed attempts to replicate with decommissioned domain controllers.

Before deleting the application directory partition, you must:

- **Identify the applications that use it**   To determine what application directory partitions are hosted on a computer, refer to the list on the Application Directory Partitions page of the Active Directory Installation Wizard.

- **Determine if it is safe to delete the last replica**   Removing the last replica of an application directory partition results in the permanent loss of any data contained in the partition. If you have identified the applications using the application directory partition, consult the documentation provided with those applications to determine if there is any reason to keep the data. If the applications that use the application directory partition are out of service, it is probably safe to remove the partition. If it is not safe to delete the last replica, or if you cannot determine whether it is safe, and you must demote the domain controller holding the last replica of a particular application directory partition, follow these steps: Add a replica of the partition on another domain controller, force the replication of the contents of the application directory partition to the domain controller holding the new replica, and then remove the replica of the partition on the domain controller to be demoted.

- **Identify the partition deletion tool provided by the application**   Most applications that create application directory partitions provide a utility to remove the partitions. When possible, always delete an application directory partition using the utility provided. Refer to the application's documentation for information about removing application directory partitions that were created and used by that application. If you cannot identify the application that created the application directory partition, or if your application does not provide a means to delete application directory partitions that it created, you can use the Ntdsutil command-line tool. To do this, refer to the section "Creating or Deleting an Application Directory Partition" later in this chapter.

> **Note**   If the domain controller holds a TAPI application directory partition, you can use the Tapicfg command-line tool to remove the TAPI application directory partition. For more information about the Tapicfg command-line tool, refer to Windows Server 2003 Help.

Security Descriptor Reference Domain

Every container and object on the network has a set of access control information attached to it. Known as a *security descriptor*, this information controls the type of access allowed by users, groups, and computers. If the object or container is not assigned a security descriptor by the application or service that created it, then it is assigned the default security descriptor for that object class as defined in the schema. This default security descriptor is ambiguous in that it may assign members of the Domain Admins group read permissions to the object, but it does not specify to what domain the domain administrators belong. When this object is created in a domain naming partition, that domain naming partition is used to specify which Domain Admins group actually is assigned read permission. For example, if the object is created in mydomain.microsoft.com, then members of the mydomain Domain Admins group would be assigned read permission.

When an object is created in an application directory partition, the definition of the default security descriptor is difficult because an application directory partition can have replicas on different domain controllers belonging to different domains. Because of this potential ambiguity, a default security descriptor reference domain is assigned when the application directory partition is created.

The default security descriptor reference domain defines what domain name to use when an object in the application directory partition needs to define a domain value for the default security descriptor. The default security descriptor reference domain is assigned at the time of creation.

If the application directory partition is a child of a domain directory partition, by default, the parent domain directory partition becomes the security descriptor reference domain. If the application directory partition is a child object of another application directory partition, the security descriptor reference domain of the parent application directory partition becomes the reference domain of the new child application directory partition. If the new application directory partition is created as the root of a new tree, then the forest root domain is used as the default security descriptor reference domain.

You can manually specify a security reference domain. However, if you plan to change the default security descriptor reference domain of a particular application directory partition, you should do so before creating the first instance of that partition. To do this, you must prepare the cross-reference object and change the default security reference domain before completing the application directory partition creation process.

Managing Application Directory Partitions

You can use the following tools to create, delete, or manage application directory partitions:

- Application-specific tools from the application vendor
- Ntdsutil command-line tool
- LDAP
- Active Directory Service Interfaces (ADSI)

This lesson provides information about using Ntdsutil to create and manage application directory partitions. To manage application directory partitions, you must be able to complete the following tasks:

- Create or delete an application directory partition.
- Add or remove an application directory partition replica.
- Display application directory partition information.
- Set a notification delay.
- Prepare a cross-reference object.
- Set an application directory partition reference domain.

To perform these tasks, you must be a member of the Domain Admins group or the Enterprise Admins group in Active Directory, or you must have been delegated the appropriate authority.

To perform these tasks, you use the domain management command within the Ntdsutil command. To open the Ntdsutil domain management command:

1. Click Start, and then click Command Prompt.
2. At the command prompt, type **ntdsutil**.
3. At the Ntdsutil command prompt, type **domain management**.

4. At the domain management command prompt, type **connection**.

5. At the connection command prompt, type **connect to server *ServerName***, where *ServerName* is the DNS name of the domain controller to which you want to connect.

6. At the connection command prompt, type **quit**.

Creating or Deleting an Application Directory Partition

When you create an application directory partition, you are creating the first instance of this partition. When you delete an application directory partition, you are removing all replicas of that partition from your forest. The deletion process must replicate to all domain controllers that contain a replica of the application directory partition before the deletion process is complete. When an application directory partition is deleted, any data that is contained in it is lost. To create or delete an application directory partition:

1. Type the appropriate commands to invoke the ntdsutil domain management command.

2. At the domain management command prompt, do one of the following:

❑   To create an application directory partition, type:

create nc *ApplicationDirectoryPartition DomainController*, where *ApplicationDirectoryPartition* is the distinguished name of the application directory partition you want to create, and *DomainController* is the DNS name of the domain controller on which you want to create the application directory partition. Type **null** to create the application directory partition on the domain controller to which you are currently connected.

❑   To delete an application directory partition, type:

delete nc *ApplicationDirectoryPartition*, where *ApplicationDirectoryPartition* is the distinguished name of the application directory partition you want to delete.

Adding or Removing an Application Directory Partition Replica

An *application directory partition replica* is an instance of a partition on another domain controller, created for redundancy or data access purposes. When you remove an application directory partition replica, any data that is contained in the replica is lost.

To add or remove an application directory partition replica:

1. Type the appropriate commands to invoke the ntdsutil domain management command.

2. At the domain management command prompt, do one of the following:

❑ To add an application directory partition replica, type:

add nc replica *ApplicationDirectoryPartition DomainController*, where *ApplicationDirectoryPartition* is the distinguished name of the application directory partition replica that you want to add, and *DomainController* is the DNS name of the domain controller on which you want to create the application directory partition replica. Type **null** to create the application directory partition replica on the domain controller to which you are currently connected.

❑ To remove an application directory partition replica, type:

remove nc replica *ApplicationDirectoryPartition DomainController*, where *ApplicationDirectoryPartition* is the distinguished name of the application directory partition replica that you want to delete, and *DomainController* is the DNS name of the domain controller on which you want to remove the application directory partition replica. Type **null** to create the application directory partition replica on the domain controller to which you are currently connected.

Displaying Application Directory Partition Information

Any domain controller that holds a replica of a particular directory partition (including application directory partitions) is said to be a member of the replica set for that directory partition. You can use Ntdsutil to list the domain controllers that are members of a particular replica set for an application directory partition. An addition of a domain controller to the replica set attribute on the cross-reference object does not create the replica, but it will display when the list nc replica command is used in Ntdsutil. The creation of the instance must replicate before the creation of the replica is complete.

To display application directory partition information:

1. Type the appropriate commands to invoke the Ntdsutil domain management command.

2. At the domain management command prompt, do one or more of the following:

❑ To show the distinguished names of known directory partitions, type: **list**.

❑ To show the reference domain and replication delays for an application directory partition, type: **list nc information** *DistinguishedName*, where *DistinguishedName* is the distinguished name of the application directory partition you want information about.

❑ To show the list of domain controllers in the replica set for an application directory partition, type: **list nc replicas** *DistinguishedName*, where *DistinguishedName* is the distinguished name of the application directory partition you want information about.

Setting Replication Notification Delays

Changes made to a particular directory partition on a particular domain controller are replicated to the other domain controllers that contain that directory partition. The domain controller on which the change was made notifies its replication partners that it has a change. You can configure how long the domain controller will wait to send the change notification to its first replication partner. You can also configure how long it waits to send the subsequent change notification to its remaining replication partners. These delays can be set for any directory partition (including domain directory partitions) on a particular domain controller.

To set a replication notification delay:

1. Type the appropriate commands to invoke the ntdsutil domain management command.

2. At the domain management command prompt, type:

   set nc replicate notification delay *ApplicationDirectoryPartition DelayIn-Seconds AdditionalDelayInSeconds*, where *ApplicationDirectoryPartition* is the distinguished name of the application directory partition for which you want to set a notification delay, *DelayInSeconds* is the number of seconds to delay before sending the change notification to the first replication partner, and *AdditionalDelayInSeconds* is the number of seconds to delay before sending subsequent change notifications to the remaining replication partners.

Delegating the Creation of Application Directory Partitions

There are two things that happen when creating an application directory partition:

- Creation of the cross-reference object
- Creation of the application directory partition root node

Normally only members of the Enterprise Admins group can create an application directory partition. However, it is possible for a member of the Enterprise Admins group to prepare a cross-reference object for the application directory partition and to delegate the rest of the process to someone with more limited permissions.

The cross-reference object for an application directory partition holds several valuable pieces of information, including the domain controllers that are to have a replica of this partition and the security descriptor reference domain. The partition root node is the Active Directory object at the root of the partition.

The Enterprise Admin can create the cross-reference object and then delegate to a person or group with less permissions the right to create the application directory partition root node. Creation of both the cross-reference object and the application directory partition root node can be accomplished using Ntdsutil.

After using Ntdsutil to create the cross-reference object, the enterprise administrator must modify the cross-reference object's access control list to allow the delegated administrator to modify this cross-reference. This will allow the delegated administrator to create the application directory partition and modify the list of domain controllers that holds replicas of this application directory partition. The delegated administrator must use the names of the application directory partition and the domain controller name that were specified during the precreation process.

To prepare a cross-reference object:

1. Type the appropriate commands to invoke the Ntdsutil domain management command.

2. At the domain management command prompt, type:

    precreate *ObjectName DomainController*, where *ObjectName* is the distinguished name of the object you want to create, and *DomainController* is the DNS name of the domain controller on which the object will reside.

Setting the Application Directory Partition Reference Domain

The security descriptor reference domain defines a domain name for the default security descriptor for objects in the application directory partition. By default, the security descriptor reference domain is the parent domain of the application directory partition. If the application directory partition is a child of another application directory partition, the default security descriptor reference domain is the security descriptor reference domain of the parent application directory partition. If the application directory partition has no parent, the forest root domain becomes the default security descriptor reference domain. You can use Ntdsutil to change the default security descriptor reference domain.

To set an application directory partition reference domain:

1. Type the appropriate commands to invoke the Ntdsutil domain management command.

2. At the domain management command prompt, type:

    set nc reference domain *ApplicationDirectoryPartition ReferenceDomain*, where *ApplicationDirectoryPartition* is the distinguished name of the application directory partition for which you want to set the reference domain, and *ReferenceDomain* is the distinguished name of the domain that you want to be the reference domain for the application directory partition.

> **Exam Tip**   Know how to create and configure application directory partitions.

Lesson Review

The following questions are intended to reinforce key information presented in this lesson. If you are unable to answer a question, review the lesson and then try the question again. Answers to the questions can be found in the "Questions and Answers" section at the end of this chapter.

1. What is an application directory partition?

   _____

   _____

2. Name the benefits of using an application directory partition.

   _____

   _____

3. What is a security descriptor and how is it used in an application directory partition?

   _____

   _____

4. What considerations should you make before deleting an application directory partition?

   _____

   _____

5. Which of the following tools can you use to delete an application directory partition? (Select all that apply.)

   a. Ntdsutil command-line tool

   b. Application-specific tools from the application vendor

   c. Active Directory Installation Wizard

   d. Active Directory Domains And Trusts console

   e. Active Directory Sites And Services console

Lesson Summary

- An application directory partition is a directory partition that is replicated only to specific domain controllers. Only domain controllers running Windows Server 2003 can host a replica of an application directory partition. Application directory partitions are usually created by the applications that use them to store and replicate data.

- An application directory partition can be a child of a domain directory partition, a child of an application directory partition, or a new tree in the forest.

- The KCC automatically generates and maintains the replication topology for all application directory partitions in the enterprise. When an application directory partition has replicas in more than one site, those replicas follow the same intersite replication schedule as the domain directory partition.

- If you must demote a domain controller, you must remove the domain controller from the replica set of the application directory partition or delete the application directory partition before you can demote the domain controller.

- For testing and troubleshooting purposes, members of the Enterprise Admins group can manually create or manage application directory partitions using the Ntdsutil command-line tool.

Lesson 6: **Monitoring and Troubleshooting Replication**

In order to maintain an effective replication configuration, you must be able to monitor and troubleshoot Active Directory replication. Monitoring and troubleshooting replication involves using the Replmon.exe: Active Directory Replication Monitor graphical tool and the Repadmin.exe: Replication Diagnostics Tool and Dsastat.exe command-line tools to handle replication-related issues.

> **Note**   The Dcdiag.exe command-line tool in Windows Server 2003 with SP1 (available in Windows Support Tools) provides new reporting on the overall health of replication and security for Active Directory. This test provides a summary of results along with detailed information for each domain controller that is tested and a diagnosis of any security errors.

After this lesson, you will be able to

- Explain the purpose of the Replmon.exe: Active Directory Replication Monitor graphical tool
- Use Replmon to perform various replication monitoring and troubleshooting tasks
- Explain the purpose of the Repadmin.exe: Replication Diagnostics Tool command-line tool
- Explain the purpose of the Dcdiag.exe utility in Windows Server 2003 with SP1
- Use Repadmin to perform various replication monitoring and troubleshooting tasks
- Explain the purpose of the Dsastat.exe command-line tool
- Use Dsastat.exe to perform various monitoring and troubleshooting tasks

Estimated lesson time: 40 minutes

Monitoring and Troubleshooting Replication

As an administrator, it will likely be your task to monitor and troubleshoot Active Directory replication. Windows Support Tools provide the following tools for monitoring and troubleshooting replication:

- Replmon.exe: Active Directory Replication Monitor
- Repadmin.exe: Replication Diagnostics Tool
- Dsastat.exe
- Dcdiag.exe in Windows Server 2003 with SP1

Replmon.exe: Active Directory Replication Monitor

The Active Directory Replication Monitor (Replmon) enables administrators to view the low-level status of Active Directory replication, force synchronization between domain controllers, view the topology in a graphical format, and monitor the status and performance of domain controller replication.

Replmon must be installed on a computer running Windows Server 2003. The computer can be a domain controller, member server, member workstation, or stand-alone computer. In addition, Replmon can be used to monitor domain controllers from different forests simultaneously.

Note   To use Replmon, you must first install the Windows Support Tools on your computer. You can find the complete installation procedure in Chapter 3, "Administering Active Directory."

To start Replmon, complete the following steps:

1. Click Start, point to Command Prompt, type **replmon**, and then press ENTER.

2. In the console tree, right-click Monitored Servers, and select Add Monitored Server.

3. On the Add Monitored Server Wizard page, select Add The Server Explicitly By Name, and then click Next.

4. On the Add Server To Monitor page, type the name of the server you want to monitor in the Enter The Name Of The Server To Monitor Explicitly box, and then click Finish.

5. In the Active Directory Replication Monitor window, shown in Figure 5-21, the server you chose for monitoring appears in the console tree. You can now monitor replication processes for this server.

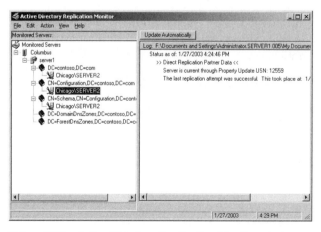

Figure 5-21   Active Directory Replication Monitor window

Features of the Active Directory Replication Monitor Window   All objects visible in the console tree support context-sensitive (right-click) menus for quick access to actions that can be performed on the node selected. The details pane displays data relevant to the node you select in the console tree. If you select a monitored server, the history of the date and time that each status refresh was initiated, along with Group Policy Objects (GPOs) and performance statistics (if those options are enabled), are displayed. Replmon also records other pertinent data regarding changes to the domain controller status in this view.

If you right-click a monitored server object, you'll see several actions you can initiate. One of those actions is to Synchronize Each Directory Partition with All Servers. If you select that option, you can initiate several different types of replication as shown in Figure 5-22.

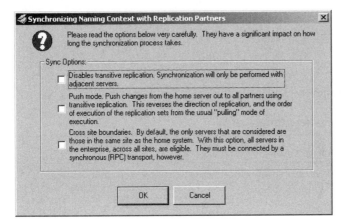

Figure 5-22   Replication Monitor Directory synchronization options

Icons enable you to determine replication status at a glance. A regular site icon represents a site. A regular server icon represents a monitored server. If the monitored server is a global catalog server, the server icon appears with a globe to the upper right. A book icon is used to represent directory partitions.

Replication partners appear under directory partitions. If the replication partner is a direct replication partner and the last replication attempt was successful, an icon representing two domain controllers on a network is used. If the replication partner is a direct replication partner and the last replication attempt failed, an icon representing two domain controllers on a network with a red "X" is used. If the replication partner is a bridgehead server, an icon representing a phone connection is used. If the last replication attempt failed, an icon representing a phone connection with a red "X" is used to denote the failure. For transitive replication partners, a single computer icon is used.

For more information about Replmon.exe: Active Directory Replication Monitor, see Windows Support Tools Help.

Repadmin.exe: Replication Diagnostics Tool

The Replication Diagnostics Tool (Repadmin), a command-line tool, allows you to view the replication topology as seen from the perspective of each domain controller. In addition, Repadmin can be used in troubleshooting to create the replication topology manually (although in normal practice this should not be necessary), to force replication events between domain controllers, and to view the replication metadata. You can also use Repadmin to see how up-to-date each domain controller is.

Note During the normal course of operations, there is no need to manually create the replication topology. Incorrect use of this tool might adversely impact the replication topology. The main use of this tool is to monitor replication so problems such as offline servers or unavailable LAN/WAN connections can be identified.

Repadmin has the following syntax:

```
repadmin command arguments [/rpc][/ ldap][/u:domain\user /pw:{password|*}]
```

Each of the command parameters is explained in Table 5-3.

Table 5-3 Repadmin Command Parameters

Parameter	Description
command arguments	Allows you to specify a command and the arguments that apply to it. For a list of commands and arguments, see Windows Support Tools Help.
/rpc	Forces Repadmin to use an RPC session for network communications.
/ldap	Forces Repadmin to use an LDAP session for network communications.
/u: domain\user	Allows you to specify an optional user as the administrator. If the user name is not specified, the credentials of the currently logged-on user are used.
/pw:[password|*]	Allows you to specify the password of the user specified by the */u:* parameter. If the password is not specified, the credentials of the currently logged-on user are used.

Using Repadmin This section describes how to perform the following replication monitoring and troubleshooting tasks using Repadmin:

- Display the replication partners for a server
- Display the highest update sequence number (USN) on a server
- Display the connection objects for a server
- Force replication between replication partners

There are additional monitoring and troubleshooting tasks you can perform using Repadmin. Refer to Windows Support Tools Help for further information.

> **Note**   To use Repadmin, you must first install the Windows Support Tools on your computer. You can find the complete installation procedure in Chapter 3, "Administering Active Directory."

To use Repadmin, complete the following steps:

1. Click Start, and then click Command Prompt.

2. At the command prompt, type the appropriate Repadmin command and parameters. The following are among the options available:

   ❑ To display the replication partners for a domain controller, type:

   repadmin /showrepl *DC_LIST*, where *DC_LIST* is the host name of the domain controller.

   For example: **repadmin /showrepl server1.contoso.com**. The object-GUID (the globally unique identifier) for the selected server and its replication partners and the InvocationID for the selected server are shown.

   ❑ To display the highest USN on a domain controller, type:

   repadmin /showutdvec *DC_LIST NamingContext*, where *DC_LIST* is the host name of the domain controller and *NamingContext* is the distinguished name of the directory partition on the domain controller.

   For example: **repadmin / showutdvect server1.contoso.com dc=contoso,dc=com**. The highest USN is shown for the specified domain controller and its replication partners.

   ❑ To display the connection objects for a domain controller, type:

   repadmin /showconn *DC_LIST*, where *DC_LIST* is the host name of the domain controller.

   For example: **repadmin /showconn server1.contoso.com**. The connection object name and replication information are shown.

   ❑ To force replication between two replication partners, type:

   repadmin /replicate *DC_LISTsource DC_LISTtarget NamingContext*, where *DC_LISTsource* is the host name of the source domain controller, *DC_LISTtarget* is the host name of the target domain controller, and *NamingContext* is the distinguished name of the directory partition on the domain controller.

   For example: **repadmin /replicate server1.contoso.com Server2.contoso.com dc=contoso,dc=com**. A message appears, stating that the sync from *server1.contoso.com* to *server2.contoso.com* was completed successfully.

For detailed information about using Repadmin.exe: Replication Diagnostics Tool, see Windows Support Tools Help.

Dsastat.exe

Dsastat.exe compares and detects differences between directory partitions on domain controllers and can be used to ensure that domain controllers are up-to-date with one another. The tool retrieves capacity statistics such as megabytes per server, objects per server, and megabytes per object class and compares the attributes of replicated objects.

Dsastat has the following syntax:

```
dsastat [/loglevel:option] [/output:option]
[/s:servername[portnumber][;servername[portnumber];...]]
[/t:option] [/sort:option] [/p:entrynumber] [/scope:option]
[/b:searchpath] [/filter:ldapfilter] [/gcattrs:option[;option;...]]
[/u:username] [/pwd:password] [/d:domain]
```

Each of the command parameters is explained in Table 5-4.

Table 5-4   Dsastat Command Parameters

Parameter	Description
/loglevel:option	Specifies the type of logging performed. Valid option values are: INFO, TRACE, and DEBUG.
/output:option	Specifies where the results of Dsastat are displayed. Valid option values are: SCREEN, FILE, or BOTH.
/s:servername[portnumber] [;servername[portnumber];...]	Specifies the names of the servers on which the comparison will be performed. Separate each server name with a semicolon.
/t:option	Specifies whether to perform a statistics comparison or a full-content comparison. Valid option values are TRUE (perform a statistical comparison) or FALSE (perform a full-content comparison). The statistical comparison merely counts the objects. It does not compare the attributes of the objects that have been retrieved from the domain controllers and it ignores the /gcattrs option. A full-content comparison retrieves every object with attribute values and performs a comparison of the attributes of the same object from different domain controllers.
/sort:option	Determines whether the search operations are performed with sorting based on objectGUID. Valid option values are TRUE (perform sorted queries) or FALSE (do not perform sorted queries). Performing a sorted query by setting this option to TRUE has a negative impact on performance; however, it complements the full-content comparison because it ensures that objects are returned in nearly the same order from different servers and improves the performance of full-content comparison.

Table 5-4   Dsastat Command Parameters

Parameter	Description
/p:pagesize	Sets page size for the LDAP search operation, indicating the number of entries to be returned per page. The valid range for pagesize is 1 to 999. The default value is 64.
/scope:option	Specifies the extent of the scope for the search operation. Valid option values are: BASE, ONELEVEL, or SUBTREE. The default option is SUBTREE.
/b:searchpath	Sets the distinguished name of the base search path, allowing Dsastat to perform the comparison against any subtree of the directory.
/filter:ldapfilter	Sets LDAP filter used in the LDAP search operation.
/gcattrs:option[;option;...]	Specifies attributes to be returned from search. This option is used only if the comparison option */t* is set to FALSE. Valid option values are: *LDAPattributes*, which displays any LDAP attribute; ObjectClass, which specifies that no attributes be displayed; auto, which specifies that only attributes replicated to the global catalog be displayed; and All, which specifies that all attributes contained in an object be displayed.
/u:username	The user name to use for the query.
/pwd:password	Password for authenticating the user name. Must be used with the */u* parameter.
/d:domain	The domain to use for authenticating the user name. Must be used with the */u* parameter.

Using Dsastat   This section describes how to perform the following replication monitoring and troubleshooting tasks using Dsastat:

- Comparison of the number of objects in the directory for the domain

- Full-content search and comparison of all the objects in the domain

- Full-content search and comparison of all the objects in a subtree of a domain

To use Dsastat, complete the following steps:

1. Click Start, and then click Command Prompt.

2. At the command prompt, type the appropriate Dsastat command and parameters. The following are among the options available:

   ❑ To compare the number of objects in the directory for the domain, type:

   ```
   dsastat [/s:servername[portnumber][;servername[portnumber];...]]
   [/b:searchpath] [/gcattrs:option[;option;...]] [/p:entrynumber]
   ```

For example: **dsastat /s:server1;server2 /b:DC=contoso,DC=com /gcattrs:objectclass /p:999**. This search keeps a count of the different types of objects in each of the replicas and then compares the count for each object class.

❑ To perform a full-content search and comparison of all the objects in the domain, type:

```
dsastat [/s:servername[portnumber] [;servername[portnumber];...]]
[/b:searchpath] [/gcattrs:option[;option;...]] [/sort:option] [/t:option]
[/p:entrynumber]
```

For example: **dsastat /s:server1;server2 /b:DC=contoso,DC=com /gcattrs:all /sort:true /t:false /p:16**. This search does a full-content search and comparison of all the objects in the *contoso.com* domain.

❑ To perform a full-content search and comparison of all the objects in a sub-tree of a domain, type:

```
dsastat [/s:servername[portnumber] [;servername[portnumber];...]]
[/b:searchpath] [/gcattrs:option[;option;...]] [/sort:option] [/t:option]
[/p:entrynumber]
```

For example: **dsastat /s:server1;server2 /b:OU=Sales,DC=contoso, DC=com /gcattrs:all /sort:true /t:false /p:16**. This search does a full-content search and comparison of all the objects in the organizational unit (OU) Sales in the *contoso.com* domain.

Dcdiag.exe in Windows Server 2003 with SP1

In Windows Server 2003 with SP1, the Dcdiag.exe command-line tool (part of the Windows Support Tools), provides new reporting on the overall health of replication and security in Active Directory. This test provides a summary of results along with detailed information for each domain controller that is tested and a diagnosis of any security errors. The new Dcdiag /Test:CheckSecurityError test can be performed on one or all domain controllers in an Active Directory forest. The test performs the following operations:

■ Checks for the availability of a Key Distribution Center (KDC) in both the destination and source domain controller's domains.

■ Verifies that the destination domain controller can transmit and receive sufficiently large User Datagram Protocol (UDP)-formatted packets (used by Kerberos).

■ Verifies that system clock of the destination domain controller is no more than 5 minutes different from the system time of the KDC in the destination and source domain, and the source domain controller.

■ Confirms that the root of each naming context on the source domain controller is configured with the necessary permission.

- Confirms that the source and destination domain controller computer accounts are not disabled, are trusted for delegation, and contain all required service principal names.

When the test has completed, Dcdiag.exe presents a summary of the results for each domain controller tested and the diagnosis of the security errors encountered.

> **Note**   Optionally, you can add the switch /ReplSource:*SourceDC* to the command to identify a specific domain controller as a source in a replication attempt.

Troubleshooting Active Directory Replication

Some of the common problems you might encounter with Active Directory replication include the following:

- New users are not recognized.

- Directory information is out-of-date.

- Service requests are not handled in a timely fashion.

- Domain controllers are unavailable.

Active Directory Replication Troubleshooting Scenarios

Table 5-5 describes some Active Directory replication troubleshooting scenarios.

Table 5-5   Active Directory Replication Troubleshooting Scenarios

Cause	Solution
Problem: Replication of directory information has stopped.	
The sites containing the clients and domain controllers are not connected by site links to domain controllers in other sites in the network, resulting in a failure to exchange directory information between sites.	Create a site link from the current site to a site that is connected to the rest of the sites in the network.
Problem: Replication of directory information has slowed but not stopped.	
Although all sites are connected by site links, your intersite replication structure is not as complete as it might be. Directory information is replicated to all domain controllers if they are all connected by site links, but this is not optimal. If there are site links but no site link bridges, changes made to domain controllers might take an unacceptably long time to be distributed to other domain controllers that are not closely linked.	Make sure Active Directory has been configured appropriately. Spanning multiple site links and creating site link bridges might provide more efficient replication.

Table 5-5   Active Directory Replication Troubleshooting Scenarios

Cause	Solution
The current network resources are insufficient to handle the amount of replication traffic. This can affect services unrelated to Active Directory because the exchange of directory information is consuming an inordinate amount of network resources.	Increase the proportion of available network resources relative to directory traffic by decreasing the frequency in the replication schedule or increasing the site link cost so a site link corresponding to a higher bandwidth network connection is used. Make network connections with more bandwidth available to Active Directory by adding site links or site link bridges.
Directory information changed at domain controllers in one site is not being updated in domain controllers in other sites in a timely fashion.	Increase the frequency of intersite replication to make up-to-date information available. If the replication is occurring over a site link bridge, check which site link is restricting replication. Increase the time range during which replication can occur or the frequency of replication within the time frame for that site link.
Clients are having to request authentication, information, and services from a domain controller with a low-bandwidth connection, resulting in a slow response for authentication, directory information, or other services.	If there is a site that will serve a client's subnet well, associate that subnet with the site. If a client who is experiencing poor service is isolated from domain controllers, and you plan to create another site that will include the client, create a new site with its own domain controller. You can also install a connection with more bandwidth.

Problem: Received Event ID 1311 in the directory service log.

Replication is configured incorrectly: One or more domain controllers are offline. Bridgehead servers are online but experiencing errors replicating a required naming context between Active Directory sites. Preferred bridgehead servers defined by an administrator are online but do not host the required naming contexts. One or more sites are not contained in site links. Site links contain all sites but the site links are not all connected. Preferred bridgehead servers defined by an administrator are offline.	Ensure all sites belong to at least one site link. Make sure the site links provide a path between all domain controllers containing a replica of a given directory partition. Make sure "Bridge All Site Links" is set correctly. If you have manually assigned preferred bridgehead servers, make sure they are online.

Table 5-5   Active Directory Replication Troubleshooting Scenarios

Cause	Solution
Problem: Received Event ID 1265 with error "DNS Lookup Failure" or "RPC server is unavailable" in the directory service log; or received "DNS Lookup Failure" or "Target account name is incorrect" from the Repadmin command.	
These messages are often the result of DNS configuration problems.	Each domain controller must register its CNAME record for the *DsaGuid._msdcs.Forestname*. Each domain controller must register its A record in the appropriate zone. The A record must map to the domain controller. The records must replicate to DNS servers used by direct replication partners. Each DNS zone must have the proper delegations to child zones. The IP configuration of the domain controllers must contain correct preferred and alternate DNS servers.
Problem: Received Event ID 1265 "Access denied" in the directory service log. Or, received "Access denied" from the repadmin command.	
These errors can occur if the local domain controller fails to authenticate against its replication partner when creating the replication link or when trying to replicate over an existing link. This often happens when the domain controller has been disconnected from the rest of the network for a long time and its computer account password is not synchronized with the computer account password stored in the directory of its replication partner.	Stop the KDC service by typing **net stop KDC**. Purge the ticket cache on the local domain controller. Reset the domain controller's account password on the PDC emulator master by typing **netdom /resetpwd**. Synchronize the domain directory partition of the replication partner with the PDC emulator master. Manually force replication between the replication partner and the PDC emulator master. Start the KCC on the local domain controller by typing **net start KDC**.
Problem: Received "Access denied" from the Active Directory Sites And Services console when manual replication was attempted.	
Using the Active Directory Sites And Services console to force replication initiates replication on all common directory partitions between the replication partners. However, a user can force manual replication only for containers on which they have been assigned the Replication Synchronization permission. The replication of other directory partitions will fail, causing the error.	Use the Repadmin or Replmon command-line tools from Windows Support Tools to manually force replication of a specific directory partition.

Practice: Monitoring and Troubleshooting Active Directory Replication

In this practice, you use Replmon, Repadmin, and Dsastat to perform routine replication monitoring and troubleshooting tasks.

> **Note** To complete this practice, you must have successfully completed the practices in Lessons 2 and 3.

Exercise 1: Using Replmon

In this exercise, you practice using Replmon to do various monitoring and troubleshooting tasks.

▶ **To use Replmon**

1. Log on to Server1 as Administrator.

2. Use the procedure provided earlier in this lesson to start Replmon. Add Server1 and Server2 as monitored servers.

3. In the console tree, find the Columbus site. Find Server1 in the Columbus site. Note how the global catalog server is represented by a domain controller icon with a globe to the upper right.

4. Select Server1. Note how the status for the server appears in the details pane. In the console tree, expand Server1. Note how the directory partitions are represented by the book icon. Expand the directory partitions for Server1. Note how the replication partners are represented by an icon resembling a phone connection, which represents a bridgehead connection. Select one of the replication partners. Note how the status for the replication partner appears in the details pane.

5. Right-click Server1, point to Show Bridgehead Servers, and click In The Enterprise. Note the results on the Show Bridgehead Servers In Site dialog box.

6. Right-click Server1 and select Generate Status Report. In the Save As dialog box, type **New** in the File Name list, and then click Save. In the Report Options dialog box, click OK. Click OK in the Report Status message box. In the Active Directory Replication Monitor window, select File, and then click Open Log. In the Open dialog box, select the New.log file you just created, and then click Open. View the results of the status report.

Exercise 2: Using Repadmin

In this exercise, you use Repadmin to display the replication partners for a server, display the highest USN on the server, determine if the server is up-to-date with another server, display the connection objects for the server, and force replication between replication partners.

▶ **To use Repadmin**

1. On Server1, click Start, and then click Command Prompt.

2. At the command prompt, type **repadmin/showrepl server1.contoso.com** to display the replication partners for Server1. The objectGUID for the selected server and its replication partners and the InvocationID for the selected server are shown.

3. Type **repadmin/showutdvec server1.contoso.com dc=contoso,dc=com** to display the highest USN on the server.

4. Type **repadmin/showconn server1.contoso.com** to display the connection objects for Server1.

5. Type **repadmin/replicate server1.contoso.com server2.contoso.com dc=contoso,dc=com** to force replication between replication partners.

Exercise 3: Using Dsastat

In this exercise, you use Dsastat to compare the number of objects in the directory for the domain.

▶ **To use Dsastat**

1. Click Start, and then click Command Prompt.

2. At the command prompt, type **dsastat -s:server1;server2 -b:DC=contoso,DC=com -gcattrs:objectclass -p:999** to compare the number of objects in the directory for the domain. This search keeps a count of the different types of objects in each of the replicas and then compares the count for each object class.

Lesson Review

The following questions are intended to reinforce key information presented in this lesson. If you are unable to answer a question, review the lesson and then try the question again. Answers to the questions can be found in the "Questions and Answers" section at the end of this chapter.

1. What is the function of Replmon.exe?

_____

_____

2. What is the function of Repadmin.exe?

_____

_____

3. What is the function of Dsastat.exe?

_____

_____

4. If replication of directory information has stopped, what should you check?

_____

_____

5. You received Event ID 1265 with the error "DNS Lookup Failure." What are some actions you might take to remedy the error? (Choose all that apply.)

a. Manually force replication.

b. Reset the domain controller's account password on the PDC emulator master.

c. Check the domain controller's CNAME record.

d. Make sure "Bridge All Site Links" is set correctly.

e. Check the domain controller's A record.

Lesson Summary

- Windows Server 2003, Standard Edition, and Windows Server 2003, Enterprise Edition, provide Replmon.exe: Active Directory Replication Monitor, Repadmin.exe: Replication Diagnostics Tool, and Dsastat.exe for monitoring and troubleshooting replication. To use these tools, you must first install the Windows Support Tools on your computer.

- The Active Directory Replication Monitor (Replmon) enables administrators to view the low-level status of Active Directory replication, force synchronization between domain controllers, view the topology in a graphical format, and monitor the status and performance of domain controller replication through a graphical interface.

- The Replication Diagnostics Tool (Repadmin) allows you to view the replication topology as seen from the perspective of each domain controller and the replication metadata and up-to-datedness vectors. This tool can be used in troubleshooting to manually create the replication topology (although in normal practice this should not be necessary), and to force replication events between domain controllers.

- Dsastat.exe compares and detects differences between directory partitions on domain controllers and can be used to ensure that domain controllers are up-to-date with one another. The tool retrieves capacity statistics such as megabytes per server, objects per server, and megabytes per object class and compares the attributes of replicated objects.

Troubleshooting Lab

You are a network administrator for Contoso Pharmaceuticals. One of your domain controllers, Server2, had a hardware failure and was offline for over a month until a replacement component was located. You start Server2 and verify that you can connect to the administrative shares (C$ and admin$) on other domain controllers from Server2. Then, you try to synchronize the domain, but the attempt fails, producing an "Access denied" error message. You look in the Event Viewer's Directory Service log and see Event ID 1265 that reads "Access Denied." You want to resolve this issue without rebuilding the domain controller.

As described earlier in this chapter, this situation is common when domain controllers have been out of communication for a while. To correct this issue, you must reset the machine account password on your domain controller. To do this, you'll require both the Windows Support Tools and the Kerbtray.exe application. You should already have the Windows Support Tools on Server2. If you haven't installed them, use the instructions in Chapter 2 to install them. To install Kerbtray, follow these steps:

1. Log on to Server2 using the administrator user name and password.

2. Place the Supplemental CD-ROM in the CD-ROM drive of Server2.

3. Assuming your CD-ROM is letter D, click Start, click Run, type: **D:\70-294\Labs \Chapter05\Kerbtray_setup.ex e**, and press ENTER. The Microsoft Web Installation Wizard opens.

4. Click Next to begin the installation of Kerbtray.exe. Read the license agreement and click "I agree" (if you agree to the terms—otherwise you cannot continue this lab). Then click Next to proceed. The destination directory screen is displayed.

5. Because Kerbtray.exe requires only 656 KB to install, you shouldn't have to worry about drive space. Click Install Now. Click Finish once the installation is complete.

You are now ready to proceed with resetting the computer account on Server2. Imagine that Server1 is one of your existing domain controllers and Server2 is your recently repaired domain controller that has been offline for over a month.

1. Stop the Key Distribution Center (KDC) service on Server2. To do so, open a command prompt, type **net stop KDC**, and press ENTER.

2. Load Kerbtray.exe. You can do so by clicking Start, clicking Run, and then typing **c:\program files\resource kit\kerbtray.exe** and pressing ENTER. You should see a little green ticket icon in your system tray in the lower right corner of your desktop.

3. Purge the ticket cache on Server2, right-click the green ticket icon in your system tray, and then click Purge Tickets. You should receive a confirmation that your ticket cache was purged. Click OK.

4. Reset the Server2 domain controller account password on Server1 (the PDC emulator). To do so, open a command prompt and type:

   netdom /resetpwd / server:server2 /userd:contoso.com\administrator/passwordd:password, and then press ENTER.

5. Synchronize the domain. To do so, open a command prompt, type **repadmin/syncall**, and then press ENTER.

6. Start the KDC service on Server2. To do so, open a command prompt, type **net start KDC**, and press ENTER.

This completes the process, and the domain controllers should be replicating successfully now.

Case Scenario Exercise

You are a network administrator for City Power & Light (*http://www.cpandl.com*). City Power & Light has five different locations named Main, North, South, East, and West. The Main location has 350 employees. The North and East locations have 150 employees each. The South location has 100 employees. The West location is fairly new and has only five employees. Each employee has a client computer on the network. The offices are connected as a WAN utilizing leased digital lines with varying speeds as shown in Figure 5-23.

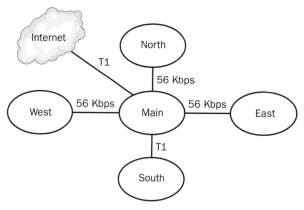

Figure 5-23 City Power & Light WAN connections

City Power & Light has a single Windows Server 2003 domain. There are two domain controllers at the Main location. No other domain controllers have been installed. There are two computers running Windows 2000 Server that are configured as member servers at each location. These servers are used for file sharing. All locations use the same applications and services. All client computers were recently upgraded from Microsoft Windows 98 to Microsoft Windows XP Professional. After the upgrade, users noticed some delay in logging on to the network.

Given this information, answer the following questions:

1. Assume that the company has only enough money to purchase two additional domain controllers. Which two locations would benefit most from those domain controllers?

   _____

   _____

2. Other than domain controllers, what services would you add to each location in order to speed up logons and directory access?

   _____

   _____

3. You've installed additional domain controllers at the North and East locations. Now you want to control replication between those new domain controllers and the domain controllers at the Main location. What should you do?

   _____

   _____

4. Backups are run every night between 10 P.M. and 4 A.M. At this time, all remote file server data is sent to the Main location. You want to ensure that Active Directory doesn't try to replicate data during those hours. What should you do?

   _____

   _____

5. The physical connection between East and Main was primarily used for logons. Now that East has its own site, the link is mainly used for replication traffic. City Power & Light pays for that connection by the minute. You just installed a new connection between East and North that doesn't carry a per-minute cost. You want replication to take place between East and North, but you cannot completely eliminate the connection between East and Main. You want the site link between East

and Main to be used only if the site link between East and North is unavailable. What should you do?

_____

_____

Chapter Summary

- A site is a set of IP subnets connected by a highly reliable and fast link (usually a LAN). Site structure mirrors the location of user communities. Sites have two main roles: to facilitate authentication and to replicate data between sites. Active Directory replicates information in two ways: intrasite (within a site) and intersite (between sites).

- For optimum network response time and application availability, place at least one domain controller in each site or two domain controllers in each domain.

- Intersite replication is replication that occurs between sites.

- A site link is a logical, transitive connection between two or more sites that mirrors the network links and allows replication to occur.

- Bridgehead servers are the contact point for exchange of directory information between sites. When two sites are connected by a site link, the KCC automatically selects bridgehead servers. You can designate bridgehead servers manually, called "preferred" bridgehead servers.

- A site link bridge is the linking of more than two sites for replication using the same transport. When more than two sites are linked for replication and use the same transport, by default, all of the site links are "bridged" in terms of cost, assuming the site links have common sites. If site link transitivity is enabled, which it is by default, creating a site link bridge has no effect. Therefore, it is seldom necessary to create site link bridges.

- A global catalog server is a domain controller that stores a full copy of all objects in the directory for its host domain and a partial copy of all objects for all other domains in the forest. For optimum network response time and application availability, designate at least one domain controller in each site as the global catalog server. To optimize replication in a multiple site environment, you might need to consider adding global catalogs for specific sites.

- Universal group membership caching, a new feature in Windows Server 2003, allows a site that does not contain a global catalog server to be configured to cache universal group memberships for users who log on to the domain controller in the site.

- An application directory partition is a directory partition that is replicated only to specific domain controllers running Windows Server 2003. Application directory partitions are usually created by the applications that use them to store and replicate data.

- Replmon.exe: Active Directory Replication Monitor, Repadmin.exe: Replication Diagnostics Tool, and Dsastat.exe are provided for monitoring and troubleshooting replication. To use these tools, you must first install the Windows Support Tools on your computer.

Exam Highlights

Before taking the exam, review the key points and terms that are presented in this chapter. You need to know this information.

Key Points

- A global catalog server is a domain controller that stores a full copy of all objects in the directory for its host domain and a partial copy of all objects for all other domains in the forest. For optimum network response time and application availability, designate at least one domain controller in each site as the global catalog server. To optimize replication in a multiple site environment, you might need to consider adding global catalogs for specific sites.

- Universal group membership caching allows a site that does not contain a global catalog server to be configured to cache universal group memberships for users who log on to the domain controller in the site. Use the universal group membership caching feature to eliminate the need to deploy global catalog servers into smaller remote office locations in order to avoid logon failures in the event that the network link connecting the remote site to the rest of the organization is disconnected.

- An application directory partition is a directory partition that is replicated only to specific domain controllers running Windows Server 2003. Use the Ntdsutil command-line tool to create or delete an application directory partition, add or remove an application directory partition replica, display application directory partition information, set a notification delay, prepare a cross-reference object, or set an application directory partition reference domain.

- To configure a site, you must create a site, create a subnet and associate it with the site, create or move a domain controller object into the site, and designate a site license server for the site.

- A site link is a logical, transitive connection between two or more sites that mirrors the network links and allows replication to occur. Site link replication frequency tells Active Directory how many minutes it should wait before using a connection to check for replication updates. Site link cost indicates the cost of the connection in relation to the speed of the link. Higher costs are used for slow links, and lower costs are used for fast links. A preferred bridgehead server is a server you manually designate to be a contact point for exchange of directory information between sites. You configure site links by using the Active Directory Sites And Services console.

■ Use Replmon.exe: Active Directory Replication Monitor, Repadmin.exe: Replication Diagnostics Tool, and Dsastat.exe to monitor and troubleshoot replication.

Key Terms

application directory partition   A directory partition that is replicated only to specific domain controllers. Only domain controllers running Windows Server 2003 can host a replica of an application directory partition. Applications and services can use application directory partitions to store application-specific data.

global catalog server   A domain controller running Windows Server 2003 that holds a copy of the global catalog for the forest.

preferred bridgehead server   A domain controller in a site, designated manually by the administrator, that is part of a group of bridgehead servers. Once designated, preferred bridgehead servers are used exclusively to replicate changes collected from the site. An administrator may choose to designate preferred bridgehead servers when there is a lot of data to replicate between sites, or to create a fault-tolerant topology. If one preferred bridgehead server is not available, the KCC automatically uses one of the other preferred bridgehead servers. If no other preferred bridgehead servers are available, replication does not occur to that site.

universal group membership caching   A feature in Windows Server 2003 that allows a site that does not contain a global catalog server to be configured to cache universal group memberships for users who log on to the domain controller in the site. This ability allows a domain controller to process user logon requests without contacting a global catalog server when a global catalog server is unavailable. The cache is refreshed periodically as determined in the replication schedule.

Questions and Answers

Page 5-9 **Lesson 1 Review**

1. What is a site?

   A site is a set of IP subnets connected by a highly reliable and fast link (usually a LAN).

2. Which directory partition replica type must be replicated to all domain controllers within the domain?

   The domain partition must be replicated to all domain controllers within the domain.

3. Which type of replication compresses data to save WAN bandwidth?

   Intersite replication compresses data to save WAN bandwidth.

4. What is the difference between a site link and a connection object?

   Site links are used by the KCC to determine replication paths between two sites and must be created manually. Connection objects actually connect domain controllers and are created by the KCC, though you can also create them manually if necessary.

5. Which of the following actions does not trigger replication?

   a. Accessing an object

   b. Creating an object

   c. Deleting an object

   d. Modifying an object

   e. Moving an object

   The correct answer is a. Creating, deleting, modifying, or moving an object triggers replication between domain controllers.

Page 5-23 **Lesson 2 Review**

1. What site is created automatically in the Sites container when you install Active Directory on the first domain controller in a domain?

   The Default-First-Site-Name site.

2. How many subnets must each site have? To how many sites can a subnet be assigned?

   Each site must have at least one subnet, but a subnet can be assigned to only one site.

3. What is the minimum number of domain controllers you should place in a site?

   For optimum network response time and application availability, place at least one domain controller for each domain available at each site.

4. What is the purpose of a site license server?

The site license server stores and replicates licensing information collected by the License Logging service on each server in a site.

5. Which of the following administrative tools is used to configure sites?

    a. Active Directory Users And Computers console

    b. Active Directory Domains And Trusts console

    c. Active Directory Sites And Services console

    d. Licensing console

The correct answer is c. The Active Directory Sites And Services console is used to configure sites.

Page
5-39
Lesson 3 Review

1. What object is created automatically in the IP container when you install Active Directory on the first DC in a domain?

The DEFAULTIPSITELINK site link.

2. You specified a preferred bridgehead server for your network. It fails and there are no other preferred bridgehead servers available. What is the result?

If no other preferred bridgehead servers are specified or no other preferred bridgehead servers are available, replication does not occur to that site even if there are servers that can act as bridgehead servers.

3. Why is it seldom necessary to create site link bridges?

If site link transitivity is enabled, which it is by default, creating a site link bridge has no effect. Therefore, it is seldom necessary to create site link bridges.

4. Which type of replication does the connection schedule control?

Intrasite replication.

5. Which of the following protocols should you use when network connections are unreliable?

    a. IP

    b. SMTP

    c. RPC

    d. DHCP

The correct answer is b. Choose SMTP replication when network connections are unreliable or not always available. SMTP site links communicate asynchronously, meaning each replication transaction does not need to complete before another can start, because the transaction can be stored until the destination server is available.

6. You have a high-speed T1 link and a dial-up network connection in case the T1 link is unavailable. You assign the T1 link to have a cost of 100. What cost value should you assign to the dial-up link?

   a. 0

   b. 50

   c. 100

   d. 150

The correct answer is d. Higher costs are used for slow links (the dial-up connection), and lower costs are used for fast links (the T1 connection). Because Active Directory always chooses the connection on a per-cost basis, the less expensive connection (T1) is used as long as it is available.

Page
5-46
Lesson 4 Review

1. What is the function of the global catalog?

   The global catalog performs three key functions:

   ❏ It enables users to log on to a network by providing universal group membership information to a domain controller when a logon process is initiated.

   ❏ It enables finding directory information regardless of which domain in the forest actually contains the data.

   ❏ It resolves UPNs when the authenticating domain controller does not have knowledge of the account.

2. What is a global catalog server?

   A global catalog server is a domain controller that stores a full copy of all objects in the directory for its host domain and a partial copy of all objects for all other domains in the forest.

3. What must you do to allow a domain controller to process user logon requests without contacting a global catalog server?

   Enable the universal group membership caching feature using Active Directory Sites And Services.

4. For optimum network response time, how many domain controllers in each site should you designate as a global catalog server?

   For optimum network response time and application availability, designate at least one domain controller in each site as the global catalog server.

5. The universal group membership caching feature is set for which of the following?

   a. Forest

   b. Domain

c. Site

d. Domain controller

The correct answer is c. The universal group membership caching feature must be set for each site and requires a domain controller to run a Windows Server 2003 operating system.

Page
5-57

Lesson 5 Review

1. What is an application directory partition?

An application directory partition is a directory partition that is replicated only to specific domain controllers. Only domain controllers running Windows Server 2003 can host a replica of an application directory partition.

2. Name the benefits of using an application directory partition.

Using an application directory partition provides redundancy, availability, or fault tolerance by replicating data to a specific domain controller or any set of domain controllers anywhere in the forest; it reduces replication traffic because the application data is only replicated to specific domain controllers; and applications or services that use LDAP can continue using it to access and store their application data in Active Directory.

3. What is a security descriptor and how is it used in an application directory partition?

A security descriptor is a set of access control information attached to a container or object that controls the type of access allowed by users, groups, and computers. When an object is created in an application directory partition, a default security descriptor reference domain is assigned when the application directory partition is created.

4. What considerations should you make before deleting an application directory partition?

Before deleting the application directory partition, you must identify the applications that use it, determine if it is safe to delete the last replica, and identify the partition deletion tool provided by the application.

5. Which of the following tools can you use to delete an application directory partition? (Choose all that apply.)

a. Ntdsutil command-line tool

b. Application-specific tools from the application vendor

c. Active Directory Installation Wizard

d. Active Directory Domains And Trusts console

e. Active Directory Sites And Services console

The correct answers are a, b, and c. To delete the application directory partition, you can use the Active Directory Installation Wizard to remove all application directory partition replicas from the domain controller, the tools provided with the application, or the Ntdsutil command-line tool.

Page
5-71 **Lesson 6 Review**

1. What is the function of Replmon.exe?

   Replmon.exe, the Active Directory Replication Monitor, enables administrators to view the low-level status of Active Directory replication, force synchronization between domain controllers, view the topology in a graphical format, and monitor the status and performance of domain controller replication through a graphical interface.

2. What is the function of Repadmin.exe?

   Repadmin.exe, the Replication Diagnostics Tool, allows you to view the replication topology as seen from the perspective of each domain controller. Repadmin.exe can be used in troubleshooting to manually create the replication topology (although in normal practice this should not be necessary), to force replication events between domain controllers, and to view the replication metadata and see how up-to-date a domain controller is.

3. What is the function of Dsastat.exe?

   Dsastat.exe compares and detects differences between directory partitions on domain controllers and can be used to ensure that domain controllers are up-to-date with one another. The tool retrieves capacity statistics such as megabytes per server, objects per server, and megabytes per object class, and compares the attributes of replicated objects.

4. If replication of directory information has stopped, what should you check?

   Site links. Make sure that a site link has been created from the current site to a site that is connected to the rest of the sites in the network.

5. You received Event ID 1265 with the error "DNS Lookup Failure." What are some actions you might take to remedy the error? (Choose all that apply.)

   a. Manually force replication.

   b. Reset the domain controller's account password on the PDC emulator master.

   c. Check the domain controller's CNAME record.

   d. Make sure "Bridge All Site Links" is set correctly.

   e. Check the domain controller's A record.

   The correct answers are c and e. This message is often the result of DNS configuration problems. Each domain controller must register its CNAME record for the *DsaGuid._msdcs.Forestname*. Each domain controller must register its A record in the appropriate zone. So, by checking the domain controller's CNAME and A records, you may be able to fix the problem.

Page
5-74 **Case Scenario Exercise**

1. Assume that the company has only enough money to purchase two additional domain controllers. Which two locations would benefit most from those domain controllers?

   The North and East locations have slow links and more users than the other locations. They could benefit most from an additional domain controller. The West and South locations may not even require additional domain controllers. The South location has a T1 link that may be sufficient for the amount of use that link receives. The West location has only five users. The five users may not be sending any more traffic over the WAN during logon than a domain controller would generate in replication traffic.

2. Other than domain controllers, what services would you add to each location in order to speed up logons and directory access?

DNS servers are used to locate domain controllers, so local DNS servers would help reduce logon delays. Because domain controllers running Windows Server 2003 can cache universal group membership information, you no longer need global catalog servers in each remote site.

3. You've installed additional domain controllers at the North and East locations. Now you want to control replication between those new domain controllers and the domain controllers at the Main location. What should you do?

Create sites for those locations. Create site links that connect each remote location to the Main location.

4. Backups are run every night between 10 P.M. and 4 A.M. At this time, all remote file server data is sent to the Main location. You want to ensure that Active Directory doesn't try to replicate data during those hours. What should you do?

Schedule the site link to be unavailable during those hours.

5. The physical connection between East and Main was primarily used for logons. Now that East has its own site, the link is mainly used for replication traffic. City Power & Light pays for that connection by the minute. You just installed a new connection between East and North that doesn't carry a per-minute cost. You want replication to take place between East and North, but you cannot completely eliminate the connection between East and Main. You want the site link between East and Main to be used only if the site link between East and North is unavailable. What should you do?

Create a site link between East and North. Configure a higher cost for the site link between East and Main than for East and North. This way, the lower cost connection between East and North will be preferred for the sake of replication.

6 Implementing an OU Structure

Exam Objectives in this Chapter:

- Plan an administrative delegation strategy.
- Plan an organizational unit (OU) structure based on delegation requirements.
- Plan an OU structure.
- Analyze the administrative requirements for an OU.
- Analyze the Group Policy requirements for an OU structure.
- Implement an OU structure.
- Create an OU.
- Move objects within an OU hierarchy.

Why This Chapter Matters

This chapter shows you how to plan and implement an OU structure. OUs are created to delegate administration, to administer Group Policy, and to hide objects. Creating OUs to delegate administration is the most important reason for creating an OU, and you should consider this before creating OUs to administer Group Policy or to hide objects. Administrative tasks for OUs, such as renaming, moving, and deleting OUs, and setting OU properties, are necessary tasks you must learn to maintain OUs.

Lessons in this Chapter:

Before You Begin

To complete the lessons in this chapter, you must

- Prepare your test environment according to the descriptions given in the "Getting Started" section of "About This Book"

- Complete the practices for installing and configuring Active Directory as discussed in Chapter 2, "Installing and Configuring Active Directory"

- Learn to use Active Directory administration tools as discussed in Chapter 3, "Administering Active Directory"

- Complete the practices for configuring sites and replication as discussed in Chapter 5, "Configuring Sites and Managing Replication"

Lesson 1: Understanding OUs

Understanding how OUs work is a prerequisite for the creation of OU structures and the administration of OUs. This lesson explains the reasons for defining OUs and introduces you to the principles of OU structure.

After this lesson, you will be able to

■ Identify the three reasons for defining an OU

■ Recognize the OU hierarchy models for delegation of administration

Estimated lesson time: 10 minutes

Understanding OUs

Recall that an *organizational unit (OU)* is a container used to organize objects within one domain into logical administrative groups. An OU can contain objects such as user accounts, groups, computers, printers, applications, shared folders, and other OUs from the same domain. OUs are represented by a folder icon with a book inside. The Domain Controllers OU is created by default when Active Directory is installed to hold new Microsoft Windows Server 2003 domain controllers. OUs can be added to other OUs to form a hierarchical structure; this process is known as *nesting OUs*. Each domain has its own OU structure—the OU structure within a domain is independent of the OU structures of other domains.

There are three reasons for defining an OU:

■ To delegate administration

■ To administer Group Policy

■ To hide objects

Defining OUs to Delegate Administration

The primary reason for defining an OU is to delegate administration. *Delegating administration* is the assignment of information technology (IT) management responsibility for a portion of the namespace, such as an OU, to an administrator, a user, or a group of administrators or users. In the Windows Server 2003 operating system, you can delegate administration for the contents of an OU (all users, computers, or resource objects in the OU) by granting administrators specific permissions for an OU on the OU's access control list. An *access control list (ACL)* is the mechanism for limiting access to certain items of information or certain controls based on users' identity and their membership in various groups. *Access control entries (ACEs)* in each ACL determine which users or groups can access the OU and what type of access they have.

ACLs and ACEs are discussed in more detail in Chapter 9, "Administering Active Directory Objects."

OU Hierarchy Models for Delegation of Administration

Once you determine the OUs needed for your organization, you can add OUs to other OUs to form a hierarchy of administrative control. Hierarchies consist of one layer of OUs, called *top-level OUs*, under which are arranged various layers of *second-level OUs*. Hierarchies for delegating administration can reflect the following organizational models:

- **Location**   This structure might be used if administration within a domain is handled by location, as shown in Figure 6-1. The top-level OUs—East and West—correspond to the regions set up for the *contoso.com* organization. The second-level OUs represent the physical locations of the company's four offices.

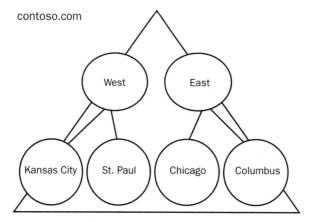

Figure 6-1   An OU structure based on location

- **Business function**   This structure might be used if administration within a domain is handled by business function, as shown in Figure 6-2. The top-level OUs—Admin, Devel, and Sales—correspond to *contoso.com*'s business divisions. The second-level OUs represent the functional divisions within the business divisions.

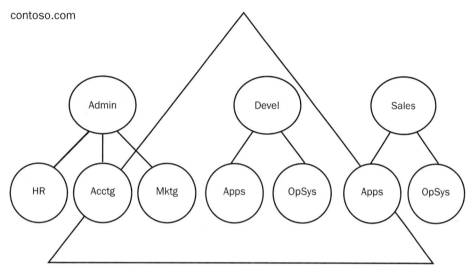

Figure 6-2   An OU structure based on business function

- **Object type**   This structure might be used if administration within a domain is handled by the types of objects being managed, as shown in Figure 6-3. The top-level OUs—Users, Computers, and Resources—correspond to the types of objects used at *contoso.com*. The second-level OUs represent further detailing of the object types.

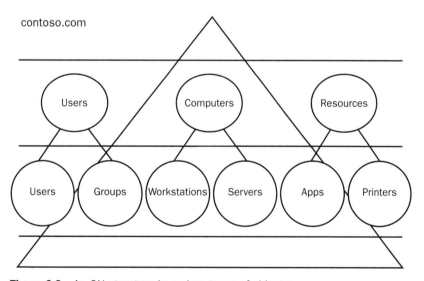

Figure 6-3   An OU structure based on types of objects

- **Combination**   This structure might be used if administration within a domain is handled by some combination of the location, business function, and object type hierarchy models, as shown in Figure 6-4. The top-level OUs—West and East—

correspond to the regions in which *contoso.com* has offices. The second-level OUs represent functional divisions within the company.

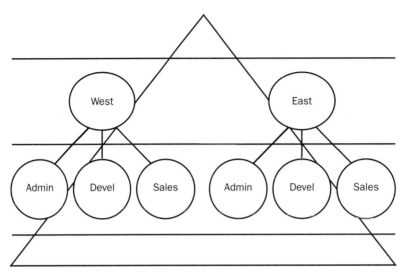

Figure 6-4   An OU structure based on location and business function

Types of Administrative Responsibility

There are two types of administrative responsibility you can delegate for an OU:

■ Full control

■ Control for object classes

By default, only domain administrators have full control over all objects in a domain. Domain administrators are responsible for creating the initial OU structure, repairing mistakes, and creating additional domain controllers. It is usually sufficient to allow only domain administrators full control over objects in a domain. However, if there are units in the organization that need to determine their own OU structure and administrative models, you can provide them with this permission by delegating full control.

> **Note**   For detailed information on delegating administrative control of Active Directory objects, including OUs, refer to Chapter 9, "Administering Active Directory Objects."

When determining whether to delegate full control for an OU, you must determine which areas in the organization need to be allowed to change OU properties and to create, delete, or modify any objects in the OU. If more restrictive control is appropriate, you can accomplish this by delegating control of specific object classes for an OU. Although there are many object classes in the schema, you need to consider only the object classes in which administrators will create objects. Such object classes typically include user account objects, computer account objects, group objects, and OU objects. When determining whether to delegate control of object classes, for each object class that your administrators will create in Active Directory, you must determine

- Which areas in the organization should be granted full control over objects of this class in the OU

- Which areas in the organization should be allowed to create objects of this class and thus have full control over these objects

- Which areas in the organization should be allowed to modify only specific attributes for or perform specific tasks pertaining to existing objects of this class

> **Note**   By default, all child objects in an OU inherit the permissions set on the OU.

Defining OUs to Administer Group Policy

Recall that *group policies* are collections of user and computer configuration settings that can be linked to computers, sites, domains, and OUs to specify the behavior of users' desktops. To create a specific desktop configuration for a particular group of users, you create *Group Policy Objects (GPOs)*, which are collections of Group Policy settings. By linking GPOs to OUs, GPOs can be applied to either users or computers in the OU. Group Policy is discussed in more detail in Chapter 11, "Administering Group Policy."

Defining OUs to Hide Objects

Your organization might require that certain domain objects, such as objects within an OU or OUs themselves, be hidden from certain users. For example, although a user might not have the permission to read an object's attributes, the user, if permitted to view the contents of the object's parent container, can still see that the object exists. You can hide objects in a domain by creating an OU for the objects and limiting the set of users who have the List Contents permission for that OU. Permissions are discussed in more detail in Chapter 9, "Administering Active Directory Objects."

> **Note**   Because there is only one way to delegate administration and there are multiple ways to administer Group Policy, you must define OU structures to delegate administration first. After an OU structure is defined to handle delegation of administration, you can define additional OUs to administer Group Policy or hide objects.

Designing OU Structures

You should design OUs for simplicity. Previous chapters emphasized the use of minimal numbers of forests and domains. However, it is likely that your domains will require a number of OUs to meet administrative requirements. The best practice is to begin with one OU and then add only those OUs that you can justify. Although you can have many levels of nested OUs, keep the number of levels to a minimum (fewer than seven) to avoid administrative and performance problems.

> **Real World   Nested OUs**
>
> You can find a wide variety of advice on how many levels down an OU structure is acceptable. Three to seven levels are probably the most common recommendations. However, some suggest that ten levels is still acceptable. The way in which you choose to configure and use the OU structure is probably of more concern than the actual number of levels. For example, a five-level nested OU structure with different group policies applied at each level would actually be more cumbersome than a seven-level OU hierarchy with fewer group policies applied. Logon and startup times increase when the system has more group policies to evaluate. Further, if you set different permissions on each OU in the hierarchy, troubleshooting could be considerably more difficult than if you had a structure with uniform (inherited) permissions applied. The point to keep in mind is to organize the OU structure to minimize the number of changes in permissions and to reduce the number of GPOs processed. When designing OU structures for your organization, it's also important to keep the following in mind:
>
> - OUs are not security principals. That is, you cannot assign access permissions based on a user's membership in an OU. Access control is the responsibility of global, domain local, or universal groups.
>
> - Users will not use the OU structure for navigation. Although users can see the OU structure of a domain, the most efficient way for users to find resources in Active Directory is to query the global catalog. Therefore, you should define OUs with administration, not users, in mind.

> **Exam Tip**   Be able to plan an OU structure. Know when to create an OU to delegate administration.

Lesson Review

The following questions are intended to reinforce key information presented in this lesson. If you are unable to answer a question, review the lesson and then try the question

again. Answers to the questions can be found in the "Questions and Answers" section at the end of this chapter.

1. What are the three reasons for defining an OU?

   _____

   _____

2. What is "delegating administration"?

   _____

   _____

3. What is the purpose of creating an OU to hide objects?

   _____

   _____

4. Can you assign access permissions based on a user's membership in an OU? Why or why not?

   _____

   _____

5. Which of the following is the primary reason for defining an OU?

   a. To delegate administration

   b. To hide objects

   c. To administer Group Policy

   d. To define the domain structure

Lesson Summary

- An OU is a container used to organize objects within one domain into logical administrative groups. OUs can be added to other OUs to form a hierarchical structure.

- There are three reasons for defining an OU: to delegate administration, to administer Group Policy, or to hide objects.

- Design OUs with administration, not users, in mind. Users will not use the OU structure for navigation. Design OUs for simplicity. The best practice is to begin with one OU and then add only those OUs that you can justify.

- OUs are not security principals—you cannot assign access permissions based on a user's membership in an OU. Access control is the responsibility of global, domain local, or universal groups.

Lesson 2: Creating an OU Structure

Each domain can implement its own OU hierarchy. If your enterprise contains several domains, you can create OU structures within each domain, independent of the structures in the other domains. This lesson walks you through the steps for creating an OU structure.

After this lesson, you will be able to

■ Create OUs

Estimated lesson time: 15 minutes

Creating OUs

Use the Active Directory Users And Computers console to create OUs.

To create OUs, complete the following steps:

1. Click Start, point to Administrative Tools, and then click Active Directory Users And Computers.

2. Right-click the location where you want to create this OU, which can be either a domain or another OU, point to New, and then click Organizational Unit.

3. In the New Object–Organizational Unit dialog box, shown in Figure 6-5, type the name of the new OU in the Name box, and then click OK.

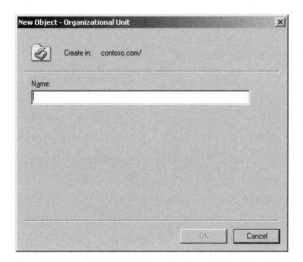

Figure 6-5   New Object–Organizational Unit dialog box

Off the Record   You can also use scripts to create, delete, and manage OUs. You can review some sample scripts for doing so on the Supplemental CD-ROM in the \70-294\Labs\Chapter06 folder. The CreateLabsOU.vbs script will create an OU named Labs in the *contoso.com* domain. The ViewDCMembers.vbs script lists the members of the Domain Controllers OU. Members of that OU are the Server1 and Server2 computer accounts. The DeleteLabsOU.vbs script removes the Labs OU from the *contoso.com* domain. To view the contents of any script, right-click the script and then click Edit.

Creating OUs to Hide Objects

Use the Active Directory Users And Computers console and the Security tab in the Properties dialog box for the OU to create OUs for the purpose of hiding objects. Only users who can modify the ACL on an OU are able to hide objects using this procedure.

To create an OU to hide objects, complete the following steps:

1. Create the OU where you will hide objects, as described in "Creating OUs."

2. Right-click the OU and select Properties.

3. In the Properties dialog box for the OU, click the Security tab.

Note   To view the Security tab in the Properties dialog box for an OU, you must select Advanced Features from the View menu on the Active Directory Users And Computers console.

4. In the Properties dialog box Security tab, shown in Figure 6-6, remove all existing permissions from the OU. Click Advanced.

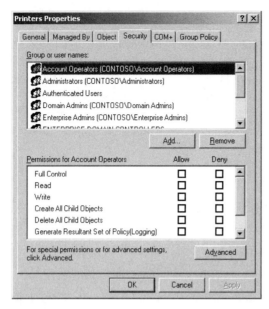

Figure 6-6   The Security tab of the Properties dialog box for an OU

5. In the Advanced Security Settings dialog box for the OU, clear the Allow Inheritable Permissions From The Parent To Propagate To This Object And All Child Objects check box.

6. In the Security message box, click Remove. Click OK.

7. In the Properties dialog box Security tab, identify the groups that you want to have full control on the OU. Grant those groups full control.

8. Identify the groups that should have generic read access on the OU and its contents. Grant those groups read access.

9. Identify any other groups that might need specific access, such as the right to create or delete a particular class of objects, on the OU. Grant those groups the specific access. Click OK.

10. Move the objects you want to hide into the OU.

Practice: Creating an OU

In this practice, you create the OU structure for the *contoso.com* domain.

Exercise 1: Planning an OU Structure

In this exercise, you plan an OU structure for Contoso Pharmaceuticals.

▶ **To plan an OU structure**

Contoso Pharmaceuticals has four locations: Chicago, Kansas City, St. Paul, and Columbus. The organization is divided into two regions, East and West, with Chicago and Columbus in the East region and Kansas City and St. Paul in the West region. The company has one domain, *contoso.com*. Some administrative decisions are handled by the IT department in each location, and each IT department reports to its regional IT department, which handles larger administrative decisions. Map the OU hierarchy for *contoso.com*.

Your map should be similar to Figure 6-1.

Exercise 2: Creating Top-Level OUs

In this exercise, you create top-level OUs for the *contoso.com* domain.

▶ **To create top-level OUs**

1. Log on to Server1 as Administrator.

2. On Server1, use the procedure provided earlier in this lesson to create the top-level OUs you planned in Exercise 1.

Exercise 3: Creating Second-Level OUs

In this exercise, you create second-level OUs for the *contoso.com* domain.

▶ **To create second-level OUs**

1. On Server1, use the procedure provided earlier in this lesson to create the second-level OUs you planned in Exercise 1.

2. The Active Directory Users And Computers console displays the OU structure for *contoso.com*, which is similar to the one shown in Figure 6-7.

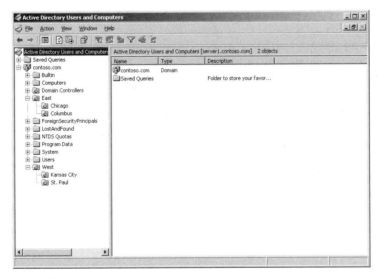

Figure 6-7   OU structure for contoso.com

Lesson Review

The following questions are intended to reinforce key information presented in this lesson. If you are unable to answer a question, review the lesson and then try the question again. Answers to the questions can be found in the "Questions and Answers" section at the end of this chapter.

1. In what two locations can you create an OU?

   _____

   _____

2. What tool do you use to create an OU?

   _____

   _____

3. What action must you take to be able to view the Security tab in the Properties dialog box for an OU?

   _____

   _____

4. How does the icon used for an OU differ from the icon used for a container?

   _____

   _____

Lesson Summary

- Use the Active Directory Users And Computers console to create an OU.

- You can create an OU within a domain or within another OU.

- Use the Active Directory Users And Computers console and the Security tab in the Properties dialog box for the OU to create OUs for the purpose of hiding objects.

Lesson 3: Administering OUs

This lesson introduces you to the tasks involved in the administration of OUs. These tasks help administrators to handle changes in the organization that affect OUs.

After this lesson, you will be able to

- ■ Rename OUs
- ■ Move OUs
- ■ Delete OUs
- ■ Set OU properties
- ■ Move objects between OUs

Estimated lesson time: 25 minutes

Administering OUs

The OU administration tasks include renaming, moving, and deleting OUs; setting OU properties; and moving objects between OUs.

Renaming, Moving, and Deleting OUs

To meet the changing needs of your organization, you might find it necessary to rename, move, or delete an OU.

> **Caution**   If you decide to delete an OU that contains objects, all of the objects that are in the OU are also deleted.

To rename an OU, complete the following steps:

1. Click Start, point to Administrative Tools, and then click Active Directory Users And Computers.

2. Expand the domain.

3. Right-click the OU you want to rename, and then click Rename.

4. Type the new OU name over the existing site name. Click in an empty part of the console tree.

To move an OU, complete the following steps:

1. Click Start, point to Administrative Tools, and then click Active Directory Users And Computers.

2. Expand the domain.

3. Click the OU you want to move, drag it to the desired location, and then release. Note that, under Windows Server 2003 with Service Pack 1 (SP1), a warning message appears explaining that moving objects in Active Directory can prevent your existing system from working the way it was designed. When you click Yes on the warning message, the OU reappears in the new location.

> **Note**   You can use the Active Directory Users And Computers console to move OUs only within a domain. To move OUs between domains, you must use Movetree.exe: Active Directory Object Manager. For more information about using Movetree.exe, refer to Windows Support Tools Help.

To delete an OU, complete the following steps:

1. Click Start, point to Administrative Tools, and then click Active Directory Users And Computers.

2. Expand the domain.

3. Right-click the OU you want to delete, and then click Delete.

4. In the Active Directory message box, click Yes.

5. If the OU contains objects, an additional Active Directory message box appears. Click Yes to delete the OU and the objects it contains.

Setting OU Properties

To provide additional information about the OU or to assist in finding the OU, you might want to set properties for an OU. The General and Managed By tabs in the Properties dialog box for each OU contain information about the OU. The General tab, shown in Figure 6-8, contains the OU's description, street address, city, state or province, ZIP code or postal code, and country or region. You can search for the OU by description if it is entered here.

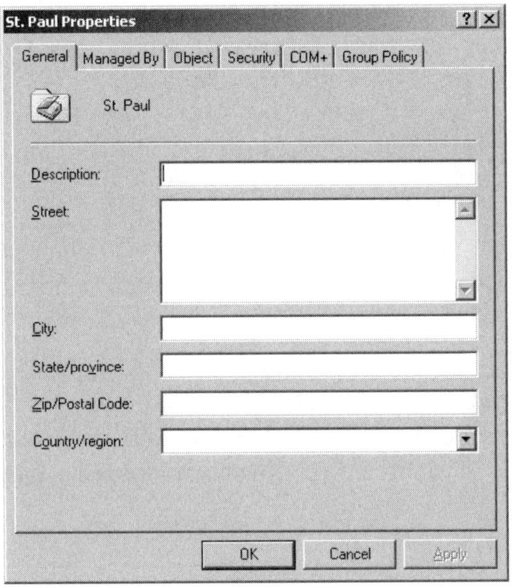

Figure 6-8   Properties dialog box for an OU, General tab

The Managed By tab, shown in Figure 6-9, contains the OU manager's name, office location, street address, city, state or province, country or region, telephone number, and fax number. If you type the manager's fully qualified domain name (FQDN) in the Name box in this tab, and you have previously entered information in the Properties dialog box for the user, the information is automatically pulled into the Managed By tab.

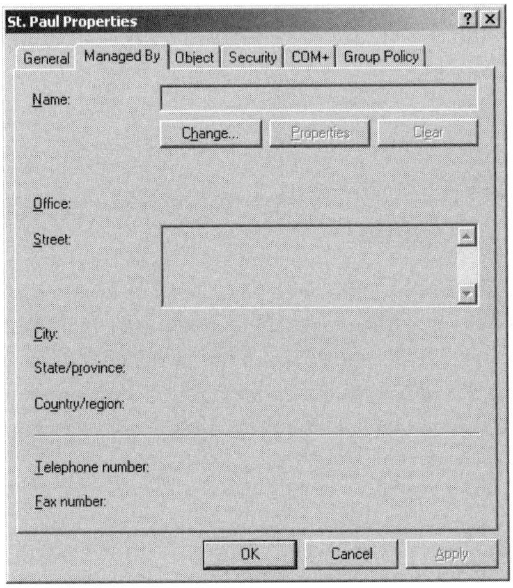

Figure 6-9   Properties dialog box for an OU, Managed By tab

To set properties for an OU, complete the following steps:

1. Click Start, point to Administrative Tools, and then click Active Directory Users And Computers.

2. Expand the domain.

3. Right-click the appropriate OU, and then click Properties.

4. Click the appropriate tab for the OU properties that you want to enter or change, and then type values for each property. Click OK.

Moving Objects Between OUs

When you move objects between OUs in a domain, permissions that are assigned directly to objects remain the same, and the objects inherit permissions from the new OU. Any permissions that were previously inherited from the old OU no longer affect the objects.

> **Note**   To simplify assignment of permissions for printers, move printers on different print servers that require identical permissions to the same OU. Printers are located in the computer object for the print server. To view a printer, click View, and then click Users, Groups, And Computers As Containers.

There are three ways to move Active Directory objects between OUs:

- Use drag and drop.
- Use the Move option on the Active Directory Users And Computers console.
- Use the Dsmove command-line tool.

Using Drag and Drop

You can move objects between OUs by selecting them in the source OU, dragging them to the target OU, and then dropping them.

> **Note**   Under Windows Server 2003 SP1, a warning message appears explaining that moving objects in Active Directory can prevent your existing system from working the way it was designed. You can dismiss the warning dialog box for the duration of the session. However, the dialog box will appear again the next time that you start Active Directory Users and Computers.

To use drag and drop to move objects between OUs, complete the following steps:

1. Click Start, point to Administrative Tools, and then click Active Directory Users And Computers.

2. Expand the domain, and then expand the source OU.

3. In the details pane, click the object you want to move in the source OU, drag it to the target OU in the console tree, and then release. Under Windows Server 2003 SP1, a warning message appears explaining that moving objects in Active Directory can prevent your existing system from working the way it was designed. When you click Yes in the warning dialog box, the object reappears in the new location.

Using the Move Option

To meet the needs of your organization, you might need to move only a few users or you might need to move entire groups between OUs. However, you use the Move option in the same way regardless of the objects you are moving.

To use the Move option to move objects between OUs, complete the following steps:

1. In Active Directory Users And Computers, right-click the object to move, and then select Move.

Note   You can move multiple objects at the same time by holding down the CTRL key as you select the objects, and then right-clicking and selecting Move.

2. In the Move dialog box, shown in Figure 6-10, select the OU or container to which you want the object to move, and then click OK.

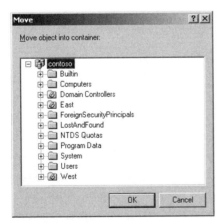

Figure 6-10   The Move dialog box

Using the Dsmove Command-Line Tool

Dsmove is a command-line tool that enables you to move objects between OUs. By using Dsmove, you can also rename a single object without moving it in the directory tree.

The syntax for Dsmove is

```
dsmove ObjectDN [-newname NewName] [- newparent ParentDN] [{-s Server | -d Domain}]
[-u UserName] [-p {Password|*}] [-q] {- uc | -uco | -uci}
```

Each of the command parameters is explained in Table 6-1.

Table 6-1   Dsmove Command Parameters

Parameter	Function
ObjectDN	Specifies the distinguished name of the object you want to move or rename. This parameter is required.
-newname *NewName*	Renames the object with a new relative distinguished name.
-newparent *ParentDN*	Specifies the new location to which you want to move the object. The new location is specified as the distinguished name of the new parent node.
{-s *Server* | -d *Domain*}	Connects to a specified remote server or domain. By default, the computer is connected to the domain controller in the logon domain.
-u *UserName*	Specifies the user name with which the user logs on to a remote server. By default, the logged on user name is used. You can specify a user name using one of the following formats: user name (such as *linda*), domain\user name (such as *contoso\linda*), user principal name (such as *linda@contoso.com*).
-p {*Password* | *}	Specifies to use either a password or a (*) to log on to a remote server. If you type *, then you are prompted for a password.
-q	Suppresses all output to standard output (quiet mode).
-uc	Specifies a Unicode format for input from or output to a pipe (|).
-uco	Specifies a Unicode format for output to a pipe (|) or a file.
-uci	Specifies a Unicode format for input from a pipe (|) or a file.

If a value that you supply contains spaces, use quotation marks around the text (for example, "CN=User One,CN=Users,DC=Contoso,DC=Com"). If you supply multiple values for a parameter, use spaces to separate the values (for example, a list of distinguished names).

■ To move User One from the Sales OU to the Marketing OU, type:

```
dsmove "CN=User One,OU=Sales,DC=Contoso,DC=Com" -newparent
OU=Marketing,DC=Contoso,DC=Com
```

- To rename a user object from User One to User Two, type:

  ```
  dsmove "CN=User One,OU=Sales,DC=Contoso,DC=Com" -newname "User Two"
  ```

- To combine the move and rename operations, type:

  ```
  dsmove "CN=User One,OU=Sales,DC=Contoso,DC=Com" -newparent
  OU=Marketing,DC=Contoso,DC=Com -newname "User Two"
  ```

To use Dsmove to move objects between OUs, complete the following steps:

1. Click Start, and then click Command Prompt.

2. At the command prompt, type **dsmove** and the appropriate parameters.

> **Exam Tip**   Be able to move objects within an OU hierarchy.

Practice: Administering OUs

In this practice, you administer OUs.

> **Note**   To complete this practice, you must have successfully completed the exercises in Lesson 2.

Exercise 1: Renaming, Deleting, and Moving OUs

In this exercise, you rename the East OU, delete and re-create the St. Paul OU, and move the Kansas City OU.

▶ **To rename, delete, and move OUs**

1. Use the procedure provided earlier in this lesson to rename the East OU as the North OU. Rename the new North OU back to the East OU.

2. Use the procedure provided earlier in this lesson to delete the St. Paul OU. Use the procedure provided in Lesson 2 to re-create the St. Paul OU.

3. Use the procedure provided earlier in this lesson to move the St. Paul OU to the East OU. Move the St. Paul OU back to the West OU.

Exercise 2: Setting OU Properties

In this exercise, you set OU properties for the East and West OUs.

▶ **To set OU properties**

1. Use the procedure provided earlier in this lesson to set OU properties for the East OU.

2. Use the procedure provided earlier in this lesson to set OU properties for the West OU.

Exercise 3: Moving Objects Between OUs

In this exercise, you move users, groups, and OUs between OUs by using the Move option and the Dsmove command-line tool.

▶ **To move objects between OUs**

1. Log on to Server1 as Administrator.

2. On Server1, use the procedure provided earlier in this lesson to perform the following moves by using drag and drop or the Move option:

   ❏ Move User11, User13, User15, User17, and User19 from the KC OU to the St. Paul OU and back to the KC OU.

   ❏ Move the West OU into the East OU as a second-level OU and back into the *contoso.com* domain as a first-level OU.

   ❏ Move User7 from the Chicago OU to the Columbus OU, and then back to the Chicago OU.

3. On Server1, use the procedure provided earlier in this lesson to move User9 from the Chicago OU to the Columbus OU by using the Dsmove command-line tool.

4. What command did you use to move User9 from the Chicago OU to the Columbus OU?

   ```
   Dsmove "CN=User Nine,OU=Chicago,OU=East,DC=Contoso,DC=Com"
   -newparent OU=Columbus,OU=East,DC=Contoso,DC=Com
   ```

Lesson Review

The following questions are intended to reinforce key information presented in this lesson. If you are unable to answer a question, review the lesson and then try the question again. Answers to the questions can be found in the "Questions and Answers" section at the end of this chapter.

1. What is the purpose of setting properties for an OU?

   _____

   _____

2. Why might you need to move an OU?

   _____

   _____

3. Which is more flexible, domain structure or OU structure?

   _____

   _____

4. What are the three ways to move Active Directory objects between OUs?

_____

_____

5. What happens to permissions when you move objects between OUs?

_____

_____

Lesson Summary

- Use the Active Directory Users And Computers console to rename, move within a domain, and delete OUs. If you delete an OU that contains objects, all of the objects that are in the OU are also deleted.

- There are three ways to move Active Directory objects between OUs: 1) use drag and drop, 2) use the Move option on the Active Directory Users And Computers console, and 3) use the Dsmove command.

- When you move objects between OUs in a domain, permissions that are assigned directly to objects remain the same, and the objects inherit permissions from the new OU. Any permissions that were previously inherited from the old OU no longer affect the objects.

Case Scenario Exercise

You are the domain administrator for City Power & Light (*http://www.cpandl.com*), as introduced in the Case Scenario Exercise of Chapter 5. City Power & Light now has three Active Directory sites, as shown in Figure 6-11. The North and East sites have one domain controller each and the Main site has two domain controllers. All locations contain client computers running Microsoft Windows XP Professional. All servers running Microsoft Windows 2000 were upgraded to Windows Server 2003. The number of employees at each location has not changed.

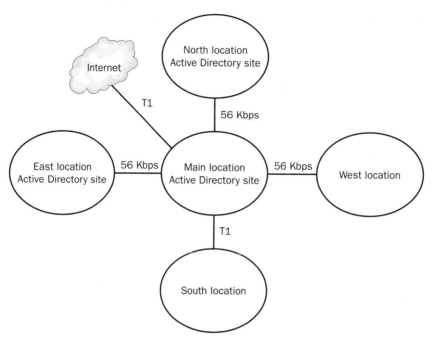

Figure 6-11   City Power & Light Active Directory infrastructure

City Power & Light still has a single Windows 2003 domain. There are three different offices in the Main location. These offices are named Accounting, Human Resources, and Operations. Each location (except Main) is also an office. The offices are named after their geographic location (North, South, East, and West).

Given this information, answer the following questions:

1. Each office with more than 100 users is allowed to hire its own network administrator. Network administrators should be allowed to create, delete, rename, reset, and manage the user accounts and computer accounts of those offices. Currently, the East, North, and Operations offices have more than 100 users apiece. What should you do?

   _____

   _____

2. The North, South, East, and West offices all require the same specialized software. However, none of the other offices require this software. What are ways in which you can organize the Active Directory structure to accommodate these requirements while distributing the software using Group Policy?

   _____

   _____

3. A total of 50 contracted employees are hired to work in the Operations office. They require different software than the rest of the users in the Operations office. Furthermore, the manager of the Operations office wants you to lock down specific portions of their desktops. The network administrator of the Operations OU needs your help. You must ensure that the network administrator of the Operations OU can manage these users and their computers. What should you do?

_____

_____

Troubleshooting Lab

You are a network administrator for Contoso Pharmaceuticals. You were recently on vacation for a week, and during your absence, two people were assigned to handle your daily tasks. One of those tasks was to create an OU named Accounting. Due to a communications error, both people performed this task. Each did so at a different domain controller. When you return to work, you are told about the situation and then shown what they believe to be corrupted data in the Active Directory database. They need your help to figure out what happened and determine what to do about it.

In order to see this issue, you must first create the problem. To do so, complete the following steps:

1. Unplug the network cable from the network card of Server2 to ensure that the servers are not able to replicate while you complete these steps.

2. Log on to Server1 using the domain administrator's user name and password.

3. Open the Active Directory Users And Computers console.

4. Create a new OU named Accounting in the _contoso.com_ domain.

5. Once you see the Accounting OU in _contoso.com_, unplug the network cable from the network interface card of Server1. Reconnect the network cable that you removed from Server2. The network cable of Server1 should be unplugged and the network cable of Server2 should be connected.

6. Log on to Server2 using the domain administrator's user name and password.

7. Open the Active Directory Users And Computers console. This will take awhile, so be patient.

8. You'll see an error indicating that naming information cannot be located. Click OK. The Active Directory Users And Computers console opens.

9. Right-click the Active Directory Users And Computers object in the console. Then click Connect To Domain Controller.

10. Type **Server2** into the Enter The Name Of Another Domain Controller text box and click OK. Click Yes to confirm that you'd like to make this connection. It will take a few moments to make the connection.

Off the Record   If you ever see an error when initializing a domain management console, you should investigate the reason for the error. You should also make arrangements to ensure that no two administrators attempt to perform the same administrative tasks at different sites (that is, on different domain controllers). Otherwise, problems might occur that are difficult to correct. For example, two administrators moving the same server object in Active Directory Sites and Services, but from two different geographical locations, are likely to cause a problem that would require Ntdsutil and Metadata cleanup. You learned about Metadata cleanup in Chapter 3.

11. Click Refresh or press the F5 key after about 60 seconds and you should see the *contoso.com* domain load.

12. Create an OU named Accounting. Although the console will run a bit slower, you should be able to perform this task. This is a different Accounting OU than you just created on Server1. You will see this once the two servers have synchronized.

13. Once the Accounting OU has been created, insert the network cable of Server1. Now both Server1 and Server2 will replicate. Wait a couple of minutes.

14. Return to Server1. Close and then reopen the Active Directory Users And Computers console. You should see two new OUs: one named Accounting and the other named Accounting with some additional characters, including a box and the letters CNF followed by a colon and 32 hexadecimal digits.

This is what happens when two administrators create objects with the same name at two different locations. This is not corrupted data, but rather a data collision. Two Lightweight Directory Access Protocol (LDAP) objects cannot have the same names in the directory structure, so Active Directory has renamed the object created last with a name that won't conflict with the object created first. You may simply delete the object with the really long name. Of course, if the object with the really long name contained other resources that were supposed to be part of your domain, you'd first move those resources to the appropriate containers.

Note   Although you caused the replication delay by unplugging the domain controllers, you'd typically find replication delays in environments utilizing sites. The default replication interval of 180 minutes and the potential for a replication schedule that prevents servers from replicating immediately make such issues more likely to occur.

Chapter Summary

- An OU is a container used to organize objects within one domain into logical administrative groups. OUs can be added to other OUs to form a hierarchical structure.

- There are three reasons for defining an OU: to delegate administration, to administer Group Policy, and to hide objects.

- Design OUs with administration, not users, in mind. Users will not use the OU structure for navigation. OUs are not security principals—you cannot assign access permissions based on a user's membership in an OU. Design OUs for simplicity. The best practice is to begin with one OU and then add only those OUs that you can justify.

- Use the Active Directory Users And Computers console to create an OU. You can create an OU within a domain or within another OU.

- The OU administration tasks include renaming, moving, and deleting OUs, setting OU properties, and delegating control of OUs.

- Use the Active Directory Users And Computers console to rename, move within a domain, and delete OUs. If you delete an OU that contains objects, all of the objects that are in the OU are also deleted.

- Use the Active Directory Users And Computers console to set properties for an OU. Properties provide additional information about the OU or assist in finding the OU.

- Use drag and drop, the Move option on the Active Directory Users And Computers console, or the Dsmove command to move Active Directory objects between OUs. When you move objects between OUs in a domain, permissions that are assigned directly to objects remain the same, and the objects inherit permissions from the new OU. Any permissions inherited from the old OU no longer affect the objects.

Exam Highlights

Before taking the exam, review the key points and terms that are presented in this chapter. You need to know this information.

Key Points

- The primary reason for defining an OU is to delegate administration. Delegating administration is the assignment of IT management responsibility for a portion of the namespace, such as an OU, to an administrator, a user, or a group of administrators or users.

- You should design OUs for simplicity. It is likely that your domains will require a number of OUs to meet administrative requirements. The best practice is to begin with one OU and then add only those OUs that you can justify. Define OUs with administration, not users, in mind.

- By linking GPOs to OUs, GPOs can be applied to either users or computers in the OU. Because there is only one way to delegate administration and there are multiple ways to administer Group Policy, you must define OU structures to delegate administration first. After an OU structure is defined to handle delegation of administration, you can define additional OUs to administer Group Policy.

- You cannot assign access permissions based on a user's membership in an OU. OUs are not security principals. Access control is the responsibility of global, domain local, or universal groups.

- You move objects within an OU hierarchy by using drag and drop, the Move option on the Active Directory Users And Computers console, or the Dsmove command.

Key Terms

access control list (ACL)   The mechanism for limiting access to certain items of information or to certain controls based on users' identity and their membership in various predefined groups. An ACL is typically used by system administrators for controlling user access to network resources such as servers, directories, and files and is typically implemented by granting permissions to users and groups for access to specific objects.

nested OUs   The creation of organizational units (OUs) within OUs.

organizational unit (OU)   An Active Directory container object used within a domain. An OU is a logical container into which you can place users, groups, computers, and other OUs. It can contain objects only from its parent domain. An OU is the smallest scope to which you can apply a Group Policy or delegate authority.

Questions and Answers

Page
6-8
Lesson 1 Review

1. What are the three reasons for defining an OU?

   The three reasons for defining an OU are to delegate administration, to administer Group Policy, or to hide objects.

2. What is "delegating administration"?

   Delegating administration is the assignment of IT management responsibility for a portion of the namespace, such as an OU, to an administrator, a user, or a group of administrators or users.

3. What is the purpose of creating an OU to hide objects?

   Although a user might not have the permission to read an object's attributes, the user can still see that the object exists by viewing the contents of the object's parent container. You can hide objects in a domain by creating an OU for the objects and limiting the set of users who have the List Contents permission for that OU.

4. Can you assign access permissions based on a user's membership in an OU? Why or why not?

   No, you cannot assign access permissions based on a user's membership in an OU. OUs are not security principals. Access control is the responsibility of global, domain local, or universal groups.

5. Which of the following is the primary reason for defining an OU?

   a. To delegate administration

   b. To hide objects

   c. To administer Group Policy

   d. To define the domain structure

   The correct answer is a. Although hiding objects and administering Group Policy are reasons for defining an OU, they are not the primary reason. You do not define an OU to define the domain structure.

Page
6-14
Lesson 2 Review

1. In what two locations can you create an OU?

   You can create an OU within a domain or within another OU.

2. What tool do you use to create an OU?

   The Active Directory Users And Computers console is used to create an OU.

3. What action must you take to be able to view the Security tab in the Properties dialog box for an OU?

You must select Advanced Features from the View menu on the Active Directory Users And Computers console.

4. How does the icon used for an OU differ from the icon used for a container?

The icon used for an OU is a folder with a book. The icon used for a container is a folder.

Page 6-22

Lesson 3 Review

1. What is the purpose of setting properties for an OU?

To provide additional information about the OU or to assist in finding the OU, you might want to set properties for an OU.

2. Why might you need to move an OU?

To accommodate the changing needs of an organization.

3. Which is more flexible, domain structure or OU structure?

Because OUs can be easily renamed, moved, and deleted, OU structure is more flexible than domain structure.

4. What are the three ways to move Active Directory objects between OUs?

There are three ways to move Active Directory objects between OUs:

❑ Use drag and drop

❑ Use the Move option on the Active Directory Users And Computers console

❑ Use the Dsmove command

5. What happens to permissions when you move objects between OUs?

Permissions that are assigned directly to objects remain the same, and the objects inherit permissions from the new OU. Any permissions that were previously inherited from the old OU no longer affect the objects.

Page 6-23

Case Scenario Exercise

1. Each office with more than 100 users is allowed to hire its own network administrator. Network administrators should be allowed to create, delete, rename, reset, and manage the user accounts and computer accounts of those offices. Currently, the East, North, and Operations offices have more than 100 users apiece. What should you do?

Create an OU for East, North, and Operations. Create a user account for each new administrator. Place all of the user and computer accounts for each office into their respective OUs. Delegate administrative rights to the new administrators to their respective office OUs.

2. The North, South, East, and West offices all require the same specialized software. However, none of the other offices require this software. What are ways in which you can organize the Active Directory structure to accommodate these requirements while distributing the software using Group Policy?

   Because you already have East and North OUs, you could create additional OUs for West and South. Then, you could distribute the software to each of these OUs by creating a single GPO and linking it to all four OUs. The other option is to place each OU inside a single OU. For example, you could create an OU named Remote and then place the North, South, East, and West OUs inside the Remote OU. Then you could assign a GPO that distributed the software to the Remote OU, which in turn would flow down to the separate locations. Probably the best way would be to use the first method, linking the GPO here to each individual OU. Flatter OU structures are easier to manage and troubleshoot. Further, Group Policy processing occurs more quickly on flat OU structures.

3. A total of 50 contracted employees are hired to work in the Operations office. They require different software than the rest of the users in the Operations office. Furthermore, the manager of the Operations office wants you to lock down specific portions of their desktops. The network administrator of the Operations OU needs your help. You must ensure that the network administrator of the Operations OU can manage these users and their computers. What should you do?

   The most efficient option is to create a new OU. For example, you could create an OU named Contractors that is subordinate to (within) the Operations OU. The network administrator of the Operations OU would then inherit the ability to manage the Contractors OU. Then, you'd use Group Policy to assign the specific software and desktop lockdown policies that are required to meet the needs of these contracted employees.

7 Administering User Accounts

Exam Objectives in this Chapter:

- Plan a user authentication strategy.
- Plan a smart card authentication strategy.

Why This Chapter Matters

This chapter shows you how to work with user accounts. As a network administrator, you'll undoubtedly have to create, modify, delete, and troubleshoot issues with user accounts. To perform these tasks effectively, you'll need to know the different types of user accounts, such as local, domain user, and built-in accounts. You must also understand the differences in the way these accounts are authenticated as well as the system rights and permissions these accounts have by default.

You may also need to establish standards for the appearance and consistency of users' desktops and data. In order to do so, you must understand how to manage user properties and user profiles. For example, you should know the differences between the types of user profiles: local, roaming, and mandatory. You should also know how and when to use each type.

User account security is an important consideration in the management of user accounts. You need to understand how to create and enforce secure password and account policies in order to help protect your network from compromise. You should understand how smart cards could be used to alleviate some of the common problems with passwords and reduce the chances of user account compromise.

Lessons in this Chapter:

Before You Begin

To complete the lessons in this chapter, you must

- Prepare your test environment according to the descriptions given in the "Getting Started" section of "About This Book"

- Complete the practices for installing and configuring Active Directory as discussed in Chapter 2, "Installing and Configuring Active Directory"

- Learn to use Active Directory administration tools as discussed in Chapter 3, "Administering Active Directory"

- Complete the practices for configuring sites and replication as discussed in Chapter 5, "Configuring Sites and Managing Replication"

- Complete the practices for implementing an organizational unit (OU) structure as discussed in Chapter 6, "Implementing an OU Structure"

Lesson 1: Understanding User Accounts

Before you can create user accounts or user profiles, you must understand the types of user accounts and the information necessary to create them. This lesson introduces you to the various types of user accounts, user account naming conventions, and user account password requirements.

After this lesson, you will be able to

- Describe the difference between a local user account and a domain user account
- Describe the purpose of the built-in accounts
- Explain the purpose of user account naming conventions
- Explain the user account password requirements
- Explain how smart cards are used to authenticate users

Estimated lesson time: 10 minutes

Understanding User Accounts

A *user account* is a record that consists of all the information that defines a user to Microsoft Windows Server 2003. This includes the user name and password required for the user to log on, the groups in which the user account has membership, and the rights and permissions the user has for using the computer and network and accessing their resources. A user account provides a user with the ability to log on to a computer to gain access to resources on that computer or to log on to a domain to gain access to network resources. Each person who regularly uses a computer or the network should have a unique user account.

In Windows Server 2003, authentication for domain users is based on user accounts in Active Directory. *Authentication* confirms the identity of any user trying to log on to a domain or to access network resources. Windows Server 2003 authentication enables single sign-on to all network resources. With single sign-on, a user can log on to the client computer once, using a single password or smart card, and authenticate to any computer in the domain. To provide security for a network running Windows Server 2003, you must provide access for legitimate users but screen out potential intruders. This means you must set up your security features to authenticate all user access to system resources. Authentication protects against intruders trying to steal identities or impersonate users.

User Account Types

Windows Server 2003 provides three types of user accounts: local user accounts, domain user accounts, and built-in user accounts. With a *local user account*, a user logs on to a specific computer to gain access to resources on that computer. With a *domain user account,* a user can log on to a domain to gain access to network resources. *Built-in user accounts* are created automatically by Windows Server 2003 for the purpose of performing administrative tasks or to gain access to network resources. This training kit focuses on domain user accounts.

Local User Accounts

Local user accounts allow users to log on to, and gain access to resources on, only the computer where the local user account is created. When you create a local user account, as shown in Figure 7-1, Windows Server 2003 creates the account only in that computer's security database, which is called the local security database. Windows Server 2003 does not replicate local user account information to domain controllers. After a local user account is created, the computer uses its local security database to authenticate the local user account, which allows the user to log on to that computer.

Figure 7-1   Local user account

Do not create local user accounts on computers that require access to domain resources, because the domain does not recognize local user accounts. Therefore, the user is unable to gain access to resources in the domain.

Domain User Accounts

Domain user accounts allow users to log on to a domain and gain access to resources anywhere on the network. The user provides his or her user name and password during the logon process. By using this information, Windows Server 2003 authenticates the user and then builds an access token that contains information about the user and security settings. The access token identifies the user to computers running Windows Server 2003 and computers running pre-Windows Server 2003 operating systems on which the user tries to gain access to resources. Windows Server 2003 provides the access token for the duration of the logon session.

You create a domain user account in a container or an OU in the copy of the Active Directory database (called the directory) on a domain controller, as shown in Figure 7-2. The domain controller replicates the new user account information to all domain controllers in the domain.

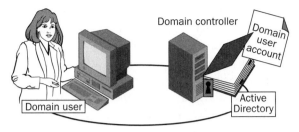

Figure 7-2   Domain user account

After Windows Server 2003 replicates the new user account information, all of the domain controllers in the domain tree can authenticate the user during the logon process.

> **Note**   It can take a few minutes to replicate the domain user account information to all domain controllers. This delay might prevent a user from immediately logging on using the newly created domain user account. By default, replication of directory information within a site occurs every five minutes.

Built-In User Accounts

Windows Server 2003 automatically creates accounts called built-in accounts. Two commonly used built-in accounts are Administrator and Guest.

> **Note**   The IUSR_computername and IWAM_computername built-in accounts are automatically created when Microsoft Internet Information Services (IIS) are installed on the domain controller. IUSR_computername is an account for anonymous access to IIS. IWAM_computername is an account for anonymous access to IIS out-of-process applications. The TsInternetUser account is automatically created when Terminal Services are installed on the domain controller. TsInternetUser is an account used by Terminal Services.

Administrator

Use the built-in Administrator account to manage the overall computer and domain configuration for such tasks as creating and modifying user accounts and groups, managing security policies, creating printers, and assigning permissions and rights to user accounts to gain access to resources. This account is assigned the password you specified during Active Directory installation and has permissions to perform all tasks in the domain. The Administrator account cannot be deleted.

Because the Administrator account has full permissions, you must protect it from penetration by intruders. First, you should always rename the Administrator account with a new name that does not connect the account to administrative tasks. Renaming makes it difficult for unauthorized users to break into the Administrator account because they do not know which user account it is. Second, you should always use a long and complex password that cannot be easily cracked for the Administrator account. Third, do not allow too many people to know the administrator password. Finally, if you are the administrator, you should create a separate user account that you use to perform nonadministrative tasks. Log on by using the Administrator account only when you perform administrative tasks. Or, log on with your user account and use the Run As program when you need to perform a few administrative tasks. For information on setting up user accounts for performing nonadministrative tasks and the Run As program, see Chapter 8, "Administering Group Accounts."

Guest

The purpose of the built-in Guest account is to provide users who do not have an account in the domain with the ability to log on and gain access to resources. For example, an employee who needs access to resources for a short time can use the Guest account. By default, the Guest account does not require a password (the password can be blank) and is disabled. You should enable the Guest account only in low-security networks and always assign it a password. If you enable the Guest account, always rename it to provide a greater degree of security. Use a name that does not identify it as the Guest account. You can rename and disable the Guest account, but you cannot delete it.

Domain User Account Naming Conventions

The domain user account naming convention you adopt establishes how users are identified in the domain. A consistent user account naming convention helps you and your users remember user logon names and locate them in lists. Table 7-1 summarizes some points you might want to consider in determining a domain user account naming convention for your organization.

Table 7-1   Domain User Account Naming Convention Considerations

Consideration	Explanation
Selecting local user account names	Local user account names must be unique on the computer where you create the local user account.
Selecting domain user account names	The user's logon name, a distinguished name (DN), must be unique to the directory. The user's full name (also referred to as the display name or account name), a relative distinguished name (RDN), must be unique within the OU where you create the domain user account. The user's Security Accounts Manager (SAM) name must be unique to the directory.

Table 7-1   Domain User Account Naming Convention Considerations

Consideration	Explanation
Determining the number of characters in user logon name	User logon names can contain up to 20 uppercase or lowercase characters. Although the field accepts more than 20 characters, Windows Server 2003 recognizes only the first 20.
Determining characters in user logon name	The following characters are invalid in user logon names if you are using pre–Microsoft Windows 2000 systems: / \ [ ] : ; | = , + * ? < > @ " You can use a combination of special and alphanumeric characters to help uniquely identify user accounts. User logon names are not case sensitive, but Windows Server 2003 preserves the case.
Accommodating duplicate names	If two users were named John Emory, you could use the first name and the last initial, and then add letters from the last name to differentiate the duplicate names. In this example, one user account logon name could be Johne and the other Johnem. Another possibility would be to number each user logon name—for example, Johne1 and Johne2.
Identifying the type of user	In some organizations, it is useful to identify temporary employees by their user account. To identify temporary employees, you can use a T and a hyphen in front of the user's logon name—for example, T-Johne. Alternatively, use parentheses in the name—for example, John Emory (Temp).
Accommodating e-mail systems	Some e-mail systems might not accept certain characters, such as spaces and parentheses. These characters should not be included in user names.

Password Requirements and Guidelines

To protect access to the domain or a computer, every user account should have a strong password. A *strong password* is a password that provides an effective defense against unauthorized access to a resource. It's important to educate users about the benefits of using strong passwords and to teach them how to create passwords that are actually strong.

Passwords can be up to 127 characters. However, if your network has computers running Microsoft Windows 95, Microsoft Windows 98, or Microsoft Windows Millennium Edition (Windows Me), you should use a maximum of 14 characters because these operating systems support passwords of up to only 14 characters. A minimum length of seven characters is recommended.

A strong password

- Is at least seven characters long.
- Does not contain a user name, real name, or company name.

- Does not contain a complete dictionary word.

- Is significantly different from previous passwords. Passwords that increment (*Password1, Password2, Password3* ...) are not strong.

- Contains characters from each of the following four groups shown in Table 7-2.

Table 7-2   Strong Password Requirement Groups

Group	Examples
Uppercase letters	A, B, C ...
Lowercase letters	a, b, c ...
Numerals	0, 1, 2, 3, 4, 5, 6, 7, 8, 9
Symbols found on the keyboard (all keyboard characters not defined as letters or numerals)	` ~ ! @ # $ % ^ & * ( ) _ + - = { } | [ ] \ : "; ' < > ? , . /

An example of a strong password is *K*c6mr93lD*. Be cautious about using keyboard symbols in passwords if your organization uses several different operating systems.

Note   Windows Server 2003 group policies can also affect passwords. You can implement a password policy setting that enforces password complexity requirements by using the Password Must Meet Complexity Requirements policy setting. For further information on using Group Policy, see Chapter 13, "Administering Security with Group Policy."

Real World   Password Security

Password security is a real problem and remains a fairly large security hole for many organizations and individuals. You can and should set a password policy at the domain level in order to enforce strong passwords. You'll learn more about this in Chapter 13, "Administering Security with Group Policy." You should also consider using a password auditing tool in order to monitor your network for weak passwords. There are several password auditing tools available. To find examples of such tools, perform a Web search on "password auditing".

Exam Tip   Know the components of a strong password.

Using Smart Cards

Windows Server 2003 supports optional smart card authentication. A *smart card* is a credit card–sized device that is used with a personal identification number (PIN) to enable certificate-based authentication and single sign-on to the enterprise. Smart cards securely store certificates, public and private keys, passwords, and other types of personal information. Smart cards provide a more secure means of user authentication than passwords. However, deploying and maintaining a smart card program requires additional overhead, including the configuration of the Microsoft Certificate Services, smart card reader devices, and the smart cards themselves. A smart card contains a chip that stores the user's private key, logon information, and public key certificate. The user inserts the card into a smart card reader attached to the computer and types in a PIN when requested. Smart cards rely on the *public key infrastructure (PKI)* of Windows Server 2003.

> **Note**   A discussion of PKI is outside the scope of this training kit. Refer to the Microsoft Windows Server 2003 Resource Kit (located on the Microsoft Web site at *http://www.microsoft.com/windows/reskits/default.asp*) for more information on this topic.

Implementing Smart Cards

In addition to PKI and the cards themselves, each computer needs a smart card reader. You must set up at least one computer as a smart card enrollment station and authorize at least one user to operate it. Although no extra hardware is required beyond a smart card reader, the user who operates the enrollment station needs to be issued an Enrollment Agent certificate. Because the holder of the Enrollment Agent certificate can generate a smart card for anyone in the organization, there must be strong security policies in place for issuing Enrollment Agent certificates.

> **Real World   Smart Card Benefit**
>
> The main problem with passwords is that the more secure a password, the more difficult it is to remember. If you require your users to create 32–character, multi-case alphanumeric passwords, they are likely to write them down. If you let your users establish any type of password they want, some people will probably decide to use a password that can be easily compromised. Smart cards can be a solution to these problems because you can implement them in place of passwords. Of course, you'll have to place smart card readers on every computer and issue smart cards to every user. However, once that is done, users won't have to use passwords anymore. Instead, they'll probably use a PIN or maybe a biometric (i.e., thumbprint or retinal scan) to gain access to their workstation and the network. Smart cards make it a lot more difficult for remote attackers to compromise network users' accounts.

Smart Card Deployment Considerations

Smart card logon is supported for Windows 2000 and Windows Server 2003. To implement smart cards, you must deploy an enterprise certification authority rather than a stand-alone or third-party certification authority to support smart card logon to Windows Server 2003 domains. Windows Server 2003 supports industry standard Personal Computer/Smart Card (PC/SC)–compliant smart cards and readers and provides drivers for commercially available plug and play smart card readers. Windows Server 2003 does not support non-PC/SC-compliant or non–plug and play smart card readers. Some manufacturers might provide drivers for non–plug and play smart card readers that work with Windows Server 2003; however, it is recommended that you purchase only plug and play PC/SC-compliant smart card readers.

The cost of administering a smart card program depends on several factors, including:

■ The number of users enrolled in the smart card program and their location.

■ Your organization's practices for issuing smart cards to users, including the requirements for verifying user identities. For example, will you require users to simply present a valid personal identification card or will you require a background investigation? Your policies affect the level of security provided as well as the actual cost.

■ Your organization's practices for users who lose or misplace their smart cards. For example, will you issue temporary smart cards, authorize temporary alternate logon to the network, or make users go home to retrieve their smart cards? Your policies affect how much worker time is lost and how much help desk support is needed.

Your smart card authentication strategy must describe the network logon and authentication methods you use, including:

■ Identify network logon and authentication strategies you want to deploy.

■ Describe smart card deployment considerations and issues.

■ Describe PKI certificate services required to support smart cards.

In addition to smart cards, third-party vendors offer a variety of security products to provide two-factor authentication, such as "security tokens" and biometric accessories. These accessories use extensible features of the Windows Server 2003 graphical logon user interface to provide alternate methods of user authentication.

> **Exam Tip**   Know what you must do to deploy smart cards.

Lesson Review

The following questions are intended to reinforce key information presented in this lesson. If you are unable to answer a question, review the lesson and then try the question again. Answers to the questions can be found in the "Questions and Answers" section at the end of this chapter.

1. Where are domain user accounts created?

_____

_____

2. What is a smart card?

_____

_____

3. Why should you always rename the built-in Administrator account?

_____

_____

4. What is the purpose of the Guest account? What is the default condition of the Guest account?

_____

_____

5. Which of the following are characteristics of a strong password?

    a. Is at least seven characters long

    b. Contains your user name

    c. Contains keyboard symbols

    d. Contains numerals

    e. Contains a dictionary word

Lesson Summary

- Windows Server 2003 provides three types of user accounts: local user accounts, domain user accounts, and built-in user accounts.

- Local user accounts are stored only in a computer's local security database. Domain user accounts are stored in Active Directory and replicated to all domain controllers in a domain. Built-in user accounts are created automatically by Windows Server

2003 for the purpose of performing administrative tasks or to gain access to network resources.

■ The user account naming convention you adopt establishes how users are identified in the domain. A consistent user account naming convention helps you and your users remember user logon names and locate them in lists.

■ To protect access to the domain or a computer, every user account should have a strong password. A strong password is a password that provides an effective defense against unauthorized access to a resource. A strong password is at least seven characters long, does not contain all or part of the user's account name, and contains at least three of the four following categories of characters: uppercase characters, lowercase characters, base 10 digits, and symbols found on the keyboard (such as !, @, #).

■ A smart card is a credit card sized device that is used with a PIN number to enable certificate-based authentication and single sign-on to the enterprise. Smart cards securely store certificates, public and private keys, passwords, and other types of personal information. Deploying and maintaining a smart card program requires additional overhead, including the configuration of the Microsoft Certificate Services, smart card reader devices, and the smart cards themselves.

Lesson 2: Creating User Accounts

Domain user accounts are created using the Active Directory Users And Computers console. To use either tool, you must have administrator privileges. This lesson takes you step-by-step through creating user accounts and setting user account properties.

After this lesson, you will be able to

- Create domain user accounts
- Modify domain user account properties

Estimated lesson time: 5 minutes

Creating Domain User Accounts

Use the Active Directory Users And Computers console to create a new domain user account. When you create the domain user account, the user logon name is by default associated with the domain in which you are creating the domain user account. However, you can associate a user logon name with any domain in which you have permissions to create domain user accounts. You must select the container in which to create the new account. Although you can create the domain user account in the Users container by default, you should add actual users to a custom OU. OUs are discussed in detail in Chapter 6, "Implementing an OU Structure."

Note   If you are using Windows Server 2003 with Service Pack 1 (SP1), the Windows Firewall might prevent you from creating user accounts using the Active Directory Users and Computers console. For example, you will get errors if the Windows Firewall is enabled on a domain controller and you are using the console from a workstation or other server.

For more information, see "Windows Firewall Settings: Remote Administration Tools" at *http://technet2.microsoft.com/WindowsServer/en/Library/e0bb5886-478e-4408-bb52-544d0ab0f4461033.mspx*.

To create domain user accounts, complete the following steps:

1. Click Start, point to Administrative Tools, and then click Active Directory Users And Computers.

2. Click the domain, right-click the OU in which the domain user account will be stored, point to New, and then click User.

3. In the New Object-User dialog box, shown in Figure 7-3, set the domain user name options as described in Table 7-3. Click Next.

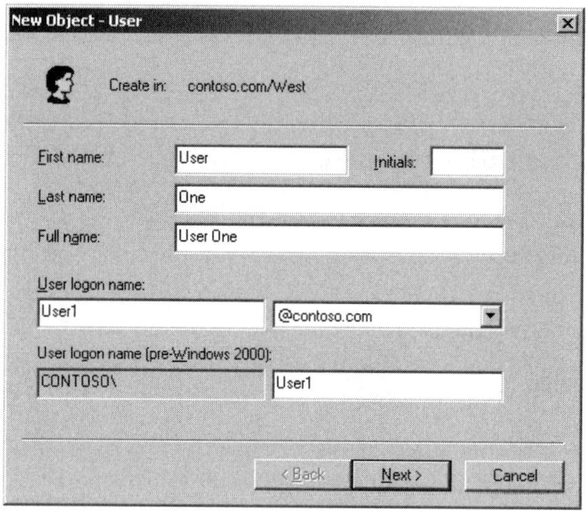

Figure 7-3   New Object–User dialog box

Table 7-3   User Name Options in the New Object-User Dialog Box

Option	Action
First Name box	Type the user's first name. An entry in this, the Initials, or the Last Name box is required.
Initials box	Type the user's initials, if applicable. An entry in this, the First Name, or the Last Name box is required. Do not use a period after the last initial; a period is entered automatically.
Last Name box	Type the user's last name. An entry in this, the Initials, or the First Name box is required.
Full Name box	No action is necessary, because the user's complete name is entered automatically from information you entered in the First Name, Initials, and Last Name boxes. The name must be unique within the OU or container where you create the user account. The full name is the one displayed in the OU or container where the user account is located in the directory.
User Logon Name box	The User Logon Name box is accompanied by a domain name list. The user logon name and the domain name together uniquely identify the user throughout the entire network. Based on your naming conventions, type the user's unique logon name in the box (on the left). The logon name is required and in combination with the domain name on the right must be unique within the domain. The current domain name is entered automatically from the list (on the right) of domains for which you have the appropriate permissions, but you may select another instead.

Table 7-3   User Name Options in the New Object-User Dialog Box

Option	Action
User Logon Name (Pre–Windows 2000) box	No action is necessary because an entry is entered automatically. The entry is the user's unique logon name that is used to log on from earlier versions of Windows, such as Microsoft Windows NT 4 or Windows NT 3.5.1. An entry is required, and must be unique within the domain. If you entered any of the following: / \ [ ] : ; | = , + * ? < > @ " in the User Logon Name box, a message appears, reminding you that these characters are not valid for pre–Windows 2000 systems and that the characters will be replaced with the underscore symbol for the pre–Windows 2000 user logon.

4. In the second New Object-User dialog box, shown in Figure 7-4, set the password requirements for the domain user account as described in Table 7-4. Click Next.

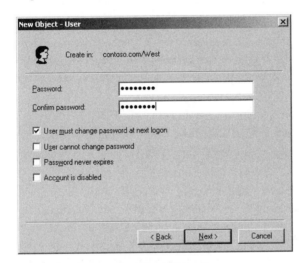

Figure 7-4   New Object-User dialog box

Table 7-4   Password Options in the New Object–User Dialog Box

Option	Action
Password box	Type the password used to authenticate the user. For greater security, assign a strong password. The password is hidden by asterisks when you type it.
Confirm Password box	Confirm the password by typing it a second time to make sure that you typed the password correctly. An entry is required if you assign a password.
User Must Change Password At Next Logon check box	Select this check box to require the user to change his or her password the first time that he or she logs on. This ensures that the user is the only person who knows the password.

Table 7-4 Password Options in the New Object–User Dialog Box

Option	Action
User Cannot Change Password check box	Select this check box if you have more than one person using the same domain user account (such as Guest) or to maintain control over user account passwords.
Password Never Expires check box	Select this check box if the password should never change—for example, for a domain user account that is used by a program or a Windows Server 2003 service. This option overrides the User Must Change Password At Next Logon option. If both check boxes are selected, the system clears the User Must Change Password At Next Logon check box.
Account Is Disabled check box	Select this check box to prevent the use of the user's account—for example, for a new employee who has not yet started.

Note It is recommended that you require new users to change their passwords the first time that they log on, so only the user knows the password. In addition, when you create the initial password for user accounts, combine letters and numbers to create a random password that will help keep the account secure.

5. In the third New Object–User dialog box, confirm that the full name and the user logon name are correct for the user. Click Finish.

Off the Record If you are ever faced with creating a large number of user accounts at one time, you might want to explore methods for automating user account creation. One way to do this is to acquire or write a script that allows you to create user accounts. To get started writing your own user creation script, you could review the Microsoft Windows 2000 Scripting Guide article titled "Creating User Accounts," available from *http://www.microsoft.com /technet/scriptcenter/guide/sas_usr_doig.mspx*. There are, of course, many books on ADSI and VB Scripting as well. For ready-made scripts, look to the TechNet Script Center, which is available on the Microsoft Web site. Also, look on Supplemental CD-ROM for this course in the \70-294\Labs\Chapter07 folder. There is a VB script that will create an OU named Trial along with 30 user accounts. The script is named 30users.vbs.

Modifying Domain User Account Properties

A set of default properties is associated with each domain user account that you create. For domain user accounts, these account properties equate to object attributes. You can use the properties that you define for a domain user account to search for users in the directory, or the properties can be used in other applications as object attributes. For this reason, you should provide detailed definitions for each domain user account that you create. For example, if a user knows a person's last name and wants to find the person's telephone number, the user can use the last name to search for the telephone number.

The tabs in the Properties dialog box for a user, shown in Figure 7-5, contain information about each user account. Table 7-5 describes the tabs in the Properties dialog box.

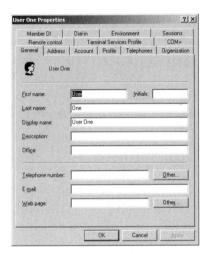

Figure 7-5   Tabs in the Properties dialog box for a user account

Table 7-5   Tabs in the Properties Dialog Box

Tab	Description
General	Documents the user's first name, initials, last name, display name, description, office location, telephone number(s), e-mail address, and Web page(s)
Address	Documents the user's street address, post office box, city, state or province, ZIP code or postal code, and country or region
Account	Documents the user's account properties, including user logon name, logon hours, computers permitted to log on to, account options, and account expiration
Profile	Sets a profile path, logon script path, and home folder
Telephones	Documents the user's home, pager, mobile, fax, and Internet Protocol (IP) telephone numbers, and contains space for notes
Organization	Documents the user's title, department, company, manager, and direct reports
Remote Control	Configures Terminal Services remote control settings
Terminal Services Profile	Configures the Terminal Services user profile
COM+	Documents the COM+ partition set of which the user is a member

Table 7-5   Tabs in the Properties Dialog Box

Tab	Description
Published Certificates*	Documents the list of X.509 certificates for the user account
Member Of	Documents the groups to which the user belongs
Dial-In	Documents the dial-in properties for the user
Environment	Configures the Terminal Services startup environment
Sessions	Sets the Terminal Services timeout and reconnection settings
Object*	Documents the fully qualified domain name (FQDN), object class, create and modified dates, the original update sequence number (USN), and the current USN
Security*	Sets permissions on the user object

* This tab is available only if Advanced Features is selected in the View menu on the Active Directory Users And Computers console.

You can also set properties on multiple user objects. To do this, select the user objects you want to modify, right-click, and then select Properties. A set of property sheets is available on which you can set or clear object attributes for the selected users.

To modify properties for domain user accounts, complete the following steps:

1. On the Administrative Tools menu, click Active Directory Users And Computers, and then click the domain.

2. Click the appropriate OU to view available domain user accounts.

3. Right-click the domain user account for which you want to modify properties, and then click Properties.

4. Click the appropriate tab for the properties that you want to enter or change, and then complete the necessary information.

5. Click OK.

Setting Up a User for Smart Card Authentication

Set up a user for smart card authentication when you have deployed smart cards in your organization.

To set up a user for smart card authentication, complete the following steps:

1. In the Properties dialog box for the user account, in the Account Options list on Account tab, click Smart Card Is Required For Interactive Logon.

2. Click OK.

Note   Setting up a user for smart card authentication is only one task required for deploying smart cards in your organization. The details for deploying smart cards are beyond the scope of this training kit. Refer to "Checklist: Deploying Smart Cards for log on to Windows" in Windows Server 2003 Help and Support Center for detailed information about deploying smart cards.

Setting Logon Hours

Set logon hours to control when a user can log on to the domain. Restricting logon hours limits the hours that users can explore the network. By default, Windows Server 2003 permits access for all hours on all days. You might want to allow users to log on only during working hours. Setting logon hours reduces the amount of time that the account is vulnerable to unauthorized access.

To set logon hours, complete the following steps:

1. In the Properties dialog box for the user account, in the Account tab, click Logon Hours.

2. In the Logon Hours dialog box for the user account, shown in Figure 7-6, select the days and hours for which you want to allow or deny access.

   ❏ To allow access, select the rectangles on the days and hours for which you want to allow access by clicking the start time, dragging to the end time, and then clicking Logon Permitted. The days and hours for which you have allowed access appear in blue.

   ❏ To deny access, select the rectangles on the days and hours for which you want to deny access by clicking the start time, dragging to the end time, and then clicking Logon Denied. The days and hours for which you have denied access appear in white.

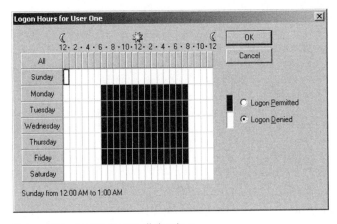

Figure 7-6   Logon hours dialog box

3. Click OK.

> **Note**   Any connections to network resources on the domain are not disconnected when the user's logon hours run out. However, the user will not be able to make any new connections.

Setting the Computers from Which Users Can Log On

By default, each user can log on from all computers in the domain. Setting the computers from which a user can log on prevents users from accessing another user's data that is stored on that user's computer.

> **Note**   To control the computers from which a user can log on to a domain, NetBIOS over Transmission Control Protocol/Internet Protocol (TCP/IP) must be enabled. If NetBIOS over TCP/IP is disabled, Windows Server 2003 is unable to determine the computer from which a user is logging on and therefore cannot restrict users to specific computers.

To set logon workstations, complete the following steps:

1. In the Properties dialog box for the user account, in the Account tab, click Log On To.

2. In the Logon Workstations dialog box, shown in Figure 7-7, select The Following Computers. Then type the name of the computer from which a user is permitted to log on in the Computer Name box. Click Add.

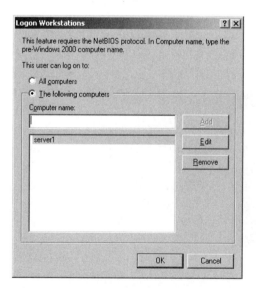

Figure 7-7   Logon Workstations dialog box

3. If necessary, type additional computer names in the Computer Name box, then click Add. Click OK.

Setting Account Expiration Date

Set the account expiration date to control when a user account expires. The account expires at the end of the day on the date you select. Setting an account expiration date ensures that users can log on only when they are supposed to and reduces the amount of time that the account is open to unauthorized access.

To set an account expiration date, complete the following steps:

1. In the Account tab of the Properties dialog box for the user account, shown in Figure 7-8, select either of the following options:

   ❏ Never, if you do not want the user account to expire

   ❏ End Of (and then enter a date in the adjoining text box), if you want Windows Server 2003 to disable the user account automatically at the end of the day on the date you specify

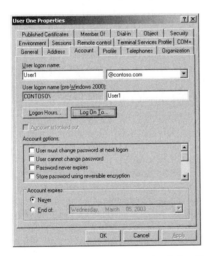

Figure 7-8   The Account tab of the Properties dialog box for a user account

2. Click OK.

Practice: Creating, Modifying, and Verifying Domain User Accounts

In this practice, you create, modify, and verify domain user accounts for the *contoso.com* domain.

Exercise 1: Creating Domain User Accounts

In this exercise, you create some domain user accounts for the *contoso.com* domain.

▶   **To create domain user accounts**

1. Log on to Server1 as Administrator.

2. On Server1, use the procedure provided earlier in this lesson to create the domain user accounts shown in Table 7-6 in the Chicago OU for *contoso.com*.

Table 7-6   Domain User Accounts for Exercise 1

First Name	Last Name	User Logon Name	Password	Change Password
User	One	User1	(blank)	Must
User	Three	User3	(blank)	Must
User	Five	User5	User5	Must
User	Seven	User7	User7	Must
User	Nine	User9	User9	Cannot

Exercise 2: Modifying User Account Properties

In this exercise, you modify user account properties for two of the user accounts you created in Exercise 1. For one account, you configure the logon hours. For the other account, you configure the account expiration settings.

▶   **To modify user account properties**

1. On Server1, use the procedure provided earlier in this lesson to modify the User Three and User Five domain user accounts you set up in Exercise 1. Use the properties specified in Table 7-7.

Table 7-7   Domain User Account Properties for Exercise 2

User Account	Logon Hours	Account Expires
User Three	6 P.M.–6 A.M., Monday-Friday	No change
User Five	No change	Yesterday

2. Close the Active Directory Users And Computers console and log off.

Exercise 3: Verifying the Creation of User Accounts

In this exercise, you attempt to log on to the domain controller using the User One account you created in Exercise 1. Then you allow users to log on at the domain controller by adding the user accounts you created in Exercise 1 and modified in Exercise 2 to the Print Operators group. Finally, you verify the password restrictions that you set up in Exercise 1 and the logon hours restrictions and account expiration settings that you set in Exercise 2.

▶ **To verify the creation of user accounts**

1. The first step in verifying the creation of a user account is to use the account to log on to a domain controller.

   a. Log on to Server1 as User1 with no password.

   b. In the Logon Message message box, click OK.

   c. In the Change Password dialog box, leave the Old Password box blank, type student in the New Password box and the Confirm New Password box, and click OK.

   d. In the Change Password message box, click OK. Were you able to successfully log on? Why or why not?

   No. By default, administrators have the right to log on to a domain controller, but regular users, like User1, do not.

2. The second step in verifying the creation of a user account is to enable users to log on at a domain controller if you have not already done so. There are several ways to allow regular users to log on at a domain controller. In the next procedure, you add the users to the Print Operators group because this group has the right to log on to a domain controller. A group is a collection of user accounts. Groups simplify administration by allowing you to assign permissions to a group of users rather than having to assign permissions to each individual user account. For more information on groups, see Chapter 8, "Administering Group Accounts."

   a. Log on to Server1 as Administrator.

   b. In the console tree of the Active Directory Users And Computers console, expand the East OU and the Chicago OU.

   c. In the details pane, right-click User One, and then click Properties.

   d. In the User One Properties dialog box, click the Member Of tab. Click Add.

   e. In the Select Groups dialog box, select Advanced.

   f. In the next Select Groups dialog box, click Find Now. Scroll down the box displaying the groups and select the Print Operators group. Click OK.

   g. In the Select Groups dialog box, click OK.

   h. Click OK to close the User One Properties window.

   i. Repeat steps 3–8 for User3, User5, User7, and User9.

   j. Close the Active Directory Users And Computers console and log off.

3. The third step in verifying the creation of a user account is to verify the operation of the password restrictions set for the account.

    a. Attempt to log on as User7 with no password. Were you able to successfully log on? Why or why not?

No, because User7 was assigned a password when the user accounts were created.

    b. Attempt to log on as User7 with a password of User7.

    c. When prompted, change the password to **student**. Were you able to log on? Why or why not?

Yes, because User7 is the correct password for the User7 user account.

    d. Press CTRL+ALT+DELETE.

    e. In the Windows Security dialog box, click Log Off.

    f. In the Log Off Windows dialog box, click Log Off to log off.

    g. Attempt to log on as User9 with a password of User9. Were you able to successfully log on? Why or why not?

Yes, because User9 is the correct password for the User9 user account.

    h. Press CTRL+ALT+DELETE.

    i. In the Windows Security dialog box, click Change Password.

    j. In the Change Password dialog box, in the Old Password box, type **User9**. In the New Password and Confirm New Password boxes, type **student**, and then click OK. Were you able to change the password? Why or why not?

No, because User9 has been restricted from changing passwords.

    k. In the Change Password message box, click OK, and then click Cancel to return to the Windows Security dialog box. Click Log Off.

    l. In the Log Off Windows dialog box, click Log Off to log off.

4. The fourth step in verifying the creation of a user account is to verify logon hour restrictions, if applicable.

    a. Attempt to log on as User3 with no password.

    b. When prompted, change the password to **student**. Were you able to successfully log on? Why or why not?

No, because User3 is only allowed to log on between 6 P.M. and 6 A.M. (The answer is Yes if you are logging on between 6 P.M. and 6 A.M.)

    c. Press CTRL+ALT+DELETE.

    d. In the Windows Security dialog box, click Log Off.

    e. In the Log Off Windows dialog box, click Log Off to log off.

5. The final step in verifying the creation of a user account is to verify the account expiration properties, if applicable.

   a. Attempt to log on as User5 with a password of **student**. Were you successful? Why or why not?

   No, because the account for User5 has expired.

Lesson Review

The following questions are intended to reinforce key information presented in this lesson. If you are unable to answer a question, review the lesson and then try the question again. Answers to the questions can be found in the "Questions and Answers" section at the end of this chapter.

1. To what type of container should you add users?

   _____

   _____

2. A user's full name must be unique to what Active Directory component?

   _____

   _____

3. A user's logon name must be unique to what Active Directory component?

   _____

   _____

4. Why should you always require new users to change their passwords the first time that they log on?

   _____

   _____

5. From which tab on a user's Properties dialog box can you set logon hours?

   a. General tab

   b. Account tab

   c. Profile tab

   d. Security tab

Lesson Summary

- To create domain user accounts, use the Active Directory Users And Computers console.

- For domain user accounts, a user's full name must be unique within the OU or container where you create the user account. A user's logon name is based on your naming conventions and must be unique within the domain.

- Always require new users to change their passwords the first time that they log on, so only the user knows the password. Be able to set the various password options.

- Provide detailed property information for each domain user account that you create so you can use this information to search for users in the directory. Be able to set logon hours, set the computer from which a user can log on, and set an account expiration date.

Lesson 3: Managing User Profiles and Home Folders

User profiles maintain consistency for users in their desktop environments by providing each user with the same desktop environment as the last time that he or she logged on to the computer. This lesson introduces user profiles and explains the differences between local user profiles, roaming user profiles, mandatory user profiles, and temporary user profiles. It also discusses the use of home folders.

After this lesson, you will be able to

- Explain the difference between a local user profile, a roaming user profile, a mandatory user profile, and a temporary user profile
- Configure a local user profile
- Manage a roaming user profile
- Manage a mandatory user profile
- Manage home folders

Estimated lesson time: 35 minutes

Understanding User Profiles

A *user profile* is a collection of folders and data that stores the user's current desktop environment, application settings, and personal data. A user profile also contains all of the network connections that are established when a user logs on to a computer, such as Start menu items and mapped drives to network servers. On computers running Windows Server 2003, user profiles automatically create and maintain the desktop settings for each user's work environment on the local computer.

Settings Saved in a User Profile

A user profile contains configuration preferences and options for each user—a snapshot of a user's desktop environment. Table 7-8 shows a sample of the settings contained in a user profile.

Table 7-8   Settings Contained in a User Profile

Parameters Saved	Source
All user-definable settings for Windows Explorer	Windows Explorer
User-stored documents	My Documents
User-stored picture items	My Pictures
Shortcuts to favorite locations on the Internet	Favorites
Any user-created mapped network drives	Mapped network drive
Links to other computers on the network	My Network Places

Table 7-8   Settings Contained in a User Profile

Parameters Saved	Source
Items stored on the Desktop and shortcut elements	Desktop contents
All user-definable computer screen colors and display text settings	Screen colors and fonts
Application data and user-defined configuration settings	Application data and registry hive
Network printer connections	Printer settings
All user-defined settings made in Control Panel	Control Panel
All user-specific program settings affecting the user's Windows environment, including Calculator, Clock, Notepad, and Paint	Accessories
Per-user program settings for programs written specifically for Windows Server 2003 and designed to track program settings	Windows Server 2003 family–based programs
Any bookmarks placed in the Windows Server 2003 family Help system	Online user education bookmarks

Contents of a User Profile Folder

Unless you have upgraded to Windows Server 2003 from Windows NT 4, local user profiles are stored in the C:\Documents and Settings folder, where C is the name of your system drive. If you have upgraded to Windows Server 2003 from Windows NT 4, local user profiles are stored in the %Systemroot%\Profiles folder. Roaming user profiles are stored in a shared folder on the server. Table 7-9 is a sample of the folders contained in a user profile folder.

Table 7-9   Sample Folders Contained in a User Profile Folder

Item	Contents
Application data folder*	Program-specific data—for example, a custom dictionary. Program vendors decide what data to store in the user profile folder.
Cookies folder	User information and preferences.
Desktop folder	Desktop items, including files, shortcuts, and folders.
Favorites folder	Shortcuts to favorite locations on the Internet.
Local Settings folder*	Application data, History, and Temporary files. Application data roams with the user by way of roaming user profiles.
My Documents folder	User documents and subfolders.
My Recent Documents folder*	Shortcuts to the most recently used documents and accessed folders.
NetHood folder*	Shortcuts to My Network Places items.

*Item is hidden

Table 7-9   Sample Folders Contained in a User Profile Folder

Item	Contents
PrintHood folder*	Shortcuts to printer folder items.
SendTo folder*	Shortcuts to document-handling utilities.
Start Menu folder	Shortcuts to program items.
Templates folder*	User template items.

*Item is hidden

Also in the User Profile Folder is the Ntuser.dat file. The Ntuser.dat file is the registry portion of the user profile. When a user logs off the computer, the system unloads the user-specific section of the registry (HKEY_CURRENT_USER) into Ntuser.dat and updates the file.

Using the My Documents folder centralizes all user settings and personal documents into a single folder that is part of the user profile. Windows Server 2003 automatically sets up the My Documents folder, and it is the default location for storing users' data for Microsoft applications. Home folders, covered later in this lesson, can also contain files and programs for a user.

User Profile Types

There are four types of user profiles:

- Local
- Roaming
- Mandatory
- Temporary

Local User Profiles

A *local user profile* is based at the local computer and is available at only the local computer. When a user logs on to the client computer running Windows Server 2003, he or she always receives his or her individual desktop settings and connections, regardless of how many users share the same client computer. Windows Server 2003 automatically creates a local user profile the first time that a user logs on to a workstation or server computer. The local user profile is stored in the C:\Documents and Settings \User_logon_name folder on the computer, where C is the name of your system drive and User_logon_name is the name the user types when logging on to the system.

A user changes his or her local user profile by changing desktop settings. For example, a user might make a new network connection or add a file to My Documents. Then, when a user logs off, Windows Server 2003 incorporates the changes into the user profile stored on the computer. The next time the user logs on to the local computer, the new network connection and the file are present.

Roaming User Profiles

To support users who work at multiple computers, you can set up roaming user profiles. A roaming user profile is based at the server and is downloaded to the local computer every time a user logs on. In contrast to a local user profile, which resides on only one client computer, a roaming user profile is available at any workstation or server computer on the network. Changes made to a user's roaming user profile are updated locally and on the server when the user logs off. This profile is created by a system administrator and is stored in a shared folder on a server.

The first time that a user logs on at a computer, Windows Server 2003 copies all documents to the local computer. Thereafter, when the user logs on to the computer, Windows Server 2003 compares the locally stored user profile files and the roaming user profile files. It copies only the files that have changed since the last time the user logged on at the computer, which makes the logon process shorter.

Mandatory User Profiles

To specify a profile for individuals or an entire group of users, you can set up mandatory user profiles. A mandatory user profile is a read-only roaming profile, based at the server and downloaded to the local computer every time a user logs on. It is available at any workstation or server computer on the network. Users can modify the desktop settings of the computer while they are logged on, but none of these changes are saved when they log off. The next time that the user logs on, the profile is the same as the last time that he or she logged on. Only system administrators can make changes to mandatory user profiles. You can assign one mandatory profile to multiple users who require the same desktop settings. If you need to change the desktop environment for this set of users, you can do so by changing only one profile.

Note   Preferably, profiles should be managed by using Group Policy. Although mandatory user profiles are permitted, they are more likely to create administration problems. For information about Group Policy, see Chapter 11, "Administering Group Policy."

Temporary User Profiles

A temporary user profile is issued any time an error condition prevents a user's profile from being loaded. Temporary profiles are deleted at the end of each session. Changes made to a user's desktop settings and files are lost when the user logs off.

User Profiles Settings in Group Policy

In Windows Server 2003, there are several Group Policy settings that affect user profiles:

- **Prevent Roaming Profile Changes From Propagating To The Server**   This policy determines if the changes a user makes to his or her roaming profile are merged with the server copy of his or her roaming profile. If this policy is set at user logon, the user receives his or her roaming profile, but any changes the user makes to his or her profile will not be merged to his or her roaming user profile at logoff.

- **Add The Administrator Security Group To Roaming User Profiles**   This policy allows an administrator to choose the same behavior as Windows NT 4 and permit the administrators group to have full control of the user's profile directories. In Windows Server 2003, the default file permissions for newly generated roaming profiles are full control, or read and write access for the user, and no file access for the Administrators group.

- **Only Allow Local User Profiles**   This setting determines whether roaming user profiles are available on a particular computer. By default, when roaming profile users log on to a computer, their roaming profile is copied to the local computer. By using this setting, an administrator can prevent users configured to use roaming profiles from receiving their roaming profile on a specific computer.

Note   For detailed information about setting Group Policies, refer to Chapter 10, "Implementing Group Policy."

Creating User Profiles

You create local user profiles simply by logging on. To create roaming user profiles, you assign a profile to a user account. To create mandatory user profiles, you must create a profile template, define a profile template storage location, define a profile, assign a profile to a user account, and configure the profile as mandatory. Temporary user profiles are created automatically by the system if there is a problem and therefore cannot be created by an administrator.

Creating Roaming User Profiles

Create roaming user profiles on a file server that you frequently back up, so that you have copies of the latest roaming user profiles. To improve logon performance for a busy network, place the roaming user profile folder on a member server instead of a domain controller. The copying of roaming user profiles between the server and client computers can use a lot of system resources, such as bandwidth and computer processing. If the profiles are on the domain controller, this can delay the authentication of users by the domain controller.

The Windows Server 2003 family does not support the use of encrypted files within the roaming user profile. Roaming user profiles that are used with Terminal Services clients are not replicated to the server until the interactive user logs off and the interactive session is closed.

Note   To create roaming user profiles for user accounts successfully, you must have permission to administer the object in which the user accounts reside.

To create a roaming user profile, complete the following steps:

1. Click Start, point to Administrative Tools, and then click Active Directory Users And Computers.

2. Expand the appropriate domain, and then click the appropriate OU.

3. In the details pane, right-click the user account for which you want to create a roaming user profile, and then click Properties.

4. In the Properties dialog box for the user, click the Profile tab.

5. In the Profile tab, shown in Figure 7-9, in the Profile Path box, type the path to the folder in which you want to store the user profile, using the format *Server_name**Shared_folder_name**%Username%*. Click OK.

Note   When you type the variable *%Username%*, Windows Server 2003 automatically replaces the variable with the user account name for the roaming user profile.

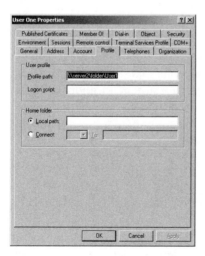

Figure 7-9   Properties dialog box for a user, Profile tab

6. Close the Active Directory Users And Computers console.

Creating Mandatory User Profiles

To create a mandatory user profile, you must complete the following tasks:

1. Create a mandatory user profile template.
2. Define a mandatory user profile template storage location.
3. Define a user profile.
4. Assign a user profile to a user account.
5. Configure the user profile as mandatory.

Creating a Mandatory User Profile Template   You create a mandatory user profile template by creating a domain user account with the profile you intend to use for the mandatory user profile; the account is created for the sole purpose of the profile. Because the domain user account is used for profile administration purposes only, you can make changes to the template without affecting an actual user.

To create a mandatory user profile template, complete the following steps:

1. Create a domain user account that can be easily identified as the account containing the mandatory user profile template.
2. Log on to the domain user account you created in step 1.
3. Customize the desktop for the user as desired.
4. Log off the domain user account.
5. Log on as Administrator.
6. Click Start, point to Control Panel, and then click System.
7. In the System Properties dialog box, click the Advanced tab. In the User Profiles box, click Settings.
8. In the User Profiles dialog box, shown in Figure 7-10, ensure that the profile for the user account you created in step 1 is listed in the Profiles Stored On This Computer box. Leave the System Properties dialog box, with the User Profiles tab open for the next procedure.

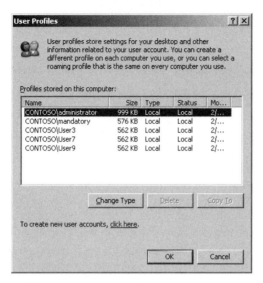

Figure 7-10   User Profiles dialog box

Defining a Mandatory User Profile Template Storage Location   You define a mandatory user profile template storage location by creating a shared folder that can be accessed when the user logs on.

To define a mandatory user profile template storage location, complete the following steps:

1. On a server, create a folder to store the folder containing the mandatory user profile template in the C drive, where C is the name of your system drive. Ensure that the folder can be easily identified as the folder containing the mandatory user profile template.

2. Share the folder you created in step 1 and give the Administrators group Change or Full Control permissions.

> **Note**   To share the folder with appropriate permissions, follow these steps: Right-click the folder, and then click Properties. In the Properties dialog box for the folder, select the Sharing tab. Click Share This Folder and ensure that the shared folder name appears in the Share Name box. Click Permissions, and in the Permissions dialog box for the folder, click Add. In the Select Users, Computers or Groups dialog box, type **Administrators**, and click OK. In the Permission dialog box for the folder, add Full Control or Change for the Administrators group, and click OK. In the Properties dialog box, click OK.

3. Open the folder and create a subfolder to store the mandatory user profile. Ensure that the subfolder can be easily identified as the folder containing the mandatory user profile.

Defining a Mandatory User Profile   You define a mandatory user profile by selecting the profile template, specifying the path to the folder you created to store the mandatory user profile, and selecting the user or group you want to be able to use the mandatory user profile in the User Profiles tab in the System Properties dialog box.

To define a mandatory user profile, complete the following steps:

1. Locate the System Properties dialog box with the User Profiles tab that you left open when creating the mandatory user profile template.

2. In the User Profiles dialog box, shown previously in Figure 7-10, select the user whose profile you want to use as the mandatory user profile, then click Copy To. The user account should be the same one you created for the mandatory user profile template in the previous procedure.

3. In the Copy To dialog box, shown in Figure 7-11, type the path to the folder you created to store the mandatory user profile in step 1, using the format *Server_name**Shared_folder_name**subfolder_name*. In the Permitted To Use box, click Change.

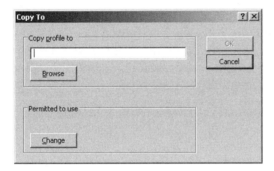

Figure 7-11   Copy To dialog box

4. In the Select Users, Computers or Groups dialog box, type the user or group that will use the mandatory profile, and click OK. In the Copy To dialog box, click OK.

5. The Confirm Copy message box appears, stating that the folder you created to store the mandatory user profile in step 1 already exists and that the current contents will be deleted. This message appears because you already created the folder for the profile. Click Yes.

6. In the User Profiles dialog box, click OK. In the System Properties dialog box, click OK.

Assigning a Mandatory User Profile to a User Account   You assign a mandatory user profile to a user account by indicating the path to the folder you created to store the mandatory user profile in the Profile tab in the Properties dialog box for the user account.

To assign a mandatory user profile to a user account, complete the following steps:

1. Click Start, point to Administrative Tools, and then click Active Directory Users And Computers.

2. Expand the appropriate domain, and then click the appropriate OU.

3. In the details pane, double-click the user account(s) to which you want to assign the mandatory user profile.

4. In the Properties dialog box for a user account, click the Profile tab.

5. In the Profile tab, shown previously in Figure 7-9, in the Profile Path box, type the path to the folder you created to store the mandatory user profile, using the format *Server_name**Shared_folder_name**subfolder_name*. Click OK.

6. Close the Active Directory Users And Computers console.

Configuring a User Profile as Mandatory   A hidden file in the profile called Ntuser.dat contains that section of the Windows Server 2003 system settings that applies to the individual user account and contains the user environment settings, such as desktop appearance. To configure a user profile as mandatory, you must make it read-only by changing the name of the Ntuser.dat file to Ntuser.man.

To configure a user profile as mandatory, complete the following steps:

1. Click Start, and then click My Computer.

2. On the C drive, where C is the name of your system drive, double-click the folder where you stored the mandatory user profile.

3. Double-click the subfolder where you stored the mandatory user profile.

4. Click the Tools menu, and then click Folder Options.

5. In the Folder Options dialog box, click the View tab.

6. In the View tab, shown in Figure 7-12, select Show Hidden Files And Folders, then clear the Hide Extensions For Known File Types check box. Click OK.

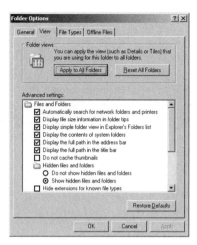

Figure 7-12   Folder Options dialog box, View tab

7. In the window for the subfolder where you stored the mandatory user profile, click Ntuser.dat. Click the File menu, then click Rename.

8. Change the extension of the Ntuser.dat file to Ntuser.man, then press ENTER.

9. Close the window for the folder.

Practice: Managing User Profiles

In this practice, you create and test a roaming user profile and a mandatory user profile.

Exercise 1: Creating and Testing a Roaming User Profile

In this exercise, you create and test a roaming user profile for User1.

▶   **To create and test a roaming user profile**

1. Log on to Server1 as Administrator.

2. On Server1, use the procedure provided earlier in this lesson to create a roaming user profile for User1.

3. Log on to Server2 as User1.

4. Right-click anywhere on the desktop, then click Properties.

5. In the Display Properties dialog box, click the Appearance tab. Notice the current color scheme.

6. In the Appearance tab, in the Scheme list, select a different color scheme, then click OK. This change takes effect immediately.

7. Log off and log on as the same user, User1. Were screen colors saved? Why or why not?

   Yes, because the screen colors are saved in the User1's roaming user profile.

8. Log off Server2.

Exercise 2: Creating and Testing a Mandatory User Profile

In this exercise, you create and test a mandatory user profile for User9.

▶ **To create and test a mandatory user profile**

1. Log on to Server1 as Administrator.

2. On Server1, use the procedures provided earlier in this lesson to create a mandatory user profile for User9.

   ❑ Create a mandatory user profile template named ProfileTemplate. Right-click anywhere on the desktop, then click Properties. In the Display Properties dialog box, click the Appearance tab. Notice the current color scheme. In the Appearance tab, in the Scheme list, select a different color scheme, and then click OK. This change takes effect immediately.

   ❑ Define the mandatory user profile template storage location by creating a subfolder named Mandatory in a folder named Profiles on your C drive, where C is the name of your system drive.

   ❑ Define the mandatory user profile. Ensure that User9 is permitted to use the mandatory user profile.

   ❑ Assign the mandatory user profile to the User9 user account.

   ❑ Configure the user profile as mandatory.

3. Log on to Server2 as User9. Were screen colors saved? Why or why not?

   Yes, because the screen colors are saved in User9's mandatory user profile.

4. Right-click anywhere on the desktop, then click Properties. In the Display Properties dialog box, click the Appearance tab. In the Scheme list, select a different color scheme, then click OK. This change takes effect immediately.

5. Log off and log on as the same user, User9. Were screen colors you set in step 4 saved? Why or why not?

   No, because the screen colors are saved in User9's mandatory user profile. The mandatory user profile is read-only and cannot be changed by users.

6. Log off Server2.

Best Practices for User Profiles

The following are the best practices for handling user profiles:

- Allow for different hardware configurations.

- Use the same type of video hardware when you create or edit a user profile for a single user.

- Create a single mandatory user profile for a group of users only if they all use computers with the same type of video hardware.

- Do not use Offline Folder caching on roaming user profile shared directories. Otherwise, you could experience synchronization problems when both Offline Folders and the roaming user profile attempt to synchronize the files in a user's profile.

- Do not use Encrypted File System (EFS) on files in a roaming user profile. EFS is not compatible with roaming user profiles.

- Do not set disk quotas too low for users with roaming user profiles. Otherwise, the roaming user profile synchronization might fail.

- When creating a roaming profile shared directory, limit access to only those users who need access. Only give users the minimum amount of permissions needed. When creating the shared directory, hide it by putting a $ after the share name. This hides the shared directory from casual browsers and it will not be visible in My Network Places.

- Use servers running Windows 2000 or later to host roaming user profile shared directories. Security features in Windows 2000 and the Windows Server 2003 family can help to secure a user's data.

- Always use the NTFS file system for volumes holding users' data. NTFS supports discretionary access control lists (DACLs) and system access control lists (SACLs), which control who can perform operations on a file and what events will trigger logging of actions performed on a file.

Home Folders

A *home folder* is an additional folder that you can provide for users to store personal documents, and for older applications, it is sometimes the default folder for saving documents. You can store a home folder on a client computer or in a shared folder on a file server. Because a home folder is not part of a roaming user profile, its size does not affect network traffic during the logon process. You can locate all users' home folders in a central location on a network server. Storing all home folders on a file server provides the following advantages:

- Users can gain access to their home folders from any client computer on the network.

- The backing up and administration of user documents is centralized.

- The home folders are accessible from a client computer running any Microsoft operating system (including MS-DOS, Windows 95, Windows 98, Windows Me, Windows 2000, and Windows Server 2003).

> **Note**   You should store home folders on an NTFS volume so that you can use NTFS permissions to secure user documents. If you store home folders on a file allocation table (FAT) volume, you can restrict home folder access only by using shared folder permissions.

You can further enhance the home folder feature by redirecting the user's My Documents pointer to the location of his or her home folder.

Creating Home Folders on a Server

To successfully complete the tasks for creating home folders, you must have permission to administer the object in which the user accounts reside.

To create home folders on a server, complete the following steps:

1. On a server, create a folder to store all home folders on a network server in the C drive, where C is the name of your system drive. The home folder for each user will reside in this shared folder. Ensure that the folder can be easily identified as the folder containing the home folders.

2. Share the folder you created in step 1 and give the Administrators group Change or Full Control permissions.

> **Note**   To share the folder, follow these steps: Right-click the folder, then click Properties. In the Properties dialog box for the folder, select the Sharing tab. Click Share This Folder and ensure that the folder name or the name users need to connect to the shared folder appears in the Share Name box. Click Permissions and, in the Permissions dialog box for the folder, click Add. In the Select Users, Computers or Groups dialog box, type **Administrators** and click OK. In the Permission dialog box for the folder, add Full Control or Change for the Administrators group and click OK. In the Properties dialog box, click OK.

3. Click Start, point to Administrative Tools, and then click Active Directory Users And Computers.

4. Expand the appropriate domain, and then click the appropriate OU.

5. In the details pane, double-click the user account(s) to which you want to assign the home folder.

6. In the Properties dialog box for a user account, click the Profile tab.

7. In the Profile tab, shown in Figure 7-13, click Connect in order to connect to the home folder on the server, and specify a drive letter to use to connect. In the To box, specify a Uniform Naming Convention (UNC) name, for example, *Server_name**Shared_folder_name**User_logon_name*. You can use the %*Username*% variable as the user's logon name to automatically name and create each user's home folder the same as the user logon name. Click OK.

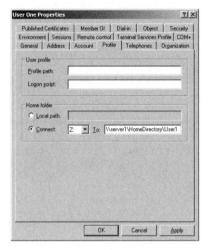

Figure 7-13   The Profile tab of the Properties dialog box

Note   If you use %*Username*% to name a folder on an NTFS volume, the user and the built-in local Administrators group are assigned the NTFS Full Control permission. All other permissions are removed for the folder.

Off the Record   You can use the %*Username*% environment variable in a template user account. A template user account is a user account that you create in order to create other similar user accounts. Typically, you'd create a user account named template (or something similar) for such a purpose. You can copy the template account each time you need to create a user with similar properties. One of those settings could be the home folder. For example, if you wanted to store all user home directories on Server1 in the Home share, you could set the home folder to \\Server1\Home\%Username%. Each new user you create by copying the template will automatically have his or her home folder created after the user name you enter.

Practice: Managing Home Folders

In this practice, you manage a home folder for a user.

Exercise 1: Creating and Testing Home Folders

In this exercise, you create and test a home folder for User1.

▶ **To create and test a home folder**

1. Log on to Server1 as Administrator.

2. On Server1, use the procedures provided earlier in this lesson to create a home folder for User1, as outlined below:

   ❑ Create a home folder storage location by creating a folder named HomeFolders on your C drive, where C is the name of your system drive. Share this folder as HomeFolders.

   ❑ Assign the HomeFolders folder to User1. Connect to the Z drive letter.

3. Log off as Administrator and log on as User1.

4. Double-click My Computer. Note that a new network drive appears, pointing to the User1 folder on \\Server1\HomeFolders with a drive assignment of Z.

5. Close the My Computer window and log off.

Lesson Review

The following questions are intended to reinforce key information presented in this lesson. If you are unable to answer a question, review the lesson and then try the question again. Answers to the questions can be found in the "Questions and Answers" section at the end of this chapter.

1. What is a user profile?

   _____

   _____

2. Describe the function of the three types of user profiles.

   _____

   _____

3. What must you do to ensure that a user on a client computer running Windows Server 2003 has a roaming user profile?

   _____

   _____

4. How can you ensure that a user has a centrally located home folder?

   _____

   _____

5. Which of the following files must be renamed to configure a user profile as mandatory?

   a. Ntuser.dat

   b. Ntuser.doc

   c. Ntuser.man

   d. Ntuser.txt

Lesson Summary

- A user profile is a collection of folders and data that stores the user's current desktop environment, application settings, and personal data. A user profile also contains all of the network connections that are established when a user logs on to a computer. There are four types of user profiles: local, roaming, mandatory, and temporary.

- A local user profile is based at the local computer and is available at only the local computer. Be able to create a local user profile.

- A roaming user profile is based at the server and is downloaded to the local computer every time a user logs on and is available at any workstation or server computer on the network. Be able to create a roaming user profile.

- A mandatory user profile is a read-only roaming profile, based at the server and downloaded to the local computer every time a user logs on and is available at any workstation or server computer on the network. Be able to create a mandatory user profile. A temporary user profile is issued anytime an error condition prevents a user's profile from being loaded. Temporary profiles are deleted at the end of each session.

- A home folder is a folder that you can provide for users to store personal documents, and for older applications, it is sometimes the default folder for saving documents. You can store a home folder on a client computer or in a shared folder on a file server. Be able to create a home folder.

Lesson 4: Maintaining User Accounts

Changes to your organization or personnel might require you to modify user accounts. These modifications include renaming, disabling, enabling, and deleting a user account. You might also need to unlock a user account or reset a user's password. This lesson takes you step-by-step through renaming, disabling, enabling, deleting, and unlocking user accounts and resetting user passwords.

After this lesson, you will be able to

- Rename, disable, enable, and delete user accounts
- Unlock user accounts
- Reset user passwords

Estimated lesson time: 5 minutes

Renaming, Disabling, Enabling, and Deleting User Accounts

Modifications that you make to user accounts that affect the functionality of the user accounts include the following:

- **Renaming a user account**   Rename a user account when you want to retain all rights, permissions, and group memberships for the user account and reassign it to a different user. For example, if there is a new company accountant replacing an accountant who has left the company, rename the account by changing the first, last, and user logon names to those of the new accountant.

- **Disabling and enabling a user account**   Disable a user account when a user does not need an account for an extended period, but will need it again. For example, if a user takes a two-month leave of absence, you would disable his or her user account at the beginning of the leave. When the user returns, you would enable his or her user account so that he or she could log on to the network again.

- **Deleting a user account**   Delete a user account when an employee leaves the organization and you are not going to rename the user account. You might decide first to disable such an account and then delete it at a later time. This allows access to any items to which the user had exclusive rights or time to assign the account to another user. In the end, if the account remains unused, you should delete it so you do not have unused accounts in Active Directory.

To modify a user account, you make changes to the user account object in Active Directory. To complete the tasks for modifying user accounts successfully, you must have permission to administer the OU or container in which the user accounts reside. The procedures for renaming, disabling, enabling, and deleting user accounts are very similar.

▶ **To rename, disable, enable, and delete user accounts**

1. Click Start, point to Administrative Tools, and then click Active Directory Users And Computers.

2. Expand the appropriate domain, and then click the appropriate OU.

3. In the details pane, select the user account that you want to rename, disable, enable, or delete. Click Action.

4. On the Action menu, click the command for the type of modification that you want to make, such as Rename, Disable Account, Enable Account, or Delete.

> **Note** If a user account is enabled, the Action menu displays the Disable Account command. If a user account is disabled, the Action menu displays the Enable Account command.

Unlocking User Accounts and Resetting Passwords

If a user cannot log on to the domain or to a local computer, you might need to unlock the user's account or reset the user's password. It is not possible to "lock" a user's account—if you need to ensure a user's account is not accessed, you must disable the account.

Unlocking User Accounts

A Windows Server 2003 group policy locks out a user account when the user violates the policy, for example, if the user exceeds the limit that a Group Policy allows for bad logon attempts. When a user account is locked out, Windows Server 2003 displays an error message. For further information on using Group Policy, see Chapter 13, "Administering Security with Group Policy."

▶ **To unlock a user's account**

1. Click Start, point to Administrative Tools, and then click Active Directory Users And Computers.

2. Expand the appropriate domain, and then click the appropriate OU.

3. In the details pane, select the locked user account that you want to unlock. Click Action.

4. On the Action menu, click Properties.

5. In the Properties dialog box, click the Account tab, where the Account Is Locked Out check box is selected. Clear the check box and click OK.

Resetting Passwords

If a user's password expires before he or she can change it, or if a user forgets his or her password, you need to reset the password. You do not need to know the old password to reset a password. After the password has been set for a user account, either by the administrator or by the user, the password is not visible to any user, including the administrator. This improves security by preventing users, including the administrator, from learning another user's password.

▶ **To reset a user password**

1. Click Start, point to Administrative Tools, and then click Active Directory Users And Computers.

2. Expand the appropriate domain, and then click the appropriate OU.

3. In the details pane, select the user account for which you want to reset a password. Click Action.

4. On the Action menu, click Reset Password.

5. In the Reset Password dialog box, shown in Figure 7-14, type a new password for the user in the New Password box. Confirm the password in the Confirm Password box. Select User Must Change Password At Next Logon to force the user to change his or her password the next time he or she logs on. Click OK.

> **Note**   If a user logs on through the Internet only, do not select the User Must Change Password At Next Logon option.

Figure 7-14   Reset Password dialog box

Practice: Administering User Accounts

In this practice, you work with disabling and enabling a user account and learn how to reset the password for a user account.

Exercise 1: Disabling and Enabling a User Account

In this exercise, you disable a user account so that it can no longer be used to log on to the domain. You then enable the same account.

▶ **To disable and enable a user account**

1. Log on to Server1 as Administrator.

2. On Server1, use the procedure provided earlier in this lesson to disable the User Three user account you created in Lesson 2. How can you tell that the user account is disabled?

   The Enable Account option appears on the Action menu, and a red X appears on the user icon for User Three in the details pane.

3. Log off Windows Server 2003.

4. Attempt to log on as User3. Were you successful? Why or why not?

   No, because the account is disabled.

5. Log on to your domain as Administrator.

6. Use the procedure provided earlier in this lesson to enable the User Three user account.

7. Click OK to return to the Active Directory Users And Computers console. How can you tell that the user account is enabled?

   The Disable Account option appears on the Action menu, and the red "X" is removed from the user icon in the details pane.

8. Log off Windows Server 2003.

9. Log on as User3. Were you successful? Why or why not?

   Yes, because the account is enabled.

10. Change your password to student.

11. Log off Windows Server 2003.

Exercise 2: Resetting the Password for a User Account

In this exercise, you reset the password for a user account.

▶ **To reset the password for a user account**

1. Log on to Server1 as Administrator.

2. On Server1, use the procedure provided earlier in this lesson to reset the password for the User Three user account you created in Lesson 2. Change the password to er$Tm7s@ and check the box labeled User Must Change Password At Next Logon.

3. Log off Windows Server 2003.

4. Log on as User3 with the changed password. When prompted for a new password, change it to User3.

5. Log off Windows Server 2003.

Lesson Review

The following questions are intended to reinforce key information presented in this lesson. If you are unable to answer a question, review the lesson and then try the question again. Answers to the questions can be found in the "Questions and Answers" section at the end of this chapter.

1. Why would you rename a user account and what is the advantage of doing so?

   _____

   _____

2. Why would you disable a user account and what is the advantage of doing so?

   _____

   _____

3. How is a disabled user account designated in the Active Directory Users And Computers console?

   _____

   _____

4. Why should you select the User Must Change Password At Next Logon check box when you reset a user's password?

   _____

   _____

Lesson Summary

- Rename a user account when you want to retain all rights, permissions, and group memberships for the user account and reassign it to a different user.

- Disable a user account when a user does not need an account for an extended period, but will need it again. Enable a user account when the user returns.

- Delete a user account when an employee leaves the organization and you are not going to rename the user account.

- Unlock a user account to allow a user who has been locked out to log on again.

- Reset a user's password if it expires before the user can change it, or if the password is forgotten.

Case Scenario Exercise

You are the domain administrator for City Power & Light, as presented in Chapter 5 and Chapter 6. City Power & Light has a single Active Directory domain named *cpandl.com*. Currently the domain has eight OUs. Table 7-10 describes the company's OUs.

Table 7-10   OUs of City Power & Light

OU Name	Number of User Accounts	Number of Client Computer Accounts	Number of Member Server Computer Accounts
Accounting	10	10	1
Human Resources	5	4	1
Operations	330	300	10
Contractors	50	45	1
North	150	100	2
South	100	75	2
East	150	100	2
West	5	5	2

The Operations OU has two administrators. The North, South, and East OUs have one administrator each. You are one of two domain administrators. Your manager, Dragan Tomic, is the other network administrator. Dragan has called a meeting of all the administrators to discuss a variety of issues.

Given the above information, answer the following questions:

1. Many of the users from the Contractors OU travel to the other locations and utilize different computers. They've complained that their desktops look different when they move from location to location. What can be done about this?

2. Many of the users from the Contractors OU say they would like a central location where they can store and share documents. They want to be able to access that location from anywhere on the network. What solutions can you offer?

3. During a recent password audit, several user accounts were discovered using simple passwords, such as "password" or a password that was identical to the user name. How can you prevent this in the future, domain-wide?

4. One of the network administrators says that you should do away with passwords altogether and implement smart cards. What are the requirements of using smart cards for authentication?

Troubleshooting Lab

You are a network administrator for Contoso Pharmaceuticals. You receive an e-mail from your manager informing you that three new employees were just hired. When these employees arrive, you are to create user accounts in the Administration OU that your manager just created. When the employees arrive, you complete this task. A few hours later you notice that the Administration OU is no longer there. Instead you see an OU named Admin. You look inside this OU, but you don't see any of the user accounts you created earlier.

You contact your manager about this issue. Your manager says that he decided the name should be Admin instead of Administration. Instead of simply changing the name, your manager deleted the Administration OU and created an Admin OU. However, he says he checked to be sure that you hadn't added any user accounts before deleting the Administration OU.

There is a replication delay between the domain controller that you were working on and the one that your manager uses. You'd like to find those user accounts, if they still exist, so you don't have to track down those employees and get all of their information again.

Before you can see what happened, you must create the issue. The following lab will take you through the process. You will create the replication delay by removing Server1 from the network for a short period. Typically, replication delays are a result of site link schedules and replication intervals, as you learned in Chapter 5.

1. Log on to Server2 using the Administrator username and password.

2. Open the Active Directory Users And Computers console.

3. Connect to Server2 with the console. To do so, right-click the Active Directory Users And Computers console object, and then click Connect To Domain Controller.

4. In the Connect To Domain Controller dialog box, select *server2.contoso.com* from the list of available domain controllers, and then click OK.

5. Create a new OU named Administration. Leave the Active Directory Users And Computers console open.

6. Log on to Server1 using the Administrator username and password.

7. Open the Active Directory Users And Computers console. Ensure that the Administration OU has replicated to Server1. If you don't want to wait, force replication using one of the techniques you learned in Chapter 5.

Tip   Ensure that the Active Directory Users And Computers console of Server1 is pointed to Server1. You should see the name *server1.contoso.com* in brackets after the Active Directory Users And Computers console object.

8. Unplug the network cable from the network card of Server1. This will prevent the systems from replicating. You are simulating a replication delay by doing this.

9. On Server1, create three new user accounts inside the Administration OU. The names and passwords of these user accounts are not really important. You can name them Test1, Test2, and Test3 or whatever you like.

10. Return to Server2.

Tip   Ensure that the Active Directory Users And Computers console of Server2 is still pointed to Server2. You should see the name *server2.contoso.com* in brackets after the Active Directory Users And Computers console object.

11. Delete the Administration OU from Server2.

12. Reinsert the network cable into the network card of Server1. Allow the two servers to replicate their changes. If you don't want to wait, force replication using one of the techniques you learned in Chapter 5.

13. On Server2, create an OU named Admin.

14. On Server2 in the Active Directory Users And Computers console, enable the Advanced Features view option. To do so, click View from the toolbar and then click Advanced Features. Expand the *contoso.com* domain object again, if necessary. You should now see several additional objects in the console hierarchy.

15. Click the LostAndFound object in the console. You should see the three user accounts you created on Server1 inside this container.

This is what happens to objects that are orphaned. Objects are orphaned when their parent container is deleted during replication. If you were faced with the actual situation described in this troubleshooting lab, you could move the user accounts from the LostAndFound container to the Admin container.

Chapter Summary

- Windows Server 2003 provides three types of user accounts: local user accounts, domain user accounts, and built-in user accounts.

- The user account naming convention you adopt establishes how users are identified in the domain. A consistent user account naming convention helps you and your users remember user logon names and locate them in lists.

- To protect access to the domain or a computer, every user account should have a strong password. A strong password is at least seven characters long, does not contain all or part of the user's account name, and contains at least three of the four following categories of characters: uppercase characters, lowercase characters, base 10 digits, and symbols found on the keyboard (such as !, @, #).

- A smart card is a credit card-sized device that is used with a PIN number to enable certificate-based authentication and single sign-on to the enterprise. Smart cards securely store certificates, public and private keys, passwords, and other types of personal information.

- To create domain user accounts, use the Active Directory Users And Computers console. Provide detailed property information for each domain user account that you create so you can use this information to search for users in the directory.

- A user profile is a collection of folders and data that stores the user's current desktop environment, application settings, and personal data. There are four types of user profiles: local, roaming, mandatory, and temporary.

- A home folder is a folder that you can provide for users to store personal documents, and for older applications, it is sometimes the default folder for saving documents. You can store a home folder on a client computer or in a shared folder on a file server.

- If there are changes to your organization, you can modify user accounts, including renaming, disabling, enabling, deleting, and unlocking a user account and resetting a user's password.

Exam Highlights

Before taking the exam, review the key points and terms that are presented in this chapter. You need to know this information.

Key Points

- To plan a user authentication strategy, you must determine whether your organization will use keyboard or smart card logon. For keyboard logon, you must determine the user account naming convention and password requirements.

- To plan a smart card authentication strategy, you must consider the cost of using smart cards, including the number of users enrolled in the smart card program and their location, your organization's practices for issuing smart cards to users, and your organization's practices for users who lose or misplace their smart cards. Your smart card authentication strategy must describe the network logon and authentication methods you use, including identifying network logon and authentication strategies you want to deploy, describing smart card deployment considerations and issues, and describing PKI certificate services required to support smart cards.

- The user account naming convention you adopt establishes how users are identified in the domain. A consistent user account naming convention helps you and your users remember user logon names and locate them in lists.

- To protect access to the domain or a computer, every user account should have a strong password. A strong password is at least seven characters long, does not contain all or part of the user's account name, and contains at least three of the four following categories of characters: uppercase characters, lowercase characters, base 10 digits, and symbols found on the keyboard (such as !, @, #).

- To create domain user accounts, use the Active Directory Users And Computers console. Provide detailed property information for each domain user account that you create so you can use this information to search for users in the directory.

Key Terms

authentication   The process by which the system validates the user's logon information. A user's name and password are compared against the list of authorized users. If the system detects a match, access is granted to the extent specified in the permissions list for that user.

smart card   A credit card–sized device that is used with an access code to enable certificate-based authentication and single sign-on to the enterprise. Smart cards securely store certificates, public and private keys, passwords, and other types of personal information. A smart card reader attached to the computer reads the smart card.

strong password   A password that provides an effective defense against unauthorized access to a resource. A strong password is at least seven characters long, does not contain all or part of the user's account name, and contains at least three of the following four categories of characters: uppercase characters, lowercase characters, base 10 digits, and symbols found on the keyboard (such as !, @, and #).

Questions and Answers

Page
7-11

Lesson 1 Review

1. Where are domain user accounts created?

Domain user accounts are created in Active Directory on a domain controller.

2. What is a smart card?

A smart card is a credit card-sized device that is used with a PIN number to enable certificate-based authentication and single sign-on to the enterprise. Smart cards securely store certificates, public and private keys, passwords, and other types of personal information.

3. Why should you always rename the built-in Administrator account?

Rename the built-in Administrator account to provide a greater degree of security; it is more difficult for unauthorized users to break into the Administrator account if they do not know which user account it is.

4. What is the purpose of the Guest account? What is the default condition of the Guest account?

The purpose of the built-in Guest account is to provide users who do not have an account in the domain with the ability to log on and gain access to resources. By default, the Guest account does not require a password (the password can be blank) and is disabled. You should enable the Guest account only in low-security networks and always assign it a password.

5. Which of the following are characteristics of a strong password?

   a. Is at least seven characters long

   b. Contains your user name

   c. Contains keyboard symbols

   d. Contains numerals

   e. Contains a dictionary word

The correct answers are a, c, and d. Strong passwords do not contain your user name or dictionary words.

Page
7-25

Lesson 2 Review

1. To what type of container should you add users?

You should add users to OUs.

2. A user's full name must be unique to what Active Directory component?

A user's full name must be unique to the OU or container where you create the user account.

3. A user's logon name must be unique to what Active Directory component?

A user's logon name must be unique to the domain where you create the user account.

4. Why should you always require new users to change their passwords the first time that they log on?

Requiring new users to change their passwords means that only they know the password, which makes the system more secure.

5. From which tab on a user's Properties dialog box can you set logon hours?

    a. General tab

    b. Account tab

    c. Profile tab

    d. Security tab

The correct answer is b. You set logon hours by clicking the Logon Hours button on the Account tab in a user's Properties dialog box.

Page
7-42

Lesson 3 Review

1. What is a user profile?

A user profile is a collection of folders and data that stores the user's current desktop environment, application settings, and personal data. A user profile also contains all of the network connections that are established when a user logs on to a computer, such as Start menu items and mapped drives to network servers.

2. Describe the function of the three types of user profiles.

A local user profile is based at the local computer and is available at only the local computer. When a user logs on to the client computer running Windows Server 2003, he or she always receives his or her individual desktop settings and connections, regardless of how many users share the same client computer.

A roaming user profile is based at the server and is downloaded to the local computer every time a user logs on and is available at any workstation or server computer on the network. Changes made to a user's roaming user profile are updated locally and on the server when the user logs off. The user always receives his or her individual desktop settings and connections, in contrast to a local user profile, which resides only on one client computer.

A mandatory user profile is a read-only roaming profile that is based at the server and downloaded to the local computer every time a user logs on. It is available at any workstation or server computer on the network. Users can modify the desktop settings of the computer while they are logged on, but none of these changes are saved when they log off.

3. What must you do to ensure that a user on a client computer running Windows Server 2003 has a roaming user profile?

First, create a shared folder on a network server that will contain the user's roaming user profile. Second, in the Profiles tab in the Properties dialog box for the user, provide a path to the shared folder on the server. The next time that the user logs on, the roaming user profile is created.

4. How can you ensure that a user has a centrally located home folder?

   First, create a shared folder on a network server that will contain the user's home folder. Second, in the Profiles tab in the Properties dialog box for the user, provide a path to the shared folder on the server. The next time that the user logs on, the home folder is available from the My Computer window.

5. Which of the following files must be renamed to configure a user profile as mandatory?

   a. Ntuser.dat

   b. Ntuser.doc

   c. Ntuser.man

   d. Ntuser.txt

   The correct answer is a. To configure a user profile as mandatory, you must make it read-only by changing the name of the Ntuser.dat file to Ntuser.man.

Page 7-48

Lesson 4 Review

1. Why would you rename a user account and what is the advantage of doing so?

   Rename a user account if you want a new user to have all of the properties of a former user, including permissions, desktop settings, and group membership. The advantage of renaming an account is that you do not have to rebuild all of the properties as you do for a new user account.

2. Why would you disable a user account and what is the advantage of doing so?

   Disable a user account when a user does not need an account for an extended period, but will need it again. The advantage of disabling a user account is that when the user returns, you can enable the user account so that the user can log on to the network again without having to rebuild a new account.

3. How is a disabled user account designated in the Active Directory Users And Computers console?

   A disabled user account is designated by a red "X."

4. Why should you select the User Must Change Password At Next Logon check box when you reset a user's password?

   Select User Must Change Password At Next Logon to force the user to change his or her password the next time he or she logs on. This way, only the user knows the password.

Case Scenario Exercise

1. Many of the users from the Contractors OU travel to the other locations and utilize different computers. They've complained that their desktops look different when they move from location to location. What can be done about this?

   To give users a consistent desktop when they change computers, you can implement roaming user profiles. You do this by providing a central server on which users can store their profiles. In their user accounts, you redirect their profile path to that central location.

2. Many of the users from the Contractors OU say they would like a central location where they can store and share documents. They want to be able to access that location from anywhere on the network. What solutions can you offer?

   One solution is to configure home folders for these users. A home folder will automatically map a drive letter to a shared folder on the network. Users can use this location to store files. Typically, the network administrator will map the folder path to the %Username% folder so that inside the central share, the user has a folder specific to his or her user name.

3. During a recent password audit, several user accounts were discovered using simple passwords, such as "password" or a password that was identical to the user name. How can you prevent this in the future, domain-wide?

   Ensure that the domain is set to enforce password complexity requirements.

4. One of the network administrators says that you should do away with passwords altogether and implement smart cards. What are the requirements of using smart cards for authentication?

   Smart cards would be required for every user. Smart card readers would need to be installed on every computer. A certificate server will also be required in order to issue certificates to the smart cards.

8 Administering Groups

Exam Objectives in this Chapter:

- Plan a security group hierarchy based on delegation requirements.
- Plan a security group strategy.

Why This Chapter Matters

As an administrator, you'll have to work with groups. Groups reduce administrative effort by allowing you to assign permissions and rights to a group of users rather than having to assign permissions to each individual user account. As a Microsoft Windows Server 2003 domain administrator, you must understand the different types of groups and which ones you can use with each domain functional level. You must certainly understand how to create and delete groups, add members to groups, and change the group scope, as these tasks are commonly performed by network administrators. You should also understand why logging on to Windows Server 2003 using an administrator account makes your system more vulnerable to Trojan horse attacks and other security risks. To address this problem, you will learn about the Run As program, which allows you to run specific tools and programs with permissions other than those provided by the account with which you are currently logged on to perform routine tasks without exposing your computer to unnecessary risk.

Lessons in this Chapter:

Before You Begin

To complete the lessons in this chapter, you must

- Prepare your test environment according to the descriptions given in the "Getting Started" section of "About This Book"
- Complete the practices for installing and configuring Active Directory as discussed in Chapter 2, "Installing and Configuring Active Directory"
- Learn to use Active Directory administration tools as discussed in Chapter 3, "Administering Active Directory"

- Complete the practices for configuring sites and replication as discussed in Chapter 5, "Configuring Sites and Managing Replication"

- Complete the practices for implementing an organizational unit (OU) structure as discussed in Chapter 6, "Implementing an OU Structure"

- Complete the practices for creating and maintaining user accounts as discussed in Chapter 7, "Administering User Accounts"

Lesson 1: Understanding Groups

Before you can create groups, you must understand the purpose of groups and how they are used to simplify administration tasks. This lesson introduces you to the group types and scopes you can create in Windows Server 2003 and the rules for group membership. You also learn about the various categories of default groups. At the end of the lesson, you learn how to plan a group strategy.

After this lesson, you will be able to

- Explain the purpose of groups
- Explain the purpose of security and distribution group types
- Explain the characteristics of domain local, global, and universal group scopes
- Explain the purpose of local groups
- Describe the types of default groups
- Plan a group strategy

Estimated lesson time: 30 minutes

Introduction to Groups

A *group* is a collection of user accounts. Groups simplify administration by allowing you to assign permissions and rights to a group of users rather than having to assign permissions to each individual user account, as shown in Figure 8-1. Users can be members of more than one group. Permissions control what users can do with a resource, such as a folder, file, or printer. When you assign permissions, you give users the capability to gain access to a resource and you define the type of access that they have. For example, if several users need to read the same file, you would add their user accounts to a group. Then you would give the group permission to read the file.

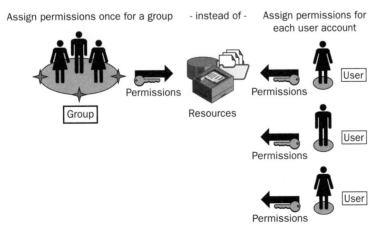

Figure 8-1   Groups simplify administration

In addition to user accounts, you can add other groups, contacts, and computers to groups. You add groups to other groups to create a consolidated group and reduce the number of times that you need to assign permissions. However, you should use caution to add only those groups that are absolutely necessary. You add computers to groups to simplify giving a system task on one computer access to a resource on another computer.

Group Types

You can create groups for security-related purposes, such as assigning permissions, or for nonsecurity purposes, such as sending e-mail messages. To facilitate this, Active Directory directory service provides for the use of two group types: *security* and *distribution*. The *group type* determines how you use the group. Both types of groups are stored in the database component of Active Directory, which allows you to use them anywhere in your network.

Security Groups

Windows Server 2003 uses only *security groups*, which you use to assign permissions to gain access to resources. Programs that are designed to search Active Directory can also use security groups for nonsecurity purposes, such as retrieving user information for use in a Web application. Thus, a security group has all the capabilities of a distribution group.

Distribution Groups

Applications use *distribution groups* as lists for nonsecurity-related functions. Use distribution groups when the only function of the group is nonsecurity related, such as sending e-mail messages to a group of users at the same time. You cannot use distribution groups to assign permissions. Only programs that are designed to work with Active Directory can use distribution groups. For example, Microsoft Exchange Server is able to use distribution groups as distribution lists for sending e-mail messages.

> **Note**   Because Windows Server 2003 uses only security groups, this chapter focuses on security groups.

Group Scopes

When you create a group, you must select a group type and a group scope. *Group scopes* allow you to use groups in different ways to assign permissions. The scope of a group determines where in the network you are able to use the group to assign permissions to the group. The three group scopes are global, domain local, and universal, as shown in Figure 8-2.

Global group
Members can come only from local domain. Members can access resources in any domain.

Domain local group
Members can come from any domain. Members access resources only in local domain.

Universal group
Members can come from any domain. Members can access resources in any domain.

Figure 8-2   Group scopes

Global Groups

Global security groups are most often used to organize users who share similar network access requirements. A global group has the following characteristics:

■ **Limited membership**   You can add members only from the domain in which you create the global group.

■ **Access to resources in any domain**   You can use a global group to assign permissions to gain access to resources that are located in any domain in the tree or forest.

Domain Local Groups

Domain local security groups are most often used to assign permissions to resources. A domain local group has the following characteristics:

■ **Open membership**   You can add members from any domain.

■ **Access to resources in one domain**   You can use a domain local group to assign permissions to gain access to resources that are located only in the same domain where you create the domain local group.

Universal Groups

The universal group is a new feature beginning in Microsoft Windows 2000. *Universal security groups* are most often used to assign permissions to related resources in multiple domains. A universal security group has the following characteristics:

■ **Open membership**   You can add members from any domain in the forest.

- **Access to resources in any domain**   You can use a universal group to assign permissions to gain access to resources that are located in any domain in the forest.

- **Available only in domains with a domain functional level set to Windows 2000 native or Windows Server 2003**   Universal security groups are not available in domains with the domain functional level set to Windows 2000 mixed.

How Universal Groups Affect Replication   Universal security groups and their members are listed in the global catalog. When you create a universal group, it temporarily resides in the domain directory partition in which the group was created until the global catalog queries the domain for changes. Once the global catalog acquires the new object, changes are replicated to other global catalogs in the forest.

In Windows 2000, when one member of a group with universal scope changes, the entire group membership is replicated to all global catalogs in the domain tree or forest, consuming a large amount of network bandwidth and processor load. Further, if group membership is updated simultaneously on two or more domain controllers, some of the membership updates could potentially be lost during replication conflict resolution. In Windows Server 2003, when the forest functional level is set to Windows Server 2003, only the member that is modified is replicated to all global catalogs, which significantly reduces global catalog replication traffic and eliminates the possibility of lost updates. For more information about Active Directory forest and domain functional levels, refer to Chapter 3, "Administering Active Directory."

Group Membership

The group scope determines the membership of a group. Membership rules define which members a group can contain. Group members include user accounts, other groups, contacts, and computers. Table 8-1 describes group membership rules.

Table 8-1   Group Scope Membership Rules

Group scope	In domains with the domain functional level set to Windows 2000 mixed, scope can contain	In domains with the domain functional level set to Windows 2000 native or Windows Server 2003, scope can contain
Global	User accounts and computer accounts from the same domain	User accounts, computer accounts, and global groups from the same domain
Domain local	User accounts, computer accounts, and global groups from any domain	User accounts, computer accounts, global groups, and universal groups from any domain; domain local groups from the same domain
Universal	Not available in domains with a domain functional level set to Windows 2000 mixed	User accounts, computer accounts, global groups, and other universal groups from any domain in the forest

Group Nesting

Adding groups to other groups, or *nesting*, helps reduce the number of times permissions need to be assigned. Create a hierarchy of groups based on the needs of the members. Windows Server 2003 allows unlimited levels of nesting in domains with a domain functional level set to Windows 2000 native or Windows Server 2003.

For example, you can create a group for each region in your organization and add managers from each region into their own group, called Regional Managers. You can then add each Regional Managers group to another group called Worldwide Managers. When all managers in the network need access to a resource, you assign permissions only to the Worldwide Managers group. Because the Worldwide Managers group contains all members of the Regional Managers groups through nesting, all managers in the network can reach the resource. This strategy allows for easy assignment of permissions and decentralized tracking of group membership.

Guidelines for group nesting include the following:

- **Minimize levels of nesting**   Tracking permissions and troubleshooting becomes more complex with multiple levels of nesting. One level of nesting is the most effective to use.

- **Document group membership to keep track of permissions assignments**   Providing documentation of group membership can eliminate the redundant assignment of user accounts to groups and reduce the likelihood of accidental group assignments.

To use nesting efficiently, you must recall the group scope membership rules:

- In domains with a domain functional level set to Windows 2000 mixed, only one type of nesting is available: global groups from any domain can be members of domain local groups. Universal groups do not exist in domains with a domain functional level set to Windows 2000 mixed.

- In domains with a domain functional level set to Windows 2000 native or Windows Server 2003, all group membership rules apply and multiple levels of nesting are allowed.

Local Groups

A *local group* is a collection of user accounts on a computer. Use local groups to assign permissions to resources residing on the computer on which the local group is created. Windows Server 2003 creates local groups in the local security database.

> **Note**   Because Active Directory groups with a "domain local" scope are sometimes referred to as "local groups," it is important to distinguish between a local group and a group with a domain local scope.

Guidelines for using local groups follow:

■ Use local groups only on the computer where you create the local groups. Local group permissions provide access to only the resources on the computer where you created the local group.

■ Use local groups on computers running Microsoft Windows XP Professional and member servers running Windows Server 2003. Local groups cannot be created on domain controllers because domain controllers cannot have a security database that is independent of the database in Active Directory.

■ Use local groups only on computers that do not belong to a domain. Using local groups on domain computers prevents you from centralizing group administration. Local groups do not appear in Active Directory, and you must administer local groups separately for each computer.

Membership rules for local groups include the following:

■ Local groups can contain local user accounts from the computer where you create the local group.

■ Local groups cannot be members of any other group.

Default Groups

Windows Server 2003 has four categories of default groups: groups in the Builtin folder, groups in the Users folder, special identity groups, and default local groups. All of the default groups are security groups and have been assigned common sets of rights and permissions that you might want to assign to the users and groups that you place into the default groups.

Groups in the Builtin Folder

Windows Server 2003 creates default security groups with a domain local scope in the Builtin folder in the Active Directory Users And Computers console. The groups in the Builtin folder are primarily used to assign default sets of permissions to users who have administrative responsibilities in the domain. Table 8-2 describes the default groups in the Builtin folder.

Table 8-2   Default Groups in the Builtin Folder

Group Name	Description
Account Operators	This group exists only on domain controllers. By default, the group has no members. By default, members can create, modify, and delete accounts for users, groups, and computers in all containers and OUs of Active Directory except the Builtin folder and the Domain Controllers OU. Members do not have permission to modify the Administrators and Domain Admins groups, nor do they have permission to modify the accounts for members of those groups.
Administrators	Members have complete and unrestricted access to the computer or domain controller, including the right to change their own permissions. If the Administrator account resides on the first domain controller configured for the domain, the Administrator account is automatically added to the Domain Admins group and complete access to the domain is granted.
Backup Operators	By default, this group has no members. Members can back up and restore all files on a computer, regardless of the permissions that protect those files. Members can also log on to the computer and shut it down.
Guests	Members have the same privileges as members of the Users group.
Incoming Forest Trust Builders	Members can create incoming, one-way trusts to this forest.
Network Configuration Operators	Members have the same default rights as members of the Users group. Members can perform all tasks related to the client side of network configuration except for installing and removing drivers and services. Members cannot configure network server services such as the Domain Name System (DNS) and Dynamic Host Configuration Protocol (DHCP) server services.
Performance Log Users	Members have remote access to schedule logging of performance counters on this computer.
Performance Monitor Users	Members have remote access to monitor this computer.
Pre–Windows 2000 Compatible Access	Members have read access on all users and groups in the domain. This group is provided for backward compatibility for computers running Microsoft Windows NT 4 and earlier.
Print Operators	This group exists only on domain controllers. Members can manage printers and document queues.
Remote Desktop Users	Members can log on to a computer from a remote location.

Table 8-2 Default Groups in the Builtin Folder

Group Name	Description
Replicator	This group supports directory replication functions and is used by the file replication service on domain controllers. By default, the group has no members. The only member should be a domain user account used to log on to the Replicator services of the domain controller. Do not add users to this group.
Server Operators	This group exists only on domain controllers. By default, the group has no members. Members can log on to a server interactively, create and delete network shares, start and stop services, back up and restore files, format the hard disk of the computer, and shut down the computer.
Terminal Service License Users	Terminal Server License Servers
Users	Members are prevented from making accidental or intentional system-wide changes. Members can run certified applications, use printers, shut down and start the computer, and use network shares for which they are assigned permissions. Members cannot share folders or install printers on the local computer. By default, the Domain Users group is a member.
Windows Authorization Access	Members have access to the computed tokenGroupsGlobalAndUniversal attribute on User objects.

Off the Record If you need to create a list of groups, you can use the Net Localgroup and Net Group commands. For example, you could open a command prompt and type **net localgroup > C:\localgroups.txt** to create a list of local groups in a file named C:\localgroups.txt. As another example of how the Net commands work, examine and run the batch file named Grouplistings.bat on the Supplemental CD-ROM in the \70-294\Labs\Chapter08 folder.

Groups in the Users Folder

Windows Server 2003 creates default security groups in the Users folder in the Active Directory Users And Computers console. The groups in the Users folder are primarily used to assign default sets of permissions to users who have administrative responsibilities in the domain. Table 8-3 describes the default groups in the Users folder.

Table 8-3 Default Groups in the Users Folder

Group Name	Description
Domain Local Groups	
Cert Publishers	Members of this group are permitted to publish certificates to Active Directory.

Table 8-3   Default Groups in the Users Folder

Group Name	Description
DnsAdmins	Members of this group are permitted administrative access to the DNS server service.
HelpServicesGroup	This group allows administrators to set rights common to all support applications. By default, the group has only one member, the account associated with Microsoft support applications, such as Microsoft Remote Assistance. Do not add users to this group, which is managed automatically by the Help And Support service.
RAS and IAS Servers	Servers in this group—for the Remote Access Service (RAS) and Internet Authentication Service (IAS)—are permitted access to the remote access properties of users.
TelnetClients	Members of this group have access to Telnet Server on this system.
Global Groups	
DnsUpdateProxy	Members of this group are DNS clients who are permitted to perform dynamic updates on behalf of some other clients (such as DHCP servers).
Domain Admins	Members of this group can perform administrative tasks on any computer anywhere in the domain.
Domain Computers	Members include all workstations and servers joined to the domain. By default, any computer account created in a domain is automatically added to this group.
Domain Controllers	Members include all domain controllers in the domain.
Domain Guests	Members include all domain guests.
Domain Users	Members include all domain users. By default, any user account created in a domain is automatically added to this group.
Group Policy Creator Owners	Members can modify group policy for the domain.
Universal Groups	
Enterprise Admins (appears only on forest root domain controllers	Members include users designated as administrators of the entire network.
Schema Admins (appears only on forest root domain controllers)	Members include users designated as administrators of the schema.

Special Identity Groups

Special identity groups, known as special groups in Microsoft Windows NT, exist on all computers running Windows Server 2003. Membership in these groups is controlled by the operating system. Although the special identity groups can be assigned rights and permission to resources, you cannot modify or view the memberships of these groups. You do not see special identity groups when you administer groups, and you cannot place them into other groups. Group scopes do not apply to special identity groups. Windows Server 2003 bases special identity group membership on how the computer is accessed, not on who uses the computer. Table 8-4 describes the most commonly used special identity groups.

Table 8-4   Commonly Used Special Identity Groups

Special Identity Group	Description
Anonymous Logon	Members include all users who log on without supplying a user name and password.
Authenticated Users	Members include all users whose identities were authenticated when they logged on. This group does not include the Guest account even if the account has a password.
Dialup	Members include all users who are logged on to the system through a dial-up connection.
Enterprise Domain Controllers	Members include all domain controllers in a forest of domains.
Everyone	On computers running Windows Server 2003, members include Authenticated Users and Domain Guests. On computers running earlier versions of the operating system, members include Authenticated Users and Domain Guests, plus Anonymous Logon.
Interactive	Members include all users who have logged on locally or through a Remote Desktop connection.
Network	Members include all users who are logged on through a network connection.
Service	Members include all security principals (users, groups, or computers) that have logged on as a service.
Terminal Server User	When Terminal Services are installed in application serving mode, this group contains any users who are currently logged on to the system using a terminal server. When Terminal Services are installed in remote administration mode, users logged on using a terminal server are not members of this group.

Anonymous User Security Enhancement   In Windows NT and Windows 2000, the operating system makes every user authenticated by the domain and all potential anonymous users members of the Everyone group because the Authenticated Users, the Anonymous Logon, and the Domain Guests groups are automatically made members of the Everyone group. This membership is provided to allow anonymous users access to Active Directory objects. To provide stricter control of access to resources, you must remember to remove the Everyone group from the access control list for the resource. Because administrators often do not realize that anonymous users are members of the Everyone group, these users might inadvertently be granted access to resources intended only for authenticated users.

In Windows Server 2003, the Anonymous Logon group is no longer a member of the Everyone group. Therefore, anonymous users attempting to access resources hosted on computers running Windows Server 2003 will be impacted. If anonymous users must be granted access to resources, you must explicitly add the Anonymous Logon security group to the access control list for the resource and provide the required permissions. If anonymous users must always be granted access to resources, you can change the new Windows Server 2003 default security setting for the Everyone group by enabling the group policy Network Access: Let Everyone Permissions Apply To Anonymous Users, located at Computer Configuration\Windows Settings\Security Settings\Local Policies\Security Options. For more information about using Group Policy, refer to Chapter 11, "Administering Group Policy."

Built-In Local Groups

All stand-alone servers, member servers, and computers running Windows XP Professional have built-in local groups. Built-in local groups give users the rights to perform system tasks on a single computer, such as backing up and restoring files, changing the system time, and administering system resources. Windows Server 2003 places the built-in local groups into the Groups folder in the Local Users and Groups snap-in in the Computer Management console. Table 8-5 describes the capabilities that members of the most commonly used built-in local groups have. Except where noted, there are no initial members in these groups.

Table 8-5   Commonly Used Built-In Local Groups

Built-in Local Group	Description
Administrators	Members can perform all administrative tasks on the computer. By default, the built-in Administrator user account for the computer is a member. When a member server or computer running Windows XP Professional joins a domain, Windows Server 2003 adds the Domain Admins predefined global group to this group.
Backup Operators	Members can use Windows Backup to back up and restore the computer.

Table 8-5   Commonly Used Built-In Local Groups

Built-in Local Group	Description
Guests	Members can perform only tasks for which you have specifically granted rights and can gain access only to resources for which you have assigned permissions; members cannot make permanent changes to their desktop environment. By default, the built-in Guest account for the computer is a member.
HelpServicesGroup	Members can set rights common to all support applications. By default, the only member is the account associated with Microsoft support applications. Do not add users to this group.
Network Configuration Operators	Members can make changes to TCP/IP settings and renew and release TCP/IP addresses. This group has no default members.
Performance Monitor Users	Members can monitor performance counters on the server locally and from remote clients without being a member of the Administrators or Performance Log Users groups.
Performance Log Users	Members can manage performance counters, logs, and alerts on the server locally and from remote clients without being a member of the Administrators or Performance Monitor Users groups.
Power Users	Members can create and modify local user accounts on the computer and share resources.
Print Operators	Members can administer domain printers.
Remote Desktop Users	Members can remotely log on to a server.
Replicator	Supports directory replication functions. The only member should be a domain user account used to log on to the Replicator services of the domain controller. Do not add the accounts of actual users to this group.
Terminal Server Users	Contains users who are currently logged on using Terminal Server.
Users	Members can perform only tasks for which you have specifically granted rights and can gain access only to resources for which you have assigned permissions. By default, Windows Server 2003 adds local user accounts that you create on the computer to the Users group. When a member server or a computer running Windows XP Professional joins a domain, Windows Server 2003 adds the Domain Users predefined global group to this group.

Exam Tip   Be familiar with the groups in each category.

Planning Groups

To use groups effectively, you must determine how you will use the groups and which types of groups you will use. It is important to have a group strategy in place before you begin creating groups.

Planning Global and Domain Local Groups

Global and domain local groups are listed in the global catalog, but their members are not. This reduces the size of the global catalog and the replication traffic associated with keeping the global catalog up to date. You can improve network performance by using groups with global or domain local scope for directory objects that change frequently. Global and domain local group implementation guidelines are identical to the group strategy recommendations for a Windows NT 4 or earlier domain. Use the following procedure, as portrayed in Figure 8-3, to plan your global and domain local group strategy:

1. **Assign users with common job responsibilities to global groups.** Identify users with common job responsibilities and add the user accounts to a global group. For example, in an accounting department, add user accounts for all accountants to a global group called Accounting.

2. **Create a domain local group for resources to be shared.** Identify the resources or group of resources, such as related files or printers, to which users need access, and then create a domain local group for that resource. For example, if you have a number of color printers in your company, create a domain local group called Color Printers.

3. **Add global groups that need access to the resources to the domain local group.** Identify all global groups that share the same access needs for resources and make them members of the appropriate domain local group. For example, add the global groups Accounting and Sales to the domain local group Color Printers.

4. **Assign resource permissions to the domain local group.** Assign the required permissions for the resource to the domain local group. For example, assign the necessary permissions to use color printers to the Color Printers group. Users in the Accounting and Sales global groups receive the required permissions because their global group is a member of the domain local group Color Printers.

This strategy gives you the most flexibility for growth and reduces permissions assignments.

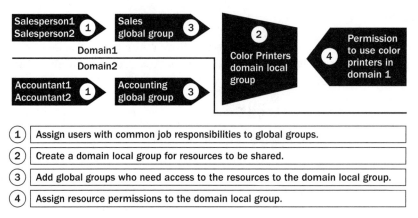

(1)	Assign users with common job responsibilities to global groups.
(2)	Create a domain local group for resources to be shared.
(3)	Add global groups who need access to the resources to the domain local group.
(4)	Assign resource permissions to the domain local group.

Figure 8-3   Planning a global and domain local group strategy

Some of the possible limitations of other strategies include the following:

■ **Placing user accounts in domain local groups and assigning permissions to the domain local groups**   This strategy does not allow you to assign permissions for resources outside of the domain. This strategy reduces the flexibility when your network grows.

■ **Placing user accounts in global groups and assigning permissions to the global groups**   This strategy can complicate administration when you are using multiple domains. If global groups from multiple domains require the same permissions, you have to assign permissions for each global group.

Planning Universal Groups

Use universal groups to grant or deny access to resources that are located in more than one domain. As discussed earlier in this lesson, when membership of any universal group changes, the changes must be replicated to every global catalog in the forest unless the Windows Server 2003 forest functional level is used. This action can cause excessive network traffic. Therefore, you should define universal groups with caution. Follow these guidelines to ensure minimal impact on replication traffic:

■ **Add global groups, not users, to universal groups**   The global groups are the members of the universal group. Keep the number of group members in universal groups as low as possible and minimize the number of individual users.

■ **Change the membership of universal groups as infrequently as possible**   By requiring all members of universal groups to be global groups and making individual membership changes in the global groups, the membership changes you make to the global groups do not affect the universal groups or replication traffic.

Practice: Planning New Group Accounts

In this practice, you plan the groups that are required for a business scenario.

Exercise 1

You are an administrator for the customer service division of a manufacturing company. You administer a domain that is part of your company's domain tree. You do not administer other domains, but you might have to give selected user accounts from other domains access to resources in your domain. Users at the company use several shared network resources. The company is also planning to implement an e-mail program that uses Active Directory.

As the administrator, you must determine

- Which groups are needed.
- The membership of each group. This can be user accounts or other groups.
- The type and scope for each group.

Use the procedure provided earlier in this lesson to plan your global and domain local group strategy. Record your planning strategy on the Group Accounts Planning Worksheet provided on pages 8-18 and 8-19. Follow these instructions to complete the worksheet:

1. On the worksheet, provide a name for each group. Record each name in the group name column.
2. Specify the type and scope of each group in the type and scope column.
3. List the members of each group in the members column.

After completing the exercise, compare your worksheet with the sample provided. The sample presents only one set of possible answers. You might have planned your groups differently.

Table 8-6 provides the job function and number of employees in each job function in the customer service division.

Table 8-6   Customer Service Division Employee Information

Job Function	Number of Employees
Product tester	20
Customer service representative	250
Maintenance worker	5
Manager	5
Sales representative	5
Network administrator	2

Table 8-7 lists the information access requirements for various employees.

Table 8-7   Employee Information Access Requirements

Employee	Access Needed
Customer service representatives and managers	Customer database, full access
Sales representatives	Customer database, read-only access
All employees	Company policies, read-only access
All employees	Receive company announcements through e-mail
Any employees in any domain who are interested in these topics	Receive periodic announcements through e-mail about important topics
All employees, except maintenance workers	Shared installation of Microsoft Office
Network administrators	Full access to all resources in the company
Sales representatives from your domain and all other domains	Sales reports

Group Accounts Planning Worksheet

Group Name	Type and Scope	Members

Group Name	Type and Scope	Members

Group Accounts Planning Worksheet (Answers)

Group Name	Type and Scope	Members
Testers	Security, global	All product testers
CSRs	Security, global	All customer service representatives
Maint	Security, global	All maintenance workers
Mgrs	Security, global	All managers
Sales	Security, global	All sales reps
NetAdmin	Security, global	All network administrators
AllEmployees	Security, global	All employees
Topics	Security, global	Employees interested in manufacturing topics
CustomerDB	Security, domain local	CSRs, Mgrs, Sales, NetAdmin global groups
Policies	Security, domain local	AllEmployees global group
MSOffice	Security, domain local	Testers, CSRs, Mgrs, Sales, NetAdmin global groups
SalesReports	Security, domain local	Sales and NetAdmin global groups
EmailAnn	Distribution, domain local	AllEmployees global group
EmailManuf	Distribution, domain local	Topics and NetAdmin global groups

Now that you've completed the worksheet, answer the following questions.

1. Does your network require local groups?

   No. The scenario presents no need to create local groups, which you can use only on a single computer.

2. Does your network require universal groups?

   No. The scenario presents no need to create universal groups. Your domain has no groups that need to have access to resources in multiple domains and also need to have members from multiple domains.

3. Sales representatives at the company frequently visit the company headquarters and other divisions. Therefore, you need to give sales representatives with user accounts in other domains the same permissions for resources that sales representatives in your domain have. You also want to make it easy for administrators in other domains to assign permissions to sales representatives in your domain. How can you accomplish this?

Create global groups for sales representatives in all other domains. Add these global groups to the appropriate domain local groups in your domain. Tell administrators in other domains about the global group that represents sales representatives in your domain. Have the administrators add the sales representatives group from your domain to the appropriate domain local groups in their domains.

Lesson Review

The following questions are intended to reinforce key information presented in this lesson. If you are unable to answer a question, review the lesson and then try the question again. Answers to the questions can be found in the "Questions and Answers" section at the end of this chapter.

1. What is the purpose of using groups?

   _____

   _____

2. When should you use security groups rather than distribution groups?

   _____

   _____

3. What strategy should you apply when you use domain and local groups?

   _____

   _____

4. Why is replication an issue with universal groups?

   _____

   _____

5. Which of the following statements about group scope membership are incorrect? (Choose all that apply.)

   a. In domains with a domain functional level set to Windows 2000 mixed, global groups can contain user accounts and computer accounts from the same domain.

   b. In domains with a domain functional level set to Windows 2000 mixed, global groups can contain user accounts and computer accounts from any domain.

c. In domains with a domain functional level set to Windows 2000 mixed, domain local groups can contain user accounts, computer accounts, and global groups from the same domain.

d. In domains with a domain functional level set to Windows 2000 mixed, domain local groups can contain user accounts, computer accounts, and global groups from any domain.

e. In domains with a domain functional level set to Windows 2000 mixed, universal groups can contain user accounts, computer accounts, global groups, and other universal groups from any domain.

f. In domains with a domain functional level set to Windows 2000 mixed, universal groups do not exist.

Lesson Summary

- A group is a collection of users, computers, contacts, and other groups. Distribution groups are used only for e-mail. Security groups are used to grant access to resources.

- Group scopes allow you to use groups in different ways to assign permissions. The three group scopes are global, domain local, and universal. Global security groups are most often used to organize users who share similar network access requirements. Domain local security groups are most often used to assign permissions to resources. Universal security groups are most often used to assign permissions to related resources in multiple domains.

- Windows Server 2003 has four categories of default groups: groups in the Builtin folder, groups in the Users folder, special identity groups, and default local groups.

- In Windows Server 2003, the Anonymous Logon group is no longer a member of the Everyone group. If anonymous users must be granted access to resources, you must explicitly add the Anonymous Logon security group to the access control list for the resource and provide the required permissions. If anonymous users must always be granted access to resources, you can change the new Windows Server 2003 default security setting for the Everyone group by enabling the group policy Network Access: Let Everyone permissions apply to anonymous users.

- Use the following strategy for planning groups: place user accounts into global groups, create a domain local groups for a group of resources to be shared in common, place the global groups into the domain local group, and then assign permissions to the domain local group.

Lesson 2: Creating and Administering Groups

After you assess user needs and have a group plan in place, you are ready to create your groups. Once you have created groups, you might find it necessary to carry out various administrative tasks to maintain them. This lesson shows you how to create groups, delete groups, add members to groups, and change the group scope.

After this lesson, you will be able to

- Create groups
- Delete groups
- Add members to groups
- Change the group scope

Estimated lesson time: 20 minutes

Note If you are using Windows Server 2003 with Service Pack 1 (SP1), the Windows Firewall might prevent you from creating and administering groups using the Active Directory Users and Computers console. For example, you will get errors if the Windows Firewall is enabled on a domain controller and you are using the console from a workstation or other server.

For more information, see "Windows Firewall Settings: Remote Administration Tools" at *http://technet2.microsoft.com/WindowsServer/en/Library/e0bb5886-478e-4408-bb52-544d0ab0f4461033.mspx*.

Creating a Group

You use the Active Directory Users And Computers console to create groups. With the necessary permissions, you can create groups in any domain in the forest, in an OU, or in a container you have created specifically for groups. The name you select for a group must be unique in the domain where you create the group.

To create a group, complete the following steps:

1. Click Start, point to Administrative Tools, and then click Active Directory Users And Computers.

2. Right-click the appropriate domain, OU, or container, point to New, and click Group.

3. In the New Object–Group dialog box, shown in Figure 8-4, type the name of the group in the Group Name box. Note that an entry automatically appears in the Group Name (Pre–Windows 2000) box, based on the group name you typed. Select the group scope in the Group Scope box. Select the group type in the Group Type box. Click OK.

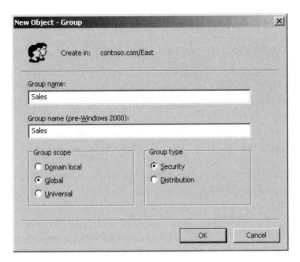

Figure 8-4   New Object–Group dialog box

Deleting a Group

As your organization grows and changes, you might discover groups that you no longer need. Be sure to delete these groups. Deleting unnecessary groups ensures you maintain security so you do not accidentally assign permissions for accessing resources to groups you no longer need. Each group you create has a unique, nonreusable identifier called the *security identifier (SID)*. Windows Server 2003 uses the SID to identify the group and the permissions assigned to it. When you delete a group, Windows Server 2003 does not use the SID for that group again, even if you create a new group with the same name as the group you deleted. Therefore, you cannot restore access to resources by recreating the group.

When you delete a group, you delete only the group and the permissions and rights associated with it. Deleting a group does not delete the user accounts that are members of the group.

To delete a group, complete the following steps:

1. Right-click the group, and then click Delete.

2. Click Yes in the Active Directory dialog box.

Off the Record   You can use a script to determine a user's group memberships. This is helpful if you'd like to make a logon script dependent upon a user's group membership. The script Chkgrps.vbs on the companion CD-ROM in the \70-294\Labs\Chapter08 folder illustrates how you can use Microsoft Visual Basic Scripting Edition (VBScript) to list a user's group memberships. In the Troubleshooting Lab, you'll learn how to use the Ifmember executable to list group membership.

Adding Members to a Group

After you create a group, you add members. Members of groups can include user accounts, contacts, other groups, and computers. You can add a computer to a group to give one computer access to a shared resource on another computer, for example, for remote backup. To add members, use the Active Directory Users And Computers console.

To add members to a group, complete the following steps:

1. Start the Active Directory Users And Computers console and expand the domain, OU, or container in which the group is contained.

2. Right-click the appropriate group, and then click Properties.

3. In the Properties dialog box for the group, click the Members tab, and then click Add.

4. In the Select Users, Contacts, Computers, Or Groups dialog box, shown in Figure 8-5, click Advanced.

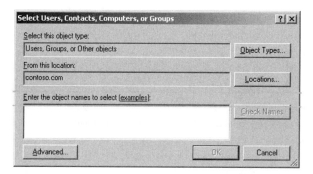

Figure 8-5   The Select Users, Contacts, Computers, Or Groups dialog box

> **Note**   If you are adding members to a global group in a domain with a domain functional level set to Windows 2000 mixed, the Select Users, Contacts, Or Computers dialog box appears because you cannot add global groups to global groups in a domain with a domain functional level set to Windows 2000 mixed.

5. In the extended Select Users, Contacts, Computers, Or Groups dialog box, shown in Figure 8-6, click Find Now. Scroll through the list at the bottom of the dialog box and select the user, contact, computer, or group that you want to add to the group. Hold down the SHIFT or CTRL key to select multiple users, contacts, computers, or groups at a time. Click OK.

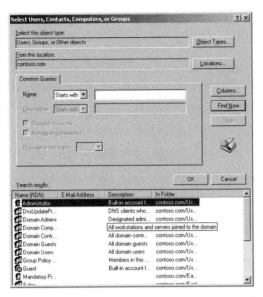

Figure 8-6   Extended Select Users, Contacts, Computers, Or Groups dialog box

6. The accounts you have selected are listed in the Enter The Object Names To Select box at the bottom of the Select Users, Contacts, Computers, Or Groups dialog box. Review the accounts to make sure that they are the accounts you wish to add to the group, and click OK to add the members.

7. In the Properties dialog box for the group, click OK.

> **Note**   You can also add a user, contact, computer, or group by using the Member Of tab in the Properties dialog box for the user, contact, computer, or group. Use this method to quickly add the same user, contact, computer, or group to multiple groups.

Changing the Group Scope

When creating a new group, by default, the new group is configured as a security group with global scope regardless of the current domain functional level. Although changing a group scope is not allowed in domains with a domain functional level set to Windows 2000 mixed, the following scope changes are allowed in domains with a domain functional level set to Windows 2000 native or Windows Server 2003.

■ Global to universal, as long as the group is not a member of another group having global scope

■ Domain local to universal, as long as the group being converted does not have another group with a domain local scope as its member

- Universal to global, as long as the group being converted does not have another universal group as its member

- Universal to domain local

To change the scope of a group, complete the following steps:

1. Start the Active Directory Users And Computers console and expand the domain, OU, or container in which the group is contained.

2. Right-click the appropriate group, and then click Properties.

3. Change the group scope in the General tab of the Properties dialog box for the group. Click OK.

Practice: Creating and Administering Groups

In this practice, you create and administer a global security group.

> **Note**   To complete this practice, you must have successfully completed the practices in Chapter 6, "Implementing an OU Structure," and Chapter 7, "Administering User Accounts."

Exercise 1: Creating a Global Group and Adding Members

In this exercise, you create a global security group and add members to the group.

▶ **To create a global group and add members**

1. Log on to Server1 as Administrator.

2. On Server1, use the procedure provided earlier in this lesson to create a global security group in the Chicago OU. Name the global group Sales.

3. Use the procedure provided earlier in this lesson to add User One and User Five as members of the Sales global group.

Exercise 2: Creating a Domain Local Group and Adding Members

In this exercise, you create a domain local group that you use to assign permissions to gain access to sales reports. Because you use the group to assign permissions, you make it a domain local group. You then add members to the group by adding the security global group you created in Exercise 1.

▶ **To create a domain local group and add members**

1. On Server1, use the procedure provided earlier in this lesson to create a domain local group in the Chicago OU. Name the domain local group Reports.

2. Use the procedure provided earlier in this lesson to add the Sales global group as a member of the Reports domain local group.

Lesson Review

The following questions are intended to reinforce key information presented in this lesson. If you are unable to answer a question, review the lesson and then try the question again. Answers to the questions can be found in the "Questions and Answers" section at the end of this chapter.

1. Where can you create groups?

   _____

   _____

2. What is deleted when you delete a group?

   _____

   _____

3. What Active Directory components can be members of groups?

   _____

   _____

4. In what domain functional level is changing the group scope allowed? What scope changes are permitted in this domain functional level?

   _____

   _____

5. The name you select for a group must be unique to which of the following Active Directory components?

   a. forest

   b. tree

   c. domain

   d. site

   e. OU

Lesson Summary

- You use the Active Directory Users And Computers console to create groups, delete groups, add members to groups, and change the group scope.

- With the necessary permissions, you can create groups in any domain in the forest, in an OU, or in a container you have created specifically for groups. The name you select for a group must be unique in the domain where you create the group.

■ When you delete a group, you delete only the group and remove the permissions and rights that are associated with it. Deleting a group does not delete the user accounts that are members of the group.

■ You cannot change the group scope for domains with a domain functional level set to Windows 2000 mixed.

■ The following scope changes are allowed in domains with the domain functional level set to Windows 2000 native or Windows Server 2003: global to universal, as long as the group is not a member of another group having global scope; domain local to universal, as long as the group being converted does not have another group with a domain local scope as its member; universal to global, as long as the group being converted does not have another universal group as its member; and universal to domain local.

Lesson 3: Administration Strategies

For optimum security, Microsoft recommends that you do not assign administrators to the Administrators group and that you avoid running your computer while logged on as an administrator. This lesson examines reasons why you should not run your computer as an administrator and the actions you should take to ensure security for administrators.

After this lesson, you will be able to

■ Explain why you should not run your computer as an administrator

■ Explain the groups administrators should use to log on

■ Explain how to use the Run As program to start a program as an administrator

Estimated lesson time: 15 minutes

Why You Should Not Run Your Computer as an Administrator

Running Windows Server 2003 as an administrator makes the system vulnerable to Trojan horse attacks and other security risks. The simple act of visiting an Internet site can be extremely damaging to the system. An unfamiliar Internet site might contain Trojan horse code that can be downloaded to the system and executed. If you are logged on with administrator privileges, a Trojan horse could possibly reformat your hard drive, delete all files, create a new user account with administrative access, and so on.

Therefore, you should not assign yourself to the Administrators group and you should avoid running your computer while logged on as an administrator. For most computer activity, you should assign yourself to the Users or Power Users group. When you log on as a member of the Users group, you can perform routine tasks, including running programs and visiting Internet sites, without exposing your computer to unnecessary risks. As a member of the Power Users group, you can perform routine tasks and also install programs, add printers, and use most Control Panel items. If you need to perform an administrator-only task, such as upgrading the operating system or configuring system parameters, you should log on as an administrator, perform the task, and then log off. If you frequently need to log on as an administrator, you can use the Run As program to start programs as an administrator.

Using the Run As Program

The Run As program allows a user to run specific tools and programs with permissions other than those provided by the account with which the user is currently logged on. Therefore, you can use the Run As program to run administrative tools with either local or domain administrator rights and permissions while logged on as a normal user. The

Run As program can be used to start any program, Microsoft Management Console (MMC) tool, or Control Panel item, as long as

- You provide the appropriate user account and password information
- The user account has the ability to log on to the computer
- The program, MMC tool, or Control Panel item is available on the system and to the user account

The Run As program is usually used to run programs as an administrator, although it is not limited to administrator accounts. Any user with multiple accounts can use Run As to run a program, MMC tool, or Control Panel item with alternate credentials. The Run As program can be invoked on the desktop or by using the Runas command.

To invoke the Run As program from the desktop, complete the following steps:

1. In Windows Explorer, or on the Start menu, right-click the program, MMC tool, or Control Panel item you want to open, and then click Run As.

2. In the Run As dialog box, shown in Figure 8-7, click The Following User.

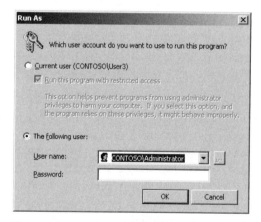

Figure 8-7   Run As dialog box

3. Type the user name and password of the account you want to use in the User Name and Password boxes, respectively. Click OK.

If you attempt to start a program, MMC tool, or Control Panel item from a network location using the Run As program, it might fail if the credentials used to connect to the network share are different from the credentials used to start the program. The credentials used to run the program might not be able to gain access to the same network share. If the Run As program fails, the Secondary Logon service might not be running. You can set the Secondary Logon service to start automatically when the system starts using the Secondary Logon Service option in the Services console.

You can also set a property on shortcuts to programs and MMC tools so that you are always prompted for alternate credentials when you use the shortcut. To set the property, right-click the shortcut, click Properties, click Advanced in the Shortcut tab, and then select the Run With Different Credentials check box in the Advanced Properties dialog box. When you start the shortcut, the Run As dialog box appears, prompting you for the alternate user name, password, and domain as described previously.

Using the Runas Command

The Runas command performs the same functions as invoking Run As from the desktop. The syntax for the Runas command is

```
runas [{/profile|/noprofile}] [/env] [/ netonly] [/savedcreds] [/smartcard]
[/showtrustlevels] [/trustlevel] / user:UserAccountName program
```

- **/profile**   Loads the user's profile. This is the default setting.

- **/noprofile**   Specifies that the user's profile is not to be loaded. This allows the application to load more quickly, but it can also cause a malfunction in some applications.

- **/env**   Specifies that the current network environment be used instead of the user's local environment.

- **/netonly**   Indicates that the user information specified is for remote access only.

- **/savedcreds**   Indicates whether the credentials have been previously saved by this user.

- **/smartcard**   Indicates whether the credentials are to be supplied from a smartcard.

- **/showtrustlevels**   Lists the /trustlevel options.

- **/trustlevel**   Specifies the level of authorization at which the application is to run.

- **/user:UserAccountName**   Specifies the name of the user account under which to run the program. The user account format should be user@domain or domain\user.

- **program**   Specifies the program or command to run using the account specified in /user.

If you want to use the Administrator account on your computer, for the /user: parameter, type:

```
/user:AdministratorAccountName@ComputerName
```

or

```
/user:ComputerName\AdministratorAccountName
```

If you want to use this command as a domain administrator, type:

```
/user:AdministratorAccountName@DomainName
```

or

```
/user:DomainName\AdministratorAccountName
```

Runas Examples

■ To start an instance of the Windows Server 2003 command prompt as an administrator on the local computer, type:

```
runas /user:localmachinename\administrator cmd
```

When prompted, type the administrator password.

■ To start an instance of the Computer Management snap-in using a domain administrator account called companydomain\domainadmin, type:

```
runas /user:companydomain\domainadmin
"mmc %windir%\system32\compmgmt.msc"
```

When prompted, type the account password.

■ To start an instance of Microsoft Notepad using a domain administrator account called user in a domain called *domain.microsoft.com*, type:

```
runas / user:user@domain.microsoft.com "notepad my_file.txt"
```

When prompted, type the account password.

■ To start an instance of a command prompt window, saved MMC console, Control Panel item, or program that administers a server in another forest, type:

```
runas /netonly / user:domain\username "command"
```

where *domain\username* must be a user with sufficient permissions to administer the server. When prompted, type the account password.

Practice: Using Run As to Start a Program as an Administrator

In this practice, use the Run As program to start a program as a domain administrator.

Exercise: Using Run As to Start a Program as an Administrator

In this exercise, you use the Run As program to start the Active Directory Users And Computers console while logged on as User9.

Note   To complete this practice, you must have successfully completed the practices in Chapter 6, "Implementing an OU Structure," and Chapter 7, "Administering User Accounts."

▶ **To use Run As to start a program as an Administrator**

1. Log on to Server1 as User9.

2. On Server1, use the procedure provided earlier in this lesson to use Run As to start Active Directory Users And Computers as the Administrator for the *contoso.com* domain. Use the Administrator password. (Hint: You can access Active Directory Users And Computers from Control Panel.)

3. Verify that you can now use Active Directory Users And Computers as a domain administrator by attempting to add a new user to the Chicago OU. If you can add a new user, you are successfully running Active Directory Users And Computers as Administrator while logged on as User9.

Lesson Review

The following questions are intended to reinforce key information presented in this lesson. If you are unable to answer a question, review the lesson and then try the question again. Answers to the questions can be found in the "Questions and Answers" section at the end of this chapter.

1. Why shouldn't administrators be assigned to the Administrators group?

2. What is the purpose of the Run As program?

3. What are the two ways of invoking the Run As Program?

Lesson Summary

- Running Windows Server 2003 as an administrator makes the system vulnerable to Trojan horse attacks and other security risks. Therefore, you should not assign yourself to the Administrators group and you should avoid running your computer while logged on as an administrator.

- For most computer activity, you should assign yourself to the Users or Power Users group. If you need to perform an administrator-only task, such as upgrading the operating system or configuring system parameters, you should log on as an administrator, perform the task, and then log off.

- If you frequently need to log on as an administrator, you can use the Run As program to start programs as an administrator. The Run As program allows you to run specific tools and programs with permissions other than those provided by the account with which you are currently logged on. The Run As program can be invoked on the desktop or by using the Runas command.

Case Scenario Exercise

You are a network administrator for Humongous Insurance. Humongous Insurance has a multi-domain forest. The forest root is *humongousinsurance.com*. There are also two child domains named *west.humongousinsurance.com* and *east.humongousinsurance.com*. The company has approximately 7,000 users, 7,000 client workstations, and 100 servers. The company's network configuration is shown in Figure 8-8.

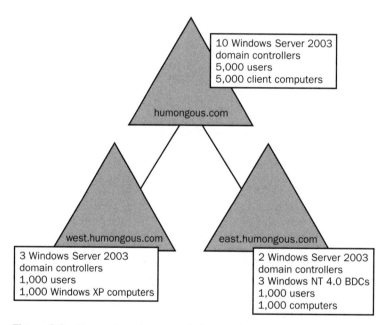

Figure 8-8   Humongous Insurance's forest structure

All domains are Windows Server 2003 domains. The forest root domain has 10 domain controllers. Five of those domain controllers are configured as DNS servers and two are configured as global catalog servers. The West domain has three domain controllers. Two of those domain controllers are configured as DNS servers. One of those domain controllers is configured as a global catalog server. The East domain has two Windows Server 2003 domain controllers and three Windows NT 4.0 backup domain controllers (BDCs).

The forest root domain is located in College Station, Texas. The East domain is located in Gainesville, Florida. The West domain is located in San Diego, California. There is also an Active Directory site configured for each of these locations. The site for College Station is named Main_Site. The Gainesville site is named East_Site. The San Diego site is named West_Site.

You are one of several network administrators assigned to handle the forest root domain and College Station site. Your manager, Jean Trenary, has called a meeting of all network and desktop administrators. She wants to address several issues.

Given this information, answer the following questions:

1. Jean says that there are four internal auditors in the forest root domain. There are two internal auditors in each of the child domains. Each set of internal auditors has been placed in a global group within each domain. These groups are named IA_Main, IA_East, and IA_West after their respective locations. Jean wants all of the members of these groups to be able to access the same resources in every domain. What is the recommended way to configure this?

   _____

   _____

2. The network administrators from the East domain want to know why the option to create a universal group is not available in their domain. What can you tell them?

   _____

   _____

3. The network administrators from the West domain want to know why everyone always recommends placing global groups into universal groups, instead of just placing the users directly into the universal groups. What should you tell them?

   _____

   _____

4. Jean approves a plan to hire assistants for each domain to create and manage user accounts. How can you give the assistants the immediate ability to help in this way without making them domain administrators?

   _____

   _____

5. Two employees have been hired to back up data, maintain the Windows Server 2003 domain controllers, and manage printers for the Main_Site. Which Builtin

groups will give these users the permissions they require to manage the domain controllers? How should you set up their accounts and group memberships?

_____

_____

6. Two security specialists have been contracted to create group policy for the *Humongous.com* domain. They have no need to perform most administrative tasks. How should you assign their group memberships?

_____

_____

Troubleshooting Lab

You are a network administrator for Contoso Pharmaceuticals. A new assistant named Amy Rusko joins your network administration team. You assign Amy to the domain Server Operators group so she can help with server management tasks. Three days later, Amy tells you that she no longer has the right to shut down the server. Your manager, Andy Ruth, thinks that he told another administrator to set up Amy's account as the new VP of Finance. Andy asks you to e-mail him a list of his group memberships as well as Amy's group memberships.

1. Log on using the Administrator name and password.

2. Insert the Supplemental CD-ROM and run the \70-294\Labs\Chapter08\Lab8.bat batch file. This batch file creates several groups and makes Amy a member of those groups. When the batch file runs, it will leave the commands it runs on-screen for you to review. Press the spacebar when you are finished reviewing what happened.

3. Open a command prompt.

4. In the command prompt window, type **net user amy > userstat.txt** and press ENTER. This command creates the file userstat.txt and sends information, including a list of group memberships of which Amy is a member to that file.

5. In the command prompt window, type **net user andy >> userstat.txt** and press ENTER. This command appends Andy's user information to the userstat.txt file.

6. Type **notepad c:\userstat.txt**. Notepad displays Amy's user information. From here you could attach the file to an e-mail and send it to Andy.

Real World   Batch Files and Group Membership

The Ifmember utility is commonly used in batch files and logon scripts to determine group membership before running a command. You can see how the Ifmember utility works by performing the following steps:

1. Insert the Supplemental CD-ROM and run the \70-294\Labs\Chapter08 \Lab8.bat batch file if you have not already. This batch file creates several groups and makes Amy a member of those groups. When the batch file runs, it will leave the commands it runs on-screen for you to review. Press the spacebar when you are finished reviewing what happened.

2. Run the IfMember_Setup.exe program from the \70-294\Labs\Chapter08 folder on the Supplemental CD-ROM. The Microsoft Web Installation Wizard appears.

3. Click Next to proceed.

4. Read the license agreement. If you do not agree, you cannot continue. If you agree, click the I Agree option button. Then, click Next to proceed. The Destination Directory opens.

5. Adjust the installation location if necessary, and click Install Now.

6. Click Finish.

7. In the new command prompt window, type **ifmember /v /l > c:\membership.txt** and press ENTER.

8. Type **notepad c:\membership.txt** and press ENTER. You'll see a list of your current group memberships displayed in Notepad.

Chapter Summary

- A group is a collection of users, computers, contacts, and other groups. Distribution groups are used only for e-mail. Security groups are used to grant access to resources.

- Group scopes allow you to use groups in different ways to assign permissions. The three group scopes are global, domain local, and universal. Global security groups are most often used to organize users who share similar network access requirements. Domain local security groups are most often used to assign permissions to resources. Universal security groups are most often used to assign permissions to related resources in multiple domains.

- Use the following strategy for planning groups: place user accounts into global groups, create a domain local group for a group of resources to be shared in common, place the global groups into the domain local group, and then assign permissions to the domain local group.

- You use the Active Directory Users And Computers console to create groups, delete groups, add members to groups, and change the group scope.

- You cannot change the group scope for domains with a domain functional level set to Windows 2000 mixed.

- The following scope changes are allowed in domains with the domain functional level set to Windows 2000 native or Windows Server 2003: global to universal, as long as the group is not a member of another group having global scope; domain local to universal, as long as the group being converted does not have another group with a domain local scope as its member; universal to global, as long as the group being converted does not have another universal group as its member; and universal to domain local.

- You should avoid running your computer while logged on as an administrator because running Windows Server 2003 as an administrator makes the system vulnerable to Trojan horse attacks and other security risks. If you frequently need to log on as an administrator, use the Run As program, which allows you to run specific tools and programs with permissions other than those provided by the account with which you are currently logged on.

Exam Highlights

Before taking the exam, review the key points and terms that are presented in this chapter. You need to know this information.

Key Points

- Global security groups are most often used to organize users who share similar network access requirements. Domain local security groups are most often used to assign permissions to resources. Universal security groups are most often used to assign permissions to related resources in multiple domains.

- You should place user accounts into global groups, create a domain local group for a group of resources to be shared in common, place the global groups into the domain local group, and then assign permissions to the domain local group.

- For global security groups, members come from only the local domain, but they can access resources in any domain.

- For domain local security groups, members can come from any domain, but they can access resources only in the local domain.

- For universal security groups, members can come from any domain in the forest and they can access resources in any domain in the forest.

Key Terms

domain local group   A security or distribution group often used to assign permissions to resources. You can use a domain local group to assign permissions to gain access to resources that are located only in the same domain where you create the domain local group. In domains with the domain functional level set to Windows 2000 mixed, domain local groups can contain user accounts, computer accounts, and global groups from any domain. In domains with the domain functional level set to Windows 2000 native or Windows Server 2003, domain local groups can contain user accounts, computer accounts, global groups, and universal groups from any domain, and domain local groups from the same domain.

global group   A security or distribution group often used to organize users who share similar network access requirements. You can use a global group to assign permissions to gain access to resources that are located in any domain in the tree or forest. In domains with the domain functional level set to Windows 2000 mixed, global groups can contain user accounts and computer accounts from the same domain. In domains with the domain functional level set to Windows 2000 native or Windows Server 2003, global groups can contain user accounts, computer accounts, and global groups from the same domain.

Run As program   A program that allows you to run administrative tools with either local or domain administrator rights and permissions while logged on as a normal user.

universal group   A security or distribution group often used to assign permissions to related resources in multiple domains. You can use a universal group to assign permissions to gain access to resources that are located in any domain in the forest. In domains with the domain functional level set to Windows 2000 mixed, universal groups are not available. In domains with the domain functional level set to Windows 2000 native or Windows Server 2003, universal groups can contain user accounts, computer accounts, global groups, and other universal groups from any domain in the forest.

Questions and Answers

Page
8-20

Lesson 1 Review

1. What is the purpose of using groups?

   Use groups to simplify administration by granting rights and assigning permissions once to the group rather than multiple times to each individual member.

2. When should you use security groups rather than distribution groups?

   Use security groups to assign permissions. Use distribution groups when the only function of the group is not security related, such as an e-mail distribution list. You cannot use distribution groups to assign permissions.

3. What strategy should you apply when you use domain and local groups?

   Place user accounts into global groups, place global groups into domain local groups, and then assign permissions to the domain local group.

4. Why is replication an issue with universal groups?

   Universal groups and their members are listed in the global catalog. Therefore, when membership of any universal group changes, the entire group membership must be replicated to every global catalog in the forest, unless the forest functional level is set to Windows Server 2003.

5. Which of the following statements about group scope membership are incorrect? (Choose all that apply.)

   a. In domains with a domain functional level set to Windows 2000 mixed, global groups can contain user accounts and computer accounts from the same domain.

   b. In domains with a domain functional level set to Windows 2000 mixed, global groups can contain user accounts and computer accounts from any domain.

   c. In domains with a domain functional level set to Windows 2000 mixed, domain local groups can contain user accounts, computer accounts, and global groups from the same domain.

   d. In domains with a domain functional level set to Windows 2000 mixed, domain local groups can contain user accounts, computer accounts, and global groups from any domain.

   e. In domains with a domain functional level set to Windows 2000 mixed, universal groups can contain user accounts, computer accounts, global groups, and other universal groups from any domain.

   f. In domains with a domain functional level set to Windows 2000 mixed, universal groups do not exist.

The correct answers are b, c, and e. In domains with a domain functional level set to Windows 2000 mixed, global groups can contain user accounts and computer accounts from the same domain. In domains with a domain functional level set to Windows 2000 mixed, domain local groups can contain user accounts, computer accounts, and global groups from any domain. In domains with a domain functional level set to Windows 2000 mixed, universal groups do not exist.

Page
8-27

Lesson 2 Review

1. Where can you create groups?

   With the necessary permissions, you can create groups in any domain in the forest, in an OU, or in a container you have created specifically for groups.

2. What is deleted when you delete a group?

   When you delete a group, you delete only the group and remove the permissions and rights that are associated with it. Deleting a group does not delete the user accounts that are members of the group.

3. What Active Directory components can be members of groups?

   Members of groups can include user accounts, contacts, other groups, and computers.

4. In what domain functional level is changing the group scope allowed? What scope changes are permitted in this domain functional level?

   You can change the scope of domains with the domain functional level set to Windows 2000 native or Windows Server 2003. The following scope changes are permitted:

   ❑ Global to universal, as long as the group is not a member of another group having global scope

   ❑ Domain local to universal, as long as the group being converted does not have another group with a domain local scope as its member

   ❑ Universal to global, as long as the group being converted does not have another universal group as its member

   ❑ Universal to domain local

5. The name you select for a group must be unique to which of the following Active Directory components?

   a. forest

   b. tree

   c. domain

   d. site

   e. OU

   The correct answer is c. The name you select for a group must be unique to the domain in which the group is created.

Page
8-33

Lesson 3 Review

1. Why shouldn't administrators be assigned to the Administrators group?

    Running Windows Server 2003 as an administrator makes the system vulnerable to Trojan horse attacks and other security risks. For most tasks, administrators should be assigned to the Users or Power Users group. To perform administrative-only tasks, administrators should log on as an administrator, perform the task, and then log off.

2. What is the purpose of the Run As program?

    The Run As program allows a user to run specific tools and programs with permissions other than those provided by the account with which the user is currently logged on. Therefore, the Run As program can be used to run administrative tools with either local or domain administrator rights and permissions while logged on as a normal user.

3. What are the two ways of invoking the Run As Program?

    The Run As program can be invoked on the desktop or by using the Runas command from the command line.

Page
8-34

Case Scenario Exercise

1. Jean says that there are four internal auditors in the forest root domain. There are two internal auditors in each of the child domains. Each set of internal auditors has been placed in a global group within each domain. These groups are named IA_Main, IA_East, and IA_West after their respective locations. Jean wants all of the members of these groups to be able to access the same resources in every domain. What is the recommended way to configure this?

    Create a universal group that all individual global groups can become a member of. This will allow each internal auditor to have access to resources granted to the universal group. Choose a name for the group that represents the entire company, such as Humongous_IA.

2. The network administrators from the East domain want to know why the option to create a universal group is not available in their domain. What can you tell them?

    Universal groups are only available to domains that have a functional level of Windows 2000 native or later. When using the mixed functional level, you cannot create universal groups. In order to change the functional level, all of the existing Windows NT 4 backup domain controllers (BDCs) must be removed or upgraded. Once the domain functional level is raised, the two Windows Server 2003 domain controllers will no longer replicate the domain database to Windows NT 4 BDCs.

3. The network administrators from the West domain want to know why everyone always recommends placing global groups into universal groups, instead of just placing the users directly into the universal groups. What should you tell them?

    Universal group membership changes cause forest-wide replication. If you use global groups in the universal groups instead of users, it is less likely that there will be membership changes to the universal groups. If instead you decided to place users in universal groups, every time a user was added to, or deleted from, a universal group, forest-wide replication would take place.

In most domains the user accounts are modified more frequently than the groups themselves. Once you are able to upgrade all the domain controllers in the forest, you'll be able to raise the domain functional level to Windows Server 2003, which would alleviate this issue and concern.

4. Jean approves a plan to hire assistants for each domain to create and manage user accounts. How can you give the assistants the immediate ability to help in this way without making them domain administrators?

   Place the assistants in the Account Operators group of the domains for which they are expected to be assistants.

5. Two employees have been hired to back up data, maintain the Windows Server 2003 domain controllers, and manage printers for the Main_Site. Which Builtin groups will give these users the permissions they require to manage the domain controllers? How should you set up their accounts and group memberships?

   These users will need permissions assigned to the Backup Operators, Print Operators, and Server Operators. You should create a global group specifically for these users. For example, create the Maintenance_Main global group. Make that group a member of the Backup Operators, Print Operators, and Server Operator domain local groups. Then place the user accounts for these new employees in that new global group.

6. Two security specialists have been contracted to create group policy for the *humongous.com* domain. They have no need to perform most administrative tasks. How should you assign their group memberships?

   Make them a member of the Group Policy Creator Owners domain group.

9 Administering Active Directory Objects

Exam Objectives in this Chapter:

- Plan a user authentication strategy.
- Delegate permissions of an organizational unit (OU) to a user or security group.

Why This Chapter Matters

The information in this chapter shows you how to locate, control access to, and delegate administrative control of Active Directory objects. It's important to be able to find Active Directory objects if you need to perform maintenance on an object or if you need to find more information about an object by viewing its attributes. After you've located an object, one of your primary administrative tasks is likely to be setting access permissions, which determine which users can access the object and the specific actions that they can perform on the object. Finally, being able to delegate administrative control allows you to provide other administrators, groups, or users with the ability to manage the functions in domains or containers according to their needs.

Lessons in this Chapter:

Before You Begin

To complete the lessons in this chapter, you must

- Prepare your test environment according to the descriptions given in the "Getting Started" section of "About This Book"
- Complete the practices for installing and configuring Active Directory as discussed in Chapter 2, "Installing and Configuring Active Directory"
- Learn to use Active Directory administration tools as discussed in Chapter 3, "Administering Active Directory"

- Complete the practices for configuring sites and replication as discussed in Chapter 5, "Configuring Sites and Managing Replication"

- Complete the practices for implementing an OU structure as discussed in Chapter 6, "Implementing an OU Structure"

- Complete the practices for creating and maintaining user accounts as discussed in Chapter 7, "Administering User Accounts"

- Complete the practices for creating and administering group accounts as discussed in Chapter 8, "Administering Groups"

Lesson 1: Locating Active Directory Objects

Active Directory directory service stores information about objects on the network. Each object is a distinct, named set of attributes that represents a specific network entity. Active Directory is designed to provide information in response to queries from users and programs about directory objects. This lesson shows you how to use the Find option in the Active Directory Users And Computers console and the Dsquery command to locate Active Directory objects.

- Identify the types of Active Directory objects

- Use the Find option to locate Active Directory objects

- Use the Dsquery command to locate Active Directory objects

- Save a query by using the saved queries feature

Locating Active Directory Objects

When you install Active Directory on your network, it becomes the main database for finding resources in your organization. The resources in your network are represented by Active Directory objects. You should be familiar with the common Active Directory objects listed in Table 9-1.

Table 9-1   Common Object Types and Their Contents

Object Type	Contents
User account	The information that allows a user to log on to Microsoft Windows Server 2003, such as user logon name.
Contact	The information about a person who has a connection to the organization.
Group	A collection of user accounts, computers, or other groups that you can create and use to simplify administration.
Shared folder	A pointer to a shared folder on a computer. A *pointer* contains the address of certain data, rather than the data itself. When you publish a shared folder or printer in Active Directory, you are creating an object that contains a pointer to the shared folder or printer.
Printer	A pointer to a printer on a computer. Windows Server 2003 automatically adds printers that you create on domain computers to Active Directory. A printer on a computer that is not in Active Directory must be manually published.
Computer	The information about a computer that is a member of the domain.

Table 9-1   Common Object Types and Their Contents

Object Type	Contents
Domain controllers	The information about a domain controller including an optional description, its Domain Name System (DNS) name, its pre–Microsoft Windows 2000 name, the version of the operating system loaded on the domain controller, the location, and who is responsible for managing the domain controller.
OU	Contains other objects, including other OUs. Used to organize Active Directory objects.

Objects are either container objects or leaf objects. A *container object* stores other objects and occupies a specific level in a subtree hierarchy. A *leaf object* does not store other objects and occupies the endpoint of a subtree. When you attempt to locate objects in Active Directory, you enter criteria for the system to use in the search. These criteria must be included in the properties for the object when the object is created. This is why it is a best practice to complete all attributes that are important to your organization when you create Active Directory objects. The more attributes you include, the greater the flexibility when you search for objects.

There are two ways to locate Active Directory objects:

- Use the Find option on the Active Directory Users And Computers console.

- Use the Dsquery command.

> **Note**   If the Windows Firewall is enabled, it might prevent you from finding Active Directory objects in the Active Directory Users And Computers console or in Dsquery. For example, you will get a Dsquery error if the Windows Firewall service is running on a domain controller and you are using this tool from a workstation or other server. The Windows Firewall is a component of Windows Server 2003 with Service Pack 1 (SP1).
>
> For more information, see "Windows Firewall Settings: Remote Administration Tools" on the Microsoft Web site at *http://technet2.microsoft.com/WindowsServer/en/Library/62d661cc-8267-4440-aacc-55358c602a081033.mspx*

Using the Find Option

If an object is published and listed in Active Directory, you can locate it by using the Find option on the Active Directory Users And Computers console. The Find option enables you to search for users, contacts, groups, computers, printers, shared folders, OUs, remote installation servers, and remote installation clients. Find also provides the capability to build custom search queries and to perform common administrative queries for users, contacts, and groups. Using Find, you enter various search criteria, which are used to create a Lightweight Directory Access Protocol (LDAP) query to search the global catalog to locate Active Directory objects. To locate Active Directory objects, complete the following steps:

1. Click Start, point to Administrative Tools, and then click Active Directory Users And Computers.

2. In the console tree, right-click the domain, OU, or container in which you want to search, and then click Find.

3. In the Find dialog box, shown in Figure 9-1, select the object type for which you want to search in the Find list. Ensure that the domain, OU, or container in which you want to search is selected in the In list. Note that the object type you select invokes a tab by the same name underneath the Find list. The contents of this tab change depending on the object type selected. If you want to begin your search now, click Find Now. Otherwise, proceed to the next step to provide additional criteria to filter your search.

Note   If you choose the Custom Search option in the Find list, the Find option builds the LDAP query or allows you to enter your own LDAP query based on parameters you enter in the Advanced tab. For example, the LDAP query **OU=*er*** searches for OU names containing "er" and returns the Domain Controllers OU.

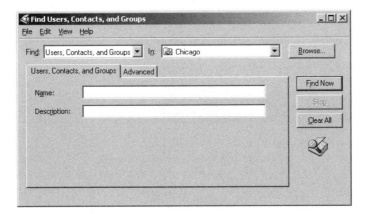

Figure 9-1   Find dialog box

4. Enter additional criteria to filter your search. There are two ways you can provide additional criteria:

   ❑ Enter the appropriate information in the tab for the object type you selected.

   ❑ Click the Advanced tab, shown in Figure 9-2, and select the attribute for which you want to search in the Field list. Select the methods available to further define the search for an attribute in the Condition list. Then type the value for the condition of the field (attribute) that you are using to search the directory in the Value box. Click Add to add the advanced search criteria to the box beneath the Add button.

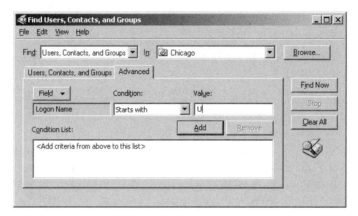

Figure 9-2 Find dialog box, Advanced tab

5. Click Find Now. The search results are displayed in the box at the bottom of the Find dialog box using the search criteria you entered, as shown in Figure 9-3.

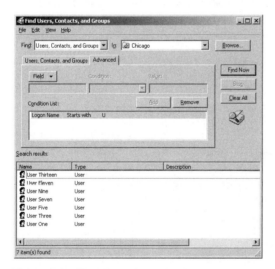

Figure 9-3 Find dialog box, showing search results

6. Click Clear All to begin a new search or close the dialog box and the Active Directory Users And Computers tool.

Using the Dsquery Command

Dsquery is a command-line tool that enables you to find computers, contacts, subnets, groups, OUs, sites, servers, and users in Active Directory according to criteria you specify. The following Dsquery commands allow you to search for the specified object types:

- **Dsquery** *   Finds any object in Active Directory by using a generic LDAP query
- **Dsquery computer**   Finds computers in the directory
- **Dsquery contact**   Finds contacts in the directory
- **Dsquery subnet**   Finds subnets in the directory
- **Dsquery group**   Finds groups in the directory
- **Dsquery ou**   Finds OUs in the directory
- **Dsquery partition**   Finds partition objects in the directory
- **Dsquery quota**   Finds quota specifications in the directory
- **Dsquery site**   Finds sites in the directory
- **Dsquery server**   Finds servers in the directory
- **Dsquery user**   Finds users in the directory

Note   You can find the syntax for each Dsquery command in Windows Server 2003 Help.

- To find all computers that have been inactive for the last four weeks, type:

  dsquery computer -inactive 4
- To find all users in the Marketing OU in the domain *microsoft.com*, type:

  dsquery user OU=Marketing,DC=Microsoft,DC=Com
- To find all users with names starting with "Mike," type:

  dsquery user -name Mike*
- To read all attributes of the object whose distinguished name is OU=Test,DC =Microsoft,DC=Com, type:

  dsquery * OU=Test,DC=Microsoft,DC=Com -scope base -attr *

To use Dsquery to find objects, complete the following steps:

1. Click Start, and then click Command Prompt.
2. At the command prompt, type the appropriate Dsquery command and parameters.

For more information about Dsquery, see Windows Server 2003 Help.

> **Real World   Using Netdom to List Domain Objects**
>
> Netdom is a useful tool for listing objects in the domain. For example, you can use **netdom query workstation** to list all of the workstations in your domain. If you want to specify a different domain, use the **/d**: switch followed by the domain name. For example, to list all of the workstations in the *contoso.com* domain, you'd type **netdom query /d:contoso.com workstation** and press ENTER. Instead of **workstation**, substitute **server**, **dc**, **pdc, fsmo** or **ou** to list servers, domain controllers, the primary domain controller (PDC) emulator, the list of operations master (also known as flexible single master operations, or FSMO) role holders, or OUs, respectively.
>
> Note that on Windows Server 2003 with SP1, Netdom will not work if the Windows Firewall service is running, unless you enable and apply both the "Windows Firewall: Allow remote administration exception" and "Windows Firewall: Allow file and printer sharing exception" Group Policy settings on the target computers.

Using Saved Queries

The saved queries feature is new in Windows Server 2003 and enables administrators to create, edit, save, organize, and e-mail saved queries. The ability to save queries enables administrators to access a specified set of directory objects in order to monitor or perform a specific task on them. Before the saved queries feature, administrators had to create custom Active Directory Services Interface (ADSI) scripts to save a query of specified objects, a lengthy process that required knowledge of how ADSI utilizes LDAP search filters to resolve a query.

Saved queries are stored in the Saved Queries container in the Active Directory Users And Computers console. These queries are preserved within the Active Directory Users And Computers console file (Dsa.msc) and are restored every time the console is opened. Once you have successfully created a customized set of queries, you can copy the console file to other Windows Server 2003 domain controllers in the same domain. You can also easily export saved queries to an .xml file and import them into other Active Directory Users And Computers consoles located on Windows Server 2003 domain controllers in the same domain.

To save a query, complete the following steps:

1. Click Start, point to Administrative Tools, and then click Active Directory Users And Computers.

2. In the console tree, right-click Saved Queries or any of its subfolders in which you want to save a query. Point to New, and then click Query.

3. In the New Query dialog box, shown in Figure 9-4, type a name for the query in the Name box. Type a description for the query in the Description box. Ensure

that the container from which you want to begin your search is listed in the Query Root box. If it is not, click Browse to locate the desired container. To search all subcontainers of the selected container, select the Include Subcontainers check box. Click Define Query.

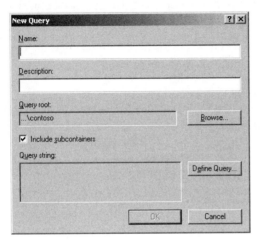

Figure 9-4   New Query dialog box

4. In the Find dialog box, shown in Figure 9-5, select the object type for which you want to search in the Find list. Note that the object type you select invokes a tab by the same name underneath the Find list. The contents of this tab change depending on the object type selected. If you want to begin your search now, click OK. Otherwise, proceed to the next step to provide additional criteria to filter your search.

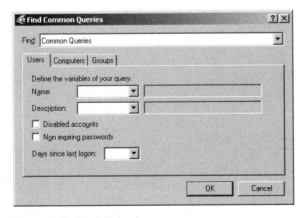

Figure 9-5   Find dialog box

5. Enter additional criteria to filter your search. There are two ways you can provide additional criteria:

   ❑ Enter the appropriate information in the tab for the object type you selected, and then click OK.

❑ Click the Advanced tab, shown previously in Figure 9-2, and select the attribute for which you want to search in the Field list. Select the methods available to further define the search for an attribute in the Condition list. Then type the value for the condition of the field (attribute) that you are using to search the directory in the Value box. Click Add to add the advanced search criteria to the box beneath the Add button, and then click OK.

6. In the New Query dialog box, click OK. The search results are displayed in the details pane using the search criteria you entered.

Tip   To organize your saved queries, you can create subfolders by right-clicking Saved Query, pointing to New, and then clicking Folder.

Practice: Locating Objects in Active Directory

In this practice, you search Active Directory for objects based on search criteria that you provide.

Note   To complete this practice, you must have successfully completed the practices in Chapter 6, "Implementing an OU Structure."

Exercise 1: Creating User Accounts for Practice

In this exercise, you create user accounts with various properties. These accounts are used to practice locating objects in Exercises 2 and 3 and saving queries in Exercise 4.

▶ **To create user accounts for practice**

1. Log on to Server1 as Administrator.

2. Create the user accounts shown in Table 9-2 in the Kansas City OU you set up in the practices in Chapter 6. Make each user a member of the Print Operators group or another group with the right to log on locally to a domain controller.

Table 9-2   User Accounts for Practice

First Name	Last Name	User Logon Name	Password	Change Password
User	Eleven	User11	Password	Default setting
User	Thirteen	User13	Password	Default setting
User	Fifteen	User15	Password	Default setting
User	Seventeen	User17	Password	Default setting
User	Nineteen	User19	Password	Default setting

3. Edit the properties of the User11 account that you created. In the General tab of the Properties dialog box, in the Telephone Number box, type **555-1234**.

4. Edit the properties of the User13, User15, and User17 accounts that you created. In the Organization tab of the Properties dialog box, in the Title box, type **CSR**. In the Department box, type **Sales**. In the Company box, type **Contoso Pharmaceuticals**. (Hint: Use the new feature that allows you to set properties on multiple user objects and set these properties only once for all three users.)

5. Edit the properties of the User19 account that you created. In the Account tab of the Properties dialog box, select the Account Is Disabled check box in the Account Options box.

Exercise 2: Locating Users Using the Find Option

In this exercise, you find various user accounts you created in Exercise 1 by using the Find option.

▶ **To locate users using the Find option**

1. On Server1, use the procedure provided earlier in this lesson to find users in the West OU with the first name of User. What is the result?

   In the Find Users, Contacts, And Groups dialog box, Windows Server 2003 displays the User11, User13, User15, User17, and User19 accounts. Results might vary on your system if additional users have been created.

2. On Server1, use the procedure provided earlier in this lesson to find users in the *contoso.com* domain with the first name of User. What is the result?

   In the Find Users, Contacts, And Groups dialog box, Windows Server 2003 displays the User11, User13, User15, User17, and User19 accounts, plus the User1, User3, User5, User7, and User9 accounts you added in Chapter 7. Results might vary on your system if additional users have been created.

3. Use the procedure provided earlier in this lesson to find users in the *contoso.com* domain with the telephone number beginning with 555. What is the result?

   In the Find Users, Contacts, And Groups dialog box, Windows Server 2003 displays the User11 account for which you typed a telephone number of 555-1234. Results might vary on your system if additional users have been created.

Exercise 3: Locating Users Using the Dsquery Command

In this exercise, you find various user accounts you created in Exercise 1 by using the Dsquery command.

▶ **To locate users using the Dsquery command**

1. Use the procedure provided earlier in this lesson and Windows Server 2003 Help to find disabled user accounts in the *contoso.com* domain. What command did you use and what is the result?

   Use the dsquery user domainroot –disabled command to find disabled user accounts in the *contoso.com* domain. The command lists the Guest, the SUPPORT, the krbtgt, and the User19 accounts as disabled. Results might vary on your system if additional users have been created.

2. Use the procedure provided earlier in this lesson and Windows Server 2003 Help to find a list of all OUs in the *contoso.com* domain, listed by their relative distinguished name. What command did you use and what is result?

   Use the dsquery ou –o rdn command to find a list of all OUs in the *contoso.com* domain, listed by their relative distinguished name. The command lists the Domain Controllers, East, West, Columbus, Chicago, St. Paul, and Kansas City OUs. Results might vary on your system if additional OUs have been created.

Exercise 4: Saving a Query

In this exercise, you save a query.

▶ **To save a query**

1. Use the procedure provided earlier in this lesson to save a query for members of the Sales Department in the *contoso.com* domain. Name the query Sales Users. Use the description "Users in the Sales Department." Include all subcontainers in your query. What is the result?

   User13, User15, and User17 are listed in the details pane. Results might vary on your system if additional users have been created.

2. Use the procedure provided earlier in this lesson to save a query for disabled user accounts in the *contoso.com* domain. Name the query Disabled Accounts. Use the description "Disabled accounts in the contoso.com domain" Include all subcontainers in your query. What is the result?

   The Guest, krbtgt, SUPPORT, and User19 accounts are listed in the details pane. Results might vary on your system if additional users have been created.

3. Disable the User17 account. Then refresh the Disabled Accounts query. View the Sales Users query. What is the result?

   User17 is included in the Disabled Accounts query. User17 is shown in the Sales Users query, but it is marked with a red X as disabled.

Lesson Review

The following questions are intended to reinforce key information presented in this lesson. If you are unable to answer a question, review the lesson and then try the question again. Answers to the questions can be found in the "Questions and Answers" section at the end of this chapter.

1. What are two ways to locate Active Directory objects?

   _____

   _____

2. Which Dsquery command should you use to find users in the directory who have been inactive for two weeks?

   _____

   _____

3. Which Dsquery command should you use to find computers in the directory that have been disabled?

   _____

   _____

4. What is the purpose of the saved queries feature?

   _____

   _____

5. Which of the following is not a valid object type in the Find option?

   a. Users, Contacts, and Groups

   b. Sites

   c. OUs

   d. Computers

Lesson Summary

- There are two ways to locate Active Directory objects: 1) use the Find option on the Active Directory Users And Computers console, and 2) use the Dsquery command.

- The Find option on the Active Directory Users And Computers console enables you to search for users, contacts, groups, computers, printers, shared folders, OUs, remote installation servers, and remote installation clients according to criteria you specify.

- The Dsquery command-line tool enables you to find computers, contacts, subnets, groups, OUs, sites, servers, and users in Active Directory according to criteria you specify.

- The saved queries feature enables administrators to create, edit, save, organize, and e-mail saved queries in order to monitor or perform a specific task on directory objects. Saved queries are stored in the Saved Queries container in the Active Directory Users And Computers console. Saved queries can be exported to an .xml file and imported into other Active Directory Users And Computers consoles located on Windows Server 2003 domain controllers in the same domain.

Lesson 2: Controlling Access to Active Directory Objects

Windows Server 2003 uses an object-based security model to implement access control for all Active Directory objects. This security model is similar to the one used to implement NTFS file system security. Every Active Directory object has a security descriptor that defines who has permission to gain access to the object and what type of access is allowed. Windows Server 2003 uses these security descriptors to control access to objects. This lesson explains how to set permissions for Active Directory objects.

After this lesson, you will be able to

- View and assign standard permissions for an object
- View, assign, and edit special permissions for an object
- View effective permissions for an object
- Set inheritance for a standard or a special permission
- Remove a security principal and its permission
- Remove special permissions for an object
- Transfer ownership of an object

Estimated lesson time: 35 minutes

Understanding Access Control

To control access to Active Directory objects, you grant or deny permissions to security principals. A *permission* is the authority to perform an operation or a set of operations on an object and is granted or denied by the object's owner. A *security principal* is a user, group, computer, or service that is assigned a unique *security identifier (SID)*. A SID uniquely identifies the user, group, computer, or service in the enterprise and is used to manage security principals. As an administrator, it is your responsibility to manage permissions for security principals. Recall from the discussion in Chapter 8 that OUs are not security principals; therefore, you cannot assign access permissions to OUs. You can set access permissions only on drives formatted to use NTFS.

Off the Record   Whoami is a command line utility that displays information about the currently logged on user. You can use this utility to learn about a specific user account before you begin to troubleshoot a resource access problem. The **Whoami /all** command can be used to the view the SID, group memberships, and specific permissions of a user account. Whoami is included in Windows Server 2003. Although the utility is not available in the default installations of Windows 2000 or Microsoft Windows XP, you can install it from the Resource Kit CD for each of those products.

Windows Server 2003 stores a list of user access permissions, called the *access control list (ACL)*, for every Active Directory object. The ACL for an object lists who can access the object and the specific actions that each user can perform on the object. Windows Server 2003 offers a fine degree of control over access to a wide variety of objects. To provide a security principal with access to an object, you add the security principal to the ACL of the object. Then you can adjust the specific permissions that the security principal has for the object.

Permissions

You set permissions to either Allow or Deny. Deny permissions take precedence over all other permissions. For example, if you deny permission to a user to gain access to an object, the user will not have that permission, even if you allow the permission for a group of which the user is a member. The object type determines which permissions you can select. For example, you can assign the Reset Password permission to a security principal for a user object but not for a printer object. For each object type, there is a group of standard permissions and a group of more detailed special permissions.

Standard permissions are the most frequently assigned. You can view the standard permissions in the Security tab in the Properties dialog box for an object, shown in Figure 9-6.

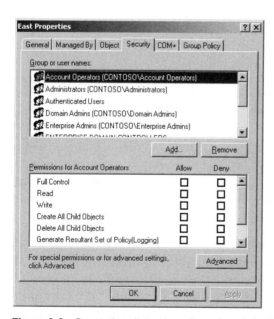

Figure 9-6   Properties dialog box, Security tab for the East OU

To view the standard permissions for an object, complete the following steps:

1. Click Start, point to Administrative Tools, and then click Active Directory Users And Computers. On the View menu, ensure that Advanced Features is selected. Right-click the object for which you want to view standard permissions and click Properties.

2. In the Properties dialog box for the object, click the Security tab. Click the appropriate security principal in the Group Or User Names box to view the assigned standard permissions.

Important   You must select Advanced Features on the View menu to be able to access the Security tab. Remember that the Active Directory Users And Computers console does not work from a remote workstation or server if the target domain controller is running the Windows Firewall service.

Table 9-3 lists the basic standard permissions that are available for most objects (some object types have additional standard permissions) and the type of access that each permission allows.

Table 9-3   Basic Standard Permissions and Type of Access Allowed

Permission	Allows the security principal to
Full Control	Take ownership, change permissions, and perform tasks allowed by all other standard permissions
Read	View objects and associated object attributes, the object owner, and Active Directory permissions
Write	Change object attributes

Standard permissions are composed of *special permissions*, which provide you with a finer degree of control for assigning access to objects. For example, the standard Write permission is composed of the Write All Properties and All Validated Writes special permissions. Special permissions are also referred to as advanced security settings. You can view the special permissions in the Permission Entry dialog box for an object, shown in Figure 9-7.

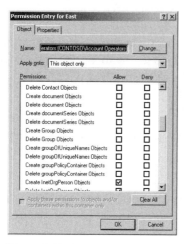

Figure 9-7   Permission Entry dialog box for the East OU

To view the special permissions for an object, complete the following steps:

1. Click Start, point to Administrative Tools, and then click Active Directory Users And Computers. On the View menu, ensure that Advanced Features is selected. Right-click the object for which you want to view special permissions, and then click Properties.

2. In the Properties dialog box for the object, click the Security tab. Click Advanced.

3. In the Advanced Security Settings dialog box for the object, select the appropriate security principal and permission in the Permission Entries list, and then click Edit.

4. In the Permission Entry dialog box for the object, select the Object tab to view special permissions for the object assigned to the security principal. Select the Properties tab to view special permissions for the properties assigned to the security principal.

> **Off the Record**   As introduced in Chapter 3, "Administering Active Directory," Acldiag.exe and Dsacls.exe are Windows Support Tools that you can use to view and edit Active Directory permissions. For example, if you want to see all of the permissions assigned to an OU named Marketing in the *contoso.com* domain, you could type **acldiag ou=marketing,dc=contoso, dc=com**. The resulting output would be a complete dump of the discretionary access control list (DACL) of the Marketing OU, including a list of special permissions.

Object Ownership

When an object is created, the user creating an object automatically becomes its owner. Administrators create and own most objects in Active Directory and on network servers when installing programs on the server. Users create and own data files in their home directories and some data files on network servers. The owner controls how permissions are set on the object and to whom permissions are granted.

Ownership can be taken by

- An administrator. By default, the Administrators group is given the Take Ownership Of Files Or Other Objects user right. User rights are discussed in Chapter 13, "Administering Security with Group Policy."

- Any user or group who has the Take Ownership permission on the object.

- A user who has the Restore Files And Directories user right.

In Windows Server 2003, quotas can be specified in Active Directory to control the number of objects a security principal (user, group, or computer) can own in a given directory partition. *Active Directory quotas* can help prevent the denial of service that can occur if a security principal creates objects until the affected domain controller runs out of storage space. Domain Administrators and Enterprise Administrators are exempt from quotas. In some cases, a security principal might be covered by multiple quotas such as a quota assigned to a user and a quota assigned to a group to which the user belongs. In this case, the effective quota is whichever is the largest quota assigned to the security principal.

If a security principal is not assigned a quota, a default quota on the partition governs the security principal. If a default quota is not explicitly set for the partition, then the partition has no limit. For quotas to be effective on a domain directory partition, all domain controllers in the domain must be running Windows Server 2003. For quotas to be effective on the configuration partition, all domain controllers in the forest must be running Windows Server 2003. The schema partition has no quotas.

To create and maintain Active Directory quotas, you use the **dsadd quota**, **dsmod quota**, and **dsquery quota** commands. For detailed information about using these commands, refer to Windows Server 2003 Help.

> **Note** When used as remote administration tools, dsquery, dsmod, or dsadd will not work if the Windows Firewall service is running on the target computer. For more information, see "Windows Firewall Settings: Remote Administration Tools" on the Microsoft Web site at *http://technet2.microsoft.com/WindowsServer/en/Library/62d661cc-8267-4440-aacc-55358c602a081033.mspx*

How Group Membership Affects Access Control

A security principal can be a member of multiple groups, each with different permissions, that provide different levels of access to objects. When you assign a permission to a security principal for access to an object and that security principal is a member of a group to which you assigned a different permission, the security principal's permissions are the combination of the security principal and group permissions. For example, if a user as an individual has Read permission and is a member of a group with Write permission, the user has both Read and Write permission. When assigning permissions to groups, you must determine which users are affected.

> **Note** Groups or users that have been granted Full Control permission for a folder can delete files and subfolders within that folder, regardless of the permissions protecting the files and subfolders.

How Inheritance Affects Access Control

There are two ways of assigning permissions to an object: assigning permissions explicitly and assigning them indirectly through inheritance. Permissions set explicitly are defined directly on an object by the object's owner. Permissions assigned through inheritance are propagated to a child object from a parent object. *Inherited permissions* ease the task of managing permissions and ensure consistency of permissions among all objects within a given container by minimizing the number of times that you need to assign permissions for objects.

> **Off the Record** The Windows Support Tools include the SDCheck utility, introduced in Chapter 3. You can use this utility to diagnose permission inheritance and permission replication issues. For example, if you run the command **sdcheck server1 administrator@contoso.com**, you'll receive a list of permissions assigned to the Administrator account of the *contoso.com* domain according to Server1. If you run the command **sdcheck server2 administrator@ contoso.com**, you'll see the same output according to Server2. You can compare the two results in an attempt to locate a discrepancy. To make the comparison more easily, you can use a file comparison utility, such as Windiff.exe, which is also part of the Windows Support Tools. In that case, you'd ensure the output of the SDCheck commands went to a file by adding **> filename.txt** to the end of the command. If you find a discrepancy, this might be an indication that there is something wrong with the replication process. For additional examples of how to use SDCheck, perform a Web search on "SDCheck examples." Note that if you run SDCheck from a remote workstation or server, this tool will not work if the Windows Firewall service is running on the target computer.

For example, as shown in Figure 9-8, if you assign Full Control permission to the Sales group for the East OU, the permission can be propagated to the child objects of the East OU, the Chicago and Columbus OUs, and their respective child objects, a shared folder named Account Information, and two users. Therefore, permissions for the Sales group in the East OU are explicit permissions, while the permissions for the Sales group in the OUs, shared folder, and users are inherited permissions.

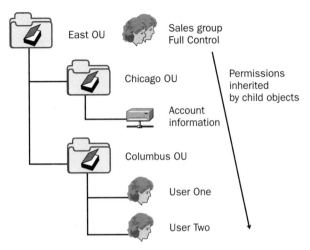

Figure 9-8   Permissions set for the parent objects can be inherited by child objects

After you set permissions on a parent object, child objects created in the parent object can inherit these permissions. There are three indicators of inherited permissions:

- **Shaded permissions check boxes**   These check boxes are located in the Security tab in the Properties dialog box for an object, shown previously in Figure 9-6, and in the Permission Entry dialog box for an object, shown previously in Figure 9-7. If a permission is inherited, a permissions check box is shaded. However, shaded special permissions check boxes do not indicate inherited permissions. These shaded check boxes merely indicate that a special permission exists.

- **The Inherited From column**   This column is located in the Permission Entries list in the Advanced Security Settings dialog box for an object, shown in Figure 9-9. If a permission is inherited, the distinguished name of the parent object is displayed. This is a new feature in Windows Server 2003.

- **Unavailable Remove button for a permission**   This button is located in the Advanced Security Settings dialog box, shown in Figure 9-9. If a permission is inherited, the Remove button is unavailable, because the permission must be removed at the parent object.

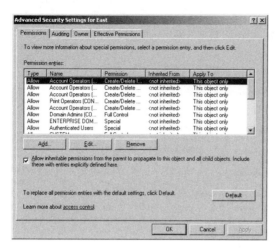

Figure 9-9   Advanced Security Settings dialog box for the East OU

Effective Permissions

Effective permissions are the overall permissions that a security principal has for an object, including group membership and inheritance from parent objects. A new feature in Windows Server 2003 enables you to view the effective permissions granted to a selected security principal for an object.

To view effective permissions granted to a security principal for an object, complete the following steps:

1. Click Start, point to Administrative Tools, and then click Active Directory Users And Computers. On the View menu, ensure that Advanced Features is selected. Right-click the object for which you want to view effective permissions and click Properties.

2. In the Properties dialog box for the object, click the Security tab, and then click Advanced.

3. In the Advanced Security Settings dialog box for the object, click the Effective Permissions tab. Click Select.

4. In the Select User, Computer, Or Group dialog box, type the name of a user or group in the Enter The Object Name To Select box, and then click OK. The selected check boxes indicate the effective permissions of the user or group for the object, as shown in Figure 9-10.

> **Tip**   The information displayed in the Effective Permissions tab is read-only. Therefore, you cannot change a user's permissions by selecting or clearing permission check boxes in this tab.

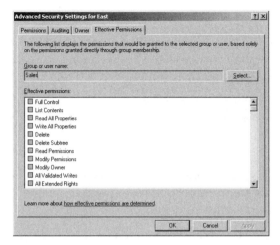

Figure 9-10   Advanced Security Settings dialog box, Effective Permissions tab

Best Practices for Assigning Permissions

The following are the best practices for assigning permissions:

- Because it is inefficient to maintain user accounts directly, you should assign permissions to groups rather than to users.

- Deny permissions sparingly. You should deny permissions only when it is necessary to exclude a subset of a group that has allowed permissions, or to exclude one special permission when you have already granted full control to a user or group. If you assign permissions correctly, you should not need to deny permissions. In most cases, denied permissions indicate mistakes that were made in assigning group membership.

- Set permissions to be inheritable to child objects.

- Assign Full Control permission, if appropriate, rather than individual permissions.

> **Caution**   Always ensure that all objects have at least one user with the Full Control permission. Failure to do so might result in some objects being inaccessible to the person using the Active Directory Users And Computers console, even an administrator, unless object ownership is changed.

Assigning Standard Permissions

Standard permissions are assigned in the Security tab in the Properties dialog box for the object, which is accessed by using the Active Directory Users And Computers console.

To assign standard permissions for an object, complete the following steps:

1. Click Start, point to Administrative Tools, and then click Active Directory Users And Computers. On the View menu, ensure that Advanced Features is selected. Right-click the object for which you want to assign permissions and click Properties.

> **Important**   You must select Advanced Features on the View menu to be able to access the Security tab and assign standard permissions for an object.

2. In the Properties dialog box for the object, click the Security tab, shown previously in Figure 9-6. Note that the permissions provided in the Properties dialog box are different for each object type. Click Add.

3. In the Select Users, Computers, Or Groups dialog box, type the name of the security principal for which you want to set permissions in the Enter The Object Name To Select box, then click OK.

4. In the Permissions For Security Principal box, select the Allow check box or the Deny check box for each permission you want to add, change, or deny. Refer to the "Setting Inheritance for a Permission" section in this lesson for details on setting inheritance, and then click OK.

Administering Special Permissions

Standard permissions are sufficient for most administrative tasks. However, you might need to assign or edit special permissions. Special permissions are assigned in the Advanced Security Settings dialog box for the object, which is accessed by using the Active Directory Users And Computers console.

To assign or edit special permissions for an object, complete the following steps:

1. Click Start, point to Administrative Tools, and then click Active Directory Users And Computers. On the View menu, ensure that Advanced Features is selected. Right-click the object for which you want to assign or edit special permissions and click Properties.

2. In the Properties dialog box for the object, click the Security tab. Click Advanced.

3. In the Advanced Security Settings dialog box for the object, do one of the following:

   ❏ To set special permissions for an additional security principal or set additional special permissions for an existing security principal, click Add. In the Enter The Object Name To Select box, type the name of the security principal, and then click OK.

❏ To change the special permissions for the object, click the entry for which you want to change special permissions in the Permission Entries list, and then click Edit.

> **Note**   To change permissions, you must be the owner of the object or have been granted permission to do so by the owner.

4. In the Permission Entry dialog box for the object, set or change the desired special permissions in the Object and Properties tabs, and then click OK. Refer to the following section, "Setting Inheritance for a Permission," for details on setting inheritance.

5. In the Advanced Security Settings dialog box for the object, click OK.

6. In the Properties dialog box for the object, click OK.

> **Note**   Avoid assigning permissions for specific attributes of objects because this can complicate system administration. Errors can result, such as Active Directory objects not being visible, preventing users from completing tasks.

Setting Inheritance for a Permission

The following three settings control permissions inheritance:

- Allow Inheritable Permissions From The Parent To Propagate To This Object And All Child Objects, Include These With Entries Explicitly Defined Here check box

  ❏ Location: Advanced Security Settings dialog box for an object.

  ❏ Function: Determines whether an object can inherit permissions.

  ❏ Default setting: The check box is selected, allowing an object to inherit permissions.

  ❏ Action to take: If you don't want an object to inherit any permissions from its parent object, clear this box.

- Apply Onto list box

  ❏ Location: Permission Entry dialog box for an object.

  ❏ Function: Determines which objects inherit permissions.

  ❏ Default setting: If permission was set in the Security tab in the Properties dialog box for the object, the list is set to "This Object Only," preventing the permission from being inherited. If permission was added from the Advanced Security Settings dialog box for the object, the list is set to "This Object And All Child Objects," allowing the permission to be inherited.

❑ Action to take: If you don't want child objects to inherit this permission, ensure that "This Object Only" is selected. If you want child objects to inherit this permission, ensure that "This Object And All Child Objects" is selected. If you want specific objects to inherit this permission, change the entry to the appropriate object in the list.

■ Apply These Permissions To Objects And/Or Containers Within This Container Only check box

❑ Location: Permission Entry dialog box for an object.

❑ Function: Prevents child objects outside of the container from inheriting permissions. This option is not available if the Apply Onto list box is set to "This Object Only."

❑ Default setting: The check box is cleared, allowing permissions inheritance to flow past the immediate children to other containers within the parent.

❑ Action to take: If you want only the immediate child objects of the container to inherit this permission, check this box.

Exam Tip Make sure you understand how each setting described here affects inheritance.

Note The settings for the Apply Onto list and the Apply These Permissions To Objects And/ Or Containers Within This Container Only check box in the Permission Entry dialog box for an object are the same in both the Object and Properties tabs, regardless of the tab in which they are set. Therefore, you don't need to make changes to both tabs.

If you choose to prevent a specific object from inheriting permissions by clearing the Allow Inheritable Permissions From The Parent To Propagate To This Object And All Child Objects, Include These With Entries Explicitly Defined Here check box, you are shown a message box that allows you to

■ Copy previously inherited permissions to the object. The new explicit permissions for the object are a copy of the permissions that it previously inherited from its parent object. Then, according to your needs, you can make any necessary changes to the permissions.

■ Remove previously inherited permissions from the object. Windows Server 2003 removes any previously inherited permissions. No permissions exist for the object. Then, according to your needs, you can assign any permissions for the object.

Note To set inheritance for a standard or special permission, you must be the owner of the object or have been granted permission to do so by the owner.

To set inheritance for a standard or special permission, complete the following steps:

1. In the Advanced Security Settings dialog box for the object, do one of the following:

   ❑ If you want this object to inherit permissions from its parent object, proceed to the next step.

   ❑ If you don't want this object to inherit any permissions from its parent object, clear the Allow Inheritable Permissions From The Parent To Propagate To This Object And All Child Objects, Include These With Entries Explicitly Defined Here check box. Then select Copy to copy the permissions or Remove to remove the permissions.

2. Select the permission in the Permission Entries box, then click Edit.

3. In the Permission Entry dialog box for the object, do one of the following:

   ❑ If you don't want child objects to inherit this permission, ensure that the Apply Onto list is set to This Object Only. Click OK.

   ❑ If you want *only* child objects to inherit this permission, ensure that the Apply Onto list is set to This Object And All Child Objects. At this point, you have two options.

   If you want permissions inheritance to flow past the immediate child objects of this object to other containers within the parent, click OK.

   If you want only the immediate child objects of this object to inherit this permission, select the Apply These Permissions To Objects And/Or Containers Within This Container Only check box. Click OK.

4. In the Advanced Security Settings dialog box for the object, click OK.

5. In the Properties dialog box for the object, click OK.

Changing Inherited Permissions

There are three ways to make changes to inherited permissions:

■ Make the changes to the parent object, and then the object inherits these permissions.

■ Assign the opposite permission (Allow or Deny) to the security principal to override the inherited permission.

■ Clear the Allow Inheritable Permissions From The Parent To Propagate To This Object And All Child Objects, Include These With Entries Explicitly Defined Here check box in the Advanced Security Settings dialog box for the object. Then, you can make changes to the permissions or remove users or groups from the Permissions Entries list. However, the object no longer inherits permissions from the parent object.

Selective Authentication

In Chapter 4, "Installing and Managing Domains, Trees, and Forests," you learned that in Windows Server 2003, you can determine the scope of authentication between two domains that are joined by an external trust or a forest trust. Recall that an external trust must be explicitly created by a systems administrator between Windows Server 2003 domains that are in different forests or between a Windows Server 2003 domain and a domain whose domain controller is running Windows NT 4 or earlier. The trust is non-transitive. A forest trust is explicitly created by a systems administrator between two forest root domains. The trust is transitive between two forests only. Both trusts can be one-way or two-way.

You can set selective authentication differently for outgoing and incoming external and forest trusts. These selective trusts allow you to make flexible access control decisions between external domains and forest-wide.

If you use domain-wide authentication on the incoming external or forest trust, users in the second domain or outside forest would have the same level of access to resources in the local domain or forest as users who belong to the local domain or forest. For example, if DomainA has an incoming external trust from DomainB and domain-wide authentication is used, any user from DomainB would be able to access any resource in DomainA (assuming that they have the required permissions). Similarly, if ForestA has an incoming forest trust from ForestB and forest-wide authentication is used, any user from ForestB would be able to access any resource in ForestA (assuming they have the required permissions).

If you set selective authentication on an incoming external or forest trust, you need to manually assign permissions on each resource to which you want users in the second domain or forest to have access. To do this, set the Allowed To Authenticate permission on an object for that particular user or group from the external domain or forest.

When a user authenticates across a trust with selective authentication enabled, an Other Organization SID is added to the user's authorization data. The presence of this SID prompts a check on the resource domain to ensure that the user is allowed to authenticate to the particular service. Once the user is authenticated, if the Other Organization SID is not already present, then the server adds the This Organization SID. Only one of these special SIDs can be present in an authenticated user's context.

Administrators in each domain or forest can add objects from one domain to ACLs on shared resources in the other domain or forest. You can use the ACL editor to add or remove objects residing in one domain or forest to ACLs on resources in the other domain.

Setting Selective Authentication

Recall from Chapter 4 that you can set selective authentication when you create an external or forest trust by using the New Trust Wizard. You can also set selective authentication for an existing external or forest trust by using the Active Directory Domains And Trusts console.

To set selective authentication for an external or forest trust, complete the following steps:

1. Click Start, point to Administrative Tools, and then click Active Directory Domains And Trusts.

2. In the console tree, right-click the domain node for the domain you want to administer, and then click Properties.

3. On the Trusts tab, under either Domains Trusted By This Domain (Outgoing Trusts) or Domains That Trust This Domain (Incoming Trusts), do one of the following:

   ❑ Click the external trust that you want to administer, and then click Properties. On the Authentication tab, click Selective Authentication, and then click OK.

   ❑ Click the forest trust that you want to administer, and then click Properties. On the Authentication tab, click Selective Authentication, and then click OK.

4. In the Properties dialog box for the domain, click OK.

5. Manually enable permissions on each domain and resource in the local domain or forest to which you want users in the second domain or forest to have access.

 Exam Tip   Know how to set selective authentication for an external trust and a forest trust.

To perform this procedure for an external or forest trust, you must be a member of the Domain Admins group (in the forest root domain) or the Enterprise Admins group in Active Directory, or you must have been delegated the appropriate authority.

Removing Security Principals and Their Permissions

If necessary, you can remove security principals and their permissions from an object in one step in the Security tab in the Properties dialog box for the object, which is accessed by using the Active Directory Users And Computers console. To remove security principals and their permissions from an object, you must be the owner of the object or have been granted permission to do so by the owner.

To remove an existing security principal and its permissions, complete the following steps:

1. Click Start, point to Administrative Tools, and then click Active Directory Users And Computers. On the View menu, ensure that Advanced Features is selected. Right-click the object for which you want to remove a security principal and click Properties.

2. In the Properties dialog box for the object, click the Security tab. In the Group Or User Names box, click the desired security principal, and then click Remove.

Removing Special Permissions

If necessary, you can remove special permissions from an object in the Security tab in the Advanced Security Settings dialog box for the object, which is accessed by using the Active Directory Users And Computers console. To remove special permissions from an object, you must be the owner of the object or have been granted permission to do so by the owner.

To remove special permissions, complete the following steps:

1. Click Start, point to Administrative Tools, and then click Active Directory Users And Computers. On the View menu, ensure that Advanced Features is selected. Right-click the object for which you want to remove special permissions and click Properties.

2. In the Properties dialog box for the object, click the Security tab, then click Advanced.

3. In the Advanced Security Settings dialog box for the object, in the Permission Entries box, select the permission you want to remove, and then click Remove.

Note   If the Remove button is unavailable, clear the Allow Inheritable Permissions From The Parent To Propagate To This Object And All Child Objects, Include These With Entries Explicitly Defined Here check box, and then click Remove. However, keep in mind that if you do this, the object no longer inherits permissions from the parent object.

Transferring Object Ownership

Object ownership can be transferred in the following ways:

■ The current owner can grant Take Ownership permission to another user, allowing that user to take ownership at any time. The user must actually take ownership to complete the transfer.

■ An administrator can take ownership of any file on the computer. However, the administrator cannot transfer ownership to others, which keeps the administrator accountable.

■ A user who has the Restore Files And Directories user right can choose any user or group to assign ownership to.

To transfer ownership of an object, complete the following steps:

1. Click Start, point to Administrative Tools, and then click Active Directory Users And Computers. On the View menu, ensure that Advanced Features is selected. Right-click the object for which you want to transfer ownership and click Properties.

2. In the Properties dialog box for the object, click the Security tab. Click Advanced.

3. In the Advanced Security Settings dialog box for the object, click the Owner tab.

4. In the Owner tab, shown in Figure 9-11, click the new owner in the Change Owner To box or, if the owner is not listed, click the Other Users Or Groups button to browse for the new owner. Click OK.

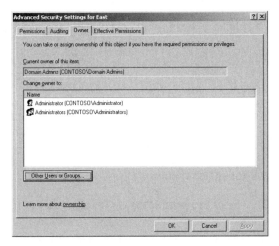

Figure 9-11   Advanced Security Settings dialog box, Owner tab

Practice: Controlling Access to Active Directory Objects

In this practice, you assign standard and special permissions for an object, set inheritance for the permissions, and remove security principals and their permissions from an object.

Exercise 1: Assigning Standard and Special Permissions

In this exercise, you assign a standard permission and a special permission to the Sales group for the East OU.

▶ **To assign standard and special permissions**

1. Log on to Server1 as Administrator.

2. On Server1, use the procedure provided earlier in this lesson to assign the Full Control standard permission to the Sales group for the East OU.

3. Use the procedure provided earlier in this lesson to edit the special permissions already assigned to the Sales group for the East OU. Change the special permissions to not allow the Modify Owner permission.

4. Access the Security tab in the Properties dialog box for the East OU. The Sales group should be listed in the Group Or User Names box.

5. Access the Security tab in the Properties dialog box for the Chicago OU. Is the Sales group listed in the Group Or User Names box? Why or why not?

   No, the Sales group is not listed for the Chicago OU because inheritance has not been set.

6. Access the Security tab in the Properties dialog box for User1 in the Chicago OU. Is the Sales group listed in the Group Or User Names box? Why or why not?

   No, the Sales group is not listed for User1 in the Chicago OU because inheritance has not been set.

Exercise 2: Setting Inheritance for a Permission

In this exercise, you set inheritance for the permissions you assigned to the Sales group for the East OU in Exercise 1. First, you set the permissions to be inherited by all child objects. Then, you set the permissions to be inherited only by immediate child objects. You check the results of your inheritance settings.

▶ **To set inheritance for a permission**

1. On Server1, use the procedures provided earlier in this lesson to apply the permissions you assigned to the Sales group in Exercise 1 to this object and all child objects.

2. Access the Security tab in the Properties dialog box for the East OU. The Sales group should still be listed in the Group Or User Names box.

3. Access the Security tab in the Properties dialog box for the Chicago OU. Is the Sales group listed in the Group Or User Names box? Why or why not?

   Yes, the Sales group is listed for the Chicago OU because inheritance has applied the permission to the East OU and all of its child objects. The Chicago OU is a child object of the East OU.

4. Access the Security tab in the Properties dialog box for User1 in the Chicago OU. Is the Sales group listed in the Group Or User Names box? Why or why not?

   Yes, the Sales group is listed for User1 because inheritance has applied the permission to the East OU and all of its child objects. User1 is a child of the Chicago OU, which is a child object of the East OU.

5. On Server1, use the procedures provided earlier in this lesson to apply the permissions you assigned to the Sales group in Exercise 1 to only the immediate child objects of the East OU.

6. Access the Security tab in the Properties dialog box for the East OU. The Sales group should still be listed in the Group Or User Names box.

7. Access the Security tab in the Properties dialog box for the Chicago OU. Is the Sales group listed in the Group Or User Names box? Why or why not?

   Yes, the Sales group is listed for the Chicago OU because inheritance has applied the permission to the East OU and its immediate child objects. The Chicago OU is an immediate child object of the East OU.

8. Access the Security tab in the Properties dialog box for User1 in the Chicago OU. Is the Sales group listed in the Group Or User Names box? Why or why not?

   No, the Sales group is not listed for User1 because inheritance has applied the permission to the East OU and its immediate child objects. User1 is a child of the Chicago OU and is not an immediate child object of the East OU.

Exercise 3: Removing Security Principals and Their Permissions

In this exercise, you remove the Sales group and the permissions assigned to it for the East OU.

▶ **To remove security principals and their permissions**

On Server1, use the procedures provided earlier in this lesson to remove the Sales security principal and its permissions from the Group Or User Names box in the Security tab in the Properties dialog box for the East OU.

Lesson Review

The following questions are intended to reinforce key information presented in this lesson. If you are unable to answer a question, review the lesson and then try the question again. Answers to the questions can be found in the "Questions and Answers" section at the end of this chapter.

   1. What is a security principal?

   _____

   _____

   2. You are trying to assign permissions to an object in its Properties dialog box, but you cannot find the Security tab. How can you fix this problem?

   _____

   _____

   3. The permissions check boxes for a security principal are shaded. What does this indicate?

   _____

   _____

   4. What are effective permissions?

   _____

   _____

   5. User X is a member of the Sales group and the Marketing group. The Sales group has Write permission for the Accounts shared folder. The Marketing group has Full Control permission for the Accounts shared folder. User X alone has Read permission for the Accounts shared folder. Which of the following permissions does User X have for the Accounts shared folder?

      a. Write permission only

      b. Read permission only

      c. Read and Write permissions only

      d. Full Control permission only

      e. All permissions

Lesson Summary

- To control access to Active Directory objects, you grant or deny permissions to security principals. You set permissions to either Allow or Deny. Deny permissions take precedence over all other permissions.

- When an object is created, the user creating it automatically becomes its owner. The owner controls how permissions are set on the object and to whom permissions are granted.

- You can set selective authentication differently for outgoing and incoming external and forest trusts. These selective trusts allow you to make flexible access control decisions between external domains and forest-wide.

- When you assign a permission to a security principal for access to an object and that security principal is a member of a group to which you assigned a different permission, the security principal's permissions are the combination of the assigned security principal and group permissions.

- Permissions assigned through inheritance are propagated to a child object from a parent object. Effective permissions are the overall permissions that a security principal has for an object, including group membership and inheritance from parent objects.

Lesson 3: Delegating Administrative Control of Active Directory Objects

To ensure that specific administrators receive the appropriate permissions for an object, you must delegate the administration of the object. In this lesson, you learn how to use the Delegation Of Control Wizard to delegate administrative control of domains, OUs, and containers.

After this lesson, you will be able to

- Delegate administrative control of domains, OUs, and containers

Estimated lesson time: 10 minutes

Delegating Administrative Control

You delegate administrative control of domains, OUs, and containers in order to provide other administrators, groups, or users with the ability to manage functions according to their needs. In small organizations, a few administrators might be responsible for managing Active Directory objects. However, larger organizations might require many more administrators, requiring administrators to manage specific domains, OUs, or containers or even specific objects within OUs or containers. To ensure that administrators receive the appropriate permissions, you must delegate the administration of the domain, OU, or container. The Delegation Of Control Wizard is provided to automate and simplify the process of setting administrative permissions for a domain or an OU. Once you've used the Delegation Of Control Wizard to set up permissions, you can view or modify permissions for an object by viewing or modifying the access control entries (ACEs) in the object's ACL.

When you delegate administrative control to users, you must ensure that the users take responsibility and can be held accountable. Provide training for users who have control of objects. If the users to whom you delegate responsibility are not performing the administrative tasks, you need to assume responsibility for their failure.

> **Note**   By default, all child objects in an OU inherit the permissions set on the OU.

> **Exam Tip**   Make sure you know the difference between access control and delegating administrative control.

The Delegation Of Control Wizard steps you through the process of assigning permissions at the domain, OU, or container level. Permissions for other objects must be manually assigned as described in Lesson 2. Table 9-4 describes the function of each of the pages in the Delegation Of Control Wizard.

Table 9-4   Pages in the Delegation Of Control Wizard

Page	Function
Users Or Groups	Enables you to select the user accounts or groups to which you want to delegate control.
Tasks To Delegate	Enables you to select the tasks to delegate. You pick common tasks from a list or indicate that you want to create custom tasks to delegate.
Active Directory Object Type (available only when custom tasks are selected in "Tasks To Delegate")	Enables you to select the objects that you want to delegate, either ■ The container, existing objects in the container, or new objects in the container, or ■ Only specific objects in the container
Permissions (available only when custom tasks are selected in "Tasks To Delegate")	Enables you to select one of the following permissions to delegate: ■ **General** The most commonly assigned permissions that are available for the object ■ **Property-Specific** The permissions that you can assign to the attributes of the object ■ **Creation/Deletion Of Specific Child Objects** The permissions that apply to the entire object

To delegate administrative control of a domain, OU, or container, complete the following steps:

1. Click Start, select Administrative Tools, and then click Active Directory Users And Computers.

2. Right-click the appropriate domain, OU, or container, and then click Delegate Control.

3. On the Welcome To The Delegation Of Control Wizard page, click Next.

4. On the Users Or Groups page, shown in Figure 9-12, click Add.

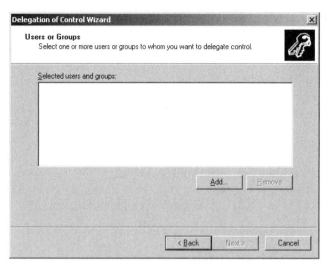

Figure 9-12 Delegation Of Control Wizard, Users Or Groups page

5. In the Select Users, Computers, Or Groups dialog box, type the user or group for which you want to delegate administration in the Enter The Object Names To Select box, and then click OK. Click Next on the Users Or Groups page.

6. On the Tasks To Delegate page, shown in Figure 9-13, do one of the following:

❑ If you want to delegate any of the tasks listed in the box, click Delegate The Following Common Tasks and select the appropriate tasks. Click Next, then proceed to step 10.

❑ If you want to delegate tasks not listed in the box, click Create A Custom Task To Delegate, then click Next.

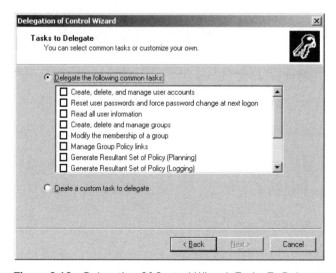

Figure 9-13 Delegation Of Control Wizard, Tasks To Delegate page

7. On the Active Directory Object Type page, shown in Figure 9-14, do one of the following:

  ❑ If you want to delegate control of the container, existing objects in the container, and objects that will be created in the container, click This Folder, Existing Objects In This Folder, And Creation Of New Objects In This Folder.

  ❑ If you want to delegate control of only specific objects in the container, click Only The Following Objects In The Folder and select the appropriate objects. If you want to restrict the user or group to creating the specified objects in the container, click Create Selected Objects In This Folder. If you want to restrict the user or group to deleting specified objects in the container, click Delete Selected Objects In This Folder. Click Next.

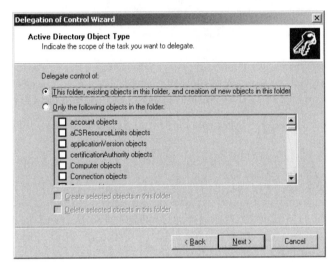

Figure 9-14   Delegation Of Control Wizard, Active Directory Object Type page

8. On the Permissions page, shown in Figure 9-15, do one of the following:

  ❑ Select General to display the general permissions (equivalent to the permissions displayed in the Security tab of the Properties dialog box for an object) in the Permissions box.

  ❑ Select Property-Specific to display the permissions that apply to specific properties (equivalent to the permissions displayed in the Properties tab of the Permission Entry dialog box for an object) in the Permissions box.

  ❑ Select Creation/Deletion Of Specific Child Objects to display the permissions that apply to the entire object (equivalent to the permissions displayed in the Object tab of the Permission Entry dialog box for an object) in the Permissions box.

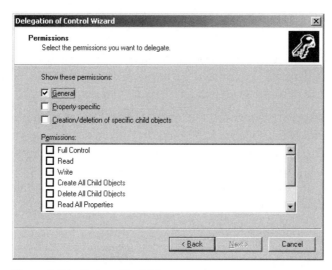

Figure 9-15 Delegation Of Control Wizard, Permissions page

9. Select the appropriate permissions you want to assign to the users or groups for the container or objects in the Permissions box, and then click Next.

10. On the Completing The Delegation Of Control Wizard page, review your selections. Click Finish.

Verifying Delegated Permissions

You can verify permissions delegated for the container or objects in the container in the Security tab in the Properties dialog box for the container and in the Advanced Security Settings dialog box for the container. Refer to the previous lesson for specific instruction on accessing these dialog boxes.

Removing Delegated Permissions

Although the Delegation Of Control Wizard can be used to grant administrative permissions to containers and the objects within them, it cannot be used to remove those privileges. If you need to remove permissions, you must do so manually in the Security tab in the Properties dialog box for the container and in the Advanced Security Settings dialog box for the container. Refer to the previous lesson for specific instruction on accessing these dialog boxes.

Note Windows Server 2003 with SP1 has improved security to help protect confidential information stored in Active Directory. This change enables you to hide certain attributes, such as an employee identification number, from some administrators while allowing Read access to other object attributes.

For more information on hiding Active Directory attributes, see "How Security Descriptors and Access Control Lists Work" on the Microsoft Web site at *http://technet2.microsoft.com /WindowsServer/en/Library/9c7bc921-2517-4e7a-ba39-d37c8b8202e31033.mspx.*

Lesson Review

The following questions are intended to reinforce key information presented in this lesson. If you are unable to answer a question, review the lesson and then try the question again. Answers to the questions can be found in the "Questions and Answers" section at the end of this chapter.

1. Why is it necessary to delegate administrative control of Active Directory objects?

2. What is the purpose of the Delegation Of Control Wizard?

3. How can you remove permissions you set by using the Delegation Of Control Wizard?

4. For which of the following Active Directory objects can you delegate administrative control by using the Delegation Of Control Wizard? (Choose all that apply.)

    a. Folder

    b. User

    c. Group

    d. Site

    e. OU

    f. Domain

    g. Shared folder

Lesson Summary

■ You delegate administrative control of domains and containers in order to provide other administrators, groups, or users with the ability to manage functions according to their needs.

■ The Delegation Of Control Wizard is provided to automate and simplify the process of setting administrative permissions for a domain, OU, or container.

Troubleshooting Lab

You are one of several network administrators for Contoso Pharmaceuticals. One of your network users tells you that they've attempted to log on several times, but they keep getting the same error message telling that the domain controller is down. You know that the domain controller is fine, so you go to the user's desktop to see the error message.

Before you can see the error message, you need to create the problem. Perform the following steps to create the problem:

1. Log on to Server2 using the domain administrator user name and password. Demote Server2 to Member Server using Dcpromo and the DemoteContoso.txt answer file. The answer file is located on the Supplemental CD-ROM in the \70-294\Labs\Chapter09 folder.

2. Log on to Server1 using the domain administrator user name and password.

3. Open Active Directory Users And Computers. Click on the Computers container. You should see SERVER2 in the right windowpane.

4. Select and right-click the SERVER2 icon and click Reset Account. When prompted about resetting the computer account, click Yes, and then click OK.

5. Go to Server2. Try to log on to the domain using the *contoso.com* domain administrator user name and password. You should see the following error message: "Windows cannot connect to the domain, either because the domain controller is down or otherwise unavailable, or because your computer account was not found. Please try again later. If this message continues to appear, contact your system administrator for assistance."

Now you've created the problem. In the Troubleshooting Lab in Chapter 4, you learned how to reset a computer password using the Netdom utility. You now realize that using the Active Directory Users And Computers interface is not the appropriate place to reset an existing computer password. The only reason to perform the steps above would be if you just reinstalled Server2 and wanted to configure a new password for that account. To fix this issue, you remove Server2 from the domain and then join the domain once again.

1. To correct this issue, you must log on as a local administrator to SERVER2 (Local).

2. Click Start, right-click My Computer, click Properties. The System Properties dialog box opens.

3. Click the Computer Name tab and then click the Change button. The Computer Name Changes dialog box opens. In the Member Of section, click Workgroup. Type the name **WORKGROUP** into the text box. Click OK. The Computer Name Changes dialog box appears.

4. Enter the local administrator name and password and click OK.

5. Click OK to confirm that your computer is now a member of the workgroup named WORKGROUP. Click OK to confirm that a restart is required.

6. Click OK in the System Properties dialog box.

7. Click Yes when prompted to restart your computer.

8. Once Server2 restarts, log on as the local administrator once again. Then join the domain *contoso.com* as described in Chapter 2, "Installing and Configuring Active Directory." Once you restart the system again, you'll be able to log on using the domain administrator name and password.

9. Promote Server2 to domain controller by using the Dcpromo command with the ContosoReplica.txt answer file. The answer file is located on the Supplemental CD-ROM in the \70-294\Labs\Chapter09 folder.

Case Scenario Exercise

You are a network administrator for City Power & Light as described in Chapters 5, 6, and 7. The company has a single domain with eight OUs directly subordinate to the domain. The company has five locations: Main, North, South, East, and West. All of the computer and user accounts for each location are in their respective OUs. All locations are connected to the Main site using T1 lines (previously many of these connections were 56 Kbps dial-up). The North, South, East, and West locations are all configured as Active Directory sites named North_Site, South_Site, East_Site, and West_Site, respectively. Each site has between 100 and 150 network users and computers, as shown in Figure 9-16.

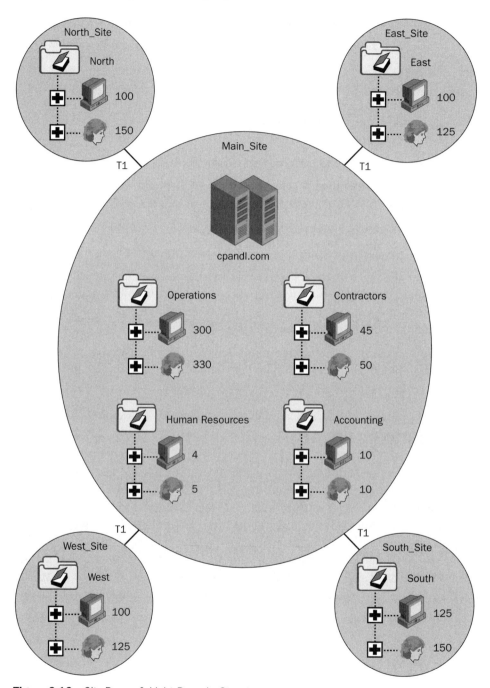

Figure 9-16 City Power & Light Domain Structure

Each site also has one domain controller. Each site's domain controller is also configured as a DNS server and global catalog server.

Your manager, Dragan Tomic, was promoted from Network Operations Manager to Chief Information Officer (CIO). You are now the Network Operations Manager. This means you are in charge of the network administration team, which includes seven other administrators. Wei Yu and Zheng Mu are administrators for the Operations OU. Ben Smith manages the Human Resources, Accounting, and Contractors OUs. The other administrators are Jim Kim (North_Site), Vamsi Kuppa (West_Site), Michael Hummer (South_Site), and Don Funk (East_Site).

You've called a meeting with all of the administrators to discuss your new role, as well as administrative issues they are facing.

Given that information, answer the following questions:

1. Vamsi is a fairly new administrator. Ben is willing to help Vamsi manage the West_Site. What should you do to ensure that Ben can fully assist Vamsi?

2. Wei tells you that Dragan delegated control of the Operations OU to Candy Spoon from the Contractors OU. Candy was helping manage the Operations OU while Zheng was on vacation. Candy is no longer helping with the Operations OU. Zheng and Wei want you to return Candy's access to that of a normal user. What should you do?

3. You've given Michael Full Control permissions to the South OU. Now he wants to allow his assistant to reset users' passwords in the South_Site. What should he do?

4. You want Jim, Vamsi, Michael, and Don to be able to log on to and shut down the domain controllers at their respective locations. However, right now when they try to log on to the domain controllers, they receive a message that reads: "The local policy of this system does not permit you to log on interactively." What should you do?

Chapter Summary

- There are two ways to locate Active Directory objects: 1) use the Find option on the Active Directory Users And Computers console, and 2) use the Dsquery command.

- The saved queries feature enables administrators to create, edit, save, organize, and e-mail saved queries to monitor or perform a specific task on directory objects.

- To control access to Active Directory objects, you grant or deny permissions to security principals. You set permissions to either Allow or Deny. Denied permissions take precedence over all other permissions.

- When an object is created, the user creating it automatically becomes its owner. The owner controls how permissions are set on the object and to whom permissions are granted.

- You can set selective authentication differently for outgoing and incoming external and forest trusts. These selective trusts allow you to make flexible access control decisions between external domains and forest-wide.

- When you assign a permission to a security principal for access to an object, and that security principal is a member of a group to which you assigned a different permission, the security principal's permissions are the combination of the assigned security principal and group permissions.

- Permissions assigned through inheritance are propagated to a child object from a parent object. Effective permissions are the overall permissions that a security principal has for an object, including group membership and inheritance from parent objects.

- You delegate administrative control of domains and containers in order to provide other administrators, groups, or users with the ability to manage functions according to their needs.

- The Delegation Of Control Wizard is provided to automate and simplify the process of setting administrative permissions for a domain, OU, or container.

Exam Highlights

Before taking the exam, review the key points and terms that are presented in this chapter. You need to know this information.

Key Points

- The ACL is the tool you use to assign users permission to access resources.

- Selective authentication allows you to make flexible access control decisions between domains in an external or forest trust. You can designate the trust authentication level for incoming or outgoing external or forest trusts as selective to control which users can access resources. If you use this option, you must manually assign permissions on each domain and resource to which you want users in the second domain or forest to have access.

- You delegate administrative control of domains and containers in order to provide other administrators, groups, or users with the ability to manage functions according to their needs. Delegating administrative control is different from access control because it enables administrative responsibility for a designated administrator, group, or user rather than providing access to objects.

- The Delegation Of Control Wizard is the tool you use to set administrative permissions for a domain, OU, or container.

Key Terms

access control   A security mechanism that determines which operations a user, group, service, or computer is authorized to perform on a computer or on a particular object.

delegation   An assignment of administrative responsibility that allows users without administrative credentials to complete specific administrative tasks or to manage specific directory objects. Responsibility is assigned through membership in a security group, the Delegation Of Control Wizard, or Group Policy settings.

permission   A rule associated with an object to regulate which users can gain access to the object and in what manner. Permissions are assigned or denied by the object's owner.

selective authentication   On domain controllers running Windows Server 2003, a method of determining the scope of authentication between two forests joined by a forest trust or two domains joined by an external trust. With these selective trusts, you can make flexible forest-wide or domain-wide access control decisions.

Questions and Answers

Page
9-13
Lesson 1 Review

1. What are two ways to locate Active Directory objects?

    There are two ways to locate Active Directory objects: 1) use the Find option on the Active Directory Users And Computers console, and 2) use the Dsquery command.

2. Which Dsquery command should you use to find users in the directory who have been inactive for two weeks?

    Dsquery user –inactive 2

3. Which Dsquery command should you use to find computers in the directory that have been disabled?

    Dsquery computer –disabled

4. What is the purpose of the saved queries feature?

    The saved queries feature enables administrators to create, edit, save, organize and e-mail saved queries in order to monitor or perform a specific task on directory objects.

5. Which of the following is not a valid object type in the Find option?

    a. Users, Contacts, and Groups

    b. Sites

    c. OUs

    d. Computers

    The correct answer is b. Sites is not an object type in the Find option.

Page
9-34
Lesson 2 Review

1. What is a security principal?

    A security principal is a user, group, computer, or service that is assigned a SID. A SID uniquely identifies the user, group, computer, or service in the enterprise and is used to manage security principals.

2. You are trying to assign permissions to an object in its Properties dialog box, but you cannot find the Security tab. How can you fix this problem?

    To view the Security tab in the Properties dialog box, you must select Advanced Features on the View menu on the Active Directory Users And Computers console.

3. The permissions check boxes for a security principal are shaded. What does this indicate?

If a permission is inherited, its check boxes (located in the Security tab in the Properties dialog box for an object, and in the Permission Entry dialog box for an object) are shaded. However, shaded special permissions check boxes do not indicate inherited permissions. These shaded check boxes merely indicate that a special permission exists.

4. What are effective permissions?

Effective permissions are the overall permissions that a security principal has for an object, including group membership and inheritance from parent objects.

5. User X is a member of the Sales group and the Marketing group. The Sales group has Write permission for the Accounts shared folder. The Marketing group has Full Control permission for the Accounts shared folder. User X alone has Read permission for the Accounts shared folder. Which of the following permissions does User X have for the Accounts shared folder?

   a. Write permission only

   b. Read permission only

   c. Read and Write permissions only

   d. Full Control permission only

   e. All permissions

The correct answer is e. When you assign a permission to a security principal for access to an object and that security principal is a member of a group to which you assigned a different permission, the security principal's permissions are the combination of the security principal and group permissions. User X has Full Control permission through membership in the Marketing group. By definition, Full Control permission contains all of the other permissions.

Page
9-41

Lesson 3 Review

1. Why is it necessary to delegate administrative control of Active Directory objects?

You delegate administrative control of domains, OUs, and containers in order to provide other administrators, groups, or users with the ability to manage functions according to their needs.

2. What is the purpose of the Delegation Of Control Wizard?

The Delegation Of Control Wizard is provided to automate and simplify the process of setting administrative permissions for a domain, OU, or container.

3. How can you remove permissions you set by using the Delegation Of Control Wizard?

Although the Delegation Of Control Wizard can be used to grant administrative permissions to containers and the objects within them, it cannot be used to remove those privileges. If you need to remove permissions, you must do so manually in the Security tab in the Properties dialog box for the container and in the Advanced Security Settings dialog box for the container.

4. For which of the following Active Directory objects can you delegate administrative control by using the Delegation Of Control Wizard? (Choose all that apply.)

   a. Folder

   b. User

   c. Group

   d. Site

   e. OU

   f. Domain

   g. Shared folder

   The correct answers are a, d, e, and f. Folders, sites, OUs, and domains are all objects for which administrative control can be delegated by using the Delegation Of Control Wizard.

Page
9-43

Case Scenario Exercise

1. Vamsi is a fairly new administrator. Ben is willing to help Vamsi manage the West_Site. What should you do to ensure that Ben can fully assist Vamsi?

   Delegate the necessary administrative permissions to Ben for the West OU. You probably want Ben to have the same access as Vamsi.

2. Wei tells you that Dragan delegated control of the Operations OU to Candy Spoon from the Contractors OU. Candy was helping manage the Operations OU while Zheng was on vacation. Candy is no longer helping with the Operations OU. Zheng and Wei want you to return Candy's access to that of a normal user. What should you do?

   In order to remove the delegated rights that Dragan implemented for Candy's account, you must modify the DACL of the Operations OU. Remove the special permissions assigned to Candy. You can probably do this by simply removing her account from the DACL. Candy will still have normal user access to the Operations OU, but she would get that access through her group memberships.

3. You've given Michael Full Control permissions to the South OU. Now he wants to allow his assistant to reset users' passwords in the South_Site. What should he do?

   Michael doesn't have the ability to delegate any permissions at the site level, but he can delegate the specific permission to reset passwords on the South OU. He can use the Delegation Of Control Wizard to accomplish this task.

4. You want Jim, Vamsi, Michael, and Don to be able to log on to and shut down the domain controllers at their respective locations. However, right now when they try to log on to the domain controllers, they receive a message that reads: "The local policy of this system does not permit you to log on interactively." What should you do?

Normal users do not have the right to log on to a domain controller. This right is available only to Account Operators, Administrators, Backup Operators, Print Operators, and Server Operators. The right to shut down the system is available only to Administrators, Backup Operators, Print Operators, and Administrators. Therefore, you can either make Jim, Vamsi, Michael, and Don members of one of these groups or specifically grant them the right to access these computers through the Default Domain Controllers Policy in Group Policy.

10 Implementing Group Policy

Exam Objectives in this Chapter:

- Plan Group Policy strategy.
- Plan a strategy for configuring the user environment with Group Policy.
- Plan a strategy for configuring the computer environment with Group Policy.
- Configure the user environment by Group Policy.
- Deploy a computer environment by Group Policy.

Why This Chapter Matters

The information in this chapter shows you how to plan and implement group policies. Planning your Group Policy strategy is essential to providing the most efficient Group Policy implementation for your organization. To effectively plan your Group Policy strategy, you must plan the settings that will be included in each Group Policy Object (GPO); whether the GPO should be applied to a site, domain, or organizational unit (OU); and administrative control of GPOs. After you've planned your Group Policy strategy, you must be able to implement GPOs for your organization. To effectively implement your Group Policy strategy, you must be able to create a GPO, create a Microsoft Management Console (MMC) for the GPO, delegate administrative control of the GPO, configure Group Policy settings for the GPO, disable unused Group Policy settings, indicate any GPO processing exceptions, filter the scope of the GPO with security groups, and link the GPO to a site, domain, or OU.

Lessons in this Chapter:

Before You Begin

To complete the lessons in this chapter, you must

- Prepare your test environment according to the descriptions given in the "Getting Started" section of "About This Book"

- Complete the practices for installing and configuring Active Directory as discussed in Chapter 2, "Installing and Configuring Active Directory"

- Learn to use Active Directory administration tools as discussed in Chapter 3, "Administering Active Directory"

- Complete the practices for configuring sites and replication as discussed in Chapter 5, "Configuring Sites and Managing Replication"

- Complete the practices for implementing an OU structure as discussed in Chapter 6, "Implementing an OU Structure"

- Complete the practices for creating and maintaining user accounts as discussed in Chapter 7, "Administering User Accounts"

- Complete the practices for creating and administering groups as discussed in Chapter 8, "Administering Groups"

Lesson 1: Understanding Group Policy

Before attempting to implement Group Policy, you must be familiar with concepts that affect Group Policy operations. This lesson defines Group Policy, explains how GPOs work, and provides an overview of the settings in a GPO. It also shows you how Group Policy affects startup and logging on, how it is applied, and how security groups are used to filter Group Policy.

After this lesson, you will be able to

- Explain the function of group policies
- Explain the function of GPOs
- Explain the function of the Group Policy Object Editor
- Discuss Group Policy settings
- Explain the function of administrative templates
- Explain how Group Policy affects startup and logging on
- Describe how Group Policy is applied
- Explain how security groups can be used to filter Group Policy

Estimated lesson time: 40 minutes

Understanding Group Policies

Group policies are collections of user and computer configuration settings that specify how programs, network resources, and the operating system work for users and computers in an organization. Group Policy can be set up for computers, sites, domains, and OUs. For example, using group policies, you can determine the programs that are available to users, the programs that appear on the user's desktop, and Start menu options. Although the name "Group Policy" suggests that you might set policies for global, domain local, or global groups, this is not the case. Instead, think of Group Policy as groupings of policy settings that are linked to computers, sites, domains, and OUs.

Off the Record   As stated in this section, group policies apply to computer and user accounts. A common misconception is that group policies can be applied to groups. Although group policies do not apply to groups, group membership can affect the application of Group Policy. For example, if a user or computer account belongs to a group that is specifically denied the ability to apply Group Policy, that account will not receive the Group Policy. This concept is known as filtering GPO scope with security groups, and is discussed in Lesson 3.

Understanding GPOs

To create a specific desktop configuration for users, you create *GPOs*, which are collections of Group Policy settings. Each computer running Microsoft Windows Server 2003 has one *local* GPO and can, in addition, be subject to any number of *nonlocal* (Active Directory–based) GPOs.

Local GPOs

One local GPO is stored on each computer whether or not the computer is part of an Active Directory environment or a networked environment. A local GPO affects only the computer on which it is stored. However, because the local GPO settings can be overridden by nonlocal GPOs, the local GPO is the least influential if the computer is in an Active Directory environment. In a non-networked environment (or in a networked environment lacking a Microsoft Windows 2000 or Windows Server 2003 domain controller), the local GPO's settings are more important because they are not overridden by nonlocal GPOs. By default, only nodes under Security Settings are configured for local GPOs; settings in other parts of a local GPO's namespace are not enabled or disabled. The local GPO is stored in %*Systemroot*%\System32\GroupPolicy.

Nonlocal GPOs

Nonlocal GPOs are created in Active Directory and must be linked to a site, domain, or OU in order to be applied to either users or computers. To use nonlocal GPOs, you must have a Windows 2000 or Windows Server 2003 domain controller installed. By default, when Active Directory directory service is set up, two nonlocal GPOs are created:

- **Default Domain Policy**   This GPO is linked to the domain, and it affects all users and computers in the domain (including computers that are domain controllers) through Group Policy inheritance. For more information, refer to the section on Group Policy inheritance later in this lesson.

- **Default Domain Controllers Policy**   This GPO is linked to the Domain Controllers OU, and it generally affects only domain controllers, because computer accounts for domain controllers are kept exclusively in the Domain Controllers OU.

Nonlocal GPOs are stored in %*Systemroot*%\SYSVOL\sysvol*Domain Name*\Policies *GPO GUID*\Adm, where *Domain Name* is the name of the domain and *GPO GUID* is the GPO's globally unique identifier. This lesson discusses nonlocal GPOs unless otherwise specified.

Off the Record   You can see a mapping of the Group Policy GUID and name in the Active Directory Replication Monitor (Replmon.exe). To see this, add a domain controller as the monitored server, and then right-click that domain controller and select Show Group Policy Object Status.

You can determine which administrative groups can administer (create, modify, delete) GPOs by defining permissions for each GPO in the GPO's Security tab, just like you would for any other object. Planning administrative control of GPOs is discussed in Lesson 2. Delegating administrative control when a GPO is implemented is discussed in Lesson 3.

> **Note**   GPOs can be applied only to Microsoft Windows XP Professional, Microsoft Windows 2000, and Windows Server 2003 and are not supported for Microsoft Windows 95, Microsoft Windows 98, Microsoft Windows Millennium Edition (Windows Me), or Microsoft Windows NT.

A GPO linked to a site affects all computers in the site. Because directory information is replicated among all the domain controllers in the site and to any domain controllers in sites for which a site link has been established, a GPO linked to a site is applied to all computers in that site, without regard to the domain containing the computers. Therefore, a GPO can be applied to multiple domains within a forest, even though the GPO exists only as a stored entity on a single domain and must be read from that domain when the affected clients read their site-linked Group Policy.

If child domains are set up across wide area network (WAN) boundaries, the site plan must consider where GPOs are linked. Otherwise, the computers in a child domain must access a site-linked GPO across a WAN link, which increases the Group Policy processing time.

Group Policy Object Editor

You use the Group Policy Object Editor to organize and manage the Group Policy settings in each GPO. The Group Policy Object Editor for the Default Domain Policy GPO is shown in Figure 10-1.

Note that the root node of the Group Policy Object Editor is displayed as the name of the GPO and the domain to which it belongs, in the format

`GPO Name DomainName Policy`

For example: Default Domain Policy [server1.contoso.com] Policy, as shown in Figure 10-1.

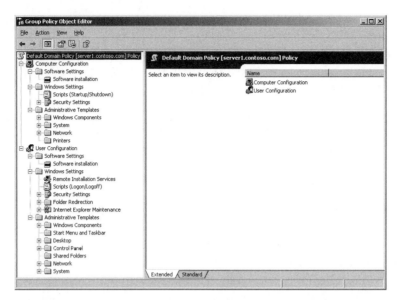

Figure 10-1   Default Domain Policy Group Policy Object Editor

How you open the Group Policy Object Editor depends on where you want to apply the GPO. Table 10-1 shows the four ways of opening the Group Policy Object Editor.

Table 10-1   Ways to Open the Group Policy Object Editor

To apply a GPO to	Do this
The local computer (local GPO)	Open the local GPO that is stored on the local computer, as described in the procedure "To open the MMC for the local GPO," which follows this table.
Another computer (local GPO)	Open the local GPO that is stored on the network computer running Windows Server 2003, as described in the procedure "To open the MMC for the local GPO," except browse to the network computer in the Select Group Policy Object dialog box. You must be an administrator of the network computer.
A site	Open a GPO as described in the procedure "To open the Group Policy Object Editor from the Active Directory Sites And Services console."
A domain or OU	Open a GPO as described in the procedure "To open the Group Policy Object Editor from the Active Directory Users And Computers console."

To open the MMC for the local GPO, complete the following steps:

1. Open the Microsoft Management Console (MMC).

2. On the MMC's menu bar, click File, and then click Add/Remove Snap-In.

3. In the Add/Remove Snap-In dialog box, in the Standalone tab, click Add.

4. In the Add Standalone Snap-In dialog box, click Group Policy Object Editor, and then click Add.

5. In the Select Group Policy Object dialog box, ensure that Local Computer appears in the Group Policy Object box.

6. Click Finish, and then click Close in the Add Standalone Snap-In dialog box.

7. In the Add/Remove Snap-In dialog box, click OK.

   The MMC for the local GPO is now available.

To open the Group Policy Object Editor from the Active Directory Sites And Services console, complete the following steps:

1. Click Start, point to Administrative Tools, and then click Active Directory Sites And Services.

2. In the console tree, right-click the site you want to set Group Policy for, and then click Properties.

3. Click the Group Policy tab, click an entry in the Group Policy Object Links list to select an existing GPO, and then click Edit. (Or, click New to create a new GPO, and then click Edit.)

   The Group Policy Object Editor for the site GPO is now available.

To open the Group Policy Object Editor from the Active Directory Users And Computers console, complete the following steps:

1. Click Start, point to Administrative Tools, and then click Active Directory Users And Computers.

2. In the console tree, right-click the domain or OU you want to set Group Policy for, and then click Properties.

3. Click the Group Policy tab, click an entry in the Group Policy Object Links list to select an existing GPO, and then click Edit. (Or, click New to create a new GPO, and then click Edit.)

   The Group Policy Object Editor for the domain or OU GPO is now available.

Group Policy Settings

Group Policy settings are contained in a GPO and determine the user's desktop environment. You can view the Group Policy settings for a GPO in the Group Policy Object Editor. There are two types of Group Policy settings: computer configuration settings and user configuration settings. They are contained in the Computer Configuration and the User Configuration nodes in a GPO.

Note   Group Policy settings override user profile settings.

Computer and User Configuration Nodes

The Computer Configuration node contains the settings used to set group policies applied to computers, regardless of who logs on to them. Computer configuration settings are applied when the operating system initializes.

The User Configuration node contains the settings used to set group policies applied to users, regardless of which computer the user logs on to. User configuration settings are applied when users log on to the computer.

> **Note** Although some settings are user interface settings—for example, the background bitmap or the ability to use the Run command on the Start menu—they can be applied to computers using settings in the Computer Configuration node.

Both the Computer Configuration and the User Configuration nodes include settings for installing software, settings for installing and accessing the Windows Server 2003 operating system, and registry settings. These settings are contained in the Software Settings, Windows Settings, and Administrative Templates nodes.

Software Settings Node

In both the Computer Configuration and the User Configuration nodes, the Software Settings node (shown in Figure 10-2) contains only the Software Installation extension by default. The Software Installation extension helps you specify how applications are installed and maintained within your organization. It also provides a place for independent software vendors to add settings.

When you configure settings in the Software Installation extension, you can manage an application within a GPO that, in turn, is associated with an Active Directory site, domain, or OU. Applications can be managed in one of two modes: assigned or published. You assign an application to a computer when you want computers or users managed by the GPO to have the application. You publish an application when you want the application to be available to users managed by the GPO, should a user want the application. You cannot publish an application to computers. More information on setting software installation using Group Policy is provided in Chapter 12, "Deploying Software with Group Policy."

Figure 10-2 Contents of Software Settings node

Windows Settings Node

In both the Computer Configuration and the User Configuration nodes, the Windows Settings node (shown in Figure 10-3) contains the Scripts extension and the Security Settings node.

Figure 10-3   Contents of Windows Settings node

The Scripts extension allows you to specify two types of scripts: startup/shutdown (in the Computer Configuration node) and logon/logoff (in the User Configuration node). Startup/shutdown scripts run at computer startup or shutdown. Logon/logoff scripts run when a user logs on or off the computer. When you assign multiple logon/logoff or startup/shutdown scripts to a user or computer, Windows Server 2003 executes the scripts from top to bottom. You can determine the order of execution for multiple scripts in the Properties dialog box. When a computer is shut down, Windows Server 2003 first processes logoff scripts, followed by shutdown scripts. By default, the timeout value for processing scripts is 10 minutes. If the logoff and shutdown scripts require more than 10 minutes to process, you must adjust the timeout value with a software policy. You can use any ActiveX scripting language to write scripts. Some possibilities include Microsoft Visual Basic Scripting Edition (VBScript), Microsoft JScript, Perl, and MS-DOS style batch files (.bat and .cmd).

> **Note**   Logon scripts on a shared network directory in another forest are supported for network logon across forests. This is a new feature of the Windows Server 2003 family.

The Security Settings node allows a security administrator to manually configure security levels assigned to a local or nonlocal GPO. This can be done after, or instead of, using a security template to set system security. For a detailed discussion of system security and the Security Settings node, refer to Chapter 13, "Administering Security with Group Policy."

In the User Configuration node only, the Windows Settings folder contains the additional nodes Remote Installation Services, Folder Redirection, and Internet Explorer

Maintenance. Remote Installation Services (RIS) is used to control the behavior of a remote operating system installation. Optionally, RIS can be used to provide customized packages for non–Windows Server 2003 clients of Active Directory. (Group Policy requires a genuine Windows 2000 or Windows Server 2003 client, not merely a pre–Windows 2000 client of Active Directory, however.) Folder Redirection allows you to redirect Windows Server 2003 special folders (Application Data, Desktop, My Documents, and Start Menu) from their default user profile location to an alternate location on the network, where they can be centrally managed. For details on folder redirection, refer to Chapter 11, "Administering Group Policy." Internet Explorer Maintenance allows you to administer and customize Microsoft Internet Explorer on computers running Windows Server 2003.

Administrative Templates Node

In both the Computer Configuration and the User Configuration nodes, the Administrative Templates node (shown in Figure 10-4) contains registry-based Group Policy settings. There are more than 550 of these settings available for configuring the user environment. As an administrator, you might spend a significant amount of time manipulating these settings. To assist you with the settings, a description of each policy setting is available in three locations:

■ In the Explain tab in the Properties dialog box for the setting. In addition, the Setting tab in the Properties dialog box for the setting lists the required operating system for the setting.

■ In Administrative Templates Help (a new feature of Windows Server 2003). The required operating system for each setting is also listed.

■ In the Extended tab (a new feature of Windows Server 2003, selected by default) in the Group Policy Object Editor. The Extended tab provides a description of each selected setting in a column between the console tree and the settings pane. The required operating system for each setting is also listed.

Figure 10-4   Contents of Administrative Templates node

Each of the settings in the Administrative Templates node can be:

- **Not Configured**   The registry is not modified.

- **Enabled**   The registry reflects that the policy setting is selected.

- **Disabled**   The registry reflects that the policy setting is not selected.

Settings in the Administrative Templates node in the Computer Configuration node are saved in the HKEY_LOCAL_MACHINE (HKLM) registry key. Settings in the Administrative Templates node in the User Configuration node are saved in the HKEY_CURRENT_USER (HKCU) registry key. HKLM and HKCU each place registry information that is specific to Group Policy in one of the following four reserved trees:

- HKEY_LOCAL_MACHINE\Software\Policies (computer settings)

- HKEY_CURRENT_USER\Software\Policies (user settings)

- HKEY_LOCAL_MACHINE\Software\Microsoft\Windows\CurrentVersion\Policies (computer settings)

- HKEY_CURRENT_USER\Software\Microsoft\Windows\CurrentVersion\Policies (user settings)

In the Computer Configuration and the User Configuration nodes, the Administrative Templates node contains the Windows Components, System, and Network nodes. The nodes in the Windows Components node enable you to administer Windows Server 2003 components including Microsoft NetMeeting, Internet Explorer, Application Compatibility, Task Scheduler, Terminal Services, Microsoft Windows Installer, Microsoft Windows Messenger, Microsoft Media Player, and Microsoft Update. For the Computer Configuration node only, the Windows Components folder also includes the Internet Information Services node. For the User Configuration node only, the nodes in the Windows Components folder also include Windows Explorer and MMC.

The settings in the System node are used to control how the Windows Server 2003 operating system is accessed and used, including settings for user profiles, scripts, logon and logoff functions, and Group Policy itself. For the Computer Configuration node only, the settings in the System node also include settings for disk quotas, the Net Logon service, remote assistance, system restore, error reporting, Windows File Protection, Remote Procedure Call, and Windows Time Service. For the User Configuration node only, the settings in the System node also include settings for CTRL+ALT+DEL options and power management.

The settings in the Network node enable you to control how the network is accessed and used, including settings for offline files, and network and dial-up connections. For the Computer Configuration node only, the settings in the Network node also include settings for the Domain Name System (DNS) client, the quality of service (QoS) packet scheduler, and Simple Network Management Protocol (SNMP).

For the Computer Configuration node only, the Administrative Templates node contains additional registry-based Group Policy settings pertaining to printers in the Printers node. For the User Configuration node only, the Administrative Templates node contains additional registry-based nodes for the Start menu and taskbar, the desktop, Control Panel, and shared folders. The settings in these nodes control a user's Start menu, taskbar, desktop, Control Panel, and shared folders.

Because there are so many settings in the Administrative Templates node, a feature that filters the view of administrative templates has been developed in Windows Server 2003 in an effort to reduce screen clutter. You might want to filter your view of administrative templates if you are inconvenienced by seeing too many administrative template settings at once in the Group Policy Object Editor. Administrative templates view filtering simply selects the settings that are visible in the editor.

Note Administrative templates view filtering does not affect whether the settings apply to users or computers. Do not confuse this feature with the procedure for filtering GPO scope according to security group membership.

To filter the view provided by administrative templates, complete the following steps:

1. Open the Group Policy Object Editor, and in the console tree, right-click the folder under Administrative Templates that contains the policy settings you want to filter. Click View, and then click Filtering.

2. In the Filtering dialog box, shown in Figure 10-5, do any of the following to filter the settings you can view:

   ❑ If you want to remove any types of settings from the GPO display, select the Filter By Requirements Information check box, and then in the Select The Items To Be Displayed list, clear any categories you do not want to see. By default, all types of settings are selected (that is, are displayed).

   ❑ If you want to hide settings that are not configured, select the Only Show Configured Policy Settings check box. If you select this check box, only Enabled or Disabled settings are visible.

   ❑ If you want to hide Windows NT 4–style system policy settings, select the Only Show Policy Settings That Can Be Fully Managed check box. Microsoft recommends selecting this check box, and it is selected by default.

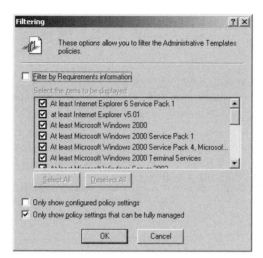

Figure 10-5   The Filtering dialog box

3. Click OK.

Administrative Templates

The previous section discussed the Administrative Templates node in a GPO, which contains the registry-based Group Policy settings you set on the Group Policy Object Editor. However, an administrative template is actually a text file used to generate the user interface for the Group Policy settings you can set on the Group Policy Object Editor. In Windows Server 2003, administrative templates have the .adm file name extension, as they did in Windows NT 4. In earlier versions of Windows, administrative templates were text files using the American National Standards Institute (ANSI) character set. They created a namespace within the System Policy Editor for convenient editing of the registry, a friendlier user interface than the Registry Editor (Regedit.exe). In Windows Server 2003 and Windows 2000, administrative templates are Unicode-based text files. The Group Policy Object Editor replaces the System Policy Editor and gives you greater control over configuration settings. Administrative templates is the only area of Group Policy (the other areas being software settings and Windows settings) that allows you to make modifications by adding new administrative templates.

There are three types of administrative templates:

■ **Default**   Administrative templates provided with Windows Server 2003, as described in Table 10-2.

■ **Vendor-supplied**   Administrative templates provided with software applications designed to run on Windows Server 2003. You might need to install these templates separately or download them from a Web site. For example, you can download the Microsoft Office 2000 or Microsoft Windows XP Resource Kit tools from the Microsoft Web site (*www.microsoft.com*) in order to implement Office 2000 or Windows XP Group Policy settings.

■ **Custom**   Templates created using the .adm language to further control computer or user settings. Custom templates are generally created by application developers.

> **Note**   A detailed discussion on creating custom administrative templates is beyond the scope of this course. You can find the details about creating your own administrative templates by searching for ".adm Language Reference" on the Microsoft TechNet Web site (*http://technet.microsoft.com/default.aspx*).

Table 10-2   Windows Server 2003 Default Administrative Templates

Administrative Template	Description
System.adm	Installed in Group Policy by default; contains system settings for Windows 2000 and Windows Server 2003 clients.
Inetres.adm	Installed in Group Policy by default; contains Internet Explorer policies for Windows 2000 and Windows Server 2003 clients.
Wmplayer.adm*	Contains Windows Media Player settings for Windows 2000 and Windows Server 2003 clients.
Conf.adm*	Contains NetMeeting settings for Windows 2000 and Windows Server 2003 clients.
Wuau.adm	Contains Windows Update settings for Windows 2000 and Windows Server 2003 clients.

* This tool is not available on the 64-bit versions of the Windows Server 2003 family.

Windows Server 2003 Service Pack 1 updates the administrative templates. The updated System.adm template adds Group Policy settings for the Windows Firewall. For more information on Windows Firewall settings, see "Windows Firewall Technical Reference" at *http://technet2.microsoft.com/WindowsServer/en/Library/6490c9fc-6c06-4304-b61c-5577af1445d01033.mspx*.

The updated Inetres.adm template incorporates registry keys and values for new Internet Explorer security features. These features were first introduced with Windows XP Service Pack 2 and are called Feature Controls. They include settings for Add-on Management and the Information Bar. For more information on Feature Controls, see the sections on Internet Explorer in "Changes to Functionality in Microsoft Windows Server 2003 Service Pack 1" at *http://www.microsoft.com/downloads/details.aspx?FamilyId =C3C26254-8CE3-46E2-B1B6-3659B92B2CDE&displaylang=en*.

The updated Wuau.adm template adds support for Windows Server Update Services (WSUS). For more information on WSUS, see "Configure Automatic Updates by Using Group Policy" at *http://technet2.microsoft.com/WindowsServer/en/Library/51c8a814-6665-4d50-a0d8-2ae27e69ca7c1033.mspx*.

How Group Policy Affects Startup and Logging On

The following sequence shows the order in which computer configuration and user configuration settings are applied when a computer starts and a user logs on.

1. The network starts. Remote Procedure Call System Service (RPCSS) and Multiple Universal Naming Convention Provider (MUP) are started.

2. An ordered list of GPOs is obtained for the computer. The list contents depend on the following factors:

   ❑ Whether the computer is part of a Windows 2000 or Windows Server 2003 domain, and is therefore subject to Group Policy through Active Directory.

   ❑ The location of the computer in Active Directory.

   ❑ If the list of GPOs has not changed, then no processing is done. You can use a Group Policy setting to change this behavior.

3. Computer configuration settings are processed. This occurs synchronously by default and in the following order: local GPO, site GPOs, domain GPOs, and OU GPOs. No user interface is displayed while computer configuration settings are being processed. See the section "How Group Policy Is Applied" for details about GPO processing.

4. Startup scripts run. This is hidden and synchronous by default; each script must complete or time out before the next one starts. The default timeout is 600 seconds (10 minutes). You can use several Group Policy settings to modify this behavior.

5. The user presses CTRL+ALT+DEL to log on.

6. After the user is validated, the user profile is loaded, governed by the Group Policy settings in effect.

7. An ordered list of GPOs is obtained for the user. The list contents depend on the following factors:

   ❑ Whether the user is part of a Windows 2000 or Windows Server 2003 domain, and is therefore subject to Group Policy through Active Directory.

   ❑ Whether loopback is enabled and the state (Merge or Replace) of the loopback policy setting. Refer to the section "How Group Policy Is Applied" for more information about loopback.

   ❑ The location of the user in Active Directory.

   ❑ If the list of GPOs to be applied has not changed, then no processing is done. You can use a policy setting to change this behavior.

8. User configuration settings are processed. This occurs synchronously by default, and in the following order: local GPO, site GPOs, domain GPOs, and OU GPOs.

No user interface is displayed while user policies are being processed. See the section "How Group Policy Is Applied" for details about GPO processing.

9. Logon scripts run. Unlike Windows NT 4 scripts, Group Policy–based logon scripts are run hidden and asynchronously by default. The user object script runs last.

10. The operating system user interface prescribed by Group Policy appears.

> **Note**   The following interactive logon tasks are supported across forests: applying Group Policy to user or computer objects across forests, and applying loopback processing across forests. This is a new feature of the Windows Server 2003 family.

How Group Policy Is Applied

Because nonlocal GPOs are applied hierarchically, the user or computer's configuration is a result of GPOs applied to its site, domain, and OU. Group Policy settings are applied in the following order:

1. Local GPO. Each computer running Windows Server 2003 has exactly one GPO stored locally.

2. Site GPOs. Any GPOs that have been linked to the site are applied next. GPO application is synchronous; the administrator specifies the order of GPOs linked to a site.

3. Domain GPOs. Multiple domain-linked GPOs are applied synchronously; the administrator specifies the order of GPOs linked to a domain.

4. OU GPOs. GPOs linked to the OU highest in the Active Directory hierarchy are applied first, followed by GPOs linked to its child OU, and so on. Finally, the GPOs linked to the OU that contains the user or computer are applied. At the level of each OU in the Active Directory hierarchy, one, many, or no GPOs can be linked. If several group policies are linked to an OU, then they are applied synchronously in an order specified by the administrator.

This order means that the local GPO is applied first, and GPOs linked to the OU of which the computer or user is a direct member are applied last, overwriting the earlier GPOs. For example, you set up a domain GPO to allow any user to log on interactively. However, an OU GPO, set up for the domain controller, prevents everyone from logging on except for certain administrative groups.

> **Note**   If there is a conflict between the computer configuration settings and the user configuration settings, the user configuration settings are applied because the user settings are more specific.

Figure 10-6 shows how Group Policy is applied for the *contoso.com* domain.

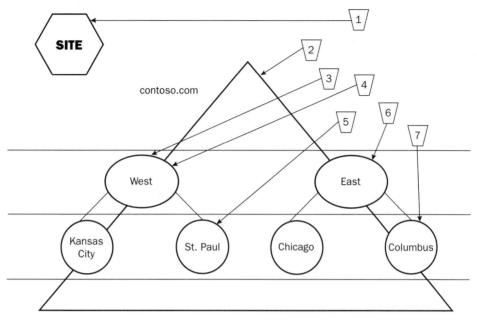

GPO processing order for the St. Paul OU = 1, 2, 3, 4, 5
GPO processing order for the Columbus OU = 1, 2, 6, 7

Figure 10-6   How Group Policy is applied for the contoso.com domain

Group Policy Inheritance

In general, Group Policy is passed down from parent to child containers within a domain. Group Policy is not inherited from parent to child domains. Group Policy is inherited in the following ways:

- If a policy setting is configured (set to Enabled or Disabled) for a parent OU, and the same policy setting *is not* already configured for its child OUs, the child OUs inherit the parent's policy setting.

- If a policy setting is configured (set to Enabled or Disabled) for a parent OU, and the same policy setting *is* configured for a child OU, the child OU's Group Policy setting overrides the setting inherited from the parent OU.

- If any of the policy settings of a parent OU are set to Not Configured, the child OU does not inherit them.

- Policy settings are inherited as long as they are compatible. If a policy setting configured for a parent OU and a policy setting configured for a child OU are compatible, the child OU inherits the parent's policy setting, and the child's policy setting is also applied. For example, if the parent OU's policy setting causes a certain folder to be placed on the desktop and the child OU's policy setting calls for an additional folder, the users in the child OU see both folders.

■ If a policy setting configured for a parent OU is incompatible with the same policy setting configured for a child OU (for example, if the setting is enabled in the parent OU and disabled in the child OU), the child OU does not inherit the policy setting from the parent OU. Only the setting configured for the child OU is applied.

 Exam Tip   Know how group polices are inherited.

Exceptions to the Application Process

The default order for the application of Group Policy settings is subject to the following exceptions:

■ **Workgroup members**   A computer that is a member of a workgroup processes only the local GPO.

■ **No Override**   Any GPO linked to a site, domain, or OU (not the local GPO) can be set to No Override so that none of its policy settings can be overridden by any other GPO during the processing of group policies. When more than one GPO has been set to No Override, the one highest in the Active Directory hierarchy (or higher in the hierarchy specified by the administrator at each fixed level in Active Directory) takes precedence. No Override is applied to the GPO link. In Figure 10-7, No Override has been applied to the GPO 4 link to the West OU. As a result, the policy settings in GPO 4 cannot be overwritten by other GPOs.

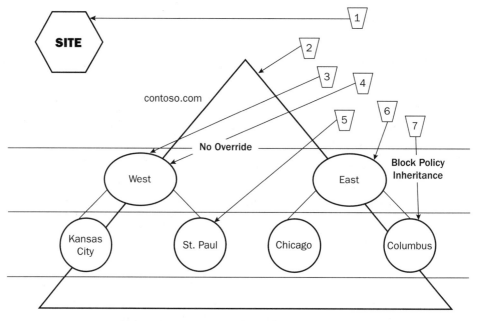

GPO processing order for the St. Paul OU = 1, 2, 3, 4, 5
GPO processing order for the Columbus OU = 6, 7

Figure 10-7   Applying No Override and Block Policy Inheritance for the contoso.com domain

- **Block Policy Inheritance**   At any site, domain, or OU, Group Policy inheritance can be selectively marked as Block Policy Inheritance. However, GPO links set to No Override are always applied and cannot be blocked. Block Policy Inheritance is applied directly to the site, domain, or OU. It is not applied to GPOs, nor is it applied to GPO links. Thus, Block Policy Inheritance deflects *all* Group Policy settings that reach the site, domain, or OU from above (by way of linkage to parents in the Active Directory hierarchy) no matter what GPOs those settings originate from. In Figure 10-7, Block Policy Inheritance has been applied to the East OU. As a result, GPOs 1 and 2, which are applied to the site and the domain, are deflected and do not apply to the East OU. Therefore, in Figure 10-7, only GPOs 6 and 7 are processed for the Columbus OU.

> **Note**   Because No Override and Block Policy Inheritance have wide-ranging effects that can cause problems with other GPOs, you should use them sparingly.

> **Exam Tip**   Know the difference between Block Policy Inheritance and No Override.

- **Loopback setting**   Loopback is an advanced Group Policy setting that is useful on computers in certain closely managed environments such as kiosks, laboratories, classrooms, and reception areas. Loopback provides alternatives to the default method of obtaining the ordered list of GPOs whose user configuration settings affect a user. By default, a user's settings come from a GPO list that depends on the user's location in Active Directory. The ordered list goes from site-linked to domain-linked to OU-linked GPOs, with inheritance determined by the location of the user in Active Directory and in an order specified by the administrator at each level. Loopback can be Not Configured, Enabled, or Disabled, as can any other Group Policy setting. In the Enabled state, loopback can be set to Merge or Replace mode.

  - *Replace mode* In this case, the GPO list for the user is replaced in its entirety by the GPO list already obtained for the computer at computer startup (during step 2 in "How Group Policy Affects Startup and Logging On"). The computer's GPOs replace the user GPOs normally applied to the user.

  - *Merge mode* In this case, the GPO list is concatenated. The GPO list obtained for the computer at computer startup (step 2 in "How Group Policy Affects Startup and Logging On") is appended to the GPO list obtained for the user when logging on (step 7 in "How Group Policy Affects Startup and Logging On"). Because the GPO list obtained for the computer is applied later, it has precedence if it conflicts with settings in the user's list.

Using Security Groups to Filter GPO Scope

By now you've learned that you can link a non-local GPO to a site, domain, or OU. However, you might need to apply GPOs only to certain groups. Although you cannot directly link a GPO to a security group, there is a way to apply GPOs to specific security groups. The policies in a non-local GPO apply only to users who have Read and Apply Group Policy permissions for the GPO set to Allow. Therefore, by setting the appropriate permissions for security groups, you can filter Group Policy to influence only the computers and users you specify. Note that the Apply Group Policy permission is not available for the local GPO. For more information on filtering GPO scope by using security groups, refer to Lesson 3.

Using WMI Queries to Filter GPO Scope

Windows Management Instrumentation (WMI) is a management infrastructure that allows administrators to monitor and control managed objects in the network. These abilities mean that the administrator can manage remote systems from a central location, controlling almost every aspect of all computers on the network. A new feature in Windows Server 2003, WMI filtering enables you to use a WMI query to filter the scope of a GPO, similar to the way security groups can be used to filter GPO scope. The GPO is applied based on properties available in WMI that are contained in the query. WMI queries are written using WMI query language (WQL). For more information about developing WMI queries for GPO filtering, see the WMI software development kit (SDK), located at *http://www.microsoft.com/*.

Delegating Control of GPOs

There are different GPO-related tasks for which you can delegate control: GPO editing, GPO creation, and GPO object linking. You delegate control of GPO editing by setting the Read and Write permissions for the selected user or groups to Allow. You delegate control of GPO creation by making users members of the Group Policy Creator Owners group and delegating to them control of GPO object linking. You delegate control of GPO object linking by setting the Manage Group Policy Links option in the Delegation Of Control Wizard for the domain or OU. For more information on delegating control of GPOs, refer to Lesson 3.

Resultant Set of Policy (RSoP)

Because an object can be affected by multiple levels of GPOs, Group Policy inheritance, and exceptions, it's often difficult to determine just what policies apply. Resultant Set of Policy (RSoP) is a new tool in Windows Server 2003 that helps you anticipate and troubleshoot Group Policy settings. RSoP polls existing and planned policies and reports the results of those queries, listing the final set of applied policies and policy precedence for an object you specify. RSoP can help you manage and troubleshoot conflicting policies. For detailed information on using RSoP, refer to Chapter 11, "Administering Group Policy."

Lesson Review

The following questions are intended to reinforce key information presented in this lesson. If you are unable to answer a question, review the lesson and then try the question again. Answers to the questions can be found in the "Questions and Answers" section at the end of this chapter.

1. What is a GPO?

_____

_____

2. What are the two types of Group Policy settings and how are they used?

_____

_____

3. In what order is Group Policy applied to components in the Active Directory structure?

_____

_____

4. What is the difference between Block Policy Inheritance and No Override?

_____

_____

5. Which of the following nodes contains the registry-based Group Policy settings?

   a. Software Settings

   b. Windows Settings

   c. Administrative Templates

   d. Security Settings

Lesson Summary

- Group policies are collections of user and computer configuration settings that can be linked to computers, sites, domains, and OUs to specify the behavior of users' desktops. You use the Group Policy Object Editor to organize and manage the Group Policy settings in each GPO.

- There are two types of Group Policy settings: computer configuration settings and user configuration settings. Computer configuration settings are used to set group policies applied to computers, regardless of who logs on to them, and are applied when the operating system initializes. User configuration settings are used to set group policies applied to users, regardless of which computer the user logs on to, and are applied when users log on to the computer.

- Group Policy is applied to Active Directory components in the following order: local computer, site, domain, and then OU.

- Group Policy is passed down from parent to child containers within a domain. If you have assigned a separate Group Policy setting to a parent container, that Group Policy setting applies to all containers beneath the parent container, including the user and computer objects in the container. However, if you specify a Group Policy setting for a child container, the child container's Group Policy setting overrides the setting inherited from the parent container.

- The default order for the application of Group Policy settings is subject to the following exceptions: No Override, Block Policy Inheritance, the Loopback setting, and a computer that is a member of a workgroup.

Lesson 2: Group Policy Planning Strategies

Before implementing group policies, you should create a plan to manage them. You can plan your Group Policy settings, GPOs, and administrative control of GPOs to provide the most efficient Group Policy implementation for your organization. This lesson examines Group Policy planning strategies.

After this lesson, you will be able to

- Plan Group Policy settings
- Plan GPOs
- Plan administrative control of GPOs

Estimated lesson time: 15 minutes

Group Policy Planning Strategies

There are three parts to planning Group Policy:

- Plan the Group Policy settings necessary for computers and users at each level (sites, domains, and OUs).

- Plan the GPOs necessary for computers and users at each level (sites, domains, and OUs).

- Plan administrative control of GPOs.

Document your Group Policy plans. Accurate and organized documentation of the Group Policy settings and GPOs needed by your organization and the administrators who control the GPOs can help when you need to revisit or modify your Group Policy configuration.

Plan Group Policy Settings

There are over 600 Group Policy settings in Windows Server 2003. The best way to familiarize yourself with these settings is to look through them on the Group Policy Object Editor. You must plan the settings necessary for computers and users for each site, domain, and OU in your organization. Plan settings sparingly—justify the selection of each setting as you would the creation of a domain or OU. Choose settings based on their ability to help you to simplify the administration of computers and users.

Planning GPOs

For each site, domain, and OU, you must determine how Group Policy settings should be arranged into GPOs. Base the arrangement of Group Policy settings on the users and computers that require them. You can arrange Group Policy settings in the following ways in a GPO:

■ **Single setting GPO** Contains a single type of Group Policy setting—for example, a GPO that includes only security settings. This model is best suited for organizations in which administrative responsibilities are task-based and delegated among several individuals.

■ **Multiple setting GPO** Contains multiple types of Group Policy settings—for example, a GPO that includes both software settings and application deployment, or a GPO that includes security and scripts settings. This model is best suited for organizations in which administrative responsibilities are centralized and an administrator might need to perform all types of Group Policy administration.

■ **Dedicated setting GPO** Contains either computer configuration or user configuration Group Policy settings. This model increases the number of GPOs that must be applied when logging on, thereby lengthening logon time, but it can aid in troubleshooting. For example, if a problem with a computer configuration GPO is suspected, an administrator can log on as a user who has no user configuration GPO assigned so user policy settings can be eliminated as a factor.

Exam Tip Be able to determine how Group Policy settings should be arranged into GPOs based on the needs and requirements of an organization.

Figure 10-8 illustrates these GPO types.

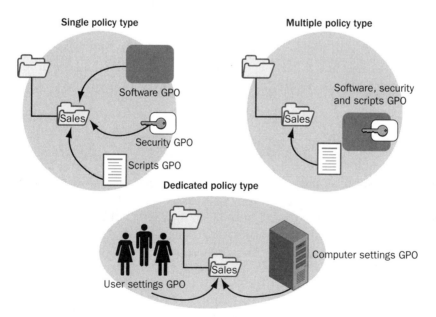

Figure 10-8 GPO setting types

Because sites and domains are the least restrictive components of Active Directory, it isn't too difficult to plan site and domain GPOs. Just remember that site and domain GPOs are applied to all child objects as a result of Group Policy inheritance, unless Block Policy Inheritance has been set for the child object. The real challenge is determining the OU GPOs. To determine the OU GPOs, you must consider the OU hierarchy set up for the domain. In Chapter 6, "Implementing an OU Structure," you learned that there are three reasons for defining an OU: to delegate administration, to hide objects, and to administer Group Policy. You were advised that because there is only one way to delegate administration and there are multiple ways to administer Group Policy, you must define OU structures to delegate administration first. Recall that the OU hierarchy structure can reflect administration handled by location, business function, object type, or a combination of the three elements. After an OU structure is defined to handle delegation of administration, you can define additional OUs to hide objects and to administer Group Policy. So, if you've defined your OU structure to accurately reflect how your domain is administered, the next step is to determine which Group Policy settings must be applied to which users and computers in each OU. Basically, you can build GPOs by using a decentralized or a centralized design.

Decentralized GPO Design

With a decentralized GPO approach (see Figure 10-9), the goal is to include a specific policy setting in as few GPOs as possible. When a change is required, only one (or a few) GPO(s) have to be changed to enforce the change. Administration is simplified at the expense of a somewhat longer logon time (due to multiple GPO processing).

To achieve this goal, create a base GPO to be applied to the domain that contains policy settings for as many users and computers in the domain as possible. For example, the base GPO could contain corporate-wide security settings such as account and password restrictions. Next, create additional GPOs tailored to the common requirements of each OU, and apply them to the appropriate OUs.

This model is best suited for environments in which different groups in the organization have common security concerns and changes to Group Policy are frequent.

Centralized GPO Design

With a centralized GPO approach (shown in Figure 10-9), the goal is to use very few GPOs (ideally only one) for any given user or computer. All of the policy settings required for a given site, domain, or OU should be implemented within a single GPO. If the site, domain, or OU has groups of users or computers with different policy requirements, consider subdividing the container into OUs and applying separate GPOs to each OU rather than to the parent. A change to the centralized GPO design involves more administration than the decentralized approach because the settings might need to be changed in multiple GPOs, but logon time is shorter. This model is best suited for environments in which users and computers can be classified into a small number of OUs for policy assignment.

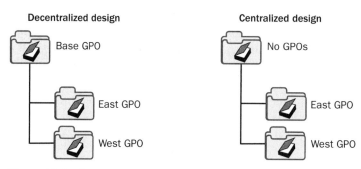

Figure 10-9   Decentralized and centralized GPO design

> **Real World   Group Policy Processing**
>
> As mentioned in earlier chapters, planning your OU structure is key to the efficient application of Group Policy. Every additional policy that you apply increases the number of settings that the individual computers must evaluate. Planning your organizational structure so that you can apply as few group policies as possible to only those containers that require them is a key to improving startup and logon performance. You might even decide to create OUs for the purpose of applying a specific Group Policy. For example, if you have several computer accounts that require a specific configuration that is unique to only those systems, you may find it more efficient to create a separate OU in order to handle that special configuration.

Planning Administrative Control of GPOs

When you plan the Group Policy settings and GPOs to be used in your organization, you should also plan who will manage them. The appropriate level of administrative control can be delegated by using a centralized, decentralized, or task-based administrative control design.

Centralized Administrative Control Design

In the centralized design, administration of Group Policy is delegated only to top-level OU administrators. In the example shown in Figure 10-10, top-level OU administrators have the ability to manage all GPOs in the domain. Second-level OU administrators do not have the ability to manage GPOs. You can accomplish this by assigning Full Control permission to top-level OU administrators. This design is best suited for organizations that want to consolidate the administration of group policies.

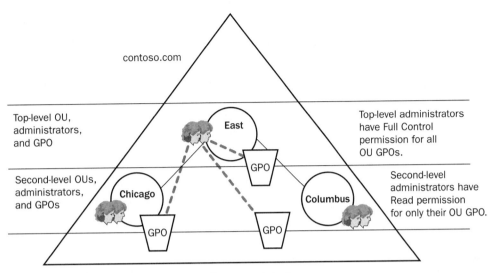

Figure 10-10   A centralized administrative control design

Decentralized Administrative Control Design

In the decentralized design, administration of Group Policy is delegated to top-level and to second-level OU administrators. In the example shown in Figure 10-11, top-level OU administrators have the ability to manage GPOs in the top-level OU. Second-level OU administrators have the ability to manage GPOs in their second-level OUs. You can accomplish this by assigning Full Control permission to top-level OU administrators for the top-level OU GPOs and Full Control permission to second-level OU administrators for their second-level OU GPOs. This design is best suited for organizations that delegate levels of administration.

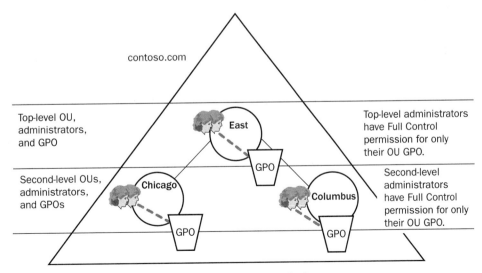

Figure 10-11   A decentralized administrative control design

Task-Based Administrative Control Design

In the task-based design, administration of specific group policies is delegated to administrators that handle the associated specific tasks, such as security or applications. In this case, the GPOs are designed to contain only a single type of Group Policy setting, as described earlier in this lesson. In the example shown in Figure 10-12, security administrators have the ability to manage security GPOs in all OUs. Applications administrators have the ability to manage applications GPOs in all OUs. You can accomplish this by assigning Full Control permission to the security administrators for the security GPOs, and Full Control permission to the applications administrators for the applications GPOs. This design is best suited for organizations in which administrative responsibilities are task-based and delegated among several individuals.

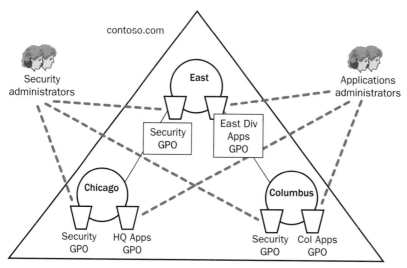

Figure 10-12   A task-based administrative control design

Lesson Review

The following questions are intended to reinforce key information presented in this lesson. If you are unable to answer a question, review the lesson and then try the question again. Answers to the questions can be found in the "Questions and Answers" section at the end of this chapter.

1. Describe a decentralized GPO design.

_____

_____

2. If administrative responsibilities in your organization are task-based and delegated among several administrators, which of the following types of GPOs should you plan to create?

    a. GPOs containing only one type of Group Policy setting

    b. GPOs containing many types of Group Policy settings

    c. GPOs containing only computer configuration settings

    d. GPOs containing only user configuration settings

Lesson Summary

- There are three parts to planning Group Policy: plan the Group Policy settings, plan GPOs, and plan administrative control of GPOs.

- Plan Group Policy settings sparingly—justify the selection of each setting as you would the creation of a domain or OU. Choose settings based on their ability to help you to simplify the administration of computers and users.

- You can build GPOs by using a decentralized or a centralized design. A decentralized design uses a base GPO applied to the domain, which contains policy settings for as many users and computers in the domain as possible. Then this design uses additional GPOs tailored to the common requirements of each OU and applied to the appropriate OUs. A centralized design uses a single GPO containing all policy settings for the associated site, domain, or OU.

- Administrative control of GPOs can be delegated by using a centralized, decentralized, or task-based administrative control design. In the centralized design, administration of Group Policy is delegated only to top-level OU administrators. In the decentralized design, administration of Group Policy is delegated to top-level and to second-level OU administrators. In the task-based design, administration of specific group policies is delegated to administrators that handle the associated specific tasks.

Lesson 3: Implementing a GPO

After you've familiarized yourself with the workings of Group Policy and planned your implementation strategy, you're ready to implement GPOs for your organization. This lesson walks you through the steps of implementing and modifying a GPO.

After this lesson, you will be able to

- Implement a GPO
- Modify a GPO

Estimated lesson time: 45 minutes

Implementing a GPO

The tasks for implementing a GPO are

1. Creating a GPO
2. Creating an MMC for the GPO
3. Delegating administrative control of the GPO
4. Configuring Group Policy settings for the GPO
5. Disabling unused Group Policy settings
6. Indicating any GPO processing exceptions
7. Filtering the scope of the GPO with security groups
8. Linking the GPO to a site, domain, or OU

Creating a GPO

The first step in implementing a Group Policy is to create a GPO. Recall that a GPO is a collection of Group Policy settings.

To create a GPO, complete the following steps:

1. Determine whether the GPO you're creating will be linked to a site, domain, or OU. Then do one of the following:

    ❑ To create a GPO linked to a domain or an OU, click Start, point to Administrative Tools, and then click Active Directory Users And Computers.

    ❑ To create a GPO linked to a site, Click Start, point to Administrative Tools, and then click Active Directory Sites And Services.

2. Right-click the site, domain, or OU for which you want to create a GPO, and then click Properties.

3. In the Properties dialog box for the object, click the Group Policy tab. In the Group Policy tab, shown in Figure 10-13, click New, then type the name you would like to use for this GPO. By default, the new GPO is linked to the site, domain, or OU that was selected in the MMC when it was created, and its settings apply to that site, domain, or OU.

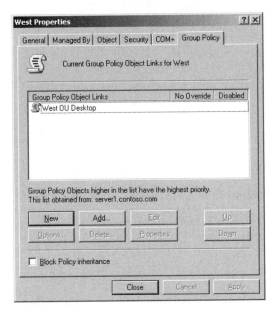

Figure 10-13   Properties dialog box for the West OU, Group Policy tab

4. Click Close.

Creating an MMC for a GPO

After you create a GPO, you should create an MMC for it. When you create an MMC for a GPO, you can open it whenever necessary from the Administrative Tools menu.

To create an MMC for a GPO, complete the following steps:

1. Click Start, and then click Run.

2. In the Run dialog box, type **mmc** in the Open box, and then click OK.

3. In the new MMC, on the File menu, click Add/Remove Snap-In.

4. In the Add/Remove Snap-In dialog box, click Add.

5. In the Add Standalone Snap-In dialog box, select Group Policy Object Editor, and then click Add.

6. In the Select Group Policy Object page, click Browse to find the GPO for which you want to create an MMC.

7. In the Browse For A Group Policy Object dialog box, click the All tab, click the GPO name, and then click OK.

8. In the Select Group Policy Object page, click Finish, and then in the Add Stand-alone Snap-In dialog box, click Close.

9. In the Add/Remove Snap-In dialog box, click OK.

10. In the MMC, on the File menu, click Save As.

11. In the Save As dialog box, type the GPO name in the File Name box and click Save. The GPO is now available on the Administrative Tools menu.

Delegating Control of a GPO

After you create a GPO, it is important to determine which groups of administrators have access permissions to the GPO. The default permissions on GPOs are shown in Table 10-3.

Table 10-3   Default GPO Permissions

Security group	Default settings
Authenticated Users	Read, Apply Group Policy, Special Permissions
Group Policy Creator Owners (also shown as Creator Owner)	Special Permissions
Domain Administrators	Read, Write, Create All Child Objects, Delete All Child Objects, Special Permissions
Enterprise Administrators	Read, Write, Create All Child Objects, Delete All Child Objects, Special Permissions
Enterprise Domain Controllers	Read, Special Permissions
System	Read, Write, Create All Child Objects, Delete All Child Objects, Special Permissions

By default, only the Domain Administrators, Enterprise Administrators, and Group Policy Creator Owner groups, and the operating system can create new GPOs. Nonadministrative users or groups can be given the ability to create GPOs by adding the users or groups to the Group Policy Creator Owners security group. Membership in the Group Policy Creator Owners group gives a user full control of only the GPOs created by the user or explicitly delegated to the user. It does not give a nonadministrative user rights over any other GPOs. If an administrator creates a GPO, the Domain Administrators group becomes the Creator Owner of the GPO.

By default, the Default Domain Policy GPO cannot be deleted by any administrator. This prevents the accidental deletion of this GPO, which contains important required settings for the domain.

GPO-related tasks for which you can delegate control are

- GPO editing

- GPO creation

- GPO object linking

Note   The Delegation Of Control Wizard is not available for automating and simplifying the process of setting administrative permissions directly for a GPO.

To delegate control of GPO editing, complete the following steps:

1. Access the Group Policy Object Editor for the GPO.

2. Right-click the root node of the GPO, and then click Properties.

3. In the Properties dialog box for the GPO, click the Security tab. In the Security tab, shown in Figure 10-14, click the security group for which you want to allow or deny administrative access to the GPO.

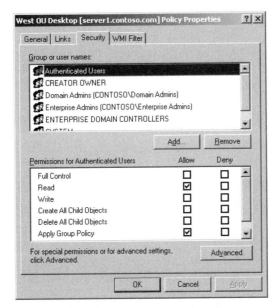

Figure 10-14   West OU Desktop GPO Properties dialog box, Security tab

If you need to change the list of security groups for which you want to allow or deny administrative access to the GPO, you can add or remove security groups using Add and Remove.

4. To provide administrative control of all aspects of the GPO, set both the Read permission and the Write permission to Allow.

> **Important**   A user or administrator who has Read permission for a GPO but does not have Write permission cannot use the Group Policy Object Editor to see the settings that it contains. Write access is required to open a GPO.

5. Click OK.

To delegate control of GPO creation, complete the following steps:

1. Click Start, point to Administrative Tools, and then click Active Directory Users And Computers.

2. In the console tree, click Users.

3. In the Name column in the details pane, double-click Group Policy Creator Owners.

4. In the Group Policy Creator Owners Properties dialog box, click the Members tab.

5. In the Members tab, click Add, and then type the name of each user or security group to whom you want to delegate creation rights in the Enter The Object Names To Select box, and then click OK.

6. In the Group Policy Creator Owners Properties dialog box, click OK.

7. Execute the procedure for delegating control of GPO object linking (shown next). By default, nonadministrators cannot manage links, and unless you execute the procedure for delegating GPO object linking, they cannot use the Active Directory Users And Computers console to create a GPO.

To delegate control of GPO object linking, complete the following steps:

1. Click Start, point to Administrative Tools, and then click Active Directory Users And Computers.

2. Right-click the OU to which you want to delegate the right to link GPOs, and then click Delegate Control.

3. On the Welcome To The Delegation Of Control Wizard page, click Next.

4. On the Users Or Groups page, click Add.

5. In the Select Users, Computers, Or Groups dialog box, type the user or group for which you want to delegate administration in the Enter The Object Names To Select box, and then click OK. Click Next on the Users Or Groups page.

6. On the Tasks To Delegate page, click Delegate The Following Common Tasks and select the Manage Group Policy Links check box, and then click Next.

7. On the Completing The Delegation Of Control Wizard page, review your selections. Click Finish.

Important   Delegated control is inherited by all child containers below the container to which control is delegated.

Note   Delegation across forests is supported for managing GPO links. Other tasks, such as creating, deleting, or modifying GPOs across forests, are not supported. This is a new feature of the Windows Server 2003 family.

Configuring Group Policy Settings

After you create a GPO and determine the administrators who have access permissions to the GPO, you can configure the Group Policy settings.

To configure Group Policy settings for a GPO, complete the following steps:

1. Access the Group Policy Object Editor for the GPO, shown in Figure 10-15.

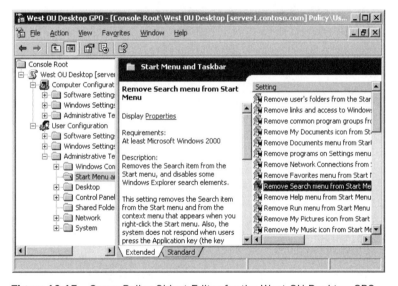

Figure 10-15   Group Policy Object Editor for the West OU Desktop GPO

2. In the console tree, expand the node that represents the policy setting you want to configure. For example, in Figure 10-15, User Configuration, Administrative Templates, and Start Menu And Taskbar nodes are expanded.

3. In the details pane, right-click the setting that you want to configure, and then click Properties.

4. In the Properties dialog box for the Group Policy setting (an example is shown in Figure 10-16), click Enabled to apply the setting to users or computers that are

subject to this GPO, and then click OK. Not Configured indicates that no change will be made to the registry regarding this setting. Disabled means that the registry will indicate that the setting does not apply to users or computers that are subject to this GPO.

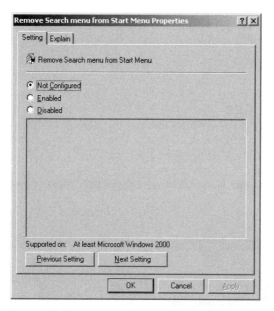

Figure 10-16   Remove Search Menu From Start Menu Properties dialog box

Disabling Unused Group Policy Settings

If the Computer Configuration or User Configuration node for a GPO has only settings that are Not Configured, then you can avoid processing those settings by disabling the node. Disabling unused Group Policy settings is recommended because it expedites startup and logging on for those users and computers subject to the GPO.

To disable the computer configuration or user configuration settings for a GPO, complete the following steps:

1. Access the Group Policy Object Editor for the GPO.

2. Right-click the root node, and then click Properties.

3. In the General tab in the Properties dialog box for the GPO, do one of the following:

   ❑ To disable the computer configuration settings, select the Disable Computer Configuration Settings check box.

   ❑ To disable the user configuration settings, select the Disable User Configuration Settings check box.

4. Click OK.

Indicating GPO Processing Exceptions

As discussed in Lesson 1, GPOs are applied according to the Active Directory hierarchy: local GPO, site GPOs, domain GPOs, and OU GPOs. However, the default order of processing Group Policy settings can be changed by modifying the order of GPOs for an object, specifying the Block Policy Inheritance option, specifying the No Override option, or by enabling the Loopback setting. This section provides procedures for accomplishing these tasks.

To modify the order of GPOs for an object, complete the following steps:

1. Open the Active Directory Users And Computers console to set the order of GPOs for a domain or OU, or open the Active Directory Sites And Services console to set the order of GPOs for a site.

2. In the console, right-click the site, domain, or OU for which you want to modify the GPO order, click Properties, and then click the Group Policy tab.

3. In the Properties dialog box for the object, in the Group Policy tab, shown in Figure 10-17, select the GPO for which you want to modify the order in the Group Policy Object Links list. Click the Up button or the Down button to change the priority for the GPO for this site, domain, or OU. Windows Server 2003 processes GPOs from the bottom of the list to the top of the list, with the topmost GPO having the final authority.

Figure 10-17   Modifying the order of GPOs in the Group Policy Object Links list

4. Click OK.

To specify the Block Policy Inheritance option, complete the following steps:

1. Open the Active Directory Users And Computers console to specify the Block Policy Inheritance option for a domain or OU, or open the Active Directory Sites And Services console to specify the Block Policy Inheritance option for a site.

2. In the console, right-click the site, domain, or OU for which you want to specify the Block Policy Inheritance option, click Properties, and then click the Group Policy tab.

3. In the Properties dialog box for the object, in the Group Policy tab, select the Block Policy Inheritance check box. By checking this box, you specify that all GPOs linked to higher level sites, domains, or OUs should be blocked from linking to this site, domain, or OU. You cannot block GPOs that use the No Override option.

4. Click OK.

To specify the No Override option, complete the following steps:

1. Open the Active Directory Users And Computers console to specify the No Override option for a domain or OU, or open the Active Directory Sites And Services console to specify the No Override option for a site.

2. In the console, right-click the site, domain, or OU to which the GPO is linked, click Properties, and then click the Group Policy tab.

3. In the Properties dialog box for the object, in the Group Policy tab, select the GPO, and then click Options.

4. In the Options dialog box for the GPO, shown in Figure 10-18, select the No Override check box to specify that other GPOs should be prevented from overriding settings in this GPO, and then click OK.

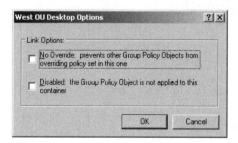

Figure 10-18   The Options dialog box for a GPO

5. In the Properties dialog box for the site, domain, or OU, click OK.

To enable the Loopback setting, complete the following steps:

1. Access the Group Policy Object Editor for the GPO.

2. In the console tree, expand Computer Configuration, Administrative Templates, System, and Group Policy.

3. In the Setting pane, double-click User Group Policy Loopback Processing Mode.

4. In the User Group Policy Loopback Processing Mode Properties dialog box, click Enabled.

5. Select one of the following modes in the Mode list:

   ❑ Replace, to replace the user settings normally applied to the user with the user settings defined in the computer's GPOs.

   ❑ Merge, to combine the user settings defined in the computer's GPOs with the user settings normally applied to the user. If the settings conflict, the user settings in the computer's GPOs take precedence over the user's normal settings.

6. Click OK.

Filtering GPO Scope with Security Groups

As discussed in Lesson 1, the policies in a GPO apply only to users who have the Read and Apply Group Policy permissions for the GPO set to Allow. However, by default, all users in the Authenticated Users group have Read and Apply Group Policy permissions set to Allow for all new GPOs. This means that by default, *all* users are affected by the GPOs set for their domain, site, or OU regardless of the other groups in which they might be members. Therefore, there are two ways of filtering GPO scope:

■ Clear the Apply Group Policy permission (currently set to Allow) for the Authenticated Users group, but do not set this permission to Deny. Then determine the groups to which the GPO should be applied and set the Read and Apply Group Policy permissions for these groups to Allow.

■ Determine the groups to which the GPO should not be applied and set the Apply Group Policy permission for these groups to Deny.

> **Note** Recall from Chapter 9, "Administering Active Directory Objects," that if you deny permission to a user to gain access to an object, the user will not have that permission, even if you allow the permission for a group of which the user is a member.

To filter the scope of a GPO, complete the following steps:

1. Access the Group Policy Object Editor for the GPO.

2. Right-click the root node, and then click Properties.

3. In the Properties dialog box for the GPO, click the Security tab, shown previously in Figure 10-14, and then click the security group through which to filter this GPO.

If you need to change the list of security groups through which to filter this GPO, you can add or remove security groups using Add and Remove.

4. Set the permissions as shown in Table 10-4, and then click OK.

Table 10-4   Permissions for GPO Scopes

GPO Scope	Set These Permissions	Result
Members of this security group should have this GPO applied to them.	■ Set Apply Group Policy to Allow. ■ Set Read to Allow.	This GPO applies to members of this security group unless they are members of at least one other security group that has Apply Group Policy set to Deny, or Read set to Deny, or both.
Members of this security group are exempt from this GPO.	■ Set Apply Group Policy to Deny. ■ Set Read to Deny. Note: Because denied permissions take precedence over all other permissions, you should Deny sparingly.	This GPO never applies to members of this security group regardless of the permissions those members have in other security groups.
Membership in this security group is irrelevant to whether the GPO should be applied.	■ Set Apply Group Policy to neither Allow nor Deny. ■ Set Read to neither Allow nor Deny.	This GPO applies to members of this security group if and only if they have both Apply Group Policy and Read set to Allow as members of at least one other security group. They also must not have Apply Group Policy or Read set to Deny as members of any other security group.

Linking a GPO

By default, a new GPO is linked to the site, domain, or OU that was selected in the MMC when it was created, as described earlier in this lesson in the procedure "Creating a GPO." Therefore its settings apply to that site, domain, or OU. However, if you want to link a GPO to additional sites, domains, or OUs, you must use the Group Policy tab in the Properties dialog box for the site, domain, or OU.

To link a GPO to a site, domain, or OU, complete the following steps:

1. Open the Active Directory Users And Computers console to link a GPO to a domain or OU, or open the Active Directory Sites And Services console to link a GPO to a site.

2. In the console, right-click the site, domain, or OU to which the GPO should be linked. Click Properties, and then click the Group Policy tab.

3. In the Properties dialog box for the object, in the Group Policy tab, click Add.

4. In the Add A Group Policy Object Link dialog box, shown in Figure 10-19, click the All tab, click the desired GPO, and then click OK.

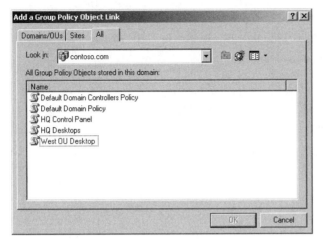

Figure 10-19   The All tab of the Add A Group Policy Object Link dialog box

5. In the Properties dialog box for the site, domain, or OU, click OK.

Modifying a GPO

The tasks for modifying a GPO are

- Removing a GPO link
- Deleting a GPO
- Editing a GPO and GPO settings
- Refreshing a GPO

Removing a GPO Link

Removing a GPO link simply unlinks the GPO from the specified site, domain, or OU. The GPO remains in Active Directory until it is deleted.

To remove a GPO link, complete the following steps:

1. Open the Active Directory Users And Computers console to unlink a GPO from a domain or OU, or open the Active Directory Sites And Services console to unlink a GPO from a site.

2. In the console, right-click the site, domain, or OU from which the GPO should be unlinked. Click Properties, and then click the Group Policy tab.

3. In the Properties dialog box for the object, in the Group Policy tab, select the GPO that you want to unlink, and then click Delete.

4. In the Delete dialog box, shown in Figure 10-20, click Remove The Link From The List. The GPO remains in Active Directory but is no longer linked.

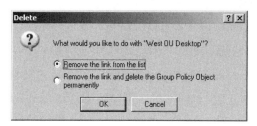

Figure 10-20   Delete dialog box

Deleting a GPO

If you delete a GPO, it is removed from Active Directory, and any sites, domains, or OUs to which it is linked are no longer affected by it. You might wish to take the less drastic step of removing the GPO link, which disassociates the GPO from its OU but leaves the GPO intact in Active Directory.

To delete a GPO, complete the following steps:

1. Open the Active Directory Users And Computers console to delete a GPO from a domain or OU, or open the Active Directory Sites And Services console to delete a GPO from a site.

2. In the console, right-click the site, domain, or OU from which the GPO should be deleted. Click Properties, and then click the Group Policy tab.

3. In the Properties dialog box for the object, in the Group Policy tab, select the GPO that you want to delete, and then click Delete.

4. In the Delete dialog box, click Remove The Link And Delete The Group Policy Object Permanently, and then click OK. The GPO is removed from Active Directory.

Editing a GPO and GPO Settings

To edit a GPO or its settings, follow the procedures outlined earlier in this lesson for creating a GPO and for specifying Group Policy settings.

Refreshing a GPO

Each GPO is refreshed when you restart your computer. When you modify the settings in a GPO, they are refreshed every 90 minutes on a workstation or server and every five minutes on a domain controller. The settings are also refreshed every 16 hours, whether or not there are any changes. In Windows Server 2003, you can refresh policy immediately by using the Gpupdate command-line tool. Gpupdate replaces the secedit.exe /refreshpolicy command used for refreshing GPOs in Windows 2000.

To refresh GPOs immediately, complete the following steps:

1. Click Start, and then click Run.

2. In the Run dialog box, type **gpupdate** in the Open box, and then click OK. You will briefly see the message "Refreshing Policy" on the command line while the policy is being refreshed.

Gpupdate also permits certain options to be specified on the command line. You can learn more about these options by searching for "gpupdate" in Windows Server 2003 Help.

Group Policy Best Practices

The following are the best practices for implementing Group Policy:

- **Disable unused parts of a GPO**   If a GPO has, under the User Configuration or Computer Configuration node of the console, only settings that are Not Configured, disable the node to expedite startup and logging on.

- **Use the Block Policy Inheritance and No Override features sparingly**   Routine use of these feature makes it difficult to troubleshoot Group Policy.

- **Do not use the same name for different GPOs**   Although using the same GPO name doesn't affect GPO function, it can be confusing to administer.

- **Filter policy based on security group membership**   Users who do not have permissions directing that a particular GPO be applied to them can avoid the associated logon delay, because the GPO is not applied for those users.

- **Use loopback only when necessary**   Use loopback only if you need the desktop configuration to be the same regardless of who logs on.

- **Override Group Policy rather than System Policy**   Use System Policy only to manage computers on an operating system earlier than Windows 2000 or if you need to manage desktops for multiple users on a stand-alone computer.

- **Avoid cross-domain GPO assignments**   The processing of GPOs delays logging on and startup if Group Policy is obtained from another domain.

- **Do not link a GPO to the same OU more than once**   When more than one link for the same OU is applied to a single object, the links may be interpreted differently and produce an unexpected RSoP.

Practice: Implementing a GPO

In this practice, you implement a GPO for your practice domain.

> **Note**   To complete this practice, you must have successfully completed the practices in Chapter 6, "Implementing an OU Structure," Chapter 7, "Administering User Accounts," and Chapter 8, "Administering Groups."

Exercise 1: Implementing a GPO

In this exercise, you implement a GPO for the West OU. You create a GPO, create an MMC for a GPO, delegate administrative control of the GPO, specify Group Policy settings for the GPO, indicate a GPO processing exception, filter the scope of the GPO, and link the GPO to an additional OU. Use the procedures provided earlier in this lesson to complete each step in the exercise.

1. Log on to Server1 as Administrator.

2. On Server1, create a GPO in the West OU. Name the GPO **West OU Desktop**.

3. Create an MMC for the West OU Desktop GPO. Name the console **West OU Desktop GPO**.

4. Specify the following Group Policy settings for the West OU Desktop GPO:

   ❑ In the User Configuration node, in the Administrative Templates node, in the Start Menu And Taskbar node, configure the Remove Search Menu From Start Menu setting to Enabled. Then configure the Remove Run Menu From Start Menu setting (still under User Configuration) to Enabled.

   ❑ In the User Configuration node, in the Administrative Templates node, in the System node, in the CTRL+ALT+DEL Options node, configure the Remove Lock Computer setting to Enabled.

5. For the West OU Desktop GPO, set the No Override option in the Group Policy tab in the Properties dialog box for the West OU to prevent other GPOs from overriding the policies set in the West OU Desktop GPO.

6. For the West OU Desktop GPO, clear the Apply Group Policy permission (currently set to Allow) for the Authenticated Users group. Do not set this permission to Deny.

7. Create a new Marketing domain local security group in the Kansas City OU. Enable the User17 and User19 accounts that were disabled in Chapter 9 and assign them to the Marketing group.

8. Ensure that the West OU Desktop GPO applies to the Marketing domain local security group by setting the group's Apply Group Policy permission for the GPO in the West OU Desktop Group Policy Object Editor to Allow.

9. By default the West OU Desktop GPO is linked to the West OU, and its settings apply to the West OU and its child OUs, Kansas City and St. Paul. Link the West OU Desktop OU to the Chicago OU you created in Chapter 6 in the Properties dialog box, the Group Policy tab for the Chicago OU.

Exercise 2: Testing a GPO

In this exercise, you view the effects of the GPO you implemented in Exercise 1.

1. Log on as User19, a member of the Marketing security group.

2. Press CTRL+ALT+DELETE. The Windows Security dialog box appears. Are you able to lock the workstation? Why?

   No, the Lock Computer option is not available. User19 is unable to lock the workstation because the West OU Desktop GPO applies to the Marketing security group, of which User19 is a member.

3. Click Cancel, and then click Start.

   a. Does the Search command appear on the Start menu?

   No.

   b. Does the Run command appear on the Start menu?

   No.

4. Log off as User19, then log on as Administrator.

5. Remove User19 from the Marketing security group.

6. Log off as Administrator, then log on as User19.

7. Press CTRL+ALT+DEL. Are you able to lock the workstation? Why?

   Yes, the Lock Computer option is available. User19 is able to lock the workstation because the West OU Desktop GPO applies only to members of the Marketing security group, of which User19 is no longer a member.

8. Log off as User19, then log on as User7.

9. Press CTRL+ALT+DEL. Are you able to lock the workstation? Why or why not?

   Yes, because the Lock Computer option is available. User7 is able to lock the workstation because the West OU Desktop GPO applies only to the Marketing security group, of which User7 is not a member. This is true even though the West OU Desktop GPO is linked to the Chicago OU, in which User7 is contained.

10. Log off as User7, then log on as Administrator.

11. Make User7 a member of the Marketing security group.

12. Log off as Administrator, then log on as User7.

13. Press CTRL+ALT+DEL. Are you able to lock the workstation? Why or why not?

No, because the Lock Computer option is not available. User7 is unable to lock the workstation because the West OU Desktop GPO is linked to the Chicago OU and applies only to the Marketing security group, of which User7 is now a member.

14. Log off as User7, then log on as Administrator.

15. Create a new GPO in the Kansas City OU. Name the GPO **KC OU Desktop**. Create an MMC for the KC OU Desktop GPO. Name the console **KC OU Desktop GPO**.

16. In the User Configuration node, in the Administrative Templates node, in the Control Panel node, configure the Prohibit Access To The Control Panel setting to Enabled.

17. Set the Block Policy Inheritance option in the Group Policy tab in the Properties dialog box for the Kansas City OU to block GPOs set in parent objects from applying to the Kansas City OU.

18. For the KC OU Desktop GPO, set the Apply Group Policy permission for the Marketing domain local security group to Allow. Clear the Apply Group Policy permission (currently set to Allow) for the Authenticated Users group. Do not set this permission to Deny.

19. Log off as Administrator, and then log on as User17. Which GPO applies and why?

The West OU Desktop and the KC OU Desktop GPOs both apply to User17 because the West OU Desktop GPO has the No Override option set. The No Override option ensures that none of a GPO's settings can be overridden by any other GPO during the processing of group policies. Even though the Block Policy Inheritance option is set for the KC OU Desktop GPO, the No Override option set for the West OU Desktop GPO overrides the KC OU Desktop GPO. Therefore, both GPOs apply to User17.

20. Log off as User17, and then log on as User7. Which GPO applies and why?

Only the West OU Desktop GPO applies to User7. Because the KC OU Desktop GPO has not been linked to the Chicago OU (in which User7 is contained) or the East OU (parent OU of the Chicago OU), the KC OU Desktop GPO does not apply to User7.

Lesson Review

The following questions are intended to reinforce key information presented in this lesson. If you are unable to answer a question, review the lesson and then try the question again. Answers to the questions can be found in the "Questions and Answers" section at the end of this chapter.

1. If you want to create a GPO for a site, what administrative tool should you use?

_____

_____

2. Why should you create an MMC for a GPO?

_____

_____

3. Besides Read permission, what permission must you assign to allow a user or administrator to see the settings in a GPO?

_____

_____

4. Why should you disable unused Group Policy settings?

_____

_____

5. How do you prevent a GPO from applying to a specific group?

_____

_____

6. What's the difference between removing a GPO link and deleting a GPO?

_____

_____

7. You want to deflect all Group Policy settings that reach the North OU from all of the OU's parent objects. To accomplish this, which of the following exceptions do you apply and where do you apply it?

   a. Block Policy Inheritance applied to the OU

   b. Block Policy Inheritance applied to the GPO

   c. Block Policy Inheritance applied to the GPO link

   d. No Override applied to the OU

   e. No Override applied to the GPO

   f. No Override applied to the GPO link

8. You want to ensure that none of the South OU Desktop settings applied to the South OU can be overridden. To accomplish this, which of the following exceptions do you apply and where do you apply it?

   a. Block Policy Inheritance applied to the OU

   b. Block Policy Inheritance applied to the GPO

   c. Block Policy Inheritance applied to the GPO link

     d. No Override applied to the OU

     e. No Override applied to the GPO

     f. No Override applied to the GPO link

Lesson Summary

- You use the Active Directory Users And Computers console to create a GPO for a domain or an OU. You use the Active Directory Sites And Services console to create a GPO for a site.

- You should create an MMC for a GPO, because you can open it whenever necessary from the Administrative Tools menu, making it easier to administer.

- You should disable unused Group Policy settings to avoid the processing of those settings and expedite startup and logging on for the users and computers subject to the GPO.

- For a GPO to apply to a specific group, that group must have the Read and Apply Group Policy permissions for the GPO set to Allow. To prevent a GPO from applying to a specific group, that group must have the Apply Group Policy permission for the GPO set to Deny.

- When you remove a GPO link to a site, domain, or OU, the GPO still remains in Active Directory. When you delete a GPO, the GPO is removed from Active Directory, and any sites, domains, or OUs to which it is linked are no longer affected by it.

Case Scenario Exercise

You are a network administrator for Humongous Insurance, as described in Chapter 8. The only change since Chapter 8 is that all of the Windows NT 4.0 backup domain controllers (BDCs) have been removed from the *east.humongous.com* domain. All domains are configured for a functional level of Windows 2000 Native. Figure 10-21 illustrates current Humongous Insurance network infrastructure.

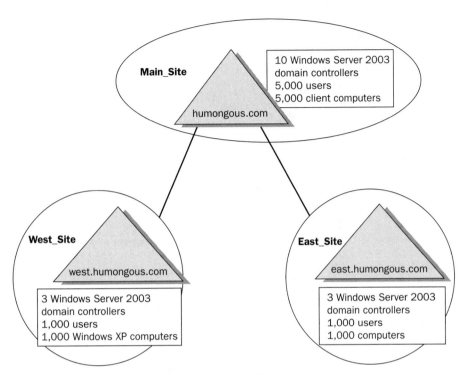

Figure 10-21   Humongous Insurance Network Structure

Five domain controllers in the Main_Site and two domain controllers in each of the other sites are configured as DNS servers. The DNS records are stored in, and replicated by, Active Directory. Each site has one global catalog server. The *humongous.com* domain has five first-level OUs: Accounting, Administration, Claims, Executives, and Marketing. The *west.humongous.com* and *east.humongous.com* domains each have three OUs: Administration, Claims, and Regional Sales. This is depicted in Figure 10-22.

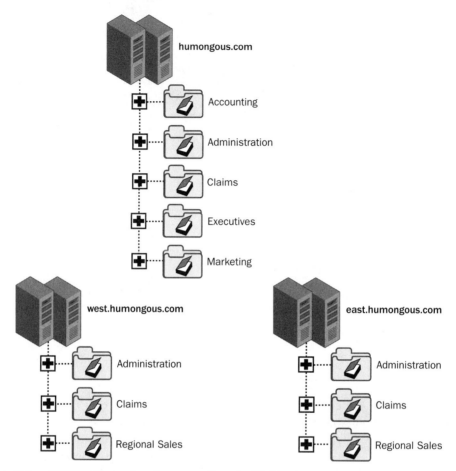

Figure 10-22   Humongous Insurance Domain OU Structure

You've been working with several other administrators to figure out how you can utilize Group Policy. Given this information, answer the following questions:

1. You link a GPO to the *humongous.com* domain, but that policy isn't inherited by the *east.humongous.com* or *west.humongous.com* domains. Why is this happening and how can you make it apply to those two domains?

   _____

   _____

2. The *east.humongous.com* administrator, Sharon Salavaria, has configured a GPO, named Required_Set, that she says is mandatory for her entire domain. She also has several GPOs that she's configured at the domain, but she doesn't consider those policies mandatory. The Administration and Regional Sales OU administrators have blocked policy inheritance to their OUs. Sharon wants to be sure that they receive at least the Required_Set GPO. What should she do?

3. Sharon realizes that three users in the Claims OU should not be receiving the Required_Set GPO, but she wants everyone else in the entire company, including other users in the Claims OU, to receive that policy. What are her options?

4. You've been asked to configure five public access computers that run the Windows XP Professional operating system in the Humongous Insurance lobby. You configure a GPO called LockDown that restricts the options that people have in operating these systems. However, you are concerned that some of your domain users might log on to these systems, which would change the appearance of the desktop. You want to be sure that the user settings that you've configured for the LockDown GPO apply to anyone who logs on to the public computers. What can you do?

Troubleshooting Lab

You are a domain administrator for Contoso Pharmaceuticals. One of the desktop administrators calls to report some peculiar results with four user accounts. Users are not supposed to have the Run command in their Start menus, but three out of four have it. The desktop administrator is puzzled. You investigate the issue and document your results, as shown in Table 10-5.

Table 10-5   Results of Your Investigation

User Account	Parent Container	Group Memberships
GPLabUser1	contoso.com	GPLabGroup1 Domain Users
GPLabUser2	*contoso.com*	GPLabGroup2 Domain Users
GPLabUser3	GPLab OU	GPLabGroup1 GPLabGroup2 Domain Users
GPLabUser4	GPLab OU	Domain Users

You learn that the GPO that doesn't seem to be working is named GPLabRemoveRun. You discover that someone has explicitly denied GPLabGroup2 the permission to

Apply Group Policy for the GPLabRemoveRun policy. You also determined that GPLabRemoveRun is linked to the GPLab OU.

To experience this issue, complete the following steps:

1. Log on to Server1 using the domain administrator name and password.

2. In the *contoso.com* domain container, create two users: GPLabUser1 and GPLabUser2.

> **Note**   When you create the user accounts in this lab, set their passwords to password.
> Clear the User Must Change Password At Next Logon box. Check the Password Never Expires
> box. (In a real-world environment, of course, you should make sure users follow proper pass-
> word procedures, such as creating complex passwords with a combination of uppercase and
> lowercase letters, numbers, and symbols.)

3. In the *contoso.com* domain container, create a new OU in *contoso.com* named GPLab.

4. In the GPLab OU, create two universal groups: GPLabGroup1 and GPLabGroup2.

5. In the GPLab OU, create two users: GPLabUser3, and GPLabUser0.

6. Add GPLabUser1, GPLabUser2, GPLabUser3, and GPLabUser0 as members of the Server Operators group. This allows these accounts to log on locally.

7. Add GPLabUser1 as a member of the GPLabGroup1 group.

8. Add GPLabUser2 as a member of the GPLabGroup2 group.

9. Add GPLabUser3 as a member of both GPLabGroup1 and GPLabGroup2.

> **Note**   GPLabUser0 was added to only the Server Operators group. By default, all new users
> are also members of Domain Users.

10. Create a new GPO for the GPLab OU. To do so, right-click GPLab, and then click Properties.

11. In the GPLab Properties dialog box, click the Group Policy tab. Click New. Type **GPLabRemoveRun** as the new policy name, and press ENTER. Click Properties.

12. In the GPLabRemoveRun Properties dialog box, click the Security tab. Click Add.

13. Type GPLabGroup1 and click OK. You should see the GPLabGroup1 appear in the Group Or User Names window.

14. Look at the Permissions For GPLabGroup1 window. Notice that GPLabGroup1 has Read permissions (the Allow box is checked) for this GPO. Check the Allow box that corresponds to the Apply Group Policy entry in this list. Click Apply.

15. Click Add again. This time type **GPLabGroup2** and click OK. The GPLabGroup2 appears in the Group Or User Names window.

16. In the Permissions For GPLabGroup2 window, check the Deny box that corresponds to the Apply Group Policy entry, and then click OK. The Security warning message box appears. Read the warning, and then click Yes.

> **Note**   You've now configured the GPLabRemoveRun GPO so members of GPLabGroup1 can apply the policy but members of GPLabGroup2 cannot.

17. In the GPLab Properties dialog box, click Edit. The Group Policy Object Editor window opens.

18. Navigate to the following policy location: User Configuration, Administrative Templates, Start Menu And Taskbar.

19. Double-click the Remove Run Menu From Start Menu setting in the details pane.

20. In the Remove Run Menu From Start Menu Properties dialog box, click Enabled, and then click OK. You've now enabled this setting, which removes the Run option from the Start menu of all affected users.

21. Close all open windows.

22. Click Start, click Run, type **gpupdate**, and then press ENTER. This ensures that the policy is immediately applied to the system.

23. Log off as Administrator. Log on as GPLabUser1. Click Start. Do you see the Run option in the Start menu?

    Yes, because the policy doesn't apply to this user.

24. Log off GPLabUser1 and log on as GPLabUser2. Do you see the Run option in the Start menu?

    Yes, because the policy doesn't apply to this user.

25. Log off GPLabUser2 and log on as GPLabUser3. Do you see the Run option in the Start menu?

    Yes, because the policy doesn't apply to this user.

26. Log off GPLabUser3 and log on as GPLabUser0. Do you see the Run option in the Start menu?

    No, because the policy applies to this user.

27. Why does the policy affect only GPLabUser0?

    GPLabUser0 is the only user account that is not specifically filtered from receiving the policy, and GPLabUser1 and GPLabUser2 are not in or subordinate to the container to which the policy is applied. GPLabUser3 is a member of a group that is specifically filtered from receiving the policy.

28. How could you configure your Active Directory objects to ensure that all four GPLabUser accounts were subject to the GPLabRemoveRun GPO?

First, you need to ensure that all user accounts are in a container that receives the GPO. You can do this by moving GPUser1 and GPUser2 to the GPLab OU. Second, you must ensure that the security filtering doesn't affect GPUser2 and GPUser3. To do this, either remove the security filtering by allowing GPLabGroup2 to apply the GPO, or remove GPUser2 and GPUser3 from GPLabGroup2.

Chapter Summary

■ Group policies are collections of user and computer configuration settings that can be linked to computers, sites, domains, and OUs to specify the behavior of users' desktops. You use the Group Policy Object Editor to organize and manage the Group Policy settings in each GPO.

■ There are two types of Group Policy settings: computer configuration settings and user configuration settings. Computer configuration settings are used to set group policies applied to computers, regardless of who logs on to them, and are applied when the operating system initializes. User configuration settings are used to set group policies applied to users, regardless of which computer the user logs on to, and are applied when users log on to the computer.

■ Group Policy is applied to Active Directory components in the following order: local computer, site, domain, and then OU.

■ Group Policy is passed down from parent to child containers within a domain. If you have assigned a separate Group Policy setting to a parent container, that Group Policy setting applies to all containers beneath the parent container, including the user and computer objects in the container. However, if you specify a Group Policy setting for a child container, the child container's Group Policy setting overrides the setting inherited from the parent container.

■ The default order for the application of Group Policy settings is subject to the following exceptions: No Override, Block Policy Inheritance, the Loopback setting, and a computer that is a member of a workgroup.

■ There are three parts to planning Group Policy: plan the Group Policy settings, plan GPOs, and plan administrative control of GPOs.

■ You use the Active Directory Users And Computers console to create a GPO for a domain or an OU. You use the Active Directory Sites And Services console to create a GPO for a site.

Exam Highlights

Before taking the exam, review the key points and terms that are presented in this chapter. You need to know this information.

Key Points

- Plan Group Policy settings sparingly—justify the selection of each setting as you would the creation of a domain or OU. Choose settings based on their ability to help you to simplify the administration of computers and users.

- Build GPOs by using a decentralized or a centralized design. A decentralized design uses a base GPO applied to the domain, which contains policy settings for as many users and computers in the domain as possible. Then this design uses additional GPOs tailored to the common requirements of each OU and applied to the appropriate OUs. A centralized design uses a single GPO containing all policy settings for the associated site, domain, or OU.

- Administrative control of GPOs can be delegated by using a centralized, decentralized, or task-based administrative control design. In the centralized design, administration of Group Policy is delegated only to top-level OU administrators. In the decentralized design, administration of Group Policy is delegated to top-level and to second-level OU administrators. In the task-based design, administration of specific group policies is delegated to administrators that handle the associated specific tasks.

Key Terms

Group Policy   A collection of user and computer configuration settings that specifies how programs, network resources, and the operating system work for users and computers in an organization. Group Policy can be linked to computers, sites, domains, and OUs.

Computer Configuration node   A node in the Group Policy Object Editor which contains the settings used to set group policies applied to computers, regardless of who logs on to them. Computer configuration settings are applied when the operating system initializes.

User Configuration node   A node in the Group Policy Object Editor which contains the settings used to set group policies applied to users, regardless of which computer the user logs on to. User configuration settings are applied when users log on to the computer.

Questions and Answers

Page
10-21

Lesson 1 Review

1. What is a GPO?

   A GPO is a Group Policy Object. Group Policy configuration settings are contained within a GPO. Each computer running Windows Server 2003 has one local GPO and can, in addition, be subject to any number of nonlocal (Active Directory–based) GPOs.

2. What are the two types of Group Policy settings and how are they used?

   The two types of Group Policy settings are computer configuration settings and user configuration settings. Computer configuration settings are used to set group policies applied to computers, regardless of who logs on to them, and are applied when the operating system initializes. User configuration settings are used to set group policies applied to users, regardless of which computer the users logs on to, and are applied when users log on to the computer.

3. In what order is Group Policy applied to components in the Active Directory structure?

   Group Policy is applied to Active Directory components in the following order: local computer, site, domain, and then OU.

4. What is the difference between Block Policy Inheritance and No Override?

   Block Policy Inheritance is applied directly to the site, domain, or OU. It is not applied to GPOs, nor is it applied to GPO links. Thus Block Policy Inheritance deflects *all* Group Policy settings that reach the site, domain, or OU from above (by way of linkage to parents in the Active Directory hierarchy) no matter what GPOs those settings originate from. GPO links set to No Override are always applied and cannot be blocked using the Block Policy Inheritance option.

   Any GPO linked to a site, domain, or OU (not the local GPO) can be set to No Override, so that none of its policy settings can be overwritten by any other GPO during the processing of group policies. When more than one GPO has been set to No Override, the one highest in the Active Directory hierarchy (or higher in the hierarchy specified by the administrator at each fixed level in Active Directory) takes precedence. No Override is applied to the GPO link.

5. Which of the following nodes contains the registry-based Group Policy settings?

   a. Software Settings

   b. Windows Settings

   c. Administrative Templates

   d. Security Settings

   The correct answer is c. The Administrative Templates node contains the registry-based Group Policy settings. The Software Settings node contains only the Software Installation extension. The Windows Settings node contains the settings for configuring the operating system, such as scripts, security settings, folder redirection, and RIS. The Security Settings node contains settings for configuring security levels.

Page
10-28

Lesson 2 Review

1. Describe a decentralized GPO design.

With a decentralized GPO design, you create a base GPO to be applied to the domain that contains policy settings for as many users and computers in the domain as possible. Next, you create additional GPOs tailored to the common requirements of each OU, and apply them to the appropriate OUs. The goal of a decentralized GPO design is to include a specific policy setting in as few GPOs as possible. When a change is required, only one (or a few) GPO(s) have to be changed to enforce the change.

2. If administrative responsibilities in your organization are task-based and delegated among several administrators, which of the following types of GPOs should you plan to create?

a. GPOs containing only one type of Group Policy setting

b. GPOs containing many types of Group Policy settings

c. GPOs containing only computer configuration settings

d. GPOs containing only user configuration settings

The correct answer is a. For example, a GPO that includes only security settings is best suited for organizations in which administrative responsibilities are task-based and delegated among several individuals.

Page
10-46

Lesson 3 Review

1. If you want to create a GPO for a site, what administrative tool should you use?

Use the Active Directory Sites And Services console to create a GPO for a site.

2. Why should you create an MMC for a GPO?

If you create an MMC for a GPO, it is easier to administer because you can open it whenever necessary from the Administrative Tools menu.

3. Besides Read permission, what permission must you assign to allow a user or administrator to see the settings in a GPO?

Write permission. A user or administrator who has Read access but not Write access to a GPO cannot use the Group Policy Object Editor to see the settings that it contains.

4. Why should you disable unused Group Policy settings?

Disabling unused Group Policy settings avoids the processing of those settings and expedites startup and logging on for the users and computers subject to the GPO.

5. How do you prevent a GPO from applying to a specific group?

You can prevent a policy from applying to a specific group by denying that group the Apply Group Policy permission for the GPO.

6. What's the difference between removing a GPO link and deleting a GPO?

When you remove a GPO link to a site, domain, or OU, the GPO still remains in Active Directory. When you delete a GPO, the GPO is removed from Active Directory, and any sites, domains, or OUs to which it is linked are not longer affected by it.

7. You want to deflect all Group Policy settings that reach the North OU from all of the OU's parent objects. To accomplish this, which of the following exceptions do you apply and where do you apply it?

   a. Block Policy Inheritance applied to the OU

   b. Block Policy Inheritance applied to the GPO

   c. Block Policy Inheritance applied to the GPO link

   d. No Override applied to the OU

   e. No Override applied to the GPO

   f. No Override applied to the GPO link

The correct answer is a. You use the Block Policy Inheritance exception to deflect all Group Policy settings from the parent objects of a site, domain, or OU. Block Policy Inheritance can only be applied directly to a site, domain, or OU, not to a GPO or a GPO link.

8. You want to ensure that none of the South OU Desktop settings applied to the South OU can be overridden. To accomplish this, which of the following exceptions do you apply and where do you apply it?

   a. Block Policy Inheritance applied to the OU

   b. Block Policy Inheritance applied to the GPO

   c. Block Policy Inheritance applied to the GPO link

   d. No Override applied to the OU

   e. No Override applied to the GPO

   f. No Override applied to the GPO link

The correct answer is f. You use the No Override exception to ensure that none of a GPO's settings can be overridden by any other GPO during the processing of group policies. No Override can only be applied directly to a GPO link.

Page
10-48

Case Scenario Exercise

1. You link a GPO to the *humongous.com* domain, but that policy isn't inherited by the *east.humongous.com* or *west.humongous.com* domains. Why is this happening and how can you make it apply to those two domains?

GPOs linked to one domain aren't inherited by other domains. The only way to affect multiple domains with a single GPO is to link the GPO to a site that includes the resources of multiple domains. Because sites and domains are independent entities, you could only be sure that a

GPO linked to the site applies to the computer and user accounts that are part of the site. At Humongous Insurance, each domain's resources are configured in three different sites. The only way to have a single GPO apply to the resources of multiple domains is to link the policy to all three domains (or all three sites).

2. The *east.humongous.com* administrator, Sharon Salavaria, has configured a GPO, named Required_Set, that she says is mandatory for her entire domain. She also has several GPOs that she's configured at the domain, but she doesn't consider those policies mandatory. The Administration and Regional Sales OU administrators have blocked policy inheritance to their OUs. Sharon wants to be sure that they receive at least the Required_Set GPO. What should she do?

Sharon should configure the Required_Set GPO for No Override. The Required Set GPO will be inherited by all the OUs, but the administrators of those OUs will not have to accept the other GPOs she has configured.

3. Sharon realizes that three users in the Claims OU should not be receiving the Required_Set GPO, but she wants everyone else in the entire company, including other users in the Claims OU, to receive that policy. What are her options?

The most likely solution is for Sharon to create a group for those who shouldn't receive the policy. She can then add specific users to that group and configure the group so that Apply Group Policy is denied. Her other options include moving the user accounts to another container that doesn't receive the GPO or configuring each user account so that each is denied the ability to apply that GPO.

4. You've been asked to configure five public access computers that run the Windows XP Professional operating system in the Humongous Insurance lobby. You configure a GPO called LockDown that restricts the options that people have in operating these systems. However, you are concerned that some of your domain users might log on to these systems, which would change the appearance of the desktop. You want to be sure that the user settings that you've configured for the LockDown GPO apply to anyone who logs on to the public computers. What can you do?

Create a new OU named Public and link the LockDown GPO to that OU. Move the computer accounts for each of those computers to the LockDown OU. Then, on the LockDown OU, enable the Computer Configuration, Administrative Templates, System, Group Policy, User Group Policy Loopback Processing Mode policy for Replace mode. This will ensure that everyone receives an identical desktop configuration.

11 Administering Group Policy

Exam Objectives in this Chapter:

- Plan a Group Policy strategy by using Resultant Set of Policy Planning mode.

- Troubleshoot issues related to Group Policy application and deployment. Tools might include RSoP and the gpresult command.

- Troubleshoot the application of Group Policy security settings. Tools might include RSoP and the gpresult command.

- Redirect folders by using Group Policy.

Why This Chapter Matters

This chapter shows you how to administer Group Policy, which is essential to meeting the needs of changing organizations. A key tool in Group Policy administration is generating Resultant Set of Policy (RSoP), a feature that simplifies policy implementation and troubleshooting. You must be able to use RSoP in Logging mode to determine the resultant effect of policy settings that have been applied to an existing user and computer based on a site, domain, and OU. You can also use RSoP in Planning mode to simulate the resultant effect of policy settings that are applied to a user and a computer. Planning your Group Policy strategy is essential to providing the most efficient Group Policy implementation for your organization. Another part of effective Group Policy administration is the ability to redirect folders, which provides users with an access point for storing and finding information and administrators with an access point for managing information. Using the Folder Redirection node in Group Policy, you can redirect the location of Application Data, Desktop, My Documents, My Pictures, and Start Menu. Finally, you must be able to provide users with access to redirected folders even when they are not connected to the network. You can do this by learning to use the Offline Files feature, which caches files accessed through folder redirection onto the hard drive of the local computer.

Lessons in this Chapter:

Before You Begin

To complete the lessons in this chapter, you must

- Prepare your test environment according to the descriptions given in the "Getting Started" section of "About This Book"

- Complete the practices for installing and configuring Active Directory as discussed in Chapter 2, "Installing and Configuring Active Directory"

- Learn to use Active Directory administration tools as discussed in Chapter 3, "Administering Active Directory"

- Complete the practices for configuring sites and replication as discussed in Chapter 5, "Configuring Sites and Managing Replication"

- Complete the practices for implementing an organizational unit (OU) structure as discussed in Chapter 6, "Implementing an OU Structure"

- Complete the practices for creating and maintaining user accounts as discussed in Chapter 7, "Administering User Accounts"

- Complete the practices for creating and administering group accounts as discussed in Chapter 8, "Administering Groups"

- Complete the practices for implementing Group Policy Objects (GPOs) as discussed in Chapter 10, "Implementing Group Policy"

Lesson 1: Managing Group Policy with RSoP

RSoP is the sum of the group policies applied to a user or computer. Determining RSoP for a computer or user can be a complex task. In Microsoft Windows Server 2003, you can generate an RSoP query to determine the policies applied to a specified user or computer. This lesson introduces you to the tools used to generate RSoP queries, the ways to save RSoP queries, and the results provided by each of the RSoP generation tools.

After this lesson, you will be able to

- Define RSoP
- Describe the three tools available for generating an RSoP query
- Use the Resultant Set Of Policy Wizard to generate an RSoP query
- Save a query generated by the Resultant Set Of Policy Wizard
- View the results of an RSoP query generated by the Resultant Set Of Policy Wizard
- Use the Gpresult command-line tool to generate an RSoP query
- View the results of an RSoP query generated by Gpresult
- Use the Advanced System Information–Policy tool to generate an RSoP query
- View the results of an RSoP query generated by the Advanced System Information–Policy tool

Estimated lesson time: 40 minutes

Understanding RSoP

As you learned in Chapter 10, GPOs are cumulative as they are applied to a local computer, site, domain, and OU hierarchy. RSoP is the sum of the policies applied to a user or computer, including the application of filters, such as through security groups and Windows Management Instrumentation (WMI), and exceptions, such as No Override and Block Policy Inheritance. Because of the cumulative effects of GPOs, filters, and exceptions, determining a user or computer's RSoP can be difficult. However, the ability to generate RSoP queries in Windows Server 2003 makes determining RSoP easier. In Windows Server 2003, an RSoP query engine is available to poll existing GPOs and report the affects of GPOs on users and computers. The query engine also checks for security groups and WMI queries used to filter GPO scope, and checks Software Installation for any applications that are associated with a particular user or computer and reports the effects of these settings as well. This information is gathered from the Common Information Management Object Model (CIMOM) database.

Note A detailed discussion of WMI is beyond the scope of this training kit. For detailed information about WMI, refer to the MSDN Library at *http://msdn.microsoft.com/library*. You can find information about WMI by pointing to Setup and System Information, Windows Management Instrumentation (WMI), and, finally, Technical Articles.

Windows Server 2003 provides the following three tools for generating RSoP queries:

- Resultant Set Of Policy Wizard
- Gpresult command-line tool
- Advanced System Information–Policy tool

Each tool uses a different interface and provides different levels of RSoP query information, as discussed in the sections that follow.

Note You can also download the Group Policy Management Console (GPMC), which provides tools to back up, restore, import, copy, and report on GPOs. GPMC with Service Pack 1 (SP1) has improved support for remote GPO management. For more information, see "Enterprise Management with the Group Policy Management Console" at *http://www.microsoft.com /windowsserver2003/gpmc/default.mspx*.

Warning After Windows Firewall in Windows Server 2003 SP1 is enabled on a server, you cannot get remote access to its RSoP data. If you wish to use the remote RSoP capabilities in the GPMC with SP1, Gpresult, or the RSoP Wizard, you need to enable and apply Windows Firewall: Allow Remote Administration Exception Group Policy setting on the target computer. If the computer you are using to obtain the RSoP is running Windows XP Service Pack 2, and also protected by Windows Firewall, you must also do the following:

- Add Unsecapp.exe to Windows Firewall exceptions list on the local computer that you are using to administer the remote computer.
- Add TCP port 135 to Windows Firewall exceptions list on the local computer that you are using to administer the remote computer.

See Also For more information, see the section on Resultant Set of Policy (RSoP) in "Changes to Functionality in Microsoft Windows Server 2003 Service Pack 1" at *http://www.microsoft.com/downloads/details.aspx?FamilyId=C3C26254-8CE3-46E2-B1B6-3659B92B2CDE&displaylang=en*.

Generating RSoP Queries with the Resultant Set Of Policy Wizard

To help you analyze the cumulative effects of GPOs, Windows Server 2003 provides the Resultant Set Of Policy Wizard, which uses existing GPO settings to report the effects of GPOs on users and computers. You can also use the Resultant Set Of Policy Wizard in an entirely different manner to simulate the effects of planned GPOs. To accomplish polling of existing GPOs and the simulation of planned GPOs, the Resultant Set Of Policy Wizard uses two modes, Logging mode and Planning mode, to create RSoP queries. Logging mode reports the existing GPO settings for a user or computer. Planning mode simulates the GPO settings that a user and computer might receive, and it enables you change the simulation.

Logging Mode

RSoP Logging mode enables you to review existing GPO settings, software installation applications, and security for a computer account or a user account. Use Logging mode to

- Find failed or overwritten policy settings
- See how security groups affect policy settings
- Find out how local policy is affecting group policies

When you create an RSoP query in Logging mode, each of the applications that are available for installation, the folders that will be redirected (and to where), and each policy setting that will be applied to the user or computer, as well as the security group's effect on those policies, are reported.

 Note In RSoP Logging mode, you can create an RSoP query only for user accounts and computer accounts. In addition, only users and computers that have logged on to the domain are available for an RSoP query.

Planning Mode

RSoP planning mode enables you to plan for growth and reorganization. Using RSoP Planning mode, you can poll existing GPOs for policy settings, software installation applications, and security, and you can use WMI filter queries to read hardware and software properties. Then, you can use the results to construct a scenario to predict the effect of changes in policy settings. Use Planning mode in the following situations:

- You want to test policy precedence in cases where
  - ❑ The user and the computer are in different security groups.
  - ❑ The user and the computer are in different OUs.
  - ❑ The user or the computer is moving to a new location.

- You want to simulate a slow link.

- You want to simulate loopback.

You can create an RSoP query in Planning mode to see what will happen to a user or a group of users if they are moved to another location or security group, or even to another computer, by setting the RSoP Planning mode options.

RSoP Planning Mode Options   There are several RSoP Planning mode options. Each option can be run separately or in conjunction with the other options, allowing for a wide range of simulation results. As you progress through the Resultant Set Of Policy Wizard, the Planning mode options are presented to you in the following order:

1. **Slow-network connection**   This option simulates a slow connection. A connection is slow if the rate at which data is transferred (from the domain controller that provides a policy update to the computers in this group) is slower than the rate that is specified by this GPO. The system's response to a slow policy connection varies among policies.

2. **Loopback processing**   This option simulates enabling of the GPO setting User Group Policy Loopback Processing Mode, located in Computer Configuration, Administrative Templates, System, Group Policy. The simulation can be set to Merge or Replace. Select Merge to simulate the appending of the GPO list obtained for the computer at computer startup to the GPO list obtained for the user. Select Replace to simulate replacement of the GPO list for the user with the GPO list already obtained for the computer at computer startup.

3. **Site name**   This option simulates the application of alternate subnets for startup or logging on, enabling you to predict the RSoP if the subnet is changed.

4. **Alternate user and computer locations**   This option simulates the application of alternate locations for both users and computers, enabling you to predict the RSoP if the user and/or computer is moved.

5. **Alternate user and computer security groups**   This option simulates the application of alternate security groups to both computer and user configurations, enabling you to predict the RSoP using security groups to filter GPO scope.

6. **WMI filters for users and computers**   This option simulates the use of WMI filters to help define the policy settings that are applied, enabling you to predict the RSoP using WMI queries to filter GPO scope.

Exam Tip   Make sure you understand the differences between using RSoP in Logging mode and in Planning mode.

Creating RSoP Queries

You create RSoP queries by first creating an RSoP query console and then configuring the RSoP query by using the Resultant Set Of Policy Wizard. You can also create an RSoP query from the Active Directory Users And Computers console (for domains, OUs, computer accounts, and user accounts) or the Active Directory Sites And Services console (for sites). However, if you create an RSoP query from the Active Directory Users And Computers or Active Directory Sites And Services consoles, you must remember to save the query to %Systemroot%\Documents and Settings\Administrator\Start Menu\Programs\Administrative Tools for the query to be available on the Administrative Tools menu.

> **Note**   To create an RSoP query from the Active Directory Users And Computers or Active Directory Sites And Services consoles, open the console, right-click the site, domain, OU, user account, or computer account for which you want to create a query, click All Tasks, and select Resultant Set Of Policy (Planning) or Resultant Set Of Policy (Logging). Note that Logging mode is available only for computer accounts and user accounts. Then run the Resultant Set Of Policy Wizard as described in the "To create an RSoP query with the Resultant Set Of Policy Wizard Logging mode" and the "To create an RSoP query with the Resultant Set Of Policy Wizard Planning mode" procedures, later in this section.

To create an RSoP query for an existing user and computer, you must be logged on to the local computer as a user; be a member of the local Administrators, Domain Administrators, or Enterprise Administrators group; or have permission to generate RSoP for the domain or OU in which the user and computer accounts are contained. You must be an enterprise administrator if the RSoP query includes site GPOs that cross domain boundaries in the same forest. This section describes how to create RSoP queries in Logging mode and Planning mode.

To create an RSoP query with the Resultant Set Of Policy Wizard Logging mode, complete the following steps:

1. Click Start, and then click Run.

2. In the Run dialog box, type **mmc** in the Open box, and then click OK.

3. In the MMC, from the File menu, click Add/Remove Snap-In.

4. In the Add/Remove Snap-In dialog box, click Add.

5. In the Add Standalone Snap-In dialog box, select Resultant Set Of Policy, click Add, and then click Close.

6. In the Add/Remove Snap-In dialog box, click OK.

7. In the MMC, right-click the Resultant Set Of Policy icon on the RSoP Wizard console, and then select Generate RSoP Data.

8. In the Welcome To The Resultant Set Of Policy Wizard page, click Next.

9. On the Mode Selection page, shown in Figure 11-1, select Logging Mode, and then click Next.

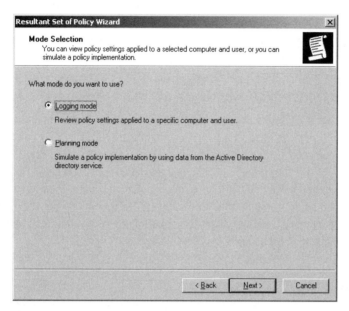

Figure 11-1   Resultant Set Of Policy Wizard, Mode Selection page

10. On the Computer Selection page in the Resultant Set Of Policy Wizard, shown in Figure 11-2, select This Computer, or to search for a different computer, click Another Computer, and then click Browse to select the appropriate computer. If you want to display user policy settings only, click the Do Not Display Policy Settings For The Selected Computer In the Results check box. Click Next.

Important   If you select Another Computer, and either the local or remote computer is running Windows Server 2003 SP1 with Windows Firewall enabled, you must configure exceptions in Windows Firewall, as described in the "Understanding RSoP" section in this chapter, to obtain the RSoP data.

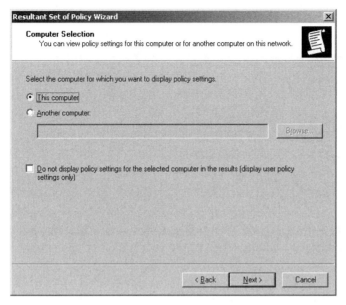

Figure 11-2   Resultant Set Of Policy Wizard, Computer Selection page

11. On the User Selection page, shown in Figure 11-3, select Current User to view policy settings for the current user, or to search for a different user, click Select A Specific User, and select a user in the list. If you want to display computer policy settings only, click the Do Not Display User Policy Settings In the Results check box. Click Next.

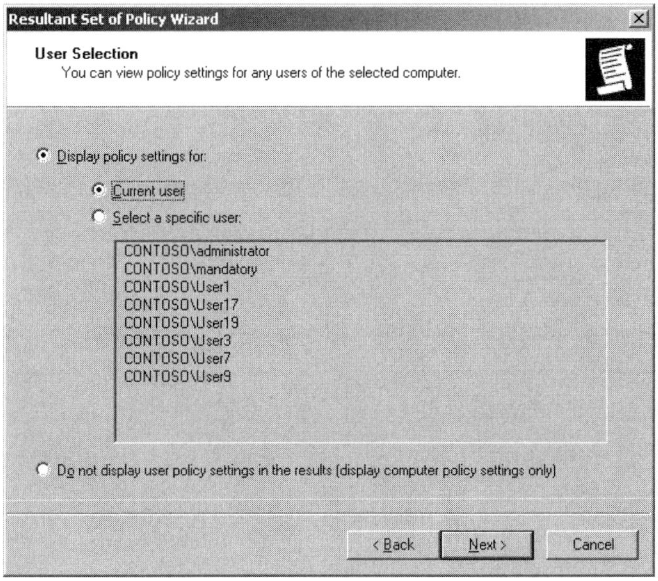

Figure 11-3   Resultant Set Of Policy Wizard, User Selection page

12. On the Summary Of Selections page, shown in Figure 11-4, review your selections. Click Next.

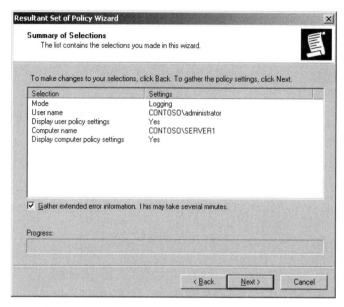

Figure 11-4   Resultant Set Of Policy Wizard, Summary Of Selections page

13. On the Completing The Resultant Set Of Policy Data Wizard page, click Finish.

14. The RSoP console opens. Click the folders in the console tree to view the data in the details pane.

To create an RSoP query with the Resultant Set Of Policy Wizard Planning mode, complete the following steps:

1. Click Start, and then click Run.

2. In the Run dialog box, type **mmc** in the Open box, and then click OK.

3. In the MMC, from the File menu, click Add/Remove Snap-In.

4. In the Add/Remove Snap-In dialog box, click Add.

5. In the Add Standalone Snap-In dialog box, select Resultant Set Of Policy, click Add, and then click Close.

6. In the Add/Remove Snap-In dialog box, click OK.

7. In the MMC, right-click the Resultant Set Of Policy icon on the RSoP Wizard console, and then select Generate RSoP Data.

8. In the Welcome To The Resultant Set Of Policy Wizard page, click Next.

9. On the Mode Selection page, shown previously in Figure 11-1, select Planning Mode, then click Next.

10. On the User And Computer Selection page, shown in Figure 11-5, type the name of the target user in the User Information box and the target computer in the Computer Information box. To search for a user or computer, click Browse. Click Next.

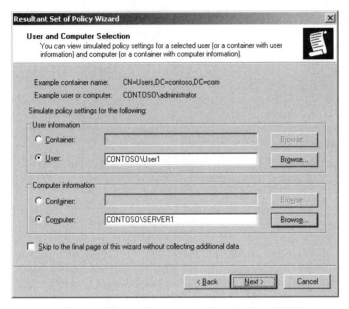

Figure 11-5   Resultant Set Of Policy Wizard, User And Computer Selection page

11. On the Advanced Simulation Options page, shown in Figure 11-6, do any or none of the following:

   ❏ If you want to simulate a slow network connection, select the Slow Network Connection check box.

   ❏ If you want to simulate the loopback processing mode, select the Loopback Processing check box. Then select Replace Mode or Merge Mode.

   Click Replace Mode to indicate that the user policies that are defined in the computer's GPOs replace the user policies that are normally applied to the user.

   Click Merge Mode to indicate that the user policies that are defined in the computer's GPOs and the user policies that are normally applied to the user are combined. Recall that if the policy settings conflict, the user policies in the computer's GPOs take precedence over the user's normal policies.

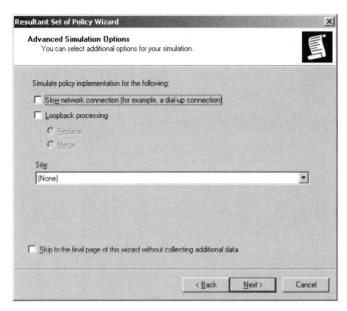

Figure 11-6   Resultant Set Of Policy Wizard, Advanced Simulation Options page

12. In the Site list, select the site that the RSoP query uses, if desired. You select a site if you want to test policy where startup or logging on occurs on another subnet than the one on which the query is currently being run. Click Next.

> **Tip**   If at any time while navigating the Resultant Set Of Policy Wizard you have finished entering information for your RSoP simulation, select the Skip To The Final Page Of This Wizard Without Collecting Additional Data check box and click Next.

13. On the Alternate Active Directory Paths page, shown in Figure 11-7, you can specify different locations for the selected user and/or computer, if desired. If you want to specify a different location for the user, enter the distinguished name of the location in the User Location box. If you want to specify a different location for a computer, enter the distinguished name of the location in the Computer Location box. Click Next.

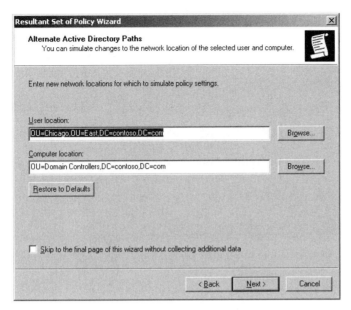

Figure 11-7   Resultant Set Of Policy Wizard, Alternate Active Directory Paths page

14. On the User Security Groups page, shown in Figure 11-8, in the Security Groups box, select the groups in which you want the user selected to be a member on the User And Computer Selection page. To add a security group, click Add, type the name of the target security group, and click OK. To remove a security group, select the security group, and click Remove. Click Next.

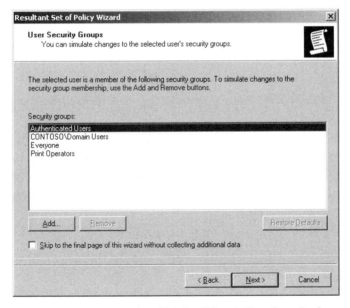

Figure 11-8   Resultant Set Of Policy Wizard, User Security Groups page

15. On the Computer Security Groups page, in the Security Groups box, select the groups in which you want the computer selected to be a member on the User And Computer Selection page. To add a security group, click Add, type the name of the target security group, and click OK. To remove a security group, select the security group, and click Remove. Click Next.

16. On the WMI Filters For Users page, shown in Figure 11-9, select the WMI filters you want to use in the simulation. If a filter is not on the list, and you want to add a WMI filter, click Only These Filters, click List Filters, and the system automatically searches for all true WMI filters. To remove WMI filters from the simulation, select the filter and click Remove. You should remove any filters that would be considered a false condition for the targeted user. Click Next.

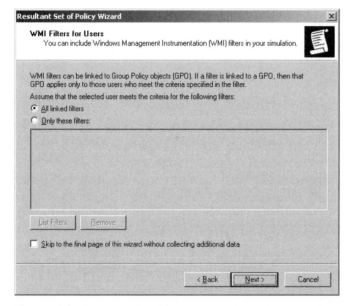

Figure 11-9   Resultant Set Of Policy Wizard, WMI Filters For Users page

17. On the WMI Filters For Computers page, select the WMI filters you want to use in the simulation. If a filter is not on the list, and you want to add a WMI filter, click Only These Filters, click List Filters, and the system automatically searches for all true WMI filters. To remove WMI filters from the simulation, select the filter and click Remove. You should remove any filters that would be considered a false condition for the targeted computer. Click Next.

18. On the Summary Of Selections page, shown in Figure 11-10, verify the domain controller (click Browse, if necessary), click Finish, and then wait for processing to complete.

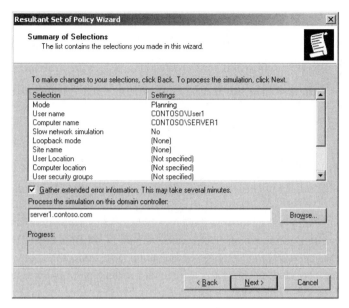

Figure 11-10   Resultant Set Of Policy Wizard, Summary Of Selections page

Saving RSoP Queries and Query Data

After you create an RSoP query with the Resultant Set Of Policy Wizard, you can save the RSoP query and you can save the RSoP query data. By saving the RSoP query, you can reuse it for processing another RSoP query later. The query is saved in the RSoP query console. By saving the RSoP query data, you can revisit the RSoP as it appeared for a particular query when the query was created. The query data is archived to an RSoP console, which you cannot use to process another RSoP query.

To save an RSoP query, complete the following steps:

1. After you have created an RSoP query, on the console for the RSoP query, in the File menu, select Save.

2. In the Save As dialog box, in the File Name box, type the name you want to use for the query console name, and then click Save. The saved RSoP query console has an .msc file name extension and appears on the Administrative Tools menu.

> **Note**   If you created an RSoP query from the Active Directory Users And Computers or Active Directory Sites And Services consoles, you must remember to save the query to %*Systemroot*% \Documents and Settings\Administrator\Start Menu\Programs\Administrative Tools for the query to be available on the Administrative Tools menu.

To save the data from an RSoP query, complete the following steps:

1. After you have created an RSoP query, on the console for the RSoP query, right-click the user account–RSoP or the computer account–RSoP node, point to View, and then select Archive Data In Console File.

2. On the File menu, click Save.

3. In the Save As dialog box, in the File Name box, type the name you want to use for the RSoP console containing the archived data, and then click Save. The saved RSoP console containing the archived data has an .msc file name extension and appears on the Administrative Tools menu.

Note If you created an RSoP query from the Active Directory Users And Computers or Active Directory Sites And Services consoles, you must remember to save the archived query data to %Systemroot%\Documents and Settings\Administrator\Start Menu\Programs \Administrative Tools for the archived query data to be available on the Administrative Tools menu.

Viewing RSoP Queries

After you create an RSoP query with the Resultant Set Of Policy Wizard and save it, the query information appears in the RSoP query console, which looks like a Group Policy Object Editor console. The RSoP query console contains four types of information that you can view:

■ Individual policy settings

■ A list of GPOs associated with the query

■ The scope of management associated with the query

■ GPO revision information

Viewing Individual Policy Settings You can view the RSoP query results for the various types of policy settings in the details pane of the RSoP query console. The details pane appears the same way that it does for the Group Policy Object Editor console, except only the settings that have been changed from the defaults appear and there might be extra columns, as described for each policy setting type in the following sections.

Software Settings Results In the Software Settings details pane, the RSoP query results are listed in the columns described in Table 11-1.

Table 11-1   Software Settings RSoP Query Results Column Descriptions

Column	Description
Name	Name of the deployed package
Version	Software version of the deployed package
Deployment State	Whether the package is assigned or published
Source	Source location of the deployed package
Origin	Name of the GPO that deployed the package

Windows Settings Results   Windows Settings contains the results for scripts settings, Internet Explorer Maintenance settings, and security settings. In the details pane for scripts, the RSoP query results are listed in the columns described in Table 11-2.

Table 11-2   Scripts RSoP Query Results Column Descriptions

Column	Description
Name	Name of the script
Parameters	Any parameters that are assigned to the script
Last Executed	Date that the script was last run
GPO Name	Name of the GPO that assigned the script

The Internet Explorer Maintenance and security settings results appear in the same manner as they do on a Group Policy Object Editor console except that there is a Precedence tab, or sometimes more than one Precedence tab, indicating which GPOs affect the settings, in order from newest to oldest.

Administrative Templates Results   In the details pane for administrative templates, the RSoP query results are listed in the details pane and the GPO Name column, which provides the name of the last GPO affecting the policy setting. To view more information about a setting, double-click the setting in the details pane. A dialog box for the setting appears with three tabs, described in Table 11-3.

Table 11-3   Administrative Templates RSoP Query Results Tab Descriptions

Tab	Description
Setting	Similar in appearance to Group Policy, but unavailable
Explain	Describes what this policy setting does
Precedence	Indicates GPO precedence, from newest to oldest

To view individual policy settings associated with an RSoP query, complete the following steps:

1. In the desired RSoP query console, in the console tree, double-click user account–RSoP or computer account–RSoP.

2. In the console tree, double-click the subfolders. The individual policy settings are visible in the details pane.

To view a list of GPOs associated with an RSoP query, complete the following steps:

1. In the desired RSoP query console, expand the user account–RSoP or the computer account–RSoP node. Right-click User Configuration or Computer Configuration, and then click Properties.

2. In the User Configuration Properties or the Computer Configuration Properties dialog box, shown in Figure 11-11, in the General tab, select the Display All GPOs And Filtering Status check box. The list of GPOs associated with the RSoP query appears in the Group Policy Object column. Filtering status appears in the Filtering column as either Applied, Not Applied (Empty), or Not Applied (Unknown).

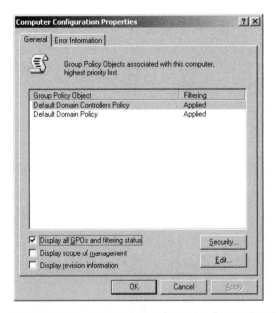

Figure 11-11 Computer Configuration Properties dialog box, displaying filtering status

To view the scope of management associated with an RSoP query, complete the following steps:

1. In the desired RSoP query console, expand the user account–RSoP or the computer account–RSoP node. Right-click User Configuration or Computer Configuration, and then click Properties.

2. In the User Configuration Properties or the Computer Configuration Properties dialog box, in the General tab, shown in Figure 11-12, select the Display Scope Of Management check box. The distinguished name of each GPO in Active Directory appears in the Scope Of Management column.

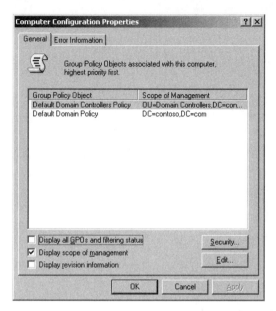

Figure 11-12   Computer Configuration Properties dialog box, displaying scope of management

To view GPO revision information associated with an RSoP query, complete the following steps:

1. In the desired RSoP query console, expand the *user account*–RSoP or the *computer account*–RSoP node. Right-click User Configuration or Computer Configuration, and then click Properties.

2. In the User Configuration Properties or the Computer Configuration Properties dialog box, in the General tab, shown in Figure 11-13, select the Display Revision Information check box. The location of the revision information for the GPOs appears in the Revision column.

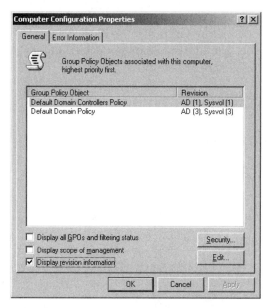

Figure 11-13   Computer Configuration Properties dialog box, displaying revision information

Reusing RSoP Queries Generated with the Resultant Set Of Policy Wizard

As discussed earlier in this lesson, you can reuse saved RSoP queries. To reuse an RSoP query, simply open the appropriate RSoP query console from the Administrative Tools menu. The query regenerates and displays the new query results on the console. If you open an RSoP console that contains archived data, you receive a message identifying the console as containing archived data.

> **Note**   If the query is generated in Logging mode, and you change the settings in a GPO and then rerun the RSoP query, you do not see the new GPO settings reflected for a user unless the user logs on after the new GPO settings are implemented.

Generating RSoP Queries with the Gpresult Command-Line Tool

The Gpresult command-line tool enables you to create and display an RSoP query on the command line. In addition, Gpresult provides general information about the operating system, user, and computer. Gpresult provides the following information about Group Policy:

- The last time Group Policy was applied and the domain controller that applied policy—for the user and for the computer

- The complete list of applied GPOs and their details, including a summary of the extensions that each GPO contains

- Registry settings that are applied and their details

- Folders that are redirected and their details

- Software management information, including details about assigned and published applications

- Disk quota information

- Internet Protocol (IP) security settings

- Scripts

Gpresult has the following syntax:

```
gpresult [/s computer [/u domain\user /p password]] [/user username] [/scope
{user|computer}] [/v] [/z]
```

Each of the command parameters is explained in Table 11-4.

Table 11-4   Gpresult Command Parameters

Parameter	Function
/s *computer*	Specifies the name or IP address of a remote computer. The default is the local computer.
/u *domain\user*	Runs the command with the account permissions of the user that is specified by *user* or *domain\user*. The default is the permissions of the current logged on user on the computer that issues the command.
/p *password*	Specifies the password of the user account that is specified in the /u parameter.
/user *username*	Specifies the user name of the user whose RSoP data is to be displayed.
/scope {user|computer}	Displays either user or computer results. Valid values for the /scope parameter are user or computer. If you omit the /scope parameter, Gpresult displays both user and computer settings.
/v	Specifies that the output displays verbose policy information.
/z	Specifies that the output displays all available information about Group Policy. Because this parameter produces more information than the /v parameter, redirect output to a text file when you use this parameter (for example, **gpresult /z > policy.txt**).

The following are examples of using the Gpresult command:

- To display RSoP query computer information for User11 on the computer issuing the command, type:

  gpresult /user User11 /scope computer

■ To display RSoP query user information for User11 on Server2 using the credentials of admin7, type:

gpresult /s server2 /u contoso\admin7 /p p@ss314 /user User11 /scope user

■ To direct all available Group Policy information for User11 on Server2 to the text file Policy.txt using the credentials of admin7, type:

gpresult /s server2 /u contoso.com\admin7 /p p@ss314 /user User11 / z > policy.txt

> **Important**   If you select a remote computer, and either the local or remote computer is running Windows Server 2003 SP1 with Windows Firewall enabled, you will get an RPC error unless you follow the steps to configure exceptions in Windows Firewall as described in the "Understanding RSoP" section in this chapter.

To create and display an RSoP query on the command line with Gpresult, complete the following steps:

1. Click Start, and then click Command Prompt.

2. At the command prompt, type **gpresult** and the appropriate parameters. In Figure 11-14, Gpresult has been used to display RSoP query computer information for User1 on Server1.

```
Command Prompt                                            _ □ X
C:\>gpresult /user User1 /scope computer

Microsoft (R) Windows (R) Operating System Group Policy Result tool v2.0
Copyright (C) Microsoft Corp. 1981-2001

Created On 4/28/2003 at 8:47:05 PM

RSOP data for CONTOSO\User1 on SERVER1 : Logging Mode

OS Type:                        Microsoft(R) Windows(R) Server 2003, Enterprise Edi
tion
OS Configuration:               Primary Domain Controller
OS Version:                     5.2.3790
Terminal Server Mode:           Remote Administration
Site Name:                      Default-First-Site-Name
Roaming Profile:
Local Profile:                  C:\Documents and Settings\User1
Connected over a slow link?: No

COMPUTER SETTINGS

    CN=SERVER1,OU=Domain Controllers,DC=contoso,DC=com
    Last time Group Policy was applied: 4/28/2003 at 8:44:03 PM
    Group Policy was applied from:      SERVER1.contoso.com
    Group Policy slow link threshold:   500 kbps
    Domain Name:                        CONTOSO
    Domain Type:                        Windows 2000

    Applied Group Policy Objects

        Default Domain Controllers Policy
```

Figure 11-14   Gpresult RSoP query information for User1 on Server1

> **Real World   Listing GPOs**
>
> Gpotool is a useful utility for obtaining information on group policies that exist on the domain. Install Gpotool on Server1 by running the Gpotool.exe from the supplemental CD-ROM from the \70-294\Labs\Chapter11 folder. Once you install the tool, open a command prompt, change to the C:\Program Files\Resource Kit folder, and follow these steps:
>
> 1. Type **gpotool /verbose > c:\gpotooloutput.txt** and press ENTER.
>
> 2. Type **notepad c:\gpotooloutput.txt** and press ENTER. Notepad opens and displays a list of group policies, including friendly names, GUIDs, and information on when these GPOs were created.

Generating RSoP Queries with the Advanced System Information–Policy Tool

The Advanced System Information–Policy tool enables you to create an RSoP query and view the results in an HTML report that appears in the Help And Support Center window. This report can be printed, and it can be saved to an .htm file. Although this report does not contain as much information as the results of RSoP queries generated with the Resultant Set Of Policy Wizard or the Gpresult command-line tool, it can be run easily by novice users who have RSoP authority. The results of the Advanced System Information–Policy tool RSoP query are obtained from RSoP Logging mode for the currently logged on user on the computer on which the query is performed. The report generated displays policy-related information for the following categories:

- Computer name, associated domain, and current site
- User name and associated domain
- Applied GPOs for the computer and user
- Security group memberships for the computer and user
- Microsoft Internet Explorer settings
- Scripts: logon, logoff, startup, shutdown
- Security settings
- Programs installed
- Folder redirection
- Registry settings

To create and display an RSoP query with the Advanced System Information–Policy tool, complete the following steps:

1. Click Start, and then click Help And Support.

2. Under Support Tasks, click Tools.

3. In the Tools pane, under Help And Support Center Tools, click Advanced System Information.

4. Under Advanced System Information, click View Group Policy Settings Applied. In Figure 11-15, the Advanced System Information–Policy tool has been used to display RSoP query computer information for Administrator on Server1. You can scroll to the results that you want to view and click the arrow in the upper-right corner of a category to hide details.

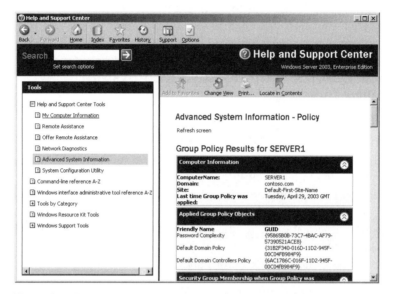

Figure 11-15   Advanced System Information–Policy RSoP query information for Administrator on Server1

Delegating Control of RSoP

Permission for generating an RSoP query is set for the domain or OU by selecting one of the Generate Resultant Set Of Policy Planning options in the Delegation Of Authority Wizard. You must be a member of the Enterprise Administrators group to delegate RSoP control at the domain and site level.

> **Important**   Delegated control is inherited by all child containers below the container to which control is delegated.

To delegate control of RSoP, complete the following steps:

1. Click Start, point to Administrative Tools, then click Active Directory Users And Computers.

2. In the console tree, right-click the domain or OU for which you want to delegate control of RSoP, and then click Delegate Control.

3. On the Welcome To The Delegation Of Control Wizard page, click Next.

4. On the Users Or Groups page, click Add.

5. In the Select Users, Computers, Or Groups dialog box, type the user or group for which you want to delegate administration in the Enter The Object Names To Select box, and then click OK. Click Next on the Users Or Groups page.

6. On the Tasks To Delegate page, click Delegate The Following Common Tasks and select the Generate Resultant Set Of Policy (Logging) check box or the Generate Resultant Set Of Policy (Planning) check box, or both, and then click Next.

7. On the Completing The Delegation Of Control Wizard page, review your selections. Click Finish.

Practice: Generating RSoP Queries

In this practice, you generate three RSoP queries.

Exercise 1: Creating an RSoP Query with the Resultant Set Of Policy Wizard Logging Mode

In this exercise, you create an RSoP query with the Resultant Set Of Policy Wizard Logging mode and view the results in the RSoP query console.

▶ **To create an RSoP query with Logging mode**

1. Log on to Server1 as Administrator.

2. On Server1, use the procedure provided earlier in this lesson to create an RSoP query with the Resultant Set Of Policy Wizard Logging mode. Create the query for the settings applied to User7 on Server1 (this computer).

3. View the results of the RSoP query on the RSoP query console in the User Configuration node, in the Administrative Templates node. The settings from the West OU Desktop GPO are shown.

4. Save the RSoP query console as User7 RSoP.

5. Open the West OU Desktop GPO. In the User Configuration node, in the Administrative Templates node, in the Desktop node, configure the Hide My Network Places Icon On Desktop setting to Enabled.

6. Open the User7 RSoP console. Is the new setting in the West OU Desktop GPO reflected in the RSoP? Why?

   No, the new setting in the West OU Desktop GPO is not reflected in the User7 RSoP because User7 has not yet logged on since the new GPO settings were implemented.

7. Log off as Administrator, and then log on as User7. Is the My Network Places icon visible on the desktop? Why?

No, the My Network Places icon is not visible on the desktop because the West OU Desktop GPO setting hides the icon.

8. Log off as User7, and then log on as Administrator. Open the User7 RSoP console. Is the new setting in the West OU Desktop GPO reflected in the RSoP? Why?

Yes, the new setting in the West OU Desktop GPO is reflected in the User7 RSoP because User7 has logged on since the new GPO settings were implemented.

Exercise 2: Creating an RSoP Query with the Gpresult Command-Line Tool

In this exercise, you create and view the results of an RSoP query on the command line with the Gpresult command-line tool.

▶   **To create an RSoP query with Gpresult**

1. On Server1, use the procedure provided earlier in this lesson to create and view the results of an RSoP query on the command line with the Gpresult command-line tool. Create the query for the settings applied to User19 on Server1 (this computer). What did you type on the command line to achieve this?

Gpresult/user user19

2. View the results of the RSoP query in the command line. What user setting GPOs were not applied to User19 and why?

KC OU Desktop and West OU Desktop GPOs were not applied because User19 has Deny permission (Apply Group Policy). Local Group Policy was not applied because it is empty.

Exercise 3: Creating an RSoP Query with the Advanced System Information–Policy Tool

In this exercise, you create an RSoP query with the Advanced System Information–Policy tool and view the results in the Help And Support Center window.

▶   **To create an RSoP query with the Advanced System Information-Policy tool**

1. On Server1, use the procedure provided earlier in this lesson to create an RSoP query with the Advanced System Information–Policy tool. Create the RSoP query for User7 on Server1. How do you create the RSoP query for User7?

Log on to Server1 as User7.

2. View the results in the Help And Support Center window. What registry key is used to hide the My Network Places icon on the desktop?

Software\Microsoft\Windows\CurrentVersion\Policies\Explorer\NoNetHood

Lesson Review

The following questions are intended to reinforce key information presented in this lesson. If you are unable to answer a question, review the lesson and then try the question again. Answers to the questions can be found in the "Questions and Answers" section at the end of this chapter.

1. What is the purpose of generating RSoP queries?

   _____

   _____

2. What are the three tools available for generating RSoP queries?

   _____

   _____

3. What is the difference between Logging mode and Planning mode?

   _____

   _____

4. What is the difference between saving an RSoP query and saving RSoP query data?

   _____

   _____

5. Which RSoP query generating tool provides RSoP query results on a console similar to a Group Policy Object Editor console?

   a. Resultant Set Of Policy Wizard

   b. Group Policy Wizard

   c. Gpupdate command-line tool

   d. Gpresult command-line tool

   e. Advanced System Information–Policy tool

   f. Advanced System Information–Services tool

Lesson Summary

- RSoP is the sum of the policies applied to the user or computer, including the application of filters (security groups, WMI) and exceptions (No Override, Block Policy Inheritance).

- Windows Server 2003 provides three tools for generating RSoP queries: the Resultant Set Of Policy Wizard, the Gpresult command-line tool, and the Advanced System Information–Policy tool.

- The Resultant Set Of Policy Wizard uses existing GPO settings to report the effects of GPOs on users and computers and can simulate the effects of planned GPOs. The wizard's Logging mode reports the existing GPO settings for a user or computer. Its Planning mode simulates the GPO settings that a user and computer might receive, and it enables you to change the simulation.

- The Gpresult command-line tool enables you to create and display an RSoP query on the command line.

- The Advanced System Information–Policy tool enables you to create an RSoP query and view the results in an HTML report that appears in the Help And Support Center window.

Lesson 2: Managing Special Folders with Group Policy

Windows Server 2003 allows you to redirect the folders containing a user's profile to a location on the network using the Folder Redirection node in the Group Policy Object Editor console. The Offline Files feature provides users with access to redirected folders even when they are not connected to the network and can be set up manually or by using the Offline Folder node in Group Policy. This lesson introduces special folder redirection and walks you through the steps for setting up folder redirection using Group Policy. It also introduces the Offline Files feature and walks you through the steps for setting up Offline Files manually.

After this lesson, you will be able to

- Explain the purpose of folder redirection
- Identify the folders that can be redirected
- Explain when to redirect My Documents to a home folder
- Redirect special folders
- Explain the purpose of the Offline Files feature
- Set up Offline Files

Estimated lesson time: 35 minutes

Folder Redirection

You redirect users' folders to provide a centralized location for key Microsoft Windows XP Professional folders on a server or servers. This centralized location, called a *share-point*, provides users with an access point for storing and finding information, and administrators with an access point for managing information. The *Folder Redirection* node in the Group Policy Object Editor console enables you to redirect certain special folders to network locations, including file shares in other forests in which two-way forests trusts have been established. Special folders are folders such as My Documents and My Pictures, which are located in *C*:\Documents and Settings (where *C* is the name of your system drive).

Windows Server 2003 allows the following special folders to be redirected:

- Application Data
- Desktop
- My Documents
- My Pictures
- Start Menu

The Folder Redirection node is located under User Configuration\Windows Settings in the Group Policy Object Editor console.

> **Caution** If Access-Based Enumeration has been enabled on the server, there might be issues when browsing for shares. Users might not see all the shares available on a server, even if these shares are not hidden. Access-Based Enumeration is a feature of Windows Server 2003 SP1-based file servers that only lists the files and folders to which users have access. This feature is not enabled by default. To use this feature, SP1 must be installed, and the Access-Based Enumeration Microsoft Installer package Abeui.msi installed. For more information, see "Windows Server 2003 Access-Based Enumeration" at *http://go.microsoft.com/fwlink/?LinkId=46228*.

Advantages of Redirecting Folders

The following benefits pertain to redirecting any folder, but redirecting My Documents can be particularly advantageous because this folder tends to become large over time.

- Even if a user logs on to various computers on the network, his or her documents are always available.

- When roaming user profiles are used, only the network path to the My Documents folder is part of the roaming user profile, not the My Documents folder itself. Therefore, its contents do not have to be copied back and forth between the client computer and the server each time the user logs on or off, and the process of logging on or off can be much faster than it was in Microsoft Windows NT 4.

- Offline File technology provides users with access to My Documents even when they are not connected to the network, and is particularly useful for people who use portable computers.

- Data stored on a shared network server can be backed up as part of routine system administration. This is safer because it requires no action on the part of the user.

- The system administrator can use Group Policy to set disk quotas, limiting the amount of space taken up by users' special folders.

- Data specific to a user can be redirected to a different hard disk on the user's local computer from the hard disk holding the operating system files. This makes the user's data safer if the operating system needs to be reinstalled.

Redirecting My Documents to Home Folders

In Windows Server 2003, a new feature enables you to redirect My Documents to a user's home folder. This option is intended only for organizations that have already deployed home folders and that want to maintain compatibility with their existing home folder environment. The ability to redirect My Documents to a user's home folder requires a Windows XP Professional client and does not function for Microsoft Windows XP Home Edition, Microsoft Windows 2000, or Windows NT clients.

When you redirect My Documents to a user's home folder, the system assumes that the administrator has set the following items correctly:

- **Security**   Security is not checked and permissions are not changed when you redirect My Documents to a user's home folder.

- **Ownership**   No ownership checks are made when you redirect My Documents to a user's home folder. Normally, folder redirection fails if a user is not the owner of the folder to which he or she is being redirected.

- **Home directory property on the user object**   When you redirect My Documents to a user's home folder, the client computer finds the path for the user's home directory from the user object in Active Directory at logon time. If this path is not set correctly for the affected users, folder redirection fails.

This relaxed security environment is why redirecting My Documents to a user's home folder is recommended only for organizations that have already deployed home folders and want to provide backward compatibility.

Note   Do not redirect My Documents to a home directory location that is subject to encryption by the Encrypting File System (EFS), because only you or a domain administrator will be able to decrypt it. The user whose My Documents folder is redirected there will not be able to decrypt it.

Default Special Folder Locations

The default locations for special folders that have not been redirected depend on the operating system that was in place previously (see Table 11-5).

Table 11-5   Default Locations for Special Folders

Operating System	Location of Special Folders
Windows Server 2003 or Windows 2000 new installation (no previous operating system) Windows Server 2003 or Windows 2000 upgrade of Microsoft Windows Me, Microsoft Windows 95, or Microsoft Windows 98 with user profiles disabled	*C*:\Documents and Settings (where *C* is the name of your system drive)
Windows Server 2003 or Windows 2000 upgrade of Windows NT 4 or Windows NT 3.51	*%Systemroot%*\Profiles; for example, C:\WinNT\Profiles
Windows Server 2003 or Windows 2000 upgrade of Windows Me, Windows 95, or Windows 98 with user profiles enabled	*%Systemroot%*\Profiles; for example, C:\Windows\System32\Profiles

Setting Up Folder Redirection

There are two ways to set up folder redirection:

- Redirect special folders to one location for everyone in the site, domain, or OU.

- Redirect special folders to a location according to security group membership.

To redirect special folders to one location for everyone in the site, domain, or OU, complete the following steps:

1. Open a GPO linked to the site, domain, or OU containing the users whose special folders you want to redirect to a network location.

2. In User Configuration, open Windows Settings, then double-click the Folder Redirection node to view the folder you want to redirect.

3. Right-click the folder you want (Application Data, Desktop, My Documents, or Start Menu), and then click Properties.

4. In the Target tab in the Properties dialog box for the redirected folder (see Figure 11-16), in the Setting list, select Basic– Redirect Everyone's Folder To The Same Location, and then click Browse.

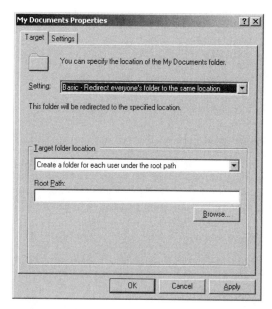

Figure 11-16   Target tab in the Properties dialog box for the redirected folder

Off the Record   Windows Server 2003 has more options for redirecting folders than Windows 2000 Server. In Windows 2000 Server, there are no selectable options for folder redirection in the target folder location section. Instead, there is only a text box where you can enter the location of the target folder. While Windows Server 2003 still offers the same features, in Windows 2000 you would have to use environment variables such as %Username% or %Userprofile% instead of being able to select from a drop-down list. Keep this in mind if you come across troubleshooting documents written for Windows 2000 folder redirection. You'll see one such example of this in the Troubleshooting Lab of this chapter.

5. In the Target Folder Location list, select the redirect location you want for this GPO from one of the following:

❑ Create A Folder For Each User Under The Root Path (not available for the Start Menu folder) creates a folder with the user's name in the root path. A new feature in Windows Server 2003, folder redirection automatically appends the user name and the folder name when the policy is applied.

❑ Redirect To The Following Location enables you to redirect the folder to a location represented by the Uniform Naming Convention (UNC) path in the form *servername**sharename* or a valid path on the user's local computer.

❑ Redirect To The Local Userprofile Location enables you to redirect the folder to the default folder location in the absence of redirection by an administrator.

❑ Redirect To The User's Home Folder (available for the My Documents folder only) enables you to redirect the user's My Documents folder to the user's home directory.

Note   Use the Redirect To The User's Home Folder option only if you have already deployed home directories in your organization. This option is intended only for organizations that want to maintain compatibility with their existing home directory environment.

6. If you have selected the Create A Folder For Each User Under The Root Path or Redirect To The Following Location options, enter the path to which the folder should be redirected, either the UNC path in the form *servername**sharename* or a valid path on the user's local computer.

7. Click the Settings tab (shown in Figure 11-17), and then set each of the following options (the default settings are recommended):

❑ Grant The User Exclusive Rights To Special Folder Type, to allow the user and the local system full rights to the folder; no one else, not even administrators, will have any rights. If this setting is disabled, no changes are made to the permissions on the folder. The permissions that apply by default remain in effect. This option is enabled by default.

❑ Move The Contents Of User's Current Special Folder To The New Location, to redirect the contents of the folder to the new location. This option is enabled by default.

> **Note** If you redirect My Documents to the home folder, domain administrators have Full Control permission over the user's My Documents folder, even if you enable the Grant The User Exclusive Rights To My Documents option.

> **Off the Record** Errors concerning Folder Redirection appear in the Application Log in the Event Viewer on the affected computers. For example, if you attempt to redirect a user's desktop and select the option Move The Contents Of The Desktop To The New Location, but you fail to give the user permission to write to that folder, the user's desktop will not be redirected. If that happens, you can find errors in the Event Viewer where the user logged on indicating that the user didn't have permission to access the folder. To solve the issue, either give the user Write permission to the desktop or clear the Move The Contents Of Desktop To The New Location check box.

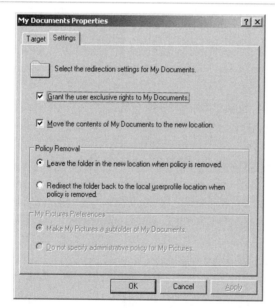

Figure 11-17 The Settings tab in the Properties dialog box for the redirected folder

8. Choose one of the following options in the Policy Removal area (the default setting is recommended):

❑ Leave The Folder In The New Location When Policy Is Removed, to leave the folder in its new location even when the GPO no longer applies. This option is enabled by default.

❏ Redirect The Folder Back To The Local Userprofile Location When Policy Is Removed, to move the folder back to its local user profile location when the GPO no longer applies.

> **Important**   See the "Policy Removal Considerations" section of this lesson for details on selecting a policy removal option.

9. Choose one of the following options (available for the My Documents folder only) in the My Pictures Preferences area:

❏ Make My Pictures A Subfolder Of My Documents, to redirect My Pictures automatically to remain a subfolder of My Documents. This option is enabled by default and is recommended.

❏ Do Not Specify Administrative Policy For My Pictures, to remove My Pictures as a subfolder of My Documents and have the user profile determine the location of My Pictures. With this option, the location of My Pictures is not dictated by Group Policy and a shortcut takes the place of the My Pictures folder in My Documents.

10. Click OK.

To redirect special folders to a location according to security group membership, complete the following steps:

1. Open a GPO linked to the site, domain, or OU containing the users whose special folders you want to redirect to a network location.

2. In User Configuration, open Windows Settings, then double-click the Folder Redirection node to view the folder you want to redirect.

3. Right-click the folder you want (Application Data, Desktop, My Documents, or Start Menu), and then click Properties.

4. In the Target tab in the Properties dialog box for the folder (shown previously in Figure 11-16), in the Setting list, select Advanced–Specify Locations For Various User Groups, and then click Add.

5. In the Specify Group And Location dialog box (see Figure 11-18), in the Security Group Membership box, click Browse.

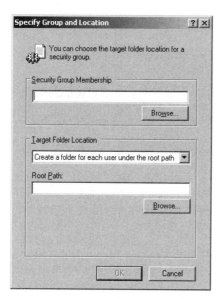

Figure 11-18   Specify Group And Location dialog box

6. In the Select Group dialog box, type the name of the security group for which you want to redirect the folder, and then click OK.

7. In the Specify Group And Location dialog box, in the Target Folder Location list, select the redirect location you want for this GPO from one of the following:

   ❑ Create A Folder For Each User Under The Root Path (not available for the Start Menu folder) creates a folder with the user's name in the root path. A new feature of Windows Server 2003, folder redirection automatically appends the user name and the folder name when the policy is applied.

   ❑ Redirect To The Following Location enables you to redirect the folder to a location represented by the UNC path in the form *servername**sharename* or a valid path on the user's local computer.

   ❑ Redirect To The Local Userprofile Location enables you to redirect the folder to the default folder location in the absence of redirection by an administrator.

   ❑ Redirect To The User's Home Folder (available for the My Documents folder only) enables you to redirect the user's My Documents folder to the user's home directory.

Note   Use the Redirect To The User's Home Folder option only if you have already deployed home directories in your organization. This option is intended only for organizations that want to maintain compatibility with their existing home directory environment.

8. If you have selected the Create A Folder For Each User Under The Root Path or Redirect To The Following Location options, enter the path to which the folder should be redirected, either the UNC path in the form *\\servername\sharename* or a valid path on the user's local computer.

9. In the Specify Group And Location dialog box, click OK.

10. If you want to redirect folders for members of other security groups, repeat steps 4 through 9 until all the groups have been entered.

11. Click the Settings tab (shown previously in Figure 11-17), and then set each of the following options (the default settings are recommended):

   ❑ Grant The User Exclusive Rights To Special Folder Type, to allow the user and the local system full rights to the folder; no one else, not even administrators, will have any rights. If this setting is disabled, no changes are made to the permissions on the folder. The permissions that apply by default remain in effect. This option is enabled by default.

   ❑ Move The Contents Of User's Current Special Folder To The New Location, to redirect the contents of the folder to the new location. This option is enabled by default.

> **Note**   If you redirect My Documents to the home folder, domain administrators have Full Control permission over the user's My Documents folder, even if you enable the Grant The User Exclusive Rights To My Documents option.

12. Choose one of the following options in the Policy Removal area (the default setting is recommended):

   ❑ Leave The Folder In The New Location When Policy Is Removed, to leave the folder in its new location even when the GPO no longer applies. This option is enabled by default.

   ❑ Redirect The Folder Back To The Local Userprofile Location When Policy Is Removed, to move the folder back to its local user profile location when the GPO no longer applies.

> **Important**   See the section "Policy Removal Considerations" for details on selecting a policy removal option.

13. Choose one of the following options (available for the My Documents folder only) in the My Pictures Preferences area:

❑ Make My Pictures A Subfolder Of My Documents, to redirect My Pictures automatically to remain a subfolder of My Documents. This option is enabled by default and is recommended.

❑ Do Not Specify Administrative Policy For My Pictures, to remove My Pictures as a subfolder of My Documents and have the user profile determine the location of My Pictures. With this option, the location of My Pictures is not dictated by Group Policy, and a shortcut takes the place of the My Pictures folder in My Documents.

14. Click OK.

Off the Record   If you redirect a user's Application Data and the user encrypts files or folders using the Encrypting File System (EFS), the user may not be able to decrypt their EFS encrypted folders when they are not connected to the network. This occurs because their encryption keys are stored in the Application Data folder structure. For Windows 2000 Professional systems, network connectivity isn't an immediate issue because the encryption keys are stored in memory. However, if the user restarts, this can become an issue if network connectivity is still not available. For Windows XP Professional systems, loss of network connectivity could become an immediate issue for users trying to decrypt EFS encrypted files because the user's encryption keys are not stored in memory.

Exam Tip   Be sure you know the two ways to set up folder redirection.

Policy Removal Considerations

Table 11-6 summarizes what happens to redirected folders and their contents when a GPO no longer applies.

Table 11-6   Effects of Policy Removal Options

When the Move The Contents Of Special Folder Type To The New Location setting is...	And the Policy Removal option is...	Results when the policy is removed are...
Enabled	Redirect The Folder Back To The Local Userprofile Location When Policy Is Removed	The special folder returns to its user profile location. The contents are copied, not moved, back to the user profile location. The contents are not deleted from the redirected location. The user continues to have access to the contents, but only on the local computer.

Table 11-6   Effects of Policy Removal Options

When the Move The Contents Of Special Folder Type To The New Location setting is...	And the Policy Removal option is...	Results when the policy is removed are...
Disabled	Redirect The Folder Back To The Userprofile Location When Policy Is Removed	The special folder returns to its user profile location. The contents are not copied or moved to the user profile location.*
Either Enabled or Disabled	Leave The Folder In The New Location When Policy Is Removed	The special folder remains at its redirected location. The contents remain at the redirected location. The user continues to have access to the contents at the redirected location.

* Caution—If the contents of a folder are not copied to the user profile location, the user can no longer see them.

Folder Redirection and Offline Files

As discussed earlier in this lesson, folder redirection provides users with central network access point for storing and finding information, and administrators with a central network access point for managing information. However, in the event of a network failure or for users who use portable computers, how will the users be able to access the information in redirected folders? The Offline Files feature provides users with access to redirected folders even when they are not connected to the network. Offline Files caches files accessed through folder redirection onto the hard drive of the local computer. When a user accesses a file in a redirected folder, the file is accessed and modified locally. When a user has finished working with the file and has logged off, only then does the file traverse the network for storage on the server.

Working Offline

Offline Files provides notification if the status of your network connection changes by displaying an informational balloon over the notification area (lower right corner of the desktop). If the informational balloon notifies you that you are offline, you might be able to continue to work with your files as you normally do, or you can click the Offline Files icon in the notification area for more information about the status of your connection.

If you are working offline (either because you are disconnected from the network or because you undocked your portable computer), you can still browse network drives and shared folders in My Computer or My Network Places. A red X appears over any disconnected network drives. You can see only those files that you made available offline and any files that you created after the network connection was lost. Your permissions on the network files and folders remain the same whether you are connected to the network or working offline. When you are disconnected from the network, you can print to local printers, but you cannot print to shared printers on the network.

Once you reconnect to the network, the Synchronization Manager updates the network files with changes that you made while working offline. When you synchronize files, the files that you opened or updated while disconnected from the network are compared to the files that are saved on the network. As long as the files you changed haven't been changed by someone else while you were offline, your changes are copied to the network.

If someone else made changes to the same network file that you updated offline, you can keep your version, the version on the network, or both. If you delete a network file on your computer while working offline but someone else on the network makes changes to that file, the file is deleted from your computer but not from the network. If you change a network file while working offline but someone else on the network deletes that file, you can save your version onto the network or delete it from your computer. If you are disconnected from the network when a new file is added to a shared network folder that you have made available offline, the new file is added to your computer when you reconnect and synchronize.

Setting Up Offline Files

If you use redirected folders of any type, it is recommended that you set up Offline Files. However, Offline Files does not depend on settings in the Folder Redirection node and is set up and configured on network shares separately from the Folder Redirection configuration. The tasks for implementing Offline Files are:

1. Configure the sharepoint.

2. Configure computers to use Offline Files.

3. Synchronize offline files and folders.

Configuring the Sharepoint   The first step in setting up Offline Files is to configure the sharepoint. You configure the sharepoint in the Sharing tab in the Properties dialog box for the shared folder.

To configure the sharepoint, complete the following steps:

1. Right-click the shared folder containing the offline files and select Sharing And Security.

2. In the Sharing tab in the Properties dialog box for the shared folder, click Offline Settings.

3. In the Offline Settings dialog box, shown in Figure 11-19, select one of the following:

   ❑ Only The Files And Programs That Users Specify Will Be Available Offline. Select this option if you want users to be able to determine which files will be available offline.

   ❑ All Files And Programs That Users Open From The Share Will Be Automatically Available Offline. Select this option if you want all files that users open from the shared resource to be automatically available offline. Select the Optimized For Performance check box if you want to automatically cache programs so they can be run locally. This option is useful for file servers that host applications because it reduces network traffic and improves server scalability.

   ❑ Files Or Programs From The Share Will Not Be Available Offline. Select this option to prevent users from storing files offline.

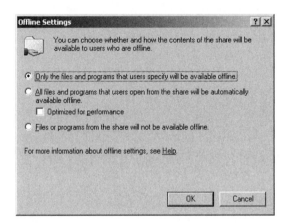

Figure 11-19   Offline Settings dialog box

4. Click OK.

5. In the Properties dialog box for the shared folder, click OK.

Configuring Computers and Servers to Use Offline Files   After you configure the sharepoint, you must configure users' computers and servers to use Offline Files. You can configure users' computers and servers to use Offline Files manually in the Offline Files tab in the Folder Options dialog box for each client computer. Or, you can configure users' computers and servers to use Offline Files by setting policies in Administrative Templates/Network/Offline Files in both the Computer Configuration and User Configuration nodes. This section provides the procedure for manually configuring computers and servers to use Offline Files.

Important   In Windows Server 2003, Remote Desktop for Administration (formerly known as Terminal Services in Remote Administration mode in Windows 2000) provides remote access to the desktop of any computer running a member of the Windows Server 2003 family. Remote Desktop for Administration is installed by default on computers running Windows Server 2003 but is not enabled by default. If Remote Desktop for Administration is enabled on a server, you cannot configure the server to use Offline Files because the Remote Desktop for Administration and Offline Files features are mutually exclusive. Therefore, before attempting to configure a server to use Offline Files, you must disable Remote Desktop for Administration. To do this on the server, right-click My Computer and select Properties. In the System Properties dialog box, select the Remote tab. In the Remote Desktop section, clear the Allow Users To Connect Remotely To This Computer check box, and then click OK. Then configure the server to use Offline Files as described in the procedure "Configuring computers and servers to use Offline Files" in this section. Because Remote Desktop for Administration is now separate from Terminal Services, it is no longer necessary to install Terminal Services For Remote Administration by using Add/Remove Programs in Control Panel.

To configure computers and servers to use Offline Files, complete the following steps:

1. Open My Computer.

2. On the Tools menu, click Folder Options.

3. In the Folder Options dialog box, click the Offline Files tab.

4. In the Offline Files tab, shown in Figure 11-20, select the Enable Offline Files check box. For computers running Windows 2000 Professional and Windows XP Professional, this box is selected by default.

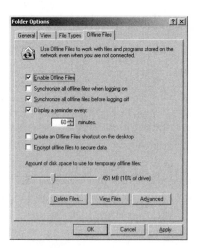

Figure 11-20   Folder Options dialog box, Offline Files tab

5. Select the Synchronize All Offline Files When Logging On check box if you want to fully synchronize offline files when a user logs on. Select the Synchronize All Offline Files Before Logging Off check box if you want to fully synchronize offline files before a user logs off. Full synchronization ensures that the network files reflect the latest changes. If you do not select these options, a quick synchronization occurs when a user logs on or off. A quick synchronization provides a complete version of online files, but might not provide the most current version.

> **Tip**   It is recommended that you always synchronize when you log on to your computer. This ensures that changes made on your computer are synchronized with changes that were made on the network while you were disconnected.

6. Select the Display A Reminder Every check box if you want to provide reminder balloons in the notification area of the desktop (lower right corner) when the computer goes offline. Specify how often (in minutes) you want the reminders to appear in the Minutes box.

7. Select the Create An Offline Files Shortcut On The Desktop check box if you want to place a shortcut to the Offline Files folder on the desktop.

8. Select the Encrypt Offline Files To Secure Data check box if you want to encrypt offline files to keep them safe from intruders who might gain unauthorized physical access to the client computer.

> **Note**   The Encrypt Offline Files To Secure Data check box is disabled if you are not an administrator on the computer, the local drive is not NTFS or does not support encryption, or your system administrator has implemented an encryption policy for Offline Files.

9. Select the amount of disk space you want to use for temporary offline files on the slider in the lower portion of the Offline Files tab.

10. Click Advanced.

11. In the Offline Files–Advanced Settings dialog box, shown in Figure 11-21, select one of the following options to indicate how a computer behaves when the connection to another computer on the network is lost:

   ❑ Notify Me And Begin Working Offline. Select this option to specify that the user can work offline if the network connection is lost, because network files will continue to be available.

   ❑ Never Allow My Computer To Go Offline, Select this option to specify that the user cannot work offline if the network connection is lost, because network files will not be available.

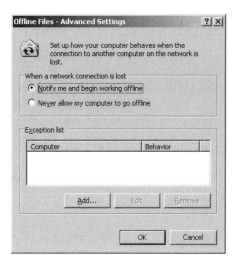

Figure 11-21   Offline Files–Advanced Settings dialog box

12. Click Add if you want a specific computer to receive a different treatment if the connection to another computer on the network is lost. If you click Add, the Offline Files–Add Custom Action dialog box appears. In the Computer box, type the name of the computer that will receive different treatment. Then select the treatment you want the computer to receive in the When A Network Connection Is Lost section. Click OK.

13. In the Offline Files–Advanced Settings dialog box, click OK.

14. In the Folder Options dialog box, click OK.

Synchronizing Offline Files and Folders   You can determine the way you want your computer to synchronize your files when you log on and off the network. There are two ways to set up synchronization of offline files and folders. You can set up synchronization manually by using the Items To Synchronize dialog box, also referred to as the Synchronization Manager in documentation and Help. Or, you can set up synchronization by setting policies in Administrative Templates/Network/Offline Files in both the Computer Configuration and User Configuration nodes. This section provides the procedure for manually setting up synchronization of offline files and folders.

To set up synchronization of offline files and folders, complete the following steps:

1. Click Start, point to All Programs, point to Accessories, and then click Synchronize.

Tip   You can also open the Items To Synchronize dialog box by typing **mobsync** on the command line.

2. In the Items To Synchronize dialog box, shown in Figure 11-22, click Setup.

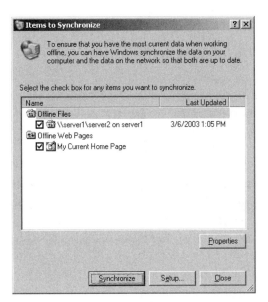

Figure 11-22   Items To Synchronize dialog box

3. In the Synchronization Settings dialog box, in the Logon/Logoff tab, shown in Figure 11-23, click the network connection that you want to use in the When I Am Using This Network Connection list.

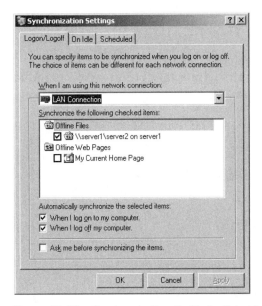

Figure 11-23   Synchronization Settings dialog box, Logon/Logoff tab

4. In the Synchronize The Following Checked Items list, select the check boxes next to the offline items that you want to synchronize, such as a folder on a mapped network drive or an Internet Explorer offline Web page.

5. Select the When I Log On To My Computer check box to synchronize the selected items when the user logs off. Select the When I Log Off My Computer check box to synchronize the selected items when the user logs off.

> **Tip**   It is recommended that you always synchronize when you log on to your computer. This ensures that changes made on your computer are synchronized with changes that were made on the network while you were disconnected.

> **Note**   The When I Log On To My Computer and the When I Log Off My Computer check boxes are selected by default if you selected the Synchronize All Offline Files When Logging On or Synchronize All Offline Files Before Logging Off options, respectively, in the Offline Files tab in the Folder Options dialog box. These options are part of the "Configure computers to use Offline Files" procedure.

6. Select the Ask Me Before Synchronizing The Items check box if you want Synchronization Manager to request permission before automatically synchronizing your offline items.

7. Click OK.

8. In the Items To Synchronize dialog box, click Close.

You can also specify items to be synchronized when a computer is idle by using the On Idle tab in the Synchronization Settings dialog box. By choosing when offline items are synchronized, you can better manage the work on your computer and on the network. Finally, you can schedule when synchronization occurs by using the Scheduled Synchronization Wizard, available from the Scheduled tab in the Synchronization Settings dialog box.

> **Note**   To manually synchronize offline files and folders immediately, right-click the file or folder you want to synchronize, and then click Synchronize.

Folder Redirection Best Practices

The following are the best practices for implementing folder redirection:

- **Allow the system to create the folders**   If you create the folders yourself, they may not have the correct permissions set.

- **Use fully qualified UNC paths, for example: *servername**sharename*** Although paths like C:*Foldername* can be used, it is not advisable because the path might not exist on the target computer.

> **Note**   If you use a UNC path with more than 260 characters, folder redirection fails because the path in truncated.

■ **Accept defaults**   In general, accept the default folder redirection settings.

■ **Place the My Pictures folder in the My Documents folder**   This is advisable unless there is a compelling reason not to, such as server scalability.

■ **Consider what will happen if the policy is removed**   Keep in mind the behavior your folder redirection policies will have if the policy is removed, as described in the "Policy Removal Considerations" section.

■ **Do not redirect My Documents to the home folder unless you have already deployed home directories in your organization**   Folder redirection to the home directory offers less security than standard folder redirection and is offered only for backward compatibility. If you redirect My Documents to the home directory, and if your users log on to the domain via Terminal Server clients, then don't specify a separate Terminal Services Home Directory.

■ **Enable Offline Files**   In the event of a network failure or for users who use portable computers, users must be able to access the information in redirected folders.

Practice: Managing Special Folders

In this practice, you set up folder redirection and Offline Files. Normally, folder redirection and Offline Files are configured for a Windows XP Professional client. However, for training purposes, this practice configures folder redirection and Offline Files for Server02, an additional domain controller in the *contoso.com* domain.

Exercise 1: Setting Up Folder Redirection

In this exercise, you redirect User One's My Documents folder to a sharepoint on Server01.

▶ **To set up folder redirection**

1. Log on to Server1 as Administrator.

2. Create a shared folder named Server2 in *C*:\ (where *C* is the name of your system drive). The share name is Server2.

3. Log on to Server2 as Administrator.

4. Create a GPO linked to the Chicago OU named My Documents Redirection. Use the procedures provided earlier in this lesson to redirect the My Documents folder to \\server1\server2. (Hint: If the GPO is not taking effect, check the No Override or Block Policy Inheritance settings on any existing GPOs linked to the Chicago OU.)

5. Log off Server2, and log on as User1. What happened in the Server2 folder on Server1?

   The User1 folder is created when User1 logs on. Inside the User1 folder is another folder, My Documents. As an administrator, you cannot view the contents of User1's My Documents folder without permission from User1.

6. On Server2, create a document using WordPad and save it as Doc1 in the My Documents folder. Create a second document using WordPad and save it as Doc2.

Exercise 2: Setting Up Offline Files

▶ **To set up Offline Files**

In this exercise, you set up Offline Files using the procedures provided earlier in this lesson.

1. On Server1, use the procedure provided earlier in this lesson to configure the shared folder C:\Server2 for Offline Files. Use the All Files And Programs That Users Open From The Share Will Be Automatically Available Offline option in the Offline Settings dialog box.

2. Log off Server2, and log on as Administrator.

3. Configure Server2 to use Offline Files.

4. Log off Server2, and log on as User1.

5. Immediately synchronize the My Documents folder on Server2. What happens to the Doc1 and Doc2 document icons in the My Documents folder?

   Two arrows are appended to the Doc1 and Doc2 icons, indicating that they have been synchronized with Server1.

6. Shut down Server1. What happens?

   The Offline Files informational balloon displays in the lower right corner of the desktop. You can view more information about working offline by clicking the display icon.

Lesson Review

The following questions are intended to reinforce key information presented in this lesson. If you are unable to answer a question, review the lesson and then try the question again. Answers to the questions can be found in the "Questions and Answers" section at the end of this chapter.

1. What is the purpose of folder redirection?

   _____

   _____

2. Which folders can be redirected?

_____

_____

3. Under what circumstances should you redirect My Documents to a home folder?

_____

_____

4. What is the purpose of the Offline Files feature?

_____

_____

5. Which of the following are true statements? (Choose three.)

a. Remote Desktop For Administration is installed by default on computers running Windows Server 2003.

b. Remote Desktop For Administration is enabled by default on computers running Windows Server 2003.

c. A server can be configured to use Offline Files and Remote Desktop For Administration at the same time.

d. A server cannot be configured to use Offline Files and Remote Desktop For Administration at the same time.

e. Before attempting to configure the computer to use Offline Files, you must disable Remote Desktop For Administration.

f. Before attempting to configure the computer to use Offline Files, you must enable Remote Desktop For Administration.

Lesson Summary

- The Folder Redirection node, located under User Configuration\Windows Settings in the Group Policy Object Editor console, enables you to redirect certain special folders to network locations. Windows Server 2003 allows the following special folders to be redirected: Application Data, Desktop, My Documents, My Pictures, and Start Menu.

- In Windows Server 2003, a new feature enables you to redirect My Documents to a user's home folder. This option is intended only for organizations that have already deployed home folders and that want to maintain compatibility with an existing home folder environment. The ability to redirect My Documents to a user's home folder requires a Windows XP Professional client.

- There are two ways to set up folder redirection:

  ❑ Redirect special folders to one location for everyone in the site, domain, or OU.

❑   Redirect special folders to a location according to security group membership.

■ The Offline Files feature provides users with access to redirected folders even when they are not connected to the network. If you use redirected folders of any type, it is recommended that you set up Offline Files.

■ The tasks for implementing Offline Files are configure the sharepoint, configure computers to use Offline Files, and set up synchronization of offline files and folders.

Lesson 3: Troubleshooting Group Policy

In order to maintain an effective Group Policy configuration, you must be able to troubleshoot Group Policy. Troubleshooting Group Policy involves using the Resultant Set Of Policy Wizard, the Gpresult and Gpupdate command-line tools, the Event Viewer, and log files to solve policy-related problems. This lesson shows you how to work with these tools to troubleshoot Group Policy for Active Directory.

After this lesson, you will be able to

■ Troubleshoot Group Policy

Estimated lesson time: 20 minutes

Troubleshooting Group Policy

As an administrator, it will likely be your task to find solutions to problems with Group Policy. If problems occur, you might need to perform some tests to verify that your Group Policy configuration is working properly, such as the following:

■ Verify that GPOs apply to the appropriate users and computers.

■ Verify that folders configured for redirection are redirected to the appropriate location.

■ Verify that files and folders configured to be available offline are available when a computer is offline.

You will also need to be able to diagnose and solve problems, including

■ GPOs are not applied.

■ GPOs cannot be accessed.

■ GPO inheritance issues cause unexpected results.

■ Folders are not redirected or are redirected to an unexpected location.

■ Files and folders are not available offline.

■ Files are not synchronized.

Windows Server 2003 provides the following Group Policy troubleshooting tools to assist you in verifying your configuration and in diagnosing and solving problems:

■ Resultant Set Of Policy Wizard

■ Gpresult

■ Gpupdate

- Event Viewer

- Log files

Troubleshooting Group Policy with the Resultant Set Of Policy Wizard and Gpresult

Recall that the Resultant Set Of Policy Wizard and the Gpresult command-line tool are both used to generate RSoP queries and provide the RSoPs for users and computers you specify. In Windows Server 2003, these tools can help you greatly reduce the amount of time you spend troubleshooting. Generating RSoP queries by using the Resultant Set Of Policy Wizard and Gpresult was discussed in detail in Lesson 1.

Troubleshooting Group Policy with Gpupdate

Recall that the Gpupdate tool, which is new in Windows Server 2003 (and also exists in Windows XP Professional), enables you to refresh policy immediately. Gpupdate replaces the Secedit /refreshpolicy command used for refreshing GPOs in Windows 2000. The Gpupdate tool is discussed in Chapter 10, "Implementing Group Policy."

Troubleshooting Group Policy with Event Viewer

By using the application event log in Event Viewer, you can view Group Policy failure and warning messages, such as the one shown in Figure 11-24. The application event log contains basic predetermined Group Policy events and is used to track problems, not for Group Policy planning. Event log records with the source Userenv pertain to Group Policy events.

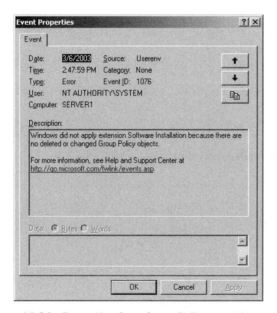

Figure 11-24 Properties for a Group Policy event log message

To avoid flooding the log, not all Group Policy failures and warnings are displayed in the event log. You can retrieve more detailed information about Group Policy processing by setting a switch in the registry to enable verbose logging for the event log.

> **Caution**   This section contains information about editing the registry. Using the Registry Editor incorrectly can cause serious damage to your operating system, so be very careful.

To enable verbose logging for the event log, complete the following steps:

1. Log on as Administrator.
2. Click Start, and then click Run.
3. In the Run dialog box, in the Open box, type **regedit**, and then click OK.
4. In the Registry Editor console, open the HKEY_LOCAL_MACHINE/Software /Microsoft/Windows NT/Current Version key, then click Edit, select New, and then select Key on the toolbar.
5. Type **Diagnostics** as the name of the new key. Right-click the new key, select New, and select DWORD Value on the toolbar.
6. In the details pane, type **RunDiagnosticLoggingGroupPolicy** as the name of the new value. Right-click the new value and select Modify.
7. In the Edit DWORD Value dialog box, type **1** in the Value Data box. Ensure that the Hexadecimal button is selected. Click OK.
8. Log off and then log on again.
9. Open the Application Log in Event Viewer and view the enhanced Group Policy event logging.

Troubleshooting Group Policy with Log Files

You can generate a diagnostic log to record detailed information about Group Policy processing to a log file named Userenv.log in the hidden folder %*Systemroot*% \Debug\Usermode. The generation of this diagnostic log is known as enabling verbose logging.

> **Caution**   This section contains information about editing the registry. Using the Registry Editor incorrectly can cause serious damage to your operating system, so be very careful.

To enable verbose logging to a log file, complete the following steps:

1. Log on as Administrator.
2. Click Start, and then click Run.

3. In the Run dialog box, in the Open box, type **regedit**, and then click OK.

4. In the Registry Editor console, open the HKEY_LOCAL_MACHINE/Software/ Microsoft/Windows NT/Current Version/Winlogon key, then click Edit, select New, and then select DWORD Value on the toolbar.

5. In the details pane, type **UserenvDebugLevel** as the name of the new value. Right-click the new value and select Modify.

6. In the Edit DWORD Value dialog box, type **30002** in the Value Data box. Ensure that the Hexadecimal button is selected. Click OK.

7. Log off and then log on again.

8. Open the %*Systemroot*%\Debug\Usermode\Userenv.log file and view the enhanced Group Policy event logging.

Note To read or copy the logs on the target machine, you must have local Administrator rights.

The Userenv.log file, shown in Figure 11-25, provides details of errors and warnings in Group Policy processing on the computer on which it is set. Reading from left to right, this log shows a process code, the time it was processed (the date is not displayed), the process name, followed by a short statement of the error. The Userenv.log file has a maximum size of 1 megabyte (MB). At system startup, if the log file exceeds 1 MB, the contents are copied into a file named Userenv.bak and a new Userenv.log file is created.

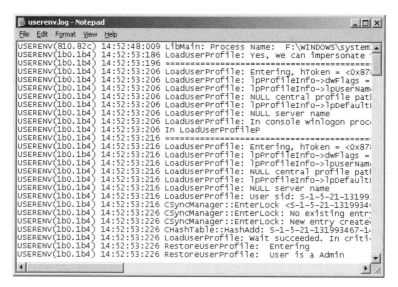

Figure 11-25 Contents of the Userenv.log file

Group Policy Troubleshooting Scenarios

Table 11-7 describes some troubleshooting scenarios related to the Group Policy Object Editor console.

Table 11-7   Group Policy Object Editor Console Troubleshooting Scenarios

Cause	Solution
Problem: The user cannot open a GPO in the console even though he or she has Read access to it.	
An administrator must have both Read permission and Write permission for the GPO to open it in the Group Policy Object Editor console.	Be a member of a security group with at least Read and Write, and preferably Full Control, permission for the GPO. For example, a domain administrator can manage nonlocal GPOs. An administrator for a computer can edit the local GPO on that computer.
Problem: When the user tries to edit a GPO, the Failed To Open The Group Policy Object message appears.	
A networking problem, specifically a problem with the Domain Name System (DNS) configuration.	Make sure DNS is working properly. Refer to help for details.
Problem: When the user tries to edit a GPO, the Missing Active Directory Container message appears.	
This is caused by Group Policy attempting to link a GPO to an OU that it cannot find. The OU might have been deleted, or it might have been created on another domain controller but not replicated to the domain controller that you are using.	Limit the number of administrators who can make structural changes to Active Directory, or who can edit a GPO at any one time. Allow changes to replicate before making changes that affect the same OU or GPO.
Problem: When the user tries to edit a GPO, the Snap-In Failed To Initialize message appears.	
This error can occur if Group Policy cannot find the file Framedyn.dll.	If you use installation scripts, make sure that your scripts place the %Systemroot%\System32\Wbem directory in the system path. By default, %Systemroot%\System32\Wbem is in the system path already; therefore, you are not likely to encounter this issue if you do not use installation scripts.

Table 11-8 describes some troubleshooting scenarios where Group Policy settings are not taking effect.

Table 11-8   Group Policy Settings Troubleshooting Scenarios

Cause	Solution
Problem: Group Policy is not being applied to users and computers in a security group that contains those users and computers, even though a GPO is linked to an OU containing that security group	
This is correct behavior. Group Policy affects only users and computers contained in sites, domains, and OUs. GPOs are not applied to security groups.	Link GPOs to sites, domains, and OUs only. Keep in mind that the location of a security group in Active Directory is unrelated to whether Group Policy applies to the users and computers in that security group.
Problem: Group Policy is not affecting users and computers in a site, domain, or OU.	
Group Policy settings can be prevented, intentionally or inadvertently, from taking effect on users and computers in several ways. A GPO can be disabled from affecting users, computers, or both. It also needs to be linked either directly to an OU containing the users and computers or to a parent domain or OU so that the Group Policy settings apply through inheritance. When multiple GPOs exist, they are applied in this order: local, site, domain, OU. By default, settings applied later have precedence. In addition, Group Policy can be blocked at the level of any OU, or enforced through a setting of No Override applied to a particular GPO link. Finally, the user or computer must belong to one or more security groups with appropriate permissions set.	Make sure that the intended policy is not being blocked. Make sure no policy set at a higher level of Active Directory has been set to No Override. If Block Policy Inheritance and No Override are both used, keep in mind that No Override takes precedence. Verify that the user or computer is not a member of any security group for which the Apply Group Policy access control entry (ACE) is set to Deny. Verify that the user or computer is a member of at least one security group for which the Apply Group Policy permission is set to Allow. Verify that the user or computer is a member of at least one security group for which the Read permission is set to Allow.
Problem: Group Policy is not affecting users and computers in an Active Directory container.	
GPOs cannot be linked to Active Directory containers other than sites, domains, and OUs.	Link a GPO to an object that is a parent to the Active Directory container. Then, by default, those settings are applied to the users and computers in the container through inheritance.
Problem: Local Group Policy is not taking effect on the computer.	
Local policies are the weakest. Any nonlocal GPO can overwrite them.	Check to see what GPOs are being applied through Active Directory and if those GPOs have settings that are in conflict with the local settings.

Table 11-9 describes some troubleshooting scenarios when redirecting folders to network locations or using Offline Files.

Table 11-9   Folder Redirection and Offline Files Troubleshooting Scenarios

Causes	Solutions
Problem: Folders are not redirected.	
The client computer is running Windows NT 4, Windows 98, or Windows 95.	Confirm that the client computer is running Windows 2000 Professional or Windows XP Professional.
Group Policy is not applied.	Verify that folder redirection Group Policy settings are applied by using Gpresult.
The network share is unavailable and Offline Files is not enabled.	If the server that contains the redirected folders is offline and Offline Files is disabled, folders cannot be redirected. Refer to Lesson 2 for details.
The user does not have access permission to the share on which the folder is redirected.	Verify that the user has access to the folder where his or her data is redirected. Users should have Full Control permission for the redirected folder.
There is a disk quota on the target folder.	If a disk quota exists for the target folder, either enlarge it or have the user delete some files.
A mapped drive has been used for the target path rather than a UNC path.	A UNC path, rather than a mapped drive, is recommended for indicating the target path.
Problem: Folder redirection is successful but files and folders are unavailable.	
Network connectivity problems.	Ping the server that stored the redirected folder to ensure network connectivity.
The network share is not available, and items are not available in the local cache.	Check user rights on the redirected folder. The user should have Full Control permission.
When using applications, open and save operations do not use the redirected path.	Check the applications the user is using; some older applications might not recognize redirected folders.
Problem: Files available when online are not available when offline.	
The files are located on a computer not running Windows 2000 Professional or Windows XP Professional.	Confirm that the files are located on a computer running Windows 2000 Professional or Windows XP Professional.
Offline Files is not enabled on the client computer.	Enable Offline Files on the client computer.
The Offline Files setting for the share is not set to automatic.	Set Offline Files setting to automatic.

Table 11-9   Folder Redirection and Offline Files Troubleshooting Scenarios

Causes	Solutions
Problem: The user cannot make files and folders available offline.	
Remote Desktop for Administration is enabled.	Check if Remote Desktop for Administration is enabled by opening Properties For My Computer, selecting the Remote tab, and clearing the Allow Users To Connect Remotely To This Computer check box. Remote Desktop for Administration is not compatible with Offline Files.
The file or folder is a local file or folder and not on a network share.	Verify that the file or folder is on a network share.
Offline Files is not configured.	Verify that Offline Files is configured.
A Group Policy setting was applied to disable Offline Files.	Verify that the Allow Or Disallow Use Of The Offline Files Feature setting in Computer Configuration\Administrative Templates\Network\ Offline Files setting is not set to Enable.
The user does not have access to the file share.	Verify that the folder is redirected successfully and is not local. Then verify that the user has the appropriate file security to read and write to the location where the folder is redirected.
Problem: Files do not synchronize.	
Files with extensions .mdb, .ldb, .mdw, .mde, and .db are not synchronized by default.	Verify extensions of files to be synchronized.
Network connection problems accessing the files to be synchronized.	Use ping to verify that the user can connect to the file share containing the files to be synchronized.
Insufficient disk space on the client computer to synchronize files.	Check the amount of free disk space on the client.
Insufficient user rights to read or write the file to be synchronized.	Check user rights and permissions to ensure that the user has the appropriate access.
A Group Policy setting was applied specifying additional file name extensions that are not synchronized.	Verify that the Files Not Cached setting in Computer Configuration\Administrative Templates\Network\Offline Files setting is not set to Enable.

Lesson Review

The following questions are intended to reinforce key information presented in this lesson. If you are unable to answer a question, review the lesson and then try the question again. Answers to the questions can be found in the "Questions and Answers" section at the end of this chapter.

1. In which Event Viewer log can you find Group Policy failure and warning messages? What type of event log records should you look for?

   _____

   _____

2. What diagnostic log file can you generate to record detailed information about Group Policy processing and in what location is this file generated?

   _____

   _____

3. Which of the following actions should you take if you attempt to open a Group Policy Object Editor console for an OU GPO and you receive the message Failed To Open The Group Policy Object?

   a. Check your permissions for the GPO.

   b. Check network connectivity.

   c. Check that the OU exists.

   d. Check that No Override is set for the GPO.

   e. Check that Block Policy Inheritance is set for the GPO.

4. Which of the following actions should you take if you attempt to edit a GPO and you receive the message Missing Active Directory Container?

   a. Check your permissions for the GPO.

   b. Check network connectivity.

   c. Check that the OU exists.

   d. Check that No Override is set for the GPO.

   e. Check that Block Policy Inheritance is set for the GPO.

5. Which of the following actions should you take if folder redirection is successful but files and folders are unavailable? Choose two.

   a. Check the user's permissions for the redirected folder.

   b. Check network connectivity.

   c. Check that the redirected folder exists.

> **d.** Check to see if Remote Desktop for Administration is enabled.
>
> **e.** Check to see if the files have extensions that are not synchronized by default.

Lesson Summary

- Windows Server 2003 provides the following Group Policy troubleshooting tools to assist you in verifying your configuration and in diagnosing and solving problems: Resultant Set Of Policy Wizard, Gpresult and Gpupdate command-line tools, Event Viewer, and log files.

- By using the application event log in Event Viewer, you can view Group Policy failure and warning messages. Event log records with the source Userenv indicate records pertaining to Group Policy events. You can retrieve more detailed information about Group Policy processing by enabling verbose logging for the event log.

- You can generate a diagnostic log to record detailed information about Group Policy processing to a log file named Userenv.log in the hidden folder %*Systemroot*% \Debug\Usermode. The generation of this diagnostic log is known as enabling verbose logging.

Case Scenario Exercise

You are a computer consultant. Linda Randall, the Chief Information Officer of Lucerne Publishing, asks for your help. The Lucerne Publishing network consists of a single Active Directory domain with four domain controllers running Windows Server 2003, three file servers, and 300 clients that are evenly divided between Windows 2000 Professional and Windows XP Professional.

Recently, several publishing projects (stored in electronic format) were lost when an employee's laptop was stolen from a publishing convention. Previously, another employee lost important publishing project files during a fire sprinkler system incident in which the employee's computer was destroyed.

Employees typically store documents in the My Documents folder on their local systems. Linda wants all employees to store their data on the network servers. The data on the network servers is backed up regularly. Linda tells you that her editors tend to work on sensitive data that requires special handling. She is especially worried about that data being backed up and secured.

All client computers have P: drive mappings that are supposed to be used for storing files. However, many employees don't really understand drive mappings. They often store files in their My Documents folder and then copy them over to the P: drive. This is also an issue because many employees forget to copy their files to the server until something (such as a data loss) occurs.

Given the concerns of Lucerne Publishing as outlined above, answer the following questions. Answers can be found in the "Questions and Answers" section at the end of this chapter.

1. How would you address Linda's concern that some employees don't understand drive mappings and others forget to store their data on the server?

_____

_____

2. How can you address the situation concerning the sensitive data that the editors work with?

_____

_____

3. How would you address the users with mobile computers so that they could work on their files while traveling?

_____

_____

4. Linda warns that some users may have huge amounts of data already stored in their My Documents folder on their local system. How might this affect your recommendations?

_____

_____

5. What tools could you use to document the policies and their effects once they are in place?

_____

_____

Troubleshooting Lab

You are a network administrator for Contoso Pharmaceuticals. You receive a call from another network administrator, John Evans, about a problem with desktop redirection. He says that he created a desktop redirection GPO for a couple of users in an OU named RedirectDesktop. He configured the folder so that both users would have the same desktop and gave them only Read, Execute, and List Folder Contents permissions to that folder.

Recently, John decided that he no longer wanted to control these users' desktops in that way. However, when he tried to make the policy redirect their desktops back to their local computers, it didn't work. He even deleted the policy, but the users' desktops are still being redirected to the shared folder. He doesn't know what else to do and needs your help.

To see how this happened, you must create the problem using the following steps:

1. Log on to Server1 using the domain administrator user name and password.

2. Create a folder on the desktop named Desktops and share it as Desktops. Configure the security permissions of this folder so that Authenticated Users have Read & Execute, List Folder Contents, and Read permission.

3. Add a couple of new text documents to this folder.

4. Create a first-level OU named DesktopRedirect.

5. Inside the DesktopRedirect OU, create two user accounts: DesktopUser1 and DesktopUser2. Set their passwords as "password". Clear the User Must Change Password At Next Logon box. Add both users to the Server Operators group. This will allow them to log on locally to the domain controllers.

Security Alert In a real-world environment, use a complex password. Microsoft recommends mixing uppercase and lowercase letters, numbers, and symbols (for example, Lp6*g9f2).

6. In the Active Directory Users And Computers console, right-click the DesktopRedirect OU and click Properties.

7. In the DesktopRedirect Properties dialog box, click the Group Policy tab. Click New. Enter the name **DesktopRedirectGPO** for the new policy, and press ENTER. Click Edit.

8. In the Group Policy Object Editor console, expand the following objects: User Configuration, Windows Settings, Folder Redirection.

9. Right-click the Desktop object and click Properties. The Desktop Properties dialog box opens.

10. Configure the Setting selection to read: Basic–Redirect Everyone's Folder To The Same Location. Additional setting boxes appear below.

11. Configure the Target folder location selection box to read: Redirect To The Following Location.

12. Type **server1****desktops** in the Root Path text box.

13. Click the Settings tab. Clear the Grant The User Exclusive Rights To Desktop check box. Also, clear the Move The Contents Of Desktop To The New Location check box. Don't change the Policy Removal option.

14. Click OK. Close the Group Policy Object Editor console. Close the DesktopRedirect Properties dialog box.

15. Run the Repadmin /syncall command to ensure that the domain policies are synchronized as soon as possible. Wait two minutes before you proceed with the next step.

16. Log off and log on as DesktopUser1. Do you see the text documents that you added to the shared Desktops folder? Can you create new objects on the desktop?

    The text documents that were added to the Desktops folder will be visible if the desktop was redirected. The user should not be able to create new files on the Desktop because permissions were set for only Read, Execute, and List Folder Contents.

17. Log on to Server2 as DesktopUser2. Do you see the text documents that you added to the shared Desktops folder? Can you create new objects on the desktop?

    Again, the text documents that were added to the Desktops folder will be visible if the desktop was redirected. The user should not be able to create new files on the Desktop because permissions were set for only Read, Execute, and List Folder Contents.

18. Log off DesktopUser1 and DesktopUser2.

19. Log on to Server1 using the domain administrator user name and password.

20. Open the DesktopRedirectGPO in the Group Policy Object Editor (using the steps described previously).

21. Open the Desktop Properties dialog box as described previously (under User Configuration, Windows Settings, Folder Redirection, Desktop).

22. Click the Settings tab on the Desktop Properties dialog box.

23. In the Policy Removal section, select Redirect The Folders Back To The Local User Profile Location When Policy Is Removed. Click OK. Close the Group Policy Object Editor. Click OK on the DesktopRedirect Properties dialog box.

Note Setting Redirect The Folders Back To The Local User Profile Location When Policy Is Removed won't redirect the user's desktop back to their local desktops. If that is the desired result, you would have had to set this option when the policy was first configured.

24. Run the Repadmin /syncall command to replicate these new settings as soon as possible.

25. Open the DesktopRedirect Properties dialog box, and click the Group Policy tab. Press Delete to delete the DesktopRedirectGPO. You will see the Delete dialog box.

26. Select Remove The Link And Delete The Group Policy Object Permanently and click OK. Click Yes in the Delete Group Policy Object dialog box. Close the DesktopRedirect Properties dialog box.

You've now configured the problem that John is facing in the scenario. Now you can begin troubleshooting this issue.

1. Log on to Server2 as DesktopUser2. Although folder redirection is still in place, the DesktopRedirectGPO policy is no longer applying to this user.

> **Note**   If you were to log on to Server1 as DesktopUser1, you'd see that the desktop is also still redirected. This is true even though the policy was completely removed. Interestingly, if you logged on to Server2 as DesktopUser1 (assuming you've never logged on there previously as DesktopUser1), you'd see that the desktop redirection policy didn't affect DesktopUser1 on Server2.

2. On Server2, open a command prompt and run the Gpresult command. You should see that the DesktopRedirectGPO is still applying to DesktopUser2.

3. Close the command prompt and log off DesktopUser2.

Now that you've verified the problem, it is time to correct it.

1. Return to Server1 (ensure that you are logged on as the domain administrator) and open the RedirectDesktop OU Properties dialog box. Click the Group Policy tab.

2. Click New and type **DesktopRedirectLocal** for the policy name and press ENTER. Click Edit and open the User Configuration, Windows Settings, Folder Redirection, Desktop, Desktop Properties dialog box.

3. Configure the Setting selection to read: Basic—Redirect Everyone's Folder To The Same Location.

4. Configure the Target folder location to read: Redirect To The Local Userprofile Location. Click OK.

> **Note**   In Windows 2000, the option to redirect to the local userprofile path was not available. However, you could type **%Userprofile%\Desktop** to achieve the same outcome.

5. Close the Group Policy Object Editor. Close the DesktopRedirect Properties dialog box.

6. Run the Repadmin /syncall command to replicate these new settings as soon as possible. Wait two minutes before moving to the next step.

7. Log on to Server2 as DesktopUser2. You should now be able to create new files and folders on the desktop. The user now has a local desktop.

You've solved the problem. Leave the DesktopRedirectLocal policy in place at least until all affected users have logged on to their affected computers. Once all users have logged on, you can delete the policy if you like.

Chapter Summary

- RSoP is the sum of the policies applied to the user or computer, including the application of filters (security groups, WMI) and exceptions (No Override, Block Policy Inheritance).

- Windows Server 2003 provides three tools for generating RSoP queries: the Resultant Set Of Policy Wizard, the Gpresult command-line tool, and the Advanced System Information–Policy tool.

- The Folder Redirection node, located under User Configuration\Windows Settings in the Group Policy Object Editor console, enables you to redirect certain special folders to network locations. Windows Server 2003 allows the following special folders to be redirected: Application Data, Desktop, My Documents, My Pictures, and Start Menu.

- The Offline Files feature provides users with access to redirected folders even when they are not connected to the network. If you use redirected folders of any type, it is recommended that you set up Offline Files.

- Windows Server 2003 provides the following Group Policy troubleshooting tools to assist you in verifying your configuration and in diagnosing and solving problems: Resultant Set Of Policy Wizard, Gpresult and Gpupdate command-line tools, Event Viewer, and log files.

Exam Highlights

Before taking the exam, review the key points and terms that are presented in this chapter. You need to know this information.

Key Points

- You can troubleshoot Group Policy application deployment and the application of Group Policy security settings by using RSoP.

- You can generate RSoP queries by using three tools: the Resultant Set Of Policy Wizard, the Gpresult command-line tool, and the Advanced System Information–Policy tool.

- Folder Redirection enables you to redirect the following special folders: Application Data, Desktop, My Documents, My Pictures, and Start Menu.

- You can also redirect My Documents to a user's home folder. This option is intended only for organizations that have already deployed home folders and that want to maintain compatibility with an existing home folder environment. The ability to redirect My Documents to a user's home folder requires a Windows XP Professional client.

- You can set up folder redirection in two ways:

  - Redirect special folders to one location for everyone in the site, domain, or OU.

  - Redirect special folders to a location according to security group membership.

Key Terms

Resultant Set of Policy (RSoP)   A feature that simplifies Group Policy implementation and troubleshooting. RSoP has two modes: Logging mode and Planning mode. Logging mode determines the resultant effect of policy settings that have been applied to an existing user and computer based on a site, domain, and OU. Planning mode simulates the resultant effect of policy settings that are applied to a user and a computer.

Sharepoint   A centralized location for key folders on a server or servers, which provides users with an access point for storing and finding information and administrators with an access point for managing information.

folder redirection   An extension within Group Policy that allows you to redirect the following special folders: Application Data, Desktop, My Documents, My Pictures, and Start Menu.

Offline Files   A feature that provides users with access to redirected folders even when they are not connected to the network. Offline Files caches files accessed through folder redirection onto the hard drive of the local computer. When a user accesses a file in a redirected folder, the file is accessed and modified locally. When a user has finished working with the file and has logged off, only then does the file traverse the network for storage on the server.

Questions and Answers

Page
11-27

Lesson 1 Review

1. What is the purpose of generating RSoP queries?

RSoP is the sum of the policies applied to the user or computer, including the application of filters (security groups, WMI) and exceptions (No Override, Block Policy Inheritance). Because of the cumulative effects of GPOs, filters, and exceptions, determining a user or computer's RSoP can be difficult. The ability to generate RSoP queries in Windows Server 2003 makes determining RSoP easier.

2. What are the three tools available for generating RSoP queries?

Windows Server 2003 provides three tools for generating RSoP queries: the Resultant Set Of Policy Wizard, the Gpresult command-line tool, and the Advanced System Information– Policy tool.

3. What is the difference between Logging mode and Planning mode?

Logging mode reports the existing GPO settings for a user or computer. Planning mode simulates the GPO settings that a user and computer might receive, and it enables you to change the simulation.

4. What is the difference between saving an RSoP query and saving RSoP query data?

By saving an RSoP query, you can reuse it for processing another RSoP query later. By saving RSoP query data, you can revisit the RSoP as it appeared for a particular query when the query was created.

5. Which RSoP query generating tool provides RSoP query results on a console similar to a Group Policy Object Editor console?

    a. Resultant Set Of Policy Wizard

    b. Group Policy Wizard

    c. Gpupdate command-line tool

    d. Gpresult command-line tool

    e. Advanced System Information–Policy tool

    f. Advanced System Information–Services tool

The correct answer is a. The Resultant Set Of Policy Wizard provides RSoP query results on a console similar to a Group Policy Object Editor console. There is no Group Policy Wizard. Gpupdate and Gpresult are command-line tools. The Advanced System Information tools provide results in an HTML report that appears in the Help And Support Center window.

Lesson 2 Review

1. What is the purpose of folder redirection?

   You redirect users' folders to provide a centralized location for key Windows XP Professional folders on a server or servers. This centralized location, called a sharepoint, provides users with an access point for storing and finding information and administrators with an access point for managing information.

2. Which folders can be redirected?

   Windows Server 2003 allows the following special folders to be redirected: Application Data, Desktop, My Documents, My Pictures, and Start Menu.

3. Under what circumstances should you redirect My Documents to a home folder?

   Redirect My Documents to a user's home folder only if you have already deployed home directories in your organization. This option is intended only for organizations that want to maintain compatibility with their existing home directory environment.

4. What is the purpose of the Offline Files feature?

   The Offline Files feature provides users with access to redirected folders even when they are not connected to the network.

5. Which of the following are true statements? (Choose three.)

   a. Remote Desktop for Administration is installed by default on computers running Windows Server 2003.

   b. Remote Desktop for Administration is enabled by default on computers running Windows Server 2003.

   c. A server can be configured to use Offline Files and Remote Desktop for Administration at the same time.

   d. A server cannot be configured to use Offline Files and Remote Desktop for Administration at the same time.

   e. Before attempting to configure the computer to use Offline Files, you must disable Remote Desktop for Administration.

   f. Before attempting to configure the computer to use Offline Files, you must enable Remote Desktop for Administration.

   The correct answers are a, d, and e. Remote Desktop for Administration is installed, but not enabled, by default on computers running Windows Server 2003. Because Remote Desktop for Administration and Offline Files are mutually exclusive, a server cannot be configured to use Offline Files and Remote Desktop for Administration at the same time. Therefore, before you can configure a computer to use Offline Files, you must disable Remote Desktop for Administration.

Lesson 3 Review

1. In which Event Viewer log can you find Group Policy failure and warning messages? What type of event log records should you look for?

   You can find Group Policy failure and warning messages in the application event log. Event log records with the Userenv source pertain to Group Policy events.

2. What diagnostic log file can you generate to record detailed information about Group Policy processing and in what location is this file generated?

   You can generate a diagnostic log to record detailed information about Group Policy processing to a log file named Userenv.log in the hidden folder %Systemroot%\Debug\Usermode.

3. Which of the following actions should you take if you attempt to open a Group Policy Object Editor console for an OU GPO and you receive the message Failed To Open The Group Policy Object?

   a. Check your permissions for the GPO.

   b. Check network connectivity.

   c. Check that the OU exists.

   d. Check that No Override is set for the GPO.

   e. Check that Block Policy Inheritance is set for the GPO.

   The correct answer is b. The message Failed To Open The Group Policy Object indicates a networking problem, specifically a problem with the Domain Name System (DNS) configuration.

4. Which of the following actions should you take if you attempt to edit a GPO and you receive the message Missing Active Directory Container?

   a. Check your permissions for the GPO.

   b. Check network connectivity.

   c. Check that the OU exists.

   d. Check that No Override is set for the GPO.

   e. Check that Block Policy Inheritance is set for the GPO.

   The correct answer is c. The message Missing Active Directory Container is caused by Group Policy attempting to link a GPO to an OU that it cannot find. The OU might have been deleted, or it might have been created on another domain controller but not replicated to the domain controller that you are using.

5. Which of the following actions should you take if folder redirection is successful but files and folders are unavailable? Choose two.

   a. Check the user's permissions for the redirected folder.

   b. Check network connectivity.

   c. Check that the redirected folder exists.

> **d.** Check to see if Remote Desktop for Administration is enabled.
>
> **e.** Check to see if the files have extensions that are not synchronized by default.

The correct answers are a and b. If folder redirection is successful but files and folders are unavailable, users might not have Full Control for the redirected folder or there might be a connectivity problem with the network. Because folder redirection is successful, the redirected folder does exist. You would check to see if Remote Desktop for Administration is enabled or if files have extensions that are not synchronized by default if you are troubleshooting Offline Files and file synchronization.

Page
11-60

Case Scenario Exercise

1. How would you address Linda's concern that some employees don't understand drive mappings and others forget to store their data on the server?

   This situation is perfectly suited to the use of Folder Redirection. Group Policy offers the ability to redirect many different special folders on a client system to an alternate location. In this case, redirecting users' My Documents folders to a network share.

2. How can you address the situation concerning the sensitive data that the editors work with?

   Redirecting the files is an excellent start, since the files will then be stored on the network and backed up regularly. If the editors' documents are deemed more valuable, one thing to consider is using Advanced Redirection. Basic Redirection redirects all users' documents to the same file share, typically storing the documents in a folder below that share. By using Advanced Redirection, it's possible to redirect files to different locations based on the security group membership of the user. You may choose to redirect the editors' documents to a file server that is more secure and/or reliable. You may also ask that the editors use EFS encryption on their documents.

3. How would you address the users with mobile computers so that they could work on their files while traveling?

   An excellent strategy would be to augment the Folder Redirection policy by configuring the files to be available offline, as well. When these users are connected to the LAN, accessing their My Documents folder would show the contents of the redirected location on the network file server. When the user is on the road, they are still able to access their My Documents folder, but they will be accessing the locally cached copy of the documents. Any changes they might make, or any new documents they create, will be synchronized with the network the next time they are connected to the LAN.

4. Linda warns that some users may have huge amounts of data already stored in their My Documents folder on their local system. How might this affect your recommendations?

   At the very least, you must ensure that there is adequate storage available on the network file servers. Furthermore, you should consider the effect on the network when the users log on for the first time when you implement this policy. The default behavior when the redirection is first implemented is for the existing contents of the local My Documents folder to be moved to the network file server. This is almost always a good idea.

If you elect not to move the contents to the new location, when users log on, their My Documents folder will appear empty. Their documents are still on their local hard drive. However, unless the user understands what has happened (and is familiar with navigating the file structure to their own local profile), the files will appear lost, which might generate panic among the users. This is why moving the contents to the new location is recommended. In this case, however, if many users have huge amounts of data, the simultaneous redirection of that amount of data could cause severe network congestion and/or overwhelm the file server. To address this issue, you could use Security Filtering to phase in the redirection, or on the Settings tab of the redirection policy, clear the check box to move contents to the new location. If you select the latter strategy, communication with the users is essential to avoid panic and a flood of calls to the help desk. The files could then be moved manually to the new location or to an alternate location.

5. What tools could you use to document the policies and their effects once they are in place?

Windows Server 2003 includes two tools that would be helpful in documenting the results of policy configurations. Resultant Set Of Policy Wizard (RSoP) in Planning mode will allow you to make RSoP queries based on chosen locations in the Active Directory structure, including the effects of security group filtering, Block Policy Inheritance settings, No Override settings, and even GPOs that reverse earlier GPOs. RSoP queries can then be archived as documentation. Alternatively, Gpresult can be used at the command line to generate RSoP queries. The result of these queries could then be saved to a text file.

12 Deploying Software with Group Policy

Exam Objectives in this Chapter:

- Distribute software by using Group Policy.
- Troubleshoot issues related to Group Policy application and deployment. Tools might include RSoP and the gpresult command.
- Maintain installed software by using Group Policy.
- Distribute updates to software distributed by Group Policy.
- Configure automatic updates for network clients using Group Policy.

Why This Chapter Matters

The information in this chapter shows you how to deploy software with Group Policy, which is essential to meet the changing application needs of organizations. When you deploy software with Group Policy, users no longer need to look for a network share, use a CD-ROM, or install, fix, and upgrade software themselves. Best of all, deploying software with Group Policy reduces the time you must spend administering users' systems. You can also use Group Policy to redeploy, upgrade, or remove applications in the same manner in which they were deployed, which further reduces administrative time.

Lessons in this Chapter:

Before You Begin

To complete the lessons in this chapter, you must

- Prepare your test environment according to the descriptions given in the "Getting Started" section of "About This Book"
- Complete the practices for installing and configuring Active Directory as discussed in Chapter 2, "Installing and Configuring Active Directory"

- Learn to use Active Directory administration tools as discussed in Chapter 3, "Administering Active Directory"

- Complete the practices for configuring sites and replication as discussed in Chapter 5, "Configuring Sites and Managing Replication"

- Complete the practices for implementing an organizational unit (OU) structure as discussed in Chapter 6, "Implementing an OU Structure"

- Complete the practices for creating and maintaining user accounts as discussed in Chapter 7, "Administering User Accounts"

- Complete the practices for creating and administering group accounts as discussed in Chapter 8, "Administering Groups"

- Complete the practices for implementing Group Policy Objects (GPOs) as discussed in Chapter 10, "Implementing Group Policy"

- Complete the practices for administering GPOs as discussed in Chapter 11, "Administering Group Policy"

Lesson 1: Understanding Software Deployment with Group Policy

The Software Installation and Maintenance feature of IntelliMirror is the administrator's primary tool for managing software within an organization. Managing software with Software Installation and Maintenance provides users with immediate access to the software they need to perform their jobs and ensures that they have an easy and consistent experience when working with software throughout its life cycle. This lesson introduces you to software deployment with Group Policy.

After this lesson, you will be able to

- Identify the hardware requirements for deploying software by using Group Policy
- Describe the tools provided for software development
- Differentiate between assigning applications and publishing applications
- Explain the purpose of Windows Installer packages
- Describe the three types of Windows Installer packages
- Explain the purpose of modifications
- Describe the two types of modifications
- Describe the steps in the software deployment process

Estimated lesson time: 15 minutes

Understanding Software Deployment with Group Policy

You use the Software Installation and Maintenance feature of IntelliMirror to create a managed software environment with the following characteristics:

- Users have access to the applications they need to do their jobs, no matter which computer they log on to.

- Computers have the required applications, without intervention from a technical support representative.

- Applications can be updated, maintained, or removed to meet the needs of the organization.

The Software Installation and Maintenance feature of IntelliMirror works in conjunction with Group Policy and Active Directory directory service, establishing a Group Policy–based software management system. To deploy software by using Group Policy, an organization must be running Microsoft Windows 2000 Server or later, with Active Directory and Group Policy on the server, and Microsoft Windows 2000 Professional or later on the client computers.

The following tools are provided for software deployment with Group Policy:

■ **Software Installation extension**   Located in the Group Policy Object Editor console on the server, this extension is used by administrators to manage software.

■ **Add Or Remove Programs**   Located in Control Panel on the client machine, this option is used by users to manage software on their own computers.

Software Installation Extension

The Software Installation extension in the Group Policy Object Editor console is the key administrative tool for deploying software, allowing administrators to centrally manage

■ Initial deployment of software

■ Upgrades, patches, and quick fixes for software

■ Removal of software

By using the Software Installation extension, you can centrally manage the installation of software on a client computer by assigning applications to users or computers or by publishing applications for users. You *assign* required or mandatory software to users or to computers. You *publish* software that users might find useful to perform their jobs. Both assigned and published software is stored in a *software distribution point (SDP)*, a network location from which users are able to get the software that they need. In Microsoft Windows Server 2003, the network location can include SDPs located in other forests in which two-way forests trusts have been established.

Exam Tip   Know the difference between assigning software and publishing software.

Assigning Applications

When you assign an application to a user, the application is advertised to the user on the Start menu the next time he or she logs on to a workstation, and local registry settings, including filename extensions, are updated. The application advertisement follows the user regardless of which physical computer he or she logs on to. This application is installed the first time the user activates the application on the computer, either by selecting the application on the Start menu or by opening a document associated with the application.

When you assign an application to the computer, the application is advertised, and the installation is performed when it is safe to do so. Typically, this happens when the computer starts up so that there are no competing processes running on the computer. Assigned software is fully installed the next time the computer is restarted.

Publishing Applications

When you publish an application to users, the application does not appear installed on the users' computers. No shortcuts are visible on the desktop or Start menu, and no updates are made to the local registry on the users' computers. Instead, published applications store their advertisement attributes in Active Directory. Then, information such as the application's name and file associations is exposed to the users in the Active Directory container. The application is available for the user to install by using Add Or Remove Programs in Control Panel or by clicking a file associated with the application (such as an .xls file for Microsoft Excel).

The Windows Installer Service

The Software Installation extension uses the Windows Installer service to systematically maintain software. The Windows Installer service runs in the background and allows the operating system to manage the installation process in accordance with the information in the Windows Installer package. The *Windows Installer package* is a file containing information that describes the installed state of the application.

Because the Windows Installer service manages the state of the installation, it always knows the state of the software. If there is a problem during software installation, Windows Installer can return the computer to its last known good state. If you need to modify features after software installation, Windows Installer allows you to do so. Because the Software Installation extension uses Windows Installer, users can take advantage of self-repairing applications. Windows Installer notes when a program file is missing and immediately reinstalls the damaged or missing files, thereby fixing the application. Finally, Windows Installer enables you to remove the software when it is no longer needed.

The Windows Installer service itself is affected by settings in Group Policy. You can find these settings in the Windows Installer node, which is located in the Windows Components node in the Administrative Templates node, for both the Computer Configuration and the User Configuration nodes.

Windows Installer Packages   A Windows Installer package is a file that contains explicit instructions on the installation and removal of specific applications. You can deploy software using the Software Installation extension by using a Windows Installer package. There are two types of Windows Installer packages:

- **Native Windows Installer package (.msi) files**   These files have been developed as a part of the application and take full advantage of Windows Installer. The author or publisher of the software can supply a natively authored Windows Installer package.

- **Repackaged application (.msi) files**   These files are used to repackage applications that do not have a native Windows Installer package. Although repackaged Windows Installer packages work the same as native Windows Installer packages, a repackaged Windows Installer package contains a single product with all the components and applications associated with that product installed as a single feature. A native Windows Installer package contains a single product with many features that can be individually installed as separate features.

Customizing Windows Installer Packages   You can customize Windows Installer packages by using modifications, also called transforms. The Windows Installer package format provides for customization by allowing you to "transform" the original package using authoring and repackaging tools. Some applications also provide wizards or templates that permit a user to create modifications.

For example, Microsoft Office XP supplies a Customization Wizard that builds modifications. Using the Office XP Customization Wizard, you can create a modification that allows you to manage the configuration of Office XP that is deployed to users. A modification might be designed to accommodate Microsoft Word as a key feature, installing it during the first installation. Less popular features, such as revision support or document translators, could install on first usage, and other features, such as clip art, might not install at all. You might have another modification that provides all of the features of Word and does not install Microsoft PowerPoint. In addition, you can make modifications to customize the installation of a Windows Installer package at the time of assignment or publication. The exact mix of which features to install and when to install them varies based on the audience for the application and how they use the software. You can use the following file types to modify an existing Windows Installer package:

- **Transform (.mst) files**   These files provide a means for customizing the installation of an application.

- **Patch (.msp) files**   These files are used to update an existing .msi file for software patches, service packs, and some software update files, including bug fixes. An .msp file provides instructions about applying the updated files and registry keys in the software patch, service pack, or software update.

> **Note**   You cannot deploy .mst or .msp files alone. They must modify an existing Windows Installer package.

Application (.zap) Files

You can also deploy software using the Software Installation extension by using an *application file*. Application files are text files that contain instructions about how to publish an application, taken from an existing setup program (Setup.exe or Install.exe). Application files use the .zap extension. Use .zap files when you can't justify developing a native Windows Installer package or repackaging the application to create a repackaged Windows Installer package. A .zap file does not support the features of Windows Installer. When you deploy an application by using a .zap file, the application is installed by using its original Setup.exe or Install.exe program. The software can only be published and users can only select it by using Add Or Remove Programs in Control Panel. It is recommended that you use .msi files to deploy software with Group Policy whenever possible.

Note   For more information on creating .zap files, see Microsoft Knowledge Base article 231747 titled "HOW TO: Publish non-MSI Programs with .zap Files," available from *http://support.microsoft.com*.

Add Or Remove Programs in Control Panel

Add Or Remove Programs in Control Panel enables users to install, modify, or remove an existing published application or repair a damaged application. You can control which software is available to users within Add Or Remove Programs in Control Panel by using Group Policy settings. Users no longer need to look for a network share, use a CD-ROM, or install, fix, and upgrade software themselves.

Software Deployment Approaches

Given that software can be either assigned or published, and targeted to users or computers, you can establish a workable combination to meet your software management goals. Table 12-1 details the different software deployment approaches.

Table 12-1   Software Deployment Approaches

Deployment Approaches	Publish (User Only)	Assign (User)	Assign (Computer)
After deployment, the software is available for installation	The next time a user logs on	The next time a user logs on	The next time the computer starts
Typically the user installs the software from	Add Or Remove Programs in Control Panel	Start menu or desktop shortcut	The software is already installed (the software automatically installs when the computer reboots)

Table 12-1 Software Deployment Approaches

Deployment Approaches	Publish (User Only)	Assign (User)	Assign (Computer)
If the software is not installed, and the user opens a file associated with the software, does the software install?	Yes (if auto-install is turned on)	Yes	Does not apply; the software is already installed
Can the user remove the software using Add Or Remove Programs in Control Panel?	Yes, and the user can choose to install it again from Add Or Remove Programs in Control Panel	Yes, and the software is available for installation again from the typical install points	No. Only the local administrator can remove the software; a user can run a repair on the software
Supported installation files	Windows Installer packages (.msi files), .zap files	Windows Installer packages (.msi files)	Windows Installer packages (.msi files)

Modifications (.mst or .msp files) are customizations applied to Windows Installer packages. A modification must be applied at the time of assignment or publication, not at the time of installation.

Software Deployment Processes

The steps in software deployment vary, depending on whether the application is published or assigned and whether the application is automatically installed by activating a document associated with the application.

Software Deployment Process for Published Applications

The following sequence shows the installation process for published applications:

1. The user logs on to a client computer running Windows 2000 or later.

2. The user opens Add Or Remove Programs in Control Panel.

3. Add Or Remove Programs obtains the list of published software from Active Directory.

4. The user selects the desired application.

5. Add Or Remove Programs obtains the location of published software from Active Directory.

6. A request for the software is sent to the SDP.

7. The Windows Installer service is started, and it installs the requested Windows Installer package.

8. The user opens the newly-installed application.

Software Deployment Process for Assigned Applications

The following sequence shows the installation process for assigned applications:

1. The user logs on to a client computer running Windows 2000 or later.

2. The WinLogon process advertises applications on the user's desktop or on the Start menu.

3. The user selects the desired application from the desktop or the Start menu.

4. The Windows Installer service gets the Windows Installer package.

5. A request for the software is sent to the SDP.

6. The Windows Installer service is started, it installs the requested Windows Installer package, and it opens the application.

Software Deployment Process for Automatically Installed Applications

The following sequence shows the installation process for automatically installed applications, whether published or assigned:

1. The user logs on to a client computer running Windows 2000 or later.

2. The user double-clicks a document with an unknown filename extension.

3. Windows Server 2003 looks for information about the application in the local computer registry.

4. One of the following steps is taken:

   ❑ If information about the application is found in the local computer registry, the registry points to the location of the application on the SDP and the corresponding Windows Installer package is started. The Windows Installer service installs the package for the user and opens the application.

   ❑ If information about the application is not found in the local computer registry, Windows Server 2003 looks for information in Active Directory. If information about the application is found in Active Directory, it points to the location of the application on the SDP. The Windows Installer service installs the package for the user and opens the application.

Distributing Windows Installer Packages

Because the Windows Installer service is part of the operating system, it does not matter how Windows Installer packages get to the client computer. If you are deploying software to many users in a large organization that is using Windows 2000 Server or later and Active Directory, and all of the workstations are using Windows 2000

Professional or later, you can deploy software with Group Policy. For large-scale deployments or deployments with computers running pre-Windows 2000 operating systems, you might also consider using the Microsoft Systems Management Server (SMS) along with Group Policy to handle software deployment.

Software deployment with Group Policy uses a *pull model*, which makes software available to users as it is needed. Applications are fully installed when a user chooses to use a user-assigned application for the first time or selects a file by choosing the file-name extension of an application. For a satisfactory end-user experience, software deployment with Group Policy requires a high-speed local area network (LAN) connection between the client computer and the distribution server containing the SDP.

SMS supports a robust distribution model that you can use when deploying software with Group Policy. You can use SMS to analyze your network infrastructure for software distribution and then use Group Policy to target users and computers and to install the software. SMS is a particularly useful tool if you are deploying software to many users in a large organization. It includes desktop management and software distribution features that significantly automate the task of upgrading software on client computers.

SMS uses a *push model* for software deployment, which you can use to coordinate and schedule software deployments, even arranging for off-hours distribution and installation, and to plan a single or multiple-phase rollout of software. It provides you with the ability to control and synchronize software deployments over multiple sites, helping to reduce compatibility issues that might otherwise occur.

The following are some of the areas where you might want to supplement software deployment with Group Policy by using SMS:

- **Non–Windows 2000–based clients**   SMS can distribute Windows Installer-based software to computers running Microsoft Windows 95 or later. Although you cannot centrally manage the non–Windows 2000–based computers with Group Policy settings, SMS allows these computers to benefit from the capabilities built into the Windows Installer service, such as self-repairing applications.

- **Deploying software over slow links**   By default, software deployment with Group Policy does not operate over slow network or dial-up connections. SMS provides options for deploying software to users who can connect only over slow network links, such as mobile users.

- **Software licensing and metering**   Software deployment with Group Policy does not have the ability to license or meter software.

- **Identification of computer configurations**   Before you distribute a managed application, you can use SMS to determine current computer configurations to

make sure that the appropriate computers have the necessary system requirements to run the application.

Configuring SMS to handle software deployment is beyond the scope of this training
kit. You can find detailed information about SMS in the Microsoft Windows Server 2003
Resource Kit, available from the Microsoft Web site at *http://www.microsoft.com*
/windowsserver2003/techinfo/reskit/resourcekit.mspx.

Lesson Review

The following questions are intended to reinforce key information presented in this
lesson. If you are unable to answer a question, review the lesson and then try the question again. Answers to the questions can be found in the "Questions and Answers" section at the end of this chapter.

1. What are the hardware requirements for deploying software by using Group Policy?

_____

_____

2. Describe the tools provided for software deployment.

_____

_____

3. What is the difference between assigning applications and publishing applications?

_____

_____

4. What is the purpose of Windows Installer packages?

_____

_____

5. Which of the following file extensions allows you to deploy software using the
Software Installation extension? (Choose two.)

    a. .mst

    b. .msi

    c. .zap

    d. .zip

    e. .msp

    f. .aas

Lesson Summary

- The Software Installation extension in the Group Policy Object Editor console enables administrators to centrally manage the installation of software on a client computer by assigning applications to users or computers or by publishing applications for users.

- When you assign an application to a user, the application is advertised to the user on the Start menu the next time he or she logs on to a workstation, and local registry settings, including filename extensions, are updated. The application advertisement follows the user regardless of which physical computer he or she logs on to. Assign required or mandatory software to users or to computers.

- When you publish the application to users, the application does not appear installed on the users' computers. No shortcuts are visible on the desktop or Start menu, and no updates are made to the local registry on the users' computers. If users choose, they can install the software from Add Or Remove Programs in Control Panel. Publish software that users might find useful to perform their jobs.

- A Windows Installer package is a file that contains explicit instructions on the installation and removal of specific applications. You can deploy software using the Software Installation extension by using a Windows Installer package. Windows Installer packages can be native or repackaged .msi files.

- Modifications enable you to customize Windows Installer packages. Modifications can be transform (.mst) or patch (.msp) files. You cannot deploy .mst or .msp files alone. They must modify an existing Windows Installer package.

Lesson 2: Deploying Software with Group Policy

After you've familiarized yourself with the software deployment tools, the Windows Installer service, and the software deployment processes, you're ready to learn how to deploy software with Group Policy. This lesson walks you through the steps of deploying software with Group Policy.

After this lesson, you will be able to

- Plan and prepare a software deployment
- Set up an SDP
- Create a GPO for software deployment
- Specify software deployment properties for a GPO
- Add Windows Installer packages to a GPO
- Set Windows Installer package properties

Estimated lesson time: 45 minutes

Deploying Software with Group Policy

The tasks for deploying software with Group Policy are:

1. Plan and prepare the software deployment

2. Set up an SDP

3. Create a GPO and a GPO console for software deployment

4. Specify the software deployment properties for the GPO

5. Add Windows Installer packages to the GPO and select package deployment method

6. Set Windows Installer package properties

Exam Tip   Know the tasks for deploying software with Group Policy.

Planning and Preparing a Software Deployment

Before you can begin deploying software with Group Policy, you must plan the deployment. When planning for software deployment, you should

- Review your organization's software requirements on the basis of your overall organizational structure within Active Directory and your available GPOs
- Determine how you want to deploy your applications

■ Create a pilot to test how you want to assign or publish software to users or computers

■ Prepare your software using a format that allows you to manage it based on what your organization requires, and test all of the Windows Installer packages or repackaged software

Table 12-2 describes strategies and considerations for deploying software. Some of these strategies might seem contradictory, but select the strategies that meet your business goals.

Table 12-2 Strategies and Considerations for Deploying Software

Strategy	Considerations
Create OUs based on software management needs.	Allows you to target applications to the appropriate set of users. Group Policy security settings are not required to target the appropriate set of users.
Deploy software close to the root in the Active Directory tree.	Makes it easy to provide all users in an organization with access to an application. This reduces administration because you can deploy a single GPO rather than having to re-create that object in multiple containers deep in the Active Directory tree.
Deploy multiple applications with a single GPO.	Reduces administration overhead by allowing you to create and manage a single GPO rather than multiple GPOs. The logon process is faster because a single GPO deploying 10 applications processes faster than 10 GPOs, each deploying one application. This is appropriate in organizations where users share the same core set of applications.
Publish or assign an application only once in the same GPO or in a series of GPOs that might apply to a single user or computer.	Makes it easier to determine which instance of the application applies to the user or computer.

Software licenses are required for software written by independent software vendors and distributed using SDPs. It is your responsibility to match the number of users who can access software to the number of licenses you have on hand. It is also your responsibility to verify that you are working within the guidelines provided by each independent software vendor with the software.

Gather the Windows Installer packages (.msi files) for the software. Perform any necessary modifications to the packages and gather the transform (.mst) or patch (.msp) files.

Setting Up an SDP

After you have planned and prepared for software management, the next step is to copy the software to one or more SDPs, network locations from which users are able to get the software that they need.

To set up an SDP, complete the following steps:

1. Create the folders for the software on the file server that will be the SDP and make the folders network shares; for example: *servername**sharename*.

2. Replicate the software to the SDP by placing or copying the software, packages, modifications, all necessary files, and components to a separate folder on the SDP.

> **Note**   Some software supports special commands to facilitate the creation of an SDP. For example, Office XP should be prepared by running **setup /a** from a command prompt. This allows you to enter the software key once for all users, and the network share (SDP) location to copy the files to. Other software might have other ways to expand any compressed files from the distribution media and transfer the files to the appropriate location.

3. Set the appropriate permissions on the folders. Administrators must be able to change the files (Full Control), and users must only view (Read) the files from the SDP folders and shares. Use Group Policy to manage the software within the appropriate GPO.

Using DFS to Manage SDPs

The Microsoft Distributed File System (DFS) provides users with convenient access to shared folders that are distributed throughout a network. With DFS, you can make files distributed across multiple servers appear to users as if they reside in one place on the network. For a software deployment with Group Policy, you can set up DFS to automatically direct users to the nearest SDP.

> **See Also**   Configuring DFS to manage SDPs is beyond the scope of this training kit. You can find detailed information about configuring DFS in the Microsoft Windows Server 2003 Resource Kit available at the Microsoft Web site at *http://www.microsoft.com /windowsserver2003/techinfo/reskit/resourcekit.mspx*.

Creating a GPO and a GPO Console for Software Deployment

In this step, you create a GPO and a GPO console for the software deployment. The procedures for creating a GPO and a GPO console are covered in Chapter 10, "Implementing Group Policy."

Specifying Software Deployment Properties for the GPO

In this step, you define the default settings for all Windows Installer packages in the GPO in the Software Installation Properties dialog box. The Software Installation Properties dialog box consists of the following tabs—General, Advanced, File Extensions, and Categories.

In the General and Advanced tabs, you specify how you want all Windows Installer packages in the GPO to be deployed and managed.

In the File Extensions tab, you specify which application users install when they select a file with an unknown extension. You can also configure a priority for installing applications when multiple applications are associated with an unknown file extension. For example, if you use a GPO to deploy both Microsoft Office XP Professional and Microsoft Office FrontPage version 2002, both of these applications can edit Spreadsheet Load Library files with the .sll extension. To configure the file extension priority so that users who are managed by this GPO always install FrontPage, set FrontPage as the application with the highest priority for the .sll extension. When a user managed by this GPO who has installed neither Microsoft Office Word version 2002 nor FrontPage 2002 receives an .sll file (by e-mail or other means) and double-clicks the .sll file, Software Installation installs FrontPage 2000 and opens the .sll file for editing. Without Software Installation, the user would see the Open With dialog box and be asked to select the best alternative from the software already present on his or her computer. File extension associations are managed on a per-GPO basis. Changing the priority order in a GPO affects only those users who have that GPO applied to them.

In the Categories tab, you can designate categories for organizing assigned and published applications to make it easier for users to locate the appropriate application from within Add Or Remove Programs in Control Panel.

> **Note** Some of the settings in the Software Installation Properties dialog box can be fine-tuned at the package level by editing the Properties dialog box for a specific Windows Installer package.

To specify software deployment properties for the GPO, complete the following steps:

1. Open the GPO console for the software deployment.

2. In the User Configuration or the Computer Configuration node, right-click the Software Installation node, and then click Properties.

3. In the General tab of the Software Installation Properties dialog box (shown in Figure 12-1), type the Uniform Naming Convention (UNC) path (*servername*

sharename) to the SDP for the Windows Installer packages (.msi files) in the GPO in the Default Package Location box.

Figure 12-1   The General tab of the Software Installation Properties dialog box

4. In the New Packages section, select one of the following:

   ❑ Display The Deploy Software Dialog Box, to specify that when you add new packages to the GPO, the Deploy Software dialog box will display, allowing you to choose whether to assign, publish, or configure package properties. This is the default setting.

   ❑ Publish, to specify that when you add new packages to the GPO, they will be published by default with standard package properties. Packages can be published only to users, not computers. If this is an installation under the Computer Configuration node of the Group Policy Object Editor console, the Publish choice is unavailable.

   ❑ Assign, to specify that when you add new packages to the GPO, they will be assigned by default with standard package properties. Packages can be assigned to users and computers.

   ❑ Advanced, to specify that when you add new packages to the GPO, the Properties dialog box for the package will display, allowing you to configure all properties for the package.

5. In the Installation User Interface Options section, select one of the following:

   ❑ Basic, to provide only a basic display for users during the installation of all packages in the GPO.

❑ Maximum, to provide all installation messages and screens for users during the installation of all packages in the GPO.

6. Click the Advanced tab. In the Advanced tab, shown in Figure 12-2, select any of the following, to be applied to all packages in the GPO:

❑ Uninstall The Applications When They Fall Out Of The Scope Of Management, to remove the application if it no longer applies to users or computers.

❑ Include OLE Information When Deploying Applications, to specify whether to deploy information about Component Object Model (COM) components with the package.

❑ Make 32-Bit X86 Windows Installer Applications Available To Win64 Machines, to specify whether 32-bit Windows Installer Applications (.msi files) can be assigned or published to 64-bit computers.

❑ Make 32-Bit X86 Down-Level (ZAP) Applications Available To Win64 Machines, to specify whether 32-bit application files (.zap files) can be assigned or published to 64-bit computers.

> **Off the Record**   In rare instances, when applications installed with Software Installation cannot be uninstalled by using Group Policy or Add/Remove Programs, you can use the MSICUU.exe (Windows Installer Cleanup Utility) or the MSIZAP.exe (Windows Installer Zapper) programs. These utilities are part of the Windows Support Tools, which you installed in Chapter 2. MSICUU is a graphical utility and MSIZAP is the command line version. MSICUU uses MSIZAP to remove applications. For detailed information about using these commands, refer to Windows Server 2003 Help.

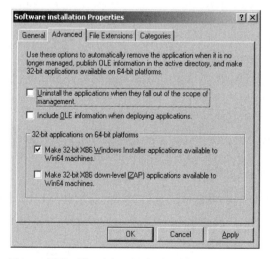

Figure 12-2   The Advanced tab of the Software Installation Properties dialog box

7. Click the File Extensions tab. In the File Extensions tab, shown in Figure 12-3, select the file extension for which you want to specify an automatic software installation from the Select File Extension list.

Figure 12-3   The File Extensions tab of the Software Installation Properties dialog box

8. In the Application Precedence list box, move the application with the highest precedence to the top of the list using the Up or Down buttons. The application at the top of the list is automatically installed if a document with the selected filename extension is invoked before the application has been installed.

9. Click the Categories tab. In the Categories tab, shown in Figure 12-4, click Add.

Figure 12-4   The Categories tab of the Software Installation Properties dialog box

10. In the Enter New Category dialog box, type the name of the application category to be used for the domain in the Category box and click OK.

> **Note** The application categories that you establish are per domain, not per GPO. You need to define them only once for the whole domain.

11. Click OK.

Adding Windows Installer Packages to the GPO and Selecting Package Deployment Method

In this step, you specify the software applications you want to deploy by adding Windows Installer packages to the GPO. Then you specify how the package is deployed (either assigned or published).

> **Note** The procedures in this step assume that you have chosen the Display The Deploy Software Dialog Box option (the default option that allows you to choose whether to assign or publish the application) in the software deployment properties for the GPO.

To modify or update the software application, any modifications must be associated with the Windows Installer package at deployment time rather than when the Windows Installer is actually using the package. Transform (.mst) and patch (.msp) files are applied to Windows Installer packages (which have the .msi extension) in an order specified by the administrator. This order must be determined before the application is assigned or published.

To add Windows Installer packages to the GPO and select package deployment method, complete the following steps:

1. Open the GPO console for the software deployment. In the Computer Configuration or User Configuration node, open Software Settings.

2. Right-click the Software Installation node, click New, and then click Package.

3. In the Open dialog box, in the File Name list, type the UNC path (***servername******sharename***) to the SDP for the Windows Installer packages (.msi files), and then click Open.

> **Caution** Be sure to enter the UNC path to the SDP in the File Name list. If you merely browse and select the Windows Installer package to be added to the GPO, you have entered only the local path and clients will not be able to find the Windows Installer package.

4. In the Deploy Software dialog box (shown in Figure 12-5), click one of the following:

❑ Published, to publish the Windows Installer package to users without applying modifications to the package.

❑ Assigned, to assign the Windows Installer package to users or computers without applying modifications to the package.

❑ Advanced, to set properties for the Windows Installer package, including published or assigned options and modifications.

> **Note**   If this is an application under the Computer Configuration node of the Group Policy Object Editor console, the Published option is unavailable, because packages can only be assigned to computers, not published.

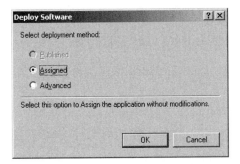

Figure 12-5   The Deploy Software dialog box

5. Click OK. If you selected Published or Assigned, the Windows Installer package has been successfully added to the GPO and appears in the details pane. If you selected Advanced, the Properties dialog box for the Windows Installer package opens, where you can set properties for the Windows Installer package, such as deployment options and modifications. Setting Windows Installer package properties is covered in the next section.

Setting Windows Installer Package Properties

In this step, you can fine-tune the deployment of each application by setting Windows Installer package properties in the Properties dialog box for the package. The Properties dialog box for the Windows Installer package contains the following tabs: General, Deployment, Upgrades, Categories, Modifications, and Security.

In the General tab, you can change the default name of the package and designate a support URL. Users can select a support URL from the Add Or Remove Programs window to be directed to a support Web page. A support URL can contain helpful information such as frequently asked questions (FAQs) and can assist in reducing calls to a help desk or support team. In the Deployment tab, you can designate the deployment type, deployment options, and installation user interface options. In the Upgrades tab, you can deploy a package that upgrades an existing package. The Upgrades tab does not appear for packages created from application files (.zap files). Using the Upgrades tab is discussed in Lesson 3. In the Categories tab, you can select the categories under which the application is listed for users in Add Or Remove Programs in Control Panel, making it easier for users to find the application. Categories you set generally pertain to published applications only, as assigned applications do not appear in Add Or Remove Programs. In the Modifications tab, you can indicate the modifications (transforms or patches) you want to apply to the package and specify the order in which the modifications apply to the package. In the Security tab, you can indicate permissions for the software installation. Permissions set for software installation pertain only to the package installation.

> **Note**   Some of the settings in the Properties dialog box for the Windows Installer package can be set at the GPO level by editing the Software Installation Properties dialog box.

To set Windows Installer package properties, complete the following steps:

1. Open the GPO console for the software deployment. In the Computer Configuration or User Configuration node, open Software Settings.

2. Click the Software Installation node.

3. In the details pane, right-click the package for which you want to set properties, and then click Properties.

4. In the General tab of the Properties dialog box for the package, shown in Figure 12-6, you can type a new name for the package in the Name box, if desired. You can also type a URL that provides user support in the URL box.

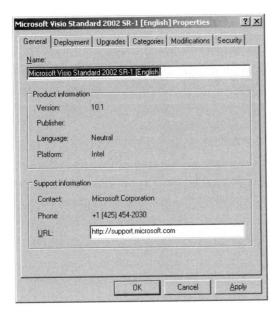

Figure 12-6   The General tab of the Properties dialog box for a package

5. Click the Deployment tab. In the Deployment tab of the Properties dialog box for the package, shown in Figure 12-7, select one of the following in the Deployment Type area:

❑ Published, to allow users in the selected site, domain, or OU to install the application using either Add Or Remove Programs in Control Panel or application installation by file activation. If this is an application under the Computer Configuration node of the Group Policy Object Editor console, the Published option is unavailable, because packages can only be assigned to computers, not published.

❑ Assigned, to allow users in the selected site, domain, or OU to receive this application the next time they log on (for assignment to users) or when the computer restarts (for assignment to computers).

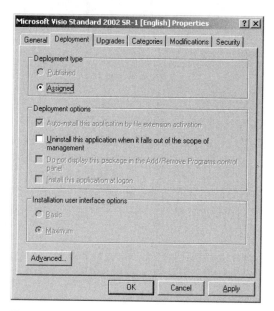

Figure 12-7   The Deployment tab of the Properties dialog box for a package

6. In the Deployment Options area, select one of the following:

❏ Auto-Install This Application By File Extension Activation, to use the application precedence for the filename extension as determined in the File Extensions tab of the Software Installation Properties dialog box. If this is an application under the Computer Configuration node of the Group Policy Object Editor console, the check box appears dimmed and selected, because by default the application is installed automatically.

❏ Uninstall This Application When It Falls Out Of The Scope Of Management, to remove the application when users log on or computers start up in the event of relocation to a site, domain, or OU for which the application is not deployed.

❏ Do Not Display This Package In The Add/Remove Programs Control Panel, to specify that this package should not be displayed in Add Or Remove Programs in Control Panel.

❏ Install This Application At Logon, to specify that this package should be fully installed rather than just advertised by a shortcut. This option is available only for assigned applications. Avoid this option if the computer or user to which the application is assigned has a slow connection because the startup and logon procedures require a large amount of time when the application is first assigned.

7. In the Installation User Interface Options area, select one of the following:

❑ Basic, to provide only a basic display to users during the install process.

❑ Maximum, to provide all installation messages and screens to users during the package installation.

8. Click Advanced to display the Advanced Deployment Options dialog box, shown in Figure 12-8. In the Advanced Deployment Options area, select any of the following check boxes:

❑ Ignore Language When Deploying This Package, to specify whether to deploy the package even if it is in a different language.

❑ Make This 32-Bit X86 Application Available To Win64 Machines, to specify whether the 32-bit program is assigned or published to 64-bit computers.

❑ Include OLE Class And Product Information, to specify whether to deploy information about COM components with the package.

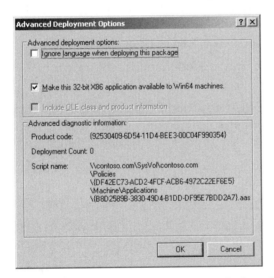

Figure 12-8   The Advanced Deployment Options dialog box

9. Click OK.

10. Click the Categories tab. In the Categories tab of the Properties dialog box for the package, shown in Figure 12-9, click the category under which you want to display this application to users from the Available Categories list, and then click Select.

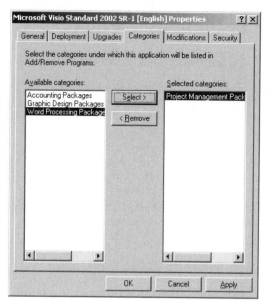

Figure 12-9 The Categories tab of the Properties dialog box for a package

11. Click the Modifications tab. In the Modifications tab, shown in Figure 12-10, do any of the following:

- ❏ To add modifications, click Add. In the Open dialog box, browse to find the transform file (.mst) or patch file (.msp), and then click Open. You can add multiple modifications.

- ❏ To remove modifications, click the modification you want to remove, and then click Remove. Repeat until each unwanted modification has been removed.

- ❏ To set the order of modifications, select a modification and then click Move Up or Move Down. Modifications are applied according to the order specified in the list.

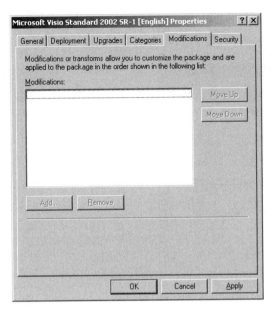

Figure 12-10   The Modifications tab of the Properties dialog box for a package

Important   Do not click OK in the Modifications tab until you have finished configuring the modifications. When you click OK, the package is assigned or published immediately. If the modifications are not properly configured, you will have to uninstall the package or upgrade the package with a correctly configured version.

12. Click the Security tab. In the Security tab of the Properties dialog box for the package, shown in Figure 12-11, click the security group on which to set permissions. Administrators who manage the application installation should have the Full Control permission set to Allow. Users who use the software assigned or published by the application should have the Read permission set to Allow.

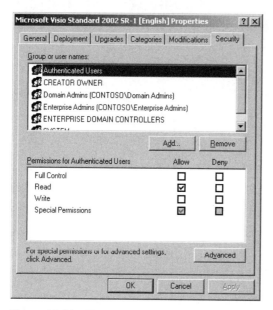

Figure 12-11   The Security tab of the Properties dialog box for a package

13. Click OK.

Software Deployment Best Practices

The following are the best practices for deploying software with Group Policy:

- **Assign or publish just once per GPO**   A Windows Installer package should be assigned or published no more than once in the same GPO. For example, if you assign Office to the computers affected by a GPO, then do not assign or publish it to users affected by the GPO.

- **Assign or publish close to the root in the Active Directory hierarchy**   Because Group Policy settings apply by default to child Active Directory containers, it is efficient to assign or publish by linking a GPO to a parent OU or domain. Use security descriptors—access control entries (ACEs)—on the GPO for finer control over who receives the software.

- **Make sure Windows Installer packages include modifications before they are published or assigned**   Remember that modifications are applied to packages at the time of assignment or publication. Therefore, you should make sure the Modifications tab in the Properties dialog box for the package is set up as you intend before you click OK. If you neglect to do this and assign or publish a modified package before you have completely configured it, you must either remove the software and republish or reassign it or upgrade the software with a completely modified version.

- **Specify application categories for your organization**   It's easier for users to find an application in Add Or Remove Programs in Control Panel when you use categories.

- **Take advantage of authoring tools**   Developers familiar with the files, registry entries, and other requirements for an application to work properly can author native Windows Installer packages using tools available from various software vendors.

- **Repackage existing software**   You can use commercially available tools to create Windows Installer packages for software that does not include natively authored .msi files. These work by comparing a computer's state before and after installation. For best results, install on a computer free of other application software.

- **Set properties for the GPO to provide widely scoped control**   This spares administrative keystrokes when assigning or publishing a large number of packages with similar properties in a single GPO—for example, when all the software is published and it all comes from the same SDP.

- **Set properties for the Windows Installer package to provide fine control**   Use the package properties for assigning or publishing a single package.

- **Know when to use Group Policy Software Installation and Systems Management Server (SMS)**   Use Group Policy Software Installation for simple software installation and deployment scenarios. Use SMS when scheduling, inventory, reporting, status, and support for installation across a wide area network (WAN) are required.

Practice: Deploying Software with Group Policy

In this practice, you deploy (assign and publish) the Windows Server 2003 Administration Tools Pack with Group Policy. Installing the Administration Tools Pack on a computer that is not a domain controller allows you to administer Active Directory remotely. Windows Server 2003, Enterprise Edition ships with the Windows Installer package Adminpak.msi, which is used for installing the Windows Server 2003 Administration Tools Pack. Use the procedures provided earlier in this lesson to complete each exercise.

Exercise 1: Preparing Server2

In this exercise, you prepare Server2 for its role as a member server in the *contoso.com* domain. To complete this practice, you must first demote Server2, which was made an additional domain controller in the *contoso.com* domain in the practice in Chapter 4. You also log on as User17 and observe the available tools in the Administrative Tools menu.

▶ **To prepare Server2**

1. Log on to Server2 as Administrator. Demote Server2. If necessary, refer to Chapter 2 for instructions on removing Active Directory from a domain controller.

2. When Server2 restarts, log on as Administrator. Click Start, right-click My Computer, and then click Properties.

3. In the System Properties dialog box, click the Computer Name tab. In the Computer Name tab, click Change.

4. In the Computer Name Changes dialog box, in the Member Of section, ensure that Domain is selected and that *contoso.com* is listed in the Domain box. Click OK. Click OK in the System Properties dialog box.

5. Log off Server2. Log on Server2 as User17 on the *contoso* domain.

6. Click Start, click Control Panel, and then double-click Administrative Tools. Make a brief note of the tools available to User17 on the Administrative Tools menu.

7. Log off Server2.

Exercise 2: Setting Up an SDP

In this exercise, you set up an SDP for the deployment of the Windows Server 2003 Administration Tools Pack.

▶ **To set up an SDP**

1. Log on to Server1 as Administrator.

2. Create a shared folder named Adminpak in C:\ (where C is the name of your system drive). Name the share **Adminpak**.

3. Search the Windows Server 2003, Enterprise Edition CD-ROM for .msi files. Copy the Adminpak.msi file to the shared Adminpak folder.

4. Set the appropriate permissions on the folder. Administrators must be able to change the files (Full Control), and Users must only view (Read) the files from the SDP folders and shares.

Exercise 3: Configure a GPO for Software Deployment (Assign)

In this exercise, you create a GPO and a GPO console for the deployment of the Windows Server 2003 Administration Tools Pack. Then, you add the Adminpak.msi Windows Installer package to the GPO and assign the package.

▶ **To configure a GPO for software deployment**

1. On Server1, create a GPO in the West OU. Name the GPO **West OU Applications**. Set the No Override option for the West OU Applications GPO in the Group Policy tab in the Properties dialog box for the West OU. This will prevent other GPOs from overriding the policies set in the West OU Applications GPO.

2. Create a console for the West OU Applications GPO. Name the console **West OU Applications GPO**.

3. For the West OU Applications GPO, set the Full Control permission for the Administrators group to Allow. Clear the Apply Group Policy permission (currently set to Allow) for the Authenticated Users group. Do not set this permission to Deny.

4. Ensure that the West OU Applications GPO applies to the Marketing domain local security group by setting the group's Apply Group Policy permission for the GPO in the West OU Applications Group Policy Object Editor console to Allow.

5. Open the West OU Applications GPO console. In the User Configuration node, Software Settings, right-click the Software Installation node, click New, and then click Package.

6. In the Open dialog box, in the File Name list, type the UNC path (**\\Server1\Adminpak**) to the SDP for the Windows Installer packages (.msi files), select the Adminpak.msi file, and then click Open.

7. When you're asked to select a deployment method, indicate that you want to assign the Adminpak.msi package to users.

8. Close and save the West OU Applications GPO console.

Exercise 4: Testing Software Deployment

In this exercise, you test the deployment of the Windows Server 2003 Administration Tools Pack that you assigned to users.

▶ **To test software deployment**

1. Log on to Server2 as User17 in the *contoso* domain.

2. Click Start, click Control Panel, and then click Administrative Tools. In addition to several other new administration tools, you should now be able to see Active Directory Users And Computers, Active Directory Sites And Services, and Active Directory Domains And Trusts in the Administrative Tools menu.

3. Log off Server2.

Exercise 5: Configure a GPO for Software Deployment (Publish)

In this exercise, you create a GPO and a GPO console for the deployment of the Windows Server 2003 Administration Tools Pack. Then, you add the Adminpak.msi Windows Installer package to the GPO and publish the package.

▶ **To configure a GPO for software deployment**

1. On Server1, create a GPO in the East OU. Name the GPO **East OU Applications**.

2. Create a console for the East OU Applications GPO. Name the console **East OU Applications GPO**.

3. For the East OU Applications GPO, set the Full Control permission for the Administrators group to Allow. Clear the Apply Group Policy permission (currently set to Allow) for the Authenticated Users group. Do not set this permission to Deny.

4. Ensure that the East OU Applications GPO applies to the Marketing domain local security group by setting the group's Apply Group Policy permission for the GPO in the East OU Applications Group Policy Object Editor console to Allow.

5. Open the East OU Applications GPO console. In the User Configuration node, in Software Settings, right-click the Software Installation node, click New, and then click Package.

6. In the Open dialog box, in the File Name list, type the UNC path (**\\Server1\Applications**) to the SDP for the Windows Installer packages (.msi files), and then click Open.

7. Indicate that you want to publish the Adminpak.msi package to users.

8. Right-click the Software Installation extension, and then select Properties. In the Software Installation Properties dialog box, click the Categories tab. In the Categories tab, add a new category named **Tools Packages**. Click OK.

9. In the details pane, right-click the package you just created, and then select Properties. In the Administration Tools Pack Properties dialog box, click the Categories tab. Select Tools Packages in the Available Categories list, and then click Select. Click OK.

10. Close and save the East OU Applications GPO console.

Exercise 6: Testing Software Deployment

In this exercise, you test the deployment of the Windows Server 2003 Administration Tools Pack that you published to users.

▶ **To test software deployment**

1. Log on to Server2 as User7.

2. Click Start, point to Run, and then point to Administrative Tools. Note that there are no new tools on the Administrative Tools menu. This is because you have published the application to users.

3. Click Start, and then click Control Panel. In Control Panel, double-click the Add Or Remove Programs icon.

4. In the Add Or Remove Programs window, click the Add New Programs button on the left.

5. In the window provided by Add New Programs, shown in Figure 12-12, note that the Administration Tools Pack is available for you to add to your network. Also note that from the Categories list, you can select Tools Packages.

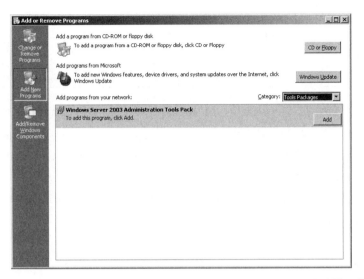

Figure 12-12   The Add Or Remove Programs window, with Add New Programs selected

6. Log off Server2.

Lesson Review

The following questions are intended to reinforce key information presented in this lesson. If you are unable to answer a question, review the lesson and then try the question again. Answers to the questions can be found in the "Questions and Answers" section at the end of this chapter.

1. Why is it necessary to set up an SDP?

   _____

   _____

2. What feature is configured in the File Extensions tab in the Software Installation Properties dialog box?

   _____

   _____

3. What feature is configured in the Categories tab in the Software Installation Properties dialog box?

   _____

   _____

4. What feature is configured in the Modifications tab in the Properties dialog box for a Windows Installer package?

_____

_____

5. You want to ensure that all users of the KC23 workstation can run FrontPage 2000. What action should you perform?

   a. Assign the application to the computer.

   b. Assign the application to users.

   c. Publish the application to the computer.

   d. Publish the application to users.

Lesson Summary

- The tasks for deploying software with Group Policy are the following: plan and prepare the software deployment, set up an SDP, create a GPO and a GPO console for software deployment, specify the software deployment properties for the GPO, add Windows Installer packages to the GPO and select package deployment method, and set Windows Installer package properties.

- For a software deployment with Group Policy, you can set up DFS to automatically direct users to the nearest SDP.

- You can define software deployment properties that affect all Windows Installer packages in a GPO.

- You can also define software deployment properties that affect individual Windows Installer packages in a GPO.

Lesson 3: Maintaining Software Deployed with Group Policy

After the deployment of software applications, it might be necessary to redeploy, upgrade, or remove them at some point in the software life cycle. This lesson shows you how to redeploy, upgrade, and remove software deployed with Group Policy.

After this lesson, you will be able to

- Redeploy an application deployed with Group Policy
- Upgrade an application deployed with Group Policy
- Remove an application deployed with Group Policy

Estimated lesson time: 15 minutes

Redeploying Applications Deployed with Group Policy

You can redeploy an application previously deployed with Group Policy if there are small changes that need to be made to the original software deployment configuration. For example, you might have deployed only Word and Excel in your original Microsoft Office software deployment. You might now need to include PowerPoint in the Office deployment. As long as you make changes to the original Office package deployed with Group Policy, you can redeploy the application to the network.

To redeploy applications deployed with Group Policy, complete the following steps:

1. Open the Group Policy Object Editor console. In the Computer Configuration or User Configuration node, open Software Settings.

2. Click the Software Installation node.

3. In the details pane, right-click the package you want to remove, click All Tasks, and then click Redeploy Application.

4. In the dialog box for the package, click Yes to redeploy the application to all computers on which it is already installed.

Upgrading Applications Deployed with Group Policy

Several events in the life cycle of the software can trigger an upgrade, including the following:

- The original developer of the software might release a new version with new and improved features.

- The organization might choose to use a different vendor's application.

Upgrades typically involve major changes to the software and normally have new version numbers. Usually a substantial number of files change for an upgrade. To establish the procedure to upgrade an existing application to the current release, you must first create a Windows Installer package that contains the upgrade and then configure the upgrade in the Upgrades tab in the Properties dialog box for the package.

> **Note**   The Upgrades tab is not available for packages created from application files (.zap files).

To upgrade applications deployed with Group Policy, complete the following steps:

1. Open the Group Policy Object Editor console. In the Computer Configuration or User Configuration node, open Software Settings.

2. Click the Software Installation node.

3. Create a new Windows Installer package that contains the upgrade. Assign or publish this new package.

4. In the details pane, right-click the Windows Installer package that will function as the upgrade (not the package to be upgraded), and then click Properties.

5. In the Upgrades tab of the Properties dialog box for the upgrade package, shown in Figure 12-13, click Add.

Figure 12-13   The Upgrades tab of the Properties dialog box for a package

6. In the Add Upgrade Package dialog box, shown in Figure 12-14, select one of the following:

❏ Current Group Policy Object (GPO), if you want to upgrade a package in the current GPO.

❏ A Specific GPO, if you want to upgrade a package in another GPO. Then click Browse, select the GPO you want, and then in the Browse For A Group Policy Object dialog box, click OK.

Figure 12-14 The Add Upgrade Package dialog box

A list of all the packages assigned or published within the selected GPO appears in the Package To Upgrade list. Depending on the GPO, this list can have zero or more entries.

7. Select the package you want to upgrade in the Package To Upgrade list.

8. Select one of the following:

❏ Uninstall The Existing Package, Then Install The Upgrade Package, to remove the existing package before the upgrade is installed. This option is used if you want to replace an application with a completely different one (perhaps from a different vendor).

❏ Package Can Upgrade Over The Existing Package, to install the upgrade without removing the previous version. This option is used if you want to install a newer version of the same product while retaining the user's application preferences, document type associations, and so on.

9. Click OK.

10. In the Upgrades tab in the Properties dialog box for the package, select the Required Upgrade For Existing Packages check box if you want the upgrade to be mandatory, and then click OK. If this is an upgrade under the Computer Configuration node of the Group Policy Object Editor console, the check box appears dimmed and selected, because packages can only be assigned to computers, not published.

> **Note**   If the Required Upgrade For Existing Packages check box is not selected, users have the option of applying the upgrade, which could cause application version variances within an organization.

11. Click OK.

Removing Applications Deployed with Group Policy

At some point, users might no longer require an application, so you might need to remove it. In Chapter 10, you learned to terminate the effects of a GPO by unlinking or deleting the GPO. However, if you delete a GPO that deploys a software application, the application cannot be uninstalled with Group Policy. If the application cannot be uninstalled with Group Policy, you (or the users) must manually uninstall the application from each client computer. To avoid this hazard, you must remove applications deployed with Group Policy in three steps:

1. Choose the software removal method you want to implement.

2. Allow the software removal to be processed.

3. Delete the GPO.

Because a great number of users and their computers can be affected by the removal of applications deployed with Group Policy, you should carefully consider the effects of removing these applications.

Software Removal Methods

There are two options for removing software deployed with Group Policy. You can immediately uninstall the software from users and computers (known as a forced removal), or you can allow users to continue to use the software, but prevent new installations (known as an optional removal).

You should choose a forced removal if a software application is no longer used. After the software is deleted, users will not be able to install or run the software. Although you specify that you want to "immediately" uninstall the software in this option, the software is actually deleted in the following fashion:

- Software assigned to computers is automatically deleted from the computer the next time the computer is rebooted or turned on.

- Software assigned to computers that are not attached to the network is automatically deleted the next time the computer is connected to the network and rebooted or turned on when the computer account logs on to Active Directory.

- Software assigned or published to users is automatically deleted from the computer the next time the user logs on.

- Software assigned or published to users on computers that are not attached to the network is automatically deleted the next time the user logs on to Active Directory.

Caution   Because the software is not "immediately" deleted, do not delete the GPO until there has been sufficient time for the software removal to be processed.

You should choose an optional removal if a version of a software application is no longer supported. The software is removed from deployment without forcing the (physical) removal of the software from the computers of users who are still using the software. Users can continue to use the software until they remove it themselves. However, no user is able to install the software (from the Start menu, from Add Or Remove Programs in Control Panel, or by document invocation).

Note   When you originally deploy the software, if you want the application to be removed when a GPO no longer applies, select the Uninstall This Application When It Falls Out Of The Scope Of Management option in the Deployment tab in the Properties dialog box for the package.

To remove applications deployed with Group Policy, complete the following steps:

1. Open the Group Policy Object Editor console. In the Computer Configuration or User Configuration node, open Software Settings.

2. Click the Software Installation node.

3. In the details pane, right-click the package you want to remove, click All Tasks, and then click Remove.

4. In the Remove Software dialog box, shown in Figure 12-15, select one of the following:

   ❑ Immediately Uninstall The Software From Users And Computers. Select this option to specify that the application should be removed the next time a user logs on to or restarts the computer (forced removal).

❑ Allow Users To Continue To Use The Software, But Prevent New Installations. Select this option to specify that users can continue to use the application if they have already installed it (optional removal). If they remove the application or have never installed it, they will not be able to install it.

Note If you select an optional removal, the package is removed from the GPO. If you determine later that you want a forced removal of the software, you must add the package to the GPO again and deploy it again, then select a forced removal. Otherwise, you (or the users) must manually uninstall the application from each client computer.

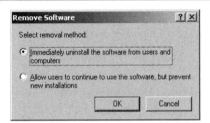

Figure 12-15 The Remove Software dialog box

5. Click OK.

Lesson Review

The following questions are intended to reinforce key information presented in this lesson. If you are unable to answer a question, review the lesson and then try the question again. Answers to the questions can be found in the "Questions and Answers" section at the end of this chapter.

1. What is the difference between redeploying and upgrading an application deployed with Group Policy?

_____

_____

2. Why shouldn't you give users the option of applying an upgrade?

_____

_____

3. What happens if you delete a GPO that deploys a software application before you choose the software removal method you want to implement and allow the software removal to be processed?

_____

_____

4. A software application deployed with Group Policy in your organization is no longer used. You no longer want users to be able to install or run the software. What action should you perform?

   a. Execute a forced removal

   b. Execute an optional removal

   c. Redeploy the application

   d. Upgrade the application

Lesson Summary

■ To maintain a software deployment, it might be necessary to redeploy, upgrade, or remove an application at some point in the software life cycle.

■ You can redeploy an application previously deployed with Group Policy if there are small changes that need to be made to the original software deployment configuration. You can redeploy an application by using the Software Installation extension.

■ To upgrade software deployed with Group Policy, you must first create a Windows Installer package that contains the upgrade and then configure the upgrade in the Upgrades tab in the Properties dialog box for the package.

■ To remove software deployed with Group Policy, you must choose whether to uninstall the software from all users and computers or to merely prevent new installations of the software by using the Software Installation extension.

Lesson 4: Troubleshooting Software Deployed with Group Policy

In order to maintain software deployed with Group Policy, you must be able to troubleshoot the software deployment. Troubleshooting a software deployment involves using the Resultant Set Of Policy Wizard, the Gpresult and Gpupdate command-line tools, the Event Viewer, and log files to solve policy-related problems. This lesson shows you how to work with these tools to troubleshoot software deployed with Group Policy.

After this lesson, you will be able to

■ Troubleshoot software deployed with Group Policy

Estimated lesson time: 20 minutes

Troubleshooting Software Deployed with Group Policy

As an administrator, it will likely be your task to find solutions to problems with software deployed with Group Policy. If problems occur, you might need to perform some tests to verify that your Group Policy configuration is working properly, and diagnose and solve problems. Windows Server 2003 provides the following Group Policy troubleshooting tools to assist you in verifying your configuration and in diagnosing and solving problems:

■ Resultant Set Of Policy Wizard

■ Gpresult

■ Gpupdate

■ Event Viewer

■ Log files

The Group Policy troubleshooting tools were discussed in detail in Chapter 11, "Administering Group Policy." You must be proficient in the use of these tools to effectively troubleshoot software deployed with Group Policy.

  Exam Tip   Know how to use Gpresult to troubleshoot software deployed with Group Policy.

Advanced Diagnostic Information

If you turn on verbose logging as discussed in Chapter 11, you can use the advanced diagnostic information provided in the Advanced Deployment Options dialog box to troubleshoot software deployed with Group Policy. The Advanced Deployment Options dialog box, shown previously in Figure 12-8, lists the following:

- **Product Code**   A globally unique identifier (GUID) that identifies the application and its version.

- **Deployment Count**   Displays the number of times the package has been redeployed.

- **Script Name**   Displays the full path to the application assignment script (.aas file). An application assignment script contains instructions associated with the assignment or publication of a package and is generated for every published or assigned application in a GPO and stored in that domain's GPO.

To view advanced diagnostic information, complete the following steps:

1. Open the Group Policy Object Editor console. In the Computer Configuration or User Configuration node, open Software Settings.

2. Click the Software Installation node.

3. In the details pane, right-click the package for which you want to view advanced diagnostic information, and then click Properties.

4. Click the Deployment tab, and then click Advanced.

Software Deployment Troubleshooting Scenarios

Table 12-3 describes some troubleshooting scenarios related to software deployed with Group Policy.

Table 12-3   Software Deployment Troubleshooting Scenarios

Causes	Solutions
Problem: Published applications do not appear for the user in Add Or Remove Programs in Control Panel.	
The client is running Terminal Services on the desktop.	Use Addiag.exe to see if Terminal Services is running on the user's desktop. Software deployed with Group Policy is not supported for Terminal Services clients.
Group Policy is not applied to this user.	Run Gpresult for the user to ensure that the GPO is applied to the user.
The user has not logged on since the GPO was created	Have the user log off and log back on. Ensure that the user is authenticated by the domain controller.
The GPO did not run.	Run Gpresult to verify that the GPO runs.
The user cannot access Active Directory.	Check to see if the user can access Active Directory.

Table 12-3   Software Deployment Troubleshooting Scenarios

Causes	Solutions
The user cannot access the SDP.	Use ping to test connectivity. Check the user's permissions on the SDP.

Problem: When a user activates a document with the extension used in a published application, the application does not install.

Auto-install is not set.	Ensure that Auto-Install This Application By File Extension Activation is checked in the Deployment tab in the Properties dialog box for the package.
Additional causes and solutions are listed in the "Published applications do not appear for the user in Add Or Remove Programs in Control Panel" problem.	

Problem: When a user activates a document with the extension used in a published application, an unexpected application automatically installs.

The precedence of filename extensions has not been set properly.	Check to see that the File Extensions tab in the Software Installation Properties dialog box has the correct application precedence set.

Problem: An application assigned to a computer does not install.

The computer has not been restarted since the application was assigned and the GPO has not been applied.	Restart the computer.
Group Policy did not run.	Check the GPO console to make sure the GPO manages the computer. Run Gpresult for the computer to ensure that the GPO is applied to the computer.
The computer is not able to access Active Directory.	Use ping to test connectivity to the domain controller.
The computer is not able to access the SDP.	Use ping to test connectivity to the SDP.

Problem: A user who has never installed a managed application selects the application to install. The installation begins and one of many error messages appears.

Problems with the Windows Installer package.	Install the package on another computer and make sure the package can be opened.
The user does not have the appropriate permissions to read the Windows Installer package from the SDP or to install the application to the installation target folder as defined in the package.	Verify the user has Read permission on the SDP and Write access to the installation target directory.

Table 12-3   Software Deployment Troubleshooting Scenarios

Causes	Solutions
Problem: A previously installed, assigned application is unexpectedly removed.	
The Uninstall Applications When They Fall Out Of The Scope Of Management check box in the Advanced tab of the Software Installation Properties dialog box is selected and the scope of management has changed.	Check to see if the GPO containing the managed application still applies to the user or computer.
The software is managed by a GPO linked to a site or OU and the computer moved to a new site or OU.	Check to see if the computer has moved to a new site or OU.
Problem: The user receives an error message such as The Feature You Are Trying To Install Cannot Be Found In The Source Directory.	
Network or permissions problems.	Make sure the network is working correctly. Ensure that the user has Read and Apply Group Policy permission for the GPO. Ensure that the folder containing the application on the SDP is shared. Ensure that the user has Read permission for the SDP. Ensure that the user has Read permission for the folder containing the application on the SDP.
Problem: After removal of an application, the shortcuts for the application still appear on the user's desktop.	
The user has created shortcuts and the Windows Installer service has no knowledge of them.	The user must remove the shortcuts manually.
Automatic upgrade of the application has left shortcuts for the application being upgraded.	Check to see if there is a new version of the application, and if so, delete the shortcuts.
Problem: The user attempts to install a published or assigned application and receives an error message such as Another Installation Is Already In Progress.	
The Windows Installer service is already running another installation.	The user should wait for the installation to complete and try again later.
Problem: The user opens an already installed application, and the Windows Installer service starts.	
An application is undergoing automatic repair. A feature is being added.	In both cases, the user must wait for the installation to complete.

Table 12-3   Software Deployment Troubleshooting Scenarios

Causes	Solutions
Problem: The administrator receives error messages such as Active Directory Will Not Allow The Package To Be Deployed or Cannot Prepare Package for Deployment.	
The Windows Installer service cannot communicate with the computer on which the SDP is located.	Use ping to test connectivity with the SDP.
The package is corrupted.	Install the package on another computer and make sure the package can be opened.

Real World   Troubleshooting Application Management Issues

If you are facing a difficult software distribution issue, and you've verified that the software deployment options are correct, you may want to enable Application Management debugging. To do this, you must go to the system experiencing the problem and log on as an administrator. You then enable Application Management debugging by editing the registry as described in the following steps:

1. Click Start, click Run, type **Regedit** and then press ENTER. In the Registry Editor, expand the following path: HKEY_LOCAL_MACHINE\Software\Microsoft\Windows NT\CurrentVersion.

2. Right-click the CurrentVersion key, point to New, and then click Key. Type **Diagnostics** as the new key name, and then press ENTER.

3. Right-click the Diagnostics key, point to New, and then click DWORD Value. Type **AppMgmtDebugLevel** as the name of the new value, and then press ENTER. Double-click the AppMgmtDebugLevel value.

4. In the Edit DWORD Value dialog box, type **4b** in the Value Data box, and then click OK. Close the Registry Editor.

Once you restart the computer (for applications assigned to the computer) or have logged on the user (for applications assigned or published to the user), you should be able to find the AppMgmt.log file in the %*Systemroot*%\debug\usermode folder. Read the entries in this file to gain insight into the problems that are occurring with the application installation. If you don't see this log file, it could be that the application deployment policy is not even reaching the local client system. This could be the case if the policy is disabled or possibly being filtered through inheritance blocking or security filtering.

After you complete your debugging, be sure to remove the AppMgmtDebugLevel key so that you don't waste system resources logging information that you don't require.

Lesson Review

The following questions are intended to reinforce key information presented in this lesson. If you are unable to answer a question, review the lesson and then try the question again. Answers to the questions can be found in the "Questions and Answers" section at the end of this chapter.

1. Which of the following actions should you perform if a user attempts to install an assigned application and receives the message Another Installation Is Already In Progress?

   a. Check your permissions for the GPO

   b. Check network connectivity

   c. Check your permissions for the SDP

   d. Wait for the installation to complete

2. Which of the following actions should you perform if a user attempts to install an assigned application and receives the message The Feature You Are Trying To Install Cannot Be Found In The Source Directory? (Choose two.)

   a. Check your permissions for the GPO

   b. Check connectivity with the SDP

   c. Check your permissions for the SDP

   d. Wait for the installation to complete

   e. Set the auto-install property for the package

3. You are preparing a package for deployment. Which of the following actions should you perform if you receive the message Cannot Prepare Package For Deployment?

   a. Check your permissions for the GPO

   b. Check connectivity with the SDP

   c. Check your permissions for the SDP

   d. Set the appropriate category for the package

   e. Set the auto-install property for the package

4. Which of the following actions should you perform if a user double-clicks a document associated with a published application and a different application than the expected one installs?

   a. Set the auto-install property for the package

   b. Clear the auto-install property for the package

   c. Adjust the precedence for the expected application in the Application Precedence list

   d. Delete the unexpected application from the Application Precedence list

Lesson Summary

   ■ Windows Server 2003 assists you in verifying your configuration and in diagnosing and solving problems related to deploying software with Group Policy with the following Group Policy troubleshooting tools: Resultant Set Of Policy Wizard, Gpresult and Gpupdate command-line tools, Event Viewer, and log files.

Case Scenario Exercise

You have been asked by Max Benson, CEO of Wide World Importers, to advise the company on some software deployment issues they are facing. Wide World Importers is an import/export company handling primarily clothing and textile products. They have offices in New York, New York, San Diego, California, and Fort Lauderdale, Florida. Wide World's network is configured as a single Active Directory domain with sites and OUs for each location. Below each top-level OU is another layer of OUs representing the functional areas of Shipping, Finance, and Marketing. The users and client computers are distributed as shown in Table 12-4.

Table 12-4   Wide World Importers Network Structure

Office/OU	Users	Computers	Operating Systems Used
NY/Shipping	15	8	Windows 2000 Professional
NY/Finance	60	60	Windows 2000 Professional, and Windows XP Professional
NY/Marketing	175	185	Windows 2000 Professional, and Windows XP Professional
CA/Shipping	55	40	Windows 2000 Professional, and Windows NT 4 Workstation
CA/Finance	110	110	Windows XP Professional
CA/Marketing	210	210	Windows 2000 Professional, and Windows XP Professional
FL/Shipping	25	15	Windows NT 4 Workstation
FL/Finance	20	20	Windows 2000 Professional
FL/Marketing	140	150	Windows 2000 Professional, and Windows XP Professional

The California and New York offices are connected by a dedicated T1 line. There are dedicated 256 Kbps Fractional T1 lines connecting the Florida office to both California and New York. Several of the Marketing users have mobile computers, and a portion of their time is spent traveling the world. Access to the main network is accomplished by dialing in to a local Internet service provider (ISP), and then establishing a Layer 2 Tunneling Protocol virtual private network (L2TP VPN) to the California office. There are three domain controllers and one file server at each location. The WAN links are used heavily during the day, but Wide World does not plan to upgrade them any time soon. It is important the software deployment strategy you suggest does not adversely affect the WAN links during business hours.

Max has indicated that he wants more control over software deployment and wants to leverage his investment in Windows Server 2003. The main software requirements of the company include Microsoft Office XP for all users, a third-party program used by the Marketing department, an application used by the Finance department for billing and accounting, and a proprietary shipping application developed for Wide World Importers. While all users utilize Office XP, they don't all use the same applications. Many users utilize only Microsoft Outlook and Word, while others also make use of Microsoft Access and PowerPoint. Still others use Excel on a daily basis.

Given the concerns of Wide World Importers as outlined above, answer the following questions:

1. Utilizing GPO for software deployment, how can you configure things so as not to negatively impact the business by saturating the WAN links during deployment?

   _____

   _____

2. Max is concerned that it would be a huge burden for mobile users to deal with software installation when they are connected to the network from remote locations. What must you do to alleviate Max's concerns?

   _____

   _____

3. With respect to the marketing, finance, and shipping applications, what are some of the options and considerations when deciding how to deploy these applications?

   _____

   _____

4. How do you recommend resolving the issue that many users utilize different parts of the Office XP suite of applications?

   _____

   _____

5. A small number of the client systems are running Windows NT 4 Workstation. How would you advise Wide World Importers regarding software installation for these systems?

_____

_____

6. The shipping application is a proprietary application that does not have an .msi file associated with it. How would you recommend using Group Policy to deploy this application to the Shipping department?

_____

_____

Troubleshooting Lab

You are a domain administrator for Contoso Pharmaceuticals. Another administrator has assigned the Microsoft Baseline Security Advisor application to all of the domain controllers in your organization. This administrator says that it has been two days and the policy has yet to appear on all the domain controllers. He asks you to look into the problem. You first check the deployment method and notice that the application is assigned to Domain Controllers OU.

To set up this scenario, complete the following steps:

1. Log on to Server1 using the domain administrator name and password.

2. Create a folder on the desktop named MBSA. Then, share that folder as MBSA.

3. Download the MBSA 2.0 Microsoft Installer package from the Microsoft Web site at _http://www.microsoft.com/technet/security/tools/mbsa2/default.mspx_. Place the MBSASetup-EN.msi file in the shared MBSA folder on the desktop.

4. Open the Active Directory Users And Computers console. Right-click the Domain Controllers OU and click Properties.

5. In the Domain Controllers Properties dialog box, click the Group Policy tab, and then click New. Type **MBSA** as the name of the new policy, and then press ENTER.

6. Ensure that MBSA is selected, and then click Edit. In the Group Policy Object Editor, expand Computer Configuration and Software Settings, and then click on Software Installation. Right-click Software Installation, point to New, and then click Package. In the Open dialog box, in the File Name box, type **\\server1\ mbsa\mbsasetup-en .msi** and then press ENTER.

7. In the Deploy Software dialog box, confirm that the software is to be Assigned and click OK. Press F5 and the new package appears in the details pane. Close the Group Policy Object Editor.

8. Ensure that MBSA is selected in the Domain Controllers Properties dialog box. Click Properties. Then, select the Disable Computer Configuration Settings check box. In the Confirm Disable message box, click Yes. Click OK. Note that there is a warning icon for the MBSA policy in the Domain Controllers Properties dialog box.

9. Click Close in the Domain Controllers Properties dialog box.

Now you've configured the scenario described above. The following steps take you through troubleshooting and resolving the issue:

1. Restart Server1 in an attempt to initiate application installation.

2. Log on to Server1 using the domain administrator user name and password.

3. Run the Gpresult command. What do you see concerning the MBSA policy?

   The MBSA policy was not applied because the GPO is disabled.

4. Open the Active Directory Users And Computers console. Open the Domain Controllers Properties dialog box, and then open the MBSA Properties dialog box. Clear the Disable Computer Configuration Settings check box. Click OK. Note that the warning icon has been removed from the MBSA policy on the Domain Controllers Properties dialog box.

5. Click OK in the Domain Controllers Properties dialog box.

6. Run the **Repadmin /syncall** command to ensure that the policy is replicated as quickly as possible. Wait two minutes before proceeding to the next step.

7. Restart Server1. Log on to Server1 using the domain administrator user name and password.

8. You should see that the Microsoft Baseline Security Advisor tool is now installed. Close all of the open MBSA windows.

Many different issues might cause an application not to be deployed. The most common reasons are policy inheritance blocking, security filtering, replication errors, network connectivity issues, or that the policy or part of the policy has been disabled. Gpresult helps you identify these problems.

> **Note** You can remove the MBSA policy once you've completed this lab. The full benefit of software distribution is not realized in this lab because you have only two computers in your test environment and only one of those computers (Server1) is in an OU. The real benefits become obvious when there are many computers in one or more OUs to which you can automatically distribute software.

Chapter Summary

- The Software Installation extension in the Group Policy Object Editor console enables administrators to centrally manage the installation of software on a client computer by assigning applications to users or computers or by publishing applications for users.

- When you assign an application to a user, the application is advertised to the user on the Start menu the next time he or she logs on to a workstation, and local registry settings, including filename extensions, are updated.

- When you publish the application to users, the application does not appear installed on the users' computers. If users choose, they can install the software from Add Or Remove Programs in Control Panel. Publish software that users might find useful to perform their jobs.

- You can deploy software using the Software Installation extension by using a Windows Installer package.

- Modifications enable you to customize Windows Installer packages. Modifications can be transform (.mst) or patch (.msp) files. You cannot deploy .mst or .msp files alone. They must modify an existing Windows Installer package.

- The tasks for deploying software with Group Policy are the following: plan and prepare the software deployment, set up an SDP, create a GPO and a GPO console for software deployment, specify the software deployment properties for the GPO, add Windows Installer packages to the GPO and select package deployment method, and set Windows Installer package properties.

- You can redeploy an application previously deployed with Group Policy if there are small changes that need to be made to the original software deployment configuration.

- To upgrade software deployed with Group Policy, you must first create a Windows Installer package that contains the upgrade and then configure the upgrade in the Upgrades tab in the Properties dialog box for the package.

- To remove software deployed with Group Policy, you must choose whether to uninstall the software from all users and computers or to merely prevent new installations of the software.

- Windows Server 2003 provides the following Group Policy troubleshooting tools to assist you in verifying your configuration and in diagnosing and solving problems related to deploying software with Group Policy: Resultant Set Of Policy Wizard, Gpresult and Gpupdate command-line tools, Event Viewer, and log files.

Exam Highlights

Before taking the exam, review the key points and terms that are presented in this chapter. You need to know this information.

Key Points

- Deploy software by using the Software Installation extension in the Group Policy Object Editor console.

- To deploy software with Group Policy, you must plan and prepare the software deployment, set up an SDP, create a GPO and a GPO console for software deployment, specify the software deployment properties for the GPO, add Windows Installer packages to the GPO and select package deployment method, and set Windows Installer package properties.

- Redeploy an application previously deployed with Group Policy by using the Software Installation extension.

- Upgrade software deployed with Group Policy by creating a Windows Installer package that contains the upgrade and then configure the upgrade in the Upgrades tab in the Properties dialog box for the package.

- Remove software deployed with Group Policy by using the Software Installation extension. Determine whether to uninstall the software from all users and computers or to merely prevent new installations of the software.

- Use the Resultant Set Of Policy Wizard, Gpresult and Gpupdate command-line tools, Event Viewer, and log files to troubleshoot Group Policy application deployment issues.

Key Terms

Software Installation extension   An extension within Group Policy that is the administrator's primary tool for managing software within an organization. Software Installation works in conjunction with Group Policy and Active Directory, establishing a Group Policy–based software management system that allows you to centrally manage the initial deployment of software, mandatory and nonmandatory upgrades, patches, quick fixes, and the removal of software.

assign   To deploy a program to members of a group where acceptance of the program is mandatory.

publish   To deploy a program to members of a group where acceptance of the program is at the discretion of the user.

software distribution point (SDP)   In Software Installation, a network location from which users are able to get the software that they need.

Windows Installer package   A file that contains explicit instructions on the installation and removal of specific applications.

Page
12-11

Lesson 1 Review

1. What are the hardware requirements for deploying software by using Group Policy?

To deploy software by using Group Policy, an organization must be running Windows 2000 Server or later, with Active Directory and Group Policy on the server, and Windows 2000 Professional or later on the client computers.

2. Describe the tools provided for software deployment.

The Software Installation extension in the Group Policy Object Editor console on the server is used by administrators to manage software. Add Or Remove Programs in Control Panel is used by users to manage software on their own computers.

3. What is the difference between assigning applications and publishing applications?

When you assign an application to a user, the application is advertised to the user the next time he or she logs on to a workstation, and local registry settings, including filename extensions, are updated. The application advertisement follows the user regardless of which physical computer he or she logs on to. When you publish the application to users, the application does not appear installed on the users' computers. No shortcuts are visible on the desktop or Start menu, and no updates are made to the local registry on the users' computers. You assign required or mandatory software to users or to computers. You publish software that users might find useful to perform their jobs.

4. What is the purpose of Windows Installer packages?

A Windows Installer package is a file that contains explicit instructions on the installation and removal of specific applications.

5. Which of the following file extensions allows you to deploy software using the Software Installation extension? (Choose two.)

    a. .mst

    b. .msi

    c. .zap

    d. .zip

    e. .msp

    f. .aas

The correct answers are b and c. Files with the extension .msi are either native Windows Installer packages or repackaged Windows Installer packages, while files with the extension .zap are application files. Files with the extensions .mst and .msp are modifications and do not allow you to deploy software on their own. Files with the extension .aas are application assignment scripts, which contain instructions associated with the assignment or publication of a package.

Page
12-33

Lesson 2 Review

1. Why is it necessary to set up an SDP?

   You must set up an SDP to provide a network location from which users can get the software that they need.

2. What feature is configured in the File Extensions tab in the Software Installation Properties dialog box?

   In the File Extensions tab in the Software Installation Properties dialog box, you specify which application users install when they open a file with an unknown extension. You can also configure a priority for installing applications when multiple applications are associated with an unknown file extension.

3. What feature is configured in the Categories tab in the Software Installation Properties dialog box?

   In the Categories tab in the Software Installation Properties dialog box, you can designate categories for organizing assigned and published applications to make it easier for users to locate the appropriate application from within Add Or Remove Programs in Control Panel.

4. What feature is configured in the Modifications tab in the Properties dialog box for a Windows Installer package?

   In the Modifications tab in the Properties dialog box for a Windows Installer package, you can add modifications, remove modifications, and set the order of modifications. If the modifications are not properly configured, you will have to uninstall the package or upgrade the package with a correctly configured version.

5. You want to ensure that all users of the KC23 workstation can run FrontPage 2000. What action should you perform?

   a. Assign the application to the computer.

   b. Assign the application to users.

   c. Publish the application to the computer.

   d. Publish the application to users.

   The correct answer is a. Assigning the application to the KC23 workstation is the only way to ensure that all users of the workstation can run FrontPage 2000.

Page
12-40

Lesson 3 Review

1. What is the difference between redeploying and upgrading an application deployed with Group Policy?

   You redeploy an application previously deployed with Group Policy if there are small changes that need to be made to the original software deployment configuration. You upgrade an application previously deployed with Group Policy if the original developer of the software releases a new version of the software or if your organization chooses to use a different vendor's application. Upgrades typically involve major changes to the software and normally have new version numbers. Usually a substantial number of files change for an upgrade.

2. Why shouldn't you give users the option of applying an upgrade?

If users have the option of applying the upgrade, they might or might not choose to apply it, which could cause application version variances within an organization.

3. What happens if you delete a GPO that deploys a software application before you choose the software removal method you want to implement and allow the software removal to be processed?

If you delete a GPO that deploys a software application before you choose the software removal method you want to implement and allow the software removal to be processed, the application cannot be uninstalled with Group Policy. If the application cannot be uninstalled with Group Policy, you (or the users) must manually uninstall the application from each client computer.

4. A software application deployed with Group Policy in your organization is no longer used. You no longer want users to be able to install or run the software. What action should you perform?

    a. Execute a forced removal

    b. Execute an optional removal

    c. Redeploy the application

    d. Upgrade the application

The correct answer is a. If you no longer want users to be able to install or run the software, you should execute a forced removal.

Page
12-47

Lesson 4 Review

1. Which of the following actions should you perform if a user attempts to install an assigned application and receives the message Another Installation Is Already In Progress?

    a. Check your permissions for the GPO

    b. Check network connectivity

    c. Check your permissions for the SDP

    d. Wait for the installation to complete

The correct answer is d. The message Another Installation Is Already In Progress indicates that Windows Installer is already running another installation. You must wait for the installation to complete and then try your installation again.

2. Which of the following actions should you perform if a user attempts to install an assigned application and receives the message The Feature You Are Trying To Install Cannot Be Found In The Source Directory? Choose two.

    a. Check your permissions for the GPO

    b. Check connectivity with the SDP

    c. Check your permissions for the SDP

    d. Wait for the installation to complete

    e. Set the auto-install property for the package

The correct answers are b and c. The message The Feature You Are Trying To Install Cannot Be Found In The Source Directory can be caused by a connectivity problem to the SDP or by insufficient user permission for the SDP. There are also other reasons for receiving this message.

3. You are preparing a package for deployment. Which of the following actions should you perform if you receive the message Cannot Prepare Package For Deployment?

    a. Check your permissions for the GPO

    b. Check connectivity with the SDP

    c. Check your permissions for the SDP

    d. Set the appropriate category for the package

    e. Set the auto-install property for the package

The correct answer is b. If you are preparing a package for deployment and you receive the message Cannot Prepare Package For Deployment, one of the actions you should take is to check connectivity with the SDP.

4. Which of the following actions should you take if a user double-clicks a document associated with a published application and a different application than the expected one installs?

    a. Set the auto-install property for the package

    b. Clear the auto-install property for the package

    c. Adjust the precedence for the expected application in the Application Precedence list

    d. Delete the unexpected application from the Application Precedence list

The correct answer is c. If a user double-clicks a document associated with a published application and a different application than the expected one installs, you should adjust the precedence for the expected application in the Application Precedence list.

Page
12-48 ## Case Scenario Exercise

1. Utilizing GPO for software deployment, how can you configure things so as not to negatively impact the business by saturating the WAN links during deployment?

On a single LAN, it is common to set up a single SDP to store the applications to be deployed using Group Policy. Bandwidth cannot be totally disregarded, but it is much less of an issue locally, since high bandwidth is assumed. When WAN links are involved, the best way to prevent a deployment scenario where the client is installing the software over the WAN link is to provide an SDP at each office. Once that is accomplished, you could keep the GPOs separate for each office, with each GPO pointing to the local SDP. A more elegant solution is to configure the three SDPs as replica links in a DFS topology. This way, all software deployment can reference the same SDP, and client machines will automatically be referred to the SDP in their own site.

2. Max is concerned that it would be a huge burden for mobile users to deal with software installation when they are connected to the network from remote locations. What must you do to alleviate Max's concerns?

Group Policy–based software deployment already includes the capability to detect slow links. When users are connected to the network over a slow link, software will not deploy. The users will get the software the next time they are in the office and they connect to the LAN. With Group Policy, we can control what constitutes a "slow" link. The default is 500 Kbps, which is often an acceptable setting. Most remote connections will fall below 500 Kbps, and certainly most LANs will be faster than 500 Kbps. However, perhaps you have some users that are able to VPN into the office at 300 Kbps, and you would like that to be treated as a fast link. You could alter the Slow Link Detection setting such that any connection faster than 250 Kbps is not considered slow.

3. With respect to the marketing, finance, and shipping applications, what are some of the options and considerations when deciding how to deploy these applications?

Although you could deploy all three applications at the domain level, and use security filtering by adding ACEs to the GPO that limit the deployment to the appropriate users, the solution would require extra administrative work. For example, you would have to implement security groups that align with the deployment goals. The best option, since these applications map nicely to the OU structure of the company, is to deploy the applications at the appropriate OUs. For example, a single GPO to deploy the sales program could be linked to all three Marketing OUs.

The other consideration is whether to assign or publish this application. You must determine whether the applications are optional or mandatory. If these applications are optional, publishing to users would make the most sense. Users would have to take the initiative in choosing to go to Add/Remove Programs (or Add Or Remove Programs, in Windows XP) and install the application. Considering that these custom applications were developed specifically to be used by these departments, it is likely that the company would consider them mandatory. Assuming that is the case, you should assign them. If users move from computer to computer in the organization, you may decide that assigning them to the users is most appropriate. If each user has his or her own computer, assigning the applications to the appropriate computers is the best solution.

4. How do you recommend resolving the issue that many users utilize different parts of the Office XP suite of applications?

Transforms are files that end with an extension of .mst. These files are deployed along with the .msi file to alter the configuration. This is an option to address this complication. It could be quite an administrative burden to develop .mst files for each of the different configurations utilized, and then deploying multiple GPOs with each of the different configurations.

It is important to understand transforms and when their use is appropriate. In this case, however, there was no indication that having extra software simply available would cause trouble. Consider assigning Office XP to users at the domain level. This will make all file extension associations on the client systems and advertise the applications by making all of the Start menu shortcuts available. Essentially, all of the applications are set to install on first use. If some users never launch Excel, for example, then the program files to run Excel will simply not be brought down for that user. A complicated set of transforms in this case would seem to be a waste of administrative effort.

5. A small number of the client systems are running Windows NT 4 Workstation. How would you advise Wide World Importers regarding software installation for these systems?

Group Policy–based software installation will not apply to Windows 95, Microsoft Windows 98, Microsoft Windows Millennium Edition (Windows Me), or Windows NT systems. One option to remedy the issue is to purchase and utilize SMS. SMS is a powerful network management application that can be used to push software to pre–Windows 2000 operating systems. However, investing in SMS might not be the best option for the sole purpose of deploying software to a few Windows 95, Windows 98, and Windows NT systems. Instead, it might make more sense to upgrade these systems to Windows 2000, Windows Server 2003, or Windows XP (as appropriate). If for some reason these options don't work for the company, installing the software manually or using some other network management tool are the remaining options.

6. The shipping application is a proprietary application that does not have an .msi file associated with it. How would you recommend using Group Policy to deploy this application to the Shipping department?

There are two options for deploying an application that does not natively have an .msi file available. The simplest, but least flexible, is to create a Zero Administration Package, or .zap file. This allows an administrator to publish this application to users, so they can select to install that application from Add/Remove Programs (or Add Or Remove Programs in Windows XP). However, a .zap file will not take advantage of Windows Installer features such as installing with elevated privileges, automatic rollback, and automatic repair of damaged or missing program files. A .zap file also cannot be assigned to users or computers, only published to users.

The other option is to use a third-party application to package the program into an .msi file. WinINSTALL, from Veritas, is one such application that can create .msi files from executable files. A limited version of WinINSTALL is included on the Windows 2000 CD-ROM. However, this application is not available on the Windows Server 2003 CD-ROM.

13 Administering Security with Group Policy

Exam Objectives in this Chapter:

- Create a password policy for domain users.
- Configure the user environment by using Group Policy.
- Automatically enroll user certificates by using Group Policy.
- Deploy a computer environment by using Group Policy.
- Automatically enroll computer certificates by using Group Policy.
- Configure computer security settings by using Group Policy.
- Troubleshoot the application of Group Policy security settings. Tools might include RSoP and the gpresult command.

Why This Chapter Matters

This chapter shows you how to administer security with Group Policy, which is essential to meet the challenge of protecting your organization from outside forces. Software restriction policies, new in Microsoft Windows XP and the Microsoft Windows Server 2003 family, are available to help govern which software can be installed on users' computers, reducing the chance of hostile code being introduced to the environment. By establishing an audit policy and administering the security log, you can monitor events you specify to ensure the environment is secure. After you've determined your organization's security goals, you can use the Security Templates, and Security Configuration and Analysis tools to establish a baseline security configuration on all computers in your organization.

Lessons in this Chapter:

Before You Begin

To complete the lessons in this chapter, you must

- Prepare your test environment according to the descriptions given in the "Getting Started" section of "About This Book"

- Complete the practices for installing and configuring Active Directory as discussed in Chapter 2, "Installing and Configuring Active Directory"

- Learn to use Active Directory administration tools as discussed in Chapter 3, "Administering Active Directory"

- Complete the practices for configuring sites and replication as discussed in Chapter 5, "Configuring Sites and Managing Replication"

- Complete the practices for implementing an organizational unit (OU) structure as discussed in Chapter 6, "Implementing an OU Structure"

- Complete the practices for creating and maintaining user accounts as discussed in Chapter 7, "Administering User Accounts"

- Complete the practices for creating and administering group accounts as discussed in Chapter 8, "Administering Groups"

- Complete the practices for implementing Group Policy Objects (GPOs) as discussed in Chapter 10, "Implementing Group Policy"

- Complete the practices for administering GPOs as discussed in Chapter 11, "Administering Group Policy"

- Complete the practices for deploying software with GPOs as discussed in Chapter 12, "Deploying Software with Group Policy"

Lesson 1: Understanding Active Directory Security

Active Directory security is determined by security groups, access control, delegation of control, and Group Policy. This lesson briefly reviews security groups, access control, and delegation of control, which were covered in previous chapters. Then, this lesson introduces auditing, security logging, and security configuration and analysis and discusses the security settings in Group Policy.

After this lesson, you will be able to

- Recognize security configuration settings in a GPO

Estimated lesson time: 15 minutes

Understanding Security Administration with Group Policy

The foundations of Active Directory security are

- Security groups
- Access control
- Delegation of control
- Group Policy

Security groups simplify administration by allowing you to assign permissions and rights to a group of users rather than having to assign permissions to each individual user account. You implement security groups by using the Active Directory Users And Computers console. Security groups are discussed in Chapter 8, "Administering Groups." Access control is the granting or denial of permissions to security principals. Access control is implemented by using the object-specific access control lists (ACL) in the Security tab of the Properties dialog box of each object. The list contains the names of user groups that have access to the object. Access control is discussed in Chapter 9, "Administering Active Directory Objects." You delegate administrative control of domains and containers in order to provide other administrators, groups, or users with the ability to manage functions according to their needs. Delegation of control is implemented by using the Delegation Of Control Wizard to automate and simplify the process of setting administrative permissions for a domain, OU, or container. Delegation of control is discussed in Chapter 6, "Implementing an OU Structure," and Chapter 9, "Administering Active Directory Objects."

Active Directory Security Provided by Group Policy

Details about Active Directory security provided by Group Policy have not yet been discussed in this training kit. There are three areas within Group Policy that handle

Active Directory security. They are security settings, auditing and security logging, and security configuration and analysis.

Security Settings   Security settings define the security behavior of the system. Through the use of GPOs in Active Directory directory service, administrators can apply security profiles to sites, domains, and OUs in the enterprise. Security settings are detailed later in this lesson and in Lesson 2.

Auditing and Security Logging   Auditing in Windows Server 2003 is the process of tracking both user activities and system activities, called events, on a computer. You can specify that information about an event be written to the security log in the Event Viewer console whenever certain actions are performed. The security log helps to detect intrusion and provides legal evidence if an intruder is caught. In addition, security logging poses an additional time-consuming task for the sophisticated intruder, making detection more likely. Auditing and administering the security log are covered in Lessons 3 and 4, respectively.

Security Configuration And Analysis   The Security Configuration And Analysis feature offers the ability to compare the security settings of a computer to a security template, view the results, and resolve any discrepancies revealed by the analysis. A security template is a physical representation of a security configuration, a single file where a group of security settings is stored, designed to streamline security administration. In addition to using security templates in the Security Configuration And Analysis feature, you can also import a security template into a GPO and apply that security profile to many computers at once. Security templates and the Security Configuration And Analysis feature are covered in Lessons 5 and 6, respectively.

Note   Windows Server 2003 with Service Pack 1 (SP1) includes the Security Configuration Wizard (SCW). You can use the SCW to create security policies based on the server's role(s). These security policies help reduce the attack surface of the server. By contrast, you use the Windows security templates and Security Configuration and Analysis snap-in, covered in Lessons 5 and 6, to implement security in more generic system configurations across both clients and servers.

For additional information on the SCW, see "Security Configuration Wizard for Windows Server 2003" at *http://go.microsoft.com/fwlink/?LinkId=45503*.

Security Settings in Group Policy

Using the Security Settings extension of the Group Policy Object Editor console, the following security areas can be configured for a nonlocal GPO:

- Account Policies
- Local Policies
- Event Log

- Restricted Groups

- System Services

- Registry

- File System

- Wireless Network (IEEE 802.11) Policies

- Public Key Policies

- Software Restriction Policies

- IP Security Policies

Account Policies

The policies in the Account Policies security area apply to user accounts in the domain to which the GPO is linked. This security area contains attributes for the following:

- **Password policy**   For domain or local user accounts, determines settings for passwords such as enforcement and lifetimes

- **Account lockout policy**   For domain or local user accounts, determines when and for whom an account is locked out of the system

Real World   Time and Kerberos

The Kerberos Policy, which is part of the Account Policies on a Windows Server 2003 domain, controls the main authentication mechanism for the domain members. Kerberos allows access based on the issuance of service tickets. These tickets have finite lifetimes and are in part based on system time clocks. If for some reason there is more than a five-minute difference between the clock of a client computer and the clock of the domain's primary domain controller (PDC) emulator, the domain member is denied access until the discrepancy is corrected.

This typically isn't a problem for computers running Microsoft Windows 2000 Professional, Windows XP Professional, Microsoft Windows 2000 Server, and Windows Server 2003 because their time clocks are automatically synchronized when they are made members of the domain. However, since Kerberos is a standard accepted by other operating systems, such as UNIX, you may find clock skew an issue when non-Microsoft operating systems use the Kerberos Key Distribution Center (KDC) that is built into your Active Directory domain controllers. Although you can modify the Kerberos Policy's Maximum Tolerance For Computer Clock Synchronization policy to allow computers a greater leeway in system time clock discrepancies, the best plan is to synchronize all systems to a single reliable time source. To learn more about issues related to time, see Microsoft Knowledge Base article 224799, entitled "Basic Operation of the Windows Time Service," available at *http://support.microsoft.com*.

Important   When setting account policies in Active Directory, keep in mind that there can be only one domain account policy. The account policy must be defined in the Default Domain policy, and it is enforced by the domain controllers that make up the domain. A domain controller always obtains the account policy from the Default Domain Policy Group Policy object (GPO), even if there is a different account policy applied to the OU that contains the domain controller.

Exam Tip   Know the function of account policies, especially password policy.

Local Policies

The policies in the Local Policies security area pertain to the security settings on the computer used by an application or user in the site, domain, or OU to which the GPO is linked. Local policies are based on the computer you are logged on to and the rights you have on that particular computer. This security area contains attributes for the following:

- **Audit policy**   Determines which security events are logged into the security log on the computer (successful attempts, failed attempts, or both). The security log is a part of the Event Viewer console. Audit policy is discussed in detail in Lesson 3.

- **User rights assignment**   Determines which users or groups have logon or task privileges on the computer in a site, domain, or OU. A *user right* is authorization to perform an operation that affects an entire computer rather than a specific object on the computer. To ease the task of user account administration, you should assign user rights primarily to group accounts rather than to individual user accounts. You can find details about user rights in Appendix C, "User Rights."

- **Security options**   Enables or disables security settings for the computer, such as digital signing of data, Administrator and Guest account names, floppy drive and CD-ROM access, driver installation, and logon prompts.

Local policies, by definition, are local to a computer. When these settings are imported to a GPO in Active Directory, they affect the local security settings of any computer accounts to which that GPO is applied.

Event Log

The Event Log security area defines attributes related to the application, security, and system logs in the Event Viewer console for computers in a site, domain, or OU. The attributes are: maximum log size, access rights for each log, and retention settings and methods. Event log size and log wrapping should be defined to match your business and security requirements.

> **Note**   You can also configure the default security log size in the Security Properties dialog box. The Security Properties dialog box is located by right-clicking Security and then clicking Properties in the Event Viewer console.

Restricted Groups

The Restricted Groups security area provides an important security feature that acts as a governor for group membership. For example, you can create a Restricted Groups policy to control membership in the Administrators group. In Restricted Groups, you specify two users, Sue and Mike, as members of the Administrators group. When policy is refreshed, only Sue and Mike remain as members of the Administrators group.

Configuring Restricted Groups ensures that group memberships are set as specified. Groups and users not specified in Restricted Groups are removed from the specific group. In addition, the reverse membership configuration option ensures that each restricted group is a member of only those groups specified in the Member Of column. For these reasons, Restricted Groups should be used primarily to configure membership of local groups on workstation or member servers.

System Services

The System Services security area is used to configure security and startup settings for services running on a computer. The security properties for the service determine what user or group accounts have permission to read/write/delete/execute, as well as inheritance settings, auditing, and ownership permission. The startup settings are the following:

- **Automatic**   Starts a service automatically at system start time
- **Manual**   Starts a service only if manually started
- **Disabled**   The service is disabled so it cannot be started

If you choose to set system service startup to Automatic, perform adequate testing to verify that the services can start without user intervention. You should track the system services used on a computer. For performance optimization, set unnecessary or unused services to Manual.

Registry and File System

The Registry security area is used to configure security on registry keys. The File System security area is used to configure security for file system objects, including access control, audit, and ownership. You can edit the security properties of the registry key or file path: what user or group accounts have permission to read/write/delete/execute, as well as inheritance settings, auditing, and ownership permission.

Wireless Network (IEEE 802.11) Policies

Wireless technology makes it possible for you to use various devices to access data from anywhere in the world. The Windows Server 2003 family provides support for 802.11 wireless networks. In the Windows Server 2003 family, only Windows Server 2003, Standard Edition supports infrared networking.

> **Note**   You can define only one wireless network policy for a domain or OU. If a wireless network policy already exists, the option to create a new wireless network policy is not available.

The Wireless Network Policy Wizard is provided to help you create a wireless network policy. Using the wizard, you can specify a name and description for the wireless network policy and configure additional wireless network policy properties such as the following:

- How often to check for policy changes
- Types of wireless networks available for connection attempts by clients
- Whether to use Windows to configure wireless network settings for clients
- Whether to automatically connect to non-preferred networks
- Networks to which clients can attempt to connect
- Wireless network key (WEP) settings
- IEEE 802.1x settings

Public Key Policies

The Public Key Policies security area, shown in Figure 13-1, is used to deploy a public key infrastructure in your organization. A *public key infrastructure (PKI)* is a system of laws, policies, standards, and software that verify and authenticate the validity of each party involved in an electronic transaction.

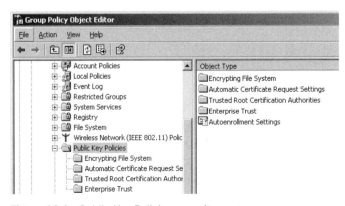

Figure 13-1   Public Key Policies security area

The Public Key Policies security area consists of the following security settings:

- **Encrypting File System**   This setting is used to add encrypted data recovery agents and change the encrypted data recovery policy settings. It is available for the Computer Configuration node only.

- **Automatic Certificate Request Settings**   A *certificate* is a digital document that is commonly used for authentication and to secure information on open networks. This setting enables computers to automatically submit a certificate request to an enterprise certification authority and install the issued certificate. This is useful for ensuring that computers have the certificates that they need to perform public key cryptographic operations. This setting is available for the Computer Configuration node only.

- **Trusted Root Certification Authorities**   A *certification authority (CA)* is an entity responsible for establishing and vouching for the authenticity of public keys belonging to subjects (usually users or computers) or other CAs. The setting is used to establish common trusted root certification authorities. You can use this policy setting to establish trust in a root certification authority that is not a part of your organization. This setting is available for the Computer Configuration node only.

- **Enterprise Trust**   This setting is used to create and distribute a certificate trust list (CTL). A *certificate trust list* is a signed list of root certification authority certificates that an administrator considers reputable for designated purposes such as client authentication or secure e-mail. This setting is available for both the Computer Configuration and the User Configuration nodes.

- **Autoenrollment Settings**   In the Autoenrollment Settings Properties dialog box, shown in Figure 13-2, you can enable or disable the automatic enrollment of computer and user certificates by using Group Policy. You can also use this dialog box to use autoenrollment to manage certificates and to request certificates based on certificate templates. The dialog box is available for both the Computer Configuration and the User Configuration nodes by opening Autoenrollment Settings.

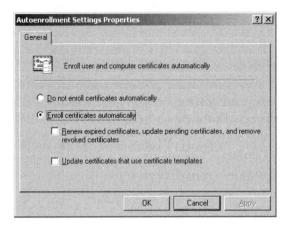

Figure 13-2 The Autoenrollment Settings Properties dialog box

> **Exam Tip** Know how to auto-enroll computer and user certificates by using Group Policy.

It is not necessary for you to use these public key policy settings in Group Policy to deploy a public key infrastructure in your organization. However, these settings give you additional flexibility and control when you establish trust in certification authorities, issue certificates to computers, and deploy the Encrypting File System (EFS) across a domain.

> **Off the Record** EFS can be controlled and disabled through Group Policy. If you choose to disable EFS for your domain, which prevents users from encrypting files, you can do so by setting an empty recovery policy at the domain level. Specific directions on how to do this are listed in Microsoft Knowledge Base Article 222022, entitled "HOW TO: Disable EFS for All Computers in a Windows 2000–Based Domain," available at *http://support.microsoft.com*.

Software Restriction Policies

The Software Restriction Policies security area is a new feature in Windows XP and Windows Server 2003 used to identify software running in a domain and to control its ability to execute. This feature can identify software that is hostile or unwanted and prevent it from executing on computers running Windows XP Professional and Windows Server 2003. Software restriction policies are discussed in detail in Lesson 2.

IP Security Policies

The IP Security Policies security area is used to configure network Internet Protocol (IP) security.

Best Practices for Security Settings

The following are the best practices for applying security settings:

■ Do not configure account policies for OUs that do not contain any computers because OUs that contain only users always receive account policy from the domain.

■ When setting account policies in Active Directory, keep in mind that there can only be one domain account policy. This account policy must be defined in the Default Domain policy, and it is enforced by all the domain controllers in the domain. A domain controller always obtains the account policy from the Default Domain Policy Group Policy object (GPO), even if there is a different account policy applied to the OU that contains the domain controller.

■ Event log size and log wrapping should be defined to match your organization's business and security requirements. Consider implementing Event Log settings at the site, domain, or OU level to take advantage of Group Policy settings.

■ Track the system services used on a computer. For performance optimization, set unnecessary or unused services to start only by manual intervention.

■ If you choose to set the system service startup to Automatic, perform adequate testing to verify that the services can start without user intervention.

■ When security settings are imported to a GPO in Active Directory, they affect the local security settings of any computer accounts to which that GPO is applied. In either case, your user account rights might no longer apply if there is a local policy setting that overrides those privileges.

■ If you create a Restricted Groups policy for a group, groups and users not specified in that policy are removed from the group specified. In addition, the reverse membership configuration option ensures that each restricted group is a member of only those groups specified. For these reasons, using Restricted Groups for security should be limited to primarily configuring membership of local groups on workstation or member servers.

Lesson Review

The following questions are intended to reinforce key information presented in this lesson. If you are unable to answer a question, review the lesson and then try the question again. Answers to the questions can be found in the "Questions and Answers" section at the end of this chapter.

1. How are account policies different from other security policies?

_____

_____

2. What is the difference between user rights and permissions?

_____

_____

3. Attributes for which logs are defined in the Event Log security area?

_____

_____

4. How can you set automatic enrollment of user certificates?

_____

_____

5. In which of the following security areas would you find the settings for determining which security events are logged in the security log on the computer?

   a. Event Log

   b. Account Policies

   c. Local Policies

   d. Restricted Groups

Lesson Summary

- Security settings define the security behavior of the system. Through the use of GPOs in Active Directory, administrators can apply security profiles to sites, domains, and OUs in the enterprise.

- The policies in the Account Policies security area can be applied only to the root domain of the domain tree and cannot be applied to sites or OUs.

- You set autoenrollment of computer and user certificates in the Autoenrollment Settings Properties dialog box, which you can access by opening Autoenrollment Settings in Computer Configuration or User Configuration/Windows Settings/Security Settings/Public Key Policies in a GPO for a site, domain, or OU.

Lesson 2: Implementing Software Restriction Policies

In the business computing environment, a wide variety of software applications are available to users from many sources. Documents and Web pages can contain executable code in scripts, and e-mail messages can contain executable code in attachments. Merely accessing such documents, Web pages, and e-mail messages forces users to make decisions about running applications. Worse, viruses and Trojan horses that might be present in the executable code can cause security breaches and damage to network files. In Windows XP and Windows Server 2003, software restriction policies have been developed to identify and control the running of software. This lesson shows you how to implement software restriction policies.

Note   Microsoft Internet Explorer security is not controlled by software restriction policies but is managed through the Administrative Templates Group Policy extension. Windows Server 2003 with SP1 incorporates new registry keys and values for Internet Explorer security features. For more information on Internet Explorer settings in Windows Server 2003 with SP1, see "Changes to Functionality in Microsoft Windows Sever 2003 Service Pack 1" at *http://www.microsoft.com/downloads/details.aspx?FamilyId=C3C26254-8CE3-46E2-B1B6-3659B92B2CDE&displaylang=en*.

After this lesson, you will be able to

- Explain the purpose of software restriction policies
- Describe the default security levels
- Describe how software is identified by software restriction policies
- Explain the function of rules
- List rule precedence
- Set the default security level
- Create rules
- Designate file types

Estimated lesson time: 25 minutes

Understanding Software Restriction Policies

Software restriction policies, new in Windows XP and Windows Server 2003, were created to address the problem of regulating unknown or untrusted code. Software restriction policies are security settings in a GPO provided to identify software and control its ability to run on a local computer, site, domain, or OU. Most organizations employ a set of known and trusted programs. However, if users install and run other programs, these programs might conflict with or change configuration data in the known and trusted programs. Or, the newly installed user programs could contain a virus or Trojan horse. Software restriction policies protect your computer environment from unknown code by enabling you to identify and specify the applications allowed to run. These policies can apply to computers or users, depending on whether you choose to modify settings in User Configuration or Computer Configuration. When software restriction policies are set, end users must adhere to the guidelines set up by administrators when executing programs.

With software restriction policies, you can

- Control the ability of programs to run on your system. For example, you can apply a policy that does not allow certain file types to run in the e-mail attachment directory of your e-mail program if you are concerned about users receiving viruses through e-mail.

- Permit users to run only specific files on multiuser computers. For example, if you have multiple users on your computers, you can set up software restriction policies and access control settings in such a way that users do not have access to any software but those specific files that are necessary for their work.

- Decide who can add trusted publishers to your computer.

- Control whether software restriction policies affect all users or just certain users on a computer.

- Prevent any files from running on your local computer, OU, site, or domain. For example, if you have a known virus, you can use software restriction policies to stop the computer from opening the file that contains the virus.

 Important   Software restriction policies should not be used as a replacement for antivirus software. Software restriction policies do not work on Microsoft Windows NT 4 or Windows 2000 systems.

Default Security Levels

Software restriction policies run on one of two default security levels:

- Unrestricted, which allows software to run with the full rights of the user who is logged on to the computer

- Disallowed, which does not allow the software to run, regardless of the access rights of the user who is logged on to the computer

If the default level is set to Unrestricted, you can identify and create rules for the set of programs that you want to prohibit from running. If the default level is set to Disallowed, you can identify and create rule exceptions for the programs that you trust to run. Either option can be set as the default security level for a GPO, but when a GPO is created, the default security level is Unrestricted.

Setting the Default Security Level to Disallowed

When you set the default security level to Disallowed, most software applications are restricted and you must apply a rule for nearly every application you want to run. Some applications must remain unrestricted for the operating system to function at all. Four registry path rules are created automatically when you set the default security level to Disallowed:

- %HKEY_LOCAL_MACHINE\SOFTWARE\Microsoft\Windows NT\CurrentVersion *Systemroot*%

- %HKEY_LOCAL_MACHINE\SOFTWARE\Microsoft\Windows NT\CurrentVersion *Systemroot*%*.exe

- %HKEY_LOCAL_MACHINE\SOFTWARE\Microsoft\Windows NT\CurrentVersion *Systemroot*%\System32*.exe

- %HKEY_LOCAL_MACHINE\SOFTWARE\Microsoft\Windows\CurrentVersion *Programfilesdir*%

These registry path rules are created as a safeguard against locking yourself and all users out of the system. Only advanced users should consider modifying or deleting these rules.

If you decide to use a default security level of Disallowed, consider the following issues:

- If a computer must run logon scripts, you must include a path rule that allows the scripts to run. For more information, refer to the Path Rule section in this lesson.

- Startup items are placed in HKEY_CURRENT_USER\Software\Microsoft\Windows \CurrentVersion\Run. If startup items must run, you must create a rule for them. For more information, refer to the Path Rule section in this lesson.

- Many applications start other programs to perform certain tasks, and you must create rules for these other programs. For example, Microsoft Word starts the Clip Organizer to manage clip art.

How Software Restriction Policies Work

When a user encounters an application to be run, software restriction policies must first identify the software. Software can be identified by its

- Hash, a series of bytes with a fixed length that uniquely identify a program or file

- Certificate, a digital document used for authentication and secure exchange of information on open networks, such as the Internet, extranets, and intranets

- Path, a sequence of folder names that specifies the location of the software within the directory tree

- Internet zone, a subtree specified through Internet Explorer: Internet, Intranet, Restricted Sites, Trusted Sites, or My Computer

Rules

Software restriction policies identify and control the running of software by using rules. There are four types of rules, which correspond to the four ways of identifying software: a hash rule, a certificate rule, a path rule, and an Internet zone rule. These rules override the default security level. After software is identified by using a rule, you can decide whether or not to allow it to run by setting a security level (Disallowed or Unrestricted) for the program associated with the rule.

Hash Rule   A *hash* is a series of bytes with a fixed length that uniquely identify a program or file. The hash is computed by a *hash algorithm*. Software restriction policies can identify files by their hash, using both the SHA-1 (Secure Hash Algorithm) and the MD5 hash algorithm. For example, you can create a hash rule and set the security level to Disallowed to prevent users from running a certain file. A file can be renamed or moved to another folder and still result in the same hash. However, any change to the file changes its hash value and allows it to bypass restrictions. Software restriction policies recognize only hashes that have been calculated by using such policies.

Certificate Rule   A *certificate rule* identifies software by its signing certificate. For example, you can use certificate rules to automatically trust software from a trusted source in a domain without prompting the user. You can also use certificate rules to run files in disallowed areas of your operating system.

Path Rule   A *path rule* identifies software by its file path. For example, if you have a computer that has a disallowed default policy, you can still grant unrestricted access to a specific folder for each user. Simply create a path rule using the file path and set the security level of the path rule to Unrestricted. Some common paths for this type of rule are *%Userprofile%*, *%Windir%*, *%Appdata%*, *%Programfiles%*, and *%Temp%*. Because these rules are specified by path, if a program is moved, the path rule no longer applies. You can also create registry path rules that use the registry key of the software as the path.

Internet Zone Rule   *Internet zone rules* apply only to Windows Installer packages. A zone rule can identify software from a zone that is specified through Internet Explorer. These zones are Internet, Intranet, Restricted Sites, Trusted Sites, and My Computer.

Rule Precedence

You can apply several rules to the same piece of software. The rules are applied in the following order of precedence, from highest to lowest:

1. Hash rule.
2. Certificate rule.

3. Path rule. When there are conflicting path rules, the most restrictive rule takes precedence. For example, if there is a path rule for C:\Windows, with a security level of Disallowed, and there is a path rule for C:\Windows\System32, with a security level of Unrestricted, the more restrictive path rule takes precedence. In this case, software programs in C:\Windows will not run, but programs in C:\Windows\System32 will run.

4. Internet zone rule.

For example, if you have a file that has a hash rule applied to it with a security level of Unrestricted, but the file resides in a folder whose path rule is set to Disallowed, the file runs because the hash rule has precedence over the path rule.

 Note   For software restriction policies to take effect, users must log off from and then log on to their computers.

Implementing Software Restriction Policies

To implement software restriction policies, you must complete the following tasks:

1. Set the default security level

2. Create rules

3. Designate file types

Setting the Default Security Level

Changing the default level affects all files on the computers that have software restriction policies applied to them. In the details pane, the current default level is indicated by a black circle with a check mark in it. Upon installation, the default security level of software restriction policies on all files on your system is set to Unrestricted.

To set the default security level of software restriction policies, complete the following steps:

1. Access the Group Policy Object Editor console for a GPO.

2. In the Group Policy Object Editor console, click Computer Configuration, double-click Windows Settings, double-click Security Settings, and then double-click Software Restriction Policies.

3. In the details pane, double-click Security Levels.

4. Right-click one of the following:

   ❑ Disallowed, which does not allow the software to run, regardless of the access rights of the user who is logged on to the computer

❑ Unrestricted, which allows software to run with the full rights of the user who is logged on to the computer

5. Click Properties.

6. In the Allowed or Disallowed Properties dialog box (depending on your choice), click Set As Default.

Creating Rules

Rules identify and control the running of software and override the default security level. You can create four types of rules: hash rules, certificate rules, path rules, and Internet zone rules.

Creating a Hash Rule   Create a hash rule to prevent a virus, Trojan horse, or other file from running on your computer. If you want others in your organization to use a hash rule to prevent a virus from running, calculate the hash of the virus using software restriction policies and e-mail the hash value to others. Do not e-mail the virus. You can also prevent a virus from running on your computer by creating a path rule to prevent execution of e-mail attachments.

To create a hash rule, complete the following steps:

1. Access the Group Policy Object Editor console for a GPO.

2. In the Group Policy Object Editor console, click Computer Configuration, double-click Windows Settings, double-click Security Settings, and then double-click Software Restriction Policies.

3. Right-click Additional Rules, and then click New Hash Rule.

4. In the New Hash Rule dialog box, shown in Figure 13-3, browse to a file, or paste a precalculated hash in the File Hash box.

5. In the Security Level list, select one of the following:

❑ Disallowed, which does not allow the software to run, regardless of the access rights of the user who is logged on to the computer

❑ Unrestricted, which allows software to run with the full rights of the user who is logged on to the computer

6. Type a description for this rule in the Description box, and then click OK.

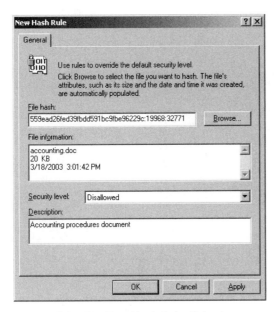

Figure 13-3   The New Hash Rule dialog box

Creating a Certificate Rule   Create a certificate rule to automatically trust software from a trusted source in a domain without prompting the user or to run files in disallowed areas of your operating system. Certificate rules can be applied to scripts and Windows Installer packages. They do not apply to files with .exe or .dll filename extensions.

To create a certificate rule, complete the following steps:

1. Access the Group Policy Object Editor console for a GPO.

2. In the Group Policy Object Editor console, click Computer Configuration, double-click Windows Settings, double-click Security Settings, and then double-click Software Restriction Policies.

3. Right-click Additional Rules, and then click New Certificate Rule.

4. In the New Certificate Rule dialog box, shown in Figure 13-4, click Browse and then select a certificate.

5. In the Security Level list, select one of the following:

   ❑ Disallowed, which does not allow the software to run, regardless of the access rights of the user who is logged on to the computer

   ❑ Unrestricted, which allows software to run with the full rights of the user who is logged on to the computer

6. Type a description for this rule, and then click OK.

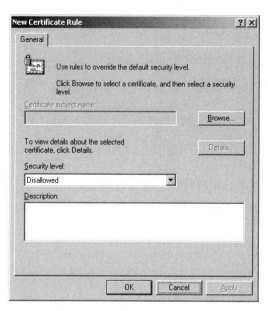

Figure 13-4   The New Certificate Rule dialog box

Creating an Internet Zone Rule   Create an Internet zone rule to identify software from a zone that is specified through Internet Explorer. Zone rules apply only to Windows Installer packages.

To create an Internet zone rule, complete the following steps:

1. Access the Group Policy Object Editor console for a GPO.

2. In the Group Policy Object Editor console, click Computer Configuration, double-click Windows Settings, double-click Security Settings, and then double-click Software Restriction Policies.

3. Right-click Additional Rules, and then click New Internet Zone Rule.

4. In the New Internet Zone Rule dialog box, shown in Figure 13-5, select a zone from the Internet Zone list.

5. In the Security Level list, select one of the following:

   ❑ Disallowed, which does not allow the software to run, regardless of the access rights of the user who is logged on to the computer

   ❑ Unrestricted, which allows software to run with the full rights of the user who is logged on to the computer

6. Type a description for this rule, and then click OK.

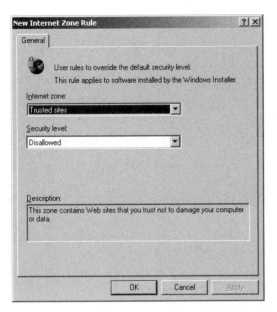

Figure 13-5   The New Internet Zone Rule dialog box

Creating a Path Rule   Create a path rule to prevent users from executing applications in a path you specify. If you create a path rule for an application and intend to prevent the program from running by setting the security level to Disallowed, note that a user can still run the software by copying it to another location. Environment variables, such as %*Programfiles*% or %*Systemroot*%, can be used in your path rule. You can also create a registry path rule for files that are not always installed in specific file folders. The wildcard characters * and ? are supported in path rules. To prevent users from executing mail attachments, create a path rule for your mail program's attachment directory that prevents users from running mail attachments.

To create a path rule, complete the following steps:

1. Access the Group Policy Object Editor console for a GPO.

2. In the Group Policy Object Editor console, click Computer Configuration, double-click Windows Settings, double-click Security Settings, and then double-click Software Restriction Policies.

3. Right-click Additional Rules, and then click New Path Rule.

4. In the New Path Rule dialog box, shown in Figure 13-6, type a path in the Path box, or browse to a file or folder.

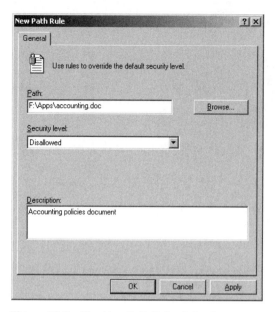

Figure 13-6   The New Path Rule dialog box

5. In the Security Level list, select one of the following:

❏ Disallowed, which does not allow the software to run, regardless of the access rights of the user who is logged on to the computer

❏ Unrestricted, which allows software to run with the full rights of the user who is logged on to the computer

6. Type a description for this rule, and then click OK.

> **Important**   For certain folders, such as the Windows folder, setting the security level to Disallowed can adversely affect the operation of your operating system. Make sure that you do not disallow a crucial component of the operating system or one of its dependent programs.

To create a registry path rule, complete the following steps:

1. Click Start, point to Run, type **regedit**, and then click OK.

2. Right-click the registry key for which you want to create a rule and click Copy Key Name. Make a note of the Value name located in the details pane.

3. Access the Group Policy Object Editor console for a GPO.

4. In the Group Policy Object Editor console, click Computer Configuration, double-click Windows Settings, double-click Security Settings, and then double-click Software Restriction Policies.

5. Right-click Additional rules, and then click New Path Rule.

6. In the New Path Rule dialog box, type the registry path in the Path box. The registry path should be formatted as follows: *%Registry Hive\Registry Key Name\Value Name%*. Notice that the registry path is enclosed in percent (%) signs. The registry path rule can contain a suffix after the closing percent sign, for example: %HKEY_CURRENT_USER\Software\Microsoft\Windows\CurrentVersion \Explorer\Shell Folders\Cache%OLK* is valid. This registry path rule identifies the folder that Microsoft Outlook XP uses to store attachments before launching them.

> **Note** The registry hive must not be abbreviated. For example, HKCU cannot be substituted for HKEY_CURRENT_USER.

7. In the Security Level list, select one of the following:

   ❑ Disallowed, which does not allow the software to run, regardless of the access rights of the user who is logged on to the computer

   ❑ Unrestricted, which allows software to run with the full rights of the user who is logged on to the computer

8. Type a description for this rule, and then click OK.

> **Note** You must be an administrator to create a registry path rule.

Designating File Types

File types that are affected by hash, certificate, path, and Internet zone rules must be listed in the Designated File Types setting in the Software Restriction Policies extension. The list of file types in the Designated File Types setting is shared by all rules. However, you can specify different designated files lists for computer policies and for user policies.

To designate or delete a file type, complete the following steps:

1. Access the Group Policy Object Editor console for a GPO.

2. In the Group Policy Object Editor console, click Computer Configuration, double-click Windows Settings, double-click Security Settings, and then double-click Software Restriction Policies.

3. In the details pane, double-click the Designated File Types setting.

4. In the Designated File Types dialog box, shown in Figure 13-7, do one of the following:

   ❑ To add a file type, type the filename extension in the File Extension box and click Add. Click OK.

❑ To delete a file type, select the file type in the Designated File Types list and click Delete. Click OK.

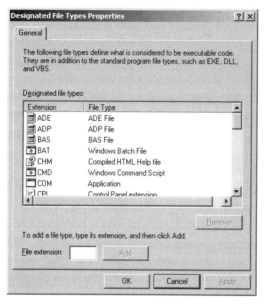

Figure 13-7   The Designated File Types dialog box

Optional Tasks for Implementing Software Restriction Policies

When implementing software restriction policies, you can optionally complete the following tasks:

- Prevent software restriction policies from applying to local administrators
- Set trusted publisher options

To prevent software restriction policies from applying to local administrators, complete the following steps:

1. Access the Group Policy Object Editor console for a GPO.

2. In the Group Policy Object Editor console, click Computer Configuration, double-click Windows Settings, double-click Security Settings, and then double-click Software Restriction Policies.

3. In the details pane, double-click the Enforcement setting.

4. In the Enforcement Properties dialog box, shown in Figure 13-8, click All Users Except Local Administrators, and then click OK.

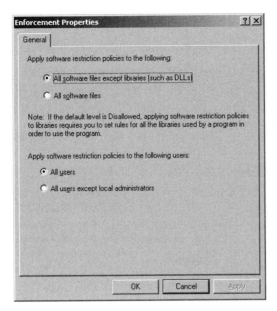

Figure 13-8   The Enforcement Properties dialog box

To set trusted publisher options, complete the following steps:

1. Access the Group Policy Object Editor console for a GPO.

2. In the Group Policy Object Editor console, click Computer Configuration, double-click Windows Settings, double-click Security Settings, and then double-click Software Restriction Policies.

3. In the details pane, double-click the Trusted Publishers setting.

4. In the Trusted Publishers Properties dialog box, shown in Figure 13-9, select the users that you want to have the right to decide what certificates will be trusted, and then click OK.

Note   Local computer administrators have the right to specify trusted publishers on the local computer, whereas enterprise administrators have the right to specify trusted publishers on an OU level.

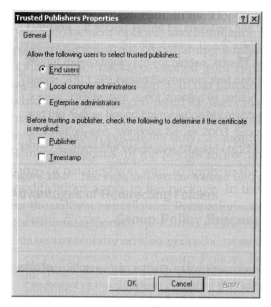

Figure 13-9   The Trusted Publishers Properties dialog box

Best Practices for Software Restriction Policies

The following are the best practices for applying software restriction policies:

- Create a separate GPO for software restriction policies so you can disable them in an emergency without affecting the rest of your security settings.

- Test a software restriction policy before applying it to other computers. Do not disallow programs or files without the proper testing. Restrictions on certain files can seriously affect the operation of your computer or network.

- If you need to edit a software restriction policy, disable it. If you apply the policy in parts, and a user refreshes the policy before all of the parts are in effect, that user's computer might be adversely affected.

- If you experience problems with applied policies, reboot in safe mode. Software restriction policies do not apply in safe mode.

- If you accidentally lock down a workstation with software restriction policies, reboot in safe mode, log on as a local administrator, modify the policy, run Gpupdate.exe, reboot the computer, and log on normally.

- Use software restriction policies in conjunction with access control settings.

- Use caution when defining a default setting of Disallowed. When you set the default security level to Disallowed, every application is restricted. A policy must be applied for every application that you want to run.

Software Restriction Policies Troubleshooting

Table 13-1 describes some troubleshooting scenarios related to software restriction policies.

Table 13-1   Software Restriction Policies Troubleshooting Scenarios

Causes	Solutions
Problem: The user receives an error message such as "Windows cannot open this program because it has been prevented by a software restriction policy. For more information, open the Event Viewer console or contact your system administrator." Or, on the command line, the message "The system cannot execute the specified program" appears.	
The default security level (or a rule) was set to Disallowed, and the software will not start.	Check the event log to see if the software program is set to Disallowed and what rule is applied.
Problem: Modified software restriction policies are not taking effect.	
Software restriction policies that are specified in a domain through Group Policy override any policies that are configured locally. This might imply that there is a policy from the domain that is overriding your setting.	Use Gpresult command-line tool to determine which policies apply. Check domain-level policies for No Override settings.
Group Policy might not have refreshed its settings. Group Policy applies policy changes periodically; therefore, it is likely that the policy changes made in the directory have not yet been refreshed.	Refresh policy with the command-line utility Gpupdate.
The local computer on which you changed software restriction policies for the network cannot contact a domain controller.	The computer on which you modify software restriction policies must be able to contact a domain controller to update policy for a network. Ensure the computer can contact a domain controller.
Problem: You have added a rule to software restriction policies, and you cannot log on to your computer.	
Your computer accesses many programs and files when it starts. You might have inadvertently set one of these programs or files to Disallowed. Because the computer cannot access the program or file, it cannot start properly.	Start your computer in safe mode, log on as a local administrator, and change software restriction policies to allow the program or file to run.
Problem: A new policy is not applying to a specific filename extension.	
The filename extension is not in the list of file types supported by the software restriction policies.	Add the filename extension to the list of supported file types.

Lesson Review

The following questions are intended to reinforce key information presented in this lesson. If you are unable to answer a question, review the lesson and then try the question again. Answers to the questions can be found in the "Questions and Answers" section at the end of this chapter.

1. What is the purpose of software restriction policies?

_____

_____

2. Explain the two default security levels.

_____

_____

3. Describe how software is identified by software restriction policies.

_____

_____

4. List the order of rule precedence.

_____

_____

5. Which of the following rule types applies only to Windows Installer packages?

    a. Hash rules

    b. Certificate rules

    c. Internet zone rules

    d. Path rules

Lesson Summary

- Software restriction policies address the problem of regulating unknown or untrusted code. Software restriction policies are security settings in a GPO provided to identify software and control its ability to run on a local computer, site, domain, or OU.

- There are two default security levels for software restriction policies: Disallowed, which does not allow the software to run, regardless of the access rights of the user who is logged on to the computer, and Unrestricted, which allows software to run with the full rights of the user who is logged on to the computer.

■ Software restriction policies identify and control the running of software by using rules. There are four types of rules, which correspond to the four ways of identifying software: a hash rule, a certificate rule, a path rule, and an Internet zone rule. These rules override the default security level.

Lesson 3: Implementing an Audit Policy

Audit policies allow you to track user activities and system-wide events in the security log in the Event Viewer console. In this lesson, you learn how to plan and set up an audit policy.

After this lesson, you will be able to

- Describe the purpose of auditing
- Plan an audit strategy and determine which events to audit
- Set up an audit policy
- Set up auditing on files, folders, and printers
- Set up auditing on Active Directory objects

Estimated lesson time: 45 minutes

Understanding Auditing

Auditing in Windows Server 2003 is the process of tracking both user activities and system activities, called *events*, on a computer. You can specify that information about an event be written to the security log in the Event Viewer console whenever certain actions are performed. Windows Server 2003 writes an event to the security log on the computer where the event occurs. For example, any time someone tries to log on to the domain using a domain user account and the logon attempt fails, Windows Server 2003 writes an event to the security log on the domain controller. The event is recorded on the domain controller rather than on the computer at which the logon attempt was made because it is the domain controller that attempted to authenticate the logon attempt and failed. The information about an event in the security log includes

- The type of event, such as error, warning, information, success audit, or failure audit
- The date the event was generated
- The time the event was logged
- The software that logged the event
- The event ID number
- The user who performed the action that generated the event
- The name of the computer on which the event occurred
- A description of the event

You can audit both successful and failed attempts at actions, so the audit can show who performed actions on the network and who tried to perform actions that are not permitted. Viewing security logs is discussed in Lesson 5.

Understanding Audit Policies

You determine the events you want to audit by setting up an audit policy in a GPO. An audit policy defines the categories of events recorded in the security log on each computer. You set the Audit Policy settings in the Computer Configuration/Windows Settings/Security Settings/Local Policies/Audit Policy extension in a GPO. You can set up an audit policy for a computer to track the success and failure of the event categories described in Table 13-2.

Table 13-2   Event Categories in the Audit Policy Extension

Event Category	Description
Account logon	A domain controller received a request to validate a user account.
Account management	An administrator created, changed, or deleted a user account or group. A user account was renamed, disabled, or enabled, or a password was set or changed.
Directory service access	A user gained access to an Active Directory object. You must configure specific Active Directory objects for auditing to log this type of event, as described in the section "Configuring Objects for Auditing" later in this lesson.
Logon events	A user logged on or logged off, or a user made or canceled a network connection to the computer.
Object access	A user gained access to a file, folder, or printer. You must configure specific files, folders, or printers for auditing, as described in the section "Configuring Objects for Auditing" later in this lesson.
Policy change	A change was made to the user security options, user rights, or audit policies.
Privilege use	A user exercised a right, such as changing the system time (this does not include rights that are related to logging on and logging off).
Process tracking	A program performed an action. This information is generally useful only for programmers who want to track details of program execution. Be aware that process tracking can generate a large number of events.
System events	A user restarted or shut down the computer, or an event occurred that affects system security or the security log (for example, the audit log is full and the system discards entries).

Off the Record   Audit Object Access, Audit Privilege Use, and Audit Process Tracking are specifically turned off in the Default Domain Controllers Policy. Although you probably won't use the latter two types of auditing, you should keep in mind that if you want to audit a file or folder that sits on a domain controller, you'll have to enable Audit Object Access in the Default Domain Controllers Policy, instead of simply enabling it in the Local Security Policy of the domain controller. Otherwise, the setting in the Default Domain Controllers Policy will prevent any type of auditing on the domain controller.

Audit Policy Guidelines

When you plan an audit policy, you must determine the computers on which you want to set up auditing. Auditing is turned off by default. As you are determining which computers to audit, you must also plan the events to audit on each computer. Windows Server 2003 records audited events on each computer separately.

After you have determined the events to audit, you must determine whether to audit the success of events, failure of events, or both. Tracking successful events can tell you how often Windows Server 2003 or users gain access to specific files, printers, or other objects. You can use this information for resource planning. Tracking failed events can alert you to possible security breaches. For example, if you notice several failed logon attempts by a certain user account, especially if these attempts are occurring outside normal business hours, you can assume that an unauthorized person is attempting to break into your system.

Other guidelines in determining your audit policy include the following:

■ Define an audit policy that is useful and manageable. Always audit sensitive and confidential data. Audit only those events that provide you with meaningful information about your network environment. This minimizes the usage of server resources and makes essential information easier to locate. Auditing too many types of events can create excess overhead for Windows Server 2003 and make it more difficult for administrators to find useful information.

■ If security breaches are an issue for your organization, set up auditing for files and folders on NTFS file system partitions by specifying the Audit Object Access event category for audit.

■ Most printers should not be audited because the Event Log might fill up with useless information. It is best to limit printer auditing to select printers that are used for printing sensitive documents or are expensive to operate.

■ Audit resource access by the Everyone group instead of the Users group. This ensures that you audit anyone who can connect to the network, not just the users for whom you create user accounts in the domain. Also audit resource access failures by the Everyone group.

■ Audit all administrative tasks performed by the administrative groups. This ensures that you audit any additions or changes made by administrators.

■ Determine if you need to track trends of system usage. Whether so, plan to archive event logs. Archiving these logs allows you to view how usage changes over time and to plan to increase system resources before they become a problem. You can learn how to archive event logs in Lesson 4.

Implementing an Audit Policy

The requirements to set up and administer an audit policy are as follows:

- You must have the Manage Auditing And Security Log user right for the computer where you want to configure an audit policy or review an audit log. By default, Windows Server 2003 grants these rights to the Administrators group. For information about user rights, see Lesson 1.

- The files and folders to be audited must be on NTFS volumes.

The tasks for implementing an audit policy are the following:

1. Specify the event categories to be audited.

2. Configure objects for auditing if you have specified the Audit Directory Service Access event category or the Audit Object Access event category to be audited.

Specifying Event Categories to be Audited

The first step in implementing auditing is selecting the categories of events that you want to audit. For each event category, you can indicate whether to track successful or failed attempts. Keep in mind that the security log is limited in size. Select the events to be audited carefully and consider the amount of disk space you are willing to devote to the security log.

To specify the event categories to be audited, complete the following steps:

1. Do one of the following:

   - To specify event categories for a local computer: Click Start, point to Administrative Tools, and then click Local Security Policy. In Security Settings, in the console tree, double-click Local Policies, and then double-click Audit Policy.

   - To specify event categories for all domain controllers when you are logged on to a domain controller: Click Start, point to Administrative Tools, and then click Active Directory Users And Computers. In the console tree, right-click the Domain Controllers OU, and then click Properties. In the Group Policy tab, add a new policy or select an existing policy in which you want set the audit policy, and then click Edit. In the Group Policy Object Editor console, in the console tree, click Computer Configuration, double-click Windows Settings, double-click Security Settings, double-click Local Policies, and then double-click Audit Policy.

   - To specify event categories for a site, domain, or OU when you are on a domain controller: Click Start, point to Administrative Tools, and then click Active Directory Users And Computers. In the console tree, right-click the site, domain, or OU for which you want to implement an audit policy, and then click Properties. In the Group Policy tab, add a new policy or select an existing policy in which you want set the audit policy, and then click Edit. In the Group Policy Object Editor console, in the console tree, click Computer Configuration, double-click Windows Settings, double-click Security Settings, double-click Local Policies, and then double-click Audit Policy.

❑ To specify event categories for a site, domain, or OU when you are on a member server or on a workstation that is joined to a domain: Click Start and then click Run. In the Open list, type **mmc** and then click OK. In the Console1 window, on the File menu, click Add/Remove Snap-In. In the Add/Remove Snap-In dialog box, click Add. In the Add Standalone Snap-In dialog box, click Group Policy, and then click Add. On the Select Group Policy Object page in the Group Policy Wizard, click Browse. In the Browse For A Group Policy Object dialog box, select a GPO in the appropriate site, domain, or OU, or create a new one, and click OK. Click Finish, click Close, and then click OK. In the resulting Group Policy Object Editor console, in the console tree, click Computer Configuration, double-click Windows Settings, double-click Security Settings, double-click Local Policies, and then double-click Audit Policy.

2. In the details pane, right-click the event category you want to audit, and then click Properties.

3. In the Properties dialog box for the event category, shown in Figure 13-10, click one or both of the following:

❑ Success, to audit successful attempts for the event category

❑ Failure, to audit failed attempts for the event category

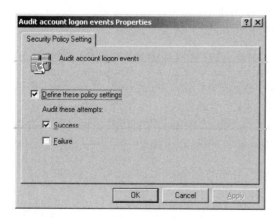

Figure 13-10 The Properties dialog box for the Audit Account Logon Events event category

4. Click OK.

5. Because the changes that you make to your computer's audit policy take effect only when the policy is propagated (applied) to your computer, do one of the following to initiate policy propagation:

- ❑ Type **gpupdate** at the command prompt, and then press ENTER.

- ❑ Restart your computer.

- ❑ Wait for automatic policy propagation. By default, setting changes are applied every 90 minutes on a workstation or server (with a 30-minute random offset) and every five minutes on a domain controller. Settings automatically refresh every 16 hours, regardless of any changes that are made.

> **Note**   Security auditing for workstations, member servers, and domain controllers can be enabled remotely only by members of the Domain Administrators and Enterprise Administrators groups.

Configuring Objects for Auditing

If you have specified the Audit Directory Service Access event category or the Audit Object Access event category to audit, you must configure the objects for auditing.

Configuring Directory Service Objects for Auditing   If you have specified the Audit Directory Service Access event category for auditing, you can audit user access to Active Directory objects.

To configure an Active Directory object for auditing, complete the following steps:

1. Click Start, point to Administrative Tools, and then click Active Directory Users And Computers. In the Active Directory Users And Computers console, click View, and then click Advanced Features.

2. Select the object that you want to audit, click Properties on the Action menu, click the Security tab, and then click Advanced.

3. In the Advanced Security Settings For dialog box for the object, in the Auditing tab, click Add, select the users or groups for whom you want to audit Active Directory object access, and then click OK.

4. In the Auditing Entry For dialog box for the object, shown in Figure 13-11, select the Successful check box, the Failed check box, or both check boxes for the events that you want to audit.

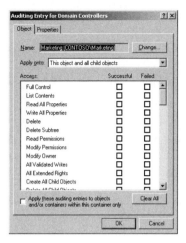

Figure 13-11 The Auditing Entry For dialog box for the Domain Controllers OU

Table 13-3 describes some of the audit events for Active Directory objects and explains what action triggers each event to occur.

Table 13-3 Some Active Directory Object Events and What Triggers Them

Event	User Activity That Triggers the Event
Full Control	Performing any type of access to the audited object
List Contents	Viewing the objects within the audited object
List Object	Viewing the audited object
Read All Properties	Viewing any attribute of the audited object
Write All Properties	Changing any attribute of the audited object
Create All Child Objects	Creating any object within the audited object
Delete All Child Objects	Deleting any object within the audited object
Read Permissions	Viewing the permissions for the audited object
Modify Permissions	Changing the permissions for the audited object
Modify Owner	Taking ownership of the audited object

5. In the Apply Onto list, specify where objects are audited. By default, this box is set to This Object And All Child Objects, so any auditing changes that you make to a parent object also apply to all child objects. Where objects are audited depends on the selection in the Apply Onto list and whether the Apply These Auditing Entries To Objects And/Or Containers Within This Container Only box is selected. These two features are enabled only for objects that act as containers.

6. Click OK to return to the Advanced Security Settings For dialog box for the object.

7. To prevent changes that are made to a parent folder from applying to the currently selected file or folder, clear the Allow Inheritable Auditing Entries From Parent To Propagate To This Object check box. If the check boxes in the Access box are shaded in the Auditing Entry For dialog box for the object, or if the Remove button is unavailable in the Advanced Security Settings For dialog box for the object, auditing has been inherited from the parent folder.

8. Click OK.

Configuring Files, Folders, and Printers for Auditing   If you have specified the Audit Object Access event category for auditing, you can audit user access to files, folders, and printers.

To configure files and folders for auditing, complete the following steps:

1. In Windows Explorer, right-click the file or folder you want to audit, and then click Properties.

2. In the Security tab in the Properties dialog box for a file or folder, click Advanced.

3. In the Advanced Security Settings For dialog box for the file or folder, in the Auditing tab, click Add, select the users and groups for whom you want to audit file and folder access, and then click OK.

4. In the Auditing Entry For dialog box for the file or folder, select the Successful check box, the Failed check box, or both check boxes for the events that you want to audit.

   Table 13-4 describes the events that can be audited for files and folders.

Table 13-4   User Events and What Triggers Them

Event	User Activity That Triggers the Event
Full Control	Performing any type of access to the audited file or folder
Traverse Folder/Execute File	Running a program or gaining access to a folder to change directories
List Folder/Read Data	Displaying the contents of a file or a folder
Read Attributes and Read Extended Attributes	Displaying the attributes of a file or folder
Create Files/Write Data and Create Folders/Append Data	Changing the contents of a file or folder or creating new folders or files in a folder
Write Attributes and Write Extended Attributes	Changing attributes of a file or folder
Delete Subfolders And Files	Deleting a file or subfolder in a folder
Delete	Deleting a file or folder

Table 13-4   User Events and What Triggers Them

Event	User Activity That Triggers the Event
Read Permissions	Viewing permissions for the file owner for a file or folder
Change Permissions	Changing permissions for a file or folder
Take Ownership	Taking ownership of a file or folder

5. In the Apply Onto list, specify where objects are audited. By default, this box is set to This Folder, Subfolders And Files, so any auditing changes that you make to a parent folder also apply to all child folders and all files in the parent and child folders. Where objects are audited depends on the selection in the Apply Onto list and whether the Apply These Auditing Entries To Objects And/Or Containers Within This Container Only check box is cleared as shown in Table 13-5.

Table 13-5   Results When the Apply These Auditing Entries To Objects And/Or Containers Within This Container Only Check Box Is Cleared

Apply Onto	Audits Current Folder	Audits Subfolders in the Current Folder	Audits Files in the Current Folder	Audits All Subsequent Folders	Audits Files in All Subsequent Folders
This Folder Only	X				
This Folder, Subfolders And Files	X	X	X	X	X
This Folder And Subfolders	X	X		X	
This Folder And Files	X		X		X
Subfolders And Files Only		X	X	X	X
Subfolders Only		X		X	
Files Only			X		X

When the Apply These Auditing Entries To Objects And/Or Containers Within This Container Only check box is selected, auditing is applied only to the selection in the Apply Onto list and its applicable child objects within the tree.

6. Click OK to return to the Advanced Security Settings dialog box for the file or folder.

7. To prevent changes that are made to a parent folder from applying to the currently selected file or folder, clear the Allow Inheritable Auditing Entries From Parent To Propagate To This Object And All Child Objects check box. If the check boxes

under Access are shaded in the Auditing Entry For dialog box for the file or folder, or if the Remove button is unavailable in the Access Control Settings For dialog box for the file or folder, auditing has been inherited from the parent folder.

8. Click OK.

To configure a printer for auditing, complete the following steps:

1. Click Start, and then click Printers And Faxes.

2. In the Printers And Faxes system folder, right-click the printer you want to audit, and then click Properties.

3. In the Properties dialog box for the printer, click the Security tab, and then click Advanced.

4. In the Advanced Security Settings For dialog box for the printer, in the Auditing tab, click Add, select the appropriate users or groups for whom you want to audit printer access, click Add, and then click OK.

5. In the Auditing Entry For dialog box for the printer, select the Successful check box, the Failed check box, or both check boxes for the events that you want to audit.

Table 13-6 describes audit events for printers and explains what action triggers the event to occur.

Table 13-6   Printer Events and What Triggers Them

Event	User Activity That Triggers the Event
Print	Printing a file
Manage Printers	Changing printer settings, pausing a printer, sharing a printer, or removing a printer
Manage Documents	Changing job settings; pausing, restarting, moving, or deleting documents; sharing a printer; or changing printer properties
Read Permissions	Viewing printer permissions
Change Permissions	Changing printer permissions
Take Ownership	Taking printer ownership

6. In the Apply Onto list, select where the auditing setting applies.

7. Click OK in the appropriate dialog boxes to exit.

Best Practices for Audit Policies

The following are the best practices for audit policies:

■ Create an audit plan. Decide what you want to audit. Consider the available resources for collecting and reviewing an audit log.

■ Collect and archive security logs across the organization. Archives can be useful in the event of an intrusion.

- Audit success and failure events in the System Events category. This audit allows you to see unusual activity that may indicate that an intruder is attempting to gain access to your computer or your network.

- Audit success events in the Policy Change event category on domain controllers. If an event is logged in this category, someone has changed the Local Security Authority (LSA) security policy configuration.

- Audit success events in the Account Management event category. This audit allows you to verify changes that are made to account properties and group properties.

- Audit success events in the Logon Events category. This audit provides a record of when each user logs on or off a computer. If a user's password is stolen and an unauthorized person logs on, you can find out when the breach of security occurred.

- Audit success events in the Account Logon Events event category. This audit allows you to see when users log on or off a domain.

- Set an appropriate size for the security log. Consider the number of events that your audit policy settings will generate and make adjustments as necessary.

Practice: Implementing Audit Policies

In this practice, you implement an audit policy for your practice domain.

Exercise 1: Planning a Domain Audit Policy

In this exercise, you plan an audit policy for your practice server.

▶ **To plan a domain audit policy**

For the *contoso.com* practice domain, determine the following:

- Which types of events to audit
- Whether to audit the success or failure of an event, or both

Use the following criteria to make your decisions:

- Record unsuccessful attempts to gain access to the network.
- Record unauthorized access to the files that make up the Customer database.
- For billing purposes, track color printer usage.
- Track whenever someone tries to tamper with the server hardware.
- Keep a record of actions that an administrator performs to track unauthorized changes.
- Track backup procedures to prevent data theft.
- Track unauthorized access to sensitive Active Directory objects.

Record your decisions to audit successful events, failed events, or both for the actions listed in the following table.

Action to Audit	Successful	Failed
Account logon events	❏	❏
Account management	❏	❏
Directory service access	❏	❏
Logon events	❏	❏
Object access	❏	❏
Policy change	❏	❏
Privilege use	❏	❏
Process tracking	❏	❏
System events	❏	❏

Action to Audit	Successful/Failed
Account logon events	Failed (for network access attempts)
Account management	Successful (for administrator actions)
Directory service access	Failed (for unauthorized access)
Logon events	Failed (for network access attempts)
Object access	Successful (for printer use) and Failed (for unauthorized access)
Policy change	Successful (for administrator actions)
Privilege use	Successful (for administrator actions and backup procedures)
Process tracking	No audits (useful primarily for developers)
System events	Successful and Failed (for attempts to breach the server)

Exercise 2: Setting Up an Audit Policy

In this exercise, you enable auditing for selected event categories.

▶ **To set up an audit policy**

1. Use the procedure provided earlier in this lesson to set the audit policy you set up in the table in Exercise 1 in a new GPO you create for the Domain Controllers OU called Domain Controllers Audit Policy.

2. Use Gpupdate to refresh Group Policy.

Exercise 3: Configuring a File for Auditing

In this exercise, you configure a file for auditing.

▶ **To configure a file for auditing**

1. In *C:* (where *C* is the name of your system drive), create a simple text file. Name the file Text.

2. Use the procedure provided earlier in this lesson to configure the Text file for auditing. Audit the success and failure for the Everyone group for each of the following events:

   ❑ Create Files/Write Data

   ❑ Delete

   ❑ Change Permissions

   ❑ Take Ownership

3. Assign Read permission to the Everyone group for the Text file. Clear the check box Allow Inheritable Permissions From The Parent To Propagate To This Object And All Child Objects. Include These With Entries Explicitly Defined Here. Click Remove to confirm that you want to clear the check box Allow Inheritable Permissions From The Parent To Propagate To This Object And All Child Objects. Include These With Entries Explicitly Defined Here. Click OK.

Exercise 4: Configuring a Printer for Auditing

In this exercise, you configure a printer for auditing.

> **Important**   To complete this exercise, you need to have a local printer installed on your computer. However, you do *not* need a printing device connected to the computer. If you do not have a local printer installed, create one now. A *printing device* refers to the physical machine that prints, and *local printer* refers to the software that Windows Server 2003 needs to send data to the printing device.

▶ **To configure a printer for auditing**

Use the procedure provided earlier in this lesson to configure a printer for auditing. Audit the success of the Everyone group for all types of access to This Printer And Documents.

Exercise 5: Configuring an Active Directory Object for Auditing

In this exercise, you configure an Active Directory object for auditing.

▶ **To configure an Active Directory object for auditing**

Use the procedure provided earlier in this lesson to configure the Users folder in the Active Directory Users And Computers console for auditing. Audit the success and failure of the Everyone group for Write All Properties and Delete for This Object Only.

Lesson Review

The following questions are intended to reinforce key information presented in this lesson. If you are unable to answer a question, review the lesson and then try the question again. Answers to the questions can be found in the "Questions and Answers" section at the end of this chapter.

1. What is the purpose of auditing?

   _____

   _____

2. Where can you view audited events?

   _____

   _____

3. What is an audit policy?

   _____

   _____

4. Which event categories require you to configure specific objects for auditing to log the events?

   _____

   _____

5. Which of the following event categories should you audit if you want to find out if an unauthorized person is trying to access a user account by entering random passwords or by using password-cracking software? (Choose all that apply.)

   a. Logon Events—success events

   b. Logon Events—failure events

   c. Account Logon—success events

   d. Account Logon—failure events

Lesson Summary

- Auditing is a tool for maintaining network security. Auditing allows you to track user activities and system-wide events.

- An audit policy defines the categories of events recorded in the security log on each computer. You set the Audit Policy settings in the Computer Configuration/ Windows Settings/Security Settings/Local Policies/Audit Policy extensions in a GPO. You use the security log in the Event Viewer console to view audited events.

- You can audit both successful and failed attempts at actions, so the audit can show who performed actions on the network and who tried to perform actions that are not permitted.

Lesson 4: Administering the Security Log

The security log contains information on security events that are specified in the audit policy. To administer the security log, you use the Event Viewer console. This lesson shows you how to view, find events in, filter, configure, and archive the security log by using the Event Viewer console.

After this lesson, you will be able to

- View the security log
- Find events in the security log
- Filter events shown in the security log
- Configure the security log
- Archive the security log

Estimated lesson time: 20 minutes

Understanding Windows Server 2003 Logs

You use the Event Viewer console to view information contained in Windows Server 2003 logs. By default, there are three logs available to view in the Event Viewer console. These logs are described in Table 13-7.

Table 13-7   Logs Maintained by Windows Server 2003

Log	Description
Application log	Contains errors, warnings, or information that programs, such as a database program or an e-mail program, generate. The program developer presets the events to record.
Security log	Contains information about the success or failure of audited events. The events that Windows Server 2003 records are a result of your audit policy.
System log	Contains errors, warnings, and information that Windows Server 2003 generates. Windows Server 2003 presets the events to record.

Application and system logs can be viewed by all users. The security log is accessible only to system administrators. As you learned in Lesson 3, security logging is turned off by default. To enable security logging, you must set up an audit policy in a GPO at the appropriate level.

Note   If additional services are installed, they might add their own event log. For example, Active Directory logs events in the Directory Service log, and the DNS service logs events in the DNS Server log. The Directory Service Log is discussed in Chapter 2, "Installing and Configuring Active Directory."

Viewing the Security Log

The security log contains information about events that are monitored by an audit policy, such as failed and successful logon attempts. Review the security log frequently. Set a schedule and regularly review the security log because configuring auditing alone does not alert you to security breaches.

To view the security log, complete the following steps:

1. Click Start, point to Administrative Tools, and then click Event Viewer.

2. In the console tree, select Security. In the details pane, the Event Viewer console displays a list of log entries and summary information for each item, as shown in Figure 13-12.

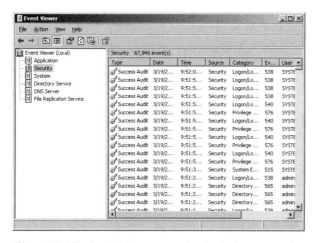

Figure 13-12   Event Viewer console displaying a sample security log

Successful events appear with a key icon and unsuccessful events appear with a lock icon. Other important information includes the date and time that the event occurred, the category of the event, and the user who generated the event. The category indicates the event category, such as Object Access, Account Management, Directory Service Access, or Logon Events.

3. To view the properties for any event, double-click the event. The properties for a logon/logoff event are shown in Figure 13-13.

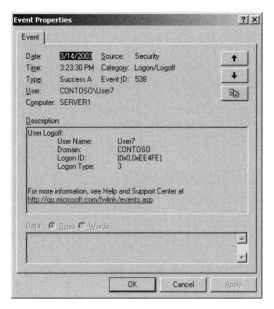

Figure 13-13   The Event Properties dialog box showing properties for a logon/logoff event

Viewing the Security Log on a Remote Computer

Windows Server 2003 records events in the security log on the computer at which the event occurred. You can view these events from any computer as long as you have administrative privileges for the computer where the events occurred.

To view the security log on a remote computer, complete the following steps:

1. Ensure that security auditing has been enabled on a remote machine. (Refer to Lesson 3 for details.)

2. Click Start, point to Administrative Tools, and then click Event Viewer.

3. Right-click the Event Viewer (Local) node and select Connect To Another Computer.

4. In the Select Computer dialog box, click Another Computer and type the network name, IP address, or DNS address for the computer for which you want to display a security log. You can also browse for the computer name.

5. Click OK.

Finding Events in the Security Log

When you first start the Event Viewer console, it automatically displays all events that are recorded in the security log. You can search for specific events in the security log by using the Find option.

To find events in the security log, complete the following steps:

1. Start Event Viewer, view the security log, and then click Find on the View menu.

2. In the Find In dialog box for the security log, shown in Figure 13-14, indicate your choices of the available search criteria.

   ❑ Select the types of events you want to locate in the Event Types area.

   ❑ Select the software or component driver that logged the event in the Event Source list.

   ❑ Select the event category in the Category list.

   ❑ Indicate the event number that identifies the event in the Event ID box.

   ❑ Indicate the user logon name in the User box.

   ❑ Indicate the computer name in the Computer box.

   ❑ Indicate the description of the event in the Description box.

   ❑ Select the direction in which to search the log (up or down) in the Search Direction area.

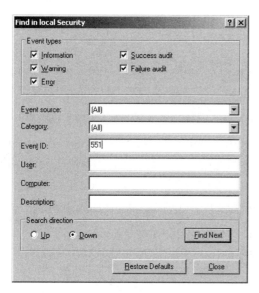

Figure 13-14   The Find In dialog box

3. Click Find Next. If an event matching the criteria you specified is found, it is highlighted in the security log.

4. Click Find Next to find the next matching event, or click Close to end your search.

Filtering Events in the Security Log

To display only specific events that appear in the security log—for example, attempting to write to a text file without the necessary permissions—you can narrow down the events to display by using the Filter option.

To filter events in the security log, complete the following steps:

1. Start the Event Viewer console, view the security log, and then click Filter on the View menu.

2. In the Filter tab in the Security Properties dialog box, shown in Figure 13-15, indicate your choices of the available filtering criteria.

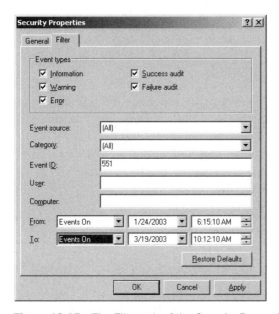

Figure 13-15   The Filter tab of the Security Properties dialog box

- ❑ Select the types of events you want to display in the Event Types area.
- ❑ Select the software or component driver that logged the event in the Event Source list.
- ❑ Select the event category in the Category list.
- ❑ Indicate the event number that identifies the event in the Event ID box.
- ❑ Indicate the user logon name in the User box.
- ❑ Indicate the computer name in the Computer box.

❑ Indicate the beginning of the range of events that you want to filter in the From list. Select First Event to see events starting with the first event in the log. Select Events On to see events that occurred starting at a specific time and date.

❑ Indicate the end of the range of events that you want to filter in the To list. Select Last Event to see events ending with the last event in the log. Select Events On to see events that occurred up to a specific time and date.

3. Click OK. The events you selected for your filtered display appear in the security log.

To remove a security log filter, complete the following steps:

1. Start the Event Viewer console, view the security log, and then click Filter on the View menu.

2. In the Filter tab in the Security Properties dialog box, click Restore Defaults, and then click OK.

Configuring the Security Log

Security logging begins when you set an audit policy for the domain controller or local computer. Logging stops when the security log becomes full and cannot overwrite itself, either because it has been set for manual clearing or because the first event in the log is not old enough. When security logging stops, an error might be written to the application log. You can avoid a full security log by logging only key events and by configuring the size of the security log.

To configure the security log size, complete the following steps:

1. Open the Event Viewer console.

2. In the console tree, right-click Security, and then click Properties.

3. In the General tab in the Security Properties dialog box, shown in Figure 13-16, type the maximum log file size, which can be from 64 kilobytes (KB) to 4,194,240 KB (4 gigabytes). The default size is 512 KB.

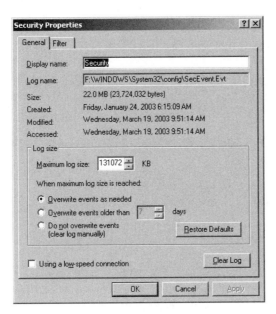

Figure 13-16   The General tab of the Security Properties dialog box

4. Under When Maximum Log File Size Is Reached, select one of the following:

❑ Overwrite Events As Needed to write all new events to the log. When the log is full, each new event replaces the oldest event. Use this option with caution; it can be used to hide undesirable events.

❑ Overwrite Events Older Than X Days and specify for X the number of days (1–365) an event is to be retained before it is overwritten. New events are not added if the maximum log size is reached and there are no events older than this period.

❑ Do Not Overwrite Events (Clear Log Manually) to specify whether existing events are retained when the log is full. If the maximum log size is reached, new events are discarded. This option requires you to manually clear the log.

Note   You also can configure security log size for computers in a site, domain, or OU by using the Event Log settings in a GPO. The Event Log settings are located in Computer Configuration/Windows Settings/Security Settings/Event Log.

Clearing the Security Log

When the log is full and no more events can be logged, you can clear the log manually. Clearing the log erases all events permanently. Reducing the amount of time you keep an event also frees the log if it allows the next record to be overwritten.

To manually clear the security log, complete the following steps:

1. Open the Event Viewer console.

2. Right-click Security in the console tree, and then click Clear All Events.

3. In the Event Viewer message box

   ❑ Click Yes to archive the log before clearing.

   ❑ Click No to permanently discard the current event records and start recording new events.

4. If you clicked Yes, in the Save As dialog box, in the File Name list, type a name for the log file to be archived.

5. In the Save As Type list, click a file format, and then click Save.

Off the Record   In a secure environment, the Event Viewer security logs on servers storing confidential data or trade secrets are often configured so that they will not overwrite events. However, with that setting alone, the server will simply stop logging new events once the log is full. This could be a problem if the events that were missed could have contained the proof that someone hacked your system. In order to truly make this setting work, you can configure the Audit: Shut Down System Immediately If Unable To Log Security Audits policy. This policy is configurable through the Group Policy Object Editor under the following path: Computer Configuration/Windows Settings/Security Settings/Local Policies/Security Options. If you enable this setting, be sure that you also have a procedure in place to archive the security log, or your server will be unable to provide services once the log is full. You'll have the opportunity to use this setting in the Troubleshooting Lab of this chapter.

Archiving the Security Log

Archiving security logs allows you to maintain a history of security-related events. Many organizations have policies on keeping archive logs for a specified period to track security-related information over time. When you archive a log, the entire log is saved, regardless of filtering options.

To archive a security log, complete the following steps:

1. Open the Event Viewer console.

2. Right-click Security in the console tree, and then click Save Log File As.

3. In the Save As dialog box, in the File Name list, type a name for the log file to be archived.

4. In the Save As Type list, click a file format, and then click Save.

If you archive a log in log-file format, you can reopen it in the Event Viewer console. Logs saved as event log files (*.evt) retain the binary data for each event recorded. If you archive a log in text or comma-delimited format (*.txt and *.csv, respectively), you can reopen the log in other programs such as word-processing or spreadsheet programs. Logs saved in text or comma-delimited format do not retain the binary data and cannot be reopened in the Event Viewer console.

To view an archived security log, complete the following steps:

1. Open the Event Viewer console.

2. Right-click the security log in the console tree, and then click Open Log File.

3. In the Open dialog box, click the file you want to open. You might need to search for the drive or folder that contains the document.

4. In the Log Type list, select Security for the type of log to be opened.

5. In the Display Name box, type the name of the file as you want it to appear in the console tree, and then click Open.

To remove an archived log file from your system, delete the file in Windows Explorer.

Practice: Administering the Security Log

In this practice, you view and manage the security log.

Important   Before attempting the exercises in this practice, you must first complete all exercises in Lesson 3.

Exercise 1: Viewing and Filtering the Security Log

In this exercise, you view the security log for your computer. Then, you filter the log to display only specific events.

▶ **To view and filter the security log**

1. Use the procedure provided earlier in this lesson to view the security log. As you scroll through the log, double-click a couple of events to view a description.

2. Use the procedure provided earlier in this lesson to filter all event types to display those with the Event ID of 576.

3. Use the procedure provided earlier in this lesson to remove the security log filter.

Exercise 2: Configuring the Security Log

In this exercise, you configure the Event Viewer console to overwrite events when the security log gets full.

▶   **To configure the security log**

Use the procedure provided earlier in this lesson to configure the security log size. Change the maximum log size to 2048 KB and overwrite older events with new events as necessary.

Exercise 3: Clearing and Archiving the Security Log

In this exercise, you clear the security log, archive a security log, and view the archived security log.

▶   **To clear and archive the security log**

1. Use the procedure provided earlier in this lesson to clear and archive the security log. Save the log in a file named Archive.evt.

2. Use the procedure provided earlier in this lesson to view the archived security log file named Archive.evt.

Lesson Review

The following questions are intended to reinforce key information presented in this lesson. If you are unable to answer a question, review the lesson and then try the question again. Answers to the questions can be found in the "Questions and Answers" section at the end of this chapter.

1. What information is logged in the security log?

   _____

   _____

2. What is the default size of the security log?

   _____

   _____

3. In which of the following file formats can you archive a security log? Choose three.

   a. .txt

   b. .doc

   c. .rtf

   d. .bmp

    e. .evt

    f. .csv

    g. .crv

4. In which of the following archived file formats can you reopen the file in the Event Viewer console?

    a. .txt

    b. .doc

    c. .rtf

    d. .bmp

    e. .evt

    f. .csv

    g. .crv

5. You filtered a security log to display only the events with Event ID 576. Then you archived this log. What information is saved?

    a. The entire log is saved

    b. The filtered log is saved

    c. The entire log and the filtered log are each saved separately

    d. No log is saved

Lesson Summary

- The security log contains information about the success or failure of audited events. Security logging is turned off by default. The events that Windows Server 2003 records are a result of the audit policy set in a GPO at the appropriate level. The security log is accessible only to system administrators.

- Use the Event Viewer console to view information contained in the security log. Use the Find option to search for specific events in the security log. Use the Filter option to display specific events that appear in the security log. Use the Clear All Events option to manually clear the security log. Use the Save Log File As option to archive the security log.

- Use the General tab in the Security Properties dialog box to configure the size of the security log. The default size is 512 KB.

Lesson 5: Using Security Templates

Windows Server 2003 provides a centralized method of configuring security by using security templates. This lesson explains how to use security templates.

After this lesson, you will be able to

- Explain the purpose of security templates
- Explain the purpose of the predefined security templates
- Manage security templates

Estimated lesson time: 25 minutes

Understanding Security Templates

A *security template* is a physical representation of a security configuration, a single file where a group of security settings is stored. Security templates are inactive until imported into a GPO or the Security Configuration And Analysis console. Locating all security settings in one place streamlines security administration. You can use security templates to define the following security settings in a GPO:

- Account Policies
- Local Policies
- Event Log
- Restricted Groups
- Registry
- File System

You cannot use security templates to define the IP Security, Public Key, Software Restriction, and Wireless Network security settings in a GPO.

Each security template is saved as a text-based .inf file. This enables you to copy, paste, or import some or all of the template attributes. You can import (apply) a security template file to a local or nonlocal GPO. All computer or user accounts in the site, domain, or OU to which the GPO is applied receive the security template settings. Importing a security template to a GPO eases domain administration by configuring security for multiple computers at once.

Predefined Security Templates

Windows Server 2003 includes a set of predefined security templates, each based on the role of a computer and common security scenarios: from security settings for workstations and servers to highly secure domain controllers. These templates can be used as provided, they can be modified, or they can serve as a basis for creating custom security templates. Apply predefined security templates to production systems only after testing to ensure that the right level of application functionality is maintained for your network and system architecture.

The predefined security templates are

- Compatible workstation or server security settings (Compatws.inf)
- Default security settings updated for domain controllers (DC security.inf)
- Highly secure domain controller security settings (Hisecdc.inf)
- Highly secure workstation or server security settings (Hisecws.inf)
- Root (Rootsec.inf)
- Secure domain controller security settings (Securedc.inf)
- Secure workstation or server security settings (Securews.inf)
- Out-of-the-box default security settings (Setup security.inf)

By default, predefined templates are stored in the %Systemroot%\Security\Templates folder.

Note   Security templates are designed to be applied to computers that use the default security settings. Security templates incrementally modify the default security settings if they are on the computer. The default security settings are not installed before performing the modifications.

Real World   Securing Systems Through OUs

As you've learned in previous chapters, OU structure is important for the efficient application of Group Policy. Since you can deploy security configurations through Group Policy, it's logical to say that OU structure is also important for security. As you develop security templates for your systems, consider grouping systems that require the same security configuration into a single OU. Not only will an OU help you keep track of those "secure" systems, but it will make it easier for you to analyze and improve their security in the future. You can deploy your security configuration by linking a custom GPO at the OU level, instead of configuring each system individually.

Compatible Template (Compatws.inf)

Default permissions for workstations and servers are primarily granted to three local groups: Administrators, Power Users, and Users. Administrators have the most privileges while Users have the least. Members of the Users group can successfully run applications that take part in the Windows Logo program for software, but may not be able to run applications that are not certified. If noncertified applications must be supported for members of the Users group, there are two options:

- Allow members of the Users group to be members of the Power Users group.

- Relax the default restrictions granted to the Users group.

Because Power Users can create users, groups, printers, and shares, some administrators would rather relax the default permissions granted to the Users group than allow members of the Users group to be members of the Power Users group. The Compatible template changes the default file and registry permissions granted to the Users group so that these members can use most noncertified applications. The Compatible template also removes all users and groups from the Power Users group, assuming that the administrator applying the Compatible template does not want end users to be Power Users.

> **Note**   Do not apply the Compatible template to domain controllers, including by importing the Compatible template to the Default Domain GPO or the Default Domain Controller GPO.

Default Security Settings Updated for Domain Controllers Template (DC security.inf)

This template is used when promoting a computer from a member server to a domain controller. It reflects the default security settings for file, registry, and system services.

Highly Secure Templates (Hisecws.inf and Hisecdc.inf)

The highly secure templates define security settings for Windows Server 2003 network communications, imposing restrictions on the levels of encryption and signing that are required for authentication and for the data that flows over secure channels and between server message block (SMB) clients and servers. These templates shut down NTLM communication and allow communication only with clients running NTLM version 2 or Kerberos. Clients that do not support NTLM version 2 include Microsoft Windows for Workgroups, Windows NT clients prior to Service Pack 4, and Microsoft Windows 95 and Microsoft Windows 98 platforms that do not have the Directory Services (DS) Client Pack installed. Microsoft Windows Me and Windows XP Professional support NTLM version 2 without additional modification.

Hisecws.inf   To apply Hisecws.inf to a computer, the following requirements must be met:

- All of the domain controllers that contain the accounts of all users that will log on to the client must run Windows NT 4 Service Pack 4 or later.

- All of the domain controllers for the domain that the client is joined to must run Microsoft Windows 2000 or later.

If a client is configured with Hisecws.inf, the following constraints apply:

- Clients cannot connect to computers that run only LAN Manager or computers running Windows NT 4 Service Pack 3 or earlier using a local account on the target server.

- Clients cannot connect to servers running Windows 2000 or Windows NT 4 Service Pack 4 using a local account defined on the target server unless the clock on the target server is within 30 minutes of the clock on the client.

- Clients cannot connect to computers running Windows XP or later using a local account defined on the target computer unless the clock on the target computer is within 20 hours of the clock on the client.

- Clients cannot connect to LAN Manager servers operating in share-level security mode.

If a server is configured with Hisecws.inf, the following constraints apply:

- A user with a local account on that server cannot connect to the server from a client that does not support NTLM version 2.

- A client with a local account on that server cannot connect to the server unless the client computer is configured to send NTLM version 2 responses.

- All clients that want to use SMB to connect to that server must enable client-side SMB packet signing. All computers running Windows 2000 or later enable client-side SMB packet signing by default.

Hisecws.inf uses Restricted Groups settings to remove all members of the Power Users group and ensure that only Domain Admins and the local Administrator account are members of the local Administrators group. Hisecws.inf defines these group restrictions under the assumption that only applications that take part in the Windows Logo Program for Software are deployed. With certified applications in place, neither the insecure Compatible template nor the insecure Power Users group is needed. Instead, users can run certified applications successfully under the secure context of a normal user as defined by the default security settings of the file system and registry.

Hisecdc.inf   In order to apply Hisecdc.inf to a domain controller, all of the domain controllers in all trusted or trusting domains must run Windows 2000 or later. If a domain controller is configured with Hisecdc.inf, the following constraints apply:

■ A user with an account in that domain cannot connect to any member server from a client unless both the client and the target server are running Windows 2000 or later and can use Kerberos-based authentication and the client is configured to send NTLM version 2 responses.

■ Lightweight Directory Access Protocol (LDAP) clients cannot bind with the Active Directory LDAP server unless data signing is negotiated. Bind requests using *ldap_simple_bind* or *ldap_simple_bind_s* are rejected. By default, all Microsoft LDAP clients that ship with Windows XP request data signing if Transport Layer Security/Secure Sockets Layer (TLS/SSL) is not already being used. If TLS/SSL is being used, then data signing is considered to be negotiated.

System Root Security Template (Rootsec.inf)

The system root security template specifies the new root permissions introduced with Windows XP. By default, Rootsec.inf defines these permissions for the root of the system drive. This template can be used to reapply the root directory permissions if they are inadvertently changed, or the template can be modified to apply the same root permissions to other volumes. The template does not overwrite explicit permissions defined on child objects; it propagates only the permissions inherited by child objects.

Secure Templates (Securedc.inf and Securews.inf)

The secure templates define enhanced security settings that are least likely to impact application compatibility, such as password, lockout, and audit settings. Additionally, the secure templates limit the use of LAN Manager and NTLM authentication protocols by configuring clients to send only NTLM version 2 responses and configuring servers to refuse LAN Manager responses. Clients that run LAN Manager include Windows for Workgroups as well as Windows 95 and Windows 98 platforms that do not have the DS Client Pack installed. If the DS Client Pack is installed on Windows 95 or Windows 98, those clients can use NTLM version 2. Windows Me and Windows XP Professional support NTLM version 2 without additional modification.

Securews.inf   To apply Securews.inf to a member computer, the following constraints apply:

■ All of the domain controllers that contain the accounts of all users that log on to the client must run Windows NT 4 Service Pack 4 or later.

■ If the member computer is joined to a domain that contains domain controllers running Windows NT 4, the clocks between the domain controllers running Windows NT 4 and the member computers must be within 30 minutes of each other.

If a client is configured with Securews.inf, the following constraints apply:

■ The client will not be able to connect to servers that use only the LAN Manager authentication protocol or that run Windows NT 4 prior to Service Pack 4 using a local account defined on the target server.

■ The client will not be able to connect to servers running Windows 2000 or Windows NT 4 using a local account defined on the target server unless the clock on the target server is within 30 minutes of the clock on the client.

■ The client will not be able to connect to a computer running Windows XP or later using a local account defined on the target server unless the clock on the target server is within 20 hours of the clock on the client.

■ The client will not be able to connect to servers running LAN Manager that are running in share-level security mode.

If a server is configured with Securews.inf, the following constraints apply:

■ A client with a local account on that server cannot connect to it from a client computer running only LAN Manager using that local account.

■ If the server is running Windows 2000, a client with a local account on the server configured to use NTLM version 2 authentication will not be able to connect unless the clocks on the two machines are within 30 minutes of each other.

■ If the server is running Windows XP, a client with a local account on the server configured to use NTLM version 2 authentication will not be able to connect unless the clocks on the two machines are within 20 hours of each other.

Securedc.inf   If a domain controller is configured with Securedc.inf, a user with an account in the domain cannot connect to any member server from a client computer running only LAN Manager using that domain account.

The secure templates also provide further restrictions for anonymous users by preventing anonymous users (such as users from untrusted domains) from enumerating account names and shares and performing SID-to-name or name-to-SID translations. Finally, the secure templates enable server-side SMB packet signing, which is disabled by default for workstations and servers. Because client-side SMB packet signing is enabled by default, SMB packet signing is always negotiated when workstations and servers are operating at the secure level.

Default Security Template (Setup security.inf)

The default security template is a computer-specific template that represents the default security settings applied during the installation of the operating system, including the file permissions for the root of the system drive. Therefore, this template is unique for each computer. You can use this template, or portions of it, for disaster recovery purposes. This template should never be applied by using Group Policy because it contains a large amount of data and can degrade performance due to the period refresh of Group Policy.

Managing Security Templates

The tasks for managing security templates are the following:

1. Accessing the Security Templates console
2. Customizing a predefined security template
3. Defining a new security template
4. Importing a security template to a local and nonlocal GPO

Accessing the Security Templates Console

The Security Templates console is the main tool for managing security templates.

To access the Security Templates console, complete the following steps:

1. Decide whether to create a new console or to add the Security Templates console to an existing console.

   ❑ To create a new console, click Start, click Run, type **mmc**, and then click OK.

   ❑ To add the Security Templates console to an existing console, open the console, and then proceed to step 2.

2. On the File menu, click Add/Remove Snap-In, and then click Add.

3. In the Add Standalone Snap-In dialog box, select Security Templates, click Add, click Close, and then click OK.

4. On the Console menu, click Save.

5. Type the name to assign to this console and click Save. The console appears on the Administrative Tools menu.

Customizing a Predefined Security Template

Customizing a predefined security template allows you to save the predefined template as a new template (to preserve the original predefined template) and then make edits to security settings to create a new template.

To customize a predefined security template, complete the following steps:

1. In the Security Templates console, shown in Figure 13-17, double-click Security Templates.

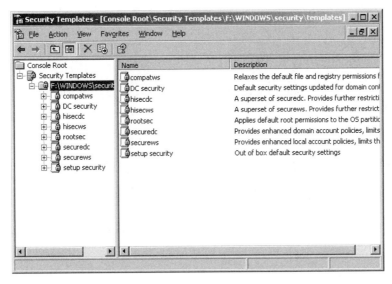

Figure 13-17   The Security Templates console

2. In the console tree, double-click the default path folder (%Systemroot%\Security\Templates), right-click the predefined template you want to modify, and then click Save As.

3. In the Save As dialog box, in the File Name list, specify a filename for the new security template, and then click Save.

4. In the console tree, right-click the new security template, and then select Set Description.

5. In the Security Template Description dialog box, type a description for the new security template, and then click OK.

6. In the console tree, double-click the new security template to display the security policies and double-click the security policy (such as Account Policies) you want to modify.

7. Click the security policy you want to customize (such as Password Policy), and then double-click the security setting to modify (such as Minimum Password Length).

8. In the Properties dialog box for the security setting, select the Define This Policy Setting In The Template check box to allow configuration, and then configure the security setting.

9. Click OK.

10. Configure other security settings as needed.

11. Close the Security Templates console.

12. In the Save Security Templates dialog box, click Yes to save the new security template file.

Defining a New Security Template

You can define a new security template and then modify the default settings to meet your requirements.

To define a new security template, complete the following steps:

1. In the Security Templates console, double-click Security Templates.

2. Right-click the template path folder where you want to store the new template and click New Template.

3. In the dialog box for the templates folder, type the name for the security template in the Template Name box. Type the description for your new security template in the Description box, and then click OK.

4. In the console tree, double-click the new security template to display the security policies and double-click the security policy (such as Account Policies) you want to define.

5. Click the security policy you want to define (such as Password Policy), and then double-click the security setting to define (such as Minimum Password Length).

6. In the Properties dialog box for the security setting, select the Define This Policy Setting In The Template check box to allow configuration, and then configure the security setting.

7. Click OK.

8. Configure other security settings as needed.

9. Close the Security Templates console.

10. In the Save Security Templates dialog box, click Yes to save the new security template file.

Importing a Security Template to a GPO

You can import a security template to local or nonlocal GPOs. Importing security templates makes administration easier because security is configured in one step for multiple computers.

To import a security template to a local or nonlocal GPO, complete the following steps:

1. In a console from which you manage local or nonlocal Group Policy settings, click the GPO to which you want to import the security template.

2. In the console tree, right-click Security Settings, and then click Import Policy.

3. In the Import Policy From dialog box, shown in Figure 13-18, click the security template you want to import, and then click Open.

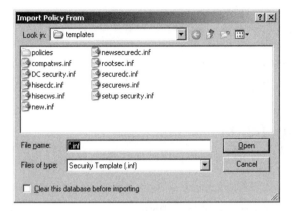

Figure 13-18   The Import Policy From dialog box

4. Because the security settings are applied only when the group policy is propagated (applied) to your computer, do one of the following to initiate policy propagation:

❑   Type **gpupdate** at the command prompt, and then press ENTER.

❑   Restart your computer.

❑   Wait for automatic policy propagation. By default, setting changes are applied every 90 minutes on a workstation or server and every five minutes on a domain controller. Settings automatically refresh every 16 hours, regardless of any changes that are made.

Best Practices for Security Templates

The following are the best practices for handling security templates:

■   Do not edit the Setup security.inf template, because it gives you the option to reapply the default security settings.

■   Do not apply the Setup security.inf template through Group Policy. The Setup security.inf template should be applied only to the local computer by using the Security Configuration and Analysis feature.

■   Do not apply the Compatible template to domain controllers.

■   Use caution when modifying predefined templates. Rather than modifying a predefined template, customize the predefined template and then save the changes under a different template name.

- Test all predefined or newly created security templates before applying them to your computer or network to ensure that the right level of application functionality is maintained.

- Importing a security template to a GPO ensures that any accounts to which the GPO is applied automatically receives the template's security settings when the Group Policy settings are refreshed. For domain controllers running Windows NT 4, you have to configure the primary domain controller policies to enable this replication.

Practice: Managing Security Templates

In this practice, you create a Security Templates console and customize a predefined security template.

Exercise 1: Creating a Security Templates Console

In this exercise, you create a new Security Templates console, the main tool for managing security templates.

▶ **To create a Security Templates console**

Use the procedure provided earlier in this lesson to create a new Security Templates console. Name the console Security Templates. The console should appear on the Administrative Tools menu.

Exercise 2: Customizing a Predefined Security Template

In this exercise, you customize a predefined security template by saving the predefined template as a new template (to preserve the original predefined template) and then making edits to security settings to create a new template.

▶ **To customize a predefined security template**

1. Use the procedure provided earlier in this lesson to customize the Securedc.inf template. Save the Securedc.inf template as a template called **New Template** with the description **New domain controller template**.

2. In New Template, in Security Settings/Account Policies/Password Policy, change the Minimum Password Length to be at least 10 characters.

3. Save New Template.

Lesson Review

The following questions are intended to reinforce key information presented in this lesson. If you are unable to answer a question, review the lesson and then try the question

again. Answers to the questions can be found in the "Questions and Answers" section at the end of this chapter.

1. What is the purpose of security templates?

_____

_____

2. For which settings can security templates not be used?

_____

_____

3. What is the purpose of the predefined security templates?

_____

_____

4. Where are the predefined security templates stored?

_____

_____

5. Which of the following predefined security templates can be used to change the default file and registry permissions granted to the Users group so that members of the group can use most noncertified applications?

   a. Compatible workstation or server security settings (Compatws.inf)

   b. Default security settings updated for domain controllers (DC security.inf)

   c. Secure domain controller security settings (Securedc.inf)

   d. Out-of-the-box default security settings (Setup security.inf)

Lesson Summary

- A security template is a physical representation of a security configuration, a single file where a group of security settings is stored. You can use security templates to define the Account Policies, Local Policies, Event Log, Restricted Groups, Registry, and File System settings in a GPO.

- You can import (apply) a security template file to a local or nonlocal GPO. Any computer or user accounts in the site, domain, or OU to which the GPO is applied receives the security template settings. Importing a security template to a GPO eases domain administration by configuring security for multiple computers at once.

■ Windows Server 2003 includes a set of predefined security templates, based on the role of a computer and common security scenarios. These templates can be used as provided, they can be modified, or they can serve as a basis for creating custom security templates.

Lesson 6: Using Security Configuration And Analysis

The Security Configuration And Analysis feature in Windows Server 2003 offers administrators the ability to configure security, analyze security, view results, and resolve any discrepancies revealed by analysis. This lesson shows you how to use the Security Configuration And Analysis feature.

After this lesson, you will be able to

- Explain the purpose of the Security Configuration And Analysis feature
- Analyze a security configuration
- Configure security by using the Security Configuration And Analysis console
- Export a security configuration to a security template

Estimated lesson time: 25 minutes

Understanding the Security Configuration And Analysis Feature

The Security Configuration And Analysis feature is a tool for analyzing and configuring local system security. This feature compares the effects of one security template or the combined effects of a number of security templates with the currently defined security settings on a local computer.

The Security Configuration And Analysis feature allows administrators to perform a quick security analysis. In the security analysis, recommendations are presented alongside current system settings and icons, or remarks are used to highlight any areas where the current settings do not match the proposed level of security. The Security Configuration And Analysis feature also offers the ability to resolve any discrepancies revealed by analysis.

The Security Configuration And Analysis feature can also be used to configure local system security. You can import security templates created with the Security Templates console and apply these templates to the GPO for the local computer. This immediately configures the system security with the levels specified in the template.

Using the Security Configuration And Analysis Feature

The tasks for using the Security Configuration And Analysis feature are the following:

1. Accessing the Security Configuration And Analysis console
2. Setting a security configuration and analysis database
3. Analyzing system security
4. Viewing security analysis results

5. Resolving security discrepancies

6. Exporting security database settings to a security template

> **Note**   To use the Security Configuration And Analysis feature, you must be logged on as an administrator or a member of the Administrators group. If your computer is connected to a network, network policy settings might prevent you from completing this procedure.

Accessing the Security Configuration And Analysis Console

The Security Configuration And Analysis console is the main tool for using the Security Configuration And Analysis feature. This procedure shows you how to add the Security Configuration And Analysis console to a Microsoft Management Console (MMC) that is accessible from the Administrative Tools menu.

To access the Security Configuration And Analysis console, complete the following steps:

1. Do one of the following:

   ❑ To add the Security Configuration And Analysis console to a new console, click Start, click Run, type **mmc**, and then click OK.

   ❑ To add the Security Configuration And Analysis console to an existing console, go directly to step 2.

2. On the Console menu, click Add/Remove Snap-In, and then click Add.

3. In the Add Standalone Snap-In dialog box, select Security Configuration And Analysis and click Add.

4. Click Close, and then click OK.

5. On the Console menu, click Save.

6. Type the name to assign to this console and click Save. The console appears on the Administrative Tools menu.

Setting a Security Configuration And Analysis Database

The Security Configuration And Analysis console uses a database to perform configuration and analysis functions. This database contains the security template that you want to compare with the settings currently defined on the computer. Before you can analyze or configure security, you must determine the database to use.

To set a security configuration and analysis database, complete the following steps:

1. In the Security Configuration And Analysis console, right-click Security Configuration And Analysis.

2. Click Open Database.

3. In the Open Database dialog box, do one of the following:

❑ If you want to use an existing database for the analysis or configuration, click the database, and then click Open. This database is now the security configuration and analysis database. The template or templates contained in this database are used for the analysis or configuration you will perform.

❑ If you want to create a new database for the analysis or configuration, type a filename in the File Name list, and then click Open. In the Import Template dialog box, shown in Figure 13-19, select the security template to load into the new security configuration and analysis database, and then click Open. This database is now the security configuration and analysis database. The template(s) contained in this database are used for the analysis or configuration you will perform.

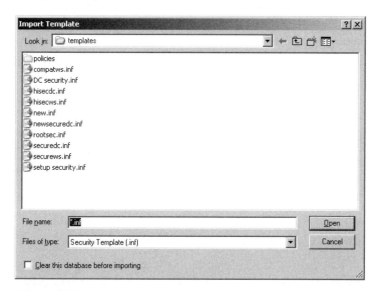

Figure 13-19   The Import Template dialog box

Analyzing System Security

The Security Configuration And Analysis feature performs security analysis by comparing the current state of system security against a security template in the security configuration and analysis database. The local computer's security settings are queried for all security areas in the database configuration. Values found are compared to the database configuration. If the current system settings match the database configuration settings, they are assumed to be correct. If not, the policies in question are displayed as potential problems that need investigation.

To analyze system security, complete the following steps:

1. In the Security Configuration And Analysis console, set a security configuration and analysis database (if one is not currently set).

2. In the console tree, right-click the Security Configuration And Analysis node, and then click Analyze Computer Now.

3. In the Perform Analysis dialog box, verify or change the path for the log file generated from the analysis in the Error Log File Path box, and then click OK. The default path for the log file is: *%Systemroot%*\Documents and Settings*UserAccount*\My Documents\Security\Logs*DatabaseName*.log. The different security areas are displayed as they are analyzed. When the security analysis completes, you can view the results.

> **Note**   You can also use the Secedit /analyze command prompt to analyze system security. Refer to Windows Server 2003 Help for further information. If you must frequently analyze a large number of computers, use Secedit.

Viewing Security Analysis Results

In the details pane, the Security Configuration And Analysis console displays the analysis results organized by security area with visual flags to indicate problems. For each security policy in the security area, the current database and computer configuration settings are displayed.

To view security analysis results, complete the following steps:

1. In the Security Configuration And Analysis console, expand the Security Configuration And Analysis node.

2. Double-click a security policies node (such as Account Policies), and then click the security area (such as Password Policy) for which you want to view results.

3. In the details pane, shown in Figure 13-20, the Policy column indicates the policy name for the analysis results, the Database Setting column indicates the security value in your template, and the Computer Setting column indicates the current security level in the system.

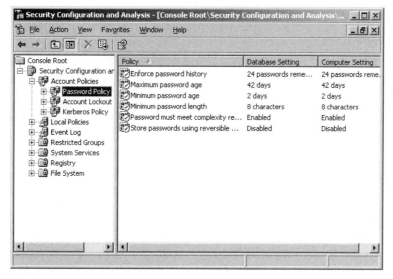

Figure 13-20   Analysis results for Password Policy

❑   A red X indicates a difference from the database configuration.

❑   A green check mark indicates consistency with the database configuration.

❑   A black question mark indicates that the entry is not defined in the analysis database and, therefore, was not analyzed. If an entry is not analyzed, it might be that it was not defined in the analysis database or that the user who is running the analysis might not have sufficient permission to perform analysis on the specific object or area.

❑   A red exclamation point indicates that the entry is defined in the analysis database but does not exist on the actual system. For example, there might be a restricted group that is defined in the analysis database but does not actually exist on the analyzed system.

❑   No icon indicates that the security policy was not included in your template and therefore not analyzed.

Viewing the Security Analysis Log File   After completing a security analysis, you can also view the security analysis log file. The log file contains all of the information about the analysis. Look for the word "mismatch" to find the differences between the template and the current security settings on the local computer.

To view the security analysis log file, in the console tree, right-click the Security Configuration And Analysis node, and then click View Log File.

> **Note** You can also view the security analysis log file in the location you specified in the Perform Analysis dialog box.

Resolving Security Discrepancies

You can resolve any security discrepancies revealed by the security analysis in the following ways:

- Accepting or changing some or all of the values flagged or not included in the security configuration and analysis database if you determine the local system security levels are valid due to the role of that computer. Refer to the section "Editing the Analysis Database" for details.

- Importing a template that is more appropriate (for the role of that computer) into the security configuration and analysis database as the new database configuration and applying it to the system. Refer to the section "Importing Additional Security Templates into a Database" for details.

- Configuring the system to the security configuration and analysis database configuration values if you determine the system is not in compliance with valid security levels. Refer to the section "Configuring System Security" for details.

Editing the Analysis Database   If you determine that the local system security levels are valid due to the role of that computer, and you want to change the analysis database to reflect this, you can edit the analysis database. These edits do not affect the actual security template, nor do they affect system security. The edits affect only the stored template in the security configuration and analysis database. The security template file will be modified only if you either return to Security Templates and edit that template or export the stored configuration to the same template file.

To edit the analysis database, complete the following steps:

1. After Security Configuration And Analysis has finished analyzing the computer, in the console tree, double-click a security policies node (such as Account Policies), and then click a security area (such as Password Policy).

2. In the details pane, double-click the security attribute you want to edit.

3. Select the Define This Policy In The Database check box.

4. Type a new value that will be recorded in the analysis database and click OK.

5. Repeat the last three steps for each security attribute you want to edit.

Importing Additional Security Templates into a Database   If you determine a need to import additional templates or a more appropriate template into the security configuration and analysis database, you can import additional security templates into the database. You can merge several different templates into one composite template that can be used for security analysis or configuration by importing each template into a security configuration and analysis database. Conflicts are resolved in the order in which the templates were imported; the settings in the last template take precedence. You can also import an additional security template without merging it with the existing template(s). In this type of import, the imported security template replaces any existing templates.

To import an additional security template into a database, complete the following steps:

1. In the Security Configuration And Analysis console, right-click the Security Configuration And Analysis node, and click Open Database.

2. In the Open Database dialog box, click the database to which you want to import the additional security template, and then click Open.

3. In the console tree, right-click Security Configuration And Analysis, and then click Import Template.

4. In the Import Template dialog box, select the file representing the additional security template you want to import, and then click Open.

5. Repeat the previous two steps for each template you want to merge into the database.

 Note   If you want to replace the template rather than merge it into the stored template, select the Clear This Database Before Importing check box in the Import Template dialog box.

Configuring System Security   If you want to configure the local computer according to the Security Configuration And Analysis database configuration values, you can configure system security. When you choose to configure system security, you apply the stored template configuration in the security configuration and analysis database to the local computer. You should configure system security only to modify security areas *not* affected by Group Policy settings, such as security on local files and folders, registry keys, and system services. Otherwise, when the Group Policy settings are applied, they take precedence over local settings—such as account policies.

In general, do not configure system security when you are configuring security for a domain or OU, because you have to configure each client individually. In this case, you should return to the Security Templates console, modify the template, and reapply it to the appropriate GPO.

To configure system security, complete the following steps:

1. In the Security Configuration And Analysis console, set a security configuration and analysis database (if one is not currently set).

2. Right-click the Security Configuration And Analysis node, and then click Configure Computer Now.

3. In the Configure System dialog box, verify or change the path for the log file generated from the analysis in the Error Log File Path box, and then click OK. The default path for the log file is: %*Systemroot*%\Documents and Settings*UserAccount*\My Documents\Security\Logs\DatabaseName.log. The different security areas are displayed as they are configured. When the configuration completes, you can view the results.

Note   You can also use the Secedit /configure command prompt to configure system security. Refer to Windows Server 2003 Help for further information.

Note   After completing a security configuration, you can view the security configuration log file in the details pane. The log file contains information about the configuration. You can also view the security configuration log file in the location you specified in the Configure System dialog box.

Exporting Security Templates

If you have a created a composite security template by importing multiple templates into one database, you can save the composite template as a separate template file. The export feature provides the ability to save a security database configuration as a new template file that can be imported into other databases, used as is to analyze or configure a system, or even redefined with the Security Templates console.

To export security database settings to a security template, complete the following steps:

1. In the Security Configuration And Analysis console, right-click the Security Configuration And Analysis node, and then click Export Template.

2. In the Export Template To dialog box, type a valid filename in the File Name box, type a path to where your template should be saved in the Save In list, and select the type of file you want to save in the Save As Type list, and then click Save.

Security Configuration And Analysis Best Practices

The following are the best practices for working with Security Configuration And Analysis:

■ If you often need to analyze a large number of computers, such as with a domain-based infrastructure, use the Secedit command-line tool.

- Use Security Configuration And Analysis to configure only security areas *not* affected by local Group Policy settings. This includes areas such as security on local files and folders, registry keys, and system services. Otherwise, the settings configured through Security Configuration And Analysis will override the local settings.

- Do not use Security Configuration And Analysis when you are configuring security for a domain or an OU. Otherwise, you must configure each client individually. In that case, you should use Security Templates to create a template and apply it to the appropriate GPO, or use the Security Settings extension to Group Policy to edit individual security settings on a GPO.

Security Configuration And Analysis Troubleshooting

Table 13-8 describes some troubleshooting scenarios related to security configuration and analysis.

Table 13-8   Security Configuration and Analysis Troubleshooting Scenarios

Causes	Solutions
Problem: The security database is corrupted.	
A hardware problem if the computer is improperly shut down or a software error.	Run **esentutl /g** to check the integrity of the security database at *%Systemroot%*\Security\Database\Secedit.sdb If the database is corrupt, attempt to recover it by running **esentutl /r** on the *%Systemroot%*\Security folder. If this fails, attempt to repair it by running **esentutl /p** on *%Systemroot%*\Security\Database\Secedit.sdb. Then delete the log files in *%Systemroot%*\Security.
Problem: Security policy is not propagating correctly.	
Any	Use RSoP to check what GPO is affecting the computer. Check the log file, located in *%Systemroot%*\Security\Logs\Winlogon.log, to identify specific errors that occur during policy propagation to the computer.
Problem: Security policies are propagated, but the user receives an error message such as "0x534: No mapping between account names and security IDs was done."	
The security policy grants rights to user or group accounts that no longer exist.	Find out which accounts are invalid. Open Microsoft Notepad and open the file at *%Systemroot%*\Security\Logs\Winlogon.log. The Windows Server 2003 family and Windows XP create this file by default during policy propagation. Search for error 1332, which indicates the account names that could not be resolved. Then remove the unresolved account names from policies in your domain. If the accounts are in the Default Domain or Domain Controller GPOs, you can edit the policies in the Security Settings node of Group Policy to remove these account names. If the accounts exist elsewhere, you might have to browse through all GPOs defined in the domain and remove them individually.

Table 13-8   Security Configuration and Analysis Troubleshooting Scenarios

Causes	Solutions
Problem: The user receives an error message such as "The system cannot log you on now because the domain *<domain_name>* is not available."	
The domain controller is unavailable and a user's logon information is not being cached because of the Interactive Logon: Number Of Previous Logons To Cache (In Case Domain Controller Is Not Available) setting in Local Policies/Security Options.	Ensure that the Interactive Logon: Number Of Previous Logons To Cache (In Case Domain Controller Is Not Available) setting is not set to zero.

> **Note**   You can find more about the Esentutl command-line tool in Windows Server 2003 Help.

Practice: Using Security Configuration and Analysis

In this practice, you access the Security Configuration And Analysis console, set a security configuration and analysis database, analyze system security, and then view the results.

Exercise 1: Accessing the Security Configuration And Analysis Console

In this exercise, you access the Security Configuration And Analysis console, the main tool for using the Security Configuration and Analysis tool.

▶ **To access the Security Configuration And Analysis console**

1. Use the procedure provided earlier in this lesson to access the Security Configuration And Analysis console. Name the console **Security Configuration And Analysis**.

2. Close and save the console. Then access the console from the Administrative Tools menu.

Exercise 2: Setting a Security Configuration and Analysis Database

In this exercise, you determine a security configuration and analysis database to use.

▶ **To set a security configuration and analysis database**

1. Use the procedure provided earlier in this lesson to set a security configuration and analysis database. Create a new database called **New Configuration**.

2. Import the Securedc.inf security template into the security configuration and analysis database. The New Configuration database is now the security configuration and analysis database, and it contains the Securedc.inf security template.

Exercise 3: Analyzing System Security and Viewing the Results

In this exercise, you analyze system security, comparing the settings in the security template Securedc.inf with the security settings currently running on your system. Then, you view the security analysis results.

▶ **To analyze system security and view the results**

1. Use the procedure provided earlier in this lesson to analyze system security.

2. Double-click the Account Policies node, and then click the Password Policy security area.

    a. In the details pane, what is indicated in the Policy column? In the Database Setting column? In the Computer Setting column?

The Policy column indicates the policy name for the analysis results. The Database Setting column indicates the security value in your template. The Computer Setting column indicates the current security level in the system.

    b. In the Policy column, what does the red X indicate? What does the green check mark indicate?

A red X indicates a difference from the database configuration. A green check mark indicates consistency with the database configuration.

Lesson Review

The following questions are intended to reinforce key information presented in this lesson. If you are unable to answer a question, review the lesson and then try the question again. Answers to the questions can be found in the "Questions and Answers" section at the end of this chapter.

1. What is the function of the Security Configuration And Analysis feature?

2. What item is contained in the security configuration and analysis database?

3. What actions are performed during a security analysis?

4. What actions are performed during a security configuration?

5. In the security analysis results, which icon represents a difference from the database configuration?

   a. A red X

   b. A red exclamation point

   c. A green check mark

   d. A black question mark

Lesson Summary

- The Security Configuration And Analysis feature is a tool for analyzing and configuring local system security. It compares the effects of one security template or the combined effects of a number of security templates with the currently defined security settings on a local computer.

- The Security Configuration And Analysis console uses a database to perform configuration and analysis functions. This database contains the security template that you want to compare with the settings currently defined on the computer.

- Security configuration applies the stored template configuration in the security configuration and analysis database to the local computer.

Case Scenario Exercise

You are a computer consultant. Lisa Jacobson, the Chief Information Officer of Tailspin Toys, has several security concerns that she's contracted you to help her solve. The Tailspin Toys network consists of two Active Directory domains: *tailspintoys.com* and *dev.tailspintoys.com*. The *tailspintoys.com* domain consists of six domain controllers running Windows Server 2003 and nine member servers, some of which are running Windows 2000 and some of which are running Windows Server 2003. There are 1,300 employees with user accounts in the *tailspintoys.com* domain, and each employee has a desktop computer running Windows XP Professional.

The child domain, *dev.tailspintoys.com*, is where the accounts and resources for employees involved in research, engineering, and support reside. This domain consists of four domain controllers running Windows Server 2003, six Windows 2000 member servers, and 300 client machines running Windows XP Professional. The member servers include three application servers and three file servers. The file servers contain large amounts of data, including many confidential development documents. These documents contain trade secrets regarding new toys.

Lisa has identified two areas of concern she would like you to address:

- She has seen many employees execute e-mail attachments directly from their e-mail messages. Although the company keeps its antivirus software up to date, Lisa wants to know if there is a way to help prevent e-mail attachments from running on client computers.

- The three file servers contain Tailspin Toys confidential information. She wants to ensure that she can track users who access or attempt to access documents stored on these servers. She plans to keep a running log of all this information and never wants to miss even one successful or unsuccessful attempt to access this data.

Given the concerns of Tailspin Toys as outlined above, answer the following questions:

1. What type of setting within Group Policy will assist you in addressing the company's concerns regarding the execution of e-mail attachments?

   _____

   _____

2. Where in Active Directory should this Group Policy be linked?

   _____

   _____

3. What kind of OU structure would assist in implementing the security requirements for the file servers that hold confidential information in *dev.tailspintoys.com*?

   _____

   _____

4. How can Security Templates and associated tools be used to assist in configuring these servers?

   _____

   _____

5. What needs to be done to track accesses or attempts to access the folders containing Tailspin's confidential documents?

   _____

   _____

6. How should the file servers that contain confidential documents be configured to meet Tailspin's requirements regarding the security log?

   _____

   _____

Troubleshooting Lab

You are a network administrator for Contoso Pharmaceuticals. Several servers in your organization store trade secrets that must be protected from attack. Firewalls and virus scanners are in place to keep these servers safe. In addition, you've configured auditing settings so that these servers will not lose any security auditing information. You are at home after the workday, and you receive a phone call from Josh Barnhill. Josh is a member of the Server Operators group. He says that Server2 stopped functioning. There is a message in the Log On To Windows box that reads The Security Log On This System Is Full. Only administrators can log on to fix the problem. Josh cannot log on. He needs your help.

In order to experience this situation, first prepare Server2.

1. Log on to Server2 using the Administrator user name and password.

2. Click Start, click Run, and type **gpedit.msc**. Server2's Local System Group Policy Object Editor opens.

3. Expand the following path: Computer Configuration, Windows Settings, Security Settings, Local Policies. Click the Security Options object. You'll see several policies in the details pane.

4. Locate and double-click the Audit: Shut Down System Immediately If Unable To Log Security Audits setting.

5. In the dialog box for the setting, click Enabled, and then click OK.

6. Click the Audit Policy object in the console tree. The audit policy settings appear in the details pane.

7. Double-click the Audit Object Access setting in the details pane.

8. In the Properties dialog box for the setting, select the Define These Policy Settings check box and the Success and Failure check boxes, and then click OK.

9. Close the Group Policy Object Editor.

10. Create a folder on the desktop named **Secure**.

11. Copy the Fileactivity.vbs file from the Supplemental CD-ROM\70-294\Labs\ Chapter 13 folder to the Secure folder. Right-click the Secure folder and click Properties.

12. In the Secure Properties dialog box, click the Security tab. Click Advanced.

13. In the Advanced Security Settings For Secure dialog box, click the Auditing tab. Click Add. In the Enter The Object Name To Select text box, type **Everyone** and then press ENTER.

14. In the Auditing Entry For Secure dialog box, in the Access list, check the two top check boxes that correspond to Full Control Successful and Failed auditing. You should see that all of the check boxes below are automatically checked. Click OK.

15. Click OK in the Advanced Security Settings For Secure dialog box. Click OK in the Secure Properties dialog box.

16. Open Event Viewer and click the Security log. Right-click the Security log and click Properties.

17. In the Security Properties dialog box, in the Log Size section, configure the Maximum log size for 64 KB and press ENTER. The Event Viewer caution message appears. Click OK.

18. Right-click the security log and click Clear All Events. The Event Viewer message box appears asking you if you'd like to save the security log. Click No. Notice a single event (Event ID 517) is placed in the log after you clear it. This is an event indicating you cleared the log. Right-click the security log and click Properties.

19. In the Security Properties dialog box, in the Log Size section, select Do Not Overwrite Events (Clear Log Manually). Click OK. Close Event Viewer.

20. Restart Server2. The restart activates the Audit: Shut Down System Immediately If Unable To Log Security Audits audit setting.

21. Log on using the domain administrator user name and password.

22. Double-click the Secure folder on the desktop.

> **Important**   You are about to cause an automated shutdown of Server2 by running the script inside the Secure folder. The script simply creates, copies, and deletes two files 500 times. This may take a few seconds, so be patient. The activity is more than enough to fill the 64 KB security log. Once that log is full, the server will shut down.

23. Double-click the Fileactivity.vbs file in the Secure folder. Server2 restarts a few seconds after you double-click the file.

You have created the problem from the scenario. Now it is time to fix the issue.

1. When Server2 restarts, press CTRL+ALT+DELETE and notice the message in the Log On To Windows dialog box. Log on using the domain administrator name and password.

2. Open Event Viewer and click the security log. In the details pane, double-click the most recent event logged (Event ID 521). The Event Properties dialog box opens.

3. Notice the description reads Unable To Log Events To Security Log. The description also indicates that the value of CrashOnAuditFail is 1. Actually, you'll see the value is now 2. Click OK.

4. Right-click the security log and click Clear All Events. The Event Viewer message box appears, asking you if you'd like to save the security log. Click No.

5. Right-click the security log and click Properties. The Security Properties dialog box opens. Select the Overwrite events as needed and configure the maximum log size for 131072 KB. Click OK. Close the Event Viewer.

6. Click Start, click Run, type **regedit**, and then press ENTER. The Registry Editor console opens.

7. Expand the following registry path: HKEY_LOCAL_MACHINE\SYSTEM \CurrentControlSet\Control and click on the LSA key.

8. In the details pane, double-click the CrashOnAuditFail value. The Edit DWORD Value appears. Change the Value data to **0**. Click OK. Close the Registry Editor.

> **Note**   By setting this value to zero, you are effectively disabling the Audit: Shut Down System Immediately If Unable To Log Security Audits setting.

9. Open the Group Policy Object Editor again (Gpedit.msc) and return to the Computer Configuration, Windows Settings, Security Settings, Local Policies, Audit Policy location. Open the Audit Open Access setting and clear the Success and Failure check boxes.

10. Delete the Secure folder from the Desktop.

You've now corrected the issue. In a secure environment, you would have left the security log set to not overwrite events. Also, you would have reset the CrashOnAudit-Fail value to 1 (instead of making it zero). To prevent the server from crashing, you would ensure that the security log could grow to a reasonable size. You would create a schedule for archiving and reviewing your security log routinely.

Chapter Summary

- Security settings define the security behavior of the system. Through the use of GPOs in Active Directory, administrators can apply security profiles to sites, domains, and OUs in the enterprise.

- Software restriction policies are security settings in a GPO provided to identify software and control its ability to run on a local computer, site, domain, or OU.

- An audit policy defines the categories of events recorded in the security log on each computer. You set the audit policy settings in the Computer Configuration/ Windows Settings/Security Settings/Local Policies/Audit Policy extensions in a GPO. You use the security log in the Event Viewer console to view audited events.

- The security log contains information about the success or failure of audited events. Security logging is turned off by default. The events that Windows Server 2003 records are a result of the audit policy set in a GPO at the appropriate level. The security log is accessible only to system administrators.

- A security template is a physical representation of a security configuration, a single file where a group of security settings is stored. You can use security templates to define the Account Policies, Local Policies, Event Log, Restricted Groups, Registry, and File System settings in a GPO.

- The Security Configuration And Analysis feature is a tool for analyzing and configuring local system security. It compares the effects of one security template or the combined effects of a number of security templates with the currently defined security settings on a local computer.

Exam Highlights

Before taking the exam, review the key points and terms that are presented in this chapter. You need to know this information.

Key Points

- You configure computer security settings using Group Policy security settings, which define the security behavior of the system.

- Software restriction policies are a new feature in Windows Server 2003, created to address the problem of regulating unknown or untrusted code.

- Password policy determines settings for domain users' passwords, such as enforcement and lifetimes.

- You auto-enroll computer and user certificates using Group Policy in the Auto-enrollment Settings Properties dialog box, available in Autoenrollment Settings in the Public Key Policies security area.

- You can troubleshoot the application of Group Policy security settings by implementing an audit policy, administering the security log, using security templates, and using Security Configuration and Analysis.

Key Terms

security template   A physical representation of a security configuration; a single file where a group of security settings is stored.

software restriction policies   Security settings in a GPO provided to identify software and control its ability to run on a local computer, site, domain, or OU.

audit policy   A policy that determines the security events to be reported to the network administrator.

Questions and Answers

Page
13-11
Lesson 1 Review

1. How are account policies different from other security policies?

   Account policies can be applied only to the root domain of the domain tree. They cannot be applied to sites or OUs.

2. What is the difference between user rights and permissions?

   User rights are assigned to user and group accounts and applied through a GPO to sites, domains, or OUs. Permissions attached to objects are assigned to user and group accounts. Additionally, because user rights are part of a GPO, user rights can be overridden depending on the GPO affecting the computer or user.

3. Attributes for which logs are defined in the Event Log security area?

   The Event Log security area defines attributes related to the application, security, and system event logs in the Event Viewer console.

4. How can you set automatic enrollment of user certificates?

   You set autoenrollment of user certificates in the Autoenrollment Settings Properties dialog box, which you can access by opening Autoenrollment Settings in Computer Configuration or User Configuration/Windows Settings/Security Settings/Public Key Policies in a GPO for a site, domain, or OU.

5. In which of the following security areas would you find the settings for determining which security events are logged in the security log on the computer?

   a. Event Log

   b. Account Policies

   c. Local Policies

   d. Restricted Groups

   The correct answer is c. You determine which security events are logged in the security log on the computer in the Audit Policy settings in the Local Policies security area.

Page
13-28
Lesson 2 Review

1. What is the purpose of software restriction policies?

   Software restriction policies address the problem of regulating unknown or untrusted code. Software restriction policies are security settings in a GPO provided to identify software and control its ability to run on a local computer, site, domain, or OU.

2. Explain the two default security levels.

   There are two default security levels for software restriction policies: Disallowed, which does not allow the software to run, regardless of the access rights of the user who is logged on to the computer, and Unrestricted, which allows software to run with the full rights of the user who is logged on to the computer. If the default level is set to Disallowed, you can identify and create rule exceptions for the programs that you trust to run. If the default level is set to Unrestricted, you can identify and create rules for the set of programs that you want to prohibit from running.

3. Describe how software is identified by software restriction policies.

Using software restriction policies, software can be identified by its

❑   Hash, a series of bytes with a fixed length that uniquely identify a program or file

❑   Certificate, a digital document used for authentication and secure exchange of information on open networks, such as the Internet, extranets, and intranets

❑   Path, a sequence of folder names that specifies the location of the software within the directory tree

❑   Internet zone, a subtree specified through Internet Explorer: Internet, Intranet, Restricted Sites, Trusted Sites, or My Computer

4. List the order of rule precedence.

Rules are applied in the following order of precedence: hash rules, certificate rules, path rules (in a conflict, the most restrictive path rule takes precedence), and Internet zone rules.

5. Which of the following rule types applies only to Windows Installer packages?

a. Hash rules

b. Certificate rules

c. Internet zone rules

d. Path rules

The correct answer is c. Internet zone rules apply only to Windows Installer packages.

Page
13-43
Lesson 3 Review

1. What is the purpose of auditing?

Auditing is a tool for maintaining network security. Auditing allows you to track user activities and system-wide events.

2. Where can you view audited events?

You use the security log in the Event Viewer console to view audited events.

3. What is an audit policy?

An audit policy defines the categories of events recorded in the security log on each computer. You set the Audit Policy settings in the Computer Configuration/Windows Settings/Security Settings/Local Policies/Audit Policy extensions in a GPO.

4. Which event categories require you to configure specific objects for auditing to log the events?

If you have specified the Audit Directory Service Access event category or the Audit Object Access event category to audit, you must configure the objects for auditing.

5. Which of the following event categories should you audit if you want to find out if an unauthorized person is trying to access a user account by entering random passwords or by using password-cracking software? Choose all that apply.

   a. Logon Events—success events

   b. Logon Events—failure events

   c. Account Logon—success events

   d. Account Logon—failure events

   The correct answers are b and d. By auditing failure events in the Logon Events category, you can monitor logon failures that might indicate that an unauthorized person is trying to access a user account by entering random passwords or by using password-cracking software. By auditing failure events in the Account Logon category, you can monitor logon failures that might indicate an unauthorized person is trying to access a domain account by using brute force.

Page
13-54
Lesson 4 Review

1. What information is logged in the security log?

   The security log contains information on security events that are specified in the audit policy.

2. What is the default size of the security log?

   The default size of the security log is 512 KB.

3. In which of the following file formats can you archive a security log? Choose three.

   a. .txt

   b. .doc

   c. .rtf

   d. .bmp

   e. .evt

   f. .csv

   g. .crv

   The correct answers are a, e, and f. Logs can be saved as text (*.txt), event log (*.evt), or comma-delimited (*.csv) file format.

4. In which of the following archived file formats can you reopen the file in the Event Viewer console?

   a. .txt

   b. .doc

   c. .rtf

d. .bmp

e. .evt

f. .csv

g. .crv

The correct answer is e. If you archive a log in log-file (*.evt) format, you can reopen it in the Event Viewer console.

5. You filtered a security log to display only the events with Event ID 576. Then you archived this log. What information is saved?

a. The entire log is saved

b. The filtered log is saved

c. The entire log and the filtered log are each saved separately

d. No log is saved

The correct answer is a. When you archive a log, the entire log is saved, regardless of filtering options.

Page
13-66

Lesson 5 Review

1. What is the purpose of security templates?

A security template is a physical representation of a security configuration, a single file where a group of security settings is stored. You can use security templates to define the Account Policies, Local Policies, Event Log, Restricted Groups, Registry, and File System settings in a GPO. You can import (apply) a security template file to a local or nonlocal GPO. All computer or user accounts in the site, domain, or OU to which the GPO is applied receive the security template settings. Importing a security template to a GPO eases domain administration by configuring security for multiple computers at once.

2. For which settings can security templates not be used?

You cannot use security templates to define the IP Security, Public Key, Software Restriction, and Wireless Network security settings in a GPO.

3. What is the purpose of the predefined security templates?

The predefined security templates are based on the role of a computer and common security scenarios. These templates can be used as provided, they can be modified, or they can serve as a basis for creating custom security templates.

4. Where are the predefined security templates stored?

By default, predefined templates are stored in the %Systemroot%\Security\Templates folder.

5. Which of the following predefined security templates can be used to change the default file and registry permissions granted to the Users group so that members of the group can use most noncertified applications?

a. Compatible workstation or server security settings (Compatws.inf)

b. Default security settings updated for domain controllers (DC security.inf)

c. Secure domain controller security settings (Securedc.inf)

d. Out-of-the-box default security settings (Setup security.inf)

The correct answer is a. Only the Compatible template changes the default file and registry permissions granted to the Users group so that these members can use most noncertified applications.

Page
13-79

Lesson 6 Review

1. What is the function of the Security Configuration And Analysis feature?

The Security Configuration And Analysis feature is a tool for analyzing and configuring local system security. This feature compares the effects of one security template or the combined effects of a number of security templates with the currently defined security settings on a local computer.

2. What item is contained in the security configuration and analysis database?

The security configuration and analysis database contains the security template that you want to compare with the settings currently defined on the computer.

3. What actions are performed during a security analysis?

Security analysis compares the current state of system security against a security template in the security configuration and analysis database. The local computer's security settings are queried for all security areas in the database configuration, and the values are compared. If the local computer settings match the database configuration settings, they are assumed to be correct. If not, the policies in question are displayed as potential problems that need investigation.

4. What actions are performed during a security configuration?

Security configuration applies the stored template configuration in the security configuration and analysis database to the local computer.

5. In the security analysis results, which icon represents a difference from the database configuration?

a. A red X

b. A red exclamation point

c. A green check mark

d. A black question mark

The correct answer is a. A red X indicates a difference from the database configuration.

Case Scenario Exercise

1. What type of setting within Group Policy will assist you in addressing the company's concerns regarding the execution of e-mail attachments?

   A new Group Policy feature available in Windows XP and Windows Server 2003 is called software restriction policies. This feature provides a flexible and powerful method of restricting what software will run on client computers. In this case, since the concern is about e-mail attachments, setting up a path rule makes the most sense. You need to determine the path where Tailspin's e-mail client software stores attachments and set up a path rule that sets the security level to Disallowed for that path. Although this will not prevent users from saving the attachments to another location and executing them, it will prevent execution while stored as an attachment.

2. Where in Active Directory should this Group Policy be linked?

   Since the concern is for all desktop machines, setting the policy at the domain level would be appropriate. Since there are two domains, you must link two different policies, one at each domain. Your other option would be to link the policy to a site that includes both domains.

3. What kind of OU structure would assist in implementing the security requirements for the file servers that hold confidential information in *dev.tailspintoys.com*?

   Although you configure the required security requirements on a server-by-server basis, it is probably best to create a separate OU for these file servers. This would ensure consistency, as well as facilitate any future changes. Place the computer accounts for the three servers in an OU. From there, you can configure the security settings required to protect these servers.

4. How can Security Templates and associated tools be used to assist in configuring these servers?

   There are several predefined security templates in Windows Server 2003. You have the option of customizing these templates as needed. Given the sensitive nature of the documents stored on these servers, you should consider starting with the Securews.inf security template. The Security Configuration And Analysis feature could be used to analyze the servers' current configuration against this template. If this template is deemed a good starting point, you could save the settings to a custom template, called DevelopmentSrv.inf, or some other descriptive name. Then, you could make changes to this template to meet Tailspin's needs. Once the custom template is complete, you could apply it to the servers using Security Configuration and Analysis. If you place all the server accounts in a single OU, you can apply the template using Group Policy. Create a new GPO based on the template and link that GPO to the OU.

5. What needs to be done to track accesses or attempts to access the folders containing Tailspin's confidential documents?

   To track access attempts at the folder level, use auditing. The folders must reside on an NTFS partition, and Object Access auditing must be enabled. This can be accomplished using Group Policy directly or by configuring our Security Template accordingly. A very important and often overlooked step is configuring the actual folder to be audited. Enabling Object Access auditing for the server is necessary but, by itself, will not cause anything to be audited! You must also configure auditing on the individual folders.

6. How should the file servers that contain confidential documents be configured to meet Tailspin's requirements regarding the security log?

Lisa Jacobson indicated that all attempts to access data *must* be audited without exception. She also indicated that the security log entries must never be overwritten. The appropriate setting for the Event Viewer security logs on these servers is Do Not Overwrite Events. By itself, this setting will cause the security log to fill up and a prompt to appear on the screen indicating that the log is full. While the log is full, no further access attempts will be audited. To alleviate this issue, raise the maximum size of the Event Viewer security log. Doing so allows more entries to be recorded. One last setting that should be considered is the Audit: Shut Down The System Immediately If Unable To Log Security Audits. Recall that if the security log fills up, and we don't allow events to be overwritten, no further audits can be made until an administrator intervenes. This setting gives up some stability in exchange for extra audit assurance. If this setting is made, it is critical that the logs be archived or cleared manually before they fill up. Otherwise, just as the setting says, the system will shut down.

14 Managing Active Directory Performance

Exam Objectives in this Chapter:

- Troubleshoot Active Directory directory service
- Monitor File Replication service replication

Why This Chapter Matters

This chapter shows you how to monitor and troubleshoot Active Directory, tasks you'll perform often as a system administrator. To effectively monitor and troubleshoot, you must know how to interpret the directory and file replication service logs in the Event Viewer console to handle errors, warnings, and informational messages generated by Active Directory and the File Replication service (FRS). You must also be able to set up System Monitor to sample Active Directory and FRS replication performance by using the NTDS, FileReplicaConn, and FileReplicaSet performance objects. The practices and labs in this chapter help you gain the skills and confidence you'll need to effectively monitor and troubleshoot Active Directory and FRS replication.

Lessons in this Chapter:

Before You Begin

To complete the lessons in this chapter, you must

- Prepare your test environment according to the descriptions given in the "Getting Started" section of "About This Book"
- Complete the practices for installing and configuring Active Directory as discussed in Chapter 2, "Installing and Configuring Active Directory"
- Learn to use Active Directory administration tools as discussed in Chapter 3, "Administering Active Directory"

Lesson 1: Monitoring Performance with Service Logs and System Monitor

Monitoring Active Directory performance is an important part of maintaining and administering your Microsoft Windows Server 2003 installation. This lesson shows you how to monitor performance by using the directory service log, the file replication service log, and System Monitor.

After this lesson, you will be able to

■ Describe the purpose of the directory service log in the Event Viewer console

■ Describe the purpose of the file replication service log in the Event Viewer console

■ Describe the purpose of System Monitor

■ Use System Monitor to monitor performance counters

Estimated lesson time: 25 minutes

Understanding the Directory and File Replication Service Logs

Windows Server 2003 provides the Event Viewer console as a way to monitor Windows-wide events such as application, security, and system events, and service-specific events such as directory service events. These events are recorded in event logs. By default, there are three logs available to view in Event Viewer: the application log, the security log, and the system log. The security log is accessible only to system administrators and is enabled only if an audit policy is set up in a Group Policy Object (GPO) at the appropriate level. If additional services are installed, the services can enable a service-specific log. When Active Directory is installed, the directory service log and the file replication service log are enabled.

The *directory service log* contains errors, warnings, and information generated by Active Directory. If you experience problems with Active Directory, use the directory service log first to locate the causes of the problem. The directory service log can help you to understand the sequence and types of events that led up to a particular Active Directory performance problem. For example, on domain controllers running Windows Server 2003 with Service Pack 1 (SP1), an event message with event ID 2089 appears when Active Directory partitions are not backed up within the tombstone lifetime (180 days).

The *File Replication service (FRS)* is a service that provides multimaster file replication for designated directory trees between designated servers running Windows Server 2003. The designated directory trees must reside on disk partitions formatted with the version of the NTFS file system used in the Windows Server 2003 family. FRS is used by Active Directory to automatically synchronize content of the system volume information across domain controllers. Therefore, you may find it necessary to monitor FRS replication. The *file replication service log* contains errors, warnings, and information generated by FRS.

> **Off the Record**   You can use the Ntfrsutl command-line utility, which is included in the Windows Support Tools, to monitor the FRS on local and remote computers. You can even configure Ntfrsutl to poll the FRS service at specific intervals. To learn more about the capabilities of Ntfrsutl, run the **ntfrsutl /?** command from a command prompt.

> **Exam Tip**   Know the purpose of the directory service log and the file replication service log.

In Chapter 13, "Administering Security with Group Policy," you learned how to administer the security log by using the Event Viewer console. The tasks for administering the directory service log and the file replication service log are identical to those tasks you learned for administering the security log. You can use the same procedures to view, find events in, filter, configure, and archive the logs.

Understanding System Monitor

System Monitor is a tool that supports detailed monitoring of the use of operating system resources. System Monitor is hosted in the Performance console. The functionality of System Monitor is based on Microsoft Windows NT Performance Monitor, not Microsoft Windows 98 System Monitor. System Monitor enables you to

- Collect real-time performance data from a local computer or from a specific computer on the network where you have permission

- View current or previously recorded performance data

- Present data in a printable graph, histogram, or report view

- Create reusable monitoring configurations that can be installed on other computers using Microsoft Management Console (MMC)

- Incorporate System Monitor functionality into applications that support ActiveX controls: for example, Web pages, Microsoft Word, or other applications in the Microsoft Office suite

- Create HTML pages from performance views

A sample System Monitor is shown in Figure 14-1.

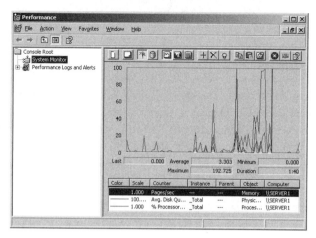

Figure 14-1 A sample System Monitor

Performance Objects and Performance Counters

To monitor performance, you select performance objects and their associated performance counters. A *performance object* is a logical collection of performance counters that is associated with a resource or service that can be monitored. A *performance counter* is a data item associated with a performance object. For each performance counter selected, System Monitor presents a value corresponding to a particular aspect of the performance that is defined for the performance object.

To monitor Active Directory, you monitor the activity of the NT Directory Services (NTDS) performance object. The counters in the NTDS performance object reflect the functions of Active Directory, including the

- Address book (AB)
- Asynchronous thread queue (ATQ)
- Directory Replication Agent (DRA)
- Directory service (DS)
- Key distribution center (KDC)
- Kerberos authentications
- Lightweight Directory Access Protocol (LDAP)
- NTLM authentications
- Security Accounts Manager (SAM)

There are more than 120 performance counters provided for the NTDS performance object. Each performance counter is described in Help. The important Active Directory System Monitor counters on the NTDS performance object are described in Table 14-1.

Table 14-1   Important Active Directory System Monitor Counters on the NTDS Performance Object

Counter	Description
DRA Inbound Bytes Compressed (Between Sites, After Compression) /Sec	The compressed size (in bytes) of inbound compressed replication data (size after compression, from Directory System Agents [DSAs] in other sites).
DRA Inbound Bytes Compressed (Between Sites, Before Compression)/Sec	The original size (in bytes) of inbound compressed replication data (size before compression, from DSAs in other sites).
DRA Inbound Bytes Not Compressed (Within Site)/Sec	The number of bytes received through inbound replication that were not compressed at the source; that is, from other DSAs in the same site.
DRA Inbound Bytes Total/Sec	The total number of bytes received through replication, per second. It is the sum of the number of uncompressed bytes (never compressed) and the number of compressed bytes (after compression).
DRA Inbound Full Sync Objects Remaining	The number of objects remaining until the full synchronization process is completed, or set.
DRA Inbound Objects/Sec	The number of objects received, per second, from replication partners through inbound replication.
DRA Inbound Objects Applied/Sec	The rate, per second, at which replication updates are received from replication partners and applied by the local directory service. This count excludes changes that are received but not applied (for example, when the change is already present). This indicates how much replication update activity is occurring on the server as a result of changes generated on other servers.
DRA Inbound Objects Filtered/Sec	The number of objects received per second from inbound replication partners that contained no updates that needed to be applied.
DRA Inbound Object Updates Remaining in Packet	The number of object updates received in the current directory replication update packet that have not yet been applied to the local server. This tells you whether the monitored server is receiving changes but taking a long time applying them to the database.
DRA Inbound Properties Applied/Sec	The number of properties applied through inbound replication as a result of reconciliation logic.
DRA Inbound Properties Filtered/Sec	The number of property changes that are already known received during the replication.
DRA Inbound Properties Total/Sec	The total number of object properties received per second from inbound replication partners.

Table 14-1   Important Active Directory System Monitor Counters on the NTDS Performance Object

Counter	Description
DRA Inbound Values (DNs Only)/Sec	The number of object property values received from inbound replication partners that are distinguished names (DNs), per second. This includes objects that reference other objects. DN values, such as group or distribution list memberships, are more expensive to apply than other kinds of values because group or distribution list objects can include hundreds and thousands of members and therefore are much bigger than a simple object with only one or two attributes. This counter might explain why inbound changes are slow to be applied to the database.
DRA Inbound Values Total/Sec	The total number of object property values received from inbound replication partners per second. Each inbound object has one or more properties, and each property has zero or more values. Zero values indicate property removal.
DRA Outbound Bytes Compressed (Between Sites, After Compression)/ Sec	The compressed size (in bytes) of outbound compressed replication data, after compression, from DSAs in other sites.
DRA Outbound Bytes Compressed (Between Sites, Before Compression)/Sec	The original size (in bytes) of outbound compressed replication data, before compression, from DSAs in other sites.
DRA Outbound Bytes Not Compressed (Within Site)/Sec	The number of bytes replicated out that were not compressed; that is, from DSAs in the same site.
DRA Outbound Bytes Total/Sec	The total number of bytes replicated out per second. The sum of the number of uncompressed bytes (never compressed) and the number of compressed bytes (after compression).
DRA Outbound Objects/Sec	The number of objects replicated out per second.
DRA Outbound Objects Filtered/Sec	The number of objects acknowledged by outbound replication that required no updates. This also represents objects that the outbound partner did not already have.
DRA Outbound Properties/Sec	The number of properties replicated out per second. This tells you whether a source server is returning objects or not.

Table 14-1   Important Active Directory System Monitor Counters on the NTDS Performance Object

Counter	Description
DRA Outbound Value (DNs Only)/Sec	The number of object property values containing DNs sent to outbound replication partners. DN values, such as group or distribution list memberships, are more expensive to read than other kinds of values because group or distribution list objects can include hundreds and thousands of members and therefore are much bigger than a simple object with only one or two attributes.
DRA Outbound Values Total/Sec	The number of object property values sent to outbound replication partners per second.
DRA Pending Replication Synchronizations	The number of directory synchronizations that are queued for this server but not yet processed. This helps in determining replication backlog; the larger the number, the larger the backlog.
DRA Sync Requests Made	The number of synchronization requests made to replication partners.
DS Directory Reads/Sec	The number of directory reads per second.
DS Directory Writes/Sec	The number of directory writes per second.
DS Security Descriptor Suboperations/Sec	The number of Security Descriptor Propagation suboperations per second. One Security Descriptor Propagation operation is made up of many suboperations. A suboperation roughly corresponds to an object the propagation causes the propagator to examine.
DS Security Descriptor Propagation Events	The number of Security Descriptor Propagation events that are queued but not yet processed.
DS Threads in Use	The current number of threads in use by the directory service (different from the number of threads in the directory service process). Threads in Use is the number of threads currently servicing client application programming interface (API) calls and can be used to indicate whether additional processors can be of benefit.
Kerberos Authentications	The number of times per second that clients use a ticket to this domain controller to authenticate to this domain controller.
LDAP Bind Time	The time (in milliseconds) taken for the last successful LDAP binding.
LDAP Client Sessions	The number of connected LDAP client sessions.
LDAP Searches/Sec	The number of search operations per second performed by LDAP clients.
LDAP Successful Binds/Sec	The number of successful LDAP binds per second.

Table 14-1   Important Active Directory System Monitor Counters on the NTDS Performance Object

Counter	Description
NTLM Authentications	The number of Windows NT LAN Manager (NTLM) authentications per second serviced by this domain controller.

To monitor FRS, you monitor the activity of the FileReplicaConn and FileReplicaSet performance objects. The FileReplicaConn performance object shows performance statistics for the Replicaconn object that defines replica connections to Distributed File System (DFS) roots. The FileReplicaSet performance object shows performance statistics for the Replicaset object that defines a replica set. The counters for these objects are available for each replica set managed by FRS while the service is running. Important FileReplicaSet counters that you can monitor to verify FRS performance are listed in Table 14-2.

Table 14-2   Important FileReplicaSet Counters

Counter	Description
Change Orders Received	Number of change notifications received from inbound partners.
Change Orders Sent	Number of change notifications sent out to outbound partners.
Files Installed	Number of replicated files installed locally.
KB of Staging Space Free	Amount of free space in the staging directory used by FRS to temporarily store files before they are replicated. The default staging space is 660 MB.
KB of Staging Space In Use	Amount of space in the staging directory currently in use. If the staging directory runs out of space, replication stops.
Packets Received	Number of FRS data or control packets (RPC calls) received by FRS.
Packets Sent	Number of FRS data and control packets sent to all outbound partners associated with this replica set member.
USN Records Accepted	Number of records that are accepted for replication. Replication is triggered by entries written to the NTFS change journal. FRS reads each file close record from the journal and determines whether to replicate the file. An accepted record generates a change order, which is then sent out. A high value on this counter (about one every five seconds) indicates a lot of replication traffic. This can cause replication latency.

Performance counters can provide baseline analysis information for capacity and performance planning. Typically, counters that are suited for capacity planning contain the word "total" in their name. These counters fall into three types: statistic counters, ratio counters, and accumulative counters. *Statistic counters* show totals per second, for example: DRA Inbound Properties Total/Sec, which is the total number of object properties received from inbound replication partners. *Ratio counters* show percentage of total, for example: DS %Writes From LDAP, which is the percentage of directory writes coming from LDAP query. *Accumulative counters* show totals since Active Directory was last started, for example: DRA Inbound Bytes Total Since Boot, which is the total number of bytes replicated in, the sum of the number of uncompressed bytes (never compressed) and the number of compressed bytes (after compression).

> **Exam Tip**   Know which performance objects are used to monitor Active Directory and FRS.

System Monitor Properties

In addition to options for defining data content, you can also determine sampling parameters and display options.

Sampling Parameters   For real-time data, System Monitor supports manual, on-demand sampling or automatic sampling based on a time interval you specify. When viewing logged data, you can also choose starting and stopping times so that you can view data spanning a specific time range.

Display Options   You have considerable flexibility in designing the appearance of your System Monitor views. You can select the type of display from graph, histogram, and report views. The graph view is shown by default. You can also select various display characteristics. For any of the three views, you can define the characteristics, colors, and fonts for the display.

Monitoring Active Directory Performance

To monitor Active Directory performance, you must first select the performance counters to monitor. Then you can set sampling parameters and display options.

To select performance counters, complete the following steps:

1. Click Start, point to Administrative Tools, and then click Performance.

2. Right-click the System Monitor details pane and click Add Counters. Alternatively, click the plus sign (+) icon on the System Monitor menu bar.

3. In the Add Counters dialog box, shown in Figure 14-2, select one of the following:

   ❑ To monitor the computer on which System Monitor is running, click Use Local Computer Counters.

❑ To monitor a specific computer, regardless of where System Monitor is running, click Select Counters From Computer and select the Uniform Naming Convention (UNC) name (the name of the local computer is selected by default) of the computer you want to monitor in the text box. Or, you can type the Internet Protocol (IP) address of the computer you want to monitor.

Note   When creating a System Monitor snap-in for export, select Use Local Computer Counters. Otherwise, System Monitor (an ActiveX control) obtains data from the computer named in the text box, regardless of where the snap-in is installed.

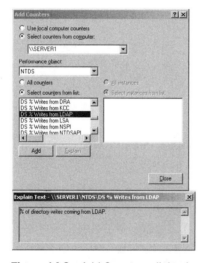

Figure 14-2   Add Counters dialog box

4. In the Performance Object list, select NTDS.

5. To select the counters to monitor, choose one of the following:

❑ To monitor all counters for the NTDS performance object, click All Counters.

❑ To monitor only selected counters, click Select Counters From List, and select the counters you want to monitor from the list. You can select multiple counters by clicking on a counter and holding the CTRL key.

Note   Because there are many counters, monitoring all counters affects processing time, provides too much information, and is not a practical solution.

> **Note**   For a description of a particular counter, select the name of the counter from the list, and then click Explain. Figure 14-2 shows the description for the DS %Writes From LDAP performance counter.

6. Click Add.

7. When you are finished adding counters, click Close. The counters that you selected appear in the lower part of the System Monitor screen; each counter is represented by its own color. Choose either the graph, histogram, or report display view by clicking the appropriate toolbar button.

To set sampling parameters and display options, complete the following steps:

1. Right-click the System Monitor details pane and click Properties. Or, on the System Monitor menu bar, click the icon showing Notepad and a pointing finger.

2. In the System Monitor Properties dialog box, in the General tab, shown in Figure 14-3, select the Sample Automatically Every check box to indicate whether the computer will sample data periodically based on the interval you set. This check box is selected by default. Type the number of seconds you want to use for the sampling interval in the Seconds box. The number of seconds is set to 1 by default.

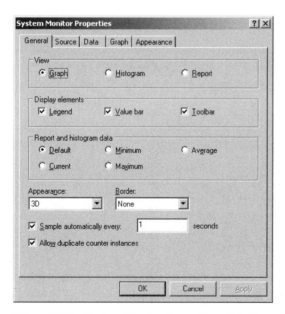

Figure 14-3   System Monitor Properties dialog box, General tab

3. In the View area, select how you want to view System Monitor data as follows:

   ❑ Select Graph to display counter data in a line graph.

❑ Select Histogram to display counter data in a bar graph.

❑ Select Report to display counter data as text in a report.

> **Note** If you are monitoring over an extended period of time, use graphs instead of reports or histograms because these views show only the last values and averages. As a result, they might not give an accurate picture of values if you are looking for spikes.

4. In the Display Elements area, select which display elements you want to appear on System Monitor.

   ❑ Select Legend to display the computer, performance object, counter, instance, and counter color and scale.

   ❑ Select Value Bar to display the last, minimum, maximum, and average values for the counter and the elapsed time shown in the graph.

   ❑ Select Toolbar to display the toolbar.

5. In the Report And Histogram Data area, select the type of value you want to display on the report or histogram from Default (for real-time monitoring, this is current data; for monitoring from a log, this is average data), Current, Minimum, Maximum, or Average.

6. If you have selected Graph or Histogram view, click the Graph tab.

7. In the Graph tab, shown in Figure 14-4, you have the option of naming the graph shown in the System Monitor by typing a name in the Title box. You can label the vertical axis of the graph by typing a name in the Vertical Axis box.

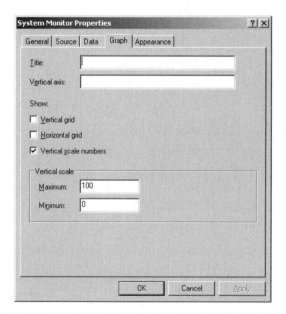

Figure 14-4 System Monitor Properties dialog box, Graph tab

8. In the Show area in the Graph tab, select the Vertical Grid check box to display a vertical grid on the graph. Select the Horizontal Grid check box to display a horizontal grid on the graph. Select the Vertical Scale Numbers check box to display vertical scale numbers on the vertical grid on the graph. Vertical Scale Numbers is selected by default.

9. In the Vertical Scale area in the Graph tab, enter the maximum value for the vertical axis for the graph in the Maximum box, and then enter the minimum value for the vertical axis for the graph in the Minimum box.

10. Click the Appearance tab.

11. In the Appearance tab, shown in Figure 14-5, select the desired graph element in the list in the Color area and click Change to change the color of the element. In the Color dialog box, select the desired color and click OK.

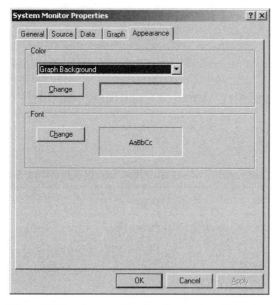

Figure 14-5   System Monitor Properties dialog box, Appearance tab

12. In the Font area in the Appearance tab, click Change to change the font. Select the desired font characteristics in the Font dialog box, and then click OK.

13. Click OK to apply your selections in the System Monitor Properties dialog box.

Monitoring Performance with the Directory Service Log and System Monitor Best Practices

The following are the best practices for monitoring performance with the directory service log and System Monitor:

■   Keep directory service log file overhead low. File size and disk space taken up by log files affect performance. To reduce file size and related disk space usage, extend the update interval. Also, log to a disk other than the one being monitored. Frequent logging also adds demand on disk input and output (I/O). During local logging of remote counters, frequent updating can slow performance due to network transport. In this case, log continuously on remote computers but upload logs infrequently—for example, once a day.

- Prepare the computer you want to monitor. Before starting System Monitor on the computer you want to monitor, stop screen saver programs, turn off services that are not relevant to monitoring, and increase the paging file to 1.5 times your computer's physical memory. If the computer you want to monitor has halted or is not responding, run System Monitor from another computer.

- Keep monitoring overhead low. The performance-monitoring tools are designed for minimal overhead. However, overhead can increase when System Monitor is running in graph view, an option other than the default (current value) for either the System Monitor graph or report views is selected, sampling is occurring at very frequent intervals (less than three seconds apart), or many objects and counters are selected. If monitoring overhead is a concern, run only the Performance Logs And Alerts service and do not monitor using a System Monitor graph.

Directory Service Log and System Monitor Troubleshooting

Table 14-3 describes some troubleshooting scenarios related to the directory service log and System Monitor.

Table 14-3   Directory Service Log and System Monitor Troubleshooting Scenarios

Causes	Solutions
Problem: System Monitor shows gaps in its line graphs.	
Data collection was subordinated to higher priority processing activity on a system with a heavy load. When the system has adequate resources to continue with data collection, the graphing resumes as usual. A message appears describing this.	Reduce the performance overhead of system monitoring.
Problem: Counter values consistently equal zero.	
The process being monitored has stopped so there is no data for the process in the performance-monitoring tools.	If you stopped the process manually, restart it to see the process in System Monitor. Otherwise, check Event Viewer for concurrent entries. You might find an error associated with this process.

Table 14-3   Directory Service Log and System Monitor Troubleshooting Scenarios

Causes	Solutions
The counter dynamic link library (DLL) was disabled after you selected the corresponding counters in a log or display. The performance tools do not detect that the counter was removed or disabled but report the counter data as zeroes.	Enable the corresponding counter DLL.
You lack permissions on the computer being monitored. If you don't have appropriate permissions to access the computer, an error message is displayed when you attempt to select the counter, and you are not able to add it to the histogram or graph.	An administrator must ensure that your user account has permissions to use the performance-monitoring tools.

Problem: Counters no longer work properly after the installation of a new application.

If you install a new application that installs performance counters on your operating system, the operating system creates a backup copy of the performance counter registry entries taken prior to the addition of the application's performance counters file. This backup is saved as a file named Perf-StringBackup.ini. If your operating system successfully adds the application's performance counters file, it then replaces the previous version of the PerfStringBackup.ini file with the file that it just created.	Restore the performance counter registry to the state described in the uncorrupted backup file by using the command **lodctr / r:*filename*** where *filename* is the name of the backup performance counter registry entry file.

Problem: Objects, counters, or instances seem to be missing or invalid.

Test routines that run when you start the Performance console have detected a problem with installed counters and have disabled the counters automatically to prevent the counters from slowing the system. Disabled objects and counters do not appear in the Add Counters dialog box.	Enable the disabled counters by using the Registry Editor. Change the value under HKEY_LOCAL_MACHINE\SYSTEM\CurrentControlSet\Services\Service_name\Performance\Disable Performance Counters from 1 for disable to 0 for enable. Note that counters that have been disabled after initial testing are likely to contain errors and might cause system problems. Turn off the counter DLL automatic testing feature or adjust the level of testing. Using the Registry Editor, locate the Configuration Flags subkey under HKEY_LOCAL_MACHINE\Software\Microsoft\Windows NT\CurrentVersion\Perflib and change the value of the REG_DWORD entry.

Table 14-3   Directory Service Log and System Monitor Troubleshooting Scenarios

Causes	Solutions
The process that starts the object counters is not started or installed.	Use Task Manager to verify that the process is running. If so, use Exctrlst.exe on the Resource Kit companion CD-ROM to verify that the counter DLL is enabled.
The counters haven't been enabled.	Make sure that the service or feature that provides the counter has been installed or configured.
The DLL that installs the counters is generating errors. An example is if the counter does not handle localization functions correctly.	Check Event Viewer to see whether the counter DLL or the Performance Data Helper reported any errors. If necessary, you can disable counter DLLs that are causing errors by using Exctrlst.exe on the *Microsoft Windows Server 2003 Resource Kit*, available on the Microsoft Web site at *http://www.microsoft.com/windowsserver2003 /techinfo/reskit/resourcekit.mspx*.
You are trying to monitor a 16-bit or MS-DOS application. Only 32-bit processes appear in the instances list. Active 16-bit processes appear as threads running in a Windows NT Virtual DOS Machine (NTVDM) process.	Monitor the application via the NTVDM process.

Practice: Using System Monitor

In this practice, you select performance counters to monitor and then view them graphically in the System Monitor as a graph, histogram, or log file data display.

Exercise 1: Verifying Performance Counters in System Monitor

1. Log on to Server1 as Administrator.

2. Use the procedure provided earlier in this lesson to select the NTDS performance object and the DRA Pending Replication Synchronizations counter and the LDAP Searches/Sec counter to monitor for Server1.

3. The counters that you selected appear in the lower part of the System Monitor screen; each counter is represented by its own color.

4. Ensure that the sampling parameters are set to sample data automatically every second.

5. Experiment with the System Monitor view. Display counter data in a histogram and in a report.

6. In the graph or histogram view, experiment by giving the view a title and naming the vertical axis. Show a vertical and a horizontal grid. Change the color of some of the graph elements.

Lesson Review

The following questions are intended to reinforce key information presented in this lesson. If you are unable to answer a question, review the lesson and then try the question again. Answers to the questions can be found in the "Questions and Answers" section at the end of this chapter.

1. Which Active Directory performance-monitoring tool should you use first to locate the causes of a problem with Active Directory?

   _____

   _____

2. What is the function of System Monitor?

   _____

   _____

3. What is the difference between a performance object and a performance counter?

   _____

   _____

4. In what format does a histogram display performance data?

   _____

   _____

5. Which of the following is not a function of System Monitor?

   a. Enables you to view current Active Directory performance data

   b. Enables you to view previously recorded Active Directory performance data

   c. Enables you to view errors and warnings generated by Active Directory

   d. Enables you to collect real-time performance data from a local computer

   e. Enables you to collect real-time performance data from a specific computer on the network where you have permission

Lesson Summary

■ Once Active Directory is installed, the directory and file replication service logs are enabled on the Event Viewer console. The directory service log contains errors, warnings, and information generated by Active Directory. If you experience problems with Active Directory, use the directory service log first to locate the causes of the problem. The file replication service log contains events logged by FRS.

■ System Monitor is a tool that supports detailed monitoring of the use of operating system resources. With System Monitor, you can collect and view real-time performance data on a local computer or from several remote computers, view data collected either currently or previously recorded in a counter log, and present data in a printable graph, histogram, or report view.

■ A performance object is a logical collection of performance counters that is associated with a resource or service that can be monitored. A performance counter is a value associated with a performance object.

■ To monitor Active Directory, you monitor the activity of the NTDS performance object. There are over 120 performance counters provided for the NTDS performance object.

Lesson 2: Monitoring Performance with Performance Logs And Alerts

Monitoring Active Directory performance is an important part of maintaining and administering your Windows Server 2003 installation. This lesson shows you how to monitor performance by using Performance Logs And Alerts.

After this lesson, you will be able to

- Describe the function of counter logs, trace logs, and alerts
- Use Performance Logs And Alerts to create counter logs, trace logs, and alerts
- View counter logs

Estimated lesson time: 25 minutes

The Performance Logs And Alerts Snap-In

The Performance Logs And Alerts snap-in provides you with the ability to create counter logs, trace logs, and system alerts automatically from local or remote computers.

Counter Logs

Counter logs record sampled data about hardware resources and system services based on performance objects and counters in the same manner as System Monitor. Counter logs collect performance counter data in a comma-separated or tab-separated format for easy import to spreadsheet or database programs. You can view logged counter data using System Monitor or export the data to a file for analysis and report generation.

Trace Logs

Trace logs collect event traces that measure performance statistics associated with events such as disk and file I/O, page faults, and thread activity. Event tracing measures activity as it happens, eliminating the inaccuracies of sampling. When the event occurs, either the default system data provider (the Windows kernel trace provider) or a nonsystem data provider designed to track these events sends the data to the Performance Logs And Alerts service. The data is measured from start to finish, rather than sampled in the manner of System Monitor. This differs from the operation of counter logs; when counter logs are in use, the service obtains data from the system when the update interval has elapsed, rather than waiting for a specific event. Because running trace logs of page faults and file I/O data incurs some performance overhead, you should log this data only for brief periods.

Off the Record   Most new hard disk controllers support simultaneous file I/O to multiple hard disks. If you have multiple physical hard disks available on an Active Directory domain controller, you should place the Active Directory database on a separate physical hard disk than the operating system files. Doing so improves the performance of Active Directory. Further, separating the Active Directory log files from the Active Directory database increases performance. You can do this with Ntdsutil, as you'll see in the Troubleshooting Lab in this chapter.

Active Directory nonsystem data providers include those for Net Logon, Kerberos, and SAM. These providers generate trace log files containing messages that can be used to track the operations performed.

A parsing tool is required to interpret the trace log output. Developers can create such a tool using APIs provided on the Microsoft Web site (*http://msdn.microsoft.com/*).

Logging Options

For both counter and trace logs you can

- Define start and stop times, filenames, file types, file sizes, and other parameters for automatic log generation and manage multiple logging sessions from a single console window.

- Start and stop logging either manually on demand or automatically based on a user-defined schedule.

- Configure additional settings for automatic logging, such as automatic file renaming, and set parameters for stopping and starting a log based on the elapsed time or the file size.

- Define a program that runs when a log is stopped.

- View logs during collection as well as after collection has stopped. Because logging runs as a service, data collection occurs regardless of whether any user is logged on to the computer being monitored.

Counter and Trace Logging Requirements

To create or modify a log, you must have Full Control permission for the registry key that controls the Performance Logs And Alerts service. This key is

HKEY_LOCAL_MACHINE\SYSTEM\CurrentControlSet\Services\SysmonLog \LogQueries

Administrators usually have this permission by default. Administrators can grant permission to users by using the Security menu in the registry editor.

To run the Performance Logs And Alerts service (which runs in the background when you configure a counter or trace log), you must have permission to start or configure services on the system. Administrators have this right by default and can grant it to users by using Group Policy. To log data on a remote computer, the Performance Logs And Alerts service must run under an account that has access to the remote system.

Creating a Counter Log

To create a counter log, you first define the counters you want to log and then set log file and scheduling parameters.

To create a counter log, complete the following steps:

1. Click Start, point to Administrative Tools, and then click Performance.

2. Double-click Performance Logs And Alerts, and then click Counter Logs. Existing logs are listed in the details pane. A green icon indicates that a log is running; a red icon indicates that a log is stopped.

3. Right-click a blank area of the details pane, and then click New Log Settings.

4. In the New Log Settings dialog box, in the Name box, type the name of the log, and then click OK.

5. In the General tab of the dialog box for a counter log, shown in Figure 14-6, ensure that the correct path and filename of the log file appear in the Current Log File Name box, and then click Add Counters.

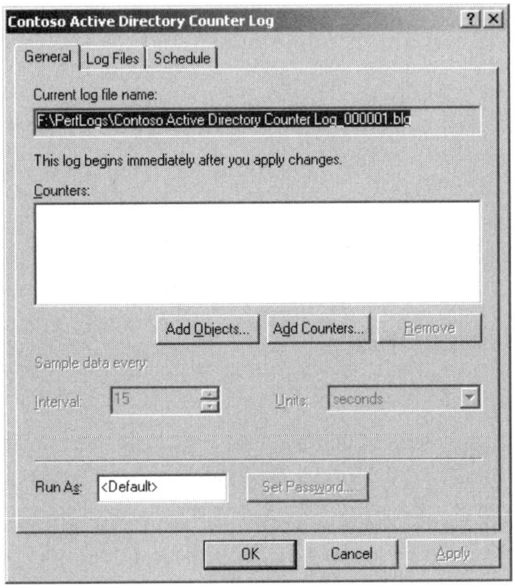

Figure 14-6   Dialog box for a counter log, General tab

6. In the Add Counters dialog box, select one of the following:

    ❑ To monitor the computer on which System Monitor is running, click Use Local Computer Counters.

    ❑ To monitor a specific computer, regardless of where System Monitor is running, click Select Counters From Computer, and select in the text box the UNC name of the computer you want to monitor (the name of the local computer is selected by default). Or, you can type the IP address of the computer you want to monitor.

> **Note**   When creating a Performance Logs And Alerts snap-in for export, make sure to select Use Local Computer Counters. Otherwise, counter logs obtain data from the computer named in the text box, regardless of where the snap-in is installed.

7. In the Performance Object list, select NTDS.

8. To select the counters to monitor, choose one of the following options:

    ❑ To monitor all counters for the NTDS performance object, click All Counters.

    ❑ To monitor only selected counters, click Select Counters From List, and select the counters you want to monitor from the list. You can select multiple counters by clicking on a counter and holding the CTRL key.

> **Note**   Because there are many counters, monitoring all counters affects processing time and is not a practical solution.

> **Tip**   For a description of a particular counter, click the name of the counter from the list, and then click Explain.

9. Click Add. When you are finished adding counters, click Close.

10. Back in the General tab, in the Sample Data Every section, specify the amount and the unit of measure for the update interval in the Interval box and the Units box, respectively.

> **Note**   Sampling should be frequent when monitoring over a short period. Similarly, for long-term planning and analysis, log for a longer period and set the update interval accordingly.

11. Click the Log Files tab, shown in Figure 14-7. In the Log File Type box, select one of the following log file types:

    ❑ Text File (Comma Delimited), to define a comma-delimited log file (.csv extension). Use this format to export the log data to a spreadsheet program.

❑ Text File (Tab Delimited), to define a tab-delimited log file (.tsv extension). Use this format to export the log data to a spreadsheet program.

❑ Binary File, to define a sequential, binary-format log file (.blg extension). Use this file format if you want to be able to record data instances that are intermittent—that is, stopping and resuming after the log has begun running. Non-binary file formats cannot accommodate instances that are not persistent throughout the duration of the log.

❑ Binary Circular File, to define a circular, binary-format log file (.blg extension). Use this file format to record data continuously to the same log file, overwriting previous records with new data.

❑ SQL Database, to define the name of an existing Structured Query Language (SQL) database and log set within the database where the performance data will be read or written. Use this file format to collect performance data at an enterprise level rather than on a per server basis.

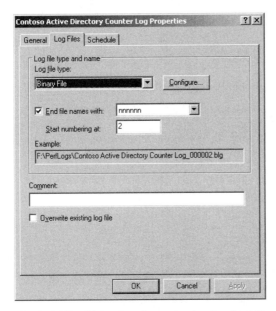

Figure 14-7   Dialog box for a counter log, Log Files tab

12. Click Configure. In the Configure Log Files dialog box, type the name of the folder where you want the log file created in the Location box, or click Browse to search for the folder.

13. Ensure that the name for the log file appears in the File Name box.

14. In the Log File Size area, select one of the following:

❑ Maximum Limit, to collect data continuously in a log file until it reaches limits set by disk quotas or the operating system. Click OK.

❑ Limit Of, to collect data up to the maximum size (in kilobytes, up to 2 gigabytes) you specify. Click OK.

15. Back in the Log Files tab, click End File Names With and choose the log file suffix style you want from the list. Enter the start number for automatic file numbering in the Start Numbering At box if you selected nnnnnn in the End File Names With list.

16. Type a comment or description for the log file in the Comment box. This comment appears in the details pane of the Performance console.

17. Select the Overwrite Existing Log File check box if you want to overwrite an existing log file with this log file.

18. Click the Schedule tab, shown in Figure 14-8. In the Schedule tab of the dialog box for the counter log, configure the options as described in Table 14-4.

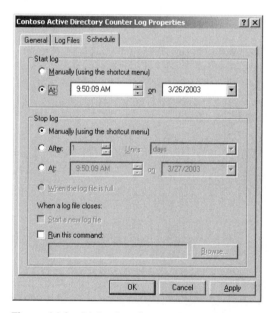

Figure 14-8 Dialog box for a counter log, Schedule tab

Table 14-4 Options in the Schedule Tab

Setting	Description
Start Log	
Manually	Logging starts manually.
At	Logging starts according to the time and date parameters you set.
Stop Log	
Manually	Logging stops manually.
After	Logging stops after the time you specify.

Table 14-4   Options in the Schedule Tab

Setting	Description
At	Logging stops at the time and date parameters you set.
When The Log File Is Full	Logging stops when the log file reaches a maximum size.
When A Log File Closes	
Start A New Log File	Logging resumes after logging stops for the current log file.
Run This Command	A command you specify is run when a log file closes.

19. Click OK.

To view a counter log, complete the following steps:

1. Click Start, point to Administrative Tools, and then click Performance.

2. Right-click the System Monitor details pane and click Properties.

3. In the System Monitor Properties dialog box, click the Source tab.

4. In the Source tab, shown in Figure 14-9, in the Data Source area, click Log Files, and then click Add.

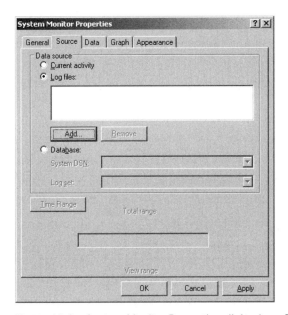

Figure 14-9   System Monitor Properties dialog box, Source tab

Note   To view data from a SQL database, click Database, and then select the system data source name (DSN) in the System DSN list and the set of log files in the Log Set list. To access the SQL database, the system DSN must be predefined, and privileges granted to write to the database. The log set must already be created in the database.

5. In the Select Log File dialog box, double-click the file you want to use as a data source.

6. In the System Monitor Properties dialog box, click Time Range to specify the time range in the log file that you want to view. Drag the bar or its handles for the appropriate starting and ending times.

> **Note** Unless you specifically want to monitor start-up events, you should exclude times that include such events from your time window because these temporary high values tend to skew overall performance results.

7. Click the Data tab. Click Add.

8. In the Add Counters dialog box, the counters you selected during log configuration are available. You can include all or some of these counters in your view of the counter log by selecting the counter and clicking Add. When you have finished selecting counters for the view, click Close.

9. In the System Monitor Properties dialog box, click OK. The view of the counter log is visible on System Monitor.

Creating a Trace Log

To create a trace log, you first define how you want events logged and then set log file and scheduling parameters.

To create a trace log, complete the following steps:

1. Click Start, point to Administrative Tools, and then click Performance.

2. Double-click Performance Logs And Alerts, and then click Trace Logs. Existing logs are listed in the details pane. A green icon indicates that a log is running; a red icon indicates that a log is stopped.

3. Right-click a blank area of the details pane, and then click New Log Settings.

4. In the New Log Settings dialog box, in the Name box, type the name of the log, and then click OK.

5. In the General tab of the dialog box for the trace log, shown in Figure 14-10, the path and filename of the log file are shown in the Current Log File Name box. By default, the log file is created in the PerfLogs folder in the root directory, a sequence number is appended to the filename you entered, and the sequential trace file type is indicated with the .etl extension.

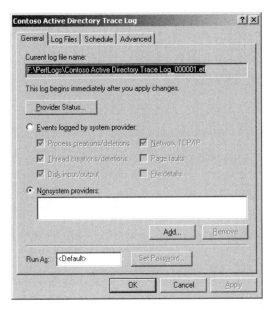

Figure 14-10   Dialog box for a trace log, General tab

6. Select one of the following to log events:

   ❑ Events Logged By System Provider, for the default provider (the Windows kernel trace provider) to monitor processes, threads, and other activity. To define events for logging, select the check boxes as appropriate. This can create some performance overhead for the system.

   ❑ Nonsystem Providers, to select the trace data providers you want—for example, if you have written your own providers. Use the Add or Remove buttons to select or remove nonsystem providers. For a list of the installed providers and their status (enabled or not), click Provider Status.

> **Note**   You can have only one trace log that uses the system provider running at a time. In addition, you cannot concurrently run multiple trace logs from the same nonsystem provider. If the system trace provider is enabled, nonsystem providers cannot be enabled, and vice versa. However, you can enable multiple nonsystem providers simultaneously.

7. In the Log Files tab of the dialog box for the trace log, configure the options as you do for counter logs, except in the Log File Type box, select one of the following:

   ❑ *Circular Trace File*. Defines a circular trace log file (with an .etl extension). Use this file format to record data continuously to the same log file, overwriting previous records with new data.

❑ *Sequential Trace File.* Defines a sequential trace log file (with an .etl extension) that collects data until it reaches a user-defined limit and then closes and starts a new file.

8. In the Schedule tab of the dialog box for the trace log, configure the options as shown for counter logs.

9. Click OK.

> **Note**   Trace logging of file details and page faults can generate an extremely large amount of data. It is recommended that you limit trace logging using the file details and page fault options to a maximum of two hours.

Alerts

An *alert* detects when a predefined counter value rises above or falls below the configured threshold and notifies a user by means of the Messenger service. Alerts enable you to define a counter value that triggers actions such as sending a network message, running a program, making an entry in the application log, or starting a log. You can start or stop an alert scan either manually, on demand, or automatically based on a user-defined schedule.

Creating an Alert

To create an alert, you first define the counters you want to monitor for the alert and then set alert triggering and scheduling parameters.

To create an alert, complete the following steps:

1. Click Start, point to Administrative Tools, and then click Performance.

2. Double-click Performance Logs And Alerts, and then click Alerts. Existing alerts are listed in the details pane. A green icon indicates that the alerts are running; a red icon indicates alerts are stopped.

3. Right-click a blank area of the details pane and click New Alert Settings.

4. In the New Alert Settings dialog box, in the Name box, type the name of the alert, and then click OK.

5. In the General tab of the dialog box for the alert, shown in Figure 14-11, type a comment to describe the alert in the Comment box, and then click Add.

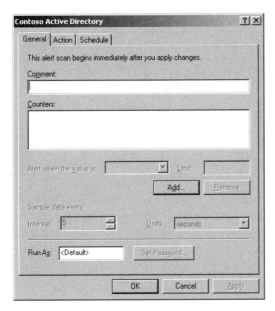

Figure 14-11   Dialog box for an alert, General tab

6. In the Add Counters dialog box, choose the computer for which you want to create an alert.

   ❑ To create an alert on the computer on which the Performance Logs And Alerts service will run, click Use Local Computer Counters.

   ❑ To create an alert on a specific computer regardless of where the service is run, click Select Counters From Computer and specify the name of the computer.

7. In the Performance Object list, select NTDS.

8. Select the counters you want to monitor, and then click Add.

9. Click Close when you have finished selecting counters to monitor for the alert.

10. Back in the General tab, specify Under or Over in the Alert When The Value Is box. In the Limit box, specify the value you want to trigger the alert.

11. In the Sample Data Every section, specify the amount and the unit of measure for the update interval in the Interval box and the Units box, respectively.

12. In the Action tab of the dialog box for the alert, shown in Figure 14-12, select when an alert is triggered as described in Table 14-5.

Table 14-5   Options in the Action Tab

Option	Description
Log An Entry In The Application Event Log	Creates an entry visible in the application log in Event Viewer
Send A Network Message To	Triggers the Messenger service to send a message to the specified computer
Start Performance Data Log	Runs a specified counter log when an alert occurs
Run This Program	Triggers the service to create a process and run a specified program when an alert occurs
Command Line Arguments	Triggers the service to copy specified command-line arguments when the Run This Program option is used

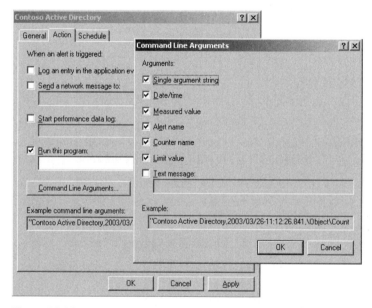

Figure 14-12   Dialog box for an alert, Action tab, and the Command Line Arguments dialog box

13. In the Schedule tab of the dialog box for the alert, configure the options as shown for counter logs.

14. Click OK.

Managing Active Directory Performance from the Command Line

In addition to using the Performance console, you can use the following command-line utilities to monitor and manage Active Directory performance:

Logman   The Logman command manages and schedules performance counter and event trace log collections on local and remote systems.

Perfmon   The Perfmon command allows you to open a Performance console configured with the System Monitor ActiveX control and Performance Logs And Alerts service.

Relog   The Relog command extracts performance counters from performance counter logs into other formats, such as text-TSV (tab-delimited text), text-CSV (comma-delimited text), binary-BIN, or SQL.

Tracerpt   The Tracerpt command processes event trace logs or real-time data from instrumented event trace providers and allows you to generate trace analysis reports and CSV files for the events generated.

Typeperf   The Typeperf command writes performance counter data to the command window or to a supported log file format.

Lodctr   The Lodctr command registers new performance counter names and Explain text for a service or device driver, and saves and restores counter settings and Explain text.

Unlodctr   The Unlodctr command removes performance counter names and Explain text for a service or device driver from the system registry.

Refer to Windows Server 2003 Help for detailed information about using these commands in performance monitoring and management.

> **Off the Record**   Excessive monitoring affects server performance, so monitor only the objects and counters required. Monitor objects and counters remotely where possible to reduce the performance impact of monitoring on the server you would like to monitor. You can also use the Logman.exe utility to configure specific logging operations from the command line, batch file, or scheduled job.

Monitoring Performance with Performance Logs And Alerts Best Practices

The following are the best practices for monitoring performance with Performance Logs And Alerts:

- Set up a monitoring configuration. Configure Performance Logs And Alerts to report data for the recommended counters at regular intervals, such as every 10 to 15 minutes. Retain logs over extended periods of time, store data in a database, and query the data to report on, and analyze, the data as needed for overall performance assessment, trend analysis, and capacity planning.

- Prepare the computer you want to monitor. Before starting Performance Logs And Alerts on the computer you want to monitor, stop screen saver programs, turn off services that are not relevant to monitoring, and increase the paging file to 1.5

times your computer's physical memory. If the computer you want to monitor has halted or is not responding, run Performance Logs And Alerts from another computer.

■ Keep log file overhead low. File size and disk space taken up by log files affect performance. To reduce file size and related disk space usage, extend the update interval. Also, log to a disk other than the one being monitored. Frequent logging also adds demand on disk I/O. During local logging of remote counters, frequent updating can slow performance due to network transport. In this case, log continuously on remote computers but upload logs infrequently—for example, once a day.

Performance Logs And Alerts Troubleshooting

Table 14-6 describes some troubleshooting scenarios related to Performance Logs And Alerts.

Table 14-6   Performance Logs And Alerts Troubleshooting Scenarios

Causes	Solutions
Problem: Values recorded in a log don't appear in the graph view.	
You did not add counters to the graph view.	Add counters to the graph view.
The graph is limited to 100 samples.	Reduce the selected time range.
Problem: An error message appears while trying to export log data to Microsoft Excel while the Performance Logs And Alerts service is actively collecting data to that log.	
Excel requires exclusive access to the log file. Other programs are not known to require this exclusive access; therefore, in general, you can work with data from a log file while the service is collecting data to that file.	Stop the Performance Logs And Alerts service before trying to use it with Excel.
Problem: The connection to a remote computer from which data was being logged has been lost and logging cannot be resumed.	
Logging data from a remote computer requires the use of Remote Registry service. If the service stops due to failure, by default the system restarts it automatically only once.	If Remote Registry service stops more than once, you must restart the service manually on the second and any subsequent failures. To change this default behavior, use the Computer Management or Services consoles (on the Administrative Tools menu) to modify the properties for Remote Registry service.
Problem: Performance counters cannot be logged from a remote computer.	
You might not have permission to view the counters on the remote machine.	Ask the administrator of the remote machine to grant you read access to the remote computer.

Table 14-6   Performance Logs And Alerts Troubleshooting Scenarios

Causes	Solutions
You might not have the correct privileges granted through Group Policy.	Ask the administrator of the remote machine to grant you access through the following user rights policies: Profile System Performance and Profile a Single Process.
The Performance Logs And Alerts service might not have permission to log on to the remote computer or to create and update the log file.	Use the Run As text box and Password button to specify the logon account name with the necessary permissions for the Performance Logs And Alerts service. You can access these features from the General tab.
The Remote Registry service is not running on the remote machine.	On the remote computer, start the Remote Registry service.
The log file size limit might not be large enough to collect your requested data.	Increase the limit of the log file size or set the file size to the maximum limit allowed.
The log update interval might be too short to allow the server to respond to each periodic data request.	Increase the log's update interval.

Practice: Using Performance Logs And Alerts

In this practice, you use Performance Logs And Alerts to create a counter log and an alert for the LDAP Searches/Sec counter.

Exercise 1: Creating a Counter Log

In this exercise, you create a counter log by first defining the counters you want to log and then setting log file and scheduling parameters.

▶ **To create a counter log**

1. Use the procedure provided earlier in this lesson to create a counter log named LDAP Searches Per Sec for Server1.

2. Select the NTDS performance object and the LDAP Searches/Sec counter to log.

3. Set the following log file options:

   ❏ Log File Type: Text File—CSV

   ❏ Location: C:\PerfLogs (where C is the name of your system drive)

   ❏ File Name: LDAP_Searches_per_sec

   ❏ Log File Size: Maximum Limit

   ❏ End File Names With: nnnnnn

   ❏ Start Numbering At: 1

4. Set the following scheduling options:

   ❑ Start Log At: a time 3 minutes from now

   ❑ Stop Log After: 2 minutes

5. When the log starts in three minutes, open the Active Directory Users And Computers console, open and close various OUs and objects, move various objects to other OUs and back again, and then close the Active Directory Users And Computers console.

6. When the log has stopped, use the procedure provided earlier in this lesson to view the counter log file C:\PerfLogs\LDAP_Searches_per_sec_00000 1.csv (where C is the name of your system drive).

Exercise 2: Creating an Alert

In this exercise, you create an alert by first defining the counters you want to monitor for the alert and then setting alert triggering and scheduling parameters.

▶ **To create an alert**

1. Use the procedure provided earlier in this lesson to create an alert named LDAP Searches Longer Than 5 Seconds for Server1. The comment for the alert is "Alerts when LDAP Searches are more than 5 per second."

2. Select the NTDS performance object and the LDAP Searches/Sec counter to monitor for the alert.

3. Set the alert to occur when the value is over five seconds and sample data every three seconds. Log the alert in the application log in Event Viewer.

4. Set the following scheduling options:

   ❑ Start Scan At: a time 3 minutes from now

   ❑ Stop Scan After: 2 minutes

5. When the log starts in three minutes, open the Active Directory Users and Computers console, open and close various OUs and objects, move various objects to other OUs and back again, and then close the Active Directory Users and Computers console.

6. When the log has stopped, you can view the alerts in the application log in Event Viewer. View the alert information by double-clicking the log entries.

Lesson Review

The following questions are intended to reinforce key information presented in this lesson. If you are unable to answer a question, review the lesson and then try the question again. Answers to the questions can be found in the "Questions and Answers" section at the end of this chapter.

1. What is the function of a counter log?

   _____

   _____

2. What is the function of a trace log?

   _____

   _____

3. In which locations can you view performance data logged in a counter log?

   _____

   _____

4. What is the function of an alert?

   _____

   _____

5. Which of the following actions can be triggered by an alert? Choose two.

   a. Logging an entry into the application log

   b. Starting logging automatically

   c. Sending a network message to a computer

   d. Stopping logging automatically

   e. Presenting data in a graph format

Lesson Summary

- The Performance Logs And Alerts snap-in provides you with the ability to create counter logs, trace logs, and system alerts automatically from local or remote computers.

- Counter logs record sampled data about hardware resources and system services based on performance objects and counters in the same manner as System Monitor. You can view logged counter data using System Monitor or export the data to a file for analysis and report generation.

- Trace logs collect event traces that measure performance statistics associated with events such as disk and file I/O, page faults, and thread activity.

- An alert detects when a predefined counter value rises above or falls below the configured threshold and notifies a user by means of the Messenger service. Alerts enable you to define a counter value that triggers actions such as sending a network message, running a program, making an entry in the application log, or starting a log.

Lesson 3: Optimizing and Troubleshooting Active Directory Performance

In order to manage Active Directory, you must be able to optimize and troubleshoot Active Directory performance. This lesson shows you how to interpret performance results to optimize and troubleshoot Active Directory performance.

After this lesson, you will be able to

- Troubleshoot Active Directory performance with the directory service log
- Troubleshoot Active Directory performance with the Performance console

Estimated lesson time: 10 minutes

Optimizing and Troubleshooting Active Directory Performance

In Lessons 1 and 2, you learned how to monitor Active Directory performance by using the directory service log in the Event Viewer console and System Monitor and Performance Logs And Alerts in the Performance console. These tools enable you to obtain up-to-date information about how Active Directory is operating. However, simply monitoring Active Directory performance does not enable you to optimize and troubleshoot performance. To effectively optimize and troubleshoot Active Directory performance, you must be able to analyze and interpret the information obtained from monitoring.

Real World   Active Directory, FRS, and Firewalls

By default, Active Directory uses FRS to replicate changes over the Remote Procedure Call (RPC) Endpoint Mapper service that utilizes TCP port 135. If there is a firewall between two domain controllers of the same domain, you will have to configure the firewall to allow replication. You do so by opening the correct ports on the firewall in order to support Active Directory replication. If you leave Active Directory domain controllers set to use the default RPC configuration, you must open TCP port 135 on the firewall in order for those domain controllers to replicate Active Directory data across the firewall. Further, the RPC client on each computer is configured to use TCP ports between 1024 and 65535. You'll have to enable dynamic ports between those ranges. If this is unacceptable, you can change the default ports that RPC uses on any given computer through the registry. The registry locations for FRS and RPC configuration are under the HKEY_LOCAL_MACHINE registry hive. The specific path to FRS configuration is \SYSTEM\CurrentControlSet\Services\NTFRS\Parameters. The specific path to RPC configuration is \SOFTWARE\Microsoft\RPC. To learn how to make specific changes to these services, see the following Microsoft Knowledge Base articles:

319553, "How to Restrict FRS Replication Traffic to a Specific Static Port"; 154596, "How to Configure RPC Dynamic Port Allocation to Work with Firewalls"; and 179442, "How to Configure a Firewall for Domains and Trusts." All are available from *http://www.microsoft.com*.

Troubleshooting Active Directory Performance with the Directory Service Log

As you learned in Lesson 1, the directory service log in the Event Viewer console contains basic errors, warnings, and information generated by Active Directory. By using the directory service log, you can view Active Directory error and warning messages. To troubleshoot problems indicated by the directory service log, you must be able to analyze and interpret these messages.

Tip   When troubleshooting Active Directory, remember to look at the DNS service. For example, if DNS lookup failures prevent a domain controller from contacting its replication partner, Active Directory update replication also fails. DNS problems are logged in the Directory Service and DNS Server logs. Note that domain controllers running Windows Server 2003 with SP1 have a more robust response to DNS name resolution failures. For more information, see "Fixing Replication DNS Lookup Problems" on the TechNet Web site at *http://www.microsoft.com/technet/prodtechnol/windowsserver2003/library/Operations /43e6f617-fb49-4bb4-8561-53310219f997.mspx*.

To troubleshoot problems indicated by error and warning messages in the directory service log, examine details about the message by double-clicking the error or warning message. An example warning message is shown in Figure 14-13. Examine the header information in the Properties dialog box for the message. In the header, you can find out the date and time the problem occurred and the user and computer affected by the problem. In the Description box in the Properties dialog box for the message, you can read a text description of the problem. You can find more information about the problem by clicking the link to the Help and Support Center, located at the bottom of the text description.

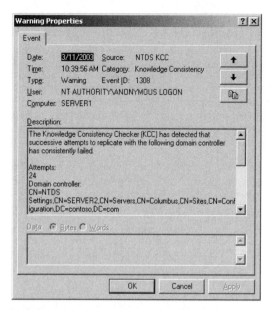

Figure 14-13 Properties dialog box for a directory service log warning message

Increasing the Directory Service Log Logging Level

By default, Active Directory records only critical error events to avoid flooding the log. You can retrieve more detailed information about directory service processing by increasing the logging level for the appropriate registry entry in the HKEY_LOCAL_MACHINE SYSTEM*CurrentControlSet*\\Services\\NTDS\\Diagnostics subkey in the registry. Each registry entry represents a type of event that Active Directory can log. The value of the entry determines the level of detail of the events that are logged and ranges from 0 (standard verbosity, records default-level errors) to 5 (most verbose, records all activity). For example, you can view messages about the replication schedule of directory partitions in the directory service log by increasing the Replication Events logging level to 2, and you can view messages about the amount of space that would be made available by offline defragmentation by increasing the Garbage Collection logging level to 1.

All of the entries in the Diagnostics subkey have the REG_DWORD data type and a default value of 0. All fatal and critical errors are logged at level 0, and no user action is required to view them.

Important Leave logging levels set to 0 unless you are investigating a problem. Increasing the logging level increases the detail of the messages and the number of messages emitted and can degrade server performance. Setting the value of entries in the Diagnostics subkey to greater than 3 is not recommended.

Table 14-7 contains a list of some of the registry entries in the Diagnostics subkey that store the directory service logging levels.

Table 14-7 Some Registry Entries in the Diagnostics Subkey

Registry Entry	Description
Knowledge Consistency Checker (KCC)	Reports if sites, servers, and site links are incorrect or missing.
Security Events	Reports events related to security, such as a user who tries to read or write an attribute with insufficient permissions, a user binding through Messaging Application Programming Interface (MAPI), or a domain that has been changed to native mode.
ExDS Interface Events	Reports events related to communication between Active Directory and Exchange clients.
MAPI Interface Events	Reports events related to communication between Active Directory and Exchange clients.
Replication Events	Reports events related to outbound replication, where changed objects are found, and inbound replication, where these changes are applied to a local database. Also logged is information about which objects and attributes were updated and why. "Normal" errors during the course of replication, such as a domain controller being down, are not logged. These errors are available through the replication tools.
Garbage Collection	Reports events generated when objects marked for deletion are actually deleted.
Internal Configuration	Interprets and displays the internal directory service operations.
Directory Access	Reads and writes directory objects from all sources.
Internal Processing	Reports events related to the internal operation of Active Directory code such as processing security descriptor propagation. Error events in this category can be an indicator of serious problems in Active Directory.
Performance Counters	Reports events related to loading and unloading the NTDS performance object and performance counters.
Initialization/Termination	Reports events related to starting and stopping Active Directory.
Service Control	Reports Active Directory service events.
Name Resolution	Reports resolved addresses and Active Directory names.
Backup	Reports events related to the backup of Active Directory. Specifically, errors occurring when Extensible Storage Engine (ESE) database records are read or written for backup purposes. Generally only logged when a backup operation is under way.
Field Engineering	Internal debugging trace.

Table 14-7 Some Registry Entries in the Diagnostics Subkey

Registry Entry	Description
LDAP Interface Events	Reports events related to LDAP, such as the LDAP server closed a socket to a client, unable to initialize LDAP Simple Bind Authentication, and LDAP over Secure Sockets Layer (SSL) is now available.
Setup	Reports events related to running the Active Directory Installation Wizard.
Global Catalog	Reports events related to the global catalog.
Inter-site Messaging	Reports messages logged by the "Intersite Message" service.

Caution This section contains information about editing the registry. Using the Registry Editor incorrectly can cause serious damage to your operating system. Use the Registry Editor at your own risk.

To increase the logging level for the directory service log in the registry, complete the following steps:

1. Log on as Administrator.

2. Click Start and then click Run.

3. In the Run dialog box, in the Open box, type **regedit** and then click OK.

4. In the Registry Editor console, open the HKEY_LOCAL_MACHINE SYSTEM\ CurrentControlSet\Services\NTDS\Diagnostics key.

5. In the details pane, double-click the DWORD value for which you would like to increase the logging level.

6. In the Edit DWORD Value dialog box, type **1** or **2** in the Value Data box. Ensure that the Hexadecimal button is selected. Click OK.

7. Log off and then log on again.

8. Open Event Viewer and view the enhanced directory service log.

Note Check the directory service log before raising the logging level. Be sure you understand the Active Directory problem and what you are looking for. To avoid clutter in the directory service log, do not set the logging level higher than 2.

Troubleshooting Active Directory Performance with the Performance Console

As you learned in Lesson 1, the Performance console provides a graphical way to view Active Directory performance by using System Monitor. The Performance console also provides a means to log activity, view logs, or send alerts by using Performance Logs And Alerts. To troubleshoot problems indicated by System Monitor, you must be able to analyze and interpret the results of each counter you have selected for monitoring.

Analyzing and Interpreting Performance-Monitoring Results

There are four steps in the process of analyzing and interpreting performance-monitoring results:

1. Establish a baseline.

2. Analyze performance-monitoring results.

3. Plan and implement changes to meet the baseline.

4. Repeat steps 2 and 3 until performance is optimized.

Establishing a Baseline   A baseline is a measurement derived from the collection of data over an extended period during varying workloads and user connections, representing acceptable performance under typical operating conditions. The baseline indicates how system resources are used during periods of normal activity and makes it easier to spot problems when they occur. You can establish a baseline for system performance by performing routine monitoring over periods ranging from days to weeks to months. During this period of routine monitoring, find out the types of work being done by the system and the days and times when the work is being done. Knowing about the work being done by the system can help you to associate types of work with resource usage and to determine the reasonable parameters of performance during those intervals. When you have gathered performance data over a period that represents the typical events in your organization, you can determine the acceptable performance levels. These performance levels comprise your baseline.

Analyzing Performance-Monitoring Results   The baseline you develop establishes the typical counter values you should expect to see when your system is performing satisfactorily. Use your baseline to detect when bottlenecks are developing or to watch for long-term changes in usage patterns that require you to increase capacity. A *bottleneck* is a condition, often involving a hardware resource, that causes the entire system to perform poorly. A bottleneck exists if a particular system component is keeping the entire system from performing more quickly. Therefore, even if a component in your system is heavily used, if other components or the system as a whole show no adverse effects, there is no bottleneck. Deviations from your baseline provide the best indicator of a bottleneck. However, occasional spikes in data might occur due to startup of a process and are not an accurate reflection of counter values for that process over time. Set alerts according to the counter values you consider to be unacceptable, as determined by your baseline.

It is not unusual to trace a bottleneck to multiple sources. Poor response time on a workstation is most likely to result from memory and processor problems. Servers are more susceptible to disk and network problems. Also, problems in one component might be the result of problems in another component, not the cause.

Planning and Implementing Changes to Meet the Baseline   If you identify a bottleneck, you must investigate the activity of the associated resource in greater detail to determine what changes must be made. Your investigation should include the following considerations:

- Analyze hardware and software configurations. Do these configurations match Microsoft recommendations for the operating system and the services you are supporting?

- Review the directory service log for the time period when you begin seeing out-of-range counter values. Do any of the entries in the log provide information on problems which could cause a bottleneck?

- Examine the kinds of applications you are running and the resources these applications require. Are the resources adequate?

- Consider network or disk utilization or other activities occurring at the times that you see increasing resource utilization. Try to understand the usage patterns. Are they associated with specific protocols or computers?

- Consider variables in your workload, such as processing different jobs at different times. What work is being done by the system?

- Approach bottleneck correction in an organized manner. Never make more than one change at a time, always repeat monitoring after a change to validate the results, eliminate results that are suspect, and keep good records of what you have done and what you have learned.

Lesson Review

The following questions are intended to reinforce key information presented in this lesson. If you are unable to answer a question, review the lesson and then try the question again. Answers to the questions can be found in the "Questions and Answers" section at the end of this chapter.

1. What action should you take to troubleshoot problems indicated by error and warning messages in the directory service log?

_____

_____

2. What registry subkey contains the entries for which you can increase the logging level to retrieve more detailed information in the directory service log?

_____

_____

3. Why should you leave logging levels set to 0 unless you are investigating a problem?

_____

_____

4. What are the four steps in the process of analyzing and interpreting performance-monitoring results?

_____

_____

5. In the process of analyzing and interpreting performance-monitoring results, what is a baseline?

_____

_____

Lesson Summary

- To troubleshoot problems indicated by error and warning messages in the directory service log, examine details about the message by double-clicking the error or warning message.

- You can retrieve more detailed information about directory service processing by increasing the logging level for the appropriate registry entry in the HKEY_LOCAL_MACHINE SYSTEM\CurrentControlSet\Services\NTDS\Diagnostics subkey in the Registry.

- All of the entries in the Diagnostics subkey have the REG_DWORD data type and a default value of 0. Leave logging levels set to 0 unless you are investigating a problem. Increasing the logging level increases the detail of the messages and the number of messages emitted and can degrade server performance.

- To troubleshoot problems indicated by System Monitor, you must be able to analyze and interpret the results of each counter you have selected for monitoring.

- There are four steps in the process of analyzing and interpreting performance-monitoring results: (1) establish a baseline, (2) analyze performance-monitoring results, (3) plan and implement changes to meet the baseline, and (4) repeat steps 2 and 3 until performance is optimized.

Case Scenario Exercise

You are a computer consultant for Margie Shoop, the owner of Margie's Travel. Margie has a single Active Directory domain structure named *margiestravel.com*. Margie has travel agencies worldwide, at 50 locations in seven countries. All locations are connected to a satellite array. Margie has signed a 10-year contract to provide satellite access to her 50 locations. Connectivity to the satellite array varies between 57 Kbps to 128 Kbps. Although each of her locations varies greatly in the number of computer and user accounts, locations with more than 15 users have their own domain controller, global catalog server, and DNS server (typically configured on the same computer). There are nine total sites in the *margiestravel.com* Active Directory infrastructure.

Given this information about Margie's Travel, answer the following questions:

1. You discuss performance monitoring with Margie. During your conversation, you learn no one has ever used System Monitor to check the performance of her domain controllers. Margie wants to know why anyone would even bother. What would you say to her?

   _____

   _____

2. Margie tells you that some of her domain controllers have multiple hard disks. She tells you that the additional one or two physical hard disks are not being used. She wants to know if they can be used in some way to improve the performance of Active Directory. What would you tell her?

   _____

   _____

3. Margie says that her local domain controllers get very slow sometimes. She theorizes that this could be due to the other domain controllers synchronizing lots of information with her local domain controllers. What could you monitor to help answer Margie's question?

   _____

   _____

4. Margie sends you to Cairo, Egypt, to troubleshoot a couple of domain controllers in her Egypt location. You find some event messages concerning replication events, but you'd like to see more detailed information than what is in the log now. What can you do?

   _____

   _____

5. Margie tells you that she wants to install new firewalls between all of the Active Directory sites that she has worldwide. She remembers that the original installers had to do something special to the firewalls because they were being used with Active Directory. She cannot remember what that special something was, so she asks if you know of anything. What would you tell her?

_____

_____

6. Margie wants you to determine whether the existing domain controllers are using default or custom ports for replication. How could you determine this?

_____

_____

Troubleshooting Lab

You are a domain administrator for Contoso Pharmaceuticals. You've noticed that one of your domain controllers is starting to run low on hard disk space. You remove all unnecessary applications and services from the server. You plan to install a couple of additional hard disks in the system as soon as possible. Right now, you just want to clean up as much space as possible on that server, until the new hard disks arrive. You decide to perform an offline compaction of the Active Directory database. This should reduce the size of Active Directory on the hard disk and increase the performance of Active Directory.

 Caution   Before you perform an offline compaction of the Active Directory database on a production server, be sure that you have a current backup of the database.

1. Perform an Active Directory database backup using Backup Or Restore Wizard. Refer to Chapter 3 if you need step-by-step instructions.

2. Restart Server1. During the startup process, as soon as Windows Server 2003 starts to load, press the F8 key. The Windows Advanced Options Menu appears.

3. Select the Directory Services Restore Mode (Windows domain controllers only) option and press ENTER. Server1 will load Windows Server 2003 in Safe Mode with the Active Directory database offline.

4. Log on using the Active Directory restore mode administrator name and password. You set this password when you installed Active Directory.

5. A desktop warning message appears during the logon process. Read it and click OK.

6. Open a command prompt, type **ntdsutil** and press ENTER. The ntdsutil prompt is displayed.

7. Type **files** and press ENTER. The file maintenance prompt is displayed.

8. Type **?** and press ENTER. Notice that you have several options at this prompt. You can check the Active Directory database integrity, you can move the database, and you can move the database log files.

9. Type **info** and press ENTER. This command displays the current location of the Active Directory database (NTDS.DIT), the backup directory, and the log files directory.

> **Note**   If you had multiple physical drives in your domain controller, you could increase Active Directory performance by placing NTDS.DIT on a different physical disk than the operating system. If you can place NTDS.DIT and the log files on different physical disks, you'll further increase Active Directory performance.

10. In order to perform offline compaction of the database, type **compact to c:** and press ENTER. The database is compacted and you are given directions on how to replace the existing database.

11. Type **quit** and press ENTER. The ntdsutil prompt appears. Type **quit** and press ENTER. You are returned to the command prompt.

12. Type **dir %systemroot%\ntds\ntds.dit** and press ENTER. You'll see statistics on the existing Active Directory database. Notice how large the file is right now.

13. Type **move c:\ntds.dit %systemroot%\ntds\ntds.dit** and press ENTER. You'll see a prompt asking if you'd like to overwrite the existing Ntds.dit file.

> **Tip**   If you have the disk space available, you may choose to make a copy of the existing Ntds.dit file before overwriting it.

14. Type **y** and then press ENTER.

15. Type **del %systemroot%\ntds*.log** and press ENTER.

16. Type **dir %systemroot%\ntds\ntds.dit** and press ENTER. You'll see statistics on the existing Active Directory database. You'll see the database is smaller now.

17. You've now successfully compacted the Active Directory database. Type **exit** and press ENTER.

18. Restart Server1. Allow the system to start up normally. If you watch the startup screen, you may notice a message stating that Active Directory is rebuilding indices. This is an indication that the newly compacted database is in use. If you have any problems with the newly compacted database, you may need to restore Active Directory from backup. See Chapter 3, "Administering Active Directory," for more information on restoring Active Directory, if necessary.

Chapter Summary

- The directory and file replication service logs are enabled on the Event Viewer console when Active Directory is installed. The directory service log contains errors, warnings, and information generated by Active Directory. The file replication service log contains errors, warnings, and information generated by FRS.

- System Monitor is a tool that supports detailed monitoring of the use of operating system resources. With System Monitor, you can collect and view real-time performance data on a local computer or from several remote computers, view data collected either currently or previously recorded in a counter log, and present data in a printable graph, histogram, or report view.

- A performance object is a logical collection of performance counters that is associated with a resource or service that can be monitored. A performance counter is a value associated with a performance object. To monitor Active Directory, you monitor the activity of the NTDS performance object.

- The Performance Logs And Alerts snap-in provides you with the ability to create counter logs, trace logs, and system alerts automatically from local or remote computers.

- Counter logs record sampled data about hardware resources and system services based on performance objects and counters. You can view logged counter data using System Monitor or export the data to a file for analysis and report generation.

- Trace logs collect event traces that measure performance statistics associated with events such as disk and file I/O, page faults, and thread activity.

- An alert detects when a predefined counter value rises above or falls below the configured threshold and notifies a user by means of the Messenger service. Alerts enable you to define a counter value that triggers actions such as sending a network message, running a program, making an entry in the application log, or starting a log.

- To troubleshoot problems indicated by error and warning messages in the directory service log, examine details about the message by double-clicking the error or warning message.

- There are four steps in the process of analyzing and interpreting performance-monitoring results: (1) establish a baseline, (2) analyze performance-monitoring results, (3) plan and implement changes to meet the baseline, and (4) repeat steps 2 and 3 until performance is optimized.

Exam Highlights

Before taking the exam, review the key points and terms that are presented in this chapter. You need to know this information.

Key Points

- The file replication service log contains errors, warnings, and information generated by FRS. You can use the file replication service log to monitor FRS replication.

- To troubleshoot problems indicated by error and warning messages in the directory and file replication service logs, examine details about the message by double-clicking the error or warning message.

- To monitor File Replication Service replication, you monitor the activity of the FileReplicaConn and FileReplicaSet performance objects in System Monitor.

- To analyze and interpret performance-monitoring results: (1) establish a baseline, (2) analyze performance-monitoring results, (3) plan and implement changes to meet the baseline, and (4) repeat steps 2 and 3 until performance is optimized.

Key Terms

directory service log   A tool that displays errors, warnings, and information generated by Active Directory. If you experience problems with Active Directory, use the directory service log first to locate the causes of the problem.

file replication service log   A tool that displays errors, warnings, and information generated by FRS.

System Monitor   A tool that allows you to collect and view extensive data about the usage of hardware resources and the activity of system services on computers you administer.

Questions and Answers

Page
14-17
Lesson 1 Review

1. Which Active Directory performance-monitoring tool should you use first to locate the causes of a problem with Active Directory?

   You should examine the directory service log in Event Viewer.

2. What is the function of System Monitor?

   System Monitor is a tool that supports detailed monitoring of the use of operating system resources.

3. What is the difference between a performance object and a performance counter?

   A performance object is a logical collection of performance counters associated with a resource or service that can be monitored. A performance counter is a value that applies to a performance object.

4. In what format does a histogram display performance data?

   A histogram displays performance data in a bar graph format.

5. Which of the following is not a function of System Monitor?

   a. Enables you to view current Active Directory performance data

   b. Enables you to view previously recorded Active Directory performance data

   c. Enables you to view errors and warnings generated by Active Directory

   d. Enables you to collect real-time performance data from a local computer

   e. Enables you to collect real-time performance data from a specific computer on the network where you have permission

   The correct answer is c. You can view errors and warnings generated by Active Directory on the directory service log, but not System Monitor.

Page
14-34
Lesson 2 Review

1. What is the function of a counter log?

   Counter logs record sampled data about hardware resources and system services based on performance objects and counters in the same manner as System Monitor.

2. What is the function of a trace log?

   Trace logs collect event traces that measure performance statistics associated with events such as disk and file I/O, page faults, and thread activity.

3. In which locations can you view performance data logged in a counter log?

   You can view logged counter data using System Monitor or export the data to a file for analysis and report generation.

4. What is the function of an alert?

An alert detects when a predefined counter value rises above or falls below the configured threshold and notifies a user by means of the Messenger service. Alerts enable you to define a counter value that triggers actions such as sending a network message, running a program, making an entry in the application log, or starting a log.

5. Which of the following actions can be triggered by an alert? (Choose two.)

   a. Logging an entry into the application log

   b. Starting logging automatically

   c. Sending a network message to a computer

   d. Stopping logging automatically

   e. Presenting data in a graph format

The correct answers are a and c. The actions that can be triggered by an alert include logging an entry in the application log in Event Viewer and sending a network message to a computer.

Page
14-42
Lesson 3 Review

1. What action should you take to troubleshoot problems indicated by error and warning messages in the directory service log?

Double-click the error or warning message and examine the header information in the Properties dialog box for the message. In the header, you can find out the date and time the problem occurred, and the user and computer affected by the problem. In the Description box in the Properties dialog box for the message, you can read a text description of the problem.

2. What registry subkey contains the entries for which you can increase the logging level to retrieve more detailed information in the directory service log?

HKEY_LOCAL_MACHINE SYSTEM\CurrentControlSet\Services\NTDS\Diagnostics

3. Why should you leave logging levels set to 0 unless you are investigating a problem?

You should leave logging levels set to 0 unless you are investigating a problem because increasing the logging level increases the detail of the messages and the number of messages emitted and can degrade server performance.

4. What are the four steps in the process of analyzing and interpreting performance-monitoring results?

The four steps are (1) establish a baseline, (2) analyze performance-monitoring results, (3) plan and implement changes to meet the baseline, and (4) repeat steps 2 and 3 until performance is optimized.

5. In the process of analyzing and interpreting performance-monitoring results, what is a baseline?

A baseline is a measurement derived from the collection of data over an extended period during varying workloads and user connections, representing acceptable performance under typical operating conditions. The baseline indicates how system resources are used during periods of normal activity and makes it easier to spot problems when they occur.

Page
14-44

Case Scenario Exercise

1. You discuss performance monitoring with Margie. During your conversation, you learn no one has ever used System Monitor to check the performance of her domain controllers. Margie wants to know why anyone would even bother. What would you say to her?

   Performance monitoring can be used to identify and troubleshoot issues. However, monitoring performance is not as useful if you don't know what acceptable or normal levels of any given counter should read. You can only determine what is normal and acceptable on a particular network by taking a performance measure when everything seems to be operating normally and acceptably. After you collect that data, you should periodically check performance. Use the information you collect to establish a baseline of performance data that indicates what "normal" operating conditions are for your network. That way, when something changes, you will hopefully be able to identify what is no longer "normal."

2. Margie tells you that some of her domain controllers have multiple hard disks. She tells you that the additional one or two physical hard disks are not being used. She wants to know if they can be used in some way to improve the performance of Active Directory. What would you tell her?

   You could improve performance by moving the Active Directory database (NTDS.DIT) to the second physical hard disk. You could further improve performance by moving the Active Directory log files to a third physical hard disk. This could be done using the Ntdsutil tool.

3. Margie says that her local domain controllers get very slow sometimes. She theorizes that this could be due to the other domain controllers synchronizing lots of information with her local domain controllers. What could you monitor to help answer Margie's question?

   You would certainly use System Monitor in this case. In addition to the typical server performance monitors, such as Server, Memory, and Pages/sec, you should look at DRA Inbound Objects Applied/sec, which indicates how much replication update activity is occurring on the server as a result of changes generated on other servers.

4. Margie sends you to Cairo, Egypt, to troubleshoot a couple of domain controllers in her Egypt location. You find some event messages concerning replication events, but you'd like to see more detailed information than what is in the log now. What can you do?

   Increase the logged information by increasing the diagnostic logging levels for replication events (and also possibly the KCC) in the registry of the domain controllers. You can also use the Replication Monitor (Replmon) or Repadmin command-line tool to learn more about replication performance. You can also use the Ntfrsutl to query the FRS services on local and remote domain controllers to determine if they are functioning correctly.

5. Margie tells you that she wants to install new firewalls between all of the Active Directory sites that she has worldwide. She remembers that the original installers had to do something special to the firewalls because they were being used with Active Directory. She cannot remember what that special something was, so she asks if you know of anything. What would you tell her?

If you need Active Directory replication to occur between domain controllers of the same site, you must allow a Remote Procedure Call (RPC) connection to occur through the firewall. You can do this by opening the RPC Endpoint mapper (TCP 135) and also allowing the dynamic RPC ports of 1024–65535. Alternately, you can configure the domain controllers to use different RPC ports.

6. Margie wants you to determine whether the existing domain controllers are using default or custom ports for replication. How could you determine this?

You could use Network Monitor (or another network packet capturing utility) to analyze the traffic on your network to determine which ports are being used for RPC and NTFRS traffic. You can also check the firewall logs or monitor the firewall to see what type of traffic is coming and going right now. Another method is to review the configuration of the domain controllers registry for the NTFRS service and RPC ports.

Part 2
Prepare for the Exam

15 Planning and Implementing an Active Directory Infrastructure (1.0)

This objective domain covers the basic skills involved in the design and planning for **domains** and **forests**, as well as the skills required for installation and configuration of **domain controllers**. Planning is critical to the successful deployment of an **Active Directory** network.

Planning must begin with a good understanding of the organization and its environment. The specific details surrounding an organization's environment will influence the planning and implementation for that organization. The elements involved in Active Directory planning will range from the network topology to organization charts. While such elements as the network topology will have an impact on the way you design the Microsoft Windows Server 2003 Active Directory infrastructure, other elements will be directly affected, such as the existing Microsoft Windows NT or Microsoft Windows 2000 Active Directory domain structures.

Installation of the domain controllers is the first part of Active Directory implementation, followed by the configuration of the various elements within each domain and forest. Once you have configured Active Directory to fit in with the organization, you will then configure it to optimize Active Directory traffic. You must be familiar with the tools and techniques that will help you throughout the implementation process.

Tested Skills and Suggested Practices

The skills that you need to successfully master the Planning and Implementing an Active Directory Infrastructure objective domain on Exam 70-294: Planning, Implementing, and Maintaining a Microsoft Windows Server 2003 Active Directory Infrastructure include:

- Plan a strategy for placement of global catalog servers.
    - ❑ Practice 1: Review several wide area network (WAN) topologies and consider the logon and authentication needs versus the traffic ramifications at each physical site in the WAN.

❑ Practice 2: Using Microsoft Network Monitor or another manufacturer's network monitoring utilities in conjunction with Performance Monitor (Perfmon), analyze the traffic during the replication process between global catalog servers.

❑ Practice 3: Implement a test network with two domains. Make certain that only one domain controller is a global catalog server. Take the global catalog server off the network. From a client station, attempt to log on the network into each domain. Bring the global catalog server back online and enable universal group membership caching on the other domain controllers. Take the global catalog server offline and attempt to log on the network from a client station again.

■ Plan a flexible operations master role placement.

❑ Practice 1: Design an imaginary network with multiple locations and multiple domains in a single forest. Select suitable placement for each of the operations masters.

❑ Practice 2: Implement a test forest with multiple domain controllers. Transfer each operations role to a single domain controller and then remove that domain controller from the network. Using the administrative tools for Active Directory, attempt to create, move, and rename objects, and then attempt to modify the schema. Using a client computer, attempt to log on. Document the affect the "failed" operations master role as on the network.

■ Implement an Active Directory forest and domain structure.

❑ Practice 1: Design an imaginary Active Directory forest with multiple domains. Consider which domain should be placed at the root of the forest. Document the domain trees.

❑ Practice 2: Install a test network with Windows Server 2003. Using the forest plan from Practice 1, run Dcpromo.exe to install Active Directory to create a new forest with a root domain.

❑ Practice 3: With the same network running from Practice 2, run Dcpromo.exe to install Active Directory on another server to create the first domain controller within a child domain.

❑ Practice 4: Using the same network in the previous practices, raise the functional level of each domain to Windows Server 2003, then raise the functional level of the forest to Windows Server 2003.

❑ Practice 5: Install two domain controllers in two separate forest root domains. Raise the domain and forest functional levels to Windows Server 2003 for each domain and forest. Establish a forest trust between the two forests. Remove the forest trust and establish a one-way external trust between the two domains.

- Implement an Active Directory site topology.

    ❑ Practice 1: Run the Active Directory Sites And Services console on a domain controller. Create several sites, then configure multiple site links to connect the sites.

- Plan an administrative delegation strategy.

    ❑ Practice 1: Using an imaginary organization with several sets of administrative groups, design an administrative delegation strategy. Then develop an organizational unit (OU) hierarchy to mirror the administrative delegation.

Further Reading

You will find reading materials listed in this section by objective that will assist you in mastering the skills tested on the exam.

Objective 1.1   Review Chapter 1, Lesson 1, "Active Directory Overview," and Chapter 5, Lesson 4, "Configuring Global Catalog Servers."

Microsoft Corporation. *Introducing Microsoft Windows Server 2003*. Redmond, Washington: Microsoft Press, 2003. Review Chapter 3, "Active Directory," and Chapter 17, "Upgrading from Windows 2000 Server."

Microsoft Corporation. *Microsoft Windows Server 2003 Administrator's Pocket Consultant*. Redmond, Washington: Microsoft Press, 2003. Review Chapter 6, "Using Active Directory," and Chapter 7, "Core Active Directory Administration."

Microsoft Corporation. Microsoft TechNet. Redmond, Washington. Review "Understanding the Global Catalog," available on the Microsoft Web site at *http:// technet2.microsoft.com/WindowsServer/en/Library/50c52ded-1703-4fe4-93a5- f5bec42619ad1033.mspx*.

Objective 1.2   Review Chapter 4, Lesson 2, "Renaming and Restructuring Domains and Renaming Domain Controllers."

Microsoft Corporation. *Microsoft Windows Server 2003 Deployment Kit, A Microsoft Resource Kit*. Redmond, Washington: Microsoft Press, 2003. Review Chapter 2, "Designing the Active Directory Logical Structure." This information can also be found on the Microsoft Web site at *http://www.microsoft.com/ windowsserver2003/techinfo/reskit/deploykit.mspx*.

Microsoft Corporation. Review "HOW TO: View and Transfer FSMO Roles in Windows Server 2003," available on the Microsoft Web site at *http://support .microsoft.com/default.aspx?scid=kb;EN-US;324801*.

Objective 1.3   Review Chapter 2, Lessons 1 and 2, "Preparing for Active Directory Installation" and "Installing and Removing Active Directory"; Chapter 3, Lesson 1,

"Using Active Directory Administration Tools"; Chapter 4, Lessons 1 and 4, "Creating Multiple Domains, Trees, and Forests" and "Managing Trust Relationships"; and Chapter 5, Lesson 5, "Configuring Application Directory Partitions."

Microsoft Corporation. *Introducing Microsoft Windows Server 2003*. Redmond, Washington: Microsoft Press, 2003. Review Chapter 17, "Upgrading from Windows 2000 Server."

Microsoft Corporation. *Microsoft Windows Server 2003 Administrator's Pocket Consultant*. Redmond, Washington: Microsoft Press, 2003. Review Chapter 6, "Using Active Directory," and Chapter 7, "Core Active Directory Administration."

Microsoft Corporation. *Microsoft Windows Server 2003 Deployment Kit, A Microsoft Resource Kit*. Redmond, Washington: Microsoft Press, 2003. Read Chapter 6, "Deploying the Windows Server 2003 Forest Root Domain," and Chapter 7, "Deploying Windows Server 2003 Regional Domains." This information can also be found on the Microsoft Web site at *http://www.microsoft.com/windowsserver2003/techinfo/reskit/deploykit.mspx*.

Microsoft Corporation. "HOW TO: Create an Active Directory Server in Windows Server 2003," available on the Microsoft Web site at *http://support.microsoft.com/default.aspx?scid=kb;EN-US;324753*.

Microsoft Corporation. "HOW TO: Manage the Application Directory Parition and Replicas in Windows Server 2003," available on the Microsoft Web site at *http://technet2.microsoft.com/WindowsServer/en/Library/5f63b4a4-1fda-41d9-bc46-b8dce55358111033.mspx*.

Objective 1.4   Review Chapter 5, Lessons 1, 2, and 3, "Understanding Sites and Replication," "Configuring Sites," and "Configuring Intersite Replication."

Microsoft Corporation. *Microsoft Windows Server 2003 Administrator's Pocket Consultant*. Redmond, Washington: Microsoft Press, 2003. Review Chapter 6, "Using Active Directory," and Chapter 7, "Core Active Directory Administration."

Microsoft Corporation. "HOW TO: Create an External Trust in Windows Server 2003," available on the Microsoft Web site at *http://technet2.microsoft.com/WindowsServer/en/Library/3209c17c-43df-4bbc-a6b4-159cbdc0feda1033.mspx*.

Objective 1.5   Review Chapter 6, "Implementing an OU Structure"; and Chapter 8, Lesson 1, "Understanding Groups."

Microsoft Corporation. *Microsoft Windows Server 2003 Administrator's Pocket Consultant*. Redmond, Washington: Microsoft Press, 2003. Review Chapter 6, "Using Active Directory," and Chapter 7, "Core Active Directory Administration."

Microsoft Corporation. Microsoft TechNet. Review the section titled "Delegating Administration," available on the Microsoft Web site at *http://technet2.microsoft.com/WindowsServer/en/Library/60096a04-8494-4551-bfd6-3aebadddc3fe1033.mspx*.

Plan a Strategy for Placing Global Catalog Servers

This objective discusses the strategy for global catalog server placement. The existing network environment will help you in formulating the overall design of Active Directory, including **forests**, **domains**, and **trust relationships**. It will also guide you in placement of **domain controllers**, **global catalog servers**, and **operations masters**, as well as the configuration of the sites and site links.

Global catalog servers are Active Directory domain controllers that have been given the added functionality of holding a copy of the **global catalog** database. The very first domain controller installed into the root domain of the forest is always given the role of global catalog server. However, subsequent domain controllers will not automatically be designated with this role and you will need to configure them manually.

There are certain situations where enabling universal group membership caching makes more sense than adding a global catalog server. If you have a small branch office that contains a domain controller for a small **domain**, and it is connected to the rest of the corporate network by a WAN link with little **available bandwidth**, that is an ideal situation for caching universal group memberships. In doing so, **authentication** and query traffic will take place locally, and **replication** traffic will be minimized since there will not be a large global catalog to replicate.

1. You have a Windows Server 2003 Active Directory network with seven global catalog servers. One of the Windows 2000 global catalog servers, 2KGC5, has failed, and you install a new server named GC8 to replace 2KGC5. You want to bring 2KGC5 back online, but you do not want it to be a global catalog server or a domain controller. You want to install Windows Server 2003, and you want to rename the server because your naming strategy requires member servers to be named differently from domain controllers. Which action should you take?

   A. Clear the Global Catalog check box on the NTDS Settings object within 2KGC5.

   B. Upgrade the server using the Windows Server 2003 WINNT32 command, selecting all defaults.

   C. Back up the data from the server, format the drive, and install Windows Server 2003 as a new server with a new name, making the server a member of the domain. Restore the data back to the server.

   D. Use the domain controller rename tool. Demote the domain controller to a member server using Dcpromo.exe.

2. You are planning your network strategy for a Windows Server 2003 forest. You currently have three Windows NT 4 domains as follows: The SALES domain encompasses all 430 members of the sales and marketing teams, who are located in 12 satellite offices, as well as users in the headquarters. The HQ domain includes all mission critical applications, 2832 users in the headquarters, and 320 administrative users located in six of the 12 satellite offices, as well as several who work from remote sites. The RESEARCH domain incorporates the three research facilities, a testing group in the headquarters, and all seven manufacturing plants, for a total of 857 users. Which of the following documents should you refer to when planning the placement of your global catalog servers?

   A. A map of the WAN topology and traffic analysis

   B. An organization chart

   C. A map of the local area network (LAN) topology

   D. A list of administrative rights

3. You are planning a network strategy for a Windows Server 2003 forest for Fabrikam, Inc. You will be upgrading Fabrikam's current Windows NT 4 domains to Windows Server 2003. The domains are separated by location. There are three main offices: one in Atlanta, one in Chicago, and one in New York, each of which is a separate domain containing at least 200 or more user accounts. Remote users dial in to the Atlanta office

to log on to their own domain, and all remote users regularly make use of the Atlanta printers because of a mission critical application residing there. There is rarely any traveling between locations. Both Atlanta and Chicago have T1 lines directly connecting to the New York office, but no direct connection between each other. You plan to place four global catalog servers in the offices—one in each office and a second global catalog server in the office that experiences the most global catalog usage. If you intend to upgrade each domain to Windows Server 2003 without changing the domain configuration, in which location will a global catalog server be used the most?

A. None of the locations will require a global catalog server.

B. Atlanta.

C. Chicago.

D. New York.

4.   Your Windows Server 2003 Active Directory forest consists of three domains: HQ has 35,000 users, Market has 8,000 users, and Sales has 300 users. The sales offices, which all belong to the Sales domain, are connected to the corporate network by slow 56 Kbps Frame Relay links. Each sales office will be given one domain controller. Which of the following will provide the users the uninterrupted ability to log on to the network without consuming too much bandwidth with replication traffic?

A. Assign the sales offices administrative rights to their own domain controller.

B. Assign the global catalog server role to the sales offices' domain controllers.

C. Configure multiple backup site links for each site.

D. Enable universal group membership caching on the sales offices' domain controllers.

Objective 1.1 Answers

1.   **Correct Answers: C**

    A. Incorrect: While this will remove the global catalog services, it will not rename the server or upgrade it, nor will it remove Active Directory and the global catalog services.

    B. Incorrect: The upgrade process will not remove the domain controller or global catalog services from 2KGC5, nor will it rename the server.

    C. Correct: This option will meet all of the objectives of bringing the server online as a member server running Windows Server 2003.

    D. Incorrect: You cannot use the domain controller rename tool unless the domain controller is running Windows Server 2003, and the domain is at the Windows Server 2003 functional level. After Dcpromo.exe removes Active Directory, the server will be a member server of the domain.

2.   **Correct Answers: A**

    A. Correct: The WAN topology map and traffic analysis will determine where global catalog servers will best serve the needs of users for authentication and queries. It will also help plan for replication traffic between global catalog servers.

    B. Incorrect: An organization chart will not provide you with the available bandwidth and capacity information, which you need to plan for the traffic impact of the Active Directory domain controllers and global catalog servers.

    C. Incorrect: The LAN topology will not provide enough information for the placement of the servers.

    D. Incorrect: Administrative rights have no effect on the placement of global catalog servers.

3.   **Correct Answers: B**

    A. Incorrect: Because there will be multiple domains, a global catalog server will be required in order to resolve logons, queries, and universal group membership information. In addition, the first domain controller installed in the root domain will automatically become a global catalog server.

    B. Correct: Since the Atlanta location receives the logons, it will require either a global catalog server or universal group membership caching in order to authenticate users. This location will have the most global catalog usage because of the remote user logons and the likelihood of queries to access Atlanta printers and its mission critical application.

C. **Incorrect:** Any global catalog servers in Chicago will experience less usage than in Atlanta, although there will probably be some usage for the rare traveler and query for the Atlanta-based resources.

D. **Incorrect:** Even though New York sits between Atlanta and Chicago because of physical connections, there is little difference between its own and Chicago's global catalog usage. New York should experience less global catalog usage than Atlanta.

4.   Correct Answers: D

A. **Incorrect:** The administrative rights to the domain controller will not ensure uninterrupted logons.

B. **Incorrect:** The global catalog server role will cause excess replication across the slow 56 Kbps links, although this option will ensure logons in the event that the WAN links fail.

C. **Incorrect:** The multiple site links will not ensure uninterrupted logons because they are logical, not actual additional physical WAN links.

D. **Correct:** Universal group membership caching will ensure that the users will be able to continue to log on even if the WAN links fail. In addition, it will ensure that there is no unnecessary global catalog replication traffic.

Objective 1.2

Plan Flexible Operations Master Role Placement

Global catalog servers are not the only special types of servers that run within Active Directory on various domain controllers. You must also plan to designate various domain controllers with one of the **operations master roles**. There are simple rules to remember when you plan your operations master roles.

■ Except in a single domain situation, the infrastructure master should not be installed on a domain controller that also acts as a global catalog server.

■ Place the operations master roles in a central location to all users, and servers, on the network.

■ Place the **domain naming master** role on a server in the site where the majority of new domain controllers are installed.

■ Place the **primary domain controller (PDC) emulator(s)**, **relative identifier (RID) master(s)**, and **infrastructure master(s)** in the location where the majority of administration for the respective domains takes place.

■ Place the infrastructure master so that it is able to contact a global catalog server. The infrastructure master compares its own information with the global catalog to determine whether its own data is up-to-date. The infrastructure master role should not be assigned to a domain controller that also holds the global catalog server role because it would always consider its own data to be up-to-date.

Objective 1.2 Questions

1. You are upgrading a Windows NT 4 domain to Windows Server 2003. You upgrade the PDC named WDC01 to Windows Server 2003 and create a new forest root domain. Your domain has a strict security policy that enforces password changes every five days. When you upgrade a backup domain controller (BDC) named WDC02 to Windows Server 2003 and enable it as a global catalog server, you decide to take WDC01 offline to upgrade hardware. Immediately after doing so, users call in to complain that they cannot change their passwords. You bring up WDC01, and users are able to change their passwords. Which operations master role should you transfer to WDC02 before taking WDC01 offline again?

    A. The domain naming master

    B. The PDC emulator

    C. The RID master

    D. The schema master

2. You have a Windows Server 2003 Active Directory forest. During a project, you realize that you are unable to install an application that integrates with Active Directory and adds new types of objects to it. Which operations master role do you check to see if it is running?

    A. The infrastructure master

    B. The domain naming master

    C. The schema master

    D. The PDC emulator

3. You are the administrator of Contoso Ltd.'s network, which has the following future domain structure in its Windows Server 2003 forest: *root.contoso.com*, *trunk.root .contoso.com*, *branch.trunk.root.contoso.com*, and *lab.contoso.local*. You have installed the root domain, *root.contoso.com*, and the research domain, *lab.contoso.local*. One of the domain controllers, *dc01.root.contoso.com*, suffers a hardware failure. After the hardware failure, you are unable to install the first domain controller for *trunk.root .contoso.com* to the domain tree. How should you correct this problem?

    A. Transfer the infrastructure master role from one of the domain controllers to another.

    B. Enable the global catalog on *dc03.root.contoso.com*.

    C. Attempt to bring *dc01.root.contoso.com* online, and if that is not possible, then seize the RID master role to another domain controller.

D. Attempt to bring *dc01.root.contoso.com* back online, and if that is not possible, then seize the domain naming master role to another domain controller. After the role has been seized, do not bring *dc01.root.contoso.com* back online.

4. You are planning the placement of the operations masters within Coho Vineyard's Active Directory network. The root domain of the forest will be *cohovineyard.com*. There will be two other domains, *bottling.cohovineyard.com* and *grape.cohovine-yard.com*, which are used by the bottling production department and the grape growers, respectively. The root domain will provide Web services as well as the administrative functions for the company. You wish to ensure absolute security on the operations master roles. In this forest, you will have three infrastructure masters, one per domain. For which operations masters will you have only one operations master role to secure for the entire *cohovineyard.com* forest?

   A. The PDC emulator

   B. The domain naming master

   C. The RID master

   D. The schema master

5. You have installed 12 domain controllers in three domains. Your naming scheme is to concatenate the letters "dc" with the number of the domain controller in sequence of installation. Therefore, the fifth domain controller that you install is DC05. The domains are named *contoso.com*, *branch.contoso.com*, and *leaf.contoso.com*. You do not transfer any of the operations master roles after installation. You attempt to rename a group of users in the root domain, but are unable to. Which of the following domain controllers is probably down or unable to communicate?

   A. *dc05.branch.contoso.com*

   B. *dc01.contoso.com*

   C. *dc03.contoso.com*

   D. *dc11.leaf.contoso.com*

Objective 1.2 Answers

1.   Correct Answers: B

   A. Incorrect: The domain naming master is used for adding and removing domains from the forest. This will not affect users who are trying to change their passwords.

   B. Correct: The PDC emulator is used in place of the former Windows NT 4 PDC. BDCs will communicate with it, obtaining updated information from the PDC emulator. This operations master role handles password changes.

   C. Incorrect: The RID master provides relative identifier information to domain controllers so that new objects can be created with unique SIDs. Users would not notice the RID master being offline unless WDC02 ran out of RIDs and they were using an application that required new objects to be created within the domain. Administrators would experience this problem first.

   D. Incorrect: The schema master determines which types of objects can exist within the Active Directory forest. Users would not notice the schema master being offline unless an application or a user was attempting to extend the schema.

2.   Correct Answers: C

   A. Incorrect: The infrastructure master will not affect an application's installation, only the movement and renaming of objects within the domain.

   B. Incorrect: The domain naming master will not affect an application's installation, only the addition or deletion of domains within the forest.

   C. Correct: An application that integrates with Active Directory will probably extend the schema of the forest. If the schema master is not functioning, the schema cannot be extended and the application will not install.

   D. Incorrect: The PDC emulator will affect all users on the network, not just the application's installation.

3.   Correct Answers: D

   A. Incorrect: The infrastructure master role is used for moving and renaming objects, not for adding domains. In addition, you would not be able to transfer the role without the domain controller that owns the role, presumably *dc01.root.contoso.com*, being online.

   B. Incorrect: The global catalog provides an index of information across the domains but will not affect the addition of a domain.

    C. Incorrect: The RID master is used for creating objects within a domain, and each domain has its own. However, any RID master being down will not affect the addition of a new domain to the forest.

    D. Correct: The domain naming master role is used to make changes to the domains within the forest, including the addition or deletion of domains. When you seize the domain naming master role, you will not be able to bring the original holder of that role back online; therefore, you should reinstall it as a new domain controller or server within the domain.

4. Correct Answers: B, D

    A. Incorrect: There is a PDC emulator for each domain within the forest.

    B. Correct: The domain naming master is in charge of changes to the domain structure in the forest. There is only one domain naming master in each forest. The first domain controller installed in the root domain, *cohovineyard.com*, will hold this role unless it is transferred to another domain controller.

    C. Incorrect: The RID master is in charge of providing the SID information to new objects in the domain. Each domain has its own RID master to provide the domain's unique SID to its own newly created objects. Coho Vineyard will have three.

    D. Correct: The schema master determines what types of objects and attributes can be held within the forest. There is only one schema master per forest. This role will be held by the first domain controller installed into *cohovineyard.com* unless it is transferred to another domain controller.

5. Correct Answers: B

    A. Incorrect: This domain controller is not in the root domain. From the information given, the root domain should be *contoso.com*.

    B. Correct: The first domain controller installed in the root domain will contain all the operations master roles, including the infrastructure master.

    C. Incorrect: This is the third domain controller in the root domain and will not contain any operations master roles.

    D. Incorrect: This domain controller is not in the root domain. From the information given, the root domain should be *contoso.com*.

Implement an Active Directory Forest and Domain Structure

This objective looks at the skills of implementing an Active Directory forest and domain. The implementation of **Active Directory** begins with the installation of the first domain controller, which is always assigned to the root domain of the forest. A child domain is created at the point that you install the first domain controller in a domain other than the ones already existing in the forest.

Application directory partitions are a new feature for Windows Server 2003 Active Directory. Application directory partitions are basically used to overcome the challenges when using a **multimaster replication** scheme and applications that use a directory of information. The information contained within an application's directory can be stored and accessed locally and not included in the entire forest's replication.

In Windows Server 2003 Active Directory, the forest has optional levels, as do the domains. You have the following **forest functional levels** available:

- Windows 2000

- Windows Server 2003 interim

- Windows Server 2003

The default forest functional level is Windows 2000. This level supports domain controllers using the Windows NT 4, Windows 2000, and Windows Server 2003 operating systems. The next level up is Windows Server 2003 interim, which supports only Windows NT 4 and Windows Server 2003 operating systems. The forest functional level of Windows Server 2003 only supports domain controllers running the Windows Server 2003 operating system.

The Windows Server 2003 interim forest functional level is intended only for upgrading Windows NT 4 domains to become a new Windows Server 2003 forest. This level cannot be used in any other situation.

The forest features are extended when the functional level is raised to Windows Server 2003. The improvements include

- The creation of a forest trust relationship.

- The faculty for renaming domains in the forest.

■ A new object called the InetOrgPerson, which is designated as an Internet administrator.

■ Global catalog replication improvements.

■ The ability to deactivate a **schema class** or **attribute**, creating defunct **schema objects**.

■ Improved replication as well as the ability to replicate linked values.

The four **domain functional levels** are

■ Windows 2000 mixed

■ Windows 2000 native

■ Windows Server 2003 interim

■ Windows Server 2003

The default functional level for a new domain is Windows 2000 mixed. This is basically the same as the Windows 2000 mixed mode domain, except that you can have Windows Server 2003 domain controllers along with Windows NT 4 and Windows 2000 domain controllers.

When raising the domain functional level to Windows 2000 native, you must have only Windows 2000 and Windows Server 2003 domain controllers. When running Windows 2000 native functional level, you have the added capabilities of

■ Using universal security groups

■ Nesting **groups**

■ Using **SID** History

The Windows Server 2003 interim domain functional level is intended for upgrading a domain directly from Windows NT 4 to Windows Server 2003. It does not support Windows 2000 domain controllers, only those running Windows NT 4 and Windows Server 2003.

The Windows Server 2003 domain functional level supports only domain controllers running Windows Server 2003. Keep in mind that when you raise a domain's functional level, you cannot install any domain controllers using unsupported operating systems. For example, a Windows Server 2003 functional level domain cannot have a Windows NT 4 or a Windows 2000 domain controller added to it. The additional features available within the Windows Server 2003 functional level are

■ Domain controller renaming, using the domain controller rename tool

■ Updating the logon timestamp

■ Ability to convert groups

- Use of SID History
- Universal groups enabled for both **distribution groups** and **security groups**
- Full nesting of groups

Within an Active Directory forest, you already have an established Kerberos transitive, two-way trust relationship between each parent and child domain. Transitive means that when DomainA trusts DomainB, and DomainB trusts DomainC, then DomainA also trusts DomainC. Two-way means that when DomainA trusts DomainB, then DomainB also trusts DomainA. There are no automatic trusts with any other entity, whether another forest, an external Windows NT 4 domain, or a Kerberos realm. In addition, in large forests with several domains, the trust relationships must be resolved up to the root domain and back down and can cause a delay. To overcome these issues, you can establish the following types of trust relationships:

- Explicit external trusts
- Forest trusts
- Shortcut trusts

Objective 1.3 Questions

1. You are the administrator of a forest with three domain trees. Users in the *sub1.child.parent.contoso.com* domain complain that they have very slow access to the resources in the *sub8.leaf.branch.root.contoso.local* domain. Which of the following actions do you perform to help fix this problem?

    A. Enable the global catalog on three domain controllers in the *sub1.child.parent .contoso.com* domain.

    B. Seize the schema master role to a new domain controller.

    C. Create a shortcut trust where *sub8.leaf.branch.root.contoso.local* trusts *sub1.child .parent.contoso.com.*

    D. Create an explicit external trust where *sub1.child.parent.contoso.com* trusts *sub8.leaf.branch.root.contoso.local.*

2. You are the administrator for a Windows NT 4 network with three domains. You upgrade the PDC of one domain to Windows Server 2003 and automatically upgrade to Active Directory. You then upgrade a BDC in that domain to Windows Server 2003. When you upgrade the BDC, which option do you select in the Active Directory Installation Wizard?

    A. A Domain Controller In An Existing Domain In An Existing Forest

    B. A Domain Controller In A New Domain Tree In An Existing Forest

    C. A Domain Controller In A New Domain In A New Forest

    D. A Domain Controller In A Child Domain In An Existing Forest

3. Contoso Ltd.'s main office is in Seattle. Branch offices are in New York, Phoenix, and Sydney. The local administrators at each branch need to be able to control local resources. You want to prevent local administrators from managing resources in the other branch offices. You want only the main office's administrators to create and manage user objects. You want to create a structure to accomplish these goals. What should you do?

    A. Create a forest with domains in each branch office, and with the root domain in the Seattle office. Each domain will contain the users and the computers for that specific office, with administrators belonging to the Domain Admins group in their respective domains.

    B. Create a forest with two domains: the root domain for the Seattle office and the child domain to be used by all other branch offices. Make the administrators members of the Domain Admins group of the child domain.

   C. Create a single domain in the forest. Develop an OU structure that provides separate OUs for each branch within an overall OU. Delegate authority to each administrator to have resource management rights within the OU that represents his or her branch. Make the Seattle administrators members of the Domain Admins group.

   D. Create a single domain in the forest. Create a group named Branches. Add all the branch administrators to this group and grant it permissions to access the resources in all the branch locations.

4.   Which of the following commands is used to install Active Directory on a new domain controller?

   A. Winnt

   B. Ntdsutil

   C. Adpromo

   D. Dcpromo.exe

5.   You are an administrator for a Windows Server 2003 forest that spans several cities. The New York office is planning to install an application that will be used only in that office. The application uses its own directory service that has the ability to integrate with Active Directory. The data for this application may grow to become quite large, so you want to ensure that it does not replicate throughout the network. Which command or Microsoft Management Console (MMC) do you use so that you can keep the application data from replicating beyond the New York office?

   A. Ntdsutil

   B. Winnt32

   C. Dcpromo

   D. Active Directory Sites And Services

6.   At Tailspin Toys, you have three Windows NT 4 domains: DOMA, DOMB, and DOMC. You decide not to upgrade the domains, but to install new servers in a new forest. After the forest is installed, you plan to migrate data and remove the Windows NT 4 servers from the network. You are able to install a server with Windows Server 2003, but when you attempt to promote it to a domain named *doma.tailspintoys.com*, you receive an error that the "domain name specified is already in use" on the network. What can you do to fix the problem?

   A. Change the domain name to *doma.tailspintoys.local*.

   B. Change the NetBIOS name of the Windows Server 2003 domain to ROOT and use *root.tailspintoys.com* for the DNS name.

    C. Change the domain controller's name to DOMA.

    D. Format the hard disk and reinstall Windows Server 2003 using the same name.

7. You are installing a new network for Contoso Pharmaceuticals. There are several subdivisions within the company, including International Sales, United States Sales, Research and Development, and Headquarters. Each of these divisions requires its own domain for security, administration, or locations purposes. You have installed a forest of four domains: *contoso.com*, *intlsales.contoso.com*, *ussales.contoso.com*, and *research.contoso.com*. Which of these domain names is also the name of the forest?

    A. *intlsales.contoso.com*

    B. *ussales.contoso.com*

    C. *research.contoso.com*

    D. *contoso.com*

8. Litware, Inc. is a company in the midst of upgrading its Windows 2000 Active Directory domains and Windows NT 4 domains to Windows Server 2003 in a single forest structure. The first domain you upgrade is the root domain named *root.litwareinc.com*. You upgrade every domain controller to Windows Server 2003 except for one in the root domain. The second domain you upgrade is a Windows NT 4 domain named LIT, which you change to *lit.root.litwareinc.com*. You upgrade the PDC, but leave three BDCs as Windows NT 4 backup domain controllers for the time being. To which of the following domain functional levels can you raise *lit.root.litwareinc.com*?

    A. Windows 2000 mixed

    B. Windows 2000 native

    C. Windows Server 2003

    D. Windows Server 2003 interim

9. You have upgraded all three Windows 2000 domain controllers in the *contoso.com* domain to Windows Server 2003. You have upgraded one Windows NT 4 BDC in that domain to Windows Server 2003. You have removed all other Windows NT 4 BDCs from the domain, and you have installed a new Windows Server 2003 domain controller in the *contoso.com* domain. There are three member servers running Windows NT 4 and eight Windows 2000 Server member servers. Which domain functional level will offer the most functionality for the *contoso.com* domain?

    A. Windows Server 2003

    B. Windows Server 2003 interim

    C. Windows 2000 native

    D. Windows 2000 mixed

10. You have attempted to raise the functional level of a forest to Windows Server 2003, but you received an error. What must you check before you raise the forest functional level?

   A. Ensure that the domain functional level of every domain in the forest is at Windows Server 2003.

   B. Check that the schema master is running.

   C. Check to see if all the domain controllers are running Windows 2000 Server.

   D. Enable the global catalog for each domain controller.

11. You have two Windows Server 2003 forests on the network. The *researchdev.local* forest has several domains containing both users and resources. The *contoso.com* forest also has several domains containing both users and resources. The users in the *researchdev.local* forest must use applications and files that exist within various domains within the *contoso.com* forest. Which of the following actions must be accomplished before you can grant the users access?

   A. You must raise the forest functional level of both forests to Windows Server 2003 and then create a forest trust where the *contoso.com* forest trusts the *researchdev.local* forest.

   B. You must create explicit external trusts between the root domain within the *researchdev.local* forest and the root domain within the *contoso.com* forest.

   C. You must create a shortcut trust between two of the domains within the *contoso.com* forest.

   D. You must raise the forest functional level of both forests to Windows Server 2003 and then create a forest trust where the *researchdev.local* forest trusts the *contoso.com* forest.

Objective 1.3 Answers

1.   Correct Answers: C

   A. Incorrect: The global catalog will not speed up access to resources; however, it will speed up the logon and query process for users.

   B. Incorrect: The schema master role is not involved in this process. Besides, you should never seize the schema master role if you can avoid it; however, you can transfer it.

   C. Correct: The shortcut trust is used within a forest to speed up resource access in forests with multiple domains and domain trees. Active Directory forests automatically include two-way, transitive trust relationships that follow the domain tree, parent to child, child to grandchild, and so on, as well as vice versa. When there are two domain trees, the trust relationship must be resolved up and down the tree before resources can be accessed. A shortcut trust reduces the time it takes to perform this process.

   D. Incorrect: The trusts within a forest are called shortcut trusts. Also, this trust relationship is in the opposite direction. In order for users in the *sub1.child.parent.contoso.com* domain to access resources in the *sub8.leaf.branch.root.contoso .local* domain, the *sub8.leaf.branch.root.contoso.local* domain must trust *sub1.child.parent.contso.com*.

2.   Correct Answers: A

   A. Correct: Because this is a BDC of a domain that is already upgraded, it will automatically become a domain controller in an existing domain within an existing forest.

   B. Incorrect: If you select this option, you will have a second domain tree in the forest.

   C. Incorrect: If you select this option, you will have two separate forests.

   D. Incorrect: If you select this option, you will have a child domain below the root domain in a single domain tree in your forest.

3.   Correct Answers: C

   A. Incorrect: This structure will permit the branch administrators to create and manage user objects in their own domain.

   B. Incorrect: This structure will not prevent the branch administrators from managing the resources in the other branch offices, nor will it prevent them from creating and managing user objects.

C. **Correct:** This structure will accomplish all the administrative goals: granting full administrative rights to the Seattle administrators, preventing branch administrators from creating and managing user objects, and allowing branch administrators to manage the resources only within their own branch.

D. **Incorrect:** This structure will not prevent the branch administrators from managing resources of other branches.

4.   Correct Answers: D

A. **Incorrect:** The Winnt command is used to install the Windows Server 2003 operating system.

B. **Incorrect:** The Ntdsutil command is used to configure aspects of Active Directory.

C. **Incorrect:** This is not a command within Windows Server 2003.

D. **Correct:** The Dcpromo.exe command is the Active Directory Installation Wizard and can be used to install a domain controller or to demote a domain controller to a member server.

5.   Correct Answers: A

A. **Correct:** The Ntdsutil command can be used to create and configure an application directory partition, which will store information for the application and prevent it from replicating outside the New York office.

B. **Incorrect:** The Winnt32 command is used to upgrade to the Windows Server 2003 operating system. The Winnt32 command will not make changes to the Active Directory configuration or to an application directory partition.

C. **Incorrect:** The Dcpromo command is used to install Active Directory. It will not configure additional application directory partitions.

D. **Incorrect:** The Active Directory Sites And Services console is used to configure the physical topology of Active Directory. However, this console is not used to create an application directory partition.

6.   Correct Answers: B

A. **Incorrect:** You will receive the same error with *doma.tailspintoys.local* as you did with *doma.tailspintoys.com* because it is the NetBIOS name, DOMA, which is the cause of the error.

B. **Correct:** The NetBIOS name is the only possible reason for a conflict because the existing network is using Windows NT which doesn't use Domain Name System (DNS) names for domains.

    C. Incorrect: The domain controller's name is not causing the conflict. In fact, you will cause a second NetBIOS name conflict by changing the name to DOMA.

    D. Incorrect: The installation of the operating system did not cause the problem. When you use the same name, the NetBIOS conflict will occur with the original Windows NT 4 domain.

7. Correct Answers: D

    A. Incorrect: The name of the forest is the name of the root domain, which is *contoso.com* because it is the top of the domain tree.

    B. Incorrect: The name of the forest is the name of the root domain, which is *contoso.com* because it is the top of the domain tree.

    C. Incorrect: The name of the forest is the name of the root domain, which is *contoso.com* because it is the top of the domain tree.

    D. Correct: The root domain of the forest is the top of the domain tree. The root domain's name is given to the forest.

8. Correct Answers: D

    A. Incorrect: The Windows 2000 mixed domain functional level is the default functional level for a new domain. You cannot raise the domain functional level to Windows 2000 mixed.

    B. Incorrect: The Windows 2000 native domain functional level does not allow Windows NT 4 domain controllers. Since you will have Windows NT 4 BDCs along with the Windows Server 2003 domain controller, you cannot raise the domain functional level to Windows 2000 native.

    C. Incorrect: The Windows Server 2003 domain functional level does not allow Windows NT 4 domain controllers, which *lit.root.litwareinc.com* still has.

    D. Correct: The Windows Server 2003 interim domain functional level is intended for Windows NT 4 to Windows Server 2003 upgrades. A Windows Server 2003 Interim functional level allows Windows NT 4 BDCs and Windows Server 2003 domain controllers. The only type of domain controller that is not allowed in this situation is the Windows 2000 domain controller, but there is no Windows 2000 domain controller within the *lit.root.litwareinc.com* domain.

9. Correct Answers: A

    A. Correct: When all the domain controllers within a domain are running Windows Server 2003, the domain functional level can be raised to Windows Server 2003, even though member servers use earlier operating systems.

    B. Incorrect: This domain functional level is used only when a Windows NT 4 domain is in the process of upgrading directly to Windows Server 2003.

C. **Incorrect:** This domain functional level is used for domains that have both Windows 2000 and Windows Server 2003 domain controllers.

D. **Incorrect:** This domain functional level is the default and will accept Windows NT 4, Windows 2000, and Windows Server 2003 operating systems as domain controllers. However, the Windows 2000 mixed domain functional level offers the least amount of capabilities of all the domain functional levels. A Windows Server 2003 domain functional level offers the highest level of functionality for the domain, and this is the best choice.

10.   Correct Answers: A

A. **Correct:** The forest functional level cannot be raised unless all domains have achieved the Windows Server 2003 domain functional level.

B. **Incorrect:** The schema master has nothing to do with the forest functional level.

C. **Incorrect:** The forest functional level cannot be raised unless all domain controllers are running Windows Server 2003 and the domain functional level of every domain is raised to Windows Server 2003.

D. **Incorrect:** The global catalog is not required to be installed on each domain controller for the forest's functional level to be raised.

11.   Correct Answers: A

A. **Correct:** The forest trust will enable you to grant permissions to access resources in the *contoso.com* forest to the users in the *researchdev.local* forest.

B. **Incorrect:** The explicit external trusts are not transitive, so this will not provide a way to grant access to resources.

C. **Incorrect:** The shortcut trust will not provide access to resources.

D. **Incorrect:** This trust relationship is one-way and going in the wrong direction. If this trust is created, you can only grant permissions to users in the *contoso.com* forest to access resources in the *researchdev.local* forest.

Implement an Active Directory Site Topology

The Active Directory **site topology** is used to manage the replication, **authentication**, and query traffic patterns in the network. The system is entirely configurable by the administrator and is not aware of the actual underlying network topology. By default, all **domain controllers** within the entire **forest** are placed within the Default-First-Site-Name site. The administrator must establish individual sites by configuring them.

Sites are considered to be a group of **well-connected IP subnets**. This means that a computer on one IP **subnet** can easily and relatively quickly access information on a computer on another IP subnet within the same **site**. The site should not contain links that are slow or have intermittent connectivity problems.

Sites are established in the **Active Directory Sites And Services console**. Once each site is configured, then you can manage how intersite communication takes place by creating **site link** objects. Site links contain information about the **replication availability**, the cost of the site link usage (used when there may be multiple routes between two sites), and the **replication frequency** across a site link. Once the site link is established, replication can take place.

Objective 1.4 Questions

1. You are a WAN administrator for Contoso, Ltd. Contoso has four locations connected by dedicated 256-Kbps leased lines. You install and configure a Windows Server 2003 domain controller at each location. You want to improve network performance by changing the bandwidth usage of replication at each location. What should you do?

   A. Create a separate site for each location and move the domain controllers to their respective sites.

   B. Create a site that spans all locations.

   C. Create and configure the frequency and replication of site links between the sites you created.

   D. Move all server objects to the Default-First-Site-Name site.

2. Which of the following is used to create and configure replication frequency?

   A. The properties dialog box of a site link object

   B. The properties of a server object

   C. The properties of an IP subnet

   D. The properties of a site link bridge

3. As the administrator of Contoso, Ltd.'s network, you have three large offices in Canada, South America, and Europe. Each of these offices is connected via a 256-Kbps fractional T1 leased line. You want to minimize the logon, query, and authentication traffic traveling across these lines. What can you do?

   A. Create a single site for the entire network.

   B. Create a separate site for each location, assign it the correct IP subnets, and move the domain controllers to the correct site. Create site links to connect the sites.

   C. Add global catalog servers to the Canada location.

   D. Create a trust relationship between the Canada and South America sites.

4. You want to make certain that your server, *DC8.contoso.com,* is used as the main server to send and receive data between sites using IP traffic. What do you do?

   A. Allow the KCC to discover and establish the preferred bridgehead servers.

   B. Use the Ntdsutil command to force the *DC8.contoso.com* server to become the preferred bridgehead server.

    C. Use the Active Directory Sites And Services console to establish *DC8.contoso.com* as a preferred bridgehead server for IP traffic.

    D. Use the Dcpromo.exe command to promote *DC8.contoso.com* to preferred bridgehead server status.

Objective 1.4 Answers

1. **Correct Answers: A, C**

    A. Correct: You will create a site at each location to localize traffic for queries and logons, as well as allow configuration of replication traffic.

    B. Incorrect: This configuration will not allow you to manage and schedule replication.

    C. Correct: The site link object properties allow you to manage the replication traffic across WAN links.

    D. Incorrect: This will not allow you to manage the replication traffic.

2. **Correct Answers: A**

    A. Correct: The site link object properties allow you to establish the cost of the link, the frequency of replication, and the availability of the link for replication.

    B. Incorrect: The server object properties do not contain replication frequency information.

    C. Incorrect: IP subnets do not include properties for replication frequency.

    D. Incorrect: The site link bridge object obtains its replication information from the site link objects that it spans.

3. **Correct Answers: B**

    A. Incorrect: In a single site, the logon, query, and authentication traffic will travel across the WAN links as a default behavior.

    B. Correct: By doing this, the logon, query, and authentication traffic will be directed to local domain controllers within the site.

    C. Incorrect: This will have no affect on localizing traffic.

    D. Incorrect: You cannot create a trust relationship between sites. You can only create site links.

4. **Correct Answers: C**

    A. Incorrect: The KCC will not select a server to be a preferred bridgehead server.

    B. Incorrect: The Ntdsutil command will not configure preferred bridgehead servers.

    C. Correct: You can establish a preferred bridgehead server in the Active Directory Sites And Services console.

    D. Incorrect: The Dcpromo command will only promote or demote domain controllers. It does not handle site traffic control such as establishing preferred bridgehead servers.

Plan an Administrative Delegation Strategy

Delegation of administration was difficult with Windows NT 4. In fact, the only way to absolutely delegate administrative authority over a set of objects—whether users or computers—was to place those objects in a separate domain. However, with Active Directory, administrative delegation is available not only for a subset of the objects within a domain, but also for a subset of administrative rights. For example, an Active Directory user can be granted the right to change passwords for users within a particular **OU** but not have any other administrative rights or the right to change passwords for users outside that OU.

An OU is a **container object** that you can create within a domain. The OUs can be nested to create a hierarchical **tree** structure. A tree structure lends itself to the delegation of administration because the higher up the tree, the larger the scope of the network that can be administered.

Active Directory makes administrative delegation easier to configure because the rights of responsibility can be inherited by the nested OUs within an upper level OU. Following this, a person who is planning the administrative delegation would design the OUs as follows:

- Create a small number of OUs at the top of the tree that represent administrative scopes in terms of users and computers.

- Create a tree structure within these OUs that matches the administrative scopes logically existing within the organization, with the largest scope at the top of the tree.

- Populate the OUs with users and computers.

- Create groups for the administrators.

- Delegate administrative authority to the top OUs, and continue with delegation for each administrative level through the OU tree.

Objective 1.5 Questions

1. You have been asked to consult on a Windows Server 2003 Active Directory migration project. The company has three main administrative groups: three people who are granted full access to everything on the network; a group that performs deskside support for users in the Detroit location; and a group that performs deskside support for users in the Cleveland location. In addition, there is a help desk that would like to perform password resets for all the users on the network. Which of the following is a good design for administrative delegation?

A. Create a forest with two domains: one for Cleveland and one for Detroit. All administrators will be granted full access to each of the domains.

B. Create a single domain with an OU hierarchy, which at the top is All Users, and the next level is Cleveland and Detroit. Make the three people with full access members of the Domain Admins group. Grant administrative rights to the Cleveland and Detroit OUs to the Cleveland and Detroit administrators, respectively. Delegate password management rights to the help desk at the All Users OU.

C. Create two domains, one which is empty except for administrators, and the other which contains users and computers. Create an OU structure in the second domain that starts with All Users, and below that, Cleveland and Detroit. Make all administrators members of the root domain's Domain Admins group.

D. Create a Cleveland domain and a Detroit domain in separate forests. Create a forest trust between the two forests. Grant the help desk users' password management permissions over both domains.

2. Contoso, Ltd. has five Windows NT 4 domains, each with separate administrator groups. The company plans to migrate to Windows Server 2003. Each administrative group needs to manage their own resources and users without other administrators accessing them. A central administrative group is going to take on full forest management across all sites. True or False? You must create a multiple domain structure to meet Contoso's administrative requirements.

A. True

B. False

3. You are the network administrator for Contoso, Ltd., and your network consists of a single domain, *contoso.com*. You have four locations: Denver, Dallas, Portland, and Mexico City. You have three major departments: Marketing, Sales, and Service. There is a rule that Group Policy must be applied only to OUs. You need to accomplish the following objectives:

    Primary Goal: Delegate control of users and resources to local administrators

    Secondary Goals:

    Make certain that you can configure user environments by location

    Be able to delegate control of the Marketing team to the help desk

    You create the following OU structure:

    1. At the top of the OU tree, you have two OUs, Corp and Admin.

    2. Within Corp, you have three OUs, Marketing, Sales, and Service.

    3. Within the Admin OU, create a Denver Net Admins OU, a Help Desk OU, and a Regional Admins OU.

    You have then achieved which of the following?

    A. You have achieved both the primary and secondary goals.

    B. You have achieved the primary goal but neither of the secondary goals.

    C. You have achieved one of the secondary goals, but not the primary goal.

    D. You have achieved neither the primary goal nor any of the secondary goals.

4. You are the network administrator of A. Datum Corporation. You have four domains in the forest: *adatum.com*, *corp.adatum.com*, *market.adatum.com*, and *research.adatum.com*. You need to establish a security group structure so that the Help Desk team can manage passwords for all users within the forest. You create a domain global group called Help Desk in each of the four domains and you have placed the Help Desk users in the domain global groups. What else must you do? (Select all that apply.)

    A. Create domain local groups named Help Desk Local in each domain and populate each one with the domain global groups

    B. Create universal groups named Help Desk Universal in each domain

    C. Assign the rights to the domain local groups for password management

    D. Assign the rights to the domain global groups for password management

Objective 1.5 Answers

1.   Correct Answers: B

A. Incorrect: The use of multiple domains will not provide the administrative delegation requested.

B. Correct: This will meet all the objectives stated. The single domain is a more cohesive structure that is easier to manage overall. The OU structure allows you to separate the Cleveland and Detroit administrative groups while allowing you to delegate password management to an OU structure for all users, rather than forcing you to delegate password management to all users in the domain. The latter options might not be desirable in the long run because you may make changes to separate certain users out of that area later.

C. Incorrect: There is no objective stated that would require a second domain. No one was granted rights to manage the users.

D. Incorrect: This will not meet the stated objectives for administrative management.

2.   Correct Answers: B

A. Incorrect: A multiple domain structure is not needed. A single domain with multiple OUs using administrative delegation can meet Contoso's requirements.

B. Correct: A single domain structure can be created with multiple OUs with appropriate delegation of administration to meet Contoso's requirements.

3.   Correct Answers: C

A. Incorrect: Because of the corporate rule that Group Policy must be applied to OUs only, you cannot achieve the secondary goal to configure user environments by location. You are not able to achieve the primary goal to delegate control of users and resources to local administrators because they are not divided by location, but by department. You are able to achieve the secondary goal of delegating control of the Marketing team to the help desk because the Marketing team has its own OU.

B. Incorrect: Because of the corporate rule that Group Policy must be applied to OUs only, you cannot achieve the secondary goal to configure user environments by location. You are not able to achieve the primary goal to delegate control of users and resources to local administrators because they are not divided by location, but by department. You are able to achieve the secondary goal of delegating control of the Marketing team to the help desk because the Marketing team has its own OU.

C. **Correct:** Because of the corporate rule that Group Policy must be applied to OUs only, you cannot achieve the secondary goal to configure user environments by location. You are not able to achieve the primary goal to delegate control of users and resources to local administrators because they are not divided by location, but by department. You are able to achieve the secondary goal of delegating control of the Marketing team to the help desk because the Marketing team has its own OU.

D. **Incorrect:** Because of the corporate rule that Group Policy must be applied to OUs only, you cannot achieve the secondary goal to configure user environments by location. You are not able to achieve the primary goal to delegate control of users and resources to local administrators because they are not divided by location, but by department. You are able to achieve the secondary goal of delegating control of the Marketing team to the help desk because the Marketing team has its own OU.

4. **Correct Answers: A, C**

A. **Correct:** You will need to create a domain local group in each domain so that the Help Desk staff will be able to be granted administrative rights in that domain.

B. **Incorrect:** You do not need a universal group in this configuration. You will need to have a domain local group populated with the existing global groups, and in addition you will need to assign rights to the domain local groups.

C. **Correct:** When you assign rights, you should assign them to the domain local groups.

D. **Incorrect:** The best practice is to assign rights to domain local groups. In fact, you may not be able to assign rights to domain global groups mainly because of backward compatibility with Windows NT domains and the Windows 2000 mixed domain functional levels.

16 Managing and Maintaining an Active Directory Infrastructure (2.0)

Active Directory directory service enables an administrator to easily manage the network. However, the Active Directory infrastructure itself requires some management and maintenance. In this domain, we will review the skills that you need to manage a **forest, domains,** and **sites**. In addition, we will look at how to monitor **replication,** diagnose and resolve problems, and restore the files that make up Active Directory.

As an organization and its network evolve over time, new trust relationships may need to be added or old ones deleted. The more complex a forest is, the more likely that users will need to access resources outside their own domain. In order to accelerate access time, you may wish to add **shortcut trust** relationships. New applications installed may extend the **schema,** while other network usage may result in the need for new **objects** or **object attributes**. Either way, the schema will require monitoring and management whenever you modify it. Forests also affect how users log on to the network through their **user principal name (UPN),** and that is another skill within the objective of managing an Active Directory forest.

Site management can be as simple or complex as you wish to make it. As the network grows, you need to monitor replication between the sites and evolve the site configuration to optimize the underlying network traffic.

Being able to recover from failures is invaluable during an emergency. Not only is restoration of Active Directory a critical component of disaster recovery, but the ability to troubleshoot **flexible single operations master** failures and replication problems is a key ability for an Active Directory administrator.

Tested Skills and Suggested Practices

The skills that you need to successfully master the Managing and Maintaining an Active Directory Infrastructure objective domain on Exam 70-294: *Planning, Implementing, and Maintaining a Microsoft Windows Server 2003 Active Directory Infrastructure* include:

- Manage an Active Directory forest and domain structure
    - ❏ Practice 1: Install a forest of at least one domain and raise the forest and domain functional levels to Microsoft Windows Server 2003. Log on as a

member of the Schema Admins group and view the schema in the Active Directory Schema console. Extend the schema by adding a new object type and attributes. You may also install an application (such as Microsoft Exchange 2000 Server or later) that will extend the schema. View the changes to the schema in the Active Directory Schema console. Using either the LDP utility or an Active Directory console, create a new object based on your schema extensions.

❑ Practice 2: Install a forest of at least one domain. Open the Active Directory Users And Computers console. Navigate to the Schema Admins group. View the permissions for this group. Create a user. Log on as that user and attempt to view and extend the schema using the Active Directory Schema console. Then log off. Add the user account as a member of the Schema Admins group. Log on as the user again and attempt to open the Active Directory Schema console. Extend the schema with a new object or attribute type.

❑ Practice 3: Install a forest of two domains with two different Domain Name System (DNS) names—for example, *fabrikam.com* and *contoso.com*. Change the UPN so that all users who log on to the forest will use the form of *user@fabrikam.com* even if those users are in the *contoso.com* domain.

❑ Practice 4: Install two forests with at least two domains apiece. Create a forest trust. Grant a user from a child domain in the first forest access to resources in a domain within the other forest. Log on as that user and attempt access to those resources. Then log off. Take the first forest's root domain offline. Log on and attempt to access the resources again. Document the response. View the trust relationships within the Active Directory Domains And Trusts console.

■ Manage an Active Directory site

❑ Practice 1: Install a forest of at least one domain on a network with at least two Internet Protocol (IP) subnets. Place a domain controller on each IP subnet. Create two sites within the forest. Assign the IP subnets to each site. Configure a site link between the two sites with the two domain controllers as replication partners. Force replication to take place. View the Active Directory Sites And Services console and verify replication took place. Configure a replication schedule to take place in five minutes. After the appointed time, verify that replication took place at the correct time.

❑ Practice 2: Install a forest of at least one domain on a network with three IP subnets that are connected in a triangular fashion. Place a domain controller on each subnet. Configure a site for each IP subnet. Create three site links. Configure the site cost for one link to be 1, another to be 5, and the third to be 99. Configure a site link bridge that encompasses the two lowest-cost site links. Force replication and monitor it using the Replication Monitor tool.

- ❑ Practice 3: Install a forest of at least one domain on a network with four IP subnets. Configure two sites with two IP subnets each. Place a domain controller on each IP subnet. Check to see how replication takes place. Move an IP subnet from one site to another. Force replication and view the changes.

- ■ Monitor Active Directory replication failures. Tools might include Replication Monitor, Event Viewer, and support tools.

  - ❑ Practice 1: Install a forest of at least one domain on two IP subnets. Configure two sites, assigning one IP subnet to each site and placing a domain controller on each subnet. Force replication and view it using Replication Monitor. Disconnect one domain controller from the network. Force replication. Use the Event Viewer and review the errors that occur.

  - ❑ Practice 2: Install a forest of at least one domain on two IP subnets. Configure the File Replication Service (FRS) to replicate a logon script. Check to make certain that the logon script has replicated at least once. Disconnect the router between the two domain controllers. Change the logon script on the other domain controller so that it includes a command that displays a message or other obvious indicator that the script executed. Force replication. Log on as a user on each IP subnet and view the results of the logon script. Re-connect the router. Force replication again and log on to see if the new logon script has replicated.

- ■ Restore Active Directory

  - ❑ Practice 1: Install two domain controllers into the root domain of a new forest. Open Active Directory Users And Computers and create an organizational unit (OU) hierarchy with at least one new user and group. Configure a site. Back up the first domain controller's system state data. Delete all the users, groups, and OUs that you created. Add a new site and IP subnets. Perform a nonauthoritative restore on the first domain controller. Allow replication to take place and view the results.

  - ❑ Practice 2: Install two domain controllers into the root domain of a new forest. Open Active Directory Users And Computers. Create a new OU hierarchy with new users and groups. Back up the first domain controller's system state data. Delete all the users, groups, and OUs that you created. Add a new site and IP subnets. Perform an authoritative restore on that first domain controller, allow replication to take place, and view the results.

- ■ Troubleshoot Active Directory

  - ❑ Practice 1: Install a forest with a single domain with two domain controllers. Take the first domain controller offline. Try to add new users to the domain. Document your results. Try to install another domain controller into a child domain. Document your results.

❑ Practice 2: Install a single domain controller in the root domain of a forest. Attempt to move and delete the NTDS.DIT file. Reboot the domain controller. Document your results.

Further Reading

You will find reading materials listed in this section by objective that will assist you in mastering the skills tested on the exam.

Objective 2.1   Review Lesson 1 in Chapter 3, "Administering Active Directory"; and Lessons 1 and 3 in Chapter 4, "Installing and Managing Domains, Trees, and Forests."

Microsoft Corporation. *Introducing Microsoft Windows Server 2003*. Redmond, Washington: Microsoft Press, 2003. Review Chapter 3, "Active Directory."

Microsoft Corporation. Redmond, Washington. Review "Manage the Schema," available on the Microsoft Web site at *http://technet2.microsoft.com/WindowsServer /en/Library/1e151f5c-474e-4e55-ae06-c0ffa41298d41033.mspx*.

Microsoft Corporation. Redmond, Washington. Review "Create an External Trust," available on the Microsoft Web site at *http://technet2.microsoft.com/WindowsServer /en/Library/b30ef067-746e-4453-b879-804259aafdd31033.mspx*.

Objective 2.2   Review Lessons 1, 2, and 3 in Chapter 5, "Configuring Sites and Managing Replication."

Microsoft Corporation. *Microsoft Windows Server 2003 Deployment Kit*, Washington: Microsoft Press, 2003. Review Chapter 3, "Designing the Site Topology" in the *Designing and Deploying Directory and Security Services* volume of this Deployment Kit. This information can also be found at *http://www.microsoft.com /windowsserver2003/techinfo/reskit/deploykit.mspx*.

Microsoft Corporation. Redmond, Washington. Review "Step by Step Guide to Active Directory Sites and Services," available on the Microsoft Web site at *http: //www.microsoft.com/technet/prodtechnol/windowsserver2003/technologies/directory /activedirectory/stepbystep/adsrv.mspx*.

Objective 2.3   Review Lesson 5 in Chapter 5, "Configuring Sites and Managing Replication"; and Lesson 1 in Chapter 14, "Managing Active Directory Performance."

Microsoft Corporation. *Microsoft Windows Server 2003 Administrator's Companion*. Redmond, Washington: Microsoft Press, 2003. Review Chapter 14, "Managing Active Directory."

Microsoft Corporation. *Introducing Microsoft Windows Server 2003*. Redmond, Washington: Microsoft Press, 2003. Review Chapter 6, "Using Active Directory."

Microsoft Corporation. Redmond, Washington. Review "Manage Application Directory Partitions," available on Microsoft's Web site at *http://technet2.microsoft.com /WindowsServer/en/Library/5f63b4a4-1fda-41d9-bc46-b8dce55358111033.mspx.*

Objective 2.4   Review Lesson 4 in Chapter 3, "Administering Active Directory."

Microsoft Corporation. *Microsoft Windows Server 2003 Administrator's Pocket Consultant.* Redmond, Washington: Microsoft Press, 2003. Review Chapter 6, "Using Active Directory," and Chapter 7, "Core Active Directory Administration."

Objective 2.5   Review Lessons 4 and 6 in Chapter 2, "Installing and Configuring Active Directory"; and Lesson 4 in Chapter 3, "Administering Active Directory."

Microsoft Corporation. "HOW TO: View and Transfer FSMO Roles in Windows Server 2003," available on the Microsoft Web site at *http://support.microsoft.com /default.aspx?scid=kb;EN-US;324801.*

Microsoft Corporation. Redmond, Washington. Review "HOW TO: Use Ntdsutil to Manage Active Directory Files from the Command Line in Windows Server 2003," available on the Microsoft Web site at *http://support.microsoft.com/default.aspx?scid= kb;en-us;816120.*

Microsoft Corporation. *Microsoft Technet.* Redmond, Washington. Review *"Active Directory Operations Guide,"* available on the Microsoft Web site at *http://www.microsoft.com/technet/prodtechnol/windows2000serv/technologies /activedirectory/maintain/opsguide/part1/adogd07.mspx.*

Objective 2.1

Manage an Active Directory Forest and Domain Structure

In this first objective of the Managing and Maintaining an Active Directory Infrastructure domain, you will be required to know how a forest interacts with external forests and domains. This objective also looks at the forest's schema management and user principal naming.

The structure of the Active Directory forest is incorporated into the trust relationships between domains both internal and external to the forest. You will need to know the types of trust relationships that you can create. In addition, you will need to know the process of creating, deleting, and troubleshooting trust relationships.

Trust relationships are intended to provide simplified management of resources across forests and domains. Because the domains and forests are separated, they can have unique and independent administration. Trust relationships ensure that network resources may still be used. The use of non-transitive trust relationships can ensure the security within each domain. You can use the **NETDOM** command-line tool to manage computer accounts, domains, and trust relationships, plus you can use the **Active Directory Domains And Trusts console** for a graphical view of the forest and for trust management.

One of the reasons for having multiple forests is to be able to maintain separate schemas. The schema is a forest-wide component that has an impact on every component within the Active Directory infrastructure. You should familiarize yourself with the groups that have the ability to make changes to the Schema Admins group, as well as the rights of the Schema Admins group. The following groups will have forest-wide administrative control:

- Domain Admins of the **forest root domain**
- Enterprise Admins
- Schema Admins

One of the schema management tasks that you should be able to perform through the **Active Directory Schema snap-in** is adding an attribute to the **global catalog**. In addition, you should be able to view **schema classes** and **schema attributes**, extend the schema, and manage permissions to secure the schema.

Within Active Directory, user accounts use logon IDs that are concatenated with a UPN suffix, and the result appears to be the same as an e-mail address. For example, a user at Litware, Inc. would log on to the network as *user@litwareinc.com*. An administrator can establish the UPN name to be different for each domain or the same throughout the forest. By default, the UPN suffix is the **DNS** name of the domain in which the user account resides. To change the UPN name, you use the Active Directory Domains And Trusts **console**.

Objective 2.1 Questions

1. As the administrator of Litware, Inc., you receive a call from the e-mail administrator to establish a trust relationship for the *litwareinc.com* domain in your Windows Server 2003 forest with a single Windows 2000 domain named *mx.litwareinc.local*. You open a ticket to document the call, taking down the appropriate name, account, password, and domain. The e-mail administrator wants to allow the users in your Windows Server 2003 forest to access and use mailboxes within *mx.litwareinc.local*, which is in its own forest. Which of the following actions do you take?

   A. Create a forest trust between *litwareinc.com* and *mx.litwareinc.local*.

   B. Create a shortcut trust between *litwareinc.com* and *mx.litwareinc.local*.

   C. Create an explicit external trust such that *mx.litwareinc.local* trusts *litwareinc.com*.

   D. Create an explicit external trust such that *litwareinc.com* trusts *mx.litwareinc.local*.

2. Contoso, Ltd. is merging with Litware, Inc. Each of the companies has a Windows Server 2003 forest. The companies intend to complete a full merger wherein Contoso will be the surviving company. The president of Contoso calls you, the administrator of Litware, Inc.'s forest, and asks you to enable all the users within Contoso's forest to access the files and data within Litware, Inc.'s network. In addition, the president wishes to have all of Litware's users to begin using Contoso's e-mail system, which is distributed across the domains within the *contoso.com* forest. What can you do to meet the president's request in the shortest period of time?

   A. Check with Contoso's administrator to ensure that the *contoso.com* forest is at the Windows Server 2003 forest functional level. Create a forest trust between the root domains of the two forests, and make certain that there is a trust relationship going in both directions. Grant Contoso users access to Litware's files and data. Request that the Contoso administrator grant Litware users access to e-mail resources.

   B. Perform a merger and migration of all users, resources, and data to the *contoso.com* forest.

   C. Check with Contoso's administrator to ensure that the *contoso.com* domain is at the Windows Server 2003 domain functional level. Create an explicit external trust relationship where the root domain of the Litware, Inc. forest trusts *contoso.com*. Grant Contoso users access to Litware's files and data. Request that the Contoso e-mail administrator grant Litware users access to e-mail resources.

D. Create an explicit external trust relationship where Litware, Inc.'s root domain trusts *contoso.com*. Create explicit external trust relationships for each of Litware, Inc.'s domains where they trust *contoso.com*. Make the *contoso.com* Enterprise Admins group a member of the Litware, Inc. root domain's Domain Admins group.

3. Fabrikam, Inc. has a Windows Server 2003 Active Directory forest. Fabrikam's research division has developed a custom expense application that integrates with Active Directory. They have added two new attributes to user and computer objects in the schema for this application. The application worked well in the research division's test forest, which consisted of one domain that the research division's programmers have extensively modified. However, when the application is installed in the root domain of the *fabrikam.com* forest, users in the *sales.fabrikam.com* and *prod.fabrikam.com* domains are unable to use the application. Which of the following actions should you take?

A. Using the Active Directory Schema console, add the two new attributes to the global catalog. Force replication and test the application as a user in each of the *sales.fabrikam.com* and *prod.fabrikam.com* domains.

B. Add the Domain Admins groups of both the *sales.fabrikam.com* and *prod .fabrikam.com* domains as members of the Schema Admins group.

C. Migrate all users to the *fabrikam.com* domain.

D. Create shortcut trusts between the root domain and *sales.fabrikam.com* and *prod.fabrikam.com*.

4. You are the administrator of a Windows Server 2003 forest for Contoso, Ltd. You are going to roll out an upgrade to your Microsoft Exchange Server systems, which will extend the schema. You want to test the rollout. Which would provide you with the most accurate experience, without interrupting daily business activities?

A. Using the Active Directory Schema console, you extend the schema of the *contoso .com* forest with each of the attributes and objects listed in the *Microsoft Exchange 2000 Server Resource Kit*.

B. You remove a domain controller from the *sales.contoso.com* domain. With the domain controller disconnected from the network, you install Exchange Server to it and then return the domain controller to the production network.

C. Create a new domain in the forest. Install Exchange Server within the new domain.

D. Create a new forest that is not connected to the production network. Back up system state data from a production forest's domain controller and restore it to the test forest so that you have a close copy of the production forest's contents. Test the Exchange Server rollout on the forest.

5.   Contoso, Ltd. is merging with Litware, Inc. Each of the companies has a Windows Server 2003 forest. The companies intend to complete a full merger wherein Contoso will be the surviving company. Users in the *contoso.com* forest currently log on to their own domains using their own IDs. Users in the *litwareinc.com* forest currently log on using UPNs of *user@litwareinc.com*. Contoso has three Mark Joneses whose IDs are mjones, each in a different domain—mjones in *contoso.com*, mjones in *sales.contoso.com*, and mjones in *prod.contoso.com*. The e-mail addresses used at Contoso are based on a different naming structure where the three Mark Joneses have unique names including numbers and all ending in *contoso.com*. You have the following objectives:

Use UPN names in both forests.

Make UPN names the same as the e-mail addresses used.

You take the following actions:

1. You change the UPN name for the *litwareinc.com* forest to *contoso.com* in the Active Directory Domains And Trusts console.

2. You implement UPN names in the *contoso.com* forest so that all users log on as **theirID@contoso.com**.

You have:

A. Achieved neither objective 1 nor objective 2

B. Achieved objective 1 but did not achieve objective 2

C. Did not achieve objective 1 but did achieve objective 2

D. Achieved both objective 1 and objective 2

Objective 2.1 Answers

1.   **Correct Answers: C**

  A. **Incorrect:** You will not be able to create a forest trust because one of the forests has a Windows 2000 domain (*mx.litwareinc.local*). Forest trusts can only be established between two Windows Server 2003 forests, which in turn require that all domains and domain controllers are running Windows Server 2003.

  B. **Incorrect:** You will not be able to create a shortcut trust between *litwareinc.com* and *mx.litwareinc.local* because the two domains are in separate forests. A shortcut trust is created between two domains in the same forest.

  C. **Correct:** The explicit external trust relationship occurs between the two domains. Since the resources are located in *mx.litwareinc.local*, it must trust *litwareinc.com*. Then the e-mail administrator can grant access to users so that they can use mailboxes in the *mx.litwareinc.local* domain.

  D. **Incorrect:** Even though this is the correct type of trust, the *mx.litwareinc.local* administrator would not be able to grant access to the mailboxes to the users in *litwareinc.com* because the direction of the trust is opposite what it needs to be.

2.   **Correct Answers: A**

  A. **Correct:** Forest trusts require both forests to be raised to the Windows Server 2003 forest functional level. A forest trust where Litware, Inc.'s forest trusts Contoso's forest will allow Contoso users to access files anywhere in the Litware, Inc. forest. The trust where Contoso's forest trusts Litware, Inc.'s forest will enable the Contoso administrators to grant Litware users access to e-mail.

  B. **Incorrect:** This action will produce the desired result, but it will be a very long and involved project.

  C. **Incorrect:** The domain functional level is not a factor in explicit external trust relationships. This particular trust relationship will not enable the Contoso users to access resources anywhere in the Litware, Inc. forest, only those in the root domain. This trust relationship will not allow Contoso users in child domains to have any access at all to the Litware, Inc. forest's resources. The trust relationship will allow no one in the Litware, Inc. forest to have e-mail access.

  D. **Incorrect:** Litware users would have no access to e-mail because none of the domains in the *contoso.com* forest trusts the domains within Litware's forest. Only the users in the *contoso.com* domain would be able to access Litware's files and data.

3.   Correct Answers: A

A. **Correct:** The Active Directory Schema snap-in is used for modifying the schema and adding attributes to the global catalog. Since there were new attributes added to the schema, the application may need to be able to query the local domain or global catalog to be able to function. Since the application works in the root domain, where it was installed, but is not able to function for users in the other domains, then adding the two new attributes to the global catalog will allow the application to find those attributes when querying any part of Active Directory outside of the root domain.

B. **Incorrect:** Adding the Domain Admins groups as members of the Schema Admins group will give those administrators the ability to make schema changes, reducing the security of the root domain. It will not enable the application for a standard user.

C. **Incorrect:** This action might fix the problem, but it would override the reason that the child domains were created in the first place, making this a poor solution.

D. **Incorrect:** There is already a parent-child trust between the root domain and each of these domains. A shortcut trust would be unnecessary because they are directly within the same domain tree. This would not fix the problem with the new expense application.

4.   Correct Answers: D

A. **Incorrect:** Manually extending the schema of the production forest can cause unanticipated problems. In addition, this option will not provide you with an accurate experience.

B. **Incorrect:** Since the domain controller is not in the *contoso.com* root domain, it will likely not have the schema master role, and you would be prevented from installing Exchange Server in the first place. If you are able to install Exchange Server, after returning the domain controller to the network, you run the risk of causing a problem to the production network. It is likely that there would be a schema conflict of some type.

C. **Incorrect:** Since the new domain is in the production forest, you run the risk of interrupting daily business through Exchange Server's extension of the production forest's schema.

D. **Correct:** When testing schema extensions of any type, you should use a non-production forest in order to avoid interrupting the daily activity of production forest users.

5.   Correct Answers: B

A. **Incorrect:** You were able to meet objective 1 because you implemented UPN names in both forests. You did not achieve objective 2 because the users will not log on with their e-mail address naming scheme but with their IDs.

B. **Correct:** You implemented UPN names in both forests but you did not change the naming scheme for the users to match their e-mail addresses.

C. **Incorrect:** You did the opposite. You achieved objective 1 by implementing UPN names in both forests, but you did not achieve objective 2 because the names were not changed to match their e-mail addresses.

D. **Incorrect:** You achieved objective 1 because you implemented the UPN names. However, you will have a conflict for the Mark Joneses because you did not achieve objective 2 in changing the naming scheme of IDs to match e-mail addresses.

Objective 2.2

Manage an Active Directory Site

Like the organizations that use them, networks are not static entities. New locations are added, while others are closed. Companies merge and subsidiaries spin off, joint ventures are established. As a result, both **local area networks (LANs)** and **wide area networks (WANs)** evolve and change. Active Directory takes advantage of the underlying network through the use of sites. An administrator can configure **sites**, **site links**, and **site link bridges** to optimize traffic and customize it to meet the needs of the organization.

Sites and the links between them are the means by which you can configure how replication traffic will take place across network links. The replication schedule has an immediate effect on replication. You have two aspects to consider with the replication schedule:

- **Replication frequency**
- Site link availability

The replication frequency setting determines how often replication can take place. By default, the frequency of replication is every 180 minutes. For a network with many changes to objects in a domain that spans multiple sites, you may wish for more frequent replication. For a network with few changes, or whose domains do not span sites, replication could easily be less frequent with little affect to network users. The minimum replication frequency is 15 minutes. The maximum is 10,080 minutes, which is the equivalent of one full week.

Site link availability prevails over the replication frequency. When you establish a site link as unavailable during a certain time period, replication cannot take place even if it is scheduled to do so. The default availability of a site link is 24 hours per day, seven days a week. However, if you have a network with a great deal of mission-critical traffic taking place during a certain time period of the day, you can set the site link as unavailable during that time period so that there is no competing traffic from replication. Keep in mind that site link availability only applies to IP. Those site links that use Simple Mail Transfer Protocol (SMTP) will ignore site link availability scheduling.

The site link cost determines which site links are used when there are multiple paths to the same site. Many networks have redundant links between locations. You can configure the site link cost so that certain paths are selected over others. Active Directory **knowledge consistency checker (KCC)** uses the site link cost to determine which site links should be preferred when performing replication. The default cost of a site link is 100. If you configure the cost of a site link to 1, it will be preferred over any site link with a higher cost.

At the boundary of each site, the KCC will assign a **bridgehead server** to handle the preferred traffic. You can change the **preferred bridgehead server** by manually configuring one of your choice. However, by doing so, the KCC will not be able to automatically recover the replication topology if your preferred bridgehead server is unavailable. Computers are assigned to sites based on their IP address and the IP subnets that are assigned to each site. You can create a **site topology** by reassigning an IP subnet from one site to another.

Objective 2.2 Questions

1.   Fabrikam, Inc. has three sites that connect to the main location, as shown in the figure below. The network has a backup link between PROD and SALES because the SALES office needs to supply sales orders directly to the PROD manufacturing plant and check on order status at all times. However, the backup link is not used for normal traffic. You decide to configure site links that mirror this network. You have HQ-SALES, HQ-MKT, HQ-PROD, and PROD-SALES site links. You also configure a site link bridge connecting the HQ-SALES and HQ-PROD site links. Which of the following actions will ensure that the replication traffic will prefer the site link bridge over the direct site link between SALES and PROD?

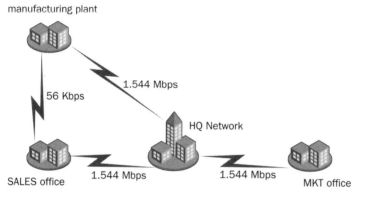

- **A.** Set the site link bridge cost to 1. Leave the site links' costs as the default.
- **B.** Set the site link cost for PROD-SALES to 150. Set the site link cost for HQ-SALES to 60. Set the site link cost for HQ-PROD to 60.
- **C.** Set the site link cost for PROD-SALES to 150.
- **D.** Set the site link cost for HQ-SALES to 60. Set the site link cost for HQ-PROD to 70. Set the site link cost for PROD-SALES to 110.

2.   You are the network administrator for Contoso, Ltd. The main campus has three buildings that are connected by Ethernet over fiber and a fourth building, named BLDG D, that is connected by a satellite link. You originally configured the campus as a single site; however, users in BLDG D complain that logons often take longer than necessary. You review the traffic and discover that more than half of all logons and queries are taking place across the satellite link rather than to the domain controllers within the building. Users often travel between buildings within the campus. You have the following objectives:

Primary objective: Force logons for users in BLDG D to prefer domain controllers in BLDG D.

Secondary objective: You want to make certain that changes are replicated as fast as possible amongst all the domain controllers.

Secondary objective: You want the replication topology to automatically reconfigure itself if there are changes to domain controllers.

You take the following actions:

1. You create a new site named BLDG D.

2. You move all IP subnets from the main site to BLDG D's new site. You reassign the domain controllers in BLDG D to the new BLDG site.

3. You configure the site link's replication frequency to 15 minutes.

A. You achieved neither the primary nor the secondary objectives.

B. You achieved the primary objective but neither of the secondary objectives.

C. You achieved the primary objective and both of the secondary objectives.

D. You achieved the primary objective and one of the secondary objectives.

3. Litware, Inc. is a book publishing company with its main office on the East Coast and two small offices on the West Coast. The West Coast offices are connected by a T1 leased line with less than half of the 1.544 Mbps capacity used at any point in time. The East Coast office is connected to one of the West Coast offices by a 256 Kbps fractional-T1 line, and not connected to the other West Coast office. This 256 Kbps is nearly at full capacity from the time the West Coast office opens at 9:00 A.M. Pacific Standard Time until the East Coast office closes at 4:00 P.M. Eastern Standard Time. To ensure that replication traffic does not interrupt this traffic, how do you configure the site link between the East and West Coast offices?

A. Set the site availability so that it is not available from 12:00 noon Eastern Standard Time to 4:00 P.M. Eastern Standard Time.

B. Set the replication frequency to 240 minutes.

C. Set the site link cost to 200.

D. Set the site availability so that it is not available from 9:00 A.M. Eastern Standard Time to 1:00 P.M. Eastern Standard Time.

4. You are the network administrator for the Contoso Pharmaceuticals network. You have 10 small pharmacy and sales offices, each in its own site, that offer services to customers 24 hours a day, seven days a week. These pharmacies are connected directly to the

main network by slow links. Each has its own domain controller. The network is very stable with few changes to user and computer objects in Active Directory. The network is busiest weekdays between 3:00 P.M. and 8:00 P.M., when the pharmacies transmit data to the main office for each new prescription. How do you configure the pharmacies to reduce the impact that replication has on the network?

   A. Set each pharmacy's site link cost to 200.

   B. Set each pharmacy's replication frequency to 60 minutes and leave the default site link availability schedule.

   C. Set each pharmacy's replication frequency to 180 minutes and change the site link cost to 10.

   D. Set the replication frequency to 360 minutes. Set the site availability so that it is not available weekdays between 3:00 P.M. and 8:00 P.M.

5. You are the network administrator for a large internetwork. You have three offices with global catalog servers: SALES, MARKET, and SERVICE. Users in the SALES office complain that they are not able to find updated information network resources in the MARKET site. You review the site link configuration and find the following:

   ■ SALES-SERVICE linkCost = 100; Availability: 10:00 P.M. to 12:00 midnight Monday through Friday, not available Saturday or Sunday; Replication frequency: 10,080 minutes.

   ■ MARKET-SERVICE link: Cost = 200; Availability: 2:00 P.M. to 5:00 P.M. Saturdays and Sundays only, not available Monday through Friday; Replication frequency: 5,040 minutes.

   ■ SALES-MKT-SVC Site link bridge configured encompassing both the site links SALES-SERVICE and MARKET-SERVICE.

Which of the following will ensure that changes will be updated on a daily basis via replication? Select two of the following:

   A. Change the cost of the SALES-SERVICE link to 50. Change the cost of the MARKET-SERVICE link to 50.

   B. Change the replication frequency of the SALES-SERVICE and MARKET-SERVICE links each to 720 minutes.

   C. Change the availability of the SALES-SERVICE and MARKET-SERVICE links so that they are available between the hours of 5:00 P.M. and 9:00 A.M. each weekday.

   D. Configure the availability of the SALES-MKT-SVC site link bridge so that it will be available between the hours of 5:00 P.M. and 9:00 A.M. each weekday.

Objective 2.2 Answers

1. **Correct Answers: B**

    A. **Incorrect:** You cannot perform this action. The site link bridge does not have a configurable cost. It inherits its costs by adding the costs of the site links that it contains.

    B. **Correct:** By setting the site link cost for PROD-SALES to 150, it will be selected last among all site links, which have a default cost of 100. However, you would also need to set the site link costs for HQ-SALES and HQ-PROD to less than 75 in order for the site link bridge, which adds the costs for its contained site links, to be selected over the PROD-SALES site link.

    C. **Incorrect:** While setting the cost for PROD-SALES to 150 will reduce its preference compared to other direct site links, it will still have a lower cost than the site link bridge, which would be 200 since it is the additive of its contained site links whose default cost is 100.

    D. **Incorrect:** This action will result in the PROD-SALES site link, with a cost of 110 to be preferred over the HQ-SALES/HQ-PROD site link bridge, with a total cost of 130 (60 + 70).

2. **Correct Answers: C**

    A. **Incorrect:** You achieved the primary objective because logons automatically prefer the domain controllers within the local site. You also achieved both of the secondary objectives because the site link's replication frequency is the fastest available, and without a preferred bridgehead server manually set, the KCC has free rein to reconfigure itself.

    B. **Incorrect:** You achieved the primary objective because logons automatically prefer the domain controllers within the local site. You also achieved both of the secondary objectives because the site link's replication frequency is the fastest available, and without a preferred bridgehead server manually set, the KCC has free rein to reconfigure itself.

    C. **Correct:** You achieved the primary objective because logons automatically prefer the domain controllers within the local site. You also achieved both of the secondary objectives because the site link's replication frequency is the fastest available, and without a preferred bridgehead server manually set, the KCC has free rein to reconfigure itself.

    D. **Incorrect:** You achieved the primary objective because logons automatically prefer the domain controllers within the local site. You also achieved both of the secondary objectives because the site link's replication frequency is the fastest available, and without a preferred bridgehead server manually set, the KCC has free rein to reconfigure itself.

3.   Correct Answers: A

    A. Correct: This will ensure that no replication will take place during the busy times specified.

    B. Incorrect: This will not prevent the site link from being used for replication during the specified time periods. It will only ensure that replication takes place once every four hours.

    C. Incorrect: Since this is the only site link between the East and West Coasts, it will be used regardless of the site link cost.

    D. Incorrect: The time is confusing since the networks are in separate time zones. This time period is incorrect for the times that the link actually needs to be unavailable.

4.   Correct Answers: D

    A. Incorrect: The site link cost will not reduce the impact of replication since there are no redundant site links mentioned.

    B. Incorrect: The default replication frequency is actually three times longer than 60 minutes, so you will be making a larger impact on replication rather than reducing it.

    C. Incorrect: These changes will have no effect on replication, since the default replication frequency is 180 minutes, and there are no redundant site links mentioned.

    D. Correct: This will reduce the impact of replication because replication will take place only half as often, plus replication will not take place during the network's busiest hours.

5.   Correct Answers: B, C

    A. Incorrect: This will only make changes to the site topology; it will not ensure that daily replication will take place.

    B. Correct: This will ensure that replication takes place every 12 hours, which means that there are two chances per day that replication updates will be made.

    C. Correct: One of the reasons that updates were not made were because the links were not available often enough for replication to take place on a daily basis.

    D. Incorrect: Site link bridges inherit their availability from site links. They cannot be configured directly.

Manage Active Directory Replicaton Failures

In this objective, we will review the process of monitoring replication. Replication is the process of ensuring that Active Directory data is updated across all **domain controllers**. It is also the process by which logon scripts and other files are updated to all domain controllers. Tools might include Replication Monitor, Event Viewer, and support tools.

The first replication process affects data within the Active Directory, including

- Domain information, replicated to domain controllers within the same domain

- **Schema partition**, replicated to all domain controllers within the same forest

- **Configuration partition**, replicated to all domain controllers within the same forest

- Global catalog, replicated to all **global catalog servers**

- **Application directory partitions**, replicated only to specified replicas

The second replication process is that of the FRS. This is intended for replication of files between domain controllers. These files are all located in the **SYSVOL** share.

When you administer an Active Directory network, you must ensure that data is kept current. Otherwise, user accounts that have been deleted from the network become a security risk in sites where replication has not taken place. To ensure that replication has taken place, you can monitor and manage it with the following tools:

- **Active Directory Sites And Services** console

- **Event Viewer**, within the directory service event log

- Replication Monitor (**REPLMON**)

- Replication Admin (**REPADMIN**)

- Domain Controller Diagnostics (**DCDIAG**)

Active Directory and FRS use the same connection setup and mechanisms, including identical replication schedules to replicate data. However, because these are two different mechanisms using the same replication topology, it is possible that FRS will fail even when directory service replication functions. You can execute the Ntfrsutil command to check FRS, ensuring that there are at least one inbound and one outbound connection.

Objective 2.3 Questions

1. You are a network administrator for Fabrikam. The company has four sites: Boston, Detroit, Tallahassee, and Atlanta, and a single domain named *fabrikam.com*. The sites are all connected by site links and a single all-encompassing site link bridge, using default availability, frequency, and site link costs. You created a special user account named Test for testing an application. You typically work in the Boston site but have traveled to the Atlanta site one day after creating the Test account in Boston. You attempt to log on to the network in Atlanta using the Test user account but are unable to do so. Which of the following actions should you take to update the domain controller's Active Directory information?

   A. Using the Active Directory Sites And Services console, you force replication to take place.

   B. Using the Event Viewer, change the Atlanta replication partner to Boston instead of Tallahassee.

   C. Using REPADMIN, change the Atlanta replication partner to Boston instead of Tallahassee.

   D. Using Active Directory Users And Computers in Atlanta, create a new Test user account in the same OU with the same name as the one that was created in Boston.

2. You are a brand new network administrator for Contoso, Ltd. Contoso has two domains in its Active Directory forest: *contoso.com* and *sales.contoso.com*. All users are located in the *contoso.com* domain, while all network resources are located in the *sales.contoso.com* domain. Users in a remote office, which is its own site, call you to complain that the new printer just added to the network cannot be found when they query the network. You suspect that the problem is with replication between global catalog servers. How do you determine which domain controllers are global catalog servers?

   A. Using Event Viewer, you look for servers that are global catalog servers.

   B. Using the Replication Monitor tool, you add monitored servers and then select the option to show global catalog servers.

   C. Using the Active Directory Domains And Trusts console, you select the option to display global catalog servers.

   D. Using Performance Monitor, you configure a chart to display traffic from global catalog servers.

3. You are one of the network administrators for Contoso, Ltd. There are over 100 sites. and you manage one of them in Chicago, which has 800 users. You have seven domain controllers, one which is a global catalog server. All of the servers are members of the *sales.contoso.com* domain. You are working on a domain controller and you run REPL-MON to see how replication is functioning. The tool displays no replication links. What is a likely cause of this problem?

   A. The domain controller is not a global catalog server.

   B. You have selected the wrong tool. You should run REPADMIN and Event Viewer.

   C. Your site, Chicago, has a site link that is configured with availability only on weekends.

   D. The domain controller is not connected to the network.

4. You are managing a network for Litware, Inc. You have two small locations, NY and Boston. They are connected by a site link with default configuration values. You have created a new logon script and placed it on DC02 in the NY site, which is one of five domain controllers. This logon script attaches a drive letter M to a folder that you moved to a new member server three days ago. An application requires drive letter M to be connected in order to function. Users from Boston call you and complain that the application does not work and has not worked since you moved the folder. All NY users can use the application. You establish that directory service replication is working and last ran two hours ago. What do you do next?

   A. Force replication using REPADMIN.

   B. Check to make certain that DC02 is connected to the network.

   C. Change the site link availability schedule.

   D. Using Event Viewer, check to see if there are FRS replication errors on each domain controller.

5. You have a problem with DC03 on the *fabrikam.com* network. The domain controller had a hardware failure, which you have fixed. You have now brought DC03 back online on the network. Replication is not working. You have performed the following actions:

   1. You checked the disk space, and there is plenty available.

   2. You checked the Event Viewer and have not found any errors.

   3. You made certain that the domain controller is online.

   4. You pinged the IP address successfully from another computer.

   5. You pinged the name *DC03.fabrikam.com* unsuccessfully.

What is the next step you should take?

A. Add a new disk to DC03.

B. Replace the network interface card.

C. Check DNS to make certain that *DC03.fabrikam.com* can be resolved.

D. Test the RPC connectivity.

Objective 2.3 Answers

1.   Correct Answers: A

   A. Correct: Forcing replication is done through the Active Directory Sites And Services console. This is the first step to take, and barring replication errors, it should succeed.

   B. Incorrect: The Event Viewer cannot be used for this purpose.

   C. Incorrect: Since the KCC will automatically configure site links and the site link bridge for replication, this is not likely to make a difference.

   D. Incorrect: This will create a conflict because the two objects are not the same but have been given the same name.

2.   Correct Answers: B

   A. Incorrect: Not only would this be tedious, but it would not provide you with the list of global catalog servers.

   B. Correct: This is the fastest method for displaying global catalog servers.

   C. Incorrect: The Active Directory Domains And Trusts console will not display this information.

   D. Incorrect: Performance Monitor cannot be used to display this type of traffic.

3.   Correct Answers: D

   A. Incorrect: All domain controllers are involved in replication, whether they are global catalog servers or not. This would not cause REPLMON to display no replication links.

   B. Incorrect: Both REPLMON and REPADMIN would display the same information because they use the same basis.

   C. Incorrect: The site link's availability schedule would not have an impact on the replication links in the REPLMON utility.

   D. Correct: Neither REPLMON nor REPADMIN will display replication links when the domain controller is disconnected from the network.

4.   Correct Answers: D

   A. Incorrect: Since you verified that directory service replication last ran two hours ago, but you also know that the logon script has not replicated for at least three days, then forcing replication will not change the current state of the network.

B. Incorrect: The users in NY are able to log on to the network and are receiving the correct logon script, so they are either connecting directly to DC02 or they are using one of the other four domain controllers in NY and receiving the correct logon script.

C. Incorrect: The site link's availability schedule is by default available all the time, so this option wouldn't make any difference.

D. Correct: The logon script is placed within the SYSVOL share, and this share is replicated using FRS. The Event Viewer will display errors, such as a lack of disk space, that can take place with FRS.

5.   Correct Answers: C

A. Incorrect: There is plenty of disk space already, so there is no need for an additional disk.

B. Incorrect: The fact that you could ping the domain controller's IP address means that the network interface card is functioning.

C. Correct: Since you were unable to successfully ping the fully qualified domain name (FQDN) of *DC03.fabrikam.com*, the likely problem is DNS configuration.

D. Incorrect: Remote procedure calls (RPCs) are required for FRS to function. However, the fact that the FQDN was unable to be pinged points to a DNS problem.

Restore Active Directory Directory Services

This objective focuses on the skills for restoring Active Directory. The nature of the Active Directory database is to be integral to the functions of a domain controller. Therefore, simply copying the Active Directory database files and restoring them will not effectively restore a domain controller to its former function. Instead, you must use a special backup and restore procedure.

The Windows Server 2003 Backup Or Restore Wizard, a graphical application, offers native backup for the system state data of a domain controller. The system state data includes the Active Directory database files, in addition to registry and configuration information. The Windows Server 2003 Backup application can also restore the system state data. There are three types of restoration methods:

- **Primary restore**
- **Nonauthoritative restore**
- **Authoritative restore**

The Primary restore method is used when restoring Active Directory data on a stand-alone domain controller. This method is also used on the first domain controller you restore when you have a completely failed forest and you must restore the entire forest.

The nonauthoritative restore is also called the normal restore method. This method should be selected when you have more than one domain controller on the network and you do not need to roll back changes that have been made to Active Directory. In this method, when replication takes place between the restored domain controller and other domain controllers on the network, the restored domain controller receives updates from its replication partners.

The authoritative restore is used when you need to roll back changes made to Active Directory. After an authoritative restore, replication partners will receive the restored data from the newly restored domain controllers. This restored data will override other changes and effectively roll back Active Directory.

Objective 2.4 Questions

1.   You are the network administrator for A. Datum Corporation, a small company with 35 users. You have a single domain controller in your Active Directory forest. Your domain controller has had a hardware failure that is unrecoverable. You install a new domain controller. Which of the following actions should you take next?

    A. Perform an authoritative restore.

    B. Perform a primary restore.

    C. Perform a nonauthoritative restore.

    D. Install a second domain controller and replicate data.

2.   A network administrator in another site calls you in a panic. While performing standard user changes using the Active Directory Users And Computers console, the administrator accidentally deleted an entire OU tree with hundreds of users in it. The administrator was connected to a domain controller named JAK003, and as soon as he realized his error, he disconnected JAK003 from the network. Replication has not taken place, and you have verified that fact. What do you advise the administrator to do?

    A. Perform a nonauthoritative restore on JAK003, then reconnect JAK003 to the network so that replication can take place.

    B. Perform a primary restore.

    C. Perform an authoritative restore on JAK003, then reconnect JAK003 to the network so that replication can take place.

    D. Reinstall the operating system on JAK003.

3.   You are the network administrator for the A. Datum Corporation network. There are six domain controllers, named DC01 through DC06 in order of original installation, in the only domain of its Windows Server 2003 forest. One of the programmers in the research department was made a member of the Domain Admins group, and then granted herself membership in the Schema Admins group. After that, the programmer developed a new application that was intended to integrate into Active Directory and extend the schema of the forest. When the programmer tested the application, it corrupted the schema and the entire forest failed. What do you do to recover from this situation? Select two.

    A. Perform an authoritative restore of DC01.

    B. Perform a primary restore of DC01.

    C. Perform a primary restore of DC02 through DC06.

    D. Perform nonauthoritative restores of DC02 through DC06.

4. You are the network administrator of a small network consisting of two sites: Dallas and Boise. Each site has two domain controllers that have full backups performed each Monday and Thursday. On Monday morning, you arrive at work to a full voice mailbox and urgent messages stating that no one can log on to the network. You discover that the OU for your site, Dallas, has completely disappeared from the Active Directory Users And Computers console. You contact the Boise administrator and discover that he accidentally deleted the OU last Friday, but when there were no complaints, he figured the OU was not used, so he didn't report the change to you. How do you recover from this error?

    A. Perform a primary restore of Thursday's backup on one of your domain controllers.

    B. Perform an authoritative restore of last Monday's backup on one of your domain controllers.

    C. Perform a nonauthoritative restore of last Thursday's backup on one of your domain controllers.

    D. Perform an authoritative restore of last Thursday's backup on one of your domain controllers.

5. You receive a call from a network administrator in the LA location. You are in Redmond. The administrator wants the system state data restored on a domain controller that suffered a hardware failure. The administrator has never performed a restore before and asks you to perform the restoration remotely. What do you advise the administrator?

    A. An administrator can restore the system state data remotely, but only as a primary restore.

    B. An administrator can restore the system state data remotely, but only in a nonauthoritative restore.

    C. The administrator must perform the restore of system state data locally in a nonauthoritative restore.

    D. The administrator must perform an authoritative restore of system state data locally.

Objective 2.4 Answers

1. **Correct Answers: B**

   A. Incorrect: The authoritative restore is used for rolling back changes that were made to Active Directory.

   B. Correct: The primary restore is used to restore a standalone domain controller or the first domain controller in the restoration of an entire forest.

   C. Incorrect: Nonauthoritative restores are used when restoring a domain controller that will then receive further updates from replication partners.

   D. Incorrect: Without restoring the data to the first domain controller, there would be nothing to replicate.

2. **Correct Answers: A**

   A. Correct: The nonauthoritative restore will restore the data to an older date on JAK003. When JAK003 is reconnected to the network, updates from other domain controllers will bring JAK003 to their own level.

   B. Incorrect: The primary restore is only used to restore a standalone domain controller or the first domain controller in the restoration of an entire forest. JAK003 is neither a standalone nor the first domain controller in the forest.

   C. Incorrect: Normally, you would perform an authoritative restore on a domain controller when you need to roll back changes made by accident. However, since JAK003 was disconnected before replication was able to take place, an authoritative restore would roll back other changes, and it is not necessary in this case.

   D. Incorrect: This is a drastic measure to take when you can perform a restore. Plus, if you reinstall the operating system without formatting the disk, the domain controller's former information may still be intact and could replicate throughout the network.

3. **Correct Answers: B, D**

   A. Incorrect: You will need to perform a primary restore of the first domain controller of the forest, then follow with nonauthoritative restores of the remaining domain controllers, and then allow replication to take place.

   B. Correct: The primary restore is used to restore a standalone domain controller or the first domain controller in the restoration of an entire forest, of which DC01 would be the first in the forest.

   C. Incorrect: DC02 through DC06 would not be the first domain controllers to be recovered in the forest, so they are not candidates for a primary restore.

D. Correct: The nonauthoritative restores of DC02 through DC06 would follow the primary restore of DC01.

4.   Correct Answers: D

A. Incorrect: You are not recovering a standalone server or the first domain controller in a forest, so you would not select a primary restore.

B. Incorrect: In selecting Monday's backup, you would be losing three days worth of Active Directory changes.

C. Incorrect: Nonauthoritative restores are used when restoring a domain controller. The domain controller would then receive updates from replication partners and the OU would disappear upon replication.

D. Correct: The authoritative restore will roll back the changes made to Active Directory to last Thursday, which is the most recent version of Active Directory backed up before the OU was deleted. The authoritative nature of the backup will force those changes to be accepted by the other domain controllers when replication next takes place.

5.   Correct Answers: C

A. Incorrect: An administrator cannot restore system state data remotely in any type of restoration.

B. Incorrect: An administrator cannot restore system state data remotely.

C. Correct: Since an administrator cannot perform the restore process remotely for system state data, you advise the administrator in LA to perform a nonauthoritative restore of the system state data. Nonauthoritative restores are used when restoring a domain controller that will then receive further updates from replication partners.

D. Incorrect: Since there is no need to roll back changes to Active Directory, you do not need to have the administrator perform an authoritative restore.

Troubleshoot Active Directory

This objective focuses on the skills needed for diagnosing and resolving the problems that can take place in an Active Directory forest. You will need to understand replication issues between domain controllers. This objective includes troubleshooting **operations master role** failures as well as problems that occur to the Active Directory files.

Replication failures have many symptoms. You may find that group policies are inconsistent across the enterprise, that there are different versions of the same logon script in the SYSVOL share, or that deleted objects still exist in Active Directory on some domain controllers. To diagnose the problems with replication, you can use Domain Controller Diagnostics (Dcdiag), Replication Monitor, Replication Administrator, Active Directory Sites And Services, and the Event Viewer. For problems with FRS, you can use the File Replication Service utility (Ntfrsutil).

While operations masters are required for Active Directory to function, they are not all necessary to the daily activities of users. In fact, you can take some operations master roles offline, such as the **Relative ID Master**, **domain naming master**, and **schema master**, and a user would likely never know the difference. However, the **PDC Emulator** has an immediate effect on users when it is taken offline, while the **infrastructure master**'s failure would affect an administrator when creating or renaming objects in the domain.

The data store for Active Directory is the **Ntds.dit** file located on a domain controller. It can be managed using the **Ntdsutil** command-line tool. However, you cannot manage the Ntds.dit file with Ntdsutil while the domain controller is operating as such. Instead, you must go into Directory Services Restore Mode, which is available when you press F8 at the startup of the domain controller.

Objective 2.5 Questions

1. You are the network administrator for the Contoso, Ltd. company. You have implemented a new security policy using group policies. When you log on to the NY site, the security policy is working. However, when you log on to Washington, you discover that the security policy is not working. What could be the problem?

    A. The operations master in charge of security has failed.

    B. FRS has failed.

    C. Active Directory replication has failed.

    D. The Ntds.dit file is corrupted.

2. You have been brought in as a consultant for Fabrikam. The company's network administrator left the company, and the company is experiencing some problems with the network. You run across the administrator's notes that state "Ran DCDIAG on DC03, failed two of the tests. REPADMIN shows no outbound connection. Directory service log shows error." What problem was the administrator trying to resolve?

    A. Replication problems

    B. A RID Master failure

    C. Disk space shortage for SYSVOL

    D. Corrupted Active Directory log files

3. You are a network administrator for Contoso, Ltd., which has a large internetwork. With hundreds of domain controllers and dozens of sites, the network has, up to this point, run very effectively. However, you have been monitoring replication and have documented that replication is taking much longer—at least 24 hours longer—for changes to be updated at your site than previously. Which of the following tools can you use to determine the problem? (Select all that apply.)

    A. REPLMON

    B. Active Directory Domains And Trusts

    C. Event Viewer

    D. Active Directory Users And Computers

4. You are a network administrator at Litware, Inc. The human resources department has sent you 65 new hire requests for user IDs on the network for temporary subcontractors who are being hired for a project. You attempt to move a group of user accounts to the subcontractor OU, then you attempt to create new user accounts for the subcontractors, but are unable to do either. What could be the problem? Select all that apply.

    A. The PDC emulator has failed.

    B. The infrastructure master has failed.

    C. The RID Master has failed.

    D. The Domain Naming Master has failed.

5. You have a domain controller that has a partition running out of space. Your directory services data store is located on this partition. You have the following objectives:

Primary objective: Keep the domain controller running uninterrupted.

Secondary objective: Recover as much space as possible on the domain controller without reinstalling or reconfiguring the partitions.

You perform the following actions:

    1. You take the domain controller into Directory Services Restore Mode.

    2. You run Ntdsutil and compact the database, then move the log files to a different partition.

    3. You empty the Recycle Bin, delete temporary files, and defragment the hard drive.

    A. You have achieved neither the primary nor secondary objective.

    B. You have achieved the primary objective, but not the secondary objective.

    C. You have achieved both the primary and secondary objectives.

    D. You have not achieved the primary objective but you have achieved the secondary objective.

Objective 2.5 Answers

1. **Correct Answers: B, C**

  A. Incorrect: There is no operations master role that deals with security.

  B. Correct: Many parts of group policies are replicated through FRS.

  C. Correct: The security policy was implemented as a Group Policy Object which is replicated as part of Active Directory.

  D. Incorrect: A corrupt Ntds.dit file would have symptoms that affect the domain controller, not a specific group policy.

2. **Correct Answers: A**

  A. Correct: DCDIAG, REPADMIN, and the directory service log in the Event Viewer are all used to diagnose and resolve replication errors.

  B. Incorrect: The only tool of these three that would be applicable to a RID Master failure is the directory service log in the Event Viewer.

  C. Incorrect: A disk space shortage for the SYSVOL share would result in FRS replication errors, but aside from Event Viewer, these tools would not be used to diagnose a disk space shortage.

  D. Incorrect: REPADMIN and DCDIAG are not used to diagnose corrupted log files.

3. **Correct Answers: A, C**

  A. Correct: REPLMON, or Replication Monitor, is one of the tools that can assist you in diagnosing and resolving replication problems.

  B. Incorrect: The Active Directory Domains And Trusts console will not provide information that applies to replication.

  C. Correct: The Event Viewer is used to display errors in the directory service, including those regarding replication.

  D. Incorrect: The Active Directory Users And Computers console will not provide information that applies to replication.

4. **Correct Answers: B, C**

  A. Incorrect: A PDC emulator failure would cause logon problems, but it would not affect the creation of new user accounts.

  B. Correct: The infrastructure master is used for moving objects and renaming them within the domain. If it fails, you would not be able to perform these functions.

C. **Correct:** The RID Master is used to provide security identifiers (SIDs) to new objects created within the domain. A domain controller that has run out of relative IDs (RIDs) would not be able to create new objects. It is more likely that the infrastructure master has failed, but the RID Master could also be a correct answer for this problem.

D. **Incorrect:** When the Domain Naming Master fails, you will not be able to add or make changes to the domain tree structure within the forest. It would not affect new object creation within an existing domain.

5.   Correct Answers: D

A. **Incorrect:** You did not achieve the primary objective because the domain controller was offline during the Ntdsutil process, but you did achieve the secondary objective to recover as much space as possible without reinstalling the server.

B. **Incorrect:** You did not achieve the primary objective because the domain controller was offline during the Ntdsutil process, but you did achieve the secondary objective to recover as much space as possible without reinstalling the server.

C. **Incorrect:** You did not achieve the primary objective because the domain controller was offline during the Ntdsutil process, but you did achieve the secondary objective to recover as much space as possible without reinstalling the server.

D. **Correct:** You did not achieve the primary objective because the domain controller was offline during the Ntdsutil process, but you did achieve the secondary objective to recover as much space as possible without reinstalling the server.

17 Planning and Implementing User, Computer, and Group Strategies (3.0)

In this domain, we will review the skills required for planning and implementing security strategies related to user, computer, and **group objects** within **Active Directory directory service**. Users, computers, and groups affect the way that each user interacts with the network. The strategy that you employ will establish **authentication**, institute password policies, organize user objects for administration, and apply group policies.

You might consider a network to be in the form of a target of three concentric circles. The bull's-eye consists of the backbone and key systems, including directory services, secure servers, and infrastructure equipment that interconnect all the rest of the network. This is the heart of the network and should be given the highest level of security. Unauthorized access to this level of the network can disable the entire network. The next layer of the network consists mainly of the systems that provide admission to the network and share files, printers, applications, services, and other network resources. This layer requires the next highest level of security. The outer layer of the target consists of the network systems that are actually used by end users. This is the layer that provides the initial access to the network. It is this set of systems, not to mention the **group** and user objects that you will be creating for the initial security strategy, which will either restrict or enable access to the inner layers of the network.

You have to balance the rights and **permissions** granted to users with the needs and objectives of the organization. Keep in mind that when users have more rights and permissions than necessary, the network's overall security is jeopardized. Backbone systems can be penetrated and misused. By contrast, when users have fewer rights and permissions than necessary, they will not be productive. They will either have no access to the resources that enable them to do their jobs, or they will have partial access that prevents them from completing tasks.

There are two different ways to organize user and computer objects so that you can apply security. You can use **organizational units (OUs)** to create a hierarchy that houses user, group, and computer objects, among others. You can also employ **security group** objects to categorize user objects for the purpose of assigning permissions. Both methods are useful in combination for applying security.

Tested Skills and Suggested Practices

The skills that you need to successfully master the Planning and Implementing User, Computer, and Group Strategies objective domain on *Exam 70:294: Planning, Implementing, and Maintaining a Microsoft Windows Server 2003 Active Directory Infrastructure* include:

- Plan a security group strategy

    □ Practice 1: On a domain controller, open the Active Directory Users And Computers console. Create a user named Test. Create a security group named All. Create a share named Share with a text file in it. Grant all rights to Share to the group All. Add the Test user to the All group and attempt to read the text file.

    □ Practice 2: Using the same user and security group in Practice 1, create another security group named Nothing. Deny all rights to Share for the group Nothing. With Test still a member of All, add Test as a user to Nothing. Attempt to read the text file in Share.

    □ Practice 3: Create a user named Testadmin. Attempt to log on to a domain controller. From any computer, log on as Testadmin and open Active Directory Users And Computers. Attempt to create a user object. Log on as an administrator and add Testadmin to the Domain Admins group. Log on again as Testadmin. Open Active Directory Users And Computers. Attempt to create a user object. Document your results.

- Plan a user authentication strategy

    □ Practice 1: Install two different forests. Create a forest trust between the forests. Create a user in Forest 1 named Test. On a computer in Forest 2, attempt to log on to the network as the user Test using the user principal name (UPN) form of the user's ID. Log off and attempt to log on as Test with the standard form of the user's ID.

    □ Practice 2: Install a forest of at least two domains. Create a user named Test in the root domain. Log on to a computer in the child domain with the Test account using the UPN form of the user's ID. Log off and attempt to log on as Test with the standard form of the user's ID.

    □ Practice 3: Install a forest of at least one domain. Install certification authority services. Enable and configure authentication for smart cards. Install smart card authentication equipment. Create a user named Test and attempt to log on using the smart card.

- Plan an OU structure

    ❑ Practice 1: Install a forest with two domains. Log on to the root domain and create an OU hierarchical structure of several nested OUs in the Active Directory Users And Computers console. Log off. Log on to the child domain and look at the OU hierarchy and note the differences between it and that of the root domain.

    ❑ Practice 2: Plan an OU structure for an imaginary organization with the following administrative groups: a main group with overall rights, two groups that have only local authority for different sites, a password management help desk, and a group that manages computer accounts.

    ❑ Practice 3: Plan an OU structure for an imaginary organization based on its needs to apply group policies as follows: all users except administrators should receive policy 1, a group of users in site 1 should receive policy 2, all salespersons should receive policy 3, and all manufacturing employees except manufacturing management should receive policy 4.

- Implement an OU structure

    ❑ Practice 1: Install a forest with a single root domain. Log on as a domain administrator. Open the Active Directory Users And Computers console and create a set of nested OUs. Assign a group policy to the top OU that will change the desktop wallpaper to a specific bitmap or that will otherwise create a visual indicator that the policy was applied. Create a user named Test in the bottom OU. Log on to a computer in the domain as user Test. Document whether the user received the policy.

    ❑ Practice 2: Install a forest with a single root domain. Log on as a domain administrator. Open the Active Directory Users And Computers console and create two trees of nested OUs. Create a user named Test in one OU at the bottom of the first tree of nested OUs. Apply a Group Policy to the top of the first tree. Move Test and its containing OU to the other tree of OUs. Note whether the Group Policy applies when you log on as Test.

    ❑ Practice 3: Install a forest with a single root domain. Log on as a domain administrator. Open the Active Directory Users And Computers console and create a tree of nested OUs. Create a user named Test. Delegate password management capabilities to the tree to the user named Test. Create a user object named Pwchange. Log off and log on again as user Test. Change the password of pwchange in the Active Directory Users And Computers console.

Further Reading

You will find reading materials listed in this section by objective that will assist you in mastering the skills tested on the exam.

Objective 3.1 Review Chapter 8, "Administering Groups."

Microsoft Corporation. *Introducing Microsoft Windows Server 2003*. Redmond, Washington: Microsoft Press, 2003. Review Chapter 3, "Active Directory."

Microsoft Corporation. Redmond, Washington. Review "HOW TO: Manage Groups in Windows Server 2003," available on the Microsoft Web site at *http://support .microsoft.com/default.aspx?scid=kb;en-us;816302.*

Objective 3.2 Review Chapter 7, Lesson 1, "Understanding User Accounts"; and Chapter 13, Lesson 1, "Understanding Active Directory Security."

Microsoft Corporation. *Microsoft Windows Server 2003 Deployment Kit, A Microsoft Resource Kit*. Redmond, Washington: Microsoft Press, 2003. Read *Designing and Deploying Directory and Security Services*, Chapter 3, "Designing a Site Topology." This information can also be found on the Microsoft Web site at *http://www.microsoft.com/windowsserver2003/techinfo/reskit/deploykit.mspx.*

Objective 3.3 Review Chapter 6, Lesson 1, "Understanding OUs."

Microsoft Corporation. *Microsoft Windows Server 2003 Administrator's Companion*. Redmond, Washington: Microsoft Press, 2003. Read Chapter 9, "Managing Users and Groups."

Microsoft Corporation. *Introducing Microsoft Windows Server 2003*. Redmond, Washington: Microsoft Press, 2003. Review Chapter 6, "Using Active Directory."

Microsoft Corporation. Redmond, Washington. Review white paper, "Administering Group Policy with the GPMC," available on the Microsoft Web site at *http:// www.microsoft.com/windowsserver2003/gpmc/gpmcwp.mspx.*

Objective 3.4 Review Chapter 6, Lessons 2, "Creating an OU Structure," and 3, "Administering OUs." Also see Chapter 9, Lesson 1, "Locating Active Directory Objects."

Microsoft Corporation. *Microsoft Windows Server 2003 Administrator's Pocket Consultant*. Redmond, Washington: Microsoft Press, 2003. Review Chapter 6, "Using Active Directory," and Chapter 7, "Core Active Directory Administration."

Microsoft Corporation. Redmond, Washington. Review "HOW TO: Create Organizational Units in Windows Server 2003," available on the Microsoft Web site at *http://technet2.microsoft.com/WindowsServer/en/Library/1ad2a3a3-b749-42b4-b606-fc6f1079d0271033.mspx.*

Plan a Security Group Strategy

This objective focuses on the skills of creating a security strategy for an entire forest and for each individual **domain** within the **forest** through the use of security groups. There are several types of groups that are engaged in a security strategy: **local groups**, **domain local groups**, domain **global groups**, and **universal groups**.

When you plan your groups, you need to determine what the needs are for the organization. Organize users into cohesive groups based on location, permission requirements, and administration. Note that users will likely be members of multiple groups. Then, as you apply rights, do so with a plan in mind that will reduce errors and administrative efforts. Groups and rights can be structured easily using the following system:

- Create universal groups for groups that contain members from multiple domains in more than one forest. Make global groups members of the universal groups. Use the universal groups when providing access to resources across multiple forests.

- Create domain global groups for groups that contain members from a single domain but that will be granted access to resources within other domains. Make universal groups members of domain global groups, as applicable. Make users members of domain global groups.

- Create domain local groups for groups that contain members from a single domain whether or not they will be granted access to resources within other domains. Make domain global groups members of the appropriate domain local groups. Grant domain-wide rights to domain local groups.

- Create local groups on **member servers** and computers. Make domain local groups members of local groups. Grant local rights to local groups.

Objective 3.1 Questions

1. You are the network administrator for Fabrikam, Inc. You have three domains in the forest: *sales.root.fabrikam.com*, *root.fabrikam.com*, and *growth.root.fabrikam.com*. You have users who are members of each domain and all users require access to resources on *dc01.root.fabrikam.com*. You have two domain controllers in *root.fabrikam.com* called DC01 and DC02. What do you do to provide the correct access to the resources?

    A. Create a local group on *dc01.root.fabrikam.com*. Create a global group in *root.fabrikam.com*. Add users to the global group. Grant rights to the global group.

    B. Create a domain local group in *sales.root.fabrikam.com*. Grant the domain local group rights to the resources on *dc01.root.fabrikam.com*. Place users in the domain local group.

    C. Create a domain local group in *growth.root.fabrikam.com*. Create a domain local group in *root.fabrikam.com*. Create a global group in *root.fabrikam.com*. Create a universal group. Add all users to the universal group. Grant access to resources to the universal group.

    D. Create a global group in each domain: *root.fabrikam.com*, *sales.root.fabrikam.com*, and *growth.root.fabrikam.com*. Place the users from each domain into the global group in the users' respective domains. Create a domain local group in *root.fabrikam.com*. Make the three global groups members of the domain local group. Grant rights to the domain local group.

2. You are the administrator of a domain in Contoso, Ltd. The sales team and the marketing team managers need access to an application. John, Mark, and Jane will need to manage passwords for users in the entire network. George will need to manage all the users in the Phoenix location. You have the following objectives:

Primary objective: Make certain that the sales team and marketing team managers can access the application.

Secondary objective: Ensure that there is a group for managing passwords for all users in the network.

Secondary objective: Ensure that if George goes on vacation or has an illness, you can easily grant the Phoenix user account management rights to another user account.

You perform the following actions:

1. You create a global group called GL-APP and add the sales team and managers of the marketing team as members.

2. You create a domain local group called LOC-APP, grant it rights to the application, and add the GL-APP group as a member.

3. You grant George the rights for managing all the users in the Phoenix location.

After performing these actions, you have achieved which of the following?

A. You have achieved neither the primary objective nor the secondary objectives.

B. You have achieved the primary objective, but not the secondary objectives.

C. You have achieved the primary objective and both of the secondary objectives.

D. You have not achieved the primary objective but you have achieved the secondary objectives.

3. You are the administrator of Litware, Inc.'s network. You have a single domain, *litwareinc.com*, and three sites—Boston, New York, and Atlanta. Janice in Atlanta will be taking on some administrative duties for that location. You do not want Janice to be able to manage users in the Boston and New York locations. You want to make certain that you can quickly grant Janice's rights to other users, or remove Janice's rights, if you ever need to. Which of the following actions will achieve your goal?

A. Create a domain global group called Global Atlanta. Make Janice a member of Global Atlanta. Create a domain local group called Local Atlanta. Make Global Atlanta a member of Local Atlanta. Delegate the rights to manage users in the Atlanta location to Local Atlanta.

B. Make Janice a member of the Administrators group.

C. Create a domain local group called Local Atlanta. Make Janice a member of Local Atlanta. Create a domain global group called Global Atlanta. Make Local Atlanta a member of Global Atlanta. Delegate the rights to manage users in the Atlanta location to Global Atlanta.

D. Make Janice a member of the Domain Admins group.

4. You have upgraded your three Windows NT 4 domains, SALES, MKT, and SVC, to Windows Server 2003. You have also restructured the three domains into a dedicated root domain and a child domain with users and groups. The former domain administrators are now going to be reorganized. The former SALES domain administrators will be granted full administrative rights to everything in the domain, including domain controllers. The former MKT domain administrators will be granted the rights to manage all user accounts, groups, and computer accounts. Half of the former SVC domain administrators will become regular users because they had accidentally been granted domain administrator rights in the SVC domain. The remaining former SVC domain administrators will be granted the rights to manage all user, group, and computer accounts. Which of the following groups can be used in this security group strategy? (Choose all that apply.)

   A. Domain Admins

   B. Account Operators

   C. Backup Operators

   D. Print Operators

5. Litware, Inc. has an Active Directory forest consisting of four domains in the same namespace tree. The root domain is named *litwareinc.com*. The forest is running at the Windows Server 2003 forest functional level. Each domain includes at least one user who provides deskside support. You have already created a domain global group called Deskside Support in each domain. In the *litwareinc.com* domain, you have created an OU called PCs containing the root domain's computer accounts. Each user in the Deskside Support group should be given the rights to manage the PCs OU. What should you do?

   A. Create a universal group called Deskside PCs. Assign the rights to manage the PCs OU to the universal group. Place the root domain Deskside Support global group in the Deskside PCs universal group.

   B. Create a domain global group called Deskside PCs. Create a universal group called Universal PCs. Place the Deskside PCs group within the Universal PCs group. Assign rights to the Universal PCs group.

   C. Create a domain local group called Deskside PCs. Add the Deskside Support global groups from each domain as members. Assign Deskside PCs the rights to manage the PCs OU.

   D. Create a domain local group named Deskside PCs in the root domain. Make this group a member of each Deskside Support global group. Assign the Deskside Support group rights to manage the PCs OU.

6.   Fabrikam, Inc. has a network with two forests: *fabrikam.com* is the production forest, and *fabrikam.local* is the lab forest. There is a forest trust between the two forests. Users in two domains within the lab forest require the ability to access resources in several domains within the production forest. What type of group should you use in the *fabrikam.local* forest?

   A. A local group

   B. A domain local group

   C. A domain global group

   D. A universal group

7.   At Contoso, Ltd., the security unit is rolling out a new application called AppSec. The security unit members are all located in the *contoso.com* domain, but new members might be added to other domains in the future. Only security unit members should be granted access to AppSec. You want to easily grant new members of the security team access to the application and remove access when security team members leave the organization. Which of the following actions should you take? Select two.

   A. Individually assign each user access rights to the application.

   B. Create a domain local group and grant the domain local group access rights to the AppSec application.

   C. Create a domain global group and populate the domain global group with users. Make the domain global group a member of a domain local group.

   D. Create a local group on a server holding the AppSec application and populate it with users.

Objective 3.1 Answers

1. **Correct Answers: D**

    A. Incorrect: Optimally, you will grant rights to a domain local group or local group. Since the resources are on a domain controller, you should use a domain local group. Rights should be granted to domain local groups or local groups.

    B. Incorrect: Domain local groups cannot be granted rights to resources outside the local domain.

    C. Incorrect: You should grant rights to a domain local group or local group. You do not need to use a universal group.

    D. Correct: This process will provide the users the rights and make it easy to manage the rights in the future.

2. **Correct Answers: B**

    A. Incorrect: You were able to achieve the primary objective in granting the sales team and marketing team managers rights to access the application. You did not achieve either of the secondary objectives for creating a password management group or ensuring that it is easy to replace George if he is away from the office. In order to achieve the secondary objective in which you create a group for managing passwords, you need to create another domain local and another global group (as a member of the domain local group) then place the password managers into the global group. The domain local group would then be provided the rights to manage passwords. The other secondary objective in which George can be easily replaced should be done through the creation of a domain local group, which is granted the rights to manage users in Phoenix, and a global group, which is the member of the domain local group, and George would be made a member of the global group. If you needed to replace George or reproduce George's rights, you would simply add another user to his group.

    B. Correct: You were able to achieve the primary objective in granting the sales team and marketing team managers rights to access the application. You did not achieve either of the secondary objectives for creating a password management group or ensuring that it is easy to replace George if he is away from the office. In order to achieve the secondary objective in which you create a group for managing passwords, you need to create another domain local and another global group (as a member of the domain local group) then place the password managers into the global group. The domain local group would then be provided the rights to manage passwords. The other secondary objective in which George can be easily replaced should be done through the creation of a domain local group, which is granted the rights to manage users in Phoenix, and a global group which is the member of the domain local group, and George, would be made a member of the global group. If you needed to replace George or reproduce George's rights, you would simply add another user to his group.

C. **Incorrect:** You were able to achieve the primary objective in granting the sales team and marketing team managers rights to access the application. You did not achieve either of the secondary objectives for creating a password management group or ensuring that it is easy to replace George if he is away from the office. In order to achieve the secondary objective in which you create a group for managing passwords, you need to create another domain local and another global group (as a member of the domain local group) then place the password managers into the global group. The domain local group would then be provided the rights to manage passwords. The other secondary objective in which George can be easily replaced should be done through the creation of a domain local group, which is granted the rights to manage users in Phoenix, and a global group which is the member of the domain local group, and George, would be made a member of the global group. If you needed to replace George or reproduce George's rights, you would simply add another user to his group.

D. **Incorrect:** You were able to achieve the primary objective in granting the sales team and marketing team managers rights to access the application. You did not achieve either of the secondary objectives for creating a password management group or ensuring that it is easy to replace George if he is away from the office. In order to achieve the secondary objective in which you create a group for managing passwords, you need to create another domain local and another global group (as a member of the domain local group) then place the password managers into the global group. The domain local group would then be provided the rights to manage passwords. The other secondary objective in which George can be easily replaced should be done through the creation of a domain local group, which is granted the rights to manage users in Phoenix, and a global group which is the member of the domain local group, and George, would be made a member of the global group. If you needed to replace George or reproduce George's rights, you would simply add another user to his group.

3.   Correct Answers: A

A. Correct: By creating this set of groups, you will be able to quickly grant Janice's rights to another user, simply by making the other user a member of Global Atlanta. You can also remove Janice's rights by deleting her user account from the membership of the Global Atlanta group.

B. Incorrect: The Administrators group is a domain local group. Users should normally be placed within domain global groups. The Administrators group will have access to manage users in the Boston and New York locations.

C. Incorrect: The use of global and local groups is backward in this example. Local groups cannot be made members of global groups.

D. Incorrect: If Janice is made a member of Domain Admins, she will be granted too many rights and will be able to manage the users in the Boston and New York locations.

4.   Correct Answers: A, B

A. Correct: The SALES domain administrators will become members of the Domain Admins group.

B. Correct: The former MKT domain administrators, along with half of the former SVC domain administrators, will become members of the Account Operators group, which will grant them the rights to manage user, group, and computer accounts.

C. Incorrect: None of the former domain administrators will require specific backup rights. As members of the Domain Admins group, the former SALES domain administrators will continue to have the rights to back up the domain controllers in addition to manage the rest of the domain.

D. Incorrect: None of the former domain administrators will require specific print operator rights. As members of the Domain Admins group, the former SALES domain administrators will also have the rights to manage any printers shared within the domain.

5.   Correct Answers: C

A. Incorrect: This will only allow the root domain Deskside Support persons the ability to manage the PCs OU. Because all members will be granted access to resources that are in a single domain, you should use a domain local group to assign rights to.

B. Incorrect: You never placed users in a group, so no one would have rights to manage the PCs.

C. Correct: This method takes advantage of the existing global groups, uses a domain local group, and ensures that the users have the appropriate rights.

D. Incorrect: A global group cannot contain a domain local group.

6.   Correct Answers: D

A. Incorrect: A local group will not be able to be used in the other forest. Local groups can only be used within a single computer.

B. Incorrect: A domain local group will not be able to be used in the other forest. Domain local groups can only be used within a single domain.

C. Incorrect: A domain global group is preferable for use within a single forest, not two forests.

D. Correct: A universal group can contain users from multiple domains and be granted access to resources within multiple domains.

7.   Correct Answers: B, C

A. Incorrect: Individually assigning rights to the application will be lengthy and require more administration for security team member changes.

B. Correct: This will create the structure that grants rights to the application. You must also populate the domain local group.

C. Correct: This will populate the domain local group and allow access to the application.

D. Incorrect: There is not enough information to state if the application is located on a single server or on multiple servers. Therefore, you should assume that the application has a wider scope, which would require a domain local group rather than a local group for rights assignment.

Objective 3.2

Plan a User Authentication Strategy

This objective discusses how to plan authentication for users within the network. **Authentication** is the process of ensuring the identity of a person or other entity and applies to **smart cards** and password management. User and computer objects in Active Directory correspond to users and computers that interact with the network. Since groups are granted rights that apply to other objects, they are classified along with user and computer objects as **security principals**. A security principal within the Active Directory domain is given a **security identifier (SID)** at its creation so that its identity can be authenticated.

When you plan your user authentication strategy, you need to consider the organization's requirements. For example, users should have individual accounts and passwords in order to maintain security. After a user is authenticated, the user should be able to access resources and administer other resources according to its rights and permissions either assigned individually or received through group memberships.

When you no longer need a user account, a best practice is to disable the account for a period of time, such as for six months. If the account is not needed within that period of time, then you can delete it. This practice will ensure that you will not need to perform an authoritative restore of old objects in case another user requires the same authority.

Smart card authentication uses **certificates** during logon to authenticate the credentials of the person logging on to the network. During the smart card authentication process, a certificate (which includes a digital signature from a **certification authority**, or **CA**) is presented to the server and the server responds with its own certificate. Each computer (the local workstation and the server) can then trust the other. A smart card stores the certificate.

Objective 3.2 Questions

1. You are the network administrator for Contoso, Ltd. You have three locations: New Orleans, Houston, and Toronto, with users from two different domains: *contoso.com* and *finance.contoso.com*, spanning them. Each location is configured as a separate site. You want to deploy smart cards to the Toronto location, but do not want to deploy smart cards to either New Orleans or Houston. Which actions should you take?

    A. Create two OUs and apply the policy to the OUs.

    B. Apply one policy to *contoso.com* and the other to *finance.contoso.com*.

    C. Apply a policy to a local group.

    D. Apply a policy for smart card authentication to the Toronto site.

2. Litware, Inc. has had several network attacks where a hacker was able to log on to the network and access resources. You have been hired as a consultant to help Litware prevent future attacks. When you review the current network policy, you see that all users are required to change their passwords every 10 days, with a minimum password length of six characters. There are no other policies. Which of the following will best verify a user's identity at logon?

    A. Require smart card authentication at logon.

    B. Create a maximum password age of five days.

    C. Create a minimum password age of 20 days.

    D. Apply a minimum password length of five characters.

3. You have a user who insists on using the same password every time he changes his password on the network. You require users to change passwords once every 90 days. When you enforce password history for five passwords, the user immediately changes his password five times and then changes it back to the original password. How can you make certain that the user uses unique passwords?

    A. Establish a maximum password age of 30 days.

    B. Establish a minimum password age of 30 days.

    C. Establish a minimum password length of seven characters.

    D. Establish an Account Lockout policy.

4. You are installing smart cards for users in a domain. You install a certificate authority and create smart cards for all users. You distribute the cards to users and install equipment. However, you discover that users are able to log on without the smart cards. What can you do?

   A. Create another smart card enrollment station.

   B. Establish an Account Lockout policy.

   C. Select the option in the user account for Smart Card Is Required For Interactive Logon.

   D. Create a universal group and add all smart card users to it.

5. Fabrikam, Inc. has a network with a single Active Directory forest consisting of two domains. In the root domain, the administrator has installed a new application for the Accounting group. This application integrates with Active Directory in order to ensure that only authenticated users are able to use the application. The application uses a special user account to log on to Active Directory. Both domains have a password policy that enforces a maximum password age of 60 days, enforces complexity requirements, and requires a minimum password length of seven characters. Which of the following options should be applied to this application's user account?

   A. A Minimum Password Age of 10 days

   B. Do Not Require Kerberos Preauthentication

   C. Password Never Expires

   D. User Cannot Change Password

6.   Contoso Pharmaceuticals has several pharmacies, a warehouse, and a research facility. There is a single domain, *contoso.com*, in the forest. You have the following objectives:

Primary objective: Ensure that all users in the Research facility have strong passwords.

Secondary objective: Create user accounts to be used by kiosks in the pharmacies that will not be able to have their passwords changed by anyone but administrators.

You take the following actions:

1. You apply a password policy to the domain which includes the OU created to contain all users at the Research facility. The policy enforces complexity requirements, has a maximum password age of 30 days and a minimum password age of three days, and requires a password history of six passwords.

2. You create a user account that will be used by all kiosks. You select the options for Password Never Expires and User Cannot Change Password on the user account.

3. You place the kiosk user account in an OU that can be managed only by members of the Domain Admins group.

After performing these actions, you have achieved which of the following?

A. You have achieved neither the primary nor the secondary objectives.

B. You have achieved the primary objective but not the secondary objective.

C. You have achieved the secondary objective but not the primary objective.

D. You have achieved both the primary and the secondary objectives.

Objective 3.2 Answers

1.   Correct Answers: D

A. Incorrect: Because there are two different domains, you would have to configure the OU structure to match the site structure within the domains, and then apply Group Policy to it. Given that this may not equate to the administrative or other requirements for the organization, this is not the appropriate action to take.

B. Incorrect: The policies would affect users from outside the Toronto location, requiring them to use smart card authentication when they don't need to.

C. Incorrect: You cannot apply a policy to a local group.

D. Correct: By applying the policy to the Toronto site, users will receive the correct smart card authentication policy regardless of the domain to which they belong.

2.   Correct Answers: A

A. Correct: Smart card authentication will require that the hacker has a smart card in addition to a user's password in order to log on.

B. Incorrect: The current maximum password age is 10 days, which is at the point of being difficult to manage for users. You would not get much value from changing the maximum password age to five days.

C. Incorrect: Making the minimum password age longer than the maximum password age will not allow users to change passwords on time.

D. Incorrect: This minimum password length is shorter than the minimum password length previously created, so it will not add much.

3.   Correct Answers: B

A. Incorrect: The user would still be able to change his password back to the original one because this will require users to change passwords only every 30 days instead of every 90 days.

B. Correct: This policy will make the user use the new password for at least 30 days before he can change the password again.

C. Incorrect: If the user is using a password that contains fewer than seven characters, this would make the user change to a new password, but only one time. The user could easily repeat the same process with a new password.

D. Incorrect: The Account Lockout policy will only lock out users who use the wrong password, and the user would still be able to change passwords back to the original password.

4. Correct Answers: C

A. Incorrect: This will only duplicate the work that you've done so far. An enrollment station will only allow you to set up a new smart card, but not to force its use.

B. Incorrect: An Account Lockout policy is not required for smart card usage.

C. Correct: This will require a user to use the smart card to log on to the network. Without selecting this option, the user will be able to log on without a smart card.

D. Incorrect: There is no need, in this situation, to create a universal group for smart card users.

5. Correct Answers: C

A. Incorrect: You cannot assign a special policy such as Minimum Password Ages to a user account.

B. Incorrect: Since the application integrates with Active Directory, it probably uses the same version of Kerberos. There is no need in this case to select this option.

C. Correct: As long as you select a password with sufficient length and complexity, you should make certain the password does not expire so that the application can continue to use the user account without interruption.

D. Incorrect: This option will not prevent the Maximum Password Age policy from interrupting the application. However, this might be an additional option to select to ensure that the user account doesn't change the password.

6. Correct Answers: D

A. Incorrect: You have achieved both the primary and the secondary objectives, because the users at the Research facility (along with all the other users in the domain) will be given a stronger password policy, and the kiosks will use a single user account that can be managed only by Domain Admins.

B. Incorrect: You have achieved both the primary and the secondary objectives, because the users at the Research facility (along with all the other users in the domain) will be given a stronger password policy, and the kiosks will use a single user account that can be managed only by Domain Admins.

C. Incorrect: You have achieved both the primary and the secondary objectives, because the users at the Research facility (along with all the other users in the domain) will be given a stronger password policy, and the kiosks will use a single user account that can be managed only by Domain Admins.

D. Correct: You have achieved both the primary and the secondary objectives, because the users at the Research facility (along with all the other users in the domain) will be given a stronger password policy, and the kiosks will use a single user account that can be managed only by Domain Admins.

Plan an OU Structure

This objective looks at the skills required to plan a hierarchy of OUs. OUs are **container objects** within a domain that help organize objects into a **tree** structure. Their structure can be used to enable administrative functions, such as delegating administration, applying **Group Policy**, and assigning rights.

OUs are often used as a method of providing administrative sections when restructuring multiple domains into a single domain. A domain can be scaled to a much larger size and remain functional for the organization through the use of OUs. By using separate OUs for each administrative unit, administrators can share a single domain yet have separate administrative areas. The use of OUs for delegating administration is even more complex in that you can delegate certain responsibilities and deny others. For example, you can delegate computer management and deny the rights to manage domain controllers. You can also delegate the ability to create user objects, but not to manage computer accounts. Using administrative delegation is more secure than adding users to administrative groups that may have more rights and capabilities than those users might need for their job. The tasks that are delegated should meet the needs of the organization.

OUs can contain any other type of object, including user objects, computer objects, and groups. The OUs can only contain objects within their own domain. For Group Policy, an OU is the smallest scope to which a Group Policy can be applied. Group Policy settings are stored in **Group Policy Objects (GPOs)**. The objects are then applied to a **site**, a **domain**, or an **OU**. The way that group policies are applied is in a layered fashion, as follows:

1. The local Group Policy is processed first.

2. The site Group Policy is processed second.

3. The domain Group Policy is processed third.

4. The top OU Group Policy is processed fourth, followed by group policies attached to **nested OUs** in the order following down the OU hierarchy.

The last Group Policy applied has precedence over any earlier group policies. For example, if a Group Policy for the domain is applied that establishes a password minimum age of 10 days, and another Group Policy for an OU is applied establishing a minimum password age of 6 days, then the minimum password age will be 6 days. However, in the case where a Group Policy for the domain establishes a minimum password age of 10 days and a Group Policy for the OU is applied establishing complexity requirements for passwords, the minimum password age will still be 10 days. This inheritance can be blocked so that an upper policy does not reach a lower OU. The inheritance can be enforced so that an upper policy always overrides a lower OU's policy. Using blocked inheritance and enforced overrides can cause confusing results, so it is best to plan your OU structure to optimize Group Policy inheritance.

Group policies have an extensive set of abilities. Group policies can be used to customize the interface that users see, such as redirecting their My Documents folder to the network so that it is then accessible from any computer regardless of where the user logs on in the network. You can deliver applications to computers and users, automatically installing the application when users log on. You can establish scripts at logon or logoff for users, and at startup and shutdown for computers. You can also establish security settings for users and computers through group policies.

1. You are the network administrator for Litware, Inc. The Active Directory forest contains two domains: *litwareinc.com* and *prod.litwareinc.com*, and three sites in Phoenix, Los Angeles, and Seattle, of which Seattle is the company's headquarters. The organization requires an application to be delivered to all users in the forest. Which of the following will achieve this goal?

    A. Create a single Group Policy and apply it to the Seattle site.

    B. Create two GPOs and apply them to the two top-level OUs in the *prod.litwareinc.com* domain.

    C. Create a single GPO and apply it to the root domain.

    D. Create two GPOs and apply them to each domain: *litwareinc.com* and *prod.litwareinc.com*.

2. You are a network administrator of the *fabrikam.com* domain. You have an OU named Sales. All the sales team members are within the Sales OU. You are deploying an application to the Sales team. You create a GPO named App and apply it to the Sales OU. You discover that none of the sales team members have had App installed on their computers. How do you fix the problem?

    A. Create a group for the Sales team, add the team as members, and apply the rights to Read and to Apply GPOs.

    B. Apply the Group Policy to the *fabrikam.com* domain.

    C. Block policy inheritance from the Sales OU.

    D. Enforce policy inheritance for the Sales OU.

3. You are upgrading two Windows NT domains to Windows Server 2003. In your Active Directory forest, you will have a single domain. In the Windows NT domains, several users were granted administrative rights because they managed a small set of users. You have the following objectives in your restructuring:

Primary objective: Allow the former administrators to have control over the same users and computers.

Secondary objective: Limit the domain administration to three people.

Secondary objective: Delegate administration of the Accounting team to an Accounting team member.

You create an OU structure with the top OU named All Users And Computers. Within this OU there are two OUs named Dom1 and Dom2 containing the accounts from the former two domains, respectively. Within Dom1, you create three OUs named Accounting, Finance, and Sales. Within Dom2, you create two OUs named Production and Warehouse.

You place three administrators within the Domain Admins group.

After performing these actions, you have achieved which of the following?

A. You have achieved neither the primary objective nor the secondary objectives.

B. You have achieved the primary objective but neither of the secondary objectives.

C. You have achieved one of the secondary objectives but not the primary objective.

D. You have achieved the primary objective and both of the secondary objectives.

4. You are the administrator of a Windows Server 2003 Active Directory forest. Users in an OU named Maintenance need to have drive letter O mapped to a server share in order for their application to run. You want to use a logon script named Maint.cmd, which includes the NET USE command to map the drive letter O. You do not want any other users to have this drive mapping. What should you do?

A. Copy Maint.cmd to SYSVOL on a domain controller. Force replication.

B. Create a Group Policy that enforces Maint.cmd at the user's logon. Assign the policy to the Maintenance OU.

C. Create a Group Policy that enforces Maint.cmd at the computer's startup. Assign the policy to the Maintenance OU.

D. Copy Maint.cmd to each computer belonging to a Maintenance user.

5. You are the administrator of a Windows 2003 domain named *fabrikam.com*. Your domain contains an OU named All Users. Within this OU, you have three OUs named Sales, Service, and Shipping. Members of the IT group need to be able to create and edit group policies that apply to the Service OU. The IT group are all members of the domain global group named IT. What should you do? (Select two.)

A. Grant the IT group Apply Group Policy permission for the Service OU.

B. Create a new group named GPO Admins and make the IT group a member.

C. Assign the IT group the ability to Read and Write the existing GPO in the Sales OU.

D. Using the Delegation Of Control Wizard, delegate the IT group the predefined task for managing Group Policy links for the Service OU.

6. You are the administrator of a Windows 2003 domain. You have two OUs, North and South, in the domain. Jan is the North administrator, and Greg is the South administrator. Both Jan and Greg need to be able to create, edit, and delete user accounts. However, you want to make certain that Jan and Greg cannot create users in each other's OU. What do you do?

A. Make both Jan and Greg members of the Account Operators group.

B. Delegate control of the North OU to Jan and delegate control of the South OU to Greg, making certain to enable only the rights needed to create, edit, and delete user accounts.

C. Delegate control of the South OU to Jan and delegate control of the North OU to Greg, making certain to enable only the rights needed to create, edit, and delete user accounts.

D. Delegate the password administration predefined task to Jan for the North OU and to Greg for the South OU.

Objective 3.3 Answers

1.   Correct Answers: D

   A. Incorrect: This will deploy the application to computers in the Seattle site, but will not deploy it to computers in the Phoenix and Los Angeles sites. In order to reach all users in the forest, you must apply the policy to each domain, or to each site.

   B. Incorrect: This will deploy the application to the *prod.litwareinc.com* computers whose users are located within those two OU hierarchies, but will not apply it to users in other OUs or to the *litwareinc.com* domain. A GPO will only apply to the users within the OU where it is applied; any users outside that OU will not be affected.

   C. Incorrect: This will deploy the application to computers in the root domain, *litwareinc.com*. A GPO will only apply to a single domain at a time, unless they are site attached, in which case the group policy is pulled from the domain where it was created but applied to users from any domain in that site.

   D. Correct: This will deploy the application to computers in the entire forest. When you apply a group policy to all users across a forest, the simplest method is to create a GPO within each domain and apply it at the domain level.

2.   Correct Answers: A

   A. Correct: Users must have the rights to Read GPOs and to Apply them in order for the policies to be applied.

   B. Incorrect: The Group Policy was applied to the OU that contained the users, which means that it was the last policy applied and took precedence over others. There is another problem preventing the policy from being applied to the users in the Sales OU, because users must have rights to read and apply GPOs before they can be applied.

   C. Incorrect: Because the Group Policy was applied to the Sales OU, it takes precedence over all other policies. There is another problem preventing users from receiving the GPO, because users must have rights to read and apply GPOs before they can be applied.

   D. Incorrect: The policy is being applied directly to the Sales OU, so enforcing inheritance will not ensure its application.

3.   **Correct Answers: C**

A. Incorrect: You have not achieved the primary objective because, while you created the OU structure, you did not delegate administration. You achieved one of the secondary objectives because you did place three people within the Domain Admins group. But you did not achieve the other secondary objective because you did not delegate administration of the Accounting OU.

B. Incorrect: You have not achieved the primary objective because, while you created the OU structure, you did not delegate administration. You achieved one of the secondary objectives because you did place three people within the Domain Admins group. But you did not achieve the other secondary objective because you did not delegate administration of the Accounting OU.

C. Correct: You have not achieved the primary objective because, while you created the OU structure, you did not delegate administration. You achieved one of the secondary objectives because you did place three people within the Domain Admins group. But you did not achieve the other secondary objective because you did not delegate administration of the Accounting OU.

D. Incorrect: You have not achieved the primary objective because, while you created the OU structure, you did not delegate administration. You achieved one of the secondary objectives because you did place three people within the Domain Admins group. But you did not achieve the other secondary objective because you did not delegate administration of the Accounting OU.

4.   **Correct Answers: B**

A. Incorrect: This will copy the command to a public area on the domain controllers, which would enable any user to implement the script and attempt the drive mapping.

B. Correct: GPOs can be used to implement custom logon scripts using this method.

C. Incorrect: For any computers in the Maintenance OU, this would execute the script prior to the user logging on to the machine, which would mean that other people would have the opportunity to receive the drive mapping.

D. Incorrect: Copying the command to the computer may make the command available to users who log on to the computer but who do not belong to the Maintenance OU.

5.   **Correct Answers: A, D**

    A. Correct: This will grant the IT group the ability to create and edit group policies in the Service OU but not any other OUs.

    B. Incorrect: New groups do not have any inherent rights, so this step will not assist the IT group in achieving the rights to create and edit group policies.

    C. Incorrect: This will not allow the IT group the ability to create a new GPO, nor is this the correct OU.

    D. Correct: This process will grant the IT group the ability to create and edit group policies in the Service OU.

6.   **Correct Answers: B**

    A. Incorrect: The Account Operators group has permissions to create, edit, and delete accounts throughout the entire domain.

    B. Correct: This will ensure that Jan and Greg have the correct permissions for the correct OUs.

    C. Incorrect: This answer has switched the OUs. Neither Jan nor Greg would be able to manage the correct OU.

    D. Incorrect: The predefined task for password management will not allow Greg or Jan to create, edit, or delete user accounts.

Implement an OU Structure

This objective covers the skills required for implementing an **OU** structure and establishes the basis for ongoing administration of OUs within a **domain**. Implementation of an OU structure requires first that the administrator has the correct permissions to create new OUs. Members of the Domain Admins and Enterprise Admins groups have the authority to create new OUs in a domain. Otherwise, users must be delegated the appropriate permissions to create OUs, either with the domain itself or within a subsection of the OU structure.

The creation of the OU structure is done within the **Active Directory Users And Computers** console. Within this **console**, you navigate the domain tree within the left pane until you reach the container (whether an OU or the domain **node**) within which you wish to place a new OU. Then right-click the container, select New from the subtopic menu, and select Organizational Unit. Type in the name of the OU.

You may use the DSADD command line to create a new object within an Active Directory domain, including a new OU. You simply open a command prompt and type **dsadd ou OU=newOUname,OU=parentOU,DC=domain,DC=com**. This will add an OU named "newOUname" in the "parentOU" of the *domain.com* domain.

When you delegate control of an OU, you can do so from within the Active Directory Users And Computers console. In this console, navigate to the OU in the left pane. Right-click the OU and select Delegate Control from the subtopic menu. This will initiate the **Delegation Of Control Wizard**, which will then walk you through the process of delegating control.

A network is never a static entity. Users might move to new locations, move to a new job within the company, or leave the company altogether. Computers, likewise, are moved, upgraded, and retired on a regular basis. Finally, an enterprise may undergo a reorganization, which can have an impact on how users and computers are organized within an Active Directory forest. To manage these changes, you can use the Active Directory Users And Computers console. Navigate in the left pane to the OU containing the object (whether it is another OU, a group, a user, or a computer) and select that OU. In the **details pane**, right-click the object and select Move from the subtopic menu. Click the destination for the object. Alternatively, you can drag and drop the object to the correct destination.

Objective 3.4 Questions

1.   You have just upgraded a Windows NT 4 domain to Windows Server 2003. You are a member of the Domain Admins group. Your new domain is the root domain of the forest. All of your users are now in a single container. You want to move the users to a new tree structure with the top OU named All, with the All OU containing two OUs named Computers and Users, and within the Users OU, you want five OUs named Accounting, Service, Finance, Maintenance, and Sales. What should you do first?

    A. Delegate rights to your user account to create new objects in the domain.

    B. Right-click a user object and select Move in the Active Directory Users And Computers console.

    C. Use the Active Directory Sites And Services console to create the Computers and Users OUs within the domain node.

    D. Use the Active Directory Users And Computers console to create the All OU within the domain node.

2.   In *litwareinc.com*, there is an OU structure as follows: There are two top-level OUs, one named Users and the other named Computers. Within the Users OU, there is an OU named Groups and a second OU named Exec. Within the Exec OU, there are four OUs named Mgmt, Prod, Svc, and Mkt. You want to move a printer that is shared by a domain controller from the Mgmt OU to the Svc OU. Which group do you need to be a member of in order to accomplish this task?

    A. Backup Operators

    B. Print Operators

    C. Domain Admins

    D. Server Operators

3.   You are an administrator for Contoso, Ltd. In the *jobs.contoso.com* domain, Marc is changing jobs and becoming the manager for the Eastern Division of the company. Marc is currently a member of the Production crew and is in the Prod OU. The Prod OU is in the Western Division OU, which is in the All OU, which is just below the domain node. Also within the All OU is the Eastern Division OU, which contains the Mgmt OU and the Sales OU. You have two objectives:

Primary objective: Move Marc's object to the Mgmt OU.

Secondary objective: Allow Marc to manage user and computer accounts for everyone in the Sales OU of the Eastern Division but not for the Mgmt OU.

You perform the following actions:

1. You move Marc's object to OU=Mgmt,OU=Eastern Division,OU=All,DC=jobs, DC=contoso,DC=com.

2. You delegate control of the Sales OU to Marc.

After performing these actions, you have achieved which of the following?

A. You have achieved both the primary and the secondary objectives.

B. You have achieved the primary objective but not the secondary objective.

C. You have achieved the secondary objective but not the primary objective.

D. You have achieved neither the primary nor the secondary objectives.

4.   You have just been informed by management that the company is being reorganized. Several users will be changing jobs and receiving new titles and different permissions for files and network resources. Administrators in your site are being split into three groups. One group will manage all users. One group will manage all computers. One group will manage the entire domain. Three users will be given administrative access to manage users in their groups, which are Sales, Marketing, and Production. What OU structure should you create?

A. A top-level OU that contains all objects, followed by two OUs for Computers and Users. Within the Users OU, three OUs for Sales, Marketing, and Production.

B. Two top-level OUs for Computers and Users. Within the Computers OU, three OUs for Sales, Marketing, and Production.

C. Three top-level OUs for Sales, Marketing, and Production. Within the Production OU, an OU for Computers and an OU for Printers.

D. One OU for Users and another OU for Computers, both within the domain node.

5. You work for a wine merchant as a network administrator. Your company has recently purchased a new vineyard in Italy. The vineyard has an existing Active Directory forest, consisting of a single domain. There is now a trust relationship between the two forests. A manager is making a temporary move to Italy to begin integrating the vineyard's operations. The manager is in the Operations OU within the All Users OU of your domain. The new vineyard's domain has three OUs: Admins, Users, and Computers. To which OU should you move the manager's account?

    A. Admins in the vineyard's forest.

    B. Stay in the Operations OU in your forest.

    C. All Users OU of your forest.

    D. Users OU of the vineyard's forest.

6. You are the manager of A. Datum Corporation's Active Directory forest. You have a single domain in the forest called *adatum.com*. Within *adatum.com*, you have the following OU structure: All OU contains Europe OU, North America OU, and Pacrim OU. Europe OU contains Germany OU and France OU. France OU contains Production OU. North America OU contains Executive OU, Management OU, Sales OU, and Service OU. The Pacrim OU is empty. You have hired three assistants to manage user and computer accounts and to provide user assistance. Jack is located in Germany. Jill is located in Toronto, Canada. Phil is located in New York. You want Jack to manage all of the European users' issues. You want Jill to handle all Executive requests and to be prepared to manage accounts for a new office being built in Sydney, Australia. You want Phil to be able to manage user and computer accounts anywhere in the *adatum.com* domain, especially in North America since he lives there. Phil should be able to continue managing all user and computer accounts even as the OU structure changes over time. What group should you add Phil to, or should you delegate control to an OU?

    A. Backup Operators.

    B. Delegate control for user account management to the North America OU.

    C. Delegate control for user and computer account management to the All OU.

    D. Account Operators.

Objective 3.4 Answers

1.   Correct Answers: D

   A. Incorrect: As a member of the Domain Admins group, you already have the rights required.

   B. Incorrect: You cannot move the users until after you create the OU structure.

   C. Incorrect: This option uses the wrong console and creates the nested OUs before the top OU, which cannot be done.

   D. Correct: This is the first step. You will then create the rest of the OUs in the structure described. Then you would move the users to their appropriate destination OUs.

2.   Correct Answers: C

   A. Incorrect: Members of the Backup Operators group do not have the rights to manage objects within the domain.

   B. Incorrect: A member of the Print Operators group would be able to manage the printer but unable to move the printer object around the OU tree structure.

   C. Correct: You must be a member of either the Domain Admins group or the Enterprise Admins group to move objects, unless you have been delegated the appropriate permissions to do so.

   D. Incorrect: Members of the Server Operators group do not have permission to move objects within the domain.

3.   Correct Answers: A

   A. Correct: You achieved the primary objective because the OU you moved Marc to is correctly named using X.500 naming. You achieved the secondary objective because Marc will be able to manage all the Sales OU. Because the Sales OU is at the same level as the Mgmt OU, there is no concern that Marc will be able to inherit permissions for the Mgmt OU.

   B. Incorrect: You achieved the primary objective because the OU you moved Marc to is correctly named using X.500 naming. You achieved the secondary objective because Marc will be able to manage all the Sales OU. Because the Sales OU is at the same level as the Mgmt OU, there is no concern that Marc will be able to inherit permissions for the Mgmt OU.

    C. Incorrect: You achieved the primary objective because the OU you moved Marc to is correctly named using X.500 naming. You achieved the secondary objective because Marc will be able to manage all the Sales OU. Because the Sales OU is at the same level as the Mgmt OU, there is no concern that Marc will be able to inherit permissions for the Mgmt OU.

    D. Incorrect: You achieved the primary objective because the OU you moved Marc to is correctly named using X.500 naming. You achieved the secondary objective because Marc will be able to manage all the Sales OU. Because the Sales OU is at the same level as the Mgmt OU, there is no concern that Marc will be able to inherit permissions for the Mgmt OU.

4. Correct Answers: A

    A. Correct: This OU structure will make it easy for you to delegate the appropriate controls to the newly structured administrative groups.

    B. Incorrect: The OUs for Sales, Marketing, and Production would not contain user accounts for the delegation required.

    C. Incorrect: This will not make delegation of control easy because it mixes up the placement of users and computers.

    D. Incorrect: This does not split up the Sales, Marketing, and Production groups to make it easy to delegate control of them.

5. Correct Answers: B

    A. Incorrect: With the trust relationship in place, the manager should not need to change to a new domain.

    B. Correct: The manager has not presented a reason for being moved within the domain, and with the trust relationship in place, he can be granted access to resources in the vineyard's domain.

    C. Incorrect: There is no need to move the manager out of the Operations OU.

    D. Incorrect: With the trust relationship in place, the manager should not need to change to the other domain.

6.   Correct Answers: D

    A. Incorrect: Members of the Backup Operators group do not have the rights to manage user accounts.

    B. Incorrect: Phil should be granted the right to manage user and computer accounts anywhere in the *adatum.com* domain, and delegating North America cuts him off from the rest of the domain.

    C. Incorrect: The All OU is too narrow of a scope for Phil. He must be able to manage the user and computer accounts throughout *adatum.com*. If another OU is created as a top-level OU next to All OU, Phil would not be able to manage its users and computers.

    D. Correct: By adding Phil as a member to the Account Operators group, he will have the right to create, modify, and delete user and computer accounts throughout the entire *adatum.com* domain, including any future OUs that are added.

18 Planning and Implementing Group Policy (4.0)

This objective domain reviews the knowledge and proficiency that you must have in planning and implementing **Group Policy Objects (GPOs)** throughout an **Active Directory** network. **Group Policy** is an administrative tool that can manage users, computers, and **domain controllers**. Through sets of rules that you establish and apply to **domains**, **sites**, and **organizational units (OUs)**, Group Policy enables you to manage detailed aspects of security, desktop configuration, software delivery, and the user environment.

One way in which Group Policy can be utilized is found in IntelliMirror. **IntelliMirror** takes advantage of a subset of Group Policy capabilities in order to provide a fully managed user environment. IntelliMirror enables users who roam around a network to have the same environment regardless of the computer they use. Through establishing user preferences, providing software applications, and **folder redirection**, a user will have all the tools required no matter where the user logs on.

Tested Skills and Suggested Practices

The skills that you need to successfully master the Planning and Implementing Group Policy objective domain on Exam 70-294: *Planning, Implementing, and Maintaining a Microsoft Windows Server 2003 Active Directory Infrastructure* include:

- Plan Group Policy strategy.
    - ❏ Practice 1: Install a domain controller within a root domain of a forest. Create an OU structure and add various GPOs with a variety of settings to several of the OU levels. In some OUs, add multiple GPOs. Create a user object in one of the OUs. Add the Resultant Set of Policy (RSoP) snap-in to the Microsoft Management Console (MMC) and begin the Resultant Set Of Policy Wizard to create a query in planning mode. Examine the policies applied to the user account you created.
    - ❏ Practice 2: Using the same OU structure in Practice 1, create a computer object in one of the OUs. Add the RSoP snap-in to the MMC and begin the Resultant Set Of Policy Wizard to create a query in planning mode. Examine the policies applied to the computer account you created.

❑ Practice 3: Using an imaginary organization, design a Group Policy structure for a nested OU structure in which the administrative and security policies are applicable to everyone except the administrators, and where three groups require different forms of folder redirection and distributed software.

■ Configure the user environment by using Group Policy.

❑ Practice 1: Using the Active Directory Users And Computers console on a domain controller, create an OU called Distribute. Add a GPO to Distribute that includes a policy for distributing the Terminal Services client to users in the Distribute OU. Create an OU within Distribute named Sub, and then create a user within Sub named Testsw. Make certain Testsw has the rights to read the GPO and access the share with the Terminal Services client software. Log on as Testsw and document your results.

❑ Practice 2: Using the Active Directory Sites And Services console, create a GPO for your site. Configure the GPO to redirect the My Documents folder to a network share. Log on to a network workstation in that site as a user and test whether the folder was redirected.

❑ Practice 3: Install a certification authority (CA) server. Using the Active Directory Users And Computers console, create an OU named Cert. Create a GPO for Cert that automatically enrolls user certificates and prompts the user during enrollment. Add a user to the Cert OU and then log on. Note your results.

■ Deploy a computer environment by using Group Policy.

❑ Practice 1: Using the Active Directory Users And Computers console on a domain controller, create an OU called Swdist. Add a GPO to Swdist which includes a policy for assigning Microsoft Office software to computers in the Swdist OU. Join a computer to the domain and place that computer object within the Swdist OU. Log on to the computer and check its software configuration.

❑ Practice 2: Create an OU named Kiosk. Add a user account named Log to this OU. Configure a GPO for computers which would allow them to log on automatically as the Log user account, and then automatically launch an application. Make sure that the Group Policy will not allow the user to access any Control Panel functions. Add a computer to the Kiosk OU. Start up the computer and note the results.

Further Reading

You will find reading materials listed in this section by objective that will assist you in mastering the skills tested on the exam.

Objective 4.1   Review Chapter 10, Lessons 1, "Understanding Group Policy," 2, "Group Policy Planning Strategies," and 3, "Implementing a GPO."

Microsoft Corporation. *Introducing Microsoft Windows Server 2003*. Redmond, Washington: Microsoft Press, 2003. Review Chapter 3, "Active Directory."

Microsoft Corporation. *Microsoft Windows Server 2003 Deployment Kit, A Microsoft Resource Kit*. Redmond, Washington: Microsoft Press, 2003. Read *Designing a Managed Environment*, Chapter 1, "Planning a Managed Environment"; and Chapter 2, "Designing a Group Policy Infrastructure." This volume can also be found on the Microsoft Web site at *http://www.microsoft.com/windowsserver2003 /techinfo/reskit/deploykit.mspx*.

Microsoft Corporation. Redmond, Washington. Review "Technical Overview of Windows Server 2003 Management Services," available on Microsoft's Web site at *http://www.microsoft.com/windowsserver2003/techinfo/overview/mgmtsrvcs.mspx*.

Microsoft Corporation. Redmond, Washington. Review "Introduction to Group Policy in Windows Server 2003," available on the Microsoft Web site at *http://www .microsoft.com/windowsserver2003/techinfo/overview/gpintro.mspx*.

Objective 4.2   Review Chapter 11, Lesson 2, "Managing Special Folders with Group Policy"; Chapter 12, "Deploying Software with Group Policy"; and Chapter 13, Lessons 1, "Understanding Active Directory Security," 2, "Implementing Software Restriction Policies," and 3, "Implementing an Audit Policy."

Microsoft Corporation. *Microsoft Windows Server 2003 Deployment Kit, A Microsoft Resource Kit*. Redmond, Washington: Microsoft Press, 2003. Read *Designing a Managed Environment*, Chapter 7, "Implementing User State Management." This volume can also be found on the Microsoft Web site at *http://www.microsoft.com /windowsserver2003/techinfo/reskit/deploykit.mspx*.

Microsoft Corporation. Redmond, Washington. Review "HOW TO: Install and Use RSoP in Windows Server 2003," available on the Microsoft Web site at *http: //support.microsoft.com/default.aspx?scid=kb;en-us;323276*.

Objective 4.3   Review Chapter 12, "Deploying Software with Group Policy"; and Chapter 13, Lessons 1, "Understanding Active Directory Security," 2, "Implementing Software Restriction Policies," and 3, "Implementing an Audit Policy."

Microsoft Corporation. *Microsoft Windows Server 2003 Administrator's Companion*. Redmond, Washington: Microsoft Press, 2003. Read Chapter 10, "Managing File Resources and Group Policy."

Microsoft Corporation. *Introducing Microsoft Windows Server 2003.* Redmond, Washington: Microsoft Press, 2003. Review Chapter 6, "Using Active Directory."

Microsoft Corporation. Redmond, Washington. Review "HOW TO: Use Software Restriction Policies in Windows Server 2003," available on the Microsoft Web site at *http://support.microsoft.com/default.aspx?scid=kb;en-us;324036.*

Plan Group Policy Strategy

This objective concentrates on the planning for **Group Policy** in **Active Directory**. Planning is a process that takes place both at the installation of Active Directory and as an ongoing response to expected changes made to the network. Networks are dynamic entities changing in response to organizational changes. Part of the planning process requires you to understand how the current configuration is functioning. You can then plan for changes that will be appropriate to the situation.

Resultant Set of Policy (RSoP) is one of the tools that can help plan for changes to Group Policy. RSoP provides for two modes:

- Logging—for troubleshooting an existing set of policies
- Planning—for review of existing policies and testing of a new set of policies

During the planning process, you can run the **Resultant Set Of Policy Wizard** to execute a query against an existing user or **computer object's** group policies, whether those policies are applied at the **site**, **domain**, or **OU**. You can also simulate the effect of new group policies on computer and user objects. This process can help to plan to avoid problems with inheritance of policies from multiple levels.

When you plan group policies, you have many options available to you. You can

- Distribute software
- Modify the registry
- Implement security settings
- Provide scripts for execution at either the startup, shutdown, logon, or logoff points

Group Policy settings are applied in the order of local policies (those configured directly on the computer itself) first. Next, site group policies are applied. Then the domain group policies, and lastly the OU group policies are applied, in order from the top node of the hierarchy to the OU containing the object. When you plan your policies, you must understand how each application can affect the next policy in line. If, for example, you have a domain-wide policy that restricts the Control Panel from being accessed, and then you have an OU Group Policy that allows the Control Panel to be accessed, the last policy "wins" and users in that OU will be able to access the Control Panel.

Every Group Policy contains a **User Configuration node** and a **Computer Configuration node**. When a user logs on to the network, that user receives the group policies in the User Configuration nodes of all the group policies that lead from the site, to domain, through each level of OU down to the one holding the user object, except in the case where the administrator has blocked or enforced inheritance of certain policies. When a computer starts up, that computer receives the group policies in the Computer Configuration nodes of all the group policies leading down to the computer object's location in the hierarchy. This means that a user may log on to two different computers and receive entirely different environments because the computer group policies are vastly dissimilar.

When you plan for user environments, you should consider the data management needs, especially regarding which folders need to be available to the user from any point in the network. This may require you to use folder redirection in your environment. You will also need to determine whether software needs to follow a user around the network, or if the software needs to be statically **assigned** to a computer regardless of its user.

Objective 4.1 Questions

1. You are the network administrator of A. Datum Corporation. The company has four departments, each within a separate OU in the forest root domain. Each of these OUs is a peer to the other. The company is reorganizing, and many users have moved to a different OU. These users have complained that they no longer can find their documents folders. What can be the problem?

   A. The users have moved to new locations, and they forgot to migrate their documents from their old computers.

   B. The users have changed domain controllers.

   C. The GPOs for the users' new site is overriding the GPOs that apply to the users' new OU.

   D. The GPOs for the users' new OU does not contain the correct information for folder redirection.

2. You are the network administrator for the *fabrikam.com* Active Directory domain. You have three sites: Los Angeles, New York, and Miami. You have several OUs named Mkt, Svc, Prod, and Sales, and each OU contains users from two or three of the sites. You are planning the group policies for the entire network. The Miami administrator wants all the Miami users, many who are in the Sales OU, to redirect their My Documents folders to the MIAM02 server. The Los Angeles and New York users travel often and will need to maintain local files, and the administrators in both locations do not want to use folder redirection. What do you do to provide the correct access to the resources?

   A. Create a GPO with the correct folder redirection path to MIAM02 and apply it to the Miami site.

   B. Create a GPO with the correct folder redirection path to MIAM02 and apply it to the Sales OU.

   C. Create a GPO with the correct folder redirection path to MIAM02 and apply it to the *fabrikam.com* domain. Block policy inheritance to the Los Angeles and New York sites.

   D. Create a GPO with the correct folder redirection path to MIAM02 and apply it to the *fabrikam.com* domain. Block policy inheritance to the Mkt, Svc, and Prod OUs.

3. You are planning to implement software distribution to your network. You need to ensure accuracy for software distribution for licensing purposes. You want to deploy application APP to all members of the Management, Executive, and Sales teams. You want to make sure that only the computers you approve of receive this software, so

that a Sales team member cannot dial in to the network and be forced to accept installation of APP to his or her home computer. You want to ensure that you can add group
policies that affect only the Executive team or only the Sales team in the future. How
do you organize this?

    A. Create an OU hierarchy for software distribution called Swdist. Add all users of the
Management, Executive, and Sales teams to this OU. Create a GPO to distribute
software to the users in this OU.

    B. Create an OU hierarchy for software distribution called Swdist. Within Swdist, create
separate OUs for the Management, Executive, and Sales teams. Apply a GPO to distribute software to computer objects in the Swdist OU hierarchy. Add the correct
users and computers to each of the Management, Executive, and Sales OUs.

    C. Apply a GPO to each site that contains Management, Executive, and Sales team
members.

    D. Apply a domain-wide GPO for distributing APP to computer objects within the
domain.

4.   A. Datum Corporation has asked you to consult on a Group Policy planning project.
The company currently has a set of group policies being used for folder redirection
and password policies. The domain uses a single OU to house user objects and another
OU to house computer objects. A. Datum Corporation wants you to create a system
that will do the following:

Primary objective: Deploy software to the Marketing team.

Secondary objective: Avoid applying any policies to the IT group.

Secondary objective: Apply password policy to all users.

You create an OU hierarchy in the domain that has a single OU at the top of the tree
named All users. Within this OU, you place an IT Group OU, a Management OU, a
Marketing OU, a Sales OU, a Service OU, and a Clerical OU to match the groups within
A. Datum Corporation You apply a software distribution GPO to the Marketing OU.
You block inheritance for the IT Group OU.

After performing these actions, you have achieved which of the following?

    A. You have achieved neither the primary objective nor the secondary objectives.

    B. You have achieved the primary objective but neither of the secondary objectives.

    C. You have achieved the primary objective and one of the secondary objectives.

    D. You have achieved the secondary objectives but not the primary objective.

5. You are working on a plan for a Group Policy structure that will ensure separate security settings for different users. You will not be changing the OU hierarchy. You want to test the security settings on each of the users. What is the best way to perform these tests?

   A. Use RSoP in planning mode to simulate the policies on existing users.

   B. Use RSoP in logging mode to simulate the policies on existing users.

   C. Create and test a new OU hierarchy.

   D. Create a new OU hierarchy in a test forest, then use RSoP in planning mode to simulate the policies on users.

6. You have a new kiosk system that is being deployed to the public. Each kiosk is equipped with a computer running Microsoft Windows XP that logs on to Active Directory. You want to ensure that the kiosks are identical in all respects. Which of the following do you use? (Select all that apply.)

   A. Enable Group Policy Loopback processing mode for the kiosks.

   B. Use a single computer account for all the kiosks to use.

   C. Place all kiosk computer accounts within the same OU.

   D. Place all kiosks within the same site.

7. You have just been hired as a network administrator for Fabrikam, Inc. Your predecessor created local policies on all computers in the network in your location of Chicago. You do not know how other locations apply group policies to computers, but the computer accounts for their computers are mingled with yours in the various OUs across the domain. Furthermore, at your site, when technicians have made changes to the computers, they have often changed the local policy settings. You want to have consistent group policies that refresh on the computer upon each startup. Which type of Group Policy should you select?

   A. Local policy

   B. Group Policy applied to OUs that contain your computer accounts

   C. Domain Group Policy

   D. Group Policy applied to the Chicago site

8. You are planning the group policies for your domain. You have six OUs in the domain. The top OU is named All. Below All, you have Computers and Users. Within Users, you have Sales, Finance, and Service. You have the following objectives:

   Primary objective: You want to make certain that the Service team has a software restriction policy to prevent installation of unapproved software.

Secondary objective: You want all others to log on with the standard security policy, which is a minimum six-character password.

Secondary objective: You want to distribute software to all computers in the company, but not to users' home computers when they dial in.

You create a domain-wide policy that requires a six-character password. You create a software distribution policy and apply it to Computers.

After performing these actions, you have achieved which of the following?

    A. You have achieved neither the primary objective nor the secondary objectives.

    B. You have achieved both of the secondary objectives but not the primary objective.

    C. You have achieved the primary objective and one of the secondary objectives.

    D. You have achieved the primary objective and both of the secondary objectives.

Objective 4.1 Answers

1. **Correct Answers: D**

   A. **Incorrect:** The scenario did not mention that there were physical moves, so this is not likely to be the issue. (However, in real life, a reorganization might mean a new location with new equipment.)

   B. **Incorrect:** Domain controllers are considered peers by design, so that any domain controller would be able to perform the same functions as any other domain controller.

   C. **Incorrect:** The question did not mention that there were physical moves, so you can disregard the issue of a new site.

   D. **Correct:** Since the users moved to a new OU, they would be affected by the new OU's GPOs. If the new GPOs did not contain the correct path for folder redirection, then the users would appear to have "lost" their documents.

2. **Correct Answers: A**

   A. **Correct:** Applying the GPO to the site will ensure that the policy is applied to the correct set of users.

   B. **Incorrect:** Because each of the OUs contains users from more than one location, you cannot apply the GPO for folder redirection to an OU.

   C. **Incorrect:** You cannot block domain Group Policy inheritance to a site because site policies are applied first.

   D. **Incorrect:** If you perform this action, you will essentially be applying a GPO to the Sales OU, which means that all the Miami users in the Mkt, Svc, and Prod OUs will not receive the folder redirection, while all the New York and Los Angeles users in the Sales OU will receive unwanted folder redirection.

3. **Correct Answers: B**

   A. **Incorrect:** This configuration will distribute software to the correct users, but not to the correct computers. Users who dial in to the network would be able to install APP on their home computers.

   B. **Correct:** Since the computer configuration was used for distributing the software, then only computer objects in the Swdist OU tree will receive the software. Furthermore, by using separate OUs for the Management, Executive, and Sales teams, you can then create new group policies that apply only to each of those teams in the future.

C. **Incorrect:** By applying the GPO to each site with those users, any user outside of these three teams would be able to install APP.

D. **Incorrect:** This will distribute APP to all computers in the domain, not only to the Management, Executive, and Sales teams, which is an undesirable result.

4.   Correct Answers: C

A. **Incorrect:** Your system will effectively deploy software to the Marketing team, which achieves the primary objective. It will also avoid applying any policies to the IT group. However, you did not create a password policy for all of the users, so you did not achieve one of the secondary objectives.

B. **Incorrect:** Your system will effectively deploy software to the Marketing team, which achieves the primary objective. It will also avoid applying any policies to the IT group. However, you did not create a password policy for all of the users, so you did not achieve one of the secondary objectives.

C. **Correct:** Your system will effectively deploy software to the Marketing team, which achieves the primary objective. It will also avoid applying any policies to the IT group. However, you did not create a password policy for all of the users, so you did not achieve one of the secondary objectives.

D. **Incorrect:** Your system will effectively deploy software to the Marketing team, which achieves the primary objective. It will also avoid applying any policies to the IT group. However, you did not create a password policy for all of the users, so you did not achieve one of the secondary objectives.

5.   Correct Answers: A

A. **Correct:** You can use RSoP to either merge the tested policies with the existing ones or to exclusively test the new policies and ignore the existing ones to simulate the effect on user accounts.

B. **Incorrect:** RSoP's logging mode is used for troubleshooting problems with existing policies, not for simulations for planned policies.

C. **Incorrect:** While creating a new OU hierarchy may be able to help determine much of the testing, it is more likely to have errors than using RSoP in planning mode. Such errors may be in upper-level GPOs that are not applied during testing, or in site GPOs not being tested, and so on.

D. **Incorrect:** Compared to using RSoP in planning mode against existing users, this is not as fast or as accurate a method for conducting this test.

6.   Correct Answers: A, C

A. Correct: Kiosks are public computers that may end up under close scrutiny by any passerby. By using Group Policy Loopback processing mode, you can ensure that any user will receive only the policies that are supposed to be used on the kiosk, rather than the policy settings that might apply on a different networked computer.

B. Incorrect: Each computer will join the domain as a separate computer account.

C. Correct: In placing all kiosk computer accounts within the same OU, they will each receive the same set of group policies for computer configuration.

D. Incorrect: It may be impossible to do this based on your company's physical network configuration.

7.   Correct Answers: D

A. Incorrect: This is the type of policy that is currently being mishandled. You should restore all local policy settings to their default state.

B. Incorrect: Since you do not know how other administrators wish to handle Group Policy, and since your computer accounts are mingled with their computer accounts in the same OUs, you should not apply group policies to OUs.

C. Incorrect: A domain Group Policy would affect the computer accounts managed by other administrators.

D. Correct: After you remove the local policy, you can apply a Group Policy to the Chicago site. From that point on, computer accounts that start up in the Chicago site will automatically have the latest policies you have applied, refreshed at each startup.

8.   Correct Answers: B

A. Incorrect: You did not apply any policy that will restrict software installations for the Service team. However, you did create a standard security policy that will require a minimum six-character password, and you were able to distribute software to all the computers in the company, but not to users who are using non-company equipment.

B. Correct: You did not apply any policy that will restrict software installations for the Service team. However, you did create a standard security policy that will require a minimum six-character password, and you were able to distribute software to all the computers in the company, but not to users who are using non-company equipment.

C. Incorrect: You did not apply any policy that will restrict software installations for the Service team. However, you did create a standard security policy that will require a minimum six-character password, and you were able to distribute software to all the computers in the company, but not to users who are using non-company equipment.

D. Incorrect: You did not apply any policy that will restrict software installations for the Service team. However, you did create a standard security policy that will require a minimum six-character password, and you were able to distribute software to all the computers in the company, but not to users who are using non-company equipment.

Configure the User Environment by Using Group Policy

This objective centers on configuration of the user's environment through GPOs. In configuring a user's environment, you will need to have the skills to identify and specify settings for the **User Configuration node** within **GPOs**.

In the User Configuration node, you have the ability to perform the following tasks (as well as many others):

- Distribute software that users will have access to regardless of the computer that they are using.

- Assign **user profiles** and configure the desktop environment.

- Apply logon and logoff scripts, then configure whether they are hidden or visible, and whether scripts run sequentially or synchronously.

- Manage user **certificates** and enable autoenrollment.

- Restrict access to files in the Windows Systemroot, to icons on the desktop or in the Start menu, and to the Control Panel.

- Restrict the use of software, or force the use of a different application in place of Explorer.exe.

- Configure how the user will interact with Microsoft Windows components such as Internet Explorer and the Windows Installer.

- Establish security settings.

Distributing software provides for two options—assigning of the application or publishing it. If you **assign** an application to a user, the user has the application installed and available after first logging on. If you **publish** an application, the user can use Add Or Remove Programs in Control Panel to install the application. Conflicts can occur between seemingly disconnected group policies. For example, the Disable Windows Installer policy can prevent a user from installing allowed applications that use the Windows Installer method, regardless of whether the software is published or assigned. Furthermore, if you publish an application and then restrict a user from accessing Control Panel or the Add Or Remove Programs icon, the user will not be able to install the application because the user cannot access the correct icon.

Autoenrollment of **certificates** can be done through Group Policy for users and computers. When using autoenrollment, users do not need to be aware of the certificates that are enrolled, retrieved, or renewed. When you select autoenrollment behavior, you can establish a silent autoenrollment that requires zero user input. You can also require a user to provide input such as when users have **smart cards** and personal identification numbers (PINs).

Folder redirection is a key to enabling easy access to data for users. When users log on to the network, they receive the Group Policy setting that tells the computer to point to a different location for certain information. This includes:

- Application data—information that configures an application for a specific person.

- Desktop—the data that a person saves to the desktop.

- My Documents—the information that a person would place in the My Documents folder on the desktop, or when saving data to My Documents.

- Start Menu—the shortcuts and data icons that appear in the Windows Start menu.

Security settings can be applied to a computer object as well as to a user object. When you deploy user-related security settings, you use the User Configuration node in Group Policy. Then, you navigate to the Windows Settings section and open Security Settings. Within this Group Policy, you can edit Public Key policies, such as autoenrolling certificates, and you can restrict software. When you restrict software, you can prevent users from being able to run certain programs or to look at files in certain paths. For example, you can prevent users from accessing files in the System32 folder within Windows in order to stop them from deleting or corrupting a critical file.

There are a lot of other settings that may be considered to be security settings, but which appear under the Administrative Templates section. These include removing icons from the desktop and Start menu, preventing access to the Control Panel, and prohibiting changes to the network configuration. Password policies are applied using the Computer Configuration node in a GPO linked to the domain only.

Objective 4.2 Questions

1.   You are the network administrator for Litware, Inc. Your organization has Legal, Marketing, Service, and Sales departments. Each of these departments has its own OU beneath the HQ OU, which is in the *litwareinc.com* domain. You have applied a folder redirection Group Policy to the HQ OU for Application data, Desktop, My Documents, and Start Menu. In this policy, all users will have their folders directed to a single, shared location. After applying this Group Policy, the Legal department users complain that they no longer have their special menu items, macros, and personal information in their Microsoft Word documents. Which policy setting is causing the problem?

   A. Application data

   B. Desktop

   C. My Documents

   D. Start Menu

2.   You have been called in to consult on a network problem being experienced by Contoso, Ltd. In the *contoso.com* domain, administrators have applied logon scripts and startup scripts to be executed at nearly every OU level in the hierarchy. These scripts map network drives, execute external programs, and write daily news items specific to the user's department and position. To make the scripts faster, they are set to run synchronously. A new OU named Application Service has been added below the Service OU. The Service OU is below the Corp OU and that is the top of the OU tree. The script applied to the Application Service OU is not deleting the drive mappings that the Corp OU script is making, even though the command to delete the drive mappings is in the script. The administrator has not blocked, and does not want to block, the upper script because it provides the new items that are necessary to be written at that level. What might be the best way to fix this problem?

   A. Copy the Group Policy to the lower OU and block inheritance.

   B. Force inheritance of the upper layer Group Policy.

   C. Disable the policy that runs logon scripts synchronously.

   D. Move the logon script to a different location.

3.   You are the network administrator for Contoso, Ltd., and you have a single domain named *contoso.com* in your forest with two locations. You have been asked to make certain that every user has the ability to install a new application named APP, which uses Windows Installer. The company does not want to install APP on any computer where the user will not use it, and the APP installation program should be available only in Control Panel. Which policy will achieve these criteria?

A. In a domain Group Policy, publish APP in the Software portion of the User Configuration node.

B. In a domain Group Policy, assign APP in the Software portion of the User Configuration node.

C. In a domain Group Policy, create a logon script in the User Configuration node that installs the APP.

D. In a site Group Policy, publish APP in the Software portion of the User Configuration node.

4. Litware, Inc. has a single domain, *litwareinc.com*, in its forest. There are seven sites. The OU hierarchy has two top OUs: one named Admin for administrators and the other named Co for the remaining users. Within Co, there are three OUs named Sales, Lit, and Finance. You have the following objectives:

Primary objective: All users in the entire network require the same security settings.

Secondary objective: Except for administrators, users require a standard desktop and folder redirection configuration.

Secondary objective: The Lit department requires a special application that no other users should receive.

You perform the following actions:

1. You create a domain Group Policy that applies security settings.

2. You create an OU Group Policy for the Lit OU to deploy the application.

3. You create an OU Group Policy for the Co OU to apply a new logon script.

After performing these actions, you have achieved which of the following?

A. You have achieved neither the primary objective nor the secondary objectives.

B. You have achieved the primary objective but not the secondary objectives.

C. You have achieved the primary objective and one of the secondary objectives.

D. You have achieved the primary objective and both of the secondary objectives.

5. You are the network administrator for a public library. You have 20 computers on the network that are available for users to browse the online library catalog or the Internet. You have decided to implement Group Policy settings within a single GPO on the OU containing only the public user accounts, as follows:

■ Configure a Group Policy setting that restricts the user from installing new applications using Windows Installer.

- Configure a Group Policy setting that restricts the user from running any file named Setup.exe.

- Configure a Group Policy setting that restricts the user from accessing any files in the Windows directories.

- Configure a Group Policy setting that prevents the user from changing desktop and Start menu settings.

- Configure a Group Policy setting that removes the History, My Favorites, My Documents, and Network Places icons from the desktop.

- Configure a Group Policy setting that restricts the user from opening the Control Panel.

- Configure a Group Policy setting that prohibits the user from changing Network Connection settings.

Given this configuration, under what circumstances will a person using a public computer at this library be able to install a new application? (Select all that apply.)

A. By publishing an application in a Group Policy so that it shows up in Add Or Remove Programs.

B. By logging on to the computer using a different user account in a different OU.

C. By assigning an application in a Group Policy so that it is available on the desktop.

D. By using a non–Windows Installer application, renaming the installation file from Setup.exe to something else, and executing it from the command line, the Run box, or Explorer.exe.

6. You are the network administrator for Fabrikam, Inc. You have several users who travel from site to site and use different network workstations. You decide to implement a Group Policy to ensure that these users can access their data both on and off the network. Which of the following should you implement on an OU containing only the traveling users? (Select two.)

A. In Administrative Templates, under Network, implement the Group Policy for Offline Files.

B. In Windows Settings, under Folder Redirection, redirect the My Documents folders to a network location.

C. In Administrative Templates, under Shared Folders, allow users to publish shares.

D. In the administrative templates, under Start Menu and Taskbar, remove the icons for the My Documents folder.

7. You are the network administrator for Fabrikam, Inc. You have implemented smart cards for a set of users on the network. You have placed these users in the Smart OU. You have two objectives:

Primary objective: Enable autoenrollment of certificates only for the users in the Smart OU.

Secondary objective: Require only the Smart OU users to use their smart cards during enrollment.

You implement a Group Policy for the *fabrikam.com* domain. In this policy, you configure the Public Key autoenrollment policy so that it prompts the user for a personal identifier.

After performing these actions, you have achieved which of the following?

You have:

    A. Achieved neither the primary objective nor the secondary objective.

    B. Achieved the primary objective but not the secondary objective.

    C. Achieved the secondary objective but not the primary objective.

    D. Achieved both the primary objective and secondary objective.

8. You are the administrator of a network that has recently experienced a security incident that caused a virus to install itself into an application that is published to all users. You have written a script that will detect whether the application has been installed, as well as its version, and if the non-secure version is being used, it will then deploy a fix to the security breach. You have replaced the files on the network share for installation so that any new installations will already have the fix. Which of the following actions do you need to perform in order to deploy the fix the fastest?

    A. Force users to log off the network, then manually run the script at each workstation.

    B. Implement a Group Policy to secure Windows Installer from being run.

    C. Implement a Group Policy to secure Add Or Remove Programs from being used.

    D. Copy the script to Sysvol. Implement a Group Policy that includes the script as a logon script.

Objective 4.2 Answers

1.   Correct Answers: A

   A. Correct: The Group Policy that redirected the Application data folder to a central location would appear to have caused changes to the Legal department's menu items and personal information for Word.

   B. Incorrect: The Desktop folder redirection would make users' desktops appear to be the same but would not have affected the application configuration.

   C. Incorrect: The users did not have a problem accessing their Word documents, just the application information that was specific to the Legal department users.

   D. Incorrect: The Start Menu folder redirection would not have manifested itself as a problem with a specific application's configuration.

2.   Correct Answers: C

   A. Incorrect: One problem that you have with duplicating a Group Policy is that when you make changes to a Group Policy, you might not remember to make the same changes to another Group Policy.

   B. Incorrect: The administrator has not blocked the upper-layer scripts, so forcing inheritance will not change the way that policy is being applied.

   C. Correct: By disabling the policy to run logon scripts synchronously, the logon scripts would execute in an order where the drive mappings would be deleted after they were made.

   D. Incorrect: Moving the logon script to a different location will not make a change in execution order.

3.   Correct Answers: A

   A. Correct: Publishing APP in a domain Group Policy will make the APP installation available in Control Panel to all users.

   B. Incorrect: Assigning APP in a domain Group Policy will install APP, not make the installation available in Control Panel, as requested.

   C. Incorrect: By performing this action, APP will be installed rather than be made available in Control Panel, as desired.

   D. Incorrect: A site Group Policy will not publish the APP to all the users if you have a site defined for each of the two locations.

4. Correct Answers: C

A. Incorrect: You were able to provide all users with security settings, meeting the primary objective. You also created a Group Policy to deploy the application to the Lit department, meeting one of the secondary objectives. However, you did not apply a Group Policy for desktop and folder redirection.

B. Incorrect: You were able to provide all users with security settings, meeting the primary objective. You also created a Group Policy to deploy the application to the Lit department, meeting one of the secondary objectives. However, you did not apply a Group Policy for desktop and folder redirection.

C. Correct: You were able to provide all users with security settings, meeting the primary objective. You also created a Group Policy to deploy the application to the Lit department, meeting one of the secondary objectives. However, you did not apply a Group Policy for desktop and folder redirection.

D. Incorrect: You were able to provide all users with security settings, meeting the primary objective. You also created a Group Policy to deploy the application to the Lit department, meeting one of the secondary objectives. However, you did not apply a Group Policy for desktop and folder redirection.

5. Correct Answers: B, D

A. Incorrect: There are two items preventing the user from installing an application that was published. First, you have a policy that prevents users from installing applications using Windows Installer. Second, you have a policy that prevents a user from opening the Control Panel, so the user will not be able to access Add Or Remove Programs.

B. Correct: By using a different user account in a different OU, the user will have different group policies that may be less restrictive for installing applications.

C. Incorrect: The group policies in place prevent the user from using Windows Installer and from executing Setup.exe files.

D. Correct: The group policies will not prevent a non–Windows Installer installation from taking place if the installation file is not named Setup.exe.

6. Correct Answers: A, B

A. Correct: Offline Files will allow the travelers to access their data when they are not connected to the network. They will be able to synchronize the data on a local computer with the data on a network share.

B. Correct: Redirecting the My Documents folder will enable the user to access his or her data from any workstation connected to the network.

C. **Incorrect:** Publishing shares in Active Directory will allow a user to let others search for files that are shared from that user's computer by using an Active Directory query. It will not enable access to files from any location.

D. **Incorrect:** Configuring the Start menu will not enable users to access files whether they are on the network or not.

7. **Correct Answers: A**

A. **Correct:** Because you applied the Group Policy to the *fabrikam.com* domain, the users across the entire domain will receive the policy, not just those within the Smart OU. Therefore, you have not achieved the primary objective or the secondary objective.

B. **Incorrect:** Because you applied the Group Policy to the *fabrikam.com* domain, the users across the entire domain will receive the policy, not just those within the Smart OU. Therefore, you have not achieved the primary objective or the secondary objective.

C. **Incorrect:** Because you applied the Group Policy to the *fabrikam.com* domain, the users across the entire domain will receive the policy, not just those within the Smart OU. Therefore, you have not achieved the primary objective or the secondary objective.

D. **Incorrect:** Because you applied the Group Policy to the *fabrikam.com* domain, the users across the entire domain will receive the policy, not just those within the Smart OU. Therefore, you have not achieved the primary objective or the secondary objective.

8. **Correct Answers: D**

A. **Incorrect:** A manually run script with forced logoffs will take more time than other options.

B. **Incorrect:** Since future installations of the software will likely need to use Windows Installer, not to mention the script, this would hinder the deployment of the fix, rather than help it.

C. **Incorrect:** Since all future installations of the software will need to use Add Or Remove Programs in Control Panel (because the application was published), this will hinder the deployment.

D. **Correct:** Using a script as a logon or logoff script is one of the faster ways of deploying a script to users.

Objective 4.3

Deploy a Computer Environment by Using Group Policy

This objective focuses on the **Computer Configuration node** within a **GPO**. When an administrator implements a Group Policy within the Computer Configuration node, that Group Policy will not affect a user who logs on to a computer that is not a member of the **OU**, **domain**, or **site** that includes that policy. Since a **user object** and a **computer object** may exist in entirely different locations within the **Active Directory** hierarchy, you must consider how you will be deploying your computer environment.

You can use the Computer Configuration node to distribute software to computers. There is a slight difference in how the computer installs software. Basically, when assigning software to a computer, the computer will install the software upon startup. When you **assign** software to a user, the user must log on first and then Group Policy will begin the assigned package installation.

In addition to distributing software to computers, you have the ability to autoenroll certificates for the computer. This is done in the Public Key Policies node within the Security Settings of Windows Settings in the computer configuration portion of the GPO. You will create a new automatic certificate request, which will prompt a wizard to help configure the request.

Whenever you deploy a Group Policy, it's always a good idea to test it in a separate OU that is a peer (at the same level) of the one to which you intend to apply the Group Policy. This will ensure that your test includes inherited group policies. When you deploy a new security setting, remember that these are refreshed every 90 minutes on members of the domain (either workstations or servers) and every 5 minutes on **domain controllers**. Even if there are no changes to security settings, they are refreshed every 16 hours.

Objective 4.3 Questions

1. You are the network administrator for Fabrikam, Inc. You have a new software package that you will be distributing to all users in the domain except the public computers used as kiosks, which are placed in their own OU named Kiosks. Administrators will require the software even on member servers of the domain. You perform the following steps:

    1. Create a network share and place the installation files on it.

    2. Create a GPO for the domain.

    3. Using the software settings in the Computer Configuration node of the GPO, you create a new package using the installation files in step 1 and make it an assigned installation.

Which of the following steps did you miss?

    A. None.

    B. Implement a startup script to install the software.

    C. Block the inheritance for all the administrators in the Admin OU.

    D. Block the inheritance for the public computers.

2. You are the network administrator for A. Datum Corporation. In your domain, you have created the following OU hierarchy: At the top of the OUs is Main. Below Main, you have All Computers and All Users. Below All Users, you have Accounting, Legal, Data, and Sales. Below Sales, you have US and Intl. You have been requested to create a special secured desktop through Group Policy settings that applies only to the Legal department. You do not want to have the policy affect any other users. To which OU should you apply the policy?

    A. None

    B. Legal

    C. Intl

    D. All Computers

3. You have been hired to implement a Group Policy for security settings for A. Datum Corporation. You have three domains: a dedicated forest root domain named *adatum.com*, a child domain named *corp.adatum.com* that holds user accounts, and another child domain called *res.adatum.com* that contains all computer accounts and member servers. You have decided to implement three GPOs:

Pol1: A GPO to restrict people from installing software on the local computer

Pol2: A GPO to establish highly secure logons

Pol3: A GPO to redirect folders

Which policies need to be applied to which domain?

A. Pol1 applied to *adatum.com*. Pol2 applied to *res.adatum.com*. Pol3 applied to *res.adatum.com*.

B. Pol1 applied to *corp.adatum.com*. Pol2 applied to *res.adatum.com*. Pol3 applied to *corp.adatum.com*.

C. Pol1 applied to *res.adatum.com*. Pol2 applied to *corp.adatum.com*. Pol3 applied to *corp.adatum.com*.

D. Pol1 applied to *corp.adatum.com*. Pol2 applied to *adatum.com*. Pol3 applied to *res.adatum.com*.

4. You are the network administrator for Blue Yonder Airlines. You maintain network connections to 17 airports, each with its own separate site. The OU structure consists of two top-level OUs: one named Admins, containing administrator accounts and computers, and the other named Blue, containing the rest of the OU hierarchy. Within Blue, there are two OUs named US and Intl. Within the Intl, you have the users and computers at international airport locations. Within the US OU, you have three OUs: Airports, Corp, and Maint. The Airports OU contains the U.S. airport users and computers. Corp holds management, executive, and marketing users and computers. Maint contains all other users and computers. You have to implement a strict level of security for all users and computers that are located at airports, applicable to both desktop settings and account password policies. Even when a user visits an airport location, you want to use the higher level of security. You want to use folder redirection for the people within the corporation who do not work at airports. These policies should apply whether a user logs on locally, remotely, or at an airport site. For the management, executive, and marketing teams, you need to deploy a marketing application. You create the following policies:

Pol1: A Group Policy to secure desktop settings

Pol2: A Group Policy to establish password policies

Pol3: A Group Policy to redirect folders

Pol4: A Group Policy that deploys the marketing application

Which policies need to be applied to which OU?

   A. Pol1 applied to US. Pol2 applied to Airports. Pol3 applied to Maint, and Pol4 applied to Corp.

   B. Pol1 and Pol2 applied to Airports. Pol3 applied to Corp. Pol4 applied to Maint.

   C. Pol1 applied to both Airports and Intl. Pol2 applied as the Default Domain policy. Pol3 applied to both Corp and Maint. Pol4 applied to Corp.

   D. Pol1 applied to Airports. Pol2 applied to Intl. Pol3 applied to US, and Pol4 applied to Corp.

5. You work for Wide World Importers. You wish to install an application to a group of computers in the warehouse, which are shared by many different users. If you create a Group Policy for the OU containing both the warehouse users and computers, which of the following will install the application before a user logs on?

   A. In the User Configuration node, publish the application.

   B. In the Computer Configuration node, publish the application.

   C. In the User Configuration node, assign the application.

   D. Assign the application in the Computer Configuration node.

6. You are the network administrator for the Baldwin Museum of Science. The network consists of 500 users and computers at the museum, with three research sites located around the world. Researchers have typically slow connection speeds and need to have the fastest possible access to their data. As a result, you have installed Terminal Services for the researchers, who dial up to the network from their laptops, then log on to one of seven Windows Server 2003 with Terminal Services member servers. You place all the researchers' user accounts in an OU named Research. You place all the researchers' computers in an OU named Rescomp. You place all the Terminal Services member servers in an OU called Resterm. All of these are below the Offsite OU, and the rest of the network users are in the Onsite OU. The Museum OU contains both the Offsite and Onsite OUs. You implement Group Policy to establish software restriction and secure desktop policies, including a special secure desktop GPO in the Computer Configuration node for the research team only. To which OU should you apply the GPO to ensure that the research team's secure desktop policy is always used?

   A. Research

   B. Offsite

   C. Museum

   D. Rescomp

7.   You are deploying group policies for Contoso, Ltd. You have three domains: *contoso.com*, *corp.contoso.com*, and *res.contoso.com*. You also have three sites: Chicago, Boston, and Las Vegas. Your users and computers are mainly in the *corp.contoso.com* and *contoso.com* domains. The *res.contoso.com* domain contains only research users and computers for the research facility in Chicago. In Las Vegas, users and some computers are in the LV OU in both the *contoso.com* domain and the *corp.contoso.com* domain, while the remaining computers are in three OUs in the *corp.contoso.com* domain. You need to autoenroll certificates for the computers in Las Vegas in order to use Internet Protocol Security (IPSec). You create a Group Policy. Where do you apply it?

   A. To the Las Vegas site

   B. To the *contoso.com* domain

   C. To the *corp.contoso.com* domain

   D. To the LV OU

8.   You are the administrator for Contoso, Ltd. You have a user named Test, who is in the tree structure OU=Sub,OU=Res,OU=Corp,OU=All,DC=contoso,DC=com. You have applied a Group Policy to all of *contoso.com* that requires users to be restricted to installing only approved software. You applied a Group Policy to the Res OU that allows users to install any software, whether approved or unapproved. You have applied a Group Policy to the All OU that restricts users from installing any software (whether approved or unapproved) using the Windows Installer. And you have blocked inheritance at the Corp OU. What software will the Test user be able to install?

   A. Only approved software

   B. Only approved software that does not use the Windows Installer

   C. Any software, whether approved or unapproved

   D. Only software that uses the Windows Installer

9.   You are the administrator for Contoso, Ltd. In the *contoso.com* domain, you have the following OU structure (as shown in the following figure): At the top of the tree is Main. Within Main, there is the Admins OU for administrators, the Power Users OU, for users with semi-administrative abilities, the Users OU for the majority of people and all computers except public computers, and the Kiosks OU for the public computers. Within Power Users, there is an OU named Helpdesk for the help desk team, and an OU named Deskside for deskside support assistants. Within Deskside, there are three OUs for Acct, Legal, and Mkt. Within the Users OU, there are Finance, Market, Sales, Service, Maintenance, and Graphics OUs. See this OU structure in the following illustration. You have applied a Group Policy to Main that deploys an application named APP A by publishing it to computers. You have applied a Group Policy to Deskside that deploys an application named APP B by assigning it to users. You have applied a Group Policy to Market that deploys an application named APP C by assigning it to computers. A user in the Legal OU logs on to a computer in the Market OU. If this is the first time the computer has ever been brought online and logged on to, which applications will install on the computer and be ready to use? (Select all that apply.)

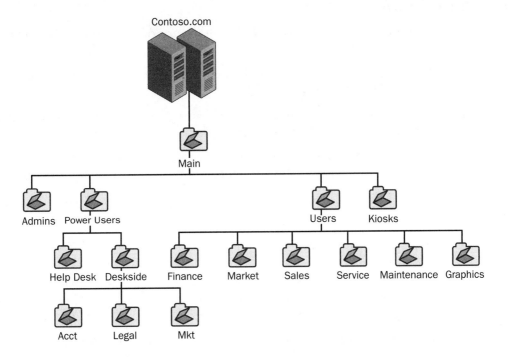

A. APP A

B. APP B

C. APP C

D. None of the above

Objective 4.3 Answers

1. **Correct Answers: D**

    A. Incorrect: You should have blocked inheritance of the policy to the public computers that are used as kiosks.

    B. Incorrect: When you assign a software package, you do not need to run another script to start the installation.

    C. Incorrect: Administrators will need to have access to the application, so you will not block inheritance for their computers.

    D. Correct: You missed the step in which the Group Policy should be blocked from being inherited by the public computers because they should not receive this policy.

2. **Correct Answers: A**

    A. Correct: You cannot apply the policy to any OU without it affecting the entire network or none of the network because there is a single OU named All Computers that would affect all of the users with new secured desktop Group Policy settings. In order to do this correctly, you should create an OU for the Legal computers below the All Computers OU and apply a policy to that OU.

    B. Incorrect: The Legal OU contains only user objects. You must apply the secured desktop policy settings to computer objects which are in the All Computers OU and not separated out by department.

    C. Incorrect: There are neither user nor computer objects in this OU that would be correct for this implementation.

    D. Incorrect: If you apply the policy to this OU, you will be affecting all the users in the network, not just the Legal department.

3. **Correct Answers: B**

    A. Incorrect: No policies need to be applied to *adatum.com*. Pol1 and Pol3 are user configuration group policies and should be applied to the *corp.adatum.com* domain. Pol2 is a computer configuration Group Policy and should be applied to the *res.adatum.com* domain.

    B. Correct: No policies need to be applied to *adatum.com*. Pol1 and Pol3 are user configuration group policies and should be applied to the *corp.adatum.com* domain. Pol2 is a computer configuration Group Policy and should be applied to the *res.adatum.com* domain.

C. **Incorrect:** No policies need to be applied to *adatum.com*. Pol1 and Pol3 are user configuration group policies and should be applied to the *corp.adatum.com* domain. Pol2 is a computer configuration Group Policy and should be applied to the *res.adatum.com* domain.

D. **Incorrect:** No policies need to be applied to *adatum.com*. Pol1 and Pol3 are user configuration group policies and should be applied to the *corp.adatum.com* domain. Pol2 is a computer configuration Group Policy and should be applied to the *res.adatum.com* domain.

4.   Correct Answers: C

A. **Incorrect:** Pol1 should be applied to the Airports and Intl OUs, or you could apply them to the 17 sites that represent airports. Pol3 should be applied to both Maint and Corp. Pol4 should be applied to Corp. Pol2 is the password policy that should be applied as the Default Domain policy.

B. **Incorrect:** Pol1 should be applied to the Airports and Intl OUs, or you could apply them to the 17 sites that represent airports. Pol3 should be applied to both Maint and Corp. Pol4 should be applied to Corp. Pol2 is the password policy that should be applied as the Default Domain policy.

C. **Correct:** Pol1 should be applied to the Airports and Intl OUs, or you could apply them to the 17 sites that represent airports. Pol3 should be applied to both Maint and Corp. Pol4 should be applied to Corp. Pol2 is the password policy that should be applied as the Default Domain policy.

D. **Incorrect:** Pol1 should be applied to the Airports and Intl OUs, or you could apply them to the 17 sites that represent airports. Pol3 should be applied to both Maint and Corp. Pol4 should be applied to Corp. Pol2 is the password policy that should be applied as the Default Domain policy.

5.   Correct Answers: D

A. **Incorrect:** Publishing the application in the User Configuration node will let each user that logs on see the application as an available option in Add Or Remove Programs.

B. **Incorrect:** Publishing the application in the Computer Configuration node will let any user who logs on to the computer see the application as an available option in Add Or Remove Programs.

C. **Incorrect:** Assigning the application in the User Configuration node will install the application for each user when that user logs on to the network.

D. **Correct:** Assigning the application in the Computer Configuration node will install the application on the computer. When the first user initializes the application, the installation will be finalized.

6. Correct Answers: B

A. Incorrect: Research contains user accounts, and these policies are applied to the Computer Configuration node.

B. Correct: By applying the policy to Offsite, it will be inherited by both Rescomp and Resterm, which contain the research team's computers and terminal servers.

C. Incorrect: The Museum OU contains more than just the research team, so the policy would be inherited by computers at the museum, rather than only the research computers, which is what you do not want.

D. Incorrect: If you apply the policy to Rescomp, the sessions running on the Terminal servers will have different requirements.

7. Correct Answers: A

A. Correct: Since you have multiple domains and multiple OUs, the simplest method is to apply the Group Policy to the Las Vegas site.

B. Incorrect: This will not apply the policy to some of the computers in Las Vegas, plus it has the undesirable effect of being applied to any computers in Chicago and Boston.

C. Incorrect: This will not apply the policy to some of the computers in Las Vegas, plus it will accidentally be applied to objects in Chicago and Boston.

D. Incorrect: The LV OU does not contain the rest of the computers in the *corp.contoso.com* domain that are in Las Vegas.

8. Correct Answers: C

A. Incorrect: The last Group Policy applied at the Res OU allows the user to install any software.

B. Incorrect: The last Group Policy applied at the Res OU allows the user to install any software.

C. Correct: The last Group Policy applied at the Res OU allows the user to install any software.

D. Incorrect: The last Group Policy applied at the Res OU allows the user to install any software.

9.   Correct Answers: B, C

    A. Incorrect: APP A was published to computers. It will not be ready to use on the computer. It will be available as an option in the Control Panel under Add Or Remove Programs.

    B. Correct: Because the user was in the Legal OU and inherited the Group Policy from Deskside, where APP B was assigned to users, at the user's logon, APP B will be installed.

    C. Correct: Because the computer was in the Market OU, it would receive the Group Policy that assigned APP C to computers. APP C will install at the computer's startup and be available when any user logs on.

    D. Incorrect: Both APP B and APP C should be available when the user logs on to that computer.

19 Managing and Maintaining Group Policy (5.0)

The Managing and Maintaining Group Policy objective domain focuses primarily on the ongoing administration of computers and users through Active Directory **Group Policy**. In this objective, we will review the methods of troubleshooting Group Policy with **Resultant Set of Policy (RSoP)**, using the Group Policy Object Editor and the **Gpresult** command. We will look at maintaining software through Group Policy's software distribution capabilities. And we will discuss the application of security settings and how to troubleshoot them using various Group Policy tools and utilities.

RSoP is a tool that is helpful in simulating the effects of group policies on user or computer objects through the use of its planning mode. Planning mode can be very useful in determining what changes must be made to group policies in order to achieve a certain user or computer environment. In addition, RSoP provides for a logging mode, which is instrumental in troubleshooting group policies.

Software distribution is an ongoing effort. Not only do you need to initially create a package to distribute, but then you need to deploy it to the users and computers that require the application. If the policy becomes corrupted, you then need to have a method for repairing the software. And finally, you should have a way to remove the software when it is no longer required to be used either for individual users, computers, or for the entire organization.

Tested Skills and Suggested Practices

The skills that you need to successfully master the Managing and Maintaining Group Policy objective domain on Exam 70-294: *Planning, Implementing, and Maintaining a Microsoft Windows Server 2003 Active Directory Infrastructure* include:

- Troubleshoot issues related to Group Policy application deployment. Tools might include RSoP and the Gpresult command.
  - ❑ Practice 1: Install a domain controller within the root domain of a forest. Using the Active Directory Users And Computers console, create an organizational unit (OU) structure. Create a user object in one of the OUs at the bottom of the OU hierarchy. Create a Group Policy Object (GPO) with Group Policy to assign a software application to users at the top of the OU hierarchy. Block inheritance at an OU between the user object and the top OU. Add the RSoP snap-in to the Microsoft Management Console (MMC) and begin the Resultant Set Of Policy Wizard to create a query. Examine the policies applied to the user account you created.

❑ Practice 2: Use the same OU structure in Practice 1. Create a computer object in one of the OUs. Create a GPO with Group Policy to assign a software application to computers at the top of the OU hierarchy. Block inheritance to computers at an OU between the computer object and the OU where the GPO was applied. Add the RSoP snap-in to the MMC and begin the Resultant Set Of Policy Wizard to create a query. Examine the policies applied to the computer account you created.

❑ Practice 3: Using the same OU structure in Practice 1, log on to a workstation that is a member of the domain as the user object you created. Execute the command **Gpresult /scope user /z >c:\mygpo.txt**, and then open C:\Mygpo.txt in Microsoft Wordpad to view the results.

■ Maintain installed software by using Group Policy.

❑ Practice 1: Using the Active Directory Users And Computers console on a domain controller, create an OU called Dist. Add a GPO to Dist that includes a policy that assigns a software application to users in the Dist OU. Create a user object named Swtest. Make certain Swtest has the rights to read the Group Policy and access the share with the software. Install the software application to a workstation. Delete the main executable file of that software application. Log on as Swtest and document your results.

❑ Practice 2: Using the Active Directory Users And Computers console on a domain controller, create an OU called Userdist and a peer OU called Compdist. Create a user object in Userdist called Apptest. Move a computer object for a workstation into Compdist. Create a GPO in Userdist called V1dist and assign an older version of your software application to computers. Create a GPO in Compdist called V2dist and assign a newer version of your software application to computers, making certain to remove all older versions in the software package. Log on to the computer as the user Apptest. View the installation results.

■ Troubleshoot the application of Group Policy security settings. Tools might include RSoP and the Gpresult command.

❑ Practice 1: Install two domain controllers into the root domain of a forest. Make certain that these two domain controllers are on two separate segments of the network. Create an OU structure of several OUs. Install a workstation and move its computer object into an OU. Create a user object named User-Disc in that OU. Disconnect the router between the two segments. On one of the domain controllers, use the Active Directory Users And Computers console to create a GPO for that same OU that will apply a special bitmap to the desktop wallpaper. Log on to the other segment as the user on that workstation. Execute the Gpotool command (from the Resource Kit tools) and view the results.

❑ Practice 2: Continue with the equipment and setup from Practice 1. Connect the two segments and wait 15 minutes. Execute the **Gpupdate /force** command from the workstation. Reboot the workstation and log on to see if the Group Policy is applied and the bitmap is used as the wallpaper.

❑ Practice 3: On a domain controller, create a set of five nested OUs. In each OU, apply a Group Policy to set a different bitmap as the wallpaper. Create a user object and move a computer object into the bottom OU. At three different OUs, either block inheritance or force inheritance of the GPO at that level. Use RSoP to see which Group Policy will "win."

Further Reading

You will find reading materials listed in this section by objective that will assist you in mastering the skills tested on the exam.

Objective 5.1   Review Chapter 12, Lesson 4, "Troubleshooting Software Deployed with Group Policy."

Microsoft Corporation. *Introducing Microsoft Windows Server 2003*. Redmond, Washington: Microsoft Press, 2003. Review Chapter 3, "Active Directory."

Microsoft Corporation. *Microsoft Windows Server 2003 Administrator's Companion*. Redmond, Washington: Microsoft Press, 2003. Review Chapter 10, "Managing File Resources and Group Policy."

Microsoft Corporation. Redmond, Washington. Review "WhitePaper: Administering Group Policy by Using the Group Policy Management Console," available on the Microsoft Web site at *http://support.microsoft.com/default.aspx?scid=kb;en-us;818735*.

Microsoft Corporation. Redmond, Washington. Review "HOW TO: Assign Software to a Specific Group by Using A Group Policy in the Windows Server 2003 Family," available on the Microsoft Web site at *http://support.microsoft.com/default.aspx?scid=kb;en-us;324750*.

Objective 5.2   Read Chapter 12, Lesson 3, "Maintaining Software Deployed with Group Policy."

Microsoft Corporation. *Microsoft Windows Server 2003 Administrator's Pocket Consultant*. Redmond, Washington: Microsoft Press, 2003. Review Chapter 4, "Automating Administrative Tasks, Policies, and Procedures."

Microsoft Corporation. Redmond, Washington. Review "White Paper: Preparation, Verification, and Deployment of Applications," available on the Microsoft Web site at *http://www.microsoft.com/windowsserver2003/techinfo/serverroles/appserver/predeploy.mspx*.

Objective 5.3 Review Chapter 13, Lessons 4, "Administering the Security Log," 5, "Using Security Templates," and 6, "Using Security Configuration and Analysis."

Microsoft Corporation. *Introducing Microsoft Windows Server 2003*. Redmond, Washington: Microsoft Press, 2003. Review Chapter 3, "Active Directory," and Chapter 4, "Management Services."

Microsoft Corporation. Redmond, Washington. Review "HOW TO: Install and Use RSoP in Windows Server 2003," available on the Microsoft Web site at *http://support.microsoft.com/default.aspx?scid=kb;en-us;323276*.

Microsoft Corporation. *Windows Server 2003 Deployment Kit: Designing a Managed Environment*. Redmond, Washington; Microsoft Press, 2003. Review Chapter 8, "Deploying a Managed Software Environment." This volume can also be found on the Microsoft Web site at *http://www.microsoft.com/windowsserver2003/techinfo/reskit/deploykit.mspx*.

Troubleshoot Issues Related to Group Policy Applicaton Deployment

This objective focuses on the issues of troubleshooting **GPOs** for application deployment. In simple application of **Group Policy**, conflicts are the main challenge to application. Multiple GPOs can contain the same Group Policy with different configuration specifications. Inheritance of Group Policy can either be blocked or forced. The combination of multiple GPOs and blocked or forced inheritance can cause unexpected results.

When troubleshooting, you must first investigate the group policies that are applied, the order of their application, and whether inheritance of any of the policies is forced or blocked. The tools that you can use in this process include **RSoP**, and the **Gpresult** command-line tool.

You have two options when you run RSoP. You can use either planning mode or logging mode. When troubleshooting, logging mode will provide you the exact data for an existing user and existing computer object. When you plan to deploy new group policy settings, you can use RSoP in planning mode to simulate the effect that loopback processing, slow network links, WMI filters and security group memberships have on the Group Policy settings. You can also invoke RSoP to discover the results of Group Policy settings when users log on to computers in different **organizational units (OUs)**.

Objective 5.1 Questions

1. You are the network administrator of A. Datum Corporation. The company has four departments, each within separate OUs in the forest root domain. You have had three users move to a new department. You move their user objects to a new OU which is nested below the OU for the department. When the users log on, they find that they do not receive the department's software application. Which of the following actions will help you discover the problem?

   A. Use the Group Policy Object Editor to view the group policies of the OU from which you moved the users.

   B. Use the Group Policy Object Editor to view the group policies of the OU to which you moved the users.

   C. Execute **Gpresult.exe /user *username*** on a domain controller.

   D. Use RSoP to look at the Group Policy results for the user objects as well as for the computer objects that the users are logging on to.

2. Litware, Inc. has three sites: London, New York, and Paris, for its single domain. Within the domain, there is an OU structure that is separated by administrative groups, and then by department. The OUs are shown in the following figure.

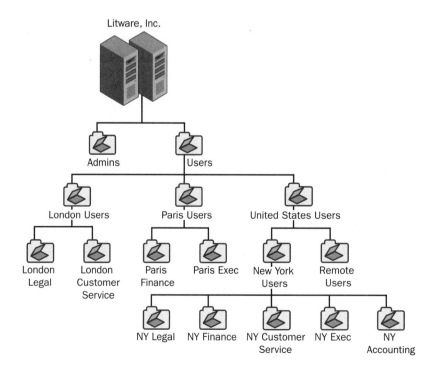

You have an application that you are deploying. The application should be available to the Accounting and Legal departments. It should not be available to anyone in the Customer Service departments or to any Remote Users. You want to avoid filtering out the GPO. Where do you apply the GPO for this application? (Select all that apply.)

   A. New York Legal

   B. New York Accounting

   C. London Legal

   D. New York Users

3. You are the network administrator of Contoso, Ltd. Across your three domains, you have 12,000 users and 12,000 computers. There are nested OU structures in each of the domains. A user named *j123@corp.contoso.com* logs on to a computer that is a member of *res.contoso.com*. The user normally logs on to a computer that is a member of *corp.contoso.com*. The user is not able to find his department's software application on the computer and cannot install it. The Internet Protocol (IP) address of the user's normal computer is 172.16.88.10. The IP address of the computer that is having the problem is 172.16.72.77. The IP address of the closest domain controller is 172.16.72.8. What command do you use from the domain controller to determine the problem with the computer object?

   A. gpresult /u j123@corp.contoso.com /scope user>c:\gp.txt

   B. gpresult /s 172.16.72.77 /u corp.contoso.com\j123 /p password /scope computer /z >c:\gp.txt

   C. gpresult /s 172.16.88.10 /u corp.contoso.com\j123 /p password /scope computer /z >c:\gp.txt

   D. gpotool /u j123@corp.contoso.com /scope user >c:\gp.txt

4. You are the network administrator for Contoso, Ltd. You have three domains. The root domain, *contoso.com*, is used only for administrators and has very few group policies placed on it. You want to make certain that all users in the *corp.contoso.com* domain are not able to change the files in the C:\Windows\System32 directory, so you apply a Group Policy software restriction policy to the *corp.contoso.com* domain. When you log on to the domain as a test user in the All OU, the Group Policy works. When you log on to the domain as a test user in the All\Research\Dev OU, the Group Policy no longer works, and you are able to view and change the files in the C:\Windows\System32 directory. You have the following objectives:

Primary objective: Use the correct tool to discover the problem.

Secondary objective: Use the correct tool to fix the problem.

You use RSoP to query the test user object in the All\Research\Dev OU. You then use the Group Policy Object Editor to fix the Group Policy application.

After performing these actions, you have achieved which of the following?

   A. You have achieved both the primary and the secondary objectives.

   B. You have achieved the primary objective but not the secondary objective.

   C. You have achieved the secondary objective but not the primary objective.

   D. You have achieved neither the primary objective nor the secondary objective.

5.   You are the administrator of Litware, Inc.'s network. In the *litwareinc.com* domain, you have five OUs in the following order: All is at the top of the tree. Within All are Exec and Corp. Within Corp are HQ and Branches. You create the following group policies:

Pol1: Defines the security policy for password length, complexity, and account lockout.

Pol2: Defines desktop and Control Panel restrictions.

Pol3: Defines software distribution for an application called App.

You have applied Pol1 to *litwareinc.com*. You have applied Pol2 to HQ. You have applied Pol3 to Corp. Before you applied these group policies, another administrator had configured other GPOs as well as inheritance blocking and forcing.

How do you best simulate the results of your new GPOs when you've added them to the old GPOs?

   A. Use the Group Policy Object Editor to view all the group policies.

   B. Run the Gpotool command.

   C. Configure auditing on Event Viewer.

   D. Use RSoP to perform a query.

6.   You are troubleshooting Group Policy for a user who travels between multiple sites in your company. At his normal site, the user's stand-alone computer has an IP address of 172.16.88.100, and the domain controller at that site has an IP address of 172.16.88.1. The user is able to install a special application named App1 from Add Or Remove Programs. However, when the user travels from his normal location, sometimes the software is not available. The user has consistent problems at one site, where the user uses a computer with an IP address of 172.16.12.12. The domain controller at that location is 172.16.12.1. You suspect that there is a problem with forced inheritance at one of the sites. To test your theory, which of the commands should you perform from your location, where your computer's IP address is 172.16.1.253?

A. gpresult /s 172.16.1.253 /u corp.contoso.com\j123 /p password /z >c:\gp.txt

B. gpresult /s 172.16.12.1 /u corp.contoso.com\j123 /p password /z >c:\gp.txt

C. gpresult /s 172.16.12.12 /u corp.contoso.com\j123 /p password /z >c:\gp.txt

D. gpresult /s 172.16.88.100 /u corp.contoso.com\j123 /p password /z >c:\gp.txt

7.   You have created a Group Policy for deploying Microsoft Office XP to users across the domain. To conserve disk space, you do not want the computers in the warehouse, which are used for a special database application, to have Office XP on them. These computers are housed in the Warehouse OU. You do want all the rest of the networked computers to have Office XP available at all times. Which of the following should you choose for the fastest deployment?

A. Assign the Group Policy to users in the domain and block inheritance in the Warehouse OU.

B. Assign the Group Policy to computers in the domain and block inheritance in the Warehouse OU.

C. Publish the Group Policy to users in the domain and block inheritance in the Warehouse OU.

D. Publish the Group Policy to computers in the domain and block inheritance in the Warehouse OU.

8.   You are running a Windows 2000 Active Directory domain. You have several Windows Server 2003 member servers in the domain, and you are planning to upgrade to Windows Server 2003. You have applied a new Group Policy that deploys a new application to a test OU in your domain. You have the following objectives:

Primary objective: You want to simulate the effect of this Group Policy on other OUs.

Secondary objective: You want to test how inheritance blocking can be used on a group of users so that they will never receive this Group Policy.

You create a test OU structure that mirrors your actual OU structure. You link the same OUs in the test structure to the GPOs of their peers in the actual OU structure.

You intend to use RSoP in planning mode.

Which of the following can you achieve?

    A. Both the primary and secondary objectives

    B. The primary objective but not the secondary objective

    C. The secondary objective but not the primary objective

    D. Neither the primary nor secondary objectives

Objective 5.1 Answers

1. **Correct Answers: D**

   A. **Incorrect:** The users' former OU will not have any affect on the user objects that have moved.

   B. **Incorrect:** Simply looking at the group policies attached to the OU where the users have moved to will give you only a partial picture of the configuration that a user or computer object should receive.

   C. **Incorrect:** While this will show the user object's Group Policy results, it will show the domain controller's group policies rather than the Group Policy results for the computer object that the users are logging on to.

   D. **Correct:** This will show you what policy will "win" for both the user objects and the computer objects and better enable you to discover the problem.

2. **Correct Answers: A, B, C**

   A. **Correct:** You should apply the GPO to each OU for both the Legal and the Accounting departments.

   B. **Correct:** You should apply the GPO to each OU for both the Legal and the Accounting departments.

   C. **Correct:** You should apply the GPO to each OU for both the Legal and the Accounting departments.

   D. **Incorrect:** If you apply the GPO to New York Users, you will have to filter out the New York Customer Service users from receiving it because they would automatically inherit the GPO from New York Users. Since you want to avoid filtering, this is not the correct choice.

3. **Correct Answers: B**

   A. **Incorrect:** This command does not look at the computer object. In addition, the syntax of this command is incorrect. The correct syntax of this Gpresult command would be **Gpresult /u corp.contoso.com\j123 >c:\gp.txt**.

   B. **Correct:** This command will provide the Group Policy results for the computer object with the problems, executed with the permissions of the user j123.

   C. **Incorrect:** This command will provide the Group Policy results for the computer object that does not have the problems, so it would not indicate the problem.

   D. **Incorrect:** You would not want to use the Gpotool command because it looks at replication problems for group policies, plus this is the incorrect syntax for the Gpotool command.

4.   **Correct Answers: A**

   A. Correct: RSoP is the correct troubleshooting tool to use when determining the Group Policy application. Group Policy Object Editor can be used to make changes to group policies.

   B. Incorrect: RSoP is the correct troubleshooting tool to use when determining the Group Policy application. Group Policy Object Editor can be used to make changes to group policies.

   C. Incorrect: RSoP is the correct troubleshooting tool to use when determining the Group Policy application. Group Policy Object Editor can be used to make changes to group policies.

   D. Incorrect: RSoP is the correct troubleshooting tool to use when determining the Group Policy application. Group Policy Object Editor can be used to make changes to group policies.

5.   **Correct Answers: D**

   A. Incorrect: This is one of the most time-consuming ways of looking at the group policies, and it will not simulate the results.

   B. Incorrect: Gpotool is useful for determining if there is a replication problem with group policies, not for simulating Group Policy results.

   C. Incorrect: Event Viewer auditing will not simulate the results of Group Policy application.

   D. Correct: RSoP will provide you with the results of the policies that are applied to user and computer objects in a graphical interface. You have the ability to receive a text file using the Gpresult command as well.

6.   **Correct Answers: C**

   A. Incorrect: You need to direct your command to the IP address where the user has consistent problems, which would be 172.16.12.12.

   B. Incorrect: You need to direct your command to the IP address where the user has consistent problems, which would be 172.16.12.12.

   C. Correct: You need to direct your command to the IP address where the user has consistent problems, which would be 172.10.12.12.

   D. Incorrect: You need to direct your command to the IP address where the user has consistent problems, which would be 172.16.12.12.

7. **Correct Answers: B**

   A. **Incorrect:** If a user who is not in the Warehouse OU logs on to the Warehouse computers, then Office XP will be installed.

   B. **Correct:** This will correctly install Office XP on all computers in the domain upon startup, except for any computers in the Warehouse OU.

   C. **Incorrect:** If a user who is not in the Warehouse OU logs on to the Warehouse computers and then selects Office XP installation from Add Or Remove Programs in Control Panel, then Office XP will be installed.

   D. **Incorrect:** This will prevent the Warehouse computers from receiving Office XP; however, it will not install Office XP on all the rest of the network computers.

8. **Correct Answers: D**

   A. **Incorrect:** To achieve your objectives, you must run RSoP, which requires you to have a Windows Server 2003 domain controller. You do not have the necessary tools to achieve either of these objectives.

   B. **Incorrect:** To achieve your objectives, you must run RSoP, which requires you to have a Windows Server 2003 domain controller. You do not have the necessary tools to achieve either of these objectives.

   C. **Incorrect:** To achieve your objectives, you must run RSoP, which requires you to have a Windows Server 2003 domain controller. You do not have the necessary tools to achieve either of these objectives.

   D. **Correct:** To achieve your objectives, you must run RSoP, which requires you to have a Windows Server 2003 domain controller. You do not have the necessary tools to achieve either of these objectives.

Objective 5.2

Maintain Installed Software by Using Group Policy

This objective looks at your ability not only to distribute software but to perform updates to that software and automate those updates through **Group Policy** application. When you use Group Policy to automate software distribution, you can take advantage of one of its most powerful administrative applications.

Because Group Policy software distribution uses Microsoft **Windows Installer**, applications can be customized upon deployment. In addition, the application can be customized later on after it has been installed to add or remove features of the program. However, Group Policy also supports non–Windows Installer software deployment through the use of an application file using the .zap file extension. This application file is a text file that uses the application's native installation method.

To deploy updates to Windows Installer–based applications, you can deploy a new Windows Installer package, or redeploy an existing Windows Installer package after making updates to the files in the installation share. To deploy updates to software applications deployed with non–Windows Installer application files, you will need to depend upon the capabilities of the application's installation process. If it is supported, you could deploy the update through a new application file, or redeploy the original application file after making changes to the files in the installation share. If all else fails, you can remove the existing software and redeploy the updated version.

Objective 5.2 Questions

1. You are the network administrator for Litware, Inc. You have a policy for distributing the App application to the users in the Legal department, and it functions properly for all new users in that OU. App uses an application file for distribution. App has a new update available which can be automatically installed through a simple silent setup command. You have applied this update by assigning it's application file to the same OU, and it does not work for any users. You assign it to a test OU, and it doesn't work there either. What could be the problem?

   A. The update has accidentally been saved with a .zap.txt extension.

   B. Replication has not occurred between the domain controllers.

   C. The Group Policy was set to disable Windows Installer for users.

   D. The domain Group Policy prevents new software from being installed.

2. You have an application named Msapp that the former administrator deployed in four separate packages to four different sites (London, New York, Boston, and Sydney) in order to overcome bandwidth problems. You have a patch available for templates to Msapp, which uses Windows Installer. The Legal department will need these new templates, but no one else will. The Legal department has users in London and New York. You have the following objectives:

   Primary objective: Apply the patch so that the Legal department receives the new templates immediately.

   Secondary objective: Apply the patch so that existing sites without a Legal department will not have existing Msapp users given the new templates.

   Secondary objective: Allow any new users who install the application, regardless of their site, to have access to the new templates.

   You perform the following steps:

   1. You copy the Msapp patch file with the .msp extension to the distribution points at all sites.

   2. You apply the patch using the Windows Installer command **Msiexec /a msapp.msi /p msapp.msp** to each distribution point.

   3. In the London and New York sites, you edit the GPO for Msapp and redeploy the application.

   4. You contact the Legal department users by e-mail and ask them to restart their computers.

After performing these actions, you have achieved which of the following?

A. You have achieved both the primary objective and the secondary objectives.

B. You have achieved the primary objective but not the secondary objectives.

C. You have achieved one of the secondary objectives but not the primary objective.

D. You have achieved neither the primary objective nor the secondary objectives.

3. You have deployed an application called Finance to your Accounting department through a GPO that you have applied to the Accounting OU. You originally deployed this application by using a repackager application called WinInstall to take before and after snapshots of a workstation. You now need to distribute an update to Finance. Which of the following methods should you use to distribute the update?

A. Create an application file and deploy it separately to the Accounting OU.

B. Use a transform to customize the .msi that was created using WinInstall and redeploy the application to the Accounting OU.

C. Create a new package for the update alone using WinInstall and deploy it as an additional software package to the Accounting OU.

D. Apply the .msp patch to the .msi file for the Finance application and then redeploy it to the Accounting OU.

4. You are the administrator for Contoso Pharmaceuticals. The Research and Development department has a custom application for tracking the results of tests directly from the equipment. This application is deployed with an application file. The department has decided to rewrite the application to improve some of its features and benefits. The department makes frequent small changes and updates to the application, which they deploy as patches. You have asked them to rewrite the application as a .msi package so that they can take advantage of Group Policy for distributing patches. They provide you with a new .msi package. You have the following objectives:

Primary objective: Make the new software available to all current users.

Secondary objective: Remove and upgrade all existing installations of the software with this package immediately.

You perform the following steps:

1. You create a GPO to deploy the new .msi package.

2. You open the software installation extension and create an upgrade relationship between this package and the application file installation of the former version.

3. You publish the new .msi software to the Research and Development users.

After performing these actions, you have achieved which of the following?

   A. You have achieved both the primary and the secondary objectives.

   B. You have achieved the primary objective but not the secondary objective.

   C. You have achieved the secondary objective but not the primary objective.

   D. You have achieved neither the primary objective nor the secondary objective.

5. You have terminated your software licensing agreement for a graphical application that is used by the Marketing department. This application was assigned to users in the Marketing OU as a single and separate GPO. The Marketing department users have frequently changed computers and worked in areas across the company. Since the software was assigned to Marketing users, it was automatically installed when they logged on to any computer, and it is now deployed in many more computers than just the ones that the Marketing department uses. Which of the following actions must you take to remove the software from all the computers? (Select two.)

   A. Attach the original GPO for the Marketing department to all the users that have computers that could be affected.

   B. Create a new .msi file that removes the software.

   C. Create a new GPO for the Marketing department, deploying the software that will affect Marketing department computers only.

   D. On the original GPO for the Marketing department, open the software installation extension for the application, and select Remove from the All Tasks menu, and then check Immediately Uninstall.

6. An antivirus application is assigned to all users in your organization. This application is deployed through an application file in a GPO named Virus. The antivirus manufacturer has supplied you with a patch for the application that uses a separate installation file. Which of the following methods do you use to deploy the patch?

   A. Create an application file and deploy it separately in a GPO named Virus Patch, assigning it to all users in a GPO that is applied directly before the Virus GPO.

   B. Create a snapshot using a repackager and deploy the patch as a .msi file in the Virus GPO.

   C. Create an application file and deploy it separately in a GPO named Virus Patch, assigning it to all users in a GPO that is applied directly after the Virus GPO.

   D. Apply a .msp patch to the application file and then redeploy the Virus GPO.

7.   You have assigned Microsoft Office 2000 to all computers in your organization through a transform and .msi file in the Office GPO. You are now upgrading to the latest version of Office, which will be installed using the same basic transform options, except that it will install into a new location on users' hard drives. You have the following objectives:

Primary objective: Allow all users to have access to the new version of Office immediately.

Secondary objective: Allow 30 days for users to upgrade their software before removing the old version.

Secondary objective: Remove the old version of Office completely.

You perform the following actions:

1. Create a new distribution point for the new version of Office.

2. Create an Office Upgrade GPO that publishes the upgrade to all users.

3. Wait 30 days.

4. Remove the Office GPO.

After performing these actions, you have achieved which of the following?

A. You have achieved the primary objective and both of the secondary objectives.

B. You have achieved the primary objective and one of the secondary objectives.

C. You have achieved the primary objective but neither of the secondary objectives.

D. You have achieved neither the primary objective nor the secondary objectives.

8.   You have just been notified that a virus is being transmitted throughout e-mail systems across the globe. The virus installs a .vbs script and runs it from the user's hard drive. It waits for several days and then e-mails itself to all listings in the user's address book. There is currently no antivirus signature for this virus. Which of the following software restriction group policies will help stave off the effects of this virus? (Select all that apply.)

A. Use a path rule to disallow all .vbs scripts.

B. Use a certificate rule to require scripts to be digitally signed before being run.

C. Create a hash rule to prevent new versions of the e-mail application from being installed.

D. Use a zone rule to restrict software from being installed from any source outside of Trusted Sites.

9.   You are replacing an application named App1 with a different application named App2 from a different vendor. App1 used an application file that was assigned in the App GPO to all domain users. The original installation file of App1 allows you to remove the software with a switch. App2 uses a .msi file. Some users are restricted from opening Control Panel. Which of the following will be the fastest methods of replacing App1 with App2?

A.   Create an application file for App2 and run an upgrade.

B.   Using the App GPO software installation extension, remove all existing App1 installations. Create a new GPO to deploy App2 and publish it to domain users.

C.   Use a repackager to create a .msi file for App1. Redeploy the .msi package for App1 and then run an upgrade to App2 by creating an upgrade relationship between the two applications.

D.   Add the software package of App2 to the App GPO. Using the software installation extension, create an upgrade relationship between App1 and App2 such that App2 will replace all App1. You can create a logon script that removes App1 using the switch.

Objective 5.2 Answers

1. **Correct Answers: A**

A. Correct: You must be careful to save your application files with a .zap extension. Most text editors will add a .txt extension, and if you have hidden the extensions on Microsoft Windows Explorer, you will not see this problem.

B. Incorrect: The application file did not work for any users, so there must be a problem with the application file itself. If the application file had worked for some users and not others, then replication might have been the source of the problem.

C. Incorrect: An application that uses an application file does not require Windows Installer, so it would be applied regardless of whether Windows Installer was enabled or disabled.

D. Incorrect: Since the original application, App, is able to be distributed to the Legal department and any new users in that OU, this option could not be true.

2. **Correct Answers: A**

A. Correct: This process will apply the patch and allow the Legal department to have immediate access to the templates, achieving the primary objective. By applying the patch to all the distribution points, you enable all new users to receive the templates. By not redeploying Msapp to Boston and Sydney, you will not change the existing templates in those sites.

B. Incorrect: This process will apply the patch and allow the Legal department to have immediate access to the templates, achieving the primary objective. By applying the patch to all the distribution points, you enable all new users to receive the templates. By not redeploying Msapp to Boston and Sydney, you will not change the existing templates in those sites.

C. Incorrect: This process will apply the patch and allow the Legal department to have immediate access to the templates, achieving the primary objective. By applying the patch to all the distribution points, you enable all new users to receive the templates. By not redeploying Msapp to Boston and Sydney, you will not change the existing templates in those sites.

D. Incorrect: This process will apply the patch and allow the Legal department to have immediate access to the templates, achieving the primary objective. By applying the patch to all the distribution points, you enable all new users to receive the templates. By not redeploying Msapp to Boston and Sydney, you will not change the existing templates in those sites.

3.   Correct Answers: C

   A.   Incorrect: Since the original application was distributed through a snapshot method, it will not use an application file for the update.

   B.   Incorrect: You do not have the ability to customize a .msi file with a transform when you repackage the application using a snapshot method.

   C.   Correct: You can create a new package using WinInstall, where you start with a "clean" computer, which has the application installed, as the "before" snapshot, and with the update as the "after" snapshot. Then deploy this update to the Accounting OU.

   D.   Incorrect: You cannot apply .msp patch files to a .msi file that was created using a repackager application such as WinInstall.

4.   Correct Answers: B

   A.   Incorrect: You achieved the primary objective by making the new software available to all current users. However, by publishing the new package rather than assigning it, and by not prompting or forcing users to reboot their workstations, the users will not receive the upgrade immediately.

   B.   Correct: You achieved the primary objective by making the new software available to all current users. However, by publishing the new package rather than assigning it, and by not prompting or forcing users to reboot their workstations, the users will not receive the upgrade immediately.

   C.   Incorrect: You achieved the primary objective by making the new software available to all current users. However, by publishing the new package rather than assigning it, and by not prompting or forcing users to reboot their workstations, the users will not receive the upgrade immediately.

   D.   Incorrect: You achieved the primary objective by making the new software available to all current users. However, by publishing the new package rather than assigning it, and by not prompting or forcing users to reboot their workstations, the users will not receive the upgrade immediately.

5.   Correct Answers: A, D

   A.   Correct: In order to make a change effective on all affected computers, you need to start by attaching the original GPO to all affected users.

   B.   Incorrect: You do not need to create a new .msi file. When the GPO prompts for removal, the original MSI publisher will remove it as long as it contains removal routines.

C. Incorrect: The problem that you have with installed software affects more than just the Marketing department's computers.

D. Correct: All users who are given this Group Policy will immediately have the software application uninstalled from their computer.

6. **Correct Answers: C**

A. Incorrect: You will need to assign the patch to users after they have the original antivirus software applied because new users will not receive the correct installation.

B. Incorrect: Repackagers may have inconsistent results. By including the .msi file in the Virus GPO, you cannot control the order of the installation as easily as you can by having separate GPOs for the antivirus software and its patch.

C. Correct: This will correctly install the patch for the antivirus software to all users, both new and existing.

D. Incorrect: You cannot apply .msp patch files to an application file, which uses the .zap file extension.

7. **Correct Answers: B**

A. Incorrect: You have achieved the primary objective by publishing the Office Upgrade GPO. You have achieved the secondary objective of allowing a 30-day grace period. You have not achieved the other secondary objective of removing the old version of Office completely because you did not create an upgrade relationship between the two versions of Office, nor did you perform a Remove action of the original Office software.

B. Correct: You have achieved the primary objective by publishing the Office Upgrade GPO. You have achieved the secondary objective of allowing a 30-day grace period. You have not achieved the other secondary objective of removing the old version of Office completely because you did not create an upgrade relationship between the two versions of Office, nor did you perform a Remove action of the original Office software.

C. Incorrect: You have achieved the primary objective by publishing the Office Upgrade GPO. You have achieved the secondary objective of allowing a 30-day grace period. You have not achieved the other secondary objective of removing the old version of Office completely because you did not create an upgrade relationship between the two versions of Office, nor did you perform a Remove action of the original Office software.

D. Incorrect: You have achieved the primary objective by publishing the Office Upgrade GPO. You have achieved the secondary objective of allowing a 30-day grace period. You have not achieved the other secondary objective of removing the old version of Office completely because you did not create an upgrade relationship between the two versions of Office, nor did you perform a Remove action of the original Office software.

8.   Correct Answers: A, B

A. **Correct:** This will prevent a user from running the virus's .vbs script.

B. **Correct:** By requiring a certificate to verify the source of a script, you can prevent unknown scripts from being run.

C. **Incorrect:** This would not affect this particular virus from wreaking havoc on your network.

D. **Incorrect:** Since the script is not a Windows Installer file and since it is not distributed through Microsoft Internet Explorer, this rule would not prevent the script from running.

9.   Correct Answers: D

A. **Incorrect:** You do not use application files (with .zap extensions) for applications that have the Windows Installer capability.

B. **Incorrect:** Publishing App2 will not automatically replace App1. App2 would not be available to anyone who was restricted from Control Panel.

C. **Incorrect:** There is no need to use a repackager to create a .msi file. You can create an upgrade relationship between applications that use different methods of installation.

D. **Correct:** You can use the Group Policy capability of creating an upgrade relationship between applications that are not from the same vendor to remove and replace software, as in this example. A script can be used to remove the old software.

Objective 5.3

Troubleshoot the Application of Group Policy Security Settings

This objective discusses the troubleshooting process for **Group Policy** security settings. When security settings are deployed, it is important that they are applied correctly. Like all group policies, conflicts from overriding group policies can cause inconsistent results with group policies that include security settings. In addition, when other issues interfere with **replication**, group policies may be applied inconsistently across the domain.

You can discover replication issues with group policies through the Gpotool command-line tool. In addition, you can use **Gpupdate** to refresh the group policies on a local workstation when you suspect that the user or workstation has not received the latest group policies.

In order to determine whether there is a Group Policy inheritance conflict, you can use **RSoP**. The Group Policy Management Console can access RSoP data to obtain the same results. For a command-line tool option, you can use the **Gpresult** command.

Objective 5.3 Questions

1. You have added a new GPO to *litwareinc.com* that follows the default domain policy to prevent users from installing non-approved software through software restrictions. You discover that the policy is not applied consistently to all users throughout the domain. What should you do to discover whether the problem is caused by blocked inheritance?

    A. Configure each computer's local policy to require software restrictions for local users.

    B. Use RSoP to query each OU containing users.

    C. Run the Gpresult command on your computer.

    D. Run the Gpotool command on your computer.

2. Litware, Inc. has three sites for its single domain: London, New York, and Paris. Within the domain there is an OU structure that is separated by administrative groups and then by department. Users in London are required to use software restrictions that prevent them from installing any software or using Windows Installer. These group policies are applied, but not all London users receive them. Which tool is best used for determining the problem? (Select all that apply.)

    A. RSoP

    B. Gpresult

    C. GPMC

    D. Gpupdate

3. You are the administrator of the *contoso.com* domain. In *contoso.com*, you have 38 sites. You do not have any site-attached GPOs. You have deployed a new Group Policy that prevents users from accessing their Windows and System32 directories. Two months later, you find out that a user has corrupted the operating system by deleting files from these directories. You investigate the problem and find out that all the users at that same site have not received the new Group Policy, even though their user objects are in the same OUs as users in other locations that are receiving the Group Policy. Which of the following tools do you use to determine the problem?

    A. RSoP

    B. Gpresult

    C. Group Policy Object Editor

    D. The Gpotool command

4. You are the administrator of the *litwareinc.com* domain. You have three sites: Detroit, Minneapolis, and Los Angeles. You have created a Group Policy named SecurityPol that restricts software installation and Control Panel access. In your network, you want administrators to be able to have full access to everything. In addition, executives and management require full access to their workstations and laptops. You have the following OU configuration in your single domain: All Users is at the top of the OU tree. Within All Users are the Administrators, Executives, and Corp OUs. Within Corp, you have the Management, Research, Finance, Legal, Service, and Sales OUs. You do not want to filter group policies. Which of the following is one of the containers to which you should apply SecurityPol?

    A. The *litwareinc.com* domain

    B. The All Users OU

    C. The Research OU

    D. The Detroit site

5. You have just been hired at Contoso, Ltd. as the new network administrator. You are reviewing the files on the former administrator's hard drive. One is a text file that lists Computer Settings, applied group policies, group policies that were filtered out, and security settings that the computer was a member of. Which tool did the former administrator use to create this text file?

    A. GPMC

    B. The Gpresult command

    C. The Gpotool command

    D. The Gpupdate command

6. You have deployed a security policy to all users by applying it to the domain, and you imported a security template and then edited it to create the GPO. After using the security policy for a while, you decide that you would like to change the requirements back to the template's defaults. Which is the fastest way to apply this change?

    A. Configure each computer separately with a new Group Policy.

    B. Delete the existing GPO. Create a new GPO by importing the template and applying it to the domain.

    C. Edit the individual policies within the GPO.

    D. Use the Gpupdate command to refresh the Group Policy defaults.

7. Your network requires a more secure workstation policy. You have the following objectives:

Primary objective: Use a security template to increase security for workstations.

Secondary objective: Apply the security template to workstations but not to member servers or domain controllers.

You perform the following actions:

1. You run the Group Policy Object Editor on a GPO at the domain level.
2. You navigate through Computer Settings to Windows Settings, and then right-click on Security Settings.
3. You select Import Policy.
4. You select Hisecws.inf and click Open.
5. You save this policy and apply it to the domain.

After performing these actions, you have achieved which of the following?

A. You have achieved both the primary and secondary objectives.

B. You have achieved the primary objective but not the secondary objective.

C. You have achieved the secondary objective but not the primary objective.

D. You have achieved neither the primary nor the secondary objectives.

8. You are the network administrator for Litware, Inc. Another administrator has called you because she is unable to install software on workstations when logging on with the administrator account. You have recently applied a software restriction policy to the entire domain. Which of the following can be changed to allow the administrator to bypass software restrictions?

A. Move all administrators to a new domain.

B. Delete the software restriction policy and apply it to the OUs instead.

C. Redeploy the software restriction policy as a site-attached policy.

D. Change the policy so that it is applied to All Users Except Administrators.

Objective 5.3 Answers

1. **Correct Answers: B**

   A. Incorrect: Not only is this time-consuming, but it will not help you discover the problem affecting domain users.

   B. Correct: By querying each OU, you can determine whether the users in that OU have had the Group Policy blocked.

   C. Incorrect: The Gpresult command will look at only one computer and user object, and the question does not state whether you have been affected by the inconsistent application of the Group Policy or not.

   D. Incorrect: The Gpotool command will tell you whether there is a problem with replication of the Group Policy, and while that may be a cause of the problem, it will not tell you whether inheritance of the domain controller Group Policy has been blocked.

2. **Correct Answers: A, B, C**

   A. Correct: RSoP has the ability to display the group policies to see where the problem may lie.

   B. Correct: Gpresult is a command-line tool that can display Group Policy results. It displays the results in a text file which may not be as easy to view as the RSoP graphical tool.

   C. Correct: GPMC is able to integrate the RSoP data in addition to the Group Policy Object editor tool, making it easy to research and troubleshoot Group Policy application from a single console.

   D. Incorrect: Gpupdate is used to trigger a refresh of the Group Policy on a computer. It will not help you discover the root of a problem.

3. **Correct Answers: D**

   A. Incorrect: Given the symptoms of the problem, the likelihood is that the site has not received the Group Policy through replication. RSoP will not help you with a replication problem.

   B. Incorrect: Since the security policy is not distributed to a single site, it is likely that there is a replication problem. Gpresult will not help with replication issues.

   C. Incorrect: The Group Policy Object Editor will not help detect a problem with Group Policy replication.

   D. Correct: The Gpotool command is used to discover a problem with replication of the Group Policy.

4.   **Correct Answers: C**

    A. Incorrect: The SecurityPol should not be assigned to the domain because it would be applied to the administrators, management, and executives.

    B. Incorrect: SecurityPol should not be assigned to the All Users OU because Administrators, Management, and Executives are all OUs nested within it.

    C. Correct: The Research OU is one of the three OUs to which you should apply SecurityPol. In addition, you should apply SecurityPol to the Finance, Legal, Service and Sales OUs.

    D. Incorrect: The SecurityPol should not be assigned to a single site because administrators, executives, and management users may be located there and would receive the policy.

5.   **Correct Answers: B**

    A. Incorrect: The Group Policy Management console is a graphical tool.

    B. Correct: The Gpresult command can create a text file that lists only computer settings.

    C. Incorrect: The Gpotool command is used to discover replication problems with Group Policy.

    D. Incorrect: The Gpupdate command is used to refresh the group policies on the local computer.

6.   **Correct Answers: B**

    A. Incorrect: Configuring each computer separately will be time-consuming.

    B. Correct: This method will be the fastest for deploying the defaults that are in the security template.

    C. Incorrect: This method would be slower than importing the security template defaults.

    D. Incorrect: The Gpupdate command will not pull in the defaults from the security template. The Gpupdate command will only refresh the policies on a local workstation.

7.   **Correct Answers: B**

    A. Incorrect: You achieved the primary objective because the security template increased security on workstations. You did not achieve the secondary objective because by applying the template to the domain, you included member servers and domain controllers. You should separate domain controllers and member servers into OUs outside the OU structure that contains computer objects. You should apply this GPO to the highest OU that contains computer objects so that it can be inherited by lower-level OUs.

B. Correct: You achieved the primary objective because the security template increased security on workstations. You did not achieve the secondary objective because by applying the template to the domain, you included member servers and domain controllers. You should separate domain controllers and member servers into OUs outside the OU structure that contains computer objects. You should apply this GPO to the highest OU that contains computer objects so that it can be inherited by lower-level OUs.

C. Incorrect: You achieved the primary objective because the security template increased security on workstations. You did not achieve the secondary objective because by applying the template to the domain, you included member servers and domain controllers. You should separate domain controllers and member servers into OUs outside the OU structure that contains computer objects. You should apply this GPO to the highest OU that contains computer objects so that it can be inherited by lower-level OUs.

D. Incorrect: You achieved the primary objective because the security template increased security on workstations. You did not achieve the secondary objective because by applying the template to the domain, you included member servers and domain controllers. You should separate domain controllers and member servers into OUs outside the OU structure that contains computer objects. You should apply this GPO to the highest OU that contains computer objects so that it can be inherited by lower-level OUs.

8.   Correct Answers: D

A. Incorrect: This will not fix the problem. There will still be administrative accounts in the domain that will be restricted.

B. Incorrect: It is possible that user accounts within the OU hierarchy are actually administrators who need the rights to install software, so applying the policy to the OUs will not necessarily fix the problem.

C. Incorrect: Site-attached policies can affect administrators. This would not avoid the problem.

D. Correct: This option is available to prevent software restrictions from affecting the administrators within the domain.

Part 3
Appendixes

Active Directory Features in the Windows Server 2003 Family

Active Directory directory service in the Microsoft Windows Server 2003 family has some improvements over the version of Active Directory employed in Microsoft Windows 2000.

System-Wide Active Directory Features

The following list summarizes the Active Directory features that are enabled by default on any domain controller running Windows Server 2003.

- **Multiple selection of directory objects**   You can modify common attributes of multiple users at one time. This includes modifying the Description attribute of multiple object types. More information about this feature is available in Chapter 9, "Administering Active Directory Objects."

- **Drag-and-drop functionality**   You can move directory objects from container to container by dragging and dropping one or more objects to a desired location in the domain hierarchy. You can also add objects to group membership lists by dragging and dropping one or more objects (including other group objects) onto the target group. More information about this feature is available in Chapter 9, "Administering Active Directory Objects."

- **Efficient search capabilities**   Search functionality is object-oriented and provides an efficient browseless search that minimizes network traffic associated with browsing objects. More information about this feature is available in Chapter 9, "Administering Active Directory Objects."

- **Saved queries**   You can save, export, reopen, and refresh Active Directory queries. You can use saved queries to find a particular set of user objects, and then edit the properties on all of them at once. You can export the results of an attribute query for reporting or analysis and then periodically refresh the query to save time when you complete management reports. More information about this feature is available in Chapter 9, "Administering Active Directory Objects."

- **Active Directory command-line tools**   You can run directory service commands provided to satisfy several remote and scripted administration scenarios. The following command-line tools can be used to manage Active Directory:

Csvde, Dsadd, Dsget, Dsmod, Dsmove, Dsquery, Dsrm, Ldifde, and Ntdsutil. More information about these tools is available in Windows Server 2003 Help.

- **InetOrgPerson class** The inetOrgPerson object class has been added to the base schema as a security principal and can be used in the same manner as the user class. The userPassword attribute can also be used to set the account password. More information about this feature is available in Chapter 7, "Administering User Accounts."

- **Application directory partitions** You can configure the replication scope for application-specific data among domain controllers running Windows Server 2003. For example, you can control the replication scope of Domain Name System (DNS) zone data stored in Active Directory so that only specific domain controllers in the forest participate in DNS zone replication. More information about this feature is available in Chapter 5, "Configuring Sites and Managing Replication."

- **Install additional domain controllers in existing domains using backup media** You can reduce the time it takes to install an additional domain controller in an existing domain by using a restored backup of another domain controller. More information about this feature is available in Chapter 2, "Installing and Configuring Active Directory."

- **Universal group membership caching** You can eliminate the need to locate a global catalog across a wide area network (WAN) during logons by storing user universal group memberships on an authenticating domain controller. More information about this feature is available in Chapter 5, "Configuring Sites and Managing Replication."

- **Domain functional levels** Domain functional levels (formerly known as domain modes) provide a way to enable domain-wide Active Directory features within your network environment. Four domain functional levels are available: Windows 2000 mixed (default), Windows 2000 native, Windows Server 2003 interim, and Windows Server 2003. More information about this feature is available in Chapter 3, "Administering Active Directory."

- **Forest functional levels** Forest functional levels provide a way to enable forest-wide Active Directory features within your network environment. Three forest functional levels are available: Windows 2000 (default), Windows Server 2003 interim, and Windows Server 2003. More information about this feature is available in Chapter 3, "Administering Active Directory."

- **Secure LDAP traffic** Active Directory administrative tools sign and encrypt all Lightweight Directory Access Protocol (LDAP) traffic by default. Signing LDAP traffic guarantees that the packaged data comes from a known source and that it has not been tampered with. More information about this feature is available in Chapter 1, "Introduction to Active Directory."

- **Active Directory quotas**   You can specify quotas in Active Directory to control the number of objects a user, group, or computer can own in a given directory partition. Domain Administrators and Enterprise Administrators are exempt from quotas. More information about this feature is available in Chapter 9, "Administering Active Directory Objects."

Change and Configuration Management Features

The following list summarizes the Active Directory change and configuration management features that are enabled by default on any domain controller running Windows Server 2003.

- **New Group Policy settings**   Windows Server 2003 includes more than 200 new Group Policy settings. The Group Policy settings in Windows 2000 function on both Windows 2000 and Windows Server 2003 clients. The settings new to Windows Server 2003 have no effect if applied to Windows 2000 clients. More information about Group Policy settings is available in Chapter 10, "Implementing Group Policy."

- **Resultant Set of Policy capability**   Windows Server 2003 enables you to determine the policies applied to a specified user or computer by using the new Resultant Set Of Policy (RSoP) Wizard. RSoP is the sum of the group policies applied to the user or computer. The wizard guides you through the steps necessary to create an appropriate target, generate RSoP data, and start the RSoP tool to use that data. More information about RSoP is available in Chapter 11, "Administering Group Policy."

- **Administrative template features**   A description of each administrative template is provided in Windows Server 2003 Help and on the Extended tab in the Group Policy console. Information about which versions of Windows are supported as clients for the setting is also provided. The view filtering feature is available to filter the view of administrative templates in an effort to reduce screen clutter. More information about these features is available in Chapter 10, "Implementing Group Policy."

- **Command-line tools**   The Gpresult and Gpupdate command-line tools are provided for Group Policy administration. The Gpresult command-line tool enables you to create and display an RSoP query on the command line. In addition, Gpresult provides general information about the operating system, user, and computer. The Gpupdate command-line tool allows you to refresh policy immediately, replacing the Secedit.exe /refreshpolicy command used for refreshing Group Policy Objects (GPOs) in Windows 2000. More information about Gpresult is available in Chapter 11, "Administering Group Policy." More information about Gpupdate is available in Chapter 10, "Implementing Group Policy."

■ **Easy use of folder redirection** In the Windows Server 2003 family, it is not necessary to type variables such as *%Username%* as part of the redirection path. In addition, you can redirect My Documents to a user's home folder. This option is intended only for organizations that have already deployed home folders and that want to maintain compatibility with the existing home folder environment. More information about folder redirection is available in Chapter 11, "Administering Group Policy."

■ **Advanced software installation options** Software installation has an advanced deployment option to enable or disable availability of 32-bit programs to 64-bit computers. Another advanced option allows administrators to choose to enable or disable (default) publication of OLE class information about a software package. Administrators also have an option to force assigned applications to be installed at deployment time. More information about this feature is available in Chapter 12, "Deploying Software with Group Policy."

■ **Cross-forest support** Group Policy features are supported in multiple forest environments allowing authenticated access to resources in separate, networked environments. Administrators can manage and enforce GPOs for user and computer objects in remote trusted forests and analyze policies using RSoP. More information about this feature is available in Chapter 11, "Administering Group Policy."

■ **The Software Restriction Policies security area** Software Restriction Policies is a security area that can identify software that is hostile or unwanted and prevent it from executing on computers running Microsoft Windows XP Professional or a member of the Windows Server 2003 family. More information about this feature is available in Chapter 13, "Administering Security with Group Policy."

Domain-Wide and Forest-Wide Active Directory Features

The following list summarizes the domain-wide and forest-wide Active Directory features that can be enabled only when all domain controllers in a domain or forest are running Windows Server 2003 and the domain or forest functionality has been set to Windows Server 2003.

■ **Domain controller renaming** You can rename domain controllers without first demoting them. More information about this feature is available in Chapter 4, "Installing and Managing Domains, Trees, and Forests."

■ **Domain renaming** You can rename any domain running Windows Server 2003 domain controllers. You can change the NetBIOS or DNS name of any child, parent, tree-root, or forest-root domain. More information about this feature is available in Chapter 4, "Installing and Managing Domains, Trees, and Forests."

- **Forest restructuring**   You can move existing domains to other locations in the domain hierarchy. More information about this feature is available in Chapter 4, "Installing and Managing Domains, Trees, and Forests."

- **Forest trusts**   You can create a forest trust to extend two-way transitivity beyond the scope of a single forest to a second forest. More information about this feature is available in Chapter 4, "Installing and Managing Domains, Trees, and Forests."

- **Replication enhancements**   Linked value replication allows individual group members to be replicated across the network instead of treating the entire group membership as a single unit of replication. Spanning tree algorithms make replication more efficient and scalable across more domains and sites in both Windows 2000 and Windows Server 2003 forests. More information about this feature is available in Chapter 8, "Administering Groups."

- **User resource access control between domains and forests**   You can block users in a domain or forest from accessing resources in another domain or forest, and then allow users selective access. More information about this feature is available in Chapter 9, "Administering Active Directory Objects."

The following list summarizes the domain-wide and forest-wide Active Directory features that can be enabled according to domain and forest functionalities. However, these features pertain to developer activities and are not covered in this training kit.

- **Deactivating defunct schema objects**   You can deactivate unnecessary classes or attributes from the schema.

- **Supporting dynamic auxiliary classes**   Support is provided for dynamically linking auxiliary classes to individual objects, and not just to entire classes of objects. In addition, auxiliary classes that have been attached to an object instance can subsequently be removed from the instance.

- **Tuning global catalog replication**   Preserves the synchronization state of the global catalog when an administrative action results in an extension of the partial attribute set. This minimizes the work generated as a result of a partial attribute set extension by only transmitting attributes that were added.

Appendix B
Active Directory Setup Answer File Parameters

This section contains the parameters for installing or removing a domain controller using an answer file, which are supported for the Microsoft Windows Server 2003 family. These parameters can be included in the DcInstall section of the answer file you create that is used to install Windows Server 2003. Alternatively, the parameters can be used in a separate answer file you create that installs only Active Directory directory service and is run after Windows Server 2003 setup is complete and you have logged on to the system. The command for running this answer file is **dcpromo/ answer:*answerfile***, where *answerfile* is the name of the answer file.

To create the answer file, refer to the instructions located in the "Microsoft Windows Preinstallation Reference," viewable by opening the Ref.chm help file on the Windows Server 2003 operating system CD. The Ref.chm help file is located in the Deploy.cab file in the \Support\Tools folder on the CD.

AdministratorPassword

Value: *admin_password*
Default: blank

This parameter sets the local administrator password for the computer during the demotion of a domain controller to a member server. This entry is valid only during a demotion. If it is not specified or has no value, a blank administrator password is used. The value is deleted from the answer file after the demotion operation is completed.

AllowAnonymousAccess

Value: *Yes* | *No*
Default: Yes

This parameter is used when any pre–Windows 2000 servers will authenticate users from this domain or any trusting domain, as follows:

- *Yes* is used with pre–Windows 2000 servers and causes the permissions to be set to permit anonymous access to user and group information.

- *No* is used when all servers in the domain are running a Microsoft Windows 2000 Server product and makes the default permissions more restrictive.

AutoConfigDNS

Value: *Yes* | *No*
Default: Yes

This parameter is used to indicate whether the Active Directory Installation Wizard configures Domain Name System (DNS) for the new domain if it detects that the DNS dynamic update protocol is not available, as follows:

- *Yes* configures DNS for the new domain if the DNS dynamic update protocol is not available.

- *No* does not configure DNS for the domain.

ChildName

Value: *child_domain_name*

This parameter specifies the DNS label to be appended to the beginning of the name of an existing directory service domain when a child domain is installed. For example, if the parent name is *parentdom.example.com* and the value of *child_domain_name* is *child-dom*, then the name of the new domain is *childdom.parentdom.example.com*. This new domain name must not be in use and DNS services must be properly configured on the computer. This value must be specified.

ConfirmGc

Value: *Yes* | *No*
Default: Yes

This parameter applies only if the *ReplicationSourcePath* parameter is specified. If restored files were created from a backup of a global catalog, then the replica can also be a global catalog of those files. Use this value to indicate whether the replica is also a global catalog, as follows:

- *Yes* makes the replica a global catalog if the backup was of a global catalog.

- *No* does not make the replica a global catalog.

CreateOrJoin

Value: *Create* | *Join*
Default: Join

This parameter is provided for backward compatibility with Windows 2000 unattended setup. For unattended setup of a member of the Windows Server 2003 family, use *NewDomain* instead. This parameter specifies that the new domain created causes the creation of a new forest of domains or is the root of a new domain tree in an existing forest of domains, as follows:

- *Create* creates a new forest of domains.
- *Join* places the new domain as the root of a new domain tree in an existing forest of domains.

CriticalReplicationOnly

Value: *Yes | No*
Default: none

This parameter specifies whether the promotion operation performs only critical replication and then continues, skipping the (potentially lengthy) noncritical portion of replication. If noncritical replication is skipped, replication automatically and silently resumes when the computer is rebooted and assumes its new role as a domain controller. The settings are configured as follows:

- *Yes* skips noncritical replication.
- *No* does not skip any replication steps.

DatabasePath

Value: *path_to_database_files*
Default: *%Systemroot%\NTDS*

This parameter specifies the fully qualified, non–Universal Naming Convention (UNC) path to a directory on a fixed disk of the local computer that contains the domain database. If the directory exists, it must be empty. If the directory does not exist, it is created. The disk must have enough free disk space available—at least 20 MB for new domains— and must have room to grow if you plan to add numerous objects to the domain. For replica domains, specify the space required in the domain size. For optimal performance, place the domain database on a different volume than the domain log files.

DisableCancelForDnsInstall

Value: *Yes | No*
Default: Yes

This parameter applies only if the answer file indicates that the wizard installs DNS on the computer if it has not already installed it. The parameter specifies whether to disable the Cancel button during a DNS installation, as follows:

- *Yes* does not display the Cancel button. During the DNS installation, the /c switch invokes the Optional Component Manager (OCM).
- *No* displays the Cancel button.

DNSOnNetwork

Value: *Yes* | *No*
Default: Yes

This parameter specifies whether to set DNS server addresses automatically. It is used when installing the first domain in a new forest and the Transmission Control Protocol/ Internet Protocol (TCP/IP) configuration has missing or incorrect DNS server addresses. Before the computer can become a domain controller, its TCP/IP stack must have a valid DNS configuration. The settings are configured as follows:

- *Yes* sets the DNS server addresses manually for the computer. The Active Directory Installation Wizard does not test the client configuration. Therefore, the user must set the server addresses manually later and may have to configure DNS manually for the new domain.

- *No* installs the DNS service, creates a valid DNS configuration, and creates a zone for the new domain with that service.

DomainNetBiosName

Value: *domain_NetBIOS_name*
Required

This parameter assigns a NetBIOS name to the new domain. The value is required, and the name specified must not already be in use as a domain or computer name. This entry is ignored when upgrading pre–Windows 2000 primary domain controllers.

IsLastDCInDomain

Value: *Yes* | *No*
Default: *No*

This parameter indicates whether the computer on which Dcpromo.exe is running is the last domain controller in the domain. This entry is valid only when demoting an existing domain controller to a member server. The settings are configured as follows:

- *Yes* designates this computer as the last domain controller in the domain.

- *No* indicates this computer is not the last domain controller in the domain.

LogPath

Value: *path_to_log_files*
Default: *%Systemroot%*\NTDS

This parameter specifies the fully qualified, non-UNC path to a directory on a fixed disk of the local computer that contains the domain log files. If the directory exists, it must be empty. If the directory does not exist, it is created. The disk must have enough free disk space available—at least 10 MB for new domains—and must have room to expand if you plan to add numerous objects to the domain. For replica domains, specify the space required in the domain size. For optimal performance, the log files are placed on a different volume than the database files.

NewDomain

Value: *Forest* | *Child* | *Tree*
Default: Forest

This parameter is used to indicate the type of the new domain, whether it is a new domain in a new forest, a child of an existing domain, or the root of a new tree in an existing forest, as follows:

- *Forest* indicates the new domain is the first domain in a new forest of domain trees.

- *Child* indicates the new domain is a child of an existing domain.

- *Tree* indicates the new domain is the root of a new tree in an existing forest.

NewDomainDNSName

Value: *DNS_name_of_domain*

This parameter specifies the required name of a new tree in an existing domain or when a new forest of domains is installed. For example, this DNS name could be *newdom.example.com.*

ParentDomainDNSName

Value: *DNS_name_of_domain*

This parameter specifies the DNS domain name of an existing directory service domain when a child domain is installed. When specifying this entry, make sure that the current user has administrative privileges to the specified domain, and that the DNS services are properly configured. The domain name must refer to an existing directory service domain.

Password

Value: *password*

This parameter specifies the password for the user name (account credentials) to be used for promoting the member server to a domain controller. The value is deleted from the answer file after the promotion operation is completed.

RebootOnSuccess

Value: *Yes* | *No* | *NoAndNoPromptEither*
Default: No

This parameter specifies whether the computer is rebooted upon successful completion. The server must be rebooted for the directory service to be started. The settings are configured as follows:

- *Yes* reboots the server upon successful completion.

- *No* does not reboot the server upon successful completion, but prompts the user to reboot.

- *NoAndNoPromptEither* does not reboot the server upon successful completion and does not prompt the user to reboot.

RemoveApplicationPartitions

Value: *Yes* | *No*
Default: No

This parameter specifies whether to remove application partitions during the demotion of a domain controller to a member server. If you remove the last replica of any application directory partition, the partition and all data it contains are destroyed. The settings are configured as follows:

- *Yes* removes application partitions on the domain controller.

- *No* does not remove application partitions on the domain controller. If the domain controller hosts the last replica of any application directory partition, you must manually confirm that you want to remove these partitions.

ReplicaDomainDNSName

Value: *DNS_name_of_domain*

This parameter specifies the DNS domain name of the domain replicate. This entry is valid only for backup domain controller (BDC) upgrades and domain controller installations. In such situations, a value must be specified or the installation fails. Normally, the user who is currently logged on has administrative privileges to the specified domain, and DNS services are properly configured. The domain name must refer to an existing directory service domain. This parameter is ignored if the *ReplicationSourcePath* parameter refers to a valid set of restored backup files. The domain name to which those files belong takes precedence.

ReplicaOrMember

Value: *Replica | Member*
Default: Member

This parameter specifies whether a Microsoft Windows NT 3.51 or Windows NT 4 BDC being upgraded is converted to a domain controller or is demoted to a member server in the domain. This entry is valid only when upgrading a BDC. The settings are configured as follows:

- *Replica* installs the BDC as a domain controller.

- *Member* installs the BDC as a member server in a domain.

ReplicaOrNewDomain

Value: *Replica | Domain*
Default: Replica

This parameter specifies whether a new domain controller is installed as the first domain controller in a new directory service domain, or whether the new domain controller is installed as a replica directory service domain controller, as follows:

- *Replica* installs the new domain controller as a replica directory service domain controller.

- *Domain* installs the new domain controller as the first domain controller in a new directory service domain. The *TreeOrChild* parameter must be specified with a valid value.

ReplicationSourceDC

Value: *DNS_name_of_DC | none*
Default: none

This parameter is used to indicate the full DNS name of the domain controller from which the domain information is to be replicated, as follows:

- *DNS_name_of_DC* indicates the full DNS name of the domain controller from which the domain information is to be replicated. This value only applies in new replica or BDC upgrade cases.

- *none* selects the closest domain controller for the domain being replicated.

ReplicationSourcePath

Value: *replication_source_path*
Default: none

This parameter indicates the location of the files to be used to create a new domain controller. The value must be the fully qualified path to a folder on the local computer where the files have been copied. The parameter is used to indicate that the bulk of the directory data replication is drawn from backup files that have been restored to a volume on the server, rather from another domain controller. However, complete replication cannot be performed entirely from copied files; access to another domain controller is still required.

If this value is present and non-empty, then data replication is performed using the restored files. If this value is not present or is empty, then replication is performed from another domain controller on the network. If the value refers to a valid set of restored backup files, then any value for the *ReplicaDomainDNSName* parameter is ignored. The domain name to which the restored files belong takes precedence.

SafeModeAdminPassword

Value: *password | none*
Default: none

This parameter is used to supply the password to be set on the administrator account used when the computer is started in safe mode or a variant of safe mode, such as DS-repair mode. The settings are configured as follows:

- *password* specifies the password that the administrator account can use when the computer is in safe mode.

- *none* does not supply a password for the administrator account to use when the computer is in safe mode.

SetForestVersion

Value: *Yes | No*
Default: No

This parameter specifies the functional level for a new forest. Use this parameter only when the destination computer is a domain controller upgraded from Windows NT 4 to a member of the Windows Server 2003 family and is the first domain controller in a new forest.

- *Yes* sets the forest functional level to Windows Server 2003 interim. If you set the functional level to Windows Server 2003 interim, you cannot change the functional level to enable Windows 2000 domain controllers later.

- *No* sets the forest functional level to Windows 2000.

SiteName

Value: *site_name*
Default: *default_first_site*

This parameter specifies the name of an existing site at which to place the new domain controller. If not specified, a suitable site is selected using the current site and subnet configuration of the forest.

Syskey

Value: *none | system key*
Default: none

This parameter only applies if the *ReplicationSourcePath* parameter is specified. This value is used if the restored files used to install a replica indicate that the system key must be supplied by the user. If the restored files indicate that the system key must be supplied on floppy disk, then the system looks for the key on drive A.

SysVolPath

Value: *path_to_database_file*
Default: *%Systemroot%*\Sysvol

This parameter specifies the fully qualified, non-UNC path to a directory on a fixed disk of the local computer. If the directory exists, it must be empty. If the directory does not exist, it is created. The disk must be formatted with NTFS version 5.

TreeOrChild

Value: *Tree | Child*
Default: Child

This parameter is provided for backward compatibility with Windows 2000 unattended setup. For unattended setup of a member of the Windows Server 2003 family, use *NewDomain* instead. This parameter specifies that the new domain is the root of a new tree or a child of an existing domain. This parameter must be specified with a valid value if "domain" is selected in the *ReplicaOrNewDomain* parameter. The settings are configured as follows:

- *Tree* specifies that the new domain is the root of a new tree. The *CreateOrJoin* or *NewDomain* parameter must be specified with a valid value.

- *Child* specifies that the new domain is a child of an existing domain.

UserDomain

Value: *domain_name*

This parameter specifies the domain name for the user name (account credentials) to be used for promoting the member server to a domain controller.

UserName

Value: *user_name*

This parameter specifies the user name (account credentials) to be used for promoting the member server to a domain controller.

Appendix C
User Rights

The User Rights Assignment settings are security settings in a Group Policy Object (GPO) that control user capabilities at the local computer in a site, domain, or organizational unit (OU). A *user right* is an authorization to perform an operation that affects a local computer. These rights authorize users to perform specific actions, such as logging on to a system interactively or backing up files and directories. User rights are different from permissions. User rights are assigned to user and group accounts and applied through a GPO to sites, domains, or OUs. Permissions attached to objects are assigned to user and group accounts. In addition, because user rights are part of a GPO, user rights can be overridden depending on the GPO affecting the computer or user. There are two types of user rights: privileges and logon rights.

Privileges

Privileges specify which users are authorized to manipulate system resources—those actions that affect the system as a whole. Table C-1 describes the privileges that can be assigned to a user or group.

Table C-1   Privileges

Privilege	Description
Act As Part Of The Operating System	Allows a process to authenticate as any user, and therefore gain access to the same resources as any user. Only low-level authentication services should require this privilege.
	The potential access is not limited to what is associated with the user by default, because the calling process may request that arbitrary additional accesses be put in the access token. Of even more concern is that the calling process can build an anonymous token that can provide any and all accesses. Additionally, this token does not provide a primary identity for tracking events in the audit log. Processes that require this privilege should use the LocalSystem account, which already includes this privilege, rather than using a separate user account with this privilege specially assigned.

Table C-1   Privileges (Continued)

Privilege	Description
Add Workstations To Domain	Allows the user to add a computer to a specific domain. For the privilege to be effective, it must be assigned to the user as part of the Default Domain Controllers Policy for the domain. A user who has this privilege can add up to 10 workstations to the domain. Users can also be allowed to join a computer to a domain by giving them Create Computer Objects permission for an OU or for the Computers container in Active Directory. Users who have the Create Computer Objects permission can add an unlimited number of workstations to the domain, regardless of whether they have been assigned the Add Workstations To Domain privilege.
Adjust Memory Quotas For A Process	Determines which accounts can use a process with Write Property access to another process to increase the processor quota assigned to the other process. This privilege is defined in the Default Domain Controller GPO and in the local security policy of workstations and servers.
Back Up Files And Directories	Allows the user to circumvent file and directory permissions to back up the system. This privilege is selected only when an application attempts access through the NTFS file system backup application programming interface (API). Otherwise, normal file and directory permissions apply. See also the Restore Files And Directories privilege.
Bypass Traverse Checking	Allows the user to pass through directories to which the user otherwise has no access, while navigating an object path in the NTFS file system or in the registry. This privilege does not allow the user to list the contents of a directory, only to traverse directories.
Change The System Time	Allows the user to set the time for the internal clock of the computer.
Create A Pagefile	Allows the user to create and change the size of a pagefile by specifying a paging file size for a given drive in Performance Options in the Advanced tab of System Properties.
Create A Token Object	Allows a process to create a token that it can then use to get access to any local resources when the process uses NtCreateToken() or other token-creation APIs. It is recommended that processes requiring this privilege use the LocalSystem account, which already includes this privilege, rather than using a separate user account with this privilege specially assigned.
Create Global Objects	Determines which accounts are allowed to create global objects in a Terminal Services session.

Table C-1   Privileges (Continued)

Privilege	Description
Create Permanent Shared Objects	Allows a process to create a directory object in the Microsoft Windows XP Professional Object Manager. This privilege is useful to kernel-mode components that plan to extend the object namespace. Because components running in kernel mode already have this privilege assigned to them, it is not necessary to specifically assign this privilege.
Debug Programs	Allows the user to attach a debugger to any process, providing powerful access to sensitive and critical system operating components.
Enable Computer And User Accounts To Be Trusted For Delegation	Allows the user to set the Trusted For Delegation setting on a user or computer object in Active Directory. The user or computer object that is granted this privilege must have write access to the account control flags on the user or computer object. Delegation of authentication is a capability that is used by multi-tier client/server applications. It allows a front-end service to use the credentials of a client in authenticating to a back-end service. For this to be possible, both client and server must be running under accounts that are trusted for delegation. Misuse of this privilege or of the Trusted For Delegation settings could make the network vulnerable to sophisticated attacks using Trojan horse programs that impersonate incoming clients and use their credentials to gain access to network resources.
Force Shutdown From A Remote System	Allows a user to shut down a computer from a remote location on the network. See also the Shut Down The System privilege.
Audits Generate Security	Allows a process to make entries in the Security log for object access auditing. The process can also generate other security audits. The Security log is used to trace unauthorized system access. See also the Manage Auditing And Security Log privilege.
Impersonate A Client After Authentication	Allows programs running on behalf of that user to impersonate a client. Requiring this setting prevents an unauthorized user from convincing a client to connect (by remote procedure call [RPC] or named pipes) to a service the unauthorized user has created and then impersonating the client, which can elevate the unauthorized user's permissions to administrative or system levels.
Increase Scheduling Priority	Allows a process with write property access to another process to increase the execution priority of that other process. A user with this privilege can change the scheduling priority of a process through the Task Manager user interface.

Table C-1   Privileges (Continued)

Privilege	Description
Load And Unload Device Drivers	Allows a user to install and uninstall Plug and Play device drivers. Device drivers that are not Plug and Play are not affected by this privilege and can only be installed by administrators. Because device drivers run as trusted (highly privileged) programs, this privilege could be misused to install hostile programs and give these programs destructive access to resources.
Lock Pages In Memory	Allows a process to keep data in physical memory, preventing the system from paging the data to virtual memory on disk. Assigning this privilege could significantly degrade system performance.
Manage Auditing And Security Log	Allows a user to specify object access auditing options for individual resources such as files, Active Directory objects, and registry keys. Object access auditing is not actually performed unless you have enabled it in the computer-wide audit policy settings under Group Policy or under Group Policy defined in Active Directory; this privilege does not grant access to the computer-wide audit policy. A user with this privilege can also view and clear the Security log from the Event Viewer.
Modify Firmware Environment Values	Allows modification of the system environment variables, either by a user through the System Properties or by a process through an API.
Perform Volume Maintenance Tasks	Determines which users are allowed to run volume maintenance tasks, such as Disk Cleanup and Disk Defragmenter.
Profile Single Process	Allows a user to utilize Windows XP Professional performance-monitoring tools to monitor the performance of nonsystem processes.
Profile System Performance	Allows a user to run performance-monitoring tools to monitor the performance of system processes.
Remove Computer From Docking Station	Allows a user of a portable computer to unlock the computer by clicking Eject PC on the Start menu.
Replace A Process Level Token	Determines which user accounts can initiate a process to replace the default token associated with a started subprocess. This privilege is defined in the Default Domain Controller GPO and in the local security policy of workstations and servers.
Restore Files And Directories	Allows a user to circumvent file and directory permissions when restoring backed-up files and directories, and to set any valid security principal as the owner of an object. See also the Back Up Files And Directories privilege.
Shut Down The System	Allows a user to shut down the local computer.

Table C-1   Privileges (Continued)

Privilege	Description
Synchronize Directory Service Data	Allows a process to provide directory synchronization services; relevant only on domain controllers.
Take Ownership Of Files Or Other Objects	Allows a user to take ownership of any securable object in the system, including Active Directory objects, NTFS files and folders, printers, registry keys, services, processes, and threads.

Some of these privileges can override permissions set on an object. For example, a user logged on to a domain account as a member of the Backup Operators group has the right to perform backup operations for all domain servers. However, this requires the ability to read all files on those servers, even files on which their owners have set permissions that explicitly deny access to all users, including members of the Backup Operators group. A user right (in this case, the right to perform a backup) takes precedence over all file and directory permissions.

Logon Rights

Logon rights specify the ways in which a user can log on to a system. Table C-2 describes the logon rights that can be assigned to a user or group.

Table C-2   Logon Rights

Logon Right	Description
Access This Computer From The Network	Allows a user to connect to the computer over the network.
Allow Logon Locally	Determines which users can interactively log on to the computer. Logons initiated by pressing Ctrl+Alt+Del require the user to have this logon right. If you define this policy for a user or group, you must also give the Administrators group the right.
Allow Logon Through Terminal Services	Determines which users are allowed to log on as a Terminal Services client. This setting will have no effect on Microsoft Windows 2000 computers that have not been updated to Service Pack 2.
Deny Access To This Computer From The Network	Prohibits a user from connecting to the computer from the network.
Deny Logon As A Batch Job	Prohibits a user from logging on through a batch-queue facility.
Deny Logon As A Service	Prohibits a user from logging on as a service.

Table C-2   Logon Rights (Continued)

Logon Right	Description
Deny Logon Locally	Prohibits a user from logging on directly at the keyboard.
Deny Logon Through Terminal Services	Determines which users are prohibited from logging on as a Terminal Services client. This setting will have no effect on Windows 2000 computers that have not been updated to Service Pack 2.
Log On As A Batch Job	Allows a user to log on using a batch-queue facility.
Log On As A Service	Allows a security principal to log on as a service, as a way of establishing a security context. Services can be configured to run under the LocalSystem, LocalService, or NetworkService accounts, which have a built-in right to log on as a service. Any service that runs under a separate user account must be assigned this logon right.

Assigning User Rights

To ease the task of user account administration, you should assign user rights primarily to group accounts, rather than to individual user accounts. When users in a group all require the same user rights, you can assign the set of user rights once to the group, rather than repeatedly assigning the same set of user rights to each individual user account. When you assign user rights to a group account, users are automatically assigned those rights when they become a member of that group. If a user is a member of multiple groups, the user's rights are cumulative, which means that the user has more than one set of rights. To remove rights from a user, simply remove the user from the group. In this case, the user no longer has the rights assigned to that group.

Glossary

A

access control A security mechanism that determines which operations a user, group, service, or computer is authorized to perform on a computer or on a particular object.

access control entry (ACE) An entry in an object's discretionary access control list (DACL) that grants permissions to a user or group. An ACE is also an entry in an object's system access control list (SACL) that specifies the security events to be audited for a user or group.

access control list (ACL) The mechanism for limiting access to certain items of information or to certain controls based on users' identity and their membership in various predefined groups. An ACL is typically used by system administrators for controlling user access to network resources such as servers, directories, and files and is typically implemented by granting permissions to users and groups for access to specific objects.

access token The user's identification for the computers in the domain or for that local computer. The access token contains the user's security settings, including the user's security identifier (SID).

account lockout A security feature that prevents a user account from logging on if a number of failed logon attempts occur within a specified amount of time, based on security policy lockout settings.

ACE *See* access control entry (ACE).

ACL *See* access control list (ACL).

Active Directory The directory service included with the Microsoft Windows 2000 and Microsoft Windows Server 2003. It stores information about objects on a network and makes this information available to users and network administrators. Active Directory gives network users access to resources anywhere on the network using a single logon process, provided the users are permitted to use these resources. It provides network administrators with an intuitive hierarchical view of the network and a single point of administration for all network objects. *See also* directory; directory service.

Active Directory Domains And Trusts console An administrative tool that allows you to manage trust relationships between Active Directory domains.

Active Directory Installation Wizard The tool that is used to install and remove Active Directory. The actual name of the command that starts the wizard is Dcpromo.exe. *See also* Dcpromo.exe.

Active Directory–integrated zone A primary Domain Name System (DNS) zone that is stored in Active Directory so that it can use multimaster replication and Active Directory security features.

Active Directory quota For domain controllers running Microsoft Windows Server 2003, a feature that determines the number of objects that can be owned in a given directory partition by a security principal. Quotas can help prevent the denial of service that can occur if a security principal accidentally, or intentionally, creates objects until the affected domain controller runs out of storage space.

Active Directory Schema snap-in An administrative tool that allows you to view and modify the Active Directory schema. You must install the Active Directory Schema console by using the Microsoft Windows Server 2003 Administration Tools on the Windows Server 2003 compact disc. On a domain controller, to install the Active Directory Schema console, you simply register the Schmmgmt.dll file.

Active Directory Service Interfaces (ADSI) A Component Object Model (COM)–based directory service model that allows ADSI-compliant client applications to access a wide variety of distinct directory protocols, including Windows Directory Services and Lightweight Directory Access Protocol (LDAP), while using a single, standard set of interfaces. ADSI shields the client application from the implementation and operational details of the underlying data store or protocol.

Active Directory Sites And Services console An administrative tool that contains information about the physical structure of a network. Active Directory uses this information to determine how to replicate directory information and handle service requests.

Active Directory Users And Computers console An administrative tool designed to perform day-to-day Active Directory administration tasks. These tasks include creating, deleting, modifying, moving, and setting permissions on objects stored in the directory. These objects include organizational units (OUs), users, contacts, groups, computers, printers, and shared file objects.

ADSI *See* Active Directory Service Interfaces (ADSI).

alert A function that detects when a predefined counter value rises above or falls below the configured threshold and notifies a user by means of the Messenger service.

answer file   A file that contains answers to questions that should be automated during installation. When used to automate Active Directory installation, the answer file must contain all of the parameters that the Active Directory Installation Wizard needs to install Active Directory.

application directory partition   An Active Directory partition that stores dynamic application-specific data in Active Directory without significantly affecting network performance by enabling you to control the scope of replication and the placement of replicas. The application directory partition can contain any type of object except security principals (users, groups, and computers).

application file   A text file that contains instructions about how to publish an application, taken from an existing setup program (Setup.exe or Install.exe). Application files use the .zap extension. A .zap file does not support the features of Microsoft Windows Installer.

assign   To deploy a program to members of a group where acceptance of the program is mandatory.

attribute   Information that indicates whether a file is read-only, hidden, ready for archiving (backing up), compressed, or encrypted, and whether the file contents should be indexed for fast file searching.

auditing   The process that tracks the activities of users by recording selected types of events in the security log of a server or a workstation.

audit policy   A policy that determines the security events to be reported to the network administrator.

authentication   The process for verifying that an entity or object is what it claims to be. Examples include confirming the source and integrity of information, such as verifying a digital signature or verifying the identity of a user or computer. *See also* trust relationship.

authoritative restore   A type of restore operation performed on an Active Directory domain controller in which the objects in the restored directory are treated as authoritative, replacing (through replication) all existing copies of those objects. Authoritative restore is applicable only to replicated System State data such as Active Directory data and File Replication Service data. You must use the Ntdsutil.exe utility to perform an authoritative restore. *See also* nonauthoritative restore.

available bandwidth   The amount of bandwidth that is actually available for use after normal network traffic is handled.

B

bandwidth   The amount of data that can be transmitted across a communications channel in a specific amount of time. In computer networks, greater bandwidth indicates faster data-transfer capability and is expressed in bits per second (bps).

base schema   A basic set of schema classes and attributes shipped with Microsoft Windows Server 2003. There are nearly 200 schema classes and more than 900 schema attributes provided in the base schema.

basic input/output system (BIOS)   On PC-compatible computers, the set of essential software routines that test hardware at startup, start the operating system, and support the transfer of data among hardware devices. The BIOS is stored in read-only memory (ROM) so that it can be executed when the computer is turned on. Although critical to performance, the BIOS is usually invisible to computer users.

Berkeley Internet Name Domain (BIND)   An implementation of the Domain Name System (DNS) written and ported to most available versions of the UNIX operating system. The Internet Software Consortium maintains the BIND software.

BIND   *See* Berkeley Internet Name Domain (BIND).

BIOS   *See* basic input/output system (BIOS).

boot volume   The volume that contains the Microsoft Windows Server 2003 operating system and its support files. The boot partition can be, but does not have to be, the same as the system partition.

bottleneck   A condition, often involving a hardware resource, which causes the entire system to perform poorly. A bottleneck exists if a particular system component is keeping the entire system from performing more quickly.

bridgehead server   A domain controller in a site, designated automatically by the knowledge consistency checker (KCC) as the contact point for exchange of directory information between this site and other sites. *See also* preferred bridgehead server.

built-in groups   The default security groups installed with the operating system. Built-in groups have been granted useful collections of rights and built-in abilities. In most cases, built-in groups provide all the capabilities needed by a particular user.

built-in user account   A user account used to perform administrative tasks or to gain access to network resources.

C

catalog service   An information store that contains selected information about every object in every domain in the directory, and which is used for performing searches across an enterprise. The catalog service provided by Active Directory is called the global catalog.

certificate   A digital document that is commonly used for authentication and to secure information on open networks. A certificate securely binds a public key to the entry that holds the corresponding private key. Certificates are digitally signed by the issuing certification authority (CA), and they can be issued for a user, computer, or service. *See also* certification authority (CA); public key infrastructure (PKI).

certificate rule   A software restriction policies rule that recognizes software that is digitally signed by an Authenticode software publisher certificate.

certificate trust list   A signed list of root certification authority certificates that an administrator considers reputable for designated purposes, such as client authentication or secure e-mail. *See also* certification authority (CA).

certification authority (CA)   An entity responsible for establishing and vouching for the authenticity of public keys belonging to subjects (usually users or computers) or other certification authorities. Activities of a certification authority can include binding public keys to distinguished names through signed certificates, managing certificate serial numbers, and certificate revocation. *See also* certificate; certificate trust list; public key infrastructure (PKI).

child domain   For the Domain Name System (DNS), a domain located in the namespace tree directly beneath another domain (the parent domain). For example, *example.microsoft.com* is a child domain of the parent domain, *microsoft.com*. A child domain is also called a subdomain.

child object   An object that resides in another object. For example, a file is a child object that resides in a folder, which is a parent object. *See also* parent object.

client   Any computer or program connecting to, or requesting the services of, another computer or program.

COM   *See* Component Object Model (COM).

Component Object Model (COM)   An object-based programming model designed to promote software interoperability. It allows two or more applications or components to easily cooperate with one another, even if they were written by different vendors, at different times, in different programming languages, or if they are running on different computers running different operating systems. COM is the foundation technology upon which broader technologies can be built. Microsoft Object Linking & Embedding (OLE) technology and ActiveX are both built on top of COM.

Computer Configuration node   A node within Group Policy that contains the settings used to set group policies applied to computers, regardless of who logs on to them. Computer configuration settings are applied when the operating system initializes.

configuration container   *See* configuration partition.

configuration partition   An Active Directory partition containing the replication topology and related metadata that is replicated to every domain controller in the forest. Directory-aware applications store information in the configuration container that applies to the entire forest.

Configure Your Server Wizard   A central location from which many services, including Active Directory, can be installed on a computer running the Microsoft Windows Server 2003 family operating system. The Configure Your Server Wizard is available from the Manage Your Server screen, which opens automatically the first time you log on to a server by using administrative permissions. You can use the Configure Your Server Wizard to install Active Directory only if the computer is the first computer on the network and has not yet been configured.

connection object   An Active Directory object that represents a replication connection from one domain controller to another. The connection object is a child of the replication destination's NTDS Settings object and identifies the replication source server, contains a replication schedule, and specifies a replication transport. Connection objects are created automatically by the knowledge consistency checker (KCC), but they can also be created manually. Connections generated automatically must not be modified by the user unless they are first converted into manual connections.

console   A collection of administrative tools.

console tree   The left pane in a Microsoft Management Console (MMC) that displays the items contained in the console. By default, it is the left pane of a console window, but it can be hidden. The items in the console tree and their hierarchical organization determine the capabilities of a console.

container object   An object that can logically contain other objects. For example, a folder is a container object. *See also* object.

contiguous namespace   A namespace where the name of the child object in an object hierarchy always contains the name of the parent domain. A tree is a contiguous namespace.

counter log   A log that collects performance counter data in a comma-separated or tab-separated format for easy import to spreadsheet programs. You can view logged counter data using System Monitor or by exporting the data to spreadsheet programs or databases for analysis and report generation.

cross-link trust   *See* shortcut trust.

cross-reference object   An object in which Active Directory stores information about directory partitions and external directory services. An example of an external directory service is another Lightweight Directory Access Protocol (LDAP)–compliant directory.

D

Dcdiag.exe   A command-line, diagnostic tool included with the Windows Support Tools on the Microsoft Windows Server 2003 Setup CD-ROM that analyzes the state of domain controllers in a forest or enterprise and reports any problems.

Dcpromo.exe   When typed in the Run dialog box, the command that starts the Active Directory Installation Wizard. *See also* Active Directory Installation Wizard.

dedicated domain   In a forest of multiple domains, a domain that does not contain any user or many computer accounts and is dedicated to the operations associated with enterprise management. This domain is created to serve as the forest root domain. A dedicated domain may be used to regulate membership in the Enterprise Admins and Schema Admins predefined universal groups in the forest root domain, to create a small forest root domain for easier replication, to avoid obsolescence of the root domain name, or when no domain can be identified as critical to the operation of an organization.

default groups   Groups that have a predetermined set of user rights or group membership. There are four categories of default groups: groups in the Builtin folder, groups in the Users folder, special identity groups, and default local groups. All of the default groups are security groups and have been assigned common sets of rights and permissions that you might want to assign to the users and groups that you place into the default groups.

delegation of administration   The ability to assign responsibility for management and administration of a portion of the namespace to another user, group, or organization.

Delegation Of Control Wizard   A wizard that steps you through the process of assigning administrative permissions at the domain, OU, or container level.

details pane   The pane in the Microsoft Management Console (MMC) that displays the details for the selected item in the console tree. The details can be a list of items or they can be administrative properties, services, and events that are acted on by a console or snap-in.

DHCP   *See* Dynamic Host Configuration Protocol (DHCP).

directory   An information source (for example, a telephone directory) that contains information about users, computer files, or other objects. In a file system, a directory stores information about files. In a distributed computing environment (such as a Microsoft Windows domain), the directory stores information about objects such as printers, fax servers, applications, databases, and other users. *See also* Active Directory; directory service.

directory database   The physical storage for each replica of Active Directory. The directory database is also called the store.

directory partition   *See* naming context.

directory service   Both the directory information source and the services that make the information available and usable. A directory service enables the user to find an object given any one of its attributes. *See also* Active Directory; directory.

directory service log   A log in Event Viewer in which Active Directory records events, including errors, warnings, and information that Active Directory generates.

directory services restore mode   A boot option that allows restores of Active Directory on a domain controller.

directory tree   A hierarchy of objects and containers in a directory that can be viewed graphically as an upside-down tree, with the root object at the top. Endpoints in the tree are usually single (leaf) objects, and nodes in the tree, or branches, are container objects. A tree shows how objects are connected in terms of the path from one object to another. A simple tree is a single container and its objects. A contiguous subtree is any unbroken path in the tree, including all the members of any container in that path.

distinguished name (DN)   A name that uniquely identifies an object by using the relative distinguished name for the object, plus the names of container objects and domains that contain the object. The distinguished name identifies the object as well as its location in a tree. Every object in Active Directory has a distinguished name. A typical distinguished name might be: CN=MyName, CN=Users, DC=microsoft,DC=com. This identifies the MyName user object in the *microsoft.com* domain.

Distributed File System (DFS)   A service that allows system administrators to organize distributed network shares into a logical namespace, enabling users to access files without specifying their physical location and providing load sharing across network shares.

distribution group   A group that is used solely for e-mail distribution and is not security enabled. Distribution groups cannot be listed in discretionary access control lists (DACLs) used to define permissions on resources and objects. Distribution groups can be used only with e-mail applications (such as Microsoft Exchange) to send e-mail to collections of users. If you do not need a group for security purposes, create a distribution group instead of a security group. *See also* security group.

DN   *See* distinguished name (DN).

DNS   *See* Domain Name System (DNS).

DNS server   A computer that runs Domain Name System (DNS) server programs containing name-to-IP (Internet Protocol) address mappings, IP address-to-name mappings, information about the domain tree structure, and other information. DNS servers also attempt to resolve client queries. A DNS server is also called a DNS name server.

domain   In Active Directory, a collection of computer, user, and group objects defined by the administrator. These objects share a common directory database, security policies, and security relationships with other domains. In Domain Name System (DNS), a domain is any tree or subtree within the DNS namespace. Although the names for DNS domains often correspond to Active Directory domains, DNS domains should not be confused with Active Directory domains.

domain controller   In an Active Directory forest, a server that contains a writable copy of the Active Directory database, participates in Active Directory replication, and controls access to network resources. Administrators can manage user accounts, network access, shared resources, site topology, and other directory objects from any domain controller in the forest. *See also* Active Directory; authentication; directory; forest.

domain functional level   A way to enable domain-wide Active Directory features within your network environment. Four domain functional levels are available: Windows 2000 Mixed (default), Windows 2000 Native, Windows Server 2003 interim, and Windows Server 2003. You can raise the domain functional level to either Windows 2000 Native or Windows Server 2003 if the domain controllers in the domain are running the appropriate version of Windows. The Windows Server 2003 interim functional level can only be used if you are upgrading a Microsoft Windows NT 4 domain.

domain hierarchy   A tree structure of parent and child domains.

domain local group A security or distribution group that can contain universal groups, global groups, and accounts from any domain in the domain tree or forest. A domain local group can also contain other domain local groups from its own domain. Rights and permissions can be assigned only at the domain containing the group.

domain name The name given by an administrator to a collection of networked computers that share a common directory. Part of the Domain Name System (DNS) naming structure, domain names consist of a sequence of name labels separated by periods. *See also* domain; Domain Name System (DNS).

Domain Name System (DNS) A hierarchical, distributed database that contains mappings of DNS domain names to various types of data, such as Internet Protocol (IP) addresses. DNS enables the location of computers and services by user-friendly names, and it also enables the discovery of other information stored in the database. *See also* domain; domain name.

domain naming master The domain controller assigned to control the addition or removal of domains in the forest. At any time, there can be only one domain naming master in the forest.

domain partition An Active Directory partition that describes the logical structure of the deployment, including data such as domain structure or replication topology. This data is common to all domains in a forest and is replicated to all domain controllers in a forest.

domain user account Allows a user to log on to the domain to gain access to network resources.

Dsastat.exe A command-line tool that compares and detects differences between directory partitions on domain controllers and can be used to ensure that domain controllers are up-to-date with one another.

Dynamic Host Configuration Protocol (DHCP) A Transmission Control Protocol/Internet Protocol (TCP/IP) service protocol that offers dynamic leased configuration of host Internet Protocol (IP) addresses and distributes other configuration parameters to eligible network clients. DHCP provides safe, reliable, and simple TCP/IP network configuration, prevents address conflicts, and helps conserve the use of client IP addresses on the network. DHCP uses a client/server model where the DHCP server centrally manages IP addresses that are used on the network. DHCP-supporting clients can then request and obtain lease of an IP address from a DHCP server as part of their network boot process.

dynamic update An updated specification to the Domain Name System (DNS) standard that permits hosts that store name information in the DNS to dynamically register and update their records in zones maintained by DNS servers that can accept and process dynamic update messages.

E

effective permissions   The overall permissions that a security principal has for an object, including group membership and inheritance from parent objects.

event   Any significant occurrence in the system, or an application that requires users to be notified or an entry to be added to a log.

Event Viewer   A Microsoft Management Console (MMC) that maintains logs about application, security, and system events on your computer.

explicit trust   A trust that is created manually.

extensions   Snap-ins that provide additional administrative functionality to another snap-in.

external trust   A trust that must be explicitly created between two Active Directory domains that are in different forests or between an Active Directory domain and a Microsoft Windows NT 4 or earlier domain. The trust is nontransitive and can be one- or two-way. *See also* shortcut trust; forest trust; realm trust.

F

File Replication service (FRS)   A service used by the Microsoft Distributed File System (DFS) to synchronize content between assigned replicas automatically, and by Active Directory to replicate topological and global catalog information across domain controllers.

flexible single-master operations (FSMO)   *See* operations master role.

folder redirection   An extension within Group Policy that allows administrators to redirect the following special folders to network locations: Application Data, Desktop, My Documents, My Pictures, and Start Menu.

forest   A collection of one or more Active Directory domains that share a common schema, configuration, and global catalog.

forest functional level   A way to enable forest-wide Active Directory features within your network environment. Three forest functional levels are available: Windows 2000 (default), Windows 2003 interim, and Windows Server 2003.

forest root domain   The first domain created in an Active Directory forest. After the forest root domain has been created, you cannot create a new forest root domain or a parent for the existing forest root domain.

forest trust   A trust that must be explicitly created by a systems administrator between two forest root domains. This trust allows all domains in one forest to transitively trust all domains in another forest. A forest trust is not transitive across three or more forests. The trust is transitive between two forests only and can be one-way or two-way. *See also* shortcut trust; external trust; realm trust.

forward lookup   In Domain Name System (DNS), a query process in which the friendly DNS domain name of a host computer is searched to find its Internet Protocol (IP) address.

G

global catalog   A domain controller that contains a partial replica of every domain in Active Directory. A global catalog holds a replica of every object in Active Directory, but with a limited number of each object's attributes. The global catalog stores those attributes most frequently used in search operations (such as a user's first and last names) and those attributes required to locate a full replica of the object. The Active Directory replication system builds the global catalog automatically. The attributes replicated into the global catalog include a base set defined by Microsoft. Administrators can specify additional properties to meet the needs of their installation.

global catalog server   A domain controller that holds a copy of the global catalog for the forest.

global group   A security or distribution group that can contain users, groups, and computers from its own domain as members. Global security groups can be granted rights and permissions for resources in any domain in the forest. *See also* local group; group.

globally unique identifier (GUID)   A 128-bit number that is guaranteed to be unique. GUIDs are assigned to objects when the objects are created. The GUID never changes, even if you move or rename the object. Applications can store the GUID of an object and use the GUID to retrieve that object regardless of its current distinguished name.

GPO   *See* Group Policy Object (GPO).

Gpresult.exe   A command-line tool that enables you to create and display a Resultant Set of Policy (RSoP) query on the command line. In addition, Gpresult provides general information about the operating system, user, and computer.

Gpupdate.exe   In Microsoft Windows Server 2003 and Microsoft Windows XP Professional, a command-line tool that enables you to refresh policy immediately. Gpupdate replaces the secedit.exe/refreshpolicy command used for refreshing Group Policy Objects (GPOs) in Microsoft Windows 2000.

group   A collection of users, computers, contacts, and other groups. Groups can be used as a security mechanism or as e-mail distribution collections. Distribution groups are used only for e-mail. Security groups are used both to grant access to resources and as e-mail distribution lists. *See also* domain local group; global group; domain functional level; universal group.

Group Policy   The component within Active Directory that enables directory-based change and configuration management of user and computer settings, including security and user data. Use Group Policy to define configurations for groups of users and computers. With Group Policy, you can specify policy settings for registry-based policies, security, software installation, scripts, folder redirection, remote installation services, and Microsoft Internet Explorer maintenance. *See also* Group Policy Object (GPO); Group Policy Object Editor.

Group Policy Object (GPO)   A collection of Group Policy settings. GPOs are essentially the documents created by the Group Policy Object Editor. GPOs are stored at the domain level, and they affect users and computers contained in sites, domains, and organizational units (OUs). In addition, each computer has exactly one group of settings stored locally, called the local Group Policy Object. *See also* Group Policy; Group Policy Object Editor; local Group Policy Object.

Group Policy Object Editor   The Microsoft Management Console (MMC) used to edit Group Policy Objects (GPOs).

group scopes   An indicator of where in the network the group can be used to assign permissions to the group. There are three group scopes: global, domain local, and universal. *See also* global group; domain local group; universal group.

group type   An indicator of how a group is used. There are two group types: security and distribution. Both types of groups are stored in the database component of Active Directory, which allows you to use them anywhere in your network. *See also* security group; distribution group.

GUID   *See* globally unique identifier (GUID).

H

hash   A series of bytes with a fixed length that uniquely identify a program or file. *See also* hash algorithm.

hash algorithm   An algorithm that produces a hash value of some piece of data, such as a message or session key. *See also* hash.

hash rule   A software restriction policies rule that recognizes specific software based on the hash of the software.

home folder   A folder (usually on a file server) that administrators can assign to individual users or groups. Administrators use home folders to consolidate user files onto specific file servers for easy backup. Home folders are used by some programs as the default folder for the Open and Save As dialog boxes. Home folders may also be referred to as home directories.

I

implicit trust   A trust created automatically.

infrastructure master   The domain controller assigned to update group-to-user references whenever group memberships are changed and to replicate these changes to any other domain controllers in the domain. At any time, there can be only one infrastructure master in a particular domain. The infrastructure master should not be located on the same computer as the global catalog if there is more than one domain controller in the forest.

inherited permissions   Permissions propagated to a child object from a parent object.

IntelliMirror   A set of change and configuration management features based on Active Directory that enable management of user and computer data and settings, including security data. IntelliMirror also provides limited ability to deploy software to Microsoft Windows 2000 and later workstations or servers.

Internet Protocol (IP)   The messenger protocol of Transmission Control Protocol/Internet Protocol (TCP/IP) that is responsible for addressing and sending IP packets over the network. IP provides a best-effort, connectionless delivery system that does not guarantee that packets arrive at their destination or in the sequence in which they were sent.

Internet zone rule   A software restriction policies rule that recognizes software based on the zone of the Internet from which the software is downloaded.

intersite replication   The replication traffic that occurs between sites.

intrasite replication   The replication traffic that occurs within a site.

IP   *See* Internet Protocol (IP).

IP address   A 32-bit address used to identify a node on an Internet Protocol (IP) internetwork. Each node on the IP internetwork must be assigned a unique IP address, which is made up of the network ID and a unique host ID. This address is typically represented in dotted-decimal notation, with the decimal value of each octet separated by a period, for example, 192.168.7.27. You can configure the IP address statically or dynamically through Dynamic Host Configuration Protocol (DHCP).

K

KCC   *See* knowledge consistency checker (KCC).

Kerberos V5   An Internet standard security protocol for handling authentication of user or system identity. With Kerberos V5, passwords that are sent across network lines are encrypted, not sent as plaintext. Kerberos V5 includes other security features as well.

knowledge consistency checker (KCC)   A built-in service that runs on all domain controllers and automatically establishes connections between individual machines in the same site, called connection objects. An administrator may establish additional connection objects or remove connection objects. At any point where replication within a site becomes impossible or has a single point of failure, the KCC will step in and establish as many new connection objects as necessary to resume Active Directory replication.

L

LAN   *See* local area network (LAN).

LDAP   *See* Lightweight Directory Access Protocol (LDAP).

Lightweight Directory Access Protocol (LDAP)   The primary access protocol for Active Directory. LDAP version 3 is defined by a set of Proposed Standard documents in Internet Engineering Task Force (IETF) RFC 2251.

local area network (LAN)   A group of computers and other devices dispersed over a relatively limited area and connected by a communications link that allows one device to interact with any other on the network.

local computer   A computer that you can access directly without using a communications line or a communications device, such as a network card or a modem.

local group   A security group that can be granted permissions and rights to only those resources on the computer on which the group resides. Local groups contain local user accounts from the computer on which the group is created. Local groups cannot be members of any other group. *See also* global group.

local Group Policy Object   A Group Policy Object (GPO) stored on each computer whether the computer is part of an Active Directory environment or a networked environment. Local GPO settings can be overwritten by nonlocal GPOs and are the least influential if the computer is in an Active Directory environment. In a non-networked environment (or in a networked environment lacking a domain controller), the local GPO's settings are more important because they are not overwritten by nonlocal GPOs.

local user account   A user account provided in a domain for a user whose global account is not in a trusted domain. A local account is not required where trust relationships exist between domains.

local user profile   A computer-based record about an authorized user that is created automatically on the computer the first time a user logs on to a workstation or server computer.

M

mandatory user profile   A user profile that is not updated when the user logs off. It is downloaded to the user's desktop each time the user logs on and is created by an administrator and assigned to one or more users to create consistent or job-specific user profiles. Only members of the Administrators group can change profiles.

member server   A server that is joined to a domain but is not a domain controller in the domain. Member servers typically function as file servers, application servers, database servers, Web servers, certificate servers, firewalls, or remote access servers. *See also* domain controller; global group; local group.

metadata   Information about the properties of data, such as the type of data in a column (numeric, text, and so on) or the length of a column.

Microsoft Management Console (MMC)   A framework for hosting administrative tools, called *consoles*. A console may contain tools, folders, or other containers, World Wide Web pages, and other administrative items. These items are displayed in the left pane of the console, called a *console tree*. A console has one or more windows that can provide views of the console tree. The main MMC window provides commands and tools for authoring consoles. The authoring features of MMC and the console tree itself may be hidden when a console is in User mode.

MMC   *See* Microsoft Management Console (MMC).

modifications   Files with the extension .mst that allow you to customize Microsoft Windows Installer packages (which have the .msi extension). Modifications are also called *transforms*. The Windows Installer package format provides for customization by allowing you to "transform" the original package using authoring and repackaging tools. Some applications also provide wizards or templates that permit a user to create modifications.

multimaster replication   A replication model in which any domain controller accepts and replicates directory changes to any other domain controller. This differs from other replication models in which one computer stores the single modifiable copy of the directory and other computers store backup copies. *See also* domain controller; replication.

N

naming context   A contiguous subtree of Active Directory that is replicated as a unit to other domain controllers in the forest that contain a replica of the same subtree. In Active Directory, a single server always holds at least three naming contexts: schema (class and attribute definitions for the directory), configuration (replication topology and related metadata), and domain (the subtree that contains the per-domain objects for one domain). The schema and configuration naming contexts are replicated to every domain controller in a specified forest. A domain naming context is replicated only to domain controllers for that domain. A naming context is also called a directory partition.

nested groups   A capability available only in the Windows 2000 Native or Windows Server 2003 domain functional levels that allows the creation of groups within groups. *See also* universal group; global group; domain local group; forest.

nested OUs   The creation of organizational units (OUs) within OUs.

NetBIOS   *See* network basic input/output system (NetBIOS).

Netdiag.exe   A command-line, diagnostic tool included with the Windows Support Tools on the Microsoft Windows Server 2003 Setup CD-ROM that helps isolate networking and connectivity problems by performing a series of tests to determine the state of a network client.

Netdom.exe   A command-line tool in Windows Domain Manager that is used to rename a domain controller. Netdom.exe is included with the Windows Support Tools on the Microsoft Windows Server 2003 Setup CD-ROM.

network basic input/output system (NetBIOS)   An application programming interface (API) that can be used by programs on a local area network (LAN). NetBIOS provides programs with a uniform set of commands for requesting the lower level services required to manage names, conduct sessions, and send datagrams between nodes on a network.

node   For tree structures, a location on the tree that can have links to one or more items below it. For local area networks (LANs), a device that is connected to the network and is capable of communicating with other network devices.

nonauthoritative restore   A restore operation performed on an Active Directory domain controller in which the objects in the restored directory are not treated as authoritative. The restored objects are updated with changes held in other domain controllers in the restored domain. *See also* authoritative restore.

nonlocal Group Policy Object A Group Policy Object (GPO) linked to Active Directory objects (sites, domains, or organizational units [OUs]) that can be applied to either users or computers. To use nonlocal GPOs, a domain controller must be installed. Following the properties of Active Directory, nonlocal GPOs are applied hierarchically from the least restrictive group (site) to the most restrictive group (OU) and are cumulative.

nontransitive trust A trust that is bound by the domains in the trust relationship.

Ntds.dit The directory database.

Ntdsutil.exe A command-line tool that provides management facilities for Active Directory. By default, the Ntdsutil.exe file is installed in the *%Systemroot%* System32 folder.

O

object An entity such as a file, folder, shared folder, printer, or Active Directory object described by a distinct, named set of attributes. For example, the attributes of a File object include its name, location, and size; the attributes of an Active Directory User object might include the user's first name, last name, and e-mail address. *See also* attribute; container object; parent object; child object.

object attributes The characteristics of objects in the directory.

object class A logical grouping of objects.

Offline Files A feature that provides users with access to redirected folders even when they are not connected to the network. Offline Files caches files accessed through folder redirection onto the hard drive of the local computer. When a user accesses a file in a redirected folder, the file is accessed and modified locally. When a user has finished working with the file and has logged off, only then does the file traverse the network for storage on the server.

operations master role A domain controller that has been assigned one or more special roles in an Active Directory domain. The domain controllers assigned these roles perform operations that are single master (not permitted to occur at different places on the network at the same time). Examples of these operations include resource identifier allocation, schema modification, primary domain controller (PDC) election, and certain infrastructure changes. The domain controller that controls the particular operation owns the operations master role for that operation. The ownership of these operations master roles can be transferred to other domain controllers. Also known as *flexible single-master operations (FSMO)*.

organizational unit (OU)   An Active Directory container object used within a domain. An OU is a logical container into which you can place users, groups, computers, and other OUs. It can contain objects only from its parent domain. An OU is the smallest scope to which you can apply a Group Policy or delegate authority.

OU   *See* organizational unit (OU).

P

parent-child trust   The two-way, transitive trust relationship created when a domain is added to an Active Directory tree. The Active Directory installation process automatically creates a transitive trust relationship between the domain you are creating (the new child domain) and the parent domain. These trust relationships make all objects in the domains of the tree available to all other domains in the tree. *See also* tree-root trust.

parent domain   For the Domain Name System (DNS), a domain that is located in the namespace tree directly above another derivative domain name (child domain). For example, *microsoft.com* is the parent domain for *example.microsoft.com*, a child domain.

parent object   The object in which another object resides. A parent object implies relation. For example, a folder is a parent object in which a file, or child object, resides. An object can be both a parent and a child object. For example, a subfolder that contains files is both the child of the parent folder and the parent folder of the files. *See also* child object; object.

partial replica   A read-only replica of a directory partition that contains a subset of the attributes of all objects in the partition. Each global catalog contains partial replicas of all domains in the forest. The attributes contained in a partial replica are defined in the schema as the attributes whose attributeSchema objects have the isMemberOfPartialAttributeSet attribute set to TRUE. *See also* global catalog.

partition   A portion of a physical disk that functions as though it were a physically separate disk. Partitions can be created only on basic disks.

path rule   A software restriction policies rule that recognizes software based on the location in which the software is stored.

PDC   *See* primary domain controller (PDC).

PDC emulator   A domain controller that holds the PDC emulator operations master role in Active Directory. The PDC emulator services network clients that do not have Active Directory client software installed, and it replicates directory changes to any Microsoft Windows NT backup domain controllers (BDCs) in the domain. The PDC emulator handles password authentication requests involving passwords that have recently changed and not yet replicated. At any time, the PDC emulator master role can be assigned to only one domain controller in each domain.

peer domain controller   A domain controller added to an existing domain. Peer domain controllers provide redundancy and reduce the load on the existing domain controllers.

performance counter   In System Monitor, a data item associated with a performance object. For each counter selected, System Monitor presents a value corresponding to a particular aspect of the performance defined for the performance object.

Performance Logs And Alerts   A tool that provides administrators with the ability to create counter logs, trace logs, and system alerts automatically from local or remote computers.

performance object   In System Monitor, a logical collection of counters that is associated with a resource or service that can be monitored.

permission   A rule associated with an object to regulate which users can gain access to the object and in what manner. *See also* object.

permissions inheritance   A mechanism that allows a given access control entry (ACE) to be copied from the container where it was applied to all children of the container. Inheritance can be combined with delegation to grant administrative rights to a whole subtree of the directory in a single update operation.

preferred bridgehead server   A domain controller in a site, designated manually by the administrator, that is part of a group of bridgehead servers. Once designated, preferred bridgehead servers are used exclusively to replicate changes collected from the site. An administrator may choose to designate preferred bridgehead servers when there is a lot of data to replicate between sites, or to create a fault-tolerant topology. If one preferred bridgehead server is not available, the knowledge consistency checker (KCC) automatically uses one of the other preferred bridgehead servers. If no other preferred bridgehead servers are available, replication does not occur to that site. *See also* bridgehead server.

primary domain controller (PDC)   In a Microsoft Windows NT Server 4 or earlier domain, the computer running Windows NT Server that authenticates logging on to a domain and maintains the directory database for a domain. The PDC tracks changes made to accounts of all computers on a domain. It is the only computer to receive these changes directly. A domain has only one PDC. In a Microsoft Windows 2000 or Microsoft Windows Server 2003 domain, the PDC emulator master supports compatibility with client computers that are not running Windows 2000 or Microsoft Windows XP Professional.

public key infrastructure (PKI)   A term generally used to describe the laws, policies, standards, and software that regulate or manipulate certificates and public and private keys. In practice, it is a system of digital certificates, certification authorities, and other registration authorities that verify and authenticate the validity of each party involved in an electronic transaction.

publish   To make data available for replication.

R

RDN   *See* relative distinguished name (RDN).

realm trust   A trust that must be explicitly created by a systems administrator between a non–Windows Kerberos realm and an Active Directory domain. This trust provides interoperability between the Active Directory domain and any realm used in Kerberos version 5 implementations. The trust can be transitive or nontransitive and one-way or two-way. *See also* shortcut trust; external trust; forest trust.

registry path rule   A software restriction policies rule that recognizes software based on the location of the software as it is stored in the registry.

relative distinguished name (RDN)   The part of an object's distinguished name that is an attribute of the object itself. For most objects, this is the Common Name attribute. For security principals, the default common name is the security principal name. For the distinguished name CN=MyName,CN=Users,DC=Microsoft,DC=com, the relative distinguished name of the MyName user object is CN=MyName. The relative distinguished name of the parent object is CN=Users.

relative ID master   The domain controller assigned to allocate sequences of relative IDs to each domain controller in its domain. Whenever a domain controller creates a security principal (user, group, or computer object), the domain controller assigns the object a unique security identifier (SID). The SID consists of a domain SID that is the same for all SIDs created in a particular domain and a relative ID that is unique for each SID created in the domain. At any time, there can be only one relative ID master in a particular domain.

Rendom.exe The domain rename utility which you can use to rename or restructure a domain. The Rendom.exe utility can be found in the \Valueadd\Msft\Mgmt\ Domren directory on the Microsoft Windows Server 2003 CD-ROM.

Repadmin.exe The replication diagnostics command-line tool, which is used to check replication consistency between replication partners, monitor replication status, display replication metadata, and force replication events and knowledge consistency checker (KCC) recalculation. This tool is included with the Windows Support Tools on the Microsoft Windows Server 2003 CD-ROM in the \Support\Tools folder.

replica In Active Directory replication, a copy of a logical Active Directory partition that is synchronized through replication between domain controllers that hold copies of the same directory partition. "Replica" can also refer to the composite set of directory partitions held by any one domain controller. These are specifically called a directory partition replica and server replica, respectively.

replication The process of copying data from a data store or file system to multiple computers to synchronize the data. Active Directory provides multimaster replication of the directory between domain controllers within a given domain. The replicas of the directory on each domain controller are writable. This allows updates to be applied to any replica of a given domain. The replication service automatically copies the changes from a given replica to all other replicas.

replication availability A schedule assigned to the site link that indicates when the link is available for replication.

replication frequency A value assigned to the site link that indicates the number of minutes Active Directory should wait before using a connection to check for replication updates.

replication partner A domain controller that acts as a replication source for a given domain controller. The knowledge consistency checker (KCC) determines which servers are best suited to replicate with each other and generates the list of domain controllers that are candidates for replication partners from the list of domain controllers in the site on the basis of connectivity, history of successful replication, and matching of full and partial replicas. A domain controller has some number of direct replication partners with whom it replicates for a given directory partition. The other domain controllers in the site replicate transitively with this domain controller.

Replmon.exe The Active Directory Replication Monitor, which enables administrators to view the low-level status of Active Directory replication, force synchronization between domain controllers, view the topology in a graphical format, and monitor the status and performance of domain controller replication. This tool is included with the Windows Support Tools on the Microsoft Windows Server 2003 CD-ROM in the \Support\Tools folder.

resource record   The standard database record used in a zone to associate Domain Name System (DNS) domain names to related data for a given type of network resource, such as a host Internet Protocol (IP) address. Most of the basic resource record types are defined in RFC 1035, but additional resource record types have been defined in other Requests for Comments (RFCs) and approved for use with DNS.

Resultant Set Of Policy (RSoP)   The sum of the policies applied to the user or computer, including the application of filters (security groups, Windows Management Instrumentation [WMI]) and exceptions (No Override, Block Policy Inheritance).

Resultant Set Of Policy Wizard   A wizard that uses existing Group Policy Object (GPO) settings to report the effects of GPOs on users and computers or simulates the effects of planned GPOs. To accomplish polling of existing GPOs and the simulation of planned GPOs, the Resultant Set Of Policy Wizard uses two modes (logging mode and planning mode) to create RSoP queries. Logging mode reports the existing GPO settings for a user or computer. Planning mode simulates the GPO settings that a user and computer might receive, and it enables you to change the simulation.

roaming user profile   A server-based user profile that is downloaded to the local computer when a user logs on, and is updated both locally and on the server when the user logs off. A roaming user profile is available from the server when logging on to a workstation or server computer. When logging on, the user can use the local user profile if it is more current than the copy on the server.

RSoP   *See* Resultant Set Of Policy (RSoP).

Run As   A program that allows you to run administrative tools with either local or domain administrator rights and permissions while logged on as a normal user.

S

safe mode   A method of starting Microsoft Windows operating systems using basic files and drivers only, without networking. Safe mode is available by pressing the F8 key when prompted during startup. This allows you to start your computer when a problem prevents it from starting normally.

SAM   *See* Security Accounts Manager (SAM).

schema   A description of the object classes and attributes stored in Active Directory. For each object class, the schema defines what attributes an object class must have, what additional attributes it may have, and what object class can be its parent. An Active Directory schema can be updated dynamically. For example, an application can extend the schema with new attributes and classes and use the extensions immediately. Schema updates are accomplished by creating or modifying the schema objects stored in Active Directory. Like every object in Active Directory, a schema object has an access control list (ACL) so that only authorized users can alter the schema.

schema attribute   In Active Directory, a single property of an object. An object is described by the values of its attributes.

schema class   A distinct, named set of attributes that represents a concrete object, such as a user, a printer, or an application. The attributes hold data describing the item that is identified by the directory object. Attributes of a user might include the user's given name, surname, and e-mail address. The terms *object class* and *class* are used interchangeably. The attributes that can be used to describe an object are determined by the content rules. For each object class, the schema defines what attributes an instance of the class must have and what additional attributes it might have.

schema master   The domain controller assigned to control all updates to the schema within a forest. At any time, there can be only one schema master in the forest.

schema objects   The informal name for schema class objects and schema attribute objects. *See also* metadata.

schema partition   A partition in Active Directory that defines the objects that can be created in the directory and the attributes those objects can have. This data is common to all domains in a forest and is replicated to all domain controllers in a forest.

Security Accounts Manager (SAM)   A Microsoft Windows service used during the logon process. SAM maintains user account information, including the list of groups to which a user belongs.

Security Configuration And Analysis   A console that offers the ability to compare the security settings of a computer to a security template, view the results, and resolve any discrepancies revealed by the analysis.

security descriptor   A data structure that contains security information associated with a protected object. Security descriptors include information about who owns the object, who may access it and in what way, and what types of access will be audited. *See also* access control list (ACL); object.

security group   A group that can be used to administer permissions for users and other domain objects.

security ID   *See* security identifier (SID).

security identifier (SID)   A unique number that identifies a user, group, or computer account. Every account on the network is issued a unique SID when the account is first created. Internal processes in Microsoft Windows refer to an account's SID rather than the account's user or group name. If you create an account, delete it, and then create an account with the same user name, the new account will not have the rights or permissions previously granted to the old account because the accounts have different SID numbers.

security log   An event log containing information on security events that are specified in the audit policy.

security principal   An account holder that is automatically assigned a security identifier (SID) to control access to resources. A security principal can be a user, group, service, or computer.

security template   A physical representation of a security configuration; a single file where a group of security settings is stored. Locating all security settings in one place eases security administration. Each template is saved as a text-based .inf file. This allows you to copy, paste, import, or export some or the entire set of template attributes.

selective authentication   A method of setting the scope of authentication differently for outgoing and incoming external and forest trusts. Selective trusts allow you to make flexible access control decisions between external domains in a forest.

shared system volume   A folder structure that exists on all domain controllers. It stores public files that must be replicated to other domain controllers, such as logon scripts and some of the Group Policy Objects (GPOs), for both the current domain and the enterprise. The default location for the shared system volume is *%Systemroot%*\Sysvol.

sharepoint   A centralized location for key folders on a server or servers, which provides users with an access point for storing and finding information and administrators with an access point for managing information.

shortcut trust   A trust that must be explicitly created by a systems administrator between two domains that are logically distant from each other in a forest or tree hierarchy. The purpose of a shortcut trust is to optimize the interdomain authentication process by shortening the trust path. All shortcut trusts are transitive and can be one- or two-way. A shortcut trust is also known as a cross-link trust. *See also* external trust; forest trust; realm trust; trust path.

SID   *See* security identifier (SID).

single-master replication   A type of replication where one domain controller is the master domain controller and operations are not permitted to occur at different places in a network at the same time. In Active Directory, one or more domain controllers can be assigned to perform single-master replication. Operations master roles are special roles assigned to one or more domain controllers in a domain to perform single-master replication. *See also* operations master role.

site   One or more well-connected (highly reliable and fast) Transmission Control Protocol/Internet Protocol (TCP/IP) subnets. A site allows administrators to configure Active Directory access and replication topology quickly and easily to take advantage of the physical network. When users log on, Active Directory clients locate Active Directory servers in the same site as the user. *See also* subnet; well-connected.

site license server   A server that contains the licensing information for a site.

site link   A link between two sites that allows replication to occur. Each site link contains the schedule that determines when replication can occur between the sites that it connects. *See also* site link cost; replication availability; replication frequency.

site link bridge   The linking of more than two sites for replication using the same transport. When site links are bridged, they are transitive; that is, all site links for a specific transport implicitly belong to a single site link bridge for that transport. A site link bridge makes disjoint networks possible. All site links within the bridge can route transitively, but they do not route outside of the bridge.

site link cost   A value assigned to the site link that indicates the cost of the connection in relation to the speed of the link. Higher costs are used for slow links, and lower costs are used for fast links.

site topology   A logical representation of a physical network.

smart card   A credit card–sized device that is used with a personal identification number (PIN) to enable certificate-based authentication and single sign-on to the enterprise. Smart cards securely store certificates, public and private keys, passwords, and other types of personal information. A smart card reader attached to the computer reads the smart card. *See also* authentication.

snap-in   A type of tool you can add to a console supported by a Microsoft Management Console (MMC). A stand-alone snap-in can be added by itself; an extension snap-in can only be added to extend the function of another snap-in.

software distribution point   In the Software Installation extension, a network location from which users are able to get the software that they need.

Software Installation   An extension within Group Policy that is the administrator's primary tool for managing software within an organization. Software Installation works in conjunction with Group Policy and Active Directory, establishing a Group Policy–based software management system that allows you to centrally manage the initial deployment of software, mandatory and nonmandatory upgrades, patches, quick fixes, and the removal of software.

software restriction policies A collection of policy settings that define what software can run on a computer, based on the default security level for a Group Policy Object (GPO). Exceptions to the default security level can then be defined by certificate rules, hash rules, path rules, registry path rules, and Internet zone rules. *See also* certificate rule; hash rule; path rule; registry path rule; Internet zone rule.

special identity groups Groups that are installed with the operating system. Membership in these groups is controlled by the operating system. Although the special identity groups can be assigned rights and permission to resources, you cannot modify or view the memberships of these groups. You do not see special identity groups when you administer groups, and you cannot place them into other groups. Group scopes do not apply to special identity groups. The operating system bases special identity group membership on how the computer is accessed, not on who uses the computer.

special permissions On NTFS volumes, a custom set of permissions. Administrators can customize permissions on files and directories by selecting the individual components of the standard sets of permissions.

standalone server A computer that runs Microsoft Windows 2000 or Microsoft Windows Server 2003 but does not participate in a domain. A standalone server has only its own database of users, and it processes logon requests by itself. It does not share account information with any other computer and cannot provide access to domain accounts, but it can participate in a workgroup.

standard permissions The permissions that are shown in the Security tab in the Properties dialog box for an object. These permissions are assigned most frequently.

standby operations master A domain controller designated by a system administrator to be used in case of failure of the operations master domain controller.

strong password A password that provides an effective defense against unauthorized access to a resource. A strong password is at least seven characters long, does not contain all or part of the user's account name, and contains at least three of the following four categories of characters: uppercase characters, lowercase characters, base 10 digits, and symbols found on the keyboard (such as !, @, and #).

subnet A portion of a network, which may be a physically independent network segment, that shares a network address with other portions of the network and is distinguished by a subnet number. A subnet is to a network what a network is to the Internet.

subnet mask A 32-bit value expressed as four decimal numbers from 0 to 255, separated by periods (for example, 255.255.0.0). This number allows the Transmission Control Protocol/Internet Protocol (TCP/IP) network stack to distinguish the network ID portion of the Internet Protocol (IP) address from the host ID portion.

System Monitor   A tool that allows you to collect and view extensive data about the usage of hardware resources and the activity of system services on computers you administer.

Systemroot   The path and folder name where the Microsoft Windows system files are located. Typically, this is C:\Windows, although you can designate a different drive or folder when you install Windows. To open your Systemroot folder, click Start, click Run, type **%Systemroot%**, and then click OK.

system state data   In Backup, a collection of system-specific data maintained by the operating system that must be backed up as a unit. It is not a backup of the entire system. The system state data includes the registry, COM+ Class Registration database, system files, boot files, and files under Windows File Protection. For servers, the system state data also includes the Certificate Services database (if the server is operating as a certificate server). If the server is a domain controller, the system state data also includes Active Directory and the Sysvol directory.

system volume   The volume that contains the hardware-specific files needed to load Microsoft Windows on x86-based computers with a basic input/output system (BIOS). The system volume can be, but does not have to be, the same volume as the boot volume. *See also* basic input/output system (BIOS).

Sysvol   A shared directory that stores the server copy of the domain's public files, which are replicated among all domain controllers in the domain.

T

TCP/IP   *See* Transmission Control Protocol/Internet Protocol (TCP/IP).

temporary user profile   A profile issued any time an error condition prevents a user's profile from being loaded. Temporary profiles are deleted at the end of each session. Changes made to a user's desktop settings and files are lost when the user logs off.

trace log   A type of log generated when the user selects a trace data provider using the Performance console. Trace logs differ from counter logs in that they measure data continuously rather than taking periodic samples.

transforms   *See* modifications.

transitive trust   A trust that is not bound by the domains in the trust relationship.

Transmission Control Protocol/Internet Protocol (TCP/IP)   A set of networking protocols used on the Internet that provides communications across interconnected networks made up of computers with diverse hardware architectures and various operating systems. TCP/IP includes standards for how computers communicate and conventions for connecting networks and routing traffic.

tree   A set of Active Directory domains connected by a two-way transitive trust, sharing a common schema, configuration, and global catalog. The domains must form a contiguous hierarchical namespace such that, for example, *a.com* is the root of the tree, *b.a.com* is a child of *a.com*, *c.b.a.com* is a child of *b.a.com*, and so on.

tree-root domain   The highest-level domain in the tree; child and grandchild domains are arranged under it. Typically, the domain you select should be the one that is most critical to the operation of the tree.

tree-root trust   The two-way, transitive trust relationship that is established when you add a new tree to an Active Directory forest. The Active Directory installation process automatically creates a transitive trust relationship between the domain you are creating (the new tree root) and the forest root. A tree-root trust can be set up only between the roots of two trees in the same forest. *See also* parent-child trust.

Trojan horse   A program that masquerades as another common program in an attempt to receive information without authorization. An example of a Trojan horse is a program that behaves like a system logon to retrieve user names and password information that the writers of the Trojan horse can later use to break into the system.

trust path   A series of trust links from one domain to another, established for the purpose of passing authentication requests.

trust relationship   A logical relationship established between domains to allow pass-through authentication, in which a trusting domain honors the logon authentications of a trusted domain. User accounts and global groups defined in a trusted domain can be given rights and permissions in a trusting domain, even though the user accounts or groups don't exist in the trusting domain's directory. *See also* authentication; domain; parent-child trust; tree-root trust; shortcut trust; external trust.

U

UNC   *See* Universal Naming Convention (UNC) name.

universal group   A security or distribution group that can contain users, groups, and computers from any domain in its forest as members. Universal security groups can be granted rights and permissions on resources in any domain in the forest. When the domain functional level is set to Windows 2000 Mixed or Windows Server 2003 Interim, universal security groups cannot be created. *See also* domain local group; forest; global catalog.

universal group membership caching   A feature in Microsoft Windows Server 2003 that allows a site that does not contain a global catalog server to be configured to cache universal group memberships for users who log on to the domain controller in the site. This ability allows a domain controller to process user logon requests without contacting a global catalog server when a global catalog server is unavailable. The cache is refreshed periodically as determined in the replication schedule.

Universal Naming Convention (UNC) name   The full name of a resource on a network. It conforms to the *Servername**Sharename* syntax, where *Servername* is the name of the server and *Sharename* is the name of the shared resource. UNC names of directories or files can also include the directory path under the share name, with the following syntax: *Servername**Sharename**Directory**Filename*.

UPN   *See* user principal name (UPN).

user account   In Active Directory, an object that consists of all the information that defines a domain user, which includes user name, password, and groups in which the user account has membership. User accounts can be stored in Active Directory or on your local computer. For computers running Microsoft Windows XP Professional and member servers, user accounts are managed with the Local Users And Groups console. For domain controllers running Microsoft Windows Server 2003, user accounts are managed with the Active Directory Users And Computers console.

User Configuration node   A node within Group Policy that contains the settings used to set group policies applied to users, regardless of which computer the user logs on to. User configuration settings are applied when users log on to the computer.

user name   A unique name identifying a user account to Microsoft Windows. An account's user name must be unique among the other group names and user names within its own domain or workgroup.

user principal name (UPN)   A user account name (sometimes referred to as the *user logon name*) and a domain name identifying the domain in which the user account is located. This is the standard usage for logging on to a Microsoft Windows domain. The format is *user@microsoft.com* (similar to an e-mail address). *See also* domain; domain name; user principal name (UPN) suffix.

user principal name (UPN) suffix   The part of the UPN to the right of the @ character. The default UPN suffix for a user account is the Domain Name System (DNS) domain name of the domain that contains the user account. Alternative UPN suffixes may be added to simplify administration and user logon processes by providing a single UPN suffix for all users. The UPN suffix is used only within the Active Directory forest, and it does not have to be a valid DNS domain name. *See also* domain; domain name; Domain Name System (DNS); forest; user account; user principal name (UPN).

user profile   A file that contains configuration information for a specific user, such as desktop settings, persistent network connections, and application settings. Each user's preferences are saved to a user profile that Microsoft Windows uses to configure the desktop each time a user logs on.

user rights   Tasks a user is permitted to perform on a computer system or domain, such as backing up files and folders, adding or deleting users in a workstation or domain, and shutting down a computer system. Rights can be granted to groups or to user accounts, but are best reserved for use by groups. User rights are set within Group Policy.

W

well-connected   Sufficient connectivity to make your network and Active Directory useful to clients on your network. The precise meaning of *well-connected* is determined by your particular needs, which may include speed and cost. *See also* site.

Windows Installer package   A file containing explicit instructions about the installation and removal of specific applications. The company or developer who produces the application provides the Windows Installer package .msi file and includes it with the application. If a Windows Installer package does not come with an application, you might need to create a Windows Installer package by using a third-party tool. *See also* Windows Installer Service.

Windows Installer Service   A component of Microsoft Windows operating systems that standardizes the way applications are installed on multiple computers. Windows Installer Service implements all the proper Setup rules in the operating system itself by using the Windows Installer package file to install the application. *See also* Windows Installer package.

Windows Server 2003 family   A family of four products: Microsoft Windows Server 2003, Standard Edition; Windows Server 2003, Enterprise Edition; Windows Server 2003, Datacenter Edition; and Windows Server 2003, Web Edition. Windows Server 2003, Web Edition, only partially supports the use of Active Directory. Windows Server 2003, Web Edition, can participate as a member server in an Active Directory–enabled network but cannot be used as an Active Directory domain controller.

Windows Support Tools   Additional tools intended for use by Microsoft support personnel and experienced users to assist in diagnosing and resolving computer problems. The Windows Support Tools are included on the Microsoft Windows Server 2003 CD-ROM in the \Support\Tools folder.

Index

Additional Windows (R2) Resources for Administrators

Published and Forthcoming Titles from Microsoft Press

Microsoft® Windows Server™ 2003 Administrator's Pocket Consultant, Second Edition
William R. Stanek • ISBN 0-7356-2245-0

Here's the practical, pocket-sized reference for IT professionals supporting Microsoft Windows Server 2003—fully updated for Service Pack 1 and Release 2. Designed for quick referencing, this portable guide covers all the essentials for performing everyday system administration tasks. Topics include managing workstations and servers, using Active Directory® directory service, creating and administering user and group accounts, managing files and directories, performing data security and auditing tasks, handling data back-up and recovery, and administering networks using TCP/IP, WINS, and DNS, and more.

MCSE Self-Paced Training Kit (Exams 70-290, 70-291, 70-293, 70-294): Microsoft Windows Server 2003 Core Requirements, Second Edition
Holme, Thomas, Mackin, McLean, Zacker, Spealman, Hudson, and Craft • ISBN 0-7356-2290-6

The Microsoft Certified Systems Engineer (MCSE) credential is the premier certification for professionals who analyze the business requirements and design and implement the infrastructure for business solutions based on the Microsoft Windows Server 2003 platform and Microsoft Windows Server System—now updated for Windows Server 2003 Service Pack 1 and R2. This all-in-one set provides in-depth preparation for the four required networking system exams. Work at your own pace through the lessons, hands-on exercises, troubleshooting labs, and review questions. You get expert exam tips plus a full review section covering all objectives and sub-objectives in each study guide. Then use the Microsoft Practice Tests on the CD to challenge yourself with more than 1500 questions for self-assessment and practice!

Microsoft Windows® Small Business Server 2003 R2 Administrator's Companion
Charlie Russel, Sharon Crawford, and Jason Gerend • ISBN 0-7356-2280-9

Get your small-business network, messaging, and collaboration systems up and running quickly with the essential guide to administering Windows Small Business Server 2003 R2. This reference details the features, capabilities, and technologies for both the standard and premium editions—including Microsoft Windows Server 2003 R2, Exchange Server 2003 with Service Pack 1, Windows SharePoint® Services, SQL Server™ 2005 Workgroup Edition, and Internet Information Services. Discover how to install, upgrade, or migrate to Windows Small Business Server 2003 R2; plan and implement your network, Internet access, and security services; customize Microsoft Exchange Server for your e-mail needs; and administer user rights, shares, permissions, and Group Policy.

Microsoft Windows Small Business Server 2003 R2 Administrator's Companion
Charlie Russel, Sharon Crawford, and Jason Gerend • ISBN 0-7356-2280-9

Here's the ideal one-volume guide for the IT professional administering Windows Server 2003. Now fully updated for Windows Server 2003 Service Pack 1 and R2, this *Administrator's Companion* offers up-to-date information on core system administration topics for Microsoft Windows, including Active Directory services, security, scripting, disaster planning and recovery, and interoperability with UNIX. It also includes all-new sections on Service Pack 1 security updates and new features for R2. Featuring easy-to-use procedures and handy work-arounds, this book provides ready answers for on-the-job results.

MCSA/MCSE Self-Paced Training Kit (Exam 70-290): Managing and Maintaining a Microsoft Windows Server 2003 Environment, Second Edition
Dan Holme and Orin Thomas • ISBN 0-7356-2289-2

MCSA/MCSE Self-Paced Training Kit (Exam 70-291): Implementing, Managing, and Maintaining a Microsoft Windows Server 2003 Network Infrastructure, Second Edition
J.C. Mackin and Ian McLean • ISBN 0-7356-2288-4

MCSE Self-Paced Training Kit (Exam 70-293): Planning and Maintaining a Microsoft Windows Server 2003 Network Infrastructure, Second Edition
Craig Zacker • ISBN 0-7356-2287-6

MCSE Self-Paced Training Kit (Exam 70-294): Planning, Implementing, and Maintaining a Microsoft Windows Server 2003 Active Directory® Infrastructure, Second Ed.
Jill Spealman, Kurt Hudson, and Melissa Craft • ISBN 0-7356-2286-8

For more information about Microsoft Press® books and other learning products, visit: **www.microsoft.com/mspress** *and* **www.microsoft.com/learning**

Additional SQL Server Resources for Administrators
Published and Forthcoming Titles from Microsoft Press

Microsoft® SQL Server™ 2005 Reporting Services *Step by Step*
Hitachi Consulting Services • ISBN 0-7356-2250-7

SQL Server Reporting Services (SRS) is Microsoft's customizable reporting solution for business data analysis. It is one of the key value features of SQL Server 2005: functionality more advanced and much less expensive than its competition. SRS is powerful, so an understanding of how to architect a report, as well as how to install and program SRS, is key to harnessing the full functionality of SQL  Server. This procedural tutorial shows how to use the Report Project Wizard, how to think about and access data, and how to build queries. It also walks the reader through the creation of charts and visual layouts to enable maximum visual understanding of the data analysis. Interactivity (enhanced in SQL Server 2005) and security are also covered in detail.

Microsoft SQL Server 2005 Administrator's Pocket Consultant
William R. Stanek • ISBN 0-7356-2107-1

Here's the utterly practical, pocket-sized reference for IT professionals who need to administer, optimize, and maintain SQL Server 2005 in their organizations. This unique guide provides essential details for using SQL Server 2005 to help protect and manage your company's data—whether automating  tasks; creating indexes and views; performing backups and recovery; replicating transactions; tuning performance; managing server activity; importing and exporting data; or performing other key tasks. Featuring quick-reference tables, lists, and step-by-step instructions, this handy, one-stop guide provides fast, accurate answers on the spot, whether you're at your desk or in the field!

Microsoft SQL Server 2005 Administrator's Companion
Marci Frohock Garcia, Edward Whalen, and Mitchell Schroeter • ISBN 0-7356-2198-5

Microsoft SQL Server 2005 Administrator's Companion is the comprehensive, in-depth guide that saves time by providing all the technical information you need to deploy, administer, optimize, and support SQL Server 2005. Using a hands-on, example-rich approach, this authoritative, one-volume reference book provides expert advice, product information, detailed solutions, procedures, and real-world troubleshooting tips from experienced SQL Server 2005 professionals. This expert guide shows you how to design high-availability database systems, prepare for installation, install and configure SQL Server 2005, administer services and features, and maintain and troubleshoot your database system. It covers how to configure your system for your I/O system and model and optimize system capacity. The expert authors provide details on how to create and use defaults, constraints, rules, indexes, views, functions, stored procedures, and triggers. This guide shows you how to administer reporting services, analysis services, notification services, and integration services. It also provides a wealth of information on replication and the specifics of snapshot, transactional, and merge replication. Finally, there is expansive coverage of how to manage and tune your SQL Server system, including automating tasks, backup and restoration of databases, and management of users and security.

Microsoft SQL Server 2005 Analysis Services *Step by Step*
Hitachi Consulting Services • ISBN 0-7356-2199-3

One of the key features of SQL Server 2005 is SQL Server Analysis Services—Microsoft's customizable analysis solution for business data modeling and interpretation. Just compare SQL Server Analysis Services to its competition to understand/grasp the great value of its enhanced features. One of the keys to harnessing the full functionality of SQL Server will be leveraging Analysis Services for the powerful tool that it is—including creating a cube, and deploying, customizing, and extending the basic calculations. This step-by-step tutorial discusses how to get started, how to build scalable analytical applications, and how to use and administer advanced features. Interactivity (which is enhanced in SQL Server 2005), data translation, and security are also covered in detail.

Microsoft SQL Server 2005 Express Edition
Step by Step
Jackie Goldstein • ISBN 0-7356-2184-5

Inside Microsoft SQL Server 2005:
The Storage Engine
Kalen Delaney • ISBN 0-7356-2105-5

Inside Microsoft SQL Server 2005:
T-SQL Programming
Itzik Ben-Gan • ISBN 0-7356-2197-7

Inside Microsoft SQL Server 2005:
Query Processing and Optimization
Kalen Delaney • ISBN 0-7356-2196-9

For more information about Microsoft Press® books and other learning products,
visit: **www.microsoft.com/mspress** and **www.microsoft.com/learning**

Prepare for Certification with Self-Paced Training Kits

Official Exam Prep Guides—
Plus Practice Tests

Ace your preparation for the skills measured by the MCP exams—and on the job. With official *Self-Paced Training Kits* from Microsoft, you'll work at your own pace through a system of lessons, hands-on exercises, troubleshooting labs, and review questions. Then test yourself with the Readiness Review Suite on CD, which provides hundreds of challenging questions for in-depth self-assessment and practice.

- **MCSE Self-Paced Training Kit (Exams 70-290, 70-291, 70-293, 70-294): Microsoft® Windows Server™ 2003 Core Requirements.** 4-Volume Boxed Set. ISBN: 0-7356-1953-0. (Individual volumes are available separately.)
- **MCSA/MCSE Self-Paced Training Kit (Exam 70-270): Installing, Configuring, and Administering Microsoft Windows® XP Professional, Second Edition.** ISBN: 0-7356-2152-7.
- **MCSE Self-Paced Training Kit (Exam 70-298): Designing Security for a Microsoft Windows Server 2003 Network.** ISBN: 0-7356-1969-7.
- **MCSA/MCSE Self-Paced Training Kit (Exam 70-350): Implementing Microsoft Internet Security and Acceleration Server 2004.** ISBN: 0-7356-2169-1.
- **MCSA/MCSE Self-Paced Training Kit (Exam 70-284): Implementing and Managing Microsoft Exchange Server 2003.** ISBN: 0-7356-1899-2.

For more information about Microsoft Press® books, visit: **www.microsoft.com/mspress**

For more information about learning tools such as online assessments, e-learning, and certification, visit:
www.microsoft.com/mspress *and* **www.microsoft.com/learning**

Microsoft Windows Server 2003 Resource Kit
The *definitive* resource

for Windows Server 2003!

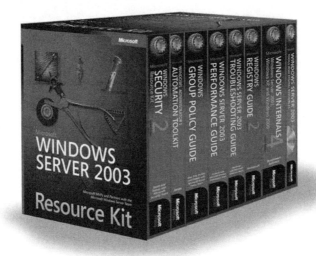

Get the in-depth technical information and tools you need to manage and optimize Microsoft® Windows Server™ 2003—with expert guidance and best practices from Microsoft MVPs, leading industry consultants, and the Microsoft Windows Server team. This official *Resource Kit* delivers seven comprehensive volumes, including:

- **Microsoft Windows® Security Resource Kit, Second Edition**
- **Microsoft Windows Administrator's Automation Toolkit**
- **Microsoft Windows Group Policy Guide**
- **Microsoft Windows Server 2003 Performance Guide**
- **Microsoft Windows Server 2003 Troubleshooting Guide**
- **Microsoft Windows Registry Guide, Second Edition**
- **Microsoft Windows Internals, Fourth Edition**

You'll find 300+ timesaving tools and scripts, an eBook of the entire *Resource Kit*, plus five bonus eBooks. It's everything you need to help maximize system performance and reliability—and help reduce ownership and support costs.

Microsoft Windows Server 2003 Resource Kit
Microsoft MVPs and Partners with the Microsoft Windows Server Team
ISBN: 0-7356-2232-9

For more information about Microsoft Press® books, visit: **www.microsoft.com/mspress**

For more information about learning tools such as online assessments, e-learning, and certification, visit: **www.microsoft.com/learning**

content●master

knowledge into understanding

Providing leading-edge content

Content Master is one of the world's leading technical authoring and consultancy organizations, working with key software vendors to provide leading-edge content to technical audiences. This content, combined with our business knowledge helps enable business decision makers, developers and IT Professionals to keep abreast of new initiatives, helping them build innovative enterprise solutions.

We also offer educational and content consultancy, identifying the most effective strategies for the development and deployment of materials. Our unique approach encompasses technical, business and educational requirements. This ensures that developed content not only offers the right level of specialist knowledge but that it addresses commercial requirements and is structured in the most effective way for the audience.

Microsoft®
GOLD CERTIFIED
Partner

What do you think of this book? We want to hear from you!

Do you have a few minutes to participate in a brief online survey? Microsoft is interested in hearing your feedback about this publication so that we can continually improve our books and learning resources for you.

To participate in our survey, please visit:

www.microsoft.com/learning/booksurvey

And enter this book's ISBN, 0-7356-2286-8. As a thank-you to survey participants in the United States and Canada, each month we'll randomly select five respondents to win one of five $100 gift certificates from a leading online merchant.* At the conclusion of the survey, you can enter the drawing by providing your e-mail address, which will be used for prize notification *only*.

Thanks in advance for your input. Your opinion counts!

Sincerely,

Microsoft Learning

Learn More. Go Further.

To see special offers on Microsoft Learning products for developers, IT professionals, and home and office users, visit: *www.microsoft.com/learning/booksurvey*

System Requirements

To complete the exercises in Part 1, your computer needs to meet the following minimum system requirements:

- Microsoft Windows Server 2003 with Service Pack 1, Enterprise Edition (180-day evaluation edition of Windows Server 2003 with SP1 and R2, Enterprise Edition, included on CD-ROM)

- Minimum CPU: 133 MHz processor (550 MHz recommended)

- Minimum RAM: 128 MB (256 MB recommended)

- Disk space for setup: 1.5 GB to 2.0 GB

- Network adapter: 100 megabits per second (Mbps)

- Display monitor capable of 800 × 600 resolution or higher

- CD-ROM or DVD-ROM drive

- Microsoft Mouse or compatible pointing device

To view the eBooks and other material that is included on the companion CD in Portable Document Format (PDF), you need Adobe Reader (*www.adobe.com*).

Uninstall Instructions

The time-limited release of Microsoft Windows Server 2003 with SP1 and R2, Enterprise Edition, will expire 180 days after installation. If you decide to discontinue the use of this software, you will need to reinstall your original operating system. You might need to reformat your drive.

$59.99

DATE			

BAKER & TAYLOR